Korean

Korean: A Comprehensive Grammar is a reference to Korean grammar, and presents a thorough overview of the language, concentrating on the real patterns of use in modern Korean.

The book moves from the alphabet and pronunciation through morphology and word classes to a detailed analysis of sentence structures and semantic features such as aspect, tense, speech styles and negation.

Updated and revised, this new edition includes lively descriptions of Korean grammar, taking into account the latest research in Korean linguistics. More lower-frequency grammar patterns have been added, and extra examples have been included throughout the text.

The unrivalled depth and range of this updated edition of *Korean: A Comprehensive Grammar* makes it an essential reference source on the Korean language.

Jaehoon Yeon is Professor of Korean Language and Linguistics at SOAS, University of London.

Lucien Brown is Senior Lecturer of Korean Studies at Monash University.

Routledge Comprehensive Grammars

Titles in this series:

Modern Welsh
A Comprehensive Grammar, 3rd Edition
Gareth King

Chinese
A Comprehensive Grammar, 2nd Edition
Yip Po-Ching, Don Rimmington

Kazakh
A Comprehensive Grammar
Raihan Muhamedowa

Panjabi
A Comprehensive Grammar
Mangat Bhardwaj

French Creoles
A Comprehensive Grammar
Anand Syea

Dutch
A Comprehensive Grammar, 3rd Edition
Bruce Donaldson

Finnish
A Comprehensive Grammar
Fred Karlsson

Persian
A Comprehensive Grammar
Saeed Yousef

Norwegian
A Comprehensive Grammar
Philip Holmes, Hans-Olav Enger

Korean
A Comprehensive Grammar, 2nd edition
Jaehoon Yeon, Lucien Brown

For more information on this series, please visit: www.routledge.com/languages/series/SE0550

Korean

A Comprehensive Grammar

Second Edition

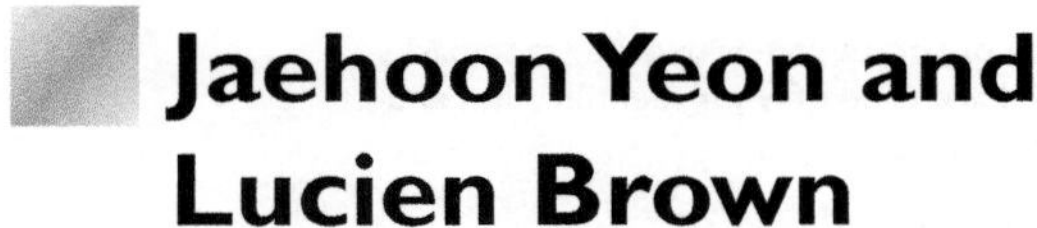

Jaehoon Yeon and Lucien Brown

LONDON AND NEW YORK

Second edition published 2019
by Routledge
2 Park Square, Milton Park, Abingdon, Oxon, OX14 4RN

and by Routledge
52 Vanderbilt Avenue, New York, NY 10017

Routledge is an imprint of the Taylor & Francis Group, an informa business

First edition published by Routledge 2011

British Library Cataloguing-in-Publication Data
A catalogue record for this book is available from the British Library

Library of Congress Cataloging-in-Publication Data
A catalog record for this book has been requested

ISBN: 978-1-138-06448-5 (hbk)
ISBN: 978-1-138-06449-2 (pbk)
ISBN: 978-1-315-16035-1 (ebk)

Typeset in Sabon and Gill Sans
by Apex CoVantage, LLC

Contents

Preface to the second edition **xix**

Chapter 1 Introduction to the Korean Language **1**

1.1 Characteristic features of Korean 1
1.1.1 Word classes 2
1.1.2 Word order: Korean is an SOV language 3
1.1.2.1 Flexible word order 3
1.1.2.2 The postpositional characteristic of Korean 5
1.1.2.3 The position of complements 6
1.1.2.4 Interrogative word order 6
1.1.3 An intricate system of honorific categories 7
1.1.4 Korean as an elliptical language 8
1.2 Korean script and pronunciation 9
1.2.1 Basic principles of Hangul writing 10
1.2.1.1 Letter names and dictionary order 10
1.2.1.2 Writing syllabically 11
1.2.2 Hangul pronunciation guide 13
1.2.2.1 Simple vowels 13
1.2.2.2 Y-vowels 14
1.2.2.3 W-vowels 15
1.2.2.4 The compound vowel 의 16
1.2.2.5 Basic consonants 17

1.2.2.6 Aspirated consonants 20
1.2.2.7 Tensed or 'Double' consonants 20
1.2.3 Pronunciation changes 21
1.2.3.1 Pronunciation of syllable-final consonants 22
1.2.3.2 Simplification of consonant clusters 23
1.2.3.3 Re-syllabification 24
1.2.3.4 Nasal assimilation 26
1.2.3.5 ㄹ *r/l* pronounced as ㄴ *n* 28
1.2.3.6 ㄴ *n* pronounced as ㄹ *l* 29
1.2.3.7 Palatalization of ㄷ *t* and ㅌ *t'* 30
1.2.3.8 ㄴ *n* addition 31
1.2.3.9 ㅎ *h* reduction 32
1.2.3.10 Aspiration 32
1.2.3.11 Reinforcement 33

Chapter 2 Nouns, nominal forms, pronouns and numbers 36

2.1 Nouns 36
2.1.1 Lack of articles, number and gender 36
2.1.1.1 Lack of articles 37
2.1.1.2 Lack of number 37
2.1.1.3 Lack of gender 38
2.1.2 Bound/dependent nouns 39
2.1.2.1 것 'thing', 'object' or 'affair' 39
2.1.2.2 겸 '-cum-' 40
2.1.2.3 곳 'place' 41
2.1.2.4 김 'occasion', 'chance' 41
2.1.2.5 대로 'in accordance with' 41
2.1.2.6 덕분 'thanks to' 41
2.1.2.7 데 'place' 42
2.1.2.8 동안 'during' 42
2.1.2.9 둥 'may or may not' 43
2.1.2.10 듯 'as if' 43
2.1.2.11 따름 'only, alone' 43
2.1.2.12 때 'when' 43
2.1.2.13 때문 'reason' 44

2.1.2.14 리 'reasons' 45
2.1.2.15 무렵 'around the time' 45
2.1.2.16 바 'thing' 45
2.1.2.17 뿐 'only', 'just', 'nothing but' 46
2.1.2.18 수 'case', 'circumstance' 46
2.1.2.19 적 'event' 46
2.1.2.20 줄 'the way', 'the fact' 47
2.1.2.21 중/도중 'the middle' 47
2.1.2.22 지 'since' 48
2.1.2.23 쪽 'side' 48
2.1.2.24 채 'just as it is' 49

2.2 Nominal forms 49

2.2.1 Nominal form –이 50
2.2.2 Nominal form –개/게 50
2.2.3 Nominal form –기 50
2.2.4 Sentence patterns with –기 52
2.2.4.1 –기 나름이– 'depending on' 52
2.2.4.2 –기 때문(에) 'because' 53
2.2.4.3 –기/게 마련이– 'be bound to' 54
2.2.4.4 –기(에) 망정이– 'fortunately . . . otherwise' 55
2.2.4.5 –기 시작하– 'start' 55
2.2.4.6 –기 십상이– 'it is easy to . . .' 56
2.2.4.7 –기 위하– 'in order to' 56
2.2.4.8 –기 이를 데 없–/그지 없– 'boundless, endless' 57
2.2.4.9 –기 일쑤이– 'be apt to' 58
2.2.4.10 –기 전 'before' 58
2.2.4.11 –기 짝이 없– 'very' 59
2.2.4.12 –기나 하– 'just' 60
2.2.4.13 –기는 'no way' 60
2.2.4.14 –기는 하– 'indeed' 61
2.2.4.15 –기(는)커녕 'far from' 62
2.2.4.16 –기도 하– 'also' 63
2.2.4.17 –기만 하– 'only' 64
2.2.4.18 –기로 하– 'decide to . . .' 64
2.2.4.19 –기로 되– 'be supposed to . . .' 65
2.2.4.20 –기를/길 바라– 'hope' 66
2.2.4.21 –기에 'upon', 'because' 68
2.2.4.22 –기에 따라 'depending on' 69
2.2.5 Nominal form –음 69

2.2.6 Using –(으)ㄴ/는 것 to create nominal forms 72
2.3 Pronouns 74
2.3.1 Personal pronouns 74
2.3.1.1 First-person pronouns 74
2.3.1.2 Second-person pronouns 75
2.3.1.3 Third-person pronouns 77
2.3.2 Demonstrative pronouns 80
2.3.3 Reflexives and reciprocals 81
2.3.4 Interrogative pronouns 82
2.4 Numbers and counting 84
2.4.1 Pure Korean and Sino-Korean numbers 84
2.4.2 Which system to use 86
2.4.3 Sentence patterns with numbers 88
2.4.4 Counting and naming periods of time 90
2.4.4.1 Years 90
2.4.4.2 Months 91
2.4.4.3 Weeks 92
2.4.4.4 Days 92
2.4.4.5 Telling the time 93
2.4.4.6 Telling the date 95

Chapter 3 Particles 96

3.1 Defining particles 96
3.2 Case particles 97
3.2.1 The subject particle 이/가 98
3.2.2 The object particle 을/를 100
3.2.3 The possessive particle 의 103
3.2.4 Particles of movement and location 106
3.2.4.1 에 'to/in/at' 106
3.2.4.2 에다(가) 'in/on' 109
3.2.4.3 에서 'from/in/at' 110
3.2.4.4 에게/한테 'to' 113
3.2.4.5 더러 'to' 115
3.2.4.6 보고 'to' 116
3.2.4.7 에게서/한테서 'from' 116
3.2.4.8 (으)로부터 'from' 117
3.2.4.9 Particle phrase (으)로 하여금 'letting/making (someone do something)' 118

3.2.5 Instrumental particles 118
3.2.5.1 (으)로 'by/with/as' 119
3.2.5.2 (으)로서 'as' 121
3.2.5.3 (으)로써 'by means of' 122
3.2.5.4 Particle phrase (으)로 인해(서) 'due to' 123
3.2.6 Comitative particles 123
3.2.6.1 과/와 'and/with' 123
3.2.6.2 하고 'and/with' 125
3.2.6.3 (이)랑 'and/with' 126
3.2.7 Vocative particle 아/야 127
3.3 Special particles 129
3.3.1 Plural particle 들 129
3.3.2 Particles of topic and focus 131
3.3.2.1 Topic particle 은/는 132
3.3.2.2 (이)야 'if it's . . .' 138
3.3.2.3 (이)야말로 'indeed' 138
3.3.3 Particles of extent 139
3.3.3.1 만 'only' 139
3.3.3.2 뿐 'only' 141
3.3.3.3 밖에 'except for' 141
3.3.3.4 부터 'from' 143
3.3.3.5 까지 'up until' 144
3.3.3.6 도 'also', 'even' 146
3.3.3.7 조차 'even' 149
3.3.3.8 마저 'even' 150
3.3.3.9 치고/치고는 'with exception', 'pretty . . . for a . . .' 150
3.3.3.10 (은/는)커녕 'far from' 151
3.3.4 Particles of frequency 152
3.3.4.1 마다 'every' 152
3.3.4.2 씩 'apiece' 153
3.3.5 Particles of approximation and optionality 154
3.3.5.1 쯤 'about' 154
3.3.5.2 (이)나 ('about', 'or', 'just') 155
3.3.6 Particles of comparison and contrast 158
3.3.6.1 처럼 'like' 158
3.3.6.2 같이 'like' 159
3.3.6.3 만큼 'as . . . as' 160

3.3.6.4 보다 'more than' 160
3.3.6.5 따라 'unusually' 162
3.3.6.6 대로 'in accordance with' 163

Chapter 4 Verbs **164**

4.1 Characteristics of Korean verbs 164
4.1.1 Types of verbs: processive and descriptive 164
4.1.2 Types of verbs: 하– verbs 167
4.1.3 Types of verbs: negative verbs 169
4.1.4 Types of verbs: the copula (equational verb) 170
4.1.5 Verb bases 172
4.1.6 The infinitive form 173
4.1.7 The dictionary form 175
4.1.8 Attaching verb endings 176
4.2 Negatives 179
4.2.1 Short negatives with 안 and 못 179
4.2.2 Long negatives with –지 않– and –지 못하– 180
4.2.3 Negative commands and proposals with –지 말– 182
4.2.4 Expressions that require negative verbs 184
4.3 Tense 185
4.3.1 Past tenses 185
4.3.1.1 Simple past –았/었– 186
4.3.1.2 Past-past or discontinuous past –았/었었– 187
4.3.1.3 Observed or perceived past tense –더 189
4.3.2 Future tenses 193
4.3.2.1 –겠– 193
4.3.2.2 –(으)ㄹ 거– 196
4.3.2.3 Other forms with future-related meanings 198
4.3.2.4 Summary of Korean futures 199
4.3.3 Continuous tense 200
4.3.3.1 Continuous states with –아/어 있– 200

4.3.3.2 Continuous actions with –고 있– 202

4.4 Derived verbs: passives, causatives and others 205

4.4.1 Passives 205

4.4.1.1 Derived passive verbs –이–/–기–/–히–/–리– 206

4.4.1.2 Passives with 되– 209

4.4.1.3 Passives with other support verbs 210

4.4.1.4 Passives with –아/어 지– 213

4.4.2 Causatives 214

4.4.2.1 Derived causative verbs 215

4.4.2.2 Causatives with –게 하– 219

4.4.2.3 Causatives with –도록 하– 221

4.4.2.4 Causatives with 시키– 222

4.4.3 Transforming descriptive verbs into processive verbs 222

4.4.3.1 Forming processive verbs with –지– 223

4.4.3.2 Forming processive verbs with –하– 223

Chapter 5 Auxiliary (support) verbs 226

5.1 Auxiliary verbs with –(아/어) 226

5.1.1 –(아/어) 가– (ongoing activity 'away') 227

5.1.2 –(아/어) 오– (ongoing activity 'towards') 227

5.1.3 –(아/어) 내– (finish, achieve) 228

5.1.4 –(아/어) 놓– (do all the way) 229

5.1.5 –(아/어) 두– (do for future reference) 230

5.1.6 –(아/어) 대– (do repeatedly) 231

5.1.7 –(아/어) 버리– (do completely for regret or relief) 232

5.1.8 –(아/어) 보– (try doing) 233

5.1.9 –(아/어) 보이– (seem) 236

5.1.10 –(아/어) 빠지– (lapse into a negative state) 236

5.1.11 –(아/어) 쌓– (do repeatedly) 237

5.1.12 –(아/어) 주– (perform a favour) 237

5.1.13 –(아/어) 치우– (do rashly) 239

5.2 Auxiliary verbs with –다 240
5.2.1 –다 말– (stop after) 240
5.2.2 –다 보– (after trying doing) 240
5.2.3 –(아/어)다 주– (run an errand) 241
5.3 Auxiliary verbs with –고 242
5.3.1 –고 나– (after finishing) 242
5.3.2 –고 말– (end up) 243
5.3.3 –고 보– (do and then realize) 244
5.3.4 –고 싶– (want to do) 245
5.4 Auxiliary verbs with –(으)ㄹ까 246
5.4.1 –(으)ㄹ까 보– (think it might) 246
5.4.2 –(으)ㄹ까 싶– (afraid it might) 247
5.4.3 –(으)ㄹ까 하– (think of doing) 248
5.5 Auxiliary verbs with –나/–(으)ㄴ가 249
5.5.1 –나/–(으)ㄴ가 보– (look like) 250
5.5.2 –나/–(으)ㄴ가 싶– (think it might) 250
5.6 Auxiliary verbs with –게 251
5.6.1 –게 되– (turn out so that) 251
5.6.2 –게 보이– (seem) 252
5.7 Auxiliary verb with –(아/어)야 253
5.7.1 –(아/어)야 되–/하– (must, have to) 253

Chapter 6 Honorifics 254

6.1 Speech styles (hearer honorifics) 255
6.1.1 The polite style 256
6.1.2 The formal style 258
6.1.3 The intimate style – *Panmal* style 261
6.1.4 The plain style 263
Plain style statements 264
Plain style questions 266
Plain style proposals 268
Plain style commands 268
6.1.5 Familiar style 270
6.1.6 Semi-formal style 272
6.2 Referent honorifics 272
6.2.1 Subject honorifics 273
6.2.1.1 The subject honorific marker –(으)시– 273
6.2.1.2 Verbs with special subject honorific forms 275

6.2.1.3 Subject honorific particle 께서 276
6.2.2 Object honorifics 277
6.2.2.1 Verbs with special object honorific forms 277
6.2.2.2 Object honorific particle 께 278
6.2.3 Honorific nouns 279
6.2.4 Putting the honorifics system together 280
6.3 Terms of address 282
6.3.1 Names 283
6.3.2 Titles 284
6.3.3 Kinship terms 286
6.3.4 How to address someone 290

Chapter 7 Clausal connectives 292

7.1 Causal connectives 292
7.1.1 –(아/어)서 293
7.1.2 –아/어 296
7.1.3 –아/어서 인지 297
7.1.4 –아/어서(는) 안 되– 297
7.1.5 –(아/어) 가지고 298
7.1.6 –(으)니까 300
7.1.7 –(으)니 304
7.1.8 –(으)ㄹ테니까 304
7.1.9 –(으)므로 305
7.1.10 –길래 306
7.1.11 –느라고 308
7.1.12 –(으)랴 309
7.1.13 –더니 and –(았/었)더니 309
7.1.14 –(으)ㄹ라 310
7.2 Contrastive connectives 311
7.2.1 –지만 311
7.2.2 –(으)나 313
7.2.3 –(으)나 마나 314
7.2.4 –(으)되 315
7.2.5 –(아/어)도 315
7.2.5.1 –(아/어)도 in permissive constructions 317
7.2.5.2 *Don't have to . . .* with –지 않아도 318

Contents

7.2.5.3 Idiomatic –(아/어)도 expressions 318
7.2.6 –더라도 319
7.2.7 –고도 320
7.2.8 –(아/어)서라도 320
7.2.9 –(으)ㄴ들 321
7.2.10 –(으)ㄹ지라도 321
7.2.11 –(으)ㄹ지언정 322
7.2.12 –(으)ㄹ망정 322
7.2.13 –거늘 323
7.2.14 –느니 323
7.2.15 –(아/어) 봤자 324
7.3 Additional and sequential connectives 325
7.3.1 –고 325
7.3.2 –고서 328
7.3.3 –고는 329
7.3.4 –고 나– 330
7.3.5 –답시고/랍시고 330
7.3.6 –거니와 331
7.3.7 –(으)면서 332
7.3.8 –(으)면서부터 333
7.3.9 –(으)며 333
7.3.10 –자(마자) 334
7.3.11 –다(가) 335
7.3.12 –(으)ㄴ/는데 339
7.3.13 –(으)ㄹ텐데 344
7.4 Optional connectives 345
7.4.1 –거나 345
7.4.2 –든지 347
7.4.3 –든가 348
7.4.4 –(으)ㄴ/는지 in oblique questions 349
7.4.5 –(으)ㄹ지 in oblique questions 351
7.4.6 –(었/았)던지 in oblique questions 352
7.4.7 –(으)ㄹ락 말락 (하–) 353
7.5 Conditional connectives 353
7.5.1 –(으)면 353
7.5.1.1 –(았/었)으면 좋– 355
7.5.1.2 –(으)면 고맙겠– 356
7.5.1.3 –(았/었)으면 하– 356
7.5.1.4 –(으)면 되– 356
7.5.1.5 –(으)면 안 되– 357

7.5.1.6 –지 않으면 안 되–/안 . . . 면 안 되– 358
7.5.2 –다면/–라면 358
7.5.3 –(으)려면 359
7.5.4 –다(가) 보면 360
7.5.5 –(았/었)더라면 360
7.5.6 –거든 361
7.5.7 –(아/어)야 362
7.5.7.1 –(아/어)야 되/하– 363
7.5.8 –(아/어)서야 364
7.5.9 –(으)면 . . . –(으)ㄹ수록 365
7.6 Causative connectives 366
7.6.1 –게 366
7.6.2 –게끔 367
7.6.3 –도록 368
7.7 Intentive connectives 369
7.7.1 –(으)러 369
7.7.2 –(으)려고 370
7.7.3 –고자 373
7.8 Comparison connectives 374
7.8.1 –듯이 374
7.8.2 –다시피 375

Chapter 8 Modifiers 377

8.1 Modifying forms 377
8.1.1 The future/prospective modifier –(으)ㄹ 378
8.1.2 The present dynamic modifier –는 380
8.1.3 The state/result modifier –(으)ㄴ 381
8.1.4 The continuous past modifier –던 384
8.1.5 The discontinuous past modifier –(았/었)던 385
8.1.6 The prospective past modifier –(았/었)을 387
8.1.7 Intentive –(으)려 with modifiers 387
8.2 Sentence patterns with modifier clauses 388
8.2.1 –는 가운데 'in the middle of ' 388
8.2.2 modifier + 것 'the fact that' 388
8.2.3 modifier + 것 같– 'it seems that' 391

8.2.4 –(으)ㄹ 겸 'with the combined purpose of' 392
8.2.5 –(으)ㄹ 계획이– 'plan to' 392
8.2.6 –(으)ㄴ|는 김에 'while you're at it', 'seeing as' 393
8.2.7 –는|던 길(에) 'on the way to' 394
8.2.8 –(으)ㄴ 나머지 'as a result' 394
8.2.9 –(으)ㄴ다음/뒤/후에 'after' 395
8.2.10 –는|–(으)ㄴ 대로 'in accordance with' 395
8.2.11 –는 데 'in the matter of' 396
8.2.12 –는 동안/사이에 'while' 396
8.2.13 –(으)ㄹ|–는|–(으)ㄴ 둥 'may or may not' 398
8.2.14 –(으)ㄹ|–는|–(으)ㄴ 듯 'just like' 398
8.2.15 –(으)ㄹ|–는|–(으)ㄴ 듯하–/듯 싶– 'seem like' 399
8.2.16 –(으)ㄹ 따름이– 'only' 399
8.2.17 –(으)ㄹ 때 'when' 400
8.2.18 –(으)ㄹ 리 없– 'no way that' 401
8.2.19 –는/ –(으)ㄴ 마당에 'in the situation where' 402
8.2.20 –(으)ㄹ 만하– 'worth' 402
8.2.21 –(으)ㄹ|–는|–(으)ㄴ 모양이– 'seem like' 403
8.2.22 –(으)ㄹ 바에(는/야) 'rather . . . than' 403
8.2.23 –(으)ㄴ|–는 바람에 'because of' 404
8.2.24 –(으)ㄴ|–는 반면(에) 'but on the other hand' 404
8.2.25 –(으)ㄹ 뻔하– 'nearly' 405
8.2.26 –(으)ㄹ 뿐 'only' 406
8.2.27 –(으)ㄹ 수 있–/없– 'can /cannot' 408
8.2.28 –(으)ㄴ|는 이상(에(는)) 'since'; 'unless' 410
8.2.29 –(으)ㄴ|–는 일/적이 있–/없– 'ever/ never' 411
8.2.30 –(으)ㄹ 정도로 'to the extent that' 411
8.2.31 –(으)ㄹ|–는|–(으)ㄴ 줄 알– /모르– 'think/know' 412
8.2.32 –는 중에/도중에 'in the middle of . . .' 414
8.2.33 –는 중– 'be in the middle of' 414
8.2.34 –(으)ㄹ 즈음(에) 'when' 415

8.2.35 –(으)ㄴ 지 'since' 416
8.2.36 –(으)려던 참이– 'just about to' 416
8.2.37 –(으)ㄴ 채(로) 'as it is' 417
8.2.38 –는 척하– 'pretend' 418
8.2.39 –는/–(으)ㄴ 탓 'due to' 419
8.2.40 –(으)ㄴ/–는 통에 'in the commotion' 419
8.2.41 –(으)ㄴ/는 한– 'as much as' 420

Chapter 9 Sentence endings **421**

9.1 –고말고 'of course' 422
9.2 –거든 'it's because', 'you see' 423
9.3 –나?/ –(으)ㄴ가? dubitative questions 424
9.4 –(는)군, –(는)구나, –(는)구려, –(는)구만/구먼 exclamations 426
9.5 –네 evidential exclamations 428
9.6 –다마다 'of course' 429
9.7 –담/람 disapproval 429
9.8 –(으)ㄹ걸 presumptions, regrets 430
9.9 –(으)ㄹ게 promise-like futures 432
9.10 –(으)ㄹ까? suggestions, tentative questions 433
9.11 –(으)ㄹ래 'feel like (doing)' 436
9.12 –(으)ㄹ텐데 'I'm afraid' 436
9.13 –(으)랴 'could . . . really?' 437
9.14 –(으)련마는/ –(으)련만 'should, must' 438
9.15 –(으)렴/–(으)려무나 granting permission; orders 439
9.16 –(으)마 promise-like futures 440
9.17 –잖아 'you know' 440
9.18 –지 tag questions 442

Chapter 10 Quotations **446**

10.1 Direct quotations 446
10.2 Indirect quotations 447
10.2.1 Quoted statements 448
10.2.2 Quoted questions 450
10.2.3 Quoted proposals 452
10.2.4 Quoted commands 453
10.2.5 The verb 주– in quoted commands 454
10.2.6 Quoting verbs 455

10.3 Reduced indirect quotations in reported speech 458
10.3.1 –다고, –냐고, –라고, –자고 459
10.3.2 –대, –내, –래, –재 461
10.4 Special patterns with indirect quotations 463
10.4.1 –다/냐/자/라니(까) 464
10.4.2 –다면/ –라면 465
10.4.3 –다/라면서 465
10.4.4 –다/라는데 466
10.4.5 –(이)라는 467
10.4.6 –단/냔/잔/란 말이– 468

Chapter 11 Other word classes 469

11.1 Adnouns 469
11.2 Adverbs 472
11.2.1 Grammatical classification of adverbs 472
11.2.1.1 Proper adverbs 472
11.2.1.2 Derived adverbs 474
11.2.1.3 Sentence adverbs 479
11.2.1.4 Conjunctive adverbs 481
11.2.2 Semantic classification of adverbs 482
11.2.2.1 Time adverbs 482
11.2.2.2 Degree adverbs 485
11.2.2.3 Manner adverbs 486
11.2.2.4 Onomatopoeic/mimetic adverbs 488
11.3 Prefixes and suffixes 494
11.3.1 Prefixes 494
11.3.2 Suffixes 498
11.3.2.1 Noun-deriving suffixes 498
11.3.2.2 Adverb-deriving suffixes 504
11.3.2.3 Verb-deriving suffixes 504
11.3.2.4 Adnominal suffix –적 506

Glossary of linguistic terms 508

Related readings and bibliography 515

Index of grammatical constructions (Korean) 519

Index of translation equivalents (English) 539

General index 547

Preface to the second edition

This revised edition of *Korean: A Comprehensive Grammar* is a thorough reference guide to Korean grammar updated based on the latest research. The level of description that the revised book offers of Korean grammatical constructions throughout is perhaps unrivalled by other English-language publications in the field. Revisions from the first edition include:

- A separate chapter on honorifics, reflecting new research in this field
- Updated descriptions of Korean grammar taking into account the latest research in functional syntax, pragmatics and language variation and change
- More low-frequency grammar patterns have been added

With the exception of chapter 1 (which provides an introduction to the Korean language), the book is organized according to grammatical categories. In turn, we look at nouns, nominal forms, pronouns and numbers (chapter 2), case particles (chapter 3), verbs (chapter 4), support (or 'auxiliary') verbs (chapter 5), honorifics and politeness (chapter 6), verbal connectives (chapter 7), modifiers (chapter 8), sentence endings (chapter 9), quotations (chapter 10) and other word classes (chapter 11). In cases where a grammatical pattern may belong to more than one category, the pattern is allotted to the category that it fits best and is then cross-referenced under the other possible category. Three indexes are included at the back of the book: a grammatical patterns index (in Korean), an English equivalents index and a general index.

As readers who already have some familiarity with the language will know, the way that Korean is spoken (or written) will vary greatly depending on whom you are talking (or writing) to. This phenomenon – and the use of honorifics and speech styles – is covered in Chapter 6. Elsewhere, the common practice has been to represent examples in the so-called 'polite' speech style wherever possible. At times, the inclusion of other speech styles is necessitated by the fact that the grammatical construction being described or the example being given is more 'natural' in another style rather than the 'polite'.

We would like to express our thanks to many people who provided us with various forms of comments and feedback on the first edition. We are particularly indebted to Professor Hyo-Sang Lee at Indiana University Bloomington for his numerous insightful comments. Thanks also to Professor Hee Rak Chae at Hankuk University of Foreign Studies for providing us with a list of corrections, and Professor Jung Soo Mok at University of Seoul for writing a useful review. We would like to thank Dr. Adam Zulawnik for his help compiling the index.

This work was supported by Laboratory Program for Korean Studies through the Ministry of Education of the Republic of Korea and Korean Studies Promotion Service of the Academy of Korean Studies (AKS-2016-LAB-2250003).

Chapter 1

Introduction to the Korean Language

1.1 Characteristic features of Korean

Overview

Korean is a language with approximately 82 million speakers which include 51 million in South Korea, 25 million in North Korea, and nearly 6 million outside of Korea – mainly in China, the US, Japan, and central Asia (the former U.S.S.R). The data used in this book represents the standard Seoul speech in the Central dialectal zone. Due to its prevalence in education and the media, Standard Seoul Korean is intelligible across South Korea. Although the post-1945 division between North and South Korea and their different language policies have made the two Koreas linguistically divergent, North and South Korean languages are mutually intelligible.

Korean has a number of characteristic features that distinguish it from other languages, particularly English and European languages. For example, Korean has neither the definite nor indefinite article (such as 'the' and 'a/an' in English). There is no sharp distinction of gender and plurality of a noun. There is no special distinction for the third-person present singular in a verb. There is no conspicuous accent for a word, although there are some accents in a sentence and these vary according to the region of the country. As a general rule, Korean usually puts stress on the first syllable of a word.

The linguistic affinity of Korean to other languages is still disputable. The most convincing hypothesis about its origin is the Altaic hypothesis, that is Korean is one of the Altaic languages along with Mongolian, Turkic and Manchu-Tungus. The difficulty of reconstructing genetic ties to other languages is mainly due to the lack of evidence of written data.

1.1.1 Word classes

As in any language, Korean words can be classified into several different classes according to the way they are used.

Korean **verbs** minimally consist of a **base** and an **ending**. The base cannot stand alone without an ending, and endings can be added to the base to alter the meaning in various ways, including the expression of tense:

먹어요.	*I am eating.*
먹었어요.	*I ate.*
먹겠어요.	*I will eat.*

In the examples above, the verb base in each sentence is the same. It means 'eat' – and its base is 먹–. However, by attaching three different endings, three different meanings are produced.

While languages such as English have a separate category of adjectives (and use these adjectives in combination with the verb 'to be' – 'He is tall', etc.), in Korean adjectives can be considered a subset of verbs. These are known as **descriptive verbs**, whereas other verbs (that typically depict an action) are known as **processive verbs**. In most ways, descriptive verbs behave the same as processive verbs and can take a lot of the same endings:

예뻐요.	*[She, it, etc.] is pretty.*
예뻤어요.	*[She, it, etc.] was pretty.*
예쁘겠어요.	*[She, it, etc.] will be pretty.*

However, there are some differences in the way that descriptive and processive verbs operate. These differences are summarized later in this book (refer to 4.1.1). The major properties of Korean verbs are discussed in Chapter 4.

Unlike verbs, Korean **nouns** can be used with no endings attached to them. Instead, **particles** are added to show the relationship between the noun and the rest of the sentence (especially the verb). In the following sentence, 가 marks 민수 as being the grammatical subject of the sentence (i.e., the person performing the action connoted in the verb) and 를 marks 오징어 'squid' as being the grammatical object (i.e., the thing having the action connoted by the verb performed on it). Without these markers, the sentence could (in context) be taken to mean that it was the squid that ate Minsu rather than the other way around!

민수가	오징어를	먹었어요	
Minsu S	squid O	ate	*Minsu ate squid.*

Korean nouns are described in more depth in Chapter 2 and particles are discussed in Chapter 3. Korean also contains more minor word classes (such as adnouns and adverbs), which are explained in Chapter 10.

1.1.2 Word order: Korean is an SOV language

The basic (i.e., most frequent, neutral and canonical) word order of Korean can be described as SOV: Subject-Object-Verb. With the verb coming after rather than before the object, this makes Korean word order quite different from English:

English:	Minsu	ate	kimchi
	SUBJECT	VERB	OBJECT
Korean:	민수가	김치를	먹었어요
	Minsu	kimchi	ate
	SUBJECT	OBJECT	VERB

As an SOV language, Korean has several other features which are typical of such languages (but different to English). These features are summarized below.

1.1.2.1 Flexible word order

Although the word order presented above is the most typical, Korean word order can actually be quite flexible. In addition to

'Minsu kimchi ate', it is quite possible to also say 'kimchi Minsu ate'.

김치는	민수가	먹었어요
Kimchi	Minsu	Ate
OBJECT	SUBJECT	VERB

As in the example above, when a non-subject element is moved to the start of the sentence, it often takes the topic particle 는 rather than the object particle 를 (refer to 3.2.2).

So how do speakers choose which word order to use? As a general rule of thumb, the noun that conveys new or added knowledge to the hearer will come closer to the verb, whereas nouns that represent already mentioned or entertained information may come at the start of the sentence. By this logic, if a speaker asks 'what did 민수 eat?', the interlocutor will put 민수 at the start of the answer and the type of food (김치) before the verb. Conversely, if a speaker asks 'who ate the kimchi?', the order of the nouns will be reversed, as shown here:

New info goes at the end.

A: 민수는 뭐 먹었어요?	WHAT did Minsu eat?
B: (민수는) 김치를 먹었어요	Minsu ate KIMCHI (new information)
A: 누가 김치를 먹었어요?	WHO ate the kimchi?
B: (김치는) 민수가 먹었어요.	MINSU ate the kimchi

Like in the above examples, as long as the verb is properly placed at the end of the sentence, the position of the remaining words is relatively free. Although, technically speaking the verb should always come last in a Korean sentence, in real speech this is not always the case. On occasions, other elements may be heard following the verb:

내 친구는 뛰어갔어요, **집으로**.	*My friend ran to his house.*
나는 영희를 보았어요, **어제 여기서**.	*I saw Yonghi, yesterday here.*

As in these examples, once a complete sentence has been uttered, it may be supplemented with further constituents which appear after the verb. This tends to happen when the speaker realizes that he/she has omitted important information from the sentence or when, judging from the hearer's reaction, he/she realizes that more clarification is needed. Although such word order is considered nonstandard and does not appear in writing, it can frequently be heard in casual speech.

1.1.2.2 *The postpositional characteristic of Korean*

Another distinctive feature of Korean which is connected to its SOV word order is the fact that it has postpositions (that come after the noun) rather than prepositions (which come before the noun). Rather than saying 'at school' as in English, Korean speakers say 'school-at':

민수가	학교에	있어요.
Minsu-subject	school-at	is

Minsu is at school.

In addition to postpositions that are the equivalent of English prepositions, Korean uses particles attached to the end of nouns to mark their grammatical function, as noted above. As well as particles coming after nouns, typical of languages with an SOV language, Korean also attaches suffixes (or verb endings) to the end of verbs. Although it is true that English also has suffixes that attach to verbs (e.g., work<u>s</u>, work<u>ed</u>, work<u>ing</u>, eat<u>en</u>), these suffixes in English are few in number, whereas in Korean they are numerous.

민수**가**	산**에서**	뱀**을**	잡**았어요**.
Minsu-**subject**	mountain-**on**	snake-**object**	catch-**past tense-polite**

Minsu caught a snake on the mountain.

선생님**은**	좋**으시었겠습니다**.
You (lit. 'teacher')-**topic**	happy-**honorific-past-must-formal**

You must have been happy.

As we can see, particles must come after the noun, and verbal suffixes must be attached behind the stem. Also, it is clear that two or more particles may follow the noun, and, as you can see in the last example above, even as many as four verb endings may attach to a verb stem. It is to this extent that in Korean important items are established at the very end of the sentence.

1.1.2.3 The position of complements

In Korean, words that complement or modify (i.e., elaborate, describe, clarify, identify, delimit) a noun always and without exception come before the noun in question:

Adnoun (refer to 11.1)	**다른** other	사람 person	*another person*
Possessive + Noun	**민호의** Minho's	담배 cigarettes	*Minho's cigarettes*
Modifying clause + Noun	**마신** drink	술 alcohol	*the alcohol that I drank*
Adverb + Verb	**빨리** quickly	갔어요 went	*went quickly*

On this point, Korean differs from Indo-European languages, in which the modifier may also follow the modified. In particular, note how the last two patterns listed above result in different word orders than those found in English.

1.1.2.4 Interrogative word order

In Korean, the word order in yes/no interrogatives (questions) does not change from that of statements. Unlike in English, the position of subject and verb does not alter. In fact, in certain styles of speech (refer to 6.1), the same sentence can be interpreted as a statement or as an interrogative purely depending on intonation:

민수가 집에 가요

Minsu is going home. (with falling intonation)

Is Minsu going home? (with rising intonation)

In so-called wh-questions, the question word (where, why, when, what, etc.) does not need to come at the beginning of the sentence (as it typically does in English). Usually, it stays in the same place where the 'missing' information being asked for would be included in the corresponding answer. In the following examples, see how the Korean word for 'what' in the question appears in the same position as 'fruit' in the answer. Also note how this is not the case in English, where 'what' moves to initial position.

A: 민수가 지금 **무엇**을 사고 있어요? ***What*** *is Minsu buying now?*

B: 민수는 지금 **과일**을 사고 있어요. *Minsu is buying* ***fruit*** *now.*

1.1.3 An intricate system of honorific categories

Although every language has different registers and levels of politeness, in few languages is this system encoded in an elaborate system of honorifics as it is in Korean. Along with Japanese, Korean is one of the few languages in which the speaker can systematically encode his/her social relationship with the hearer and people he/she is talking about (and between different people he/she is talking about) through the addition of grammatical markers and special sets of vocabulary. When speaking Korean, it is practically impossible to utter a single sentence without bearing in mind your social position in relation to the hearer and people you are referring to (i.e., comparative age and rank, level of intimacy, etc.).

Honorifics can commonly be broken into two groups: hearer honorifics and referent honorifics. Hearer honorifics – more frequently referred to as 'speech styles' in the case of Korean (refer to 6.1) index the relationship between the speaker and the hearer (and/or immediate audience). In Korean, this is achieved by a range of six different 'speech styles'. As a taster of this, when addressing an intimate of similar age or younger (or a child), the speaker may apply the 'intimate' speech style as in the sentence below, which consists of the –어 verb ending:

버스가 벌써 갔**어** *The bus has gone* (*intimate speech style*)

However, when speaking to a non-intimate or someone of superior age or rank, the –어요 ending of the 'polite' speech style would be more appropriate:

버스가 벌써 갔**어요** *The bus has gone* *(polite speech style)*

Referent honorifics (refer to 6.2) mark the relationship between the speaker and the grammatical subject/object of the sentence. This may either be the hearer him/herself or a third person. In the most complex of cases, this can result in an 'honorific' sentence that looks quite different to its 'non-honorific counterpart':

선생님**께서** **진지**를 **잡수십**니다.	*The teacher is eating a meal. (honorific)*
제 친구**가** **밥**을 **먹**습니다.	*My friend is eating a meal.*

In the 'honorific' sentence, respect is shown to the teacher by using the honorific subject particle –께서, the honorific noun for meal 진지 and the honorific verb for eat 잡수시– (which incorporates the honorific marker –시–). In the 'non-honorific sentence', when discussing one's friend, the plain counterparts of these words may be used instead. Although the two sentences have the same meaning, they are composed of two totally different vocabulary sets.

The reasons why Korean and Japanese have developed such elaborate systems of honorifics are not totally clear. However, the perpetuation of the Korean system has seemingly been influenced by the hierarchical structure of Korean society. Even in modern-day South Korea, families, companies, schools, etc. have rigid vertical social structures in which younger parties are expected to show deference and compliance towards elders and seniors. In some situations, an age difference of only one year may be enough to trigger a non-reciprocal pattern of honorifics (in which the younger party uses honorifics, but receives plain forms).

1.1.4 Korean as an elliptical language

Every language has full sentences in which all constituents are present, and elliptical sentences in which certain words are dropped. However, a peculiar feature of Korean is that major constituents such as the subject and the object can readily be dropped from the sentence. On this point Korean differs from Indo-European languages, in which – apart from certain grammatically sanctioned drops (for example, 'you' does not need to be included in English imperatives such as 'go home!') – the subject should normatively be present in order to produce a well-formed sentence. To be sure, English speakers sometimes drop major constituents too (consider examples such as 'Hope this helps!' or 'Going home?'), but such utterances always sound casual and may not be considered as complete, well-formed sentences. In Korean, however, dropping major constituents is highly frequent and usually does not result in any question that the sentence is incomplete or poorly formed.

The general rule is that major constituents such as subjects and objects can be dropped when these can easily be worked out from context. For example, when two acquaintances meet by chance on the street, the following question is understood as meaning 'where are you going?' even though there is no explicit mention of 'you':

어디 가요? *Where are [you] going?*

With this dropping of constituents, many Korean sentences contain nothing but a verb. In the following, unless a different contextual frame is in operation, the sentence will normally be understood as referring to the first person:

먹었어요. *I've eaten.*

Although including the subject (and/or object) is hardly ever incorrect, in many cases it seems superfluous and could even sound clumsy.

1.2 Korean script and pronunciation

Overview

Korean is written using an alphabetic writing system known both in South Korea and internationally as Hangul (한글) but in North Korea as *Chosŏngul* (조선글). Unlike the majority of writing systems that came into being through a process of evolution, Hangul is a deliberate invention dating back to the 15th century (1443). The invention of Hangul is attributed to

King Sejong the Great, who was the fourth King of the Chosŏn dynasty (1392–1910).

Although Korean people today exclusively use Hangul in most everyday writing activities, Korean can also be written in a mixed script combining this phonemic system with logographic Chinese characters, known in Korean as *Hancha* (한자; 漢字). In South Korea, the use of *Hancha* has greatly decreased in recent years and is now mainly limited to sporadic use in broadsheet newspapers and some academic publications. North Korea does not use Chinese characters at all.

There are several different systems for rendering Korean in the Roman script. When Romanizations are given in this book (such as for the word *Hancha* above), they typically appear in the McCune-Reischauer system, as this is generally the most convenient for native English speakers. It should be noted however that South Korea has now stopped using this system in favour of the Revised Romanization system.

The current section provides a concise introduction to Hangul and the sounds of Korean that are associated to it. It should be noted that the pronunciations given are based on the 'standard' language of Seoul. This may at times differ from the pronunciations you will hear in real everyday conversation, particularly from Koreans who speak regional dialects.

1.2.1 Basic principles of Hangul writing

Hangul is an alphabetic writing system. This means that vowels and consonants are represented with letter-like symbols. Modern Korean has a total of 24 basic letter shapes, which extends to 40 when one includes compound letters.

The current section introduces the names of the characters and the way that they are written syllabically.

1.2.1.1 Letter names and dictionary order

The Hangul letters are summarized in the following table, with their names and sorted by the normal South Korean dictionary order.

Regarding the names of consonants, note that these are normatively composed of two syllables that are most commonly formed as follows, taking ㅂ as an example:

First syllable: Character in question, followed by the vowel 'ㅣ' (e.g., for ㅂ, '비')

Second syllable: The Character in question, preceded by the vowel 'ㅡ' (e.g., for ㅂ, '읍')

Note that the consonant names 기역, 디귿 and 시옷 are exceptions to this formula. However, in North Korea, these exceptions have been abolished and the regular 기윽, 디읃 and 시읏 are used instead.

Regarding the dictionary order of characters, note that consonants and vowels have separate sequences. The consonant sequence has priority, and letters in the same line appear in sequence after the left-most letter:

Consonant signs (with names)			*Vowels*						
ㄱ	(기역)	ㄲ (쌍기역)	ㅏ				ㅐ	ㅑ	ㅒ
ㄴ	(니은)		ㅓ				ㅔ	ㅕ	ㅖ
ㄷ	(디귿)	ㄸ (쌍디귿)	ㅗ	ㅘ	ㅙ	ㅚ		ㅛ	
ㄹ	(리을)		ㅜ	ㅝ	ㅞ	ㅟ		ㅠ	
ㅁ	(미음)		ㅡ			ㅢ			
ㅂ	(비읍)	ㅃ (쌍비읍)	ㅣ						
ㅅ	(시옷)	ㅆ (쌍시옷)							
ㅇ	(이응)								
ㅈ	(지읒)	ㅉ (쌍지읒)							
ㅊ	(치읓)								
ㅋ	(키읔)								
ㅌ	(티읕)								
ㅍ	(피읖)								
ㅎ	(히읗)								

1.2.1.2 *Writing syllabically*

Although Hangul has individual letters for consonants and vowels, these 'letters' are not written in a linear fashion such as in the

Roman alphabet. Instead, they are grouped together into square syllable blocks according to the following principles:

1 Each syllable block must begin with a consonant sign. Where a spoken syllable begins with a vowel, the absence of the initial consonant is written with the 'zero' letter ㅇ:

Spoken	*Written*	*Meaning*
[a-u]	아우	*younger brother/sister*
[o-i]	오이	*Cucumber*

2 The consonant letter (represented below as 'C') is placed either to the left or above the sign for the following vowel ('V'), depending on the vowel sign's shape, resulting in two possible patterns:

when vowel sign is vertical	CV	아 버 지
when vowel sign is horizontal	C over V	주 유 소

Note that in the case of [Horizontal + Vertical] vowel letter compounds (ㅘ, ㅙ, ㅚ, ㅝ, ㅞ, ㅟ, ㅢ), where the horizontal letter represents a w-like sound, the initial consonant sign appears in the empty top left corner:

when vowel sign is vertical and horizontal	C over V, V	외 과

3 A syllable-final consonant letter is always written underneath the initial consonant-vowel grouping, with height adjustments for a square end product:

when vowel sign is vertical	CV over C	정 말
when vowel sign is horizontal	C over V over C	음 운
when vowel sign is vertical and horizontal	CV over V over C	원

4 There are no Hangul blocks with two initial consonant signs (except for the double consonant letters ㄲ, ㄸ, ㅃ, ㅆ, ㅉ). There are, however, some Hangul blocks with two final consonant signs written at the bottom:

when vowel sign is vertical	CV / CC	삶	닭
when vowel sign is horizontal	C / V / CC	몫	굶

Note, however, that due to restrictions against consonant clusters, both of these consonants can only be pronounced if they are followed by a vowel (refer to 1.2.3.1, 1.2.3.2).

1.2.2 Hangul pronunciation guide

The current section provides basic guidelines regarding how each of the 40 Hangul letter shapes should most normally be pronounced. Note, however, that there are a number of changes between the way that Korean is written and the way that it is pronounced. Although some basic sound changes are dealt with in this section, the majority of irregular pronunciations are described in the next section (refer to 1.2.3).

1.2.2.1 Simple vowels

In terms of their graphic representation, it can be said that Korean has six simple vowel shapes (ㅏ, ㅓ, ㅗ, ㅜ, ㅡ, ㅣ). However, in terms of phonetics, ㅐ and ㅔ should also be included as simple vowels since they are pronounced as such in contemporary Korean even though they historically originate in the combinations [ㅏ+ㅣ] and [ㅓ+ㅣ]. This means that phonetically Korean has eight vowels, although this typically reduces to seven since most speakers pronounce ㅐ and ㅔ identically (see below).

Since any Hangul block must begin with a consonant symbol, syllables that begin with a vowel in pronunciation are written with the zero symbol 'ㅇ' to the left or above the vowel sign. Written in syllable-block form, the eight simple vowels are as follows.

For each vowel, we give an English equivalent, the relevant phonetic symbol and how the vowel is represented in the McCune-Reischauer system of Romanization:

	English parallels	*Phonetic symbol*	*McCune-Reischauer*
아	A in *father*	[ɑ]	a
어	British English: O in *often* American English: U in *burn*	[ʌ]	ŏ
오	O in *core*	[o]	o
우	like OO in *moon*	[u]	u
으	like U in *urgh!*	[ɯ]	ŭ
이	EE in *feet* (but usually shorter!)	[i]	i
애	British English: A in care American English: A in apple	[æ]	ae
에	E in *bed*	[ɛ]	e

It should be noted that many native speakers of Korean (particularly younger generations) do not differentiate between 애 and 에 and pronounce both of these as a sound somewhere between the two.

1.2.2.2 *Y-vowels*

Korean has six Y-vowels that consist of a 'y'-like sound before a simple vowel. The Y vowels are written by adding one additional short stroke to the relevant simple vowel signs. Written in syllable-block form, the Y vowels are as follows:

Hangul sign		*English Parallels*	*Phonetic symbol*	*McCune-Reischauer*
Simple	***Y-vowel***			
아	야	YA in *yahoo*	[jɑ]	ya
어	여	British English: Yo in *yob* American Eng: YEA in *yearn*	[jʌ]	yŏ

오	요	YO in *yoga*	[jo]	yo
우	유	YOU in *youth*	[ju]	yu
애	얘	British English: YA in *yay!* American Eng: YA in *yak*	[jæ]	yae
에	예	like YE in *yet* or *yes*	[jɛ]	ye

Many native speakers of Korean (particularly younger generations) do not differentiate between 얘 and 예 and pronounce both of these as a sound somewhere between the two.

1.2.2.3 W-vowels

Korean has six W-vowels that consist of a 'w'-like sound (as in English *was*) before a simple vowel. The W vowels are written by combining the horizontal letters ㅗ [o] or ㅜ [u] with one of the vertical letters ㅏ, ㅓ, ㅐ, ㅔ and ㅣ. Their pronunciation is generally what one would expect from these combinations, except for the W vowel that is written as [ㅗ+ㅣ] but usually pronounced as [wɛ].

Hangul sign		*English parallels*	*Phonetic symbol*	*McCune-Reischauer*
Elements	***W-vowel***			
오+아	와	British Eng: WA in *wag* Am Eng: WA in *swan*	[wɑ]	wa
우+어	워	like WO in *wonder*	[wʌ]	wŏ
오+애	왜	like WEA in *wear*	[wæ]	wæ
우+에	웨	like WE in *wet*	[wɛ]	we
오+이	외	usually like WE in *wet*	[wɛ]	oe
우+이	위	like WEE in *weep*	[wi]	wi

Not only do native speakers tend to pronounce 웨 and 외 the same, but many speakers (particularly younger generations) do not differentiate between these two and 왜.

Note that, although 외 and 위 are pronounced as [wɛ] and [wi] by the majority of speakers of Seoul Korean, these are not the original pronunciations of these vowels. Historically, 외 and 위 were pronounced in accordance with the way that they are written as combinations of [o] and [u] followed by a 'y'-like sound [j]. These complex vowels then transformed into the simple vowels [ö] (similar to the German ö umlaut) and 위 as [ü] (similar to the vowel sound in French 'rue' or 'tu'), before finally changing into the pronunciations we know today. You may still hear 외 and 위 pronounced as [ö] and [ü] by some older speakers.

1.2.2.4 *The compound vowel 의*

Korean has one complex vowel, 의, which consists of a glide from 으 [ɨ] to 이 [i] (and which is romanized in the McCune-Reischauer system as ŭi). However, this vowel is only ever pronounced in this way when it occurs at the start of a word without being preceded by any consonant. In other positions, it is pronounced the same as '이' (i.e., like EE in feet). These two pronunciations are summarized below:

Position	*Pronunciation*	*Examples*
Word-initial (at the start of a word, with no preceding consonant)	Quick glide from [으] to [이]	의자 = [**으이**자]/ [**ii**-ja]
Not word-initial (after consonant or in second or later syllable)	[이] only	띄고 = [**띠**고]/ [**tti**-ko] 거의 = [거**이**]/[kʌ-**i**]

Also, bear in mind that 의 typically takes on the irregular pronunciation of 에 (i.e., like E in *bed*) when it appears as the possessive particle 의 (refer to 3.2.3). In the most complex of examples, 의 may be pronounced in three different ways within one short phrase:

written as: 민주주의의 의의 **pronounced as:** [민주주이에 의이]

the significance of democracy

Even when 의 appear in initial position, you may sometimes hear it pronounced as a simple vowel (i.e., like 으 or 이), particularly in dialectal speech.

1.2.2.5 Basic consonants

Korean has ten basic consonants that are presented in the table below. As can be seen, the first four consonants have separate 'voiced' and 'unvoiced' pronunciations. These will be explained below.

Sign	*(Name)*	*English Parallels*		*Phonetic symbol(s)*	*McCune-Reischauer*
		When unvoiced:	*When voiced:*		
ㅂ	(비읍)	P, as in *park*, but more relaxed	B, as in *about*	[p]/[b]	p, b
ㄷ	(디귿)	T, as in *tall*, but more relaxed	D, as in *idea*	[t]/[d]	t, d
ㅈ	(지읒)	CH, as in *child*, but more relaxed	J, as in *injury*	[ʧ]/[ʤ]	ch, j
ㄱ	(기역)	K, as in *kill*, but more relaxed	G, as in *again*	[k]/[g]	k, g
ㅅ	(시옷)	S, as in *sky*, but more relaxed **or** SH as in *shin* (see below)		[s] [ʃ]	s sh
ㅁ	(미음)	M, as in *mother*		[m]	m
ㄴ	(니은)	N, as in *net*		[n]	n
ㅇ	(이응)	NG, as in *sing*		[ŋ]	ng
ㄹ	(리을)	Tongue-flap R as in Scottish *rock* or *Mary* **or** Tongue-tip L in British *let* or *lip* (see below)		[ɾ] [l]	r l
ㅎ	(히읗)	H, as in *hack* or *hope*, but with much heavier breath release		[h]	h

Further notes regarding the pronunciation of these consonants are as follows:

1. Pronunciation of ㅂ, ㄷ, ㅈ, ㄱ

As shown in the above table, the primary pronunciation of these is similar to English P, T, CH and K. Like P, T, CH and K, they are unvoiced (i.e., pronounced without voice sounds in the vocal cords). However, **unlike** English P, T, CH and K, they are unaspirated (pronounced followed by no or very little release of air). To approximate the Korean pronunciations, attempt to pronounce the corresponding English sounds **without** a following puff of air.

However, the table also shows that these consonants can – in some environments – become voiced (i.e., pronounced **with** voice sounds in the vocal cords) and thus sound similar to the English B, D, J and G respectively. This happens under the following conditions:

1 When the consonant occurs between two vowels. Note how, in the following examples, the first appearance of the consonant is unvoiced and the second (between two vowels) is voiced:

Hangul	*McCune-Reischauer*	*Meaning*
바보	pabo	*fool*
도둑	toduk	*thief*
자주	chaju	*often*
고기	kogi	*meat*

2 When the consonant occurs after the voiced consonants ㅁ, ㄴ, ㅇ and ㄹ:

갈비	kalbi	*ribs*
침대	ch'imdae	*bed*
안주	anju	*appetizers*
경기	kyŏngi	*game, match*

2. Pronunciation of ㅅ

The basic pronunciation of ㅅ is akin to that of S in English, if somewhat weaker. Whereas in English the tongue is grooved, making a narrow path for the airflow and producing more hissing, in Korean the tongue is flattened out and relaxed. Perhaps due to this more relaxed tongue shape, when ㅅ occurs before 'ㅣ', any of the Y-vowels or 위, its pronunciation softens to SH:

사실	sashil	*truth, fact*
샤워	shawŏ	*shower*
쉼표	shwimp'yo	*a pause*

3. Pronunciation of ㅇ

As previously noted, when ㅇ occurs at the start of syllable, it is a 'zero consonant' that is not pronounced. The pronunciation as NG [ŋ] only applies when it occurs at the bottom of a syllable block:

영양	Yŏngyang	*nutrition*
잉어	ing-ŏ	*a carp*

4. Pronunciation of ㄹ

ㄹ has multiple pronunciations depending on where it appears in a word:

1 When it occurs between vowels (such as in 보라 *purple or* 머리 *head*), it is pronounced as 'tongue-flap' R. 'Tongue-flap' R is pronounced by briefly tapping the front of the tongue against the bone ridge behind the teeth, slightly behind the position used for [t] or [d]. Although there is no equivalent sound in most varieties of English, Scottish English, Japanese and Spanish have similar sounds.
2 When it is pronounced at the end of a syllable (비율 *ratio*) or when it occurs twice in succession (빌려요 *borrow*), it is pronounced as 'tongue-tip' L. 'Tongue-tip' L is pronounced by pressing the front of the tongue against the bone ridge behind the teeth, as in British *let* or *lip* (but not *lack* or *all*, which involve the whole tongue).
3 ㄹ does not tend to occur at the start of Korean words. In fact when Sino-Korean words starting with a character featuring an initial ㄹ, this ㄹ drops (for example, 이론 *theory*) or changes to ㄴ (for example, 노동 *labour*). Note that this rule does not apply in North Korea (where you will see words such as 리론 and 로동). Any words that do start with initial ㄹ tend to be

of foreign origins, such as 라면 *ramen* and 립스틱 *lipstick*. In such cases, ㄹ is most typically pronounced as 'tongue-flap' R, but you may also hear it pronounced as 'tongue-tip' L (particularly in words such as 립스틱 *lipstick* where the underlying English word starts with an L).

1.2.2.6 *Aspirated consonants*

In addition to its simple consonants, Korean has two other consonant sets. The first are the four Aspirated Consonants ㅍ, ㅌ, ㅊ, and ㅋ. These are the aspirated equivalents of ㅂ, ㄷ, ㅈ and ㄱ. Traditional descriptions claim that ㅍ/ㅌ/ㅊ/ㅋ are differentiated from ㅂ/ㄷ/ㅈ/ㄱ since they are pronounced accompanied by a heavy puff of air (this is what 'aspirated' means). However, more recent descriptions (for example, refer to Kang 2014) show that many speakers (particularly younger generations) pronounce both ㅂ/ㄷ/ㅈ/ㄱ and ㅍ/ㅌ/ㅊ/ㅋ with similar levels of air output and that the more important distinction is that ㅍ/ㅌ/ㅊ/ㅋ are pronounced with higher pitch on the following vowel.

Unlike ㅂ/ㄷ/ㅈ/ㄱ, ㅍ/ㅌ/ㅊ/ㅋ never become voiced.

Sign	*(Name)*	*English parallels*	*Phonetic symbol*	*MR Romanization*
ㅍ	(피읖)	P, as in *park*	[pʰ]	p'
ㅌ	(티읕)	T, as in *talk*	[tʰ]	t'
ㅊ	(치읓)	CH, as in *chat*	[ʧʰ]	ch'
ㅋ	(키읔)	K, as in *kill*	[kʰ]	k'

1.2.2.7 *Tensed or 'Double' consonants*

Korean also has five tensed consonants, which are written with the five 'double' consonant letters ㅃ, ㄸ, ㅉ, ㅆ, and ㄲ. These are pronounced by putting the mouth into the same position as that for the simple counterpart, holding the mouth tense and tight in that position, and then suddenly releasing the sound with virtually no voice and little aspiration (breath release). The following vowel takes high pitch.

The tensed 'double' consonants of Korean have no close parallel in English. They are, however, somewhat similar to Italian double consonants (PP, TT, CC) and to Japanese tensed consonants. As for English pronunciation, the closest we get to Korean ㅃ, ㄸ, ㄲ are English P, T, K when they appear after S (as in 'spy', 'style' and 'sky'), which are also pronounced without aspiration (breath release), but much less tensing. Korean ㅉ is also somewhat similar to English TCH in words such as 'matching', but more tense and with no puff of air. As for Korean ㅆ, the best parallel is a succession of English words finishing and starting on S, such as 'mass suicide', with a strong volume increase on the second S.

Sign	*(Name)*	*English parallels*	*Phonetic symbol*	*MR Romanization*
ㅃ	(쌍비읍)	P, as in *spy*, but with more tensing	[pp]/[p̤]	pp
ㄸ	(쌍디귿)	T, as in *style*, but with much more tensing	[tt]/[t̤]	tt
ㅉ	(쌍지읒)	TCH, as in *matching*, but with tensing and no breath release	[tʧ]/[ʧ̤]	tch
ㅆ	(쌍시옷)	S+S, as in *mas<u>s</u> <u>s</u>uicide*, but with initial tensing and later volume increase	[ss]/[s̤]	ss
ㄲ	(쌍기역)	K, as in *sky*, but with much more tensing	[kk]/[k̤]	kk

1.2.3 Pronunciation changes

The pronunciation of Korean is complicated by a number of changes between how it is written and how it is actually pronounced. The reason for these spelling-pronunciation irregularities is that modern Hangul spellings are not supposed to be strict transcriptions of pronunciations, but representations of underlying forms.

1.2.3.1 Pronunciation of syllable-final consonants

Generally speaking Korean consonants may appear both at the beginning or the end of a syllable. However, they are only pronounced fully according to the pronunciations detailed above (refer to 1.2.2.4, 1.2.2.5, 1.2.2.6) when they appear at the start of a syllable. When they are pronounced at the end of a syllable, they lose much of their sound mass and distinctiveness.

The reason for this is that Korean final consonants are never released. Non-release means that the speaker puts his/her mouth into the position for the consonant, but then tenses up the mouth, and finishes by relaxing it again without producing any sound. With the consonants ㅂ *p*, ㄷ *t* and ㄱ *k* this produces pronunciations quite different from English, where the corresponding sounds rely on the release of sound (and a puff of air). If you ask a Korean speaker to read the Korean words below, you should immediately feel this difference. In fact, you may find it hard to hear the final consonants at all.

Korean word		*Compare with the English . . .*
국	*soup*	cook
밥	*rice*	pap
곧	*immediately*	cot

The non-release of final consonants means that many of the distinctions between consonant sounds are lost. Without being released, many of the distinctive features of consonant sounds simply cannot be realized. This includes the plain consonants ㅈ *ch*, ㅅ *s* and ㅎ *h* and all of the aspirated and tensed consonants. Thus, although these consonants may be *written* in final position (except for ㅃ *pp*, ㄸ *tt* and ㅉ *tch*), they can never be *pronounced* in final position. Instead, as shown in the table below, these consonants are pronounced according to the closest possible non-released sound (i.e. the sound which is produced by the same part of the mouth).

Written consonant	*Pronunciation in final position*	*Example*
ㄹ	ㄹ	팔 *arm*
ㄴ	ㄴ	은 *silver*

ㅁ	ㅁ	몸 *body*
ㅇ	ㅇ	용 *dragon*
ㅂ	ㅂ	집 *house*
ㅍ		짚 [집] *straw*
ㄷ	ㄷ	받– *receive*
ㅌ		같– [갇] *be the same*
ㅈ		갖– [갇] *have, hold*
ㅊ		살갗 [살갇] *complexion, skin*
ㅅ		등갓 [등갇] *lampshade*
ㅆ		갔– [갇] *went [past stem of 'go']*
ㅎ		히읗 [히읃] *(name of letter ㅎ)*
ㄱ	ㄱ	역 *station*
ㄲ		엮– [역] *compile, weave*
ㅋ		녘 [녁] *around, about*

Note that although ㅎ is conventionally listed as being pronounced as ㄷ in final position, the only word where this is actually the case is 히읗. This should be considered as a convention for pronouncing the name of this letter, rather than as a general sound rule. In other cases where ㅎ occurs at the end of a syllable (e.g., in verb bases such as 좋– 'good' and 많– 'many') it is not pronounced at all (refer to 1.2.3.9), although it may affect the pronunciation of any consonants that follow it (refer to 1.2.3.10).

What is written as a final consonant of one syllable block can in some cases be pronounced as the opening sound of the *next* syllable block (refer to 1.2.3.3). In such cases, the full pronunciation can be maintained.

1.2.3.2 *Simplification of consonant clusters*

A 'consonant cluster' refers to instances in which two or more consonants appear in succession without any vowel sounds between them (examples in English include strike, helps, crisps).

In Korean pronunciation, consonant clusters are not allowed. However, clusters of two consonants do sometimes appear in writing in final consonant position. In such cases, one of the sounds must always drop (or otherwise move to another syllable through 're-syllabification' (refer to 1.2.3.3)). Luckily, knowing which consonant drops and which is pronounced is usually totally predictable, as shown in the following table. Note however, that for the combinations ㄺ *lk* and ㄼ *lp*, some speakers may pronounce the ㄹ *l* rather than the prescribed ㄱ *k* or ㅂ *p* in certain words.

Consonant cluster	*Sound pronounced*	*Example*
ㄳ	ㄱ	넋 [넉] *soul, spirit*
ㄶ	ㄴ	많– [만-] *be many*
ㄻ	ㅁ	삶– [삼] *boil*
ㄽ	ㄹ	외곬 [외골] *single way track*
ㄿ	ㅍ [ㅂ]	읊– [읍] *recite*
ㅄ	ㅂ	값 [갑] *price*
ㄵ	ㄴ	앉– [안] *sit*
ㄺ	ㄱ	읽– [익] *read*
		맑– [막] *clear* – but frequently pronounced as [말]
ㄼ	ㅂ	밟– [밥] *step on*
		넓– [넙] *wide* – but frequently pronounced as [널]
ㄾ	ㄹ	핥– [할] *lick*
ㅀ	ㄹ	뚫– [뚤] *bore [a hole]*

1.2.3.3 *Re-syllabification*

Re-syllabification refers to the process whereby a consonant is written at the end of one syllable block but pronounced at the start of the next syllable. This happens whenever one syllable block ends in a consonant and the following syllable has no opening consonant sound. The two exceptions to this rule are ㅇ *ng* and ㅎ *h*. ㅇ *ng* cannot become the opening sound of the following syllable block because *ng* can only appear as a final consonant sound. As for ㅎ, it does not get pronounced at all in such cases (for example, 좋아요 'good' is pronounced as *cho-a-yo*, not *cho-ha-yo*).

Here are some basic examples of nouns that show re-syllabification:

How it is written	*How it is pronounced*	*Meaning*
독일	[도길]	*Germany*
언어	[어너]	*language*
신인	[시닌]	*new person (i.e., newcomer, 'new face', etc.)*

As in the above examples, most nouns that show re-syllabification are Sino-Korean words composed of compounds of two or more elements originating from separate Chinese characters (for example, 신인 'new person' is composed of the elements 신 (新) 'new' and 인 (人) 'person'). The words are written to reflect the base forms of these two separate elements (i.e., 신-인) rather than pronunciation (i.e. 시-닌).

Re-syllabification also occurs when particles (refer to Chapter 3) (with no opening consonant sound) and the copula (refer to 4.1.4) are attached to nouns (ending in a consonant) and when verb endings (with no opening consonant sound) are attached to verb stems (ending in a consonant):

Written	*Pronunciation*	*Meaning*
한국**이**	[한구기]	*Korea-**subject***
물**을**	[무를]	*water-**object***
약**이에요**	[야기에요]	*medicine-**copula***
입**어서**	[이버서]	*wear –아/어서 verb ending* (refer to 7.1.1)
입**으면**	[이브면]	*wear –(으)면 verb ending* (refer to 7.5.1)

The rule of re-syllabification can be said to override the rules regarding the pronunciation of syllable-final consonants described above (refer to 1.2.3.1). If a consonant can be re-syllabified, it can naturally be rendered according to its full pronunciation. For this reason, adding a particle (with no opening consonant sound) or the copula to a noun (ending in a consonant) and adding verb endings (with no opening consonant sound) to verb stems (ending in a consonant) allow the final nouns to 'recover' their original pronunciation.

Original noun	*Noun + particle/copula*
짚 [집] *straw*	짚**<u>이</u>** [지피] *straw-**<u>subject</u>***
낫 [낟] *sickle*	낫**<u>으로</u>** [나스로] *sickle-**<u>instrumental</u>***
Verb stem	*Verb + ending*
같– *be the same*	같**<u>아서</u>** [가타서] *be the same –아/어서* (refer to 7.1.1)
갔– *went [past stem of 'go']*	갔**<u>으면</u>** [가쓰면] *went –(으)면* (refer to 7.5.1)

The rule of re-syllabification also overrides the rules regarding the simplification of consonant clusters. If a consonant cluster is followed by a vowel at the start of the next syllable, the first consonant of the cluster can be pronounced as the final sound of the current syllable and the second consonant of the cluster can simply move across to the next syllable. This also allows for sounds at the end of nouns and verb stems to be 'recovered' when certain particles, the copula and verb endings are added:

Original noun	*Noun + particle/copula*
넋 [넉] *soul, spirit*	넋**<u>을</u>** [넉슬] *spirit-**<u>object</u>***
값 [갑] *price*	값**<u>으로</u>** [갑스로] *price-**<u>instrumental</u>***
Verb stem	*Verb + ending*
삶– *boil*	삶**<u>아서</u>** [살마서] *boil –아/어서* verb *ending* (refer to 7.1.1)
읽– *read*	읽**<u>으면</u>** [일그면] *read –(으)면* verb *ending* (refer to 7.5.1)

1.2.3.4 Nasal assimilation

'Assimilation' refers to a phonological change whereby a sound 'assimilates' to become similar to a neighbouring sound.

What is known as nasal assimilation happens when a stop consonant (i.e., a consonant whose sound is formed by slowing down or stopping the flow of air through the mouth before being released with an expulsion of breath and sound – in Korean, ㄱ *k*, ㅋ *k'*, ㄲ *kk*, ㄷ *t*, ㅌ *t'*, ㄸ *tt*, ㅂ *p*, ㅍ *p'*, ㅃ *pp*) occurs before a nasal consonant (i.e., a consonant produced through the nose with the mouth closed – in Korean ㄴ *n*, ㅁ *m*, ㅇ *ng*, although ㅇ *ng* does not apply here as it never appears in initial position). When this happens, the stop consonant assimilates to the nasal sound that is produced using the same point of articulation:

ㄱ *k*, ㅋ *k'*, ㄲ *kk*	→	ㅇ *ng*
ㄷ *t*, ㅌ *t'*, ㄸ *tt*	→	ㄴ *n*
ㅂ *p*, ㅍ *p'*, ㅃ *pp*	→	ㅁ *m*

Here are some examples of these changes:

ㄱ *k*, ㅋ *k'*, ㄲ *kk*	→	**ㅇ *ng***	
국물	→	[궁물]	*broth*
먹는다	→	[멍는다]	*eat*
부엌만	→	[부엉만]	*kitchen-**<u>only</u>***
묶는다	→	[뭉는다]	*tie*
ㄷ *t*, ㅌ *t'*, ㄸ *tt*	→	**ㄴ *n***	
받는다	→	[반는다]	*receive*
붙는다	→	[분는다]	*stick to*
ㅂ *p*, ㅍ *p'*, ㅃ *pp*	→	**ㅁ *m***	
법망	→	[범망]	*net of the law*
돕는다	→	[돔는다]	*help* *[plain speech style]*
앞마당	→	[암마당]	*front yard*
없는	→	[엄는]	*not exist-**<u>modifier</u>*** (refer to 8.1.2)

The final example shows the results of two pronunciation changes. The consonant cluster at the end of the first syllable first simplifies to ㅂ *p* (없는 → 업는) (refer to 1.2.3.2). Then, ㅂ *p* assimilates to ㅁ *m* (업는 → 엄는).

In casual speech, one further type of nasal assimilation may occur. This involves the nasal ㄴ *n* changing to another nasal sound, either ㅇ *ng* ㅁ or *m*. This happens when ㄴ *n* occurs before consonants pronounced using the same point of articulation as ㅇ *ng* or ㅁ *m*, namely ㄱ *k* (in the case of ㅇ *ng*) and ㅂ *p* and ㅁ *m* itself (in the case of ㅁ). Put more simply, ㄴ *n* changes to ㅇ *ng* before ㄱ *k*, and ㄴ *n* changes to ㅁ before ㅂ *p* or ㅁ *m*:

ㄴ *n*	→	**ㅇ *ng***	
한국어	→	[항구거]	*Korean language*
ㄴ *n*	→	**ㅁ *m***	
난방	→	[남방]	*heating*
신문	→	[심문]	*newspaper*

1.2.3.5 ㄹ r/l *pronounced as* ㄴ n

The appearance and pronunciation of ㄹ *r/l* is quite restricted in Korean. As noted above (refer to 1.2.2.5), ㄹ r/*l* rarely occurs at the start of Korean words. In addition, when it occurs in the middle of words, ㄹ *r/l* only tends to be retain its original pronunciation after vowels, after another ㄹ *r/l* and after ㄴ (refer to 1.2.3.6). When it occurs after consonants such as ㅁ *m* and ㅇ *ng*, its pronunciation changes to ㄴ *n*:

ㅁㄹ	→	**ㅁㄴ**	
금리	→	[금니]	*interest on money*
담론	→	[담논]	*discussion*
ㅇㄹ	→	**ㅇㄴ**	
등록	→	[등녹]	*registration*
영리	→	[영니]	*profit, gain*

In cases where the preceding consonant is ㅂ*p*, ㄱ *k* or ㄷ (or any other consonants that neutralize toㅂ*p*, ㄱ *k* or ㄷ (refer to 1.2.3.1)), the change from ㄹ l to ㄴ n (or the anticipation of it) triggers nasal assimilation (refer to 1.2.3.4) on the preceding consonant. This means that ㅂ*p* is pronounced as ㅁ *m*, ㄷ t is pronounced as ㄴ n and ㄱ *k* is pronounced as ㅇ *ng*:

ㄱㄹ	→	ㅇㄴ	
독립	→	[동닙]	*independence*
ㄷㄹ	→	ㄴㄴ	
꽃룸	→	[꼰눔]*	*flower-room*
ㅂㄹ	→	ㅁㄴ	
압력	→	[암녁]	*pressure*

*The ㄷㄹ combination is not commonly found in contemporary Korean.

1.2.3.6 ㄴ n *pronounced as* ㄹ l

One important exception to the rule described in the previous section (whereby ㄹ *r/l* changes to ㄴ *n* after other consonants) occurs when ㄹ *r/l* meetsㄴ *n* itself. In these cases, it is ㄴ *n* that changes to ㄹ *r/l*. In other words, the combination ㄴㄹ is pronounced as ㄹㄹ:

ㄴㄹ	→	ㄹㄹ	
난로	→	[날로]	*heater*
신라	→	[실라]	*Shilla (name of Kingdom on Korean peninsula)*

This change also occurs when the order of ㄴ *n* and ㄹ *l/r* is reversed. ㄹㄴ is also pronounced as ㄹㄹ:

ㄹㄴ	→	ㄹㄹ	
칼날	→	[칼랄]	*knife blade*
핥는다	→	[할른다]*	*lick*

*The ㄾ consonant cluster simplifies to ㄹ

It should be noted, however, that the rule whereby ㄴㄹ is pronounced as ㄹㄹ only applies to word-internal cases (i.e., when ㄴ precedes ㄹ within a word). When ㄴ *n* occurs at the end of a word and this word then takes a suffix beginning with ㄹ, the combination is most commonly pronounced as ㄴㄴ (although you may here some speakers use ㄹㄹ).

Original word ending in ㄴ	*Word plus suffix starting with* ㄹ	*Pronunciation*
입원 *hospitalization*	입원료 *hospital expenses*	[이뷘뇨]
신문 *newspaper*	신문로 *'newspaper street'*	[신문노]

1.2.3.7 *Palatalization of* ㄷ t *and* ㅌ t'

When ㄷ *t* or ㅌ *t'* occurs before the vowel ㅣ *i*, the pronunciation becomes 'palatalized'. Basically, this means that ㄷ *t* and ㅌ *t'* change to ㅈ *ch* and ㅊ *ch'* respectively. Note however, that this change *only* occurs when the ㄷ *t* or ㅌ *t'* is at the end of a word or stem and the ㅣ is part of a suffix, verb ending, particle or the copula. It does *not* occur elsewhere (for example, in words such 어디 *where*, 마디 *joint*, 티 *speck*).

ㄷ → ㅈ

해돋이 → [해도지] *sunrise [해 sun + 돋– rise + suffix –이]*
맏이 → [마지] *first born [맏– eldest + 이 person]*
굳이 → [구지] *firmly [굳– firm + adverb ending –이]*

ㅌ → ㅊ

밭이 → [바치] *field (subject) [밭 field + subject particle 이]*
솥이면 → [소치면] *if it's a kettle [솥 kettle + copula 이 + (으)면]*
같이 → [가치] *together [같– 'be the same' + adverb ending –이]*

As well as occurring before ㅣ *i*, this process also occurs before y-vowels:

ㅌ → ㅊ

붙여요 → [부쳐요] *stick [붙– be stuck + causative 이 + 어요]*

A slightly more complicated thing happens when a final-position ㄷ *t* is followed by a suffix starting in 히 *hi*. The combination of ㄷ *t* and ㅎ *h* creates the aspirated ㅌ *t'* through a process of aspiration (refer to 1.2.3.10). This then becomes palatalized to produce ㅊ *ch'*:

ㄷㅎ	→	ㅊ	
닫히-	→	[다치-]	*be shut [닫- shut + passive -히]*
굳히-	→	[구치-]	*harden [굳- be hard + causative -히]*

1.2.3.8 ㄴ n *addition*

In some complex words (i.e., words made up of two or more meaningful units such as the English *flowerpot* (*flower+pot*) or *undo* (*un+do*)) in which the second part of the compound begins with ㅣ *i* or any of the y-vowels, an extra ㄴ *n* is added in pronunciation.

For some words, the addition of ㄴ *n* is reflected in Hangul spelling (for example, 앞니 *front tooth*). In other cases, there is no clue in the spelling that tells us that ㄴ *n* has to be added:

담요	→	[담뇨]	*blanket*
한여름	→	[한녀름]	*midsummer*
면양말	→	[면냥말]	*cotton socks*

When the first element of the compound ends in a stop consonant (i.e., ㄱ *k*, ㅋ *k'*, ㄲ *kk*, ㄷ *t*, ㅌ *t'*, ㄸ *tt*, ㅂ *p*, ㅍ *p'*, ㅃ *pp*), the addition of ㄴ *n* triggers nasal assimilation (refer to 1.2.3.4):

ㄱ/ㅋ/ㄲ + ㄴ	→	ㅇㄴ	
내복약	→	[내봉냑]	*internal medicine*
부엌일	→	[부엉닐]	*kitchen work*
ㄷ/ㅌ/ㄸ + ㄴ	→	ㄴㄴ	
꽃잎	→	[꼰닙]*	*petal*
깻잎	→	[깬닙]*	*sesame leaf*

* Here, ㅊ and ㅅ at the end of the respective first syllables are both pronounced as ㄷ in the original components 꽃 and 깻- respectively. (refer to 1.2.3.1)

ㅂ/ㅍ/ㅃ+ ㄴ	→	ㅁㄴ	
앞일	→	[암닐]	*the future*
영업용	→	[영엄뇽]	*business use/purposes*

1.2.3.9 ㅎ h *reduction*

Full deletion of ㅎ *h* is obligatory when it occurs at the end of a verb base in front of a vowel sound. In words such as the following, ㅎ is never pronounced.

좋아요	→	[조아요]	*is good*
많아요	→	[마나요]	*is many*

Note, however, that the presence of ㅎ *h* at the end of the base will trigger aspiration when verb endings starting with certain consonants are added (refer to 1.2.3.10).

In addition, when ㅎ occurs between voiced sounds (i.e., all vowels and/or the consonants ㅁ *m* ㄴ *n*, ㅇ *ng*, ㄹ *r*), it is pronounced very weakly or is even lost entirely in fast everyday speech:

영화	→	[영와]	*film, movie*
여행	→	[여앵]	*travel*
미안합니다	→	[미아납니다]	*I'm sorry*
전화	→	[저놔]	*telephoning*

1.2.3.10 *Aspiration*

When ㅎ *h* occurs next to the basic consonants ㄱ *k*, ㄷ *t*, ㅂ *p* and ㅈ *ch*, it causes them to change into their aspirated counterparts ㅋ *k'*, ㅌ *t'*, ㅍ *p'* and ㅊ *ch'* respectively (ㅎ *h* is then not pronounced as a separate sound).

This aspiration process can occur both when ㅎ *h* precedes or follows the basic consonant in question. In the first set of examples, ㅎ *h* precedes the consonant:

ㅎㄱ	→	**ㅋ**	
그렇게	→	[그러케]	*like that*
ㅎㄷ	→	**ㅌ**	
좋다	→	[조타]	*is good*
ㅎㅂ	→	**ㅍ**	[this combination is not found in modern Korean]

ㅎㅈ	→	ㅊ	
그렇지만	→	[그러치만]	*like that*

In the next set of examples, ㅎ *h* follows the consonants:

ㄱㅎ	→	ㅋ	
백화점	→	[배콰점]	*department store*
ㄷㅎ	→	ㅌ	
맏형	→	[마텽]	*the eldest brother*
ㅂㅎ	→	ㅍ	
급히	→	[그피]	*urgently*
ㅈㅎ	→	ㅊ	
맞히–	→	[마치–]	*hit [the mark]*

1.2.3.11 Reinforcement

Reinforcement refers to the process by which the basic consonants ㄱ *k*, ㄷ *t*, ㅂ *p* and ㅈ *ch* become pronounced as their tensed or 'double' counterparts ㄲ *kk*, ㄸ *tt*, ㅃ *pp* and ㅉ *tch*. There are several situations in which this may occur.

The first situation in which reinforcement occurs is when two of the basic consonants (ㄱ *k*, ㄷ *t*, ㅂ *p* and ㅈ *ch*) occur together in a word (one ending the one syllable block and the other starting the next). When this happens, the second consonant will always be pronounced with reinforcement:

Reinforcement of ㄱ	받고	→	[받꼬]	*receive* + –고 *(refer to* 7.3.1)
Reinforcement of ㄷ	법대	→	[법때]	*law school*
Reinforcement of ㅂ	국밥	→	[국빱]	*soup with rice*
Reinforcement of ㅈ	곧장	→	[곧짱]	*straight away*

This kind of reinforcement will also take place when the final consonant of the first syllable is not written as ㄱ *k*, ㄷ *t*, ㅂ *p* and ㅈ *ch* but is pronounced as such due to the rules regarding the pronunciation of final consonants (refer to 1.2.3.1) or simplification of consonant clusters (refer to 1.2.3.2):

Spelling		*Sound change*		*Reinforcement*	
옆집	→	엽집	→	[엽찝]	*next door*
꽃바구니	→	꼳바구니	→	[꼳빠구니]	*flower basket*

Spelling		*Simplified cluster*		*Reinforcement*	
닭살	→	닥살	→	[닥쌀]	*goose bumps*
없다	→	업다	→	[업따]	*not exist*

Reinforcement does not usually occur after a nasal consonant (i.e., ㄴ *n*, ㅁ *m*, ㅇ *ng*). However, the exception to this is when the nasal sound in question occurs at the end of a verb stem and an ending beginning with a plain consonant is added to it:

신고	→	[신꼬]	*report* + –고 *(refer to* 7.3.1)
다듬다가	→	[다듬따가]	*trim, refine* + –다가 *(refer to* 7.3.11*)*

A more complicated variety of reinforcement can occur in complex nouns (i.e., nouns composed of two or more morphemes). This first of all happens in complex nouns in which the two elements are linked together by the addition of the so-called 'genitive s' (사이시옷) – an additional ㅅ *s* written at the bottom of the syllable. Although written as ㅅ *s*, it is never pronounced as such (at least not in the modern language). All that it does is to cause the following plain consonants to become reinforced:

사잇길	→	[사이낄]	*the way between*
뱃길	→	[배낄]	*shipping route*
종잇장	→	[종이짱]	*sheet of paper*
텃밭	→	[터빧]	*backyard vegetable plot*

The 'genitive s' can only be written when the first element in the complex noun ends in a vowel. However, 'genitive s' may be phonologically present in complex nouns that end in a consonant as well (although Hangul orthography does not allow it to be written). Due to this, other compounds may also see tensing on the second element with no indication at all in the spelling:

안방	→	[안빵]	*inner room*
안과	→	[안꽈]	*opticians; eye clinic*
눈동자	→	[눈똥자]	*pupil (of eye)*
잠보	→	[잠뽀]	*sleepyhead*
김밥	→	[김빱]	*rice rolled in seaweed*
강가	→	[강까]	*riverside*

Non-predictable tensing may also occur in other complex nouns where there is no etymological evidence of there being a 'genitive s':

한자	→	[한짜]	*Chinese characters*
글자	→	[글짜]	*letters*
문법	→	[문뻡]	*grammar*
산보	→	[산뽀]	*a stroll*
조건	→	[조껀]	*condition*
인기	→	[인끼]	*popularity*
결정	→	[결쩡]	*decision*

Chapter 2

Nouns, nominal forms, pronouns and numbers

2.1 Nouns

Overview

The current sub-chapter provides important information regarding the grammatical appearance of Korean nouns.

Section one considers three points on which Korean nouns differ greatly from their counterparts in English and other European languages: the absence of articles, the limited appearance of number and the lack of importance of gender. Section two then considers an important category of noun that requires further comment: bound nouns.

One important feature of Korean nouns not covered in this chapter is the fact that some Korean nouns have a separate 'honorific' form. This situation is discussed in the chapter on honorifics (6.2.3)

2.1.1 *Lack of articles, number and gender*

Unlike many European languages, Korean does not have articles (such as 'a/an' and 'the' in English), does not typically mark number (i.e., whether a noun is singular or plural) and does not usually mark gender (as in European languages such as French, German, Spanish and Russian). On these points, however, Korean is similar to other East Asian languages such as Chinese and Japanese.

Although the lack of these categories can sometimes be disorienting to European learners, Korean has ways to express these meanings where necessary.

2.1.1.1 *Lack of articles*

Due to the lack of articles, a Korean sentence such as the following can be ambiguous regarding whether the 'man' that Yumi met is a specific man ('the man') or an unspecified man ('a man')

어제 유미가 **남자**를 만났어요.
Yesterday, Yumi met the man. / Yesterday, Yumi met a man.

However, where need be, Korean can use other resources to tell us whether a specific man or an unspecified man is being talked about. For definite reference ('the man'), 그 'that' (or, according to context, 이 'this') can be used:

어제 유미가 **그 남자**를 만났어요.
Yesterday, Yumi met the man.

For indefinite reference ('a man'), 한 'one' or 어떤 'some (kind of)' can be used:

어제 유미가 **어떤 남자**를 만났어요.
Yesterday, Yumi met a man.

2.1.1.2 *Lack of number*

Since Korean nouns are not normally marked for number, it is often unclear (unless there is a clarifying context), whether the speaker is talking about a single item or plural items. In the following sentence, '책' could translate as 'book' or 'books':

책이 있어요. *I've got a book. / I've got some books.*

However, if it is necessary to specify that what is being talked about is not a single item but plural items, Korean does have a grammatical marker that can fulfil this function: the plural marker 들 (refer to 3.3.1). The following sentence can only mean that I have 'books', not that I have 'a book':

책들이 있어요. *I've got some books.*

Another way to make a noun plural is to use a number expression (refer to 2.4). Note that when one of these number expressions is used, since this makes it obvious that what you are talking about is plural (or singular), the plural marker is not normally used.

2.1.1.3 Lack of gender

Korean does not mark gender on the noun such as in French, Russian and other European languages. In addition, the majority of job names and/or work titles are not 'gendered' as they tend to be in English. In the following list, whereas the corresponding English expressions are gender-marked, the Korean expressions do not contain such bias:

소방수	*fireman*
경찰관	*policeman*
판매원	*salesman*
회장	*chairman (of the board)*

When it is necessary to distinguish that the person being referred to is male or female, the words 남자 'man' and 여자 'woman' must be inserted before the noun:

여자 선생님	*a female teacher*
남자 판매원	*a male salesperson*

In some cases, 여자 and 남자 can be shortened to 여– and 남– and this can be attached as a prefix to the front of the noun:

남학생	*male student*	여학생	*female student*
남선생	*male teacher*	여선생	*female teacher*

The use of 남(자) or 여(자) before the noun is particularly common in cases where the gender of the person in question goes against stereotypical gender roles, such as when talking about a female police officer (여자 경찰관) or a male nurse (남자 간호사).

Some other expressions in Korean may contain a gender bias. Notably, the noun '사람', originally meaning 'person', is typically understood as meaning 'man' in the pronoun-like phrase '그 사람' 'that person', 'he'. If a woman is being talked about, '그 여자' 'that woman', 'she' would normally be applied instead. To make it 100% specific that you are talking about a man, you can also use '그 남자' 'that man'.

Although not the same as grammatical gender, Korean family terms display a gender distinction different to anything found in

English. For some expressions, a different vocabulary item is used depending on whether the family member in question is being talked about as a relative of a man or of a woman (refer to 6.3.3).

2.1.2 Bound/dependent nouns

Korean contains a special set of nouns that are known as 'bound nouns or dependent nouns'. Unlike the majority of nouns that are freestanding ('free/independent nouns'), 'bound/dependent nouns' cannot occur on their own and always require an accompanying element. This element precedes the noun phrase and comprises of a modifier (refer to Chapter 8) (i.e., a word or phrases used to elaborate, describe, clarify, identify or delimit).

The following sections introduce a few of the more important bound nouns that appear in Korean.

2.1.2.1 것 *'thing', 'object' or 'affair'*

것 is the most commonly occurring bound noun and has the rough meaning of 'thing', 'object' or 'affair'. It is frequently shortened to '거' in colloquial Korean and may also take on the following abbreviated forms when it is combined with a particle:

	Full form	*Abbreviated form*
것 + subject particle (refer to 3.2.1)	것이	게
것 + object particle (refer to 3.2.2)	것을	걸
것 + topic particle (refer to 3.3.2.1)	것은	건

This bound noun first of all occurs with the demonstratives 이 'this', 그 'that' and 저 'that . . . over there' to create 이것 'this (thing)', 그것 'that (thing)' and 저것 'that (thing) over there':

이**것**이 프랑스 와인이에요.	*This is French wine.*
그**것**이 호주 와인이에요.	*That is Australian wine.*
저**것**이 칠레 와인이에요.	*That one over there is Chilean wine.*

것 may also appear with pronouns used in a possessive meaning (such as 내 'my', 제 'my (humble)', 네 'your') or other terms of address to give possessive meanings corresponding to the English 'mine', 'yours', etc. In this context, it is pronounced as [꺼]

이 신문은 제 **거**예요.	*This newspaper is mine.*
이 볼펜은 내 **거**야.	*This pen is mine.*
이 잡지는 유미 씨 **거**예요.	*This magazine is Yumi's.*
이 책은 교수님 **거**예요.	*This book is the professor's.*

Furthermore, 것 may occur preceded by the question words 어느 'which' or 어떤 'what kind of; which' or 누구 'who' to give the meanings 'which (one)', 'what kind of; which (one)' or 'whose':

어느 **것**을 추천하시겠어요?	*Which one do you recommend?*
어떤 **것**을 더 선호하세요?	*Which one do you prefer?*
이 우산이 누구 **거**예요?	*Whose umbrella is this?*

Finally and of most importance, 것 occurs preceded by modifier expressions containing a verb. This pattern is covered in detail elsewhere (refer to 2.2.6, 8.2.2).

2.1.2.2 *겸 '-cum-'*

The bound Sino-Korean noun 겸 (兼) is used to depict addition, combination, concurrence or dual purpose. It can occur first of all between two nouns, behaving similar to English ' . . .-cum- . . .'.

아침 **겸** 점심	*breakfast-cum-lunch (brunch)*
거실 **겸** 침실	*a living room-cum-bedroom*
편집인 **겸** 발행인	*an editor-cum-publisher*

겸 can also be used for talking about two actions that take place simultaneously (refer to 8.2.4).

Note that, unrelated to its use as a bound noun, 겸(兼) may also appear in Sino-Korean compound words such as 겸상 'a table for two', 겸직 'additional work (outside of your regular job)', and 겸하다 'hold an additional position'.

2.1.2.3 곳 *'place'*

This bound noun has the meaning of 'place' and is similar in meaning and usage to 데 (refer to 2.1.2.7).

여기가 내가 사는 **곳**이에요.
This is the place where I live.

미나 씨는 그 **곳**에 자주 가요.
Mina often goes to that place.

어느 **곳**에 가면 좋을지 모르겠어요.
I don't know where it would be best to go.

2.1.2.4 김 *'occasion', 'chance'*

The bound noun 김 only occurs in the modifying pattern –(으)ㄴ/는 김에 'as long as you're at it' (refer to 8.2.6).

2.1.2.5 대로 *'in accordance with'*

대로 is primarily a particle meaning 'in accordance with' or 'in conformity with' (refer to 3.3.6.6). However, 대로 can also be used as a bound noun. In this case, it occurs preceded by modifier clauses (refer to 8.2.10).

2.1.2.6 덕분 *'thanks to'*

덕분 is a bound noun that has the meaning of 'thanks to' or 'owing to' and which is normally preceded by another noun or modifier. It appears either followed by the particle 에 (refer to 3.2.4.1) or otherwise by the copula (refer to 4.1.4).

자네 **덕분에** 잘 놀았네.	*Thanks to you, I had a good time.*
모두 부모님 **덕분이에요**.	*It's all thanks to my parents.*
열심히 노력하신 **덕분이지요**.	*It's all thanks to your hard efforts.*

아이들 **덕분에** 트와이스 노래를 다 배웠어요.
Thanks to the kids, I have learned all of the 'Twice' songs.

낮잠을 잔 **덕분에** 이 시간까지 말똥말똥 하답니다.
Thanks to having taken a nap, I am wide awake until now.

Although 덕분 generally behaves as a bound noun that has to be preceded by another noun or a modifying expression, there is one important exception. In the expression 'thanks to you', it is possible to omit any address term corresponding to 'you' and thus for '덕분에' to appear on its own. This occurs at particularly high frequency in greeting expressions such as the following:

덕분에 잘 다녀왔습니다. *Thanks to you, I had a good trip.*

덕분에 잘 지냅니다. *Thanks to you, I am doing fine.*

2.1.2.7 *데 'place'*

데 is a bound noun with the meaning of 'place' and occurs preceded either by an adnoun such as 다른 or 딴 'other' (refer to 11.1) or by a modifying clause (refer to Chapter 8). This 데 is frequently followed by a particle such as 에 'to, in, at' (refer to 3.2.4.1) or 에서 'in, at, from'. The latter (데에서) is regularly contracted to 데서:

먼 **데**서 자동차 소리가 들려요.
From a faraway place, I can hear the sound of a car.

여기는 청소년들이 오는 **데**가 아니에요
This is not a place for young people to come.

콩 심은 **데** 콩 나요.
Where you plant beans, beans grow (= You reap what you sow).

2.1.2.8 *동안 'during'*

동안 has the basic meaning of 'during'. It may appear either preceded by a modifying clause (refer to 8.2.12) or by a time expression or other noun:

방학 **동안** *during the school holidays*

10분 **동안** *for ('during') ten minutes*

5년 **동안** *for ('during') five years*

수업 **동안** *during the lesson*

2.1.2.9 둥 *'may or may not'*

The bound noun 둥 appears exclusively in the modifier pattern –(으)ㄹ/–는/–(으)ㄴ 둥, translating as 'may or may not' (refer to 8.2.13).

책을 **보는 둥 마는 둥** 해요.
He is reading a book half-heartedly.

밥을 **먹는 둥 마는 둥** 합니다.
She is just making a gesture of eating rice.

2.1.2.10 듯 *'as if'*

듯 is a bound noun that occurs in the modifier pattern –(으)ㄹ/–는/–(으)ㄴ 듯 (refer to 8.2.14). It also combines with 하– or 싶– in the pattern –(으)ㄹ/–는/–(으)ㄴ 듯하–/듯 싶– (refer to 8.2.15) and features as an integral part of the connective –듯이 (refer to 7.8.1). All of these sentence patterns contain some element of comparison and/or realization:

집은 아무도 없**는 듯** 조용했어요.
The house is quiet, as if no one is there.

모든 파일이 삭제**된 듯해요**.
It looks like all of the files have been erased.

구름은 춤을 추**듯이** 움직였어요.
The clouds moved just like they were dancing.

2.1.2.11 따름 *'only, alone'*

따름 indicates singularity – that there is nothing other than what is being mentioned. It occurs in the sentence pattern –(으)ㄹ 따름이– (refer to 8.2.16).

그저 감사할 **따름**입니다. *I am just thankful.*

그것은 정말 놀라울 **따름**이에요. *It is just amazing.*

2.1.2.12 때 *'when'*

때 has the basic meaning of 'time' or 'when' and occurs most commonly with modifying clauses (refer to 8.2.17). However, 때 can also be used following nouns that refer to days or periods of time (where it takes on the meaning 'at/in'):

크리스마스 **때**
at Christmas/when it is Christmas

방학 **때**
in the school holidays/when it is the school holidays

2002 년 월드컵 **때**
at the time of the 2002 World Cup/when it was the 2002 World Cup

As noted in the main entry on –(으)ㄹ 때 (refer to 8.2.17), this bound noun may also occur after nouns where the corresponding English expression would be incomplete without the addition of the verb 'be':

학생 **때** *when I was a student*

다섯 살 **때** *when I was five years old*

Note that 때 can be used as an independent noun as in the following example:

지금은 때가 아니다/안 좋다.
Now is not the right time [to do something].

2.1.2.13 *때문 'reason'*

때문 is a bound noun with the meaning of 'reason' which occurs in constructions that link a cause with its effect. It must always be preceded either by a noun or a nominal clause and be followed either by the particle 에 (refer to 3.2.4.1) or by the copula (refer to 4.1.4)

사업 **때문에** 영국에 왔어요.
I came to England because of my business.

날씨 **때문에** 방학이 별로 재미없었어요.
My vacation wasn't much fun because of the weather.

나 **때문에** 그 사람이 못 갔어요.
He couldn't go because of me.

A: 왜 사람을 죽였어? *Why did he commit murder?*

B: 그건 돈 **때문이야**! *Because of the money!*

Use of 때문 following a nominal clause is discussed elsewhere (refer to 2.2.4.2).

2.1.2.14 *리 'reasons'*

The bound Sino-Korean noun 리 (理) means 'grounds' or 'reasons'. It is applied preceded by a modifying construction in the pattern –(으)ㄹ 리 없– 'there is no grounds/reasons for . . .' (refer to 8.2.18).

선생님이 그것을 모를 **리** 없어요.
It is not possible that the teacher doesn't know about it.

늦을 **리**가 없어요.
There is no reason for delay.

2.1.2.15 *무렵 'around the time'*

무렵 is a bound noun that takes on the meaning of 'around the time'. It must be preceded either by a noun, demonstrative or a modifying clause (refer to Chapter 8) and is often followed by the particle 에 (refer to 3.2.4.1) or otherwise 부터 (refer to 3.3.3.4) or 까지 (refer to 3.3.3.5).

저녁 **무렵**에	*around evening time*
그 **무렵**에	*at around that time; in those days*
2000년 **무렵**부터	*from around the year 2000*
여름이 끝날 **무렵**	*at around the time when summer was ending*
해 질 **무렵**에	*at around the time when the sun was setting*

2.1.2.16 *바 'thing'*

The bound noun 바, meaning 'thing' or 'what' is in essence applied the same as certain uses of 것 (refer to 2.1.2.1). However, the usage is restricted to written language (or to formal speech), as discussed elsewhere (refer to 8.2.22):

군대 **갈 바에(는/야)** 차라리 죽고 싶어요.
I would rather die than go to the army.

어찌 **할 바**를 모르겠어요
I am at a loss what to do.

제가 **아는 바**에 따르면 . . .
According to what I know. . . .

2.1.2.17 뿐 *'only', 'just', 'nothing but'*

뿐 has the basic meaning of 'only, just, nothing but'. When it appears as a bound noun, it occurs preceded by modifier constructions (refer to 8.2.26).

일년에 한두 번 만**날 뿐**이에요.	*I only meet him/her once or twice a year.*
시간과 돈 낭비**일 뿐**이에요.	*It's just a waste of time and money.*

뿐 can also function as a particle, as discussed elsewhere (refer to 3.3.3.2). In addition, it may function as an independent noun in expressions such as 뿐만 아니라 'in addition, moreover'.

2.1.2.18 수 *'case', 'circumstance'*

The bound noun 수 literally means 'case, circumstance; way, means'. It is used in the modifier pattern –을/ㄹ 수 있–/없– which is used to express ability (refer to 8.2.27).

김치를 잘 담**글 수 있어요**.	*I can make kimchi well.*
운전**할 수 있어요**?	*Can you drive?*

2.1.2.19 적 *'event'*

The bound noun 적 means 'event', 'act' or 'experience' and appears primarily in the modifier pattern –(으)ㄴ/–는 적이 있–/없– (refer to 8.2.29):

한국에 가 **본 적이 있어요**?	*Have you ever been to Korea?*
어릴 적에 시골에서 살았어요.	*I lived in the countryside when I was a child.*

2.1.2.20 줄 *'the way', 'the fact'*

줄 is a bound noun that occurs proceeded by a modifying clause and followed by cognitive verbs, most typically 알– 'know' and 모르– 'not know' (refer to 8.2.31):

자**는 줄** 알았어요.	*I thought you were sleeping.*
아무 것도 **할 줄** 몰라요.	*There's nothing she can do well.*

2.1.2.21 중/도중 *'the middle'*

The Sino-Korean 중 (中) is a bound noun with the meaning of 'middle'. It may appear followed either by the particle 에 (refer to 3.2.4.1) or by the copula (refer to 4.1.4) in constructions that translate as 'in the middle of' or simply 'during'. When it is followed by 에, it may appear in the alternative form 도중 (途中).

오늘 영어 수업 **중**에 선생님이 핏대를 올리시더군요.
Today during English class the teacher got really worked up.

회의 **도중**에 문자가 도착했어요.
I received a text message in the middle of the meeting.

연애 **중**에 절대로 해서는 안 되는 말이 있잖아요.
There are certain things you should not say while you are dating, you know.

지금 회의 **중**이에요.	*I'm in the middle of a meeting now.*
통화 **중**이에요.	*He/she is in the middle of a phone call (= His/her phone is engaged).*

When 중 is followed by 에서 (refer to 3.2.4.3) it may take on one more additional function. Namely 중에서 can be used like 'from' or 'between' in English when discussing what (or who) 'from' a given group or range of entities performs a particular action, has a particular attribute, etc. Note that the final '서' (or even the complete 에서) may be dropped with no change in meaning.

'이달의 소녀' **중에서** 누가 제일 예뻐요?
Who is the prettiest from the group 'Loona'?

엄마 아빠 **중에** 누가 더 좋아?
Who do you like best between your mommy and daddy?

동물 **중에서** 가장 오래 사는 동물은 어떤 동물인가요?
From all the animals, which is the one that lives the longest?

중 also frequently appears in modifier constructions, as discussed elsewhere in this book (refer to 8.2.32, 8.2.33).

2.1.2.22 *지 'since'*

지 is a bound noun that appears preceded by a modifying construction and typically followed by a time expression when discussing the amount of time that has elapsed since an event occurred (refer to 8.2.35).

한국에 **온 지** 2 년이 됐어요.
It's been 2 years since I came to Korea.

그 회사는 생**긴 지** 20년 됐어요.
The company has been in existence for 20 years.

2.1.2.23 *쪽 'side'*

쪽 has the basic meaning of 'side' or 'direction'. Note that some common combinations with 쪽 (such as at the top of the following list) may be written as one word (and are recognized as such):

북/동/남/서쪽	*the North/East/South/West (side/direction)*
이쪽	*this side/direction*
그쪽	*that side/direction*
저쪽	*that side/direction (over there)*
반대 쪽	*the opposite side/direction*
다른/딴 쪽	*another side/direction*

어느 쪽 *which side/direction*

서울 쪽 *the direction/side of Seoul*

Note that if you want to say 'in the direction of', the instrumental particle (으)로 (refer to 3.2.5.1) must be used (rather than a particle of movement and location (refer to 3.2.4))

동쪽으로 갈까요? **서쪽으로** 갈까요?
Shall we go to the East? Or to the West?

이야기가 **딴 쪽으로** 흘러갔어요.
Our chat went off in another direction.

서울 쪽으로 가는 길은 항상 막혀요.
The road going in the direction of Seoul is always jammed.

2.1.2.24 *채 'just as it is'*

The bound noun 채 takes on meanings such as 'just as it is', 'as it stands', 'with no change' and 'in the existing state'. Although it most commonly occurs in the modifier pattern -(으)ㄴ 채(로) (refer to 8.2.37), it may also follow preceded by nouns as in the following examples:

통 채로 삼켰어요. *I swallowed it whole.*

뿌리 채로 뽑았어요. *I pulled it out, roots and all.*

뼈 채로 먹었어요. *I ate it, bones and all.*

사과를 **껍질 채** 먹었어요. *I ate an apple without peeling it.*

2.2 Nominal forms

Overview

Nominal forms are used when you want to talk about or in relation to the act of doing things (i.e., what is normally expressed by using verbs) as if they were nouns. Put another way, nominal forms are grammatical means for converting verbs into noun forms. In English, the most common way to change a verb into a noun is to add *-ing* (*read* → *reading*; *eat* → *eating*, etc.). In Korean, there are five separate ways to nominalize a verb phrase: -이, -개/게, -기, -음 and -는 것. This chapter looks at these forms in turn and also looks at verbal expressions that combine these nominalized forms (and particularly –기) as an integral part:

2.2.1 Nominal form –이

A small number of verbs can be changed into nouns by the addition of –이. The resulting forms are relatively fossilized; in other words, they are thought of as separate nouns rather than something derived from verbs (and are listed in dictionaries as such).

Original verb		*Nominalized form*	
먹–	*eat*	먹이	*food*
놀–	*play*	놀이	*game*
넓–	*be wide*	넓이	*width*
길–	*be long*	길이	*length*
높–	*be high*	높이	*height*
깊–	*be deep*	깊이	*depth*

2.2.2 Nominal form –개/게

An even small number set of verbs can be changed into nouns by the addition of –개 or –게. The resulting forms are independent nouns that take on meanings that are not always totally predictable from looking at the original verb:

Original verb		*Nominalized form*	
덮–	*to cover*	덮개	*a cover*
지우–	*rub out*	지우개	*eraser*
찌–	*steam, cook (with water)*	찌개	*Korean stew*
지–	*carry (on the back)*	지게	*Korean carrying frame*
집–	*pick*	집게	*tweezers*

2.2.3 Nominal form –기

–기 is formed according to the normal patterns of one-shape verb endings (refer to 4.1.8).

Nominal forms with –기 firstly occur when referring to an activity concept. For instance, in a (Korean) language class the activity types of 'speaking', 'listening', 'reading' and 'writing' are referred to as 말하기, 듣기, 읽기 and 쓰기, respectively. Similar examples to these include 걷기, 'walking', 뛰기 'running' and 먹기 'eating'. All of these examples are with processive verbs (refer to 4.1.1) without tense marking and the resultant forms are relatively fossilized.

In addition, –기 can be used productively to nominalize any kind of verb, processive or descriptive verbs (refer to 4.1.1). In these cases, it can occur with past bases (refer to 4.3.1.1), future bases with –겠– (refer to 4.3.2.1) and honorific bases with –시– (refer to 6.2.1.1):

Past base	*Future base*	*Honorific base*	
갔기	가겠기	가시기	*going*
했기	하겠기	하시기	*doing*

Nominalizer forms on past and future bases are only used with certain 'sentence patterns with –기' covered in a separate section below (refer to 2.2.4); the use of the future base is somewhat unusual.

In principle, nominal forms with –기 behave just like other nouns. That is, they occur in the same sentence positions as normal nouns and can be marked with the same particles:

공부하기**가** 재미있어요 *Studying is interesting.*

공부하기**를** 싫어해요. *I hate studying.*

More often, what appears in the noun slot is not just the nominal form but a longer sentence-like phrase. Notice that, as in the following examples, sentences with nominalized phrases may contain two subject (or two object) particles (refer to 3.2.1, 3.2.2).

내가 먹**기**가 싫어요.
I don't want to eat.

내가 학교 식당에서 먹**기**가 싫어요.
I don't want to eat at the school cafeteria.

내가 학교 식당에서 유미랑 밥을 먹**기**를 싫어해요.
I don't like eating with Yumi at the school cafeteria.

Verb forms that occur following a –기 nominalized phrase tend to be of certain types. They tend to either be emotive verbs (싫– 'be hateful', ' . . . don't want to', 좋– 'be good', 재미있– 'be interesting/fun', etc.), verbs of ease or frequency (어렵– 'be difficult', 쉽–, 'be easy', 일쑤– 'be customary', etc.) or verbs that mark temporal boundaries (시작하– 'start', '끝나– ', 'end', etc.).

Here are some examples of –기 occurring with these verbs:

고기가 먹**기**가 좋아요.
The meat is good (or easy) to eat.

일본말 가르치**기**가 쉬워요.
Teaching Japanese is easy.

모든 것을 다 잘 하**기**가 어려워요.
It's hard to do everything well.

가수가 나오**기**를 기다리고 있어요.
We are waiting for the pop-singer to appear.

There are also verbs that can occur with –기 followed by the instrumental particle (으)로 such as 유명하– 'famous', 소문나– 'be rumored/talked about/renowned':

그 배우는 성질이 더럽**기로** 유명해요.
That actor is famous for having a dirty character.

우리 아파트는 겉모양이 아름답**기로** 소문난 아파트예요.
Our apartment is a building that is renowned for having a beautiful outward appearance.

2.2.4 Sentence patterns with –기

We now look at some set sentence patterns that combine –기 as an integral element.

2.2.4.1 –기 나름이– 'depending on'

In this pattern, –기 is followed by the expression 나름이–, which has the meaning 'depending on, resting on, being conditional on'. The resulting construction means 'it depends on how (much) . . .':

모든 일은 노력하**기 나름이에요**.
[The success of] all work depends on how much you try.

좋으냐 나쁘냐는 생각하**기 나름이지요**.
Whether it's good or bad depends on how you look at it.

독자가 받아들이**기 나름이에요**.
It depends on the reception of the reader.

The pattern may also appear with the negative copula 아니– :

교육하**기 나름 아닐까요**? *Doesn't that depend on education?*

In addition to nominalized expressions with –기, 나름이– also frequently occurs after normal nouns:

그것은 사람 **나름이에요**. *That depends on the person.*

2.2.4.2 *–기 때문(에)* 'because'

In this pattern, which occurs more commonly in writing and formal speech rather than casual conversation, –기 is directly followed by the bound noun 때문 (refer to 2.1.2.13) 'reason' to create a construction expressing cause and effect. 때문 is then followed either by the particle 에 and then another sentence-like clause (i.e., ' . . ., so . . .') or otherwise by the copula (i.e., 'it's because . . .' or ' the reason is . . .'):

–기 때문 + 에	풍경이 멋지**기 때문에** 사람들이 많이 와요. *Many people come because the scenery is fantastic.*
–기 때문 + copula	풍경이 멋지**기 때문이에요**. *It's because the scenery is fantastic.*

While –기 때문에 functions as a kind of connective that expresses the cause before the effect, the pattern –기 때문 is used to supply the reason for something that has already been mentioned:

A: 그런데 다른 애들을 왜 자꾸 때리는지 모르겠어요.
I don't understand though why he keeps hitting the other kids.

B: 말로는 표현을 잘 못 하**기 때문이지요**.
That's because he can't express himself verbally.

만일 여자가 반장을 맡고 남자가 부반장이라면 어색하고 우스꽝스러운 이유는 무엇인가? 현실과 다르**기 때문이다**.
And if we imagine that a woman becomes the leader and a man her deputy, what is the reason that makes this an awkward and comical idea? The reason is precisely that it is different from reality.

The –기 때문 pattern may be used with any verb and may be preceded by past tense marking (–았/었기 때문에). Future tense is typically formed with –(으)ㄹ 거– (refer to 4.3.2.2) (–을 것이기 때문에). Here are examples that show tense marking:

불어를 **몰랐기 때문에** 문제를 많이 겪었어요.
Because I didn't know French, I encountered a lot of problems.

이번 경기침체가 상당히 오래**갈 것이기 때문에** 상당수의 건설사 정리는 불가피합니다.
Because this economic slump is going to continue for a long time, the liquidation of a large number of construction firms is unavoidable.

Similar to the causal connective –아/어서 (refer to 7.1.1), –기 때문에 cannot be used when the second clause contains a command, proposal, suggestion, invitation or request. In such cases, –(으)니까 (refer to 7.1.6) is used instead. Although –기 때문에 generally operates in a similar way to –아/어서, note that only –아/어서 and not –기 때문에 can be used with expressions of thanks, apology and with excuses (refer to 7.1.1). In addition, whereas –아/어서 may sound awkward when the two events being linked actually happen in reverse order (i.e., when the event depicted in the second clause actually occurs before the one in the first clause), no such restriction applies to –기 때문에. For this reason, –기 때문에 would be preferred in the following example:

수업이 10시에 시작하**기 때문에** 집에서 9시 반에 나와요
Since the class starts at 10, I leave the house at 9:30.

Note that 때문 may also appear preceded by simple nouns, as discussed elsewhere (refer to 2.1.2.13).

2.2.4.3 *–기/게 마련이– 'be bound to'*

This pattern combines a nominalized form with the noun 마련 and the copula (refer to 4.1.4). The noun 마련, as an independent noun, originally means 'preparation' or 'arrangement'. It can also be combined with –하– to form the verb 마련하– 'to prepare'. When used with a nominalizer, it takes on the meaning of 'is bound to', 'is doomed to', 'is expected to' or 'is normal to'. This pattern is used to express that the matter in question comes about as a matter of course according to normal shared common knowledge. Note that, in this pattern, the –기 ending of the nominalized form may be replaced by the adverbial ending –게 (refer to 10.2.1.2) with no perceptible change in meaning:

사람은 누구나 죽**기 마련이다**. *All people are doomed to die.*

술을 많이 마시다 보면 취하**기 마련이에요**.
If you drink a lot, it is only natural that you get drunk.

부모는 자식에게 관대하**기 마련이에요**.
It is only to be expected that parents are lenient towards their children.

사랑은 언젠가 식**기 마련이에요**.
Love is bound to grow cold with time.

2.2.4.4 *–기(에) 망정이–* *'fortunately . . . otherwise'*

The pattern –기(에) 망정이– expresses a fortunate decision or turn of events in the first clause, linked with a danger that was averted in the second clause:

일찍 돌아왔**기에 망정이지** 하마터면 비를 맞을 뻔했다
Fortunately, we returned early, otherwise we would have been caught in the rain.

택시를 탔**기 망정이지** 하마터면 늦을 뻔했다.
Fortunately we took a taxi, since we were nearly late.

2.2.4.5 *–기 시작하–* *'start'*

In this pattern, the plain nominal form on -기 is followed by the verb 시작하– 'start'. No past or future tense marking is allowed.

비가 오**기 시작했어요**. *It began to rain.*

한국말은 언제부터 배우**기 시작했어요**?
When did you start learning Korean?

어제부터 수영을 배우**기 시작했어요**.
From yesterday, I began to learn swimming.

2.2.4.6 *–기 십상이– 'it is easy to . . .'*

In this pattern, –기 is followed by the noun 십상 and the copula (refer to 4.1.4). The word 십상 originally means 'the right thing (for)' as a noun and 'right, exactly, perfectly' as an adverb. The expression is used to connote ease, in other words, that the state of affairs in question comes about 'easily', 'quickly' or 'naturally':

과도한 다이어트는 건강을 해치**기 십상이**에요.
If you over-diet, it is easy to harm your health.

생선은 더운 날씨에서는 상하**기 십상이**에요.
Fish can go off quickly in hot weather.

외국 여행 할 때 바가지 쓰**기 십상이**지요.
It's easy to get ripped off when you travel abroad, you see.

이런 음식을 대접하면 욕먹**기 십상이**에요.
If you treat people to this kind of food, you should expect to be criticized.

In sentences such as the above, 십상이– can often be replaced by '쉽– ' 'easy' with little change in meaning.

Note that the noun 십상, although most commonly occurring in the pattern –기 십상이–, may occur in other sentences:

하이킹 날씨로는 **십상이**에요. *This weather is made for hiking.*

네게는 그 모자가 **십상이**다. *That hat was made for you.*

2.2.4.7 *–기 위하– 'in order to'*

In this pattern, –기 is followed by the verb 위하– (爲–) whose original meaning is 'to serve, to devote oneself'. The expression that is created takes on the meaning of 'in order to' or 'for the sake of' or simply 'for'. Tense cannot be marked before –기.

To incorporate this into a sentence, –기 위하– then has to be followed either by the causal connectives –아/어서 (refer to 7.1.1) or –아/어 (refer to 7.1.2) or the modifier form on ㄹ(으)ㄴ (refer to 8.1.3) to create the following forms:

–기 위해서

–기 위해/–기 위하여

–기 위한

The first two patterns (–기 위해서 and –기 위해/–기 위하여) are then followed by a sentence-like clause to create sentences such as the following:

세계평화를 이루**기 위해서** 오래 싸워야 돼요.
In order to achieve world peace, we must struggle for a long time.

나라를 구하**기 위하여** 몸을 바친 사람들이 정말 훌륭해요.
Those who offered their lives for the sake of the country are truly great.

The pattern –기 위한 must be followed directly by a noun. Typically, these are nouns that describe efforts, methods or plans:

1904년 유신회라는 단체를 만들어 **나라를 구하기 위한 활동**을 했어요.
In 1904 he founded a group called 'Yushinhoe' and engaged in activities aimed at saving the country [from Japanese colonization].

꿈을 실현하**기 위한** 계획을 세우면 꿈이 이루어질 거예요.
If you make a plan for realizing your dreams, then your dreams will come true.

Finally, note that the verb 위하– may also appear after regular nouns, which are then usually marked with the object particle 을/를:

건강**을 위해서** 날마다 운동을 해요.
I exercise every day for my health.

가난한 이웃**을 위해** 돈을 모읍시다.
Let's collect money for our poor neighbours.

2.2.4.8 *–기 이를 데 없–/그지 없–* 'boundless, endless'

This pattern has two alternative forms: –기 이를 데 없– and –기 그지 없–. They share the same basic meaning: that the state of affairs depicted by the descriptive verb to which the form attaches applies to a superlative degree:

정말 **기쁘기 이를 데 없어요**.	*I am only too glad.*
안타깝**기 그지없네요**.	*It is just too distressing.*
사랑스럽**기 그지없는** 조그만 강아지.	*An absolutely lovable little puppy.*

2.2.4.9 *–기 일쑤이– 'be apt to'*

Here, –기 is combined with the noun 일쑤 and the copula (refer to 4.1.4). The resultant pattern expresses that the action in question happens 'frequently' or 'customarily' or that the person being talked about 'tends to' or 'is apt to' carry out the behaviour in question. The state of affairs being talked about normally has negative connotations.

민호는 거짓말하**기 일쑤이지요**. *Minho is a compulsive liar.*

저는 차멀미를 하**기 일쑤예요**. *I tend to get motion sickness.*

몸에 해롭다는 것을 알면서도 툭하면 과음하**기 일쑤예요**.
Even though I know it is bad for health, I tend to drink too much.

유미는 건망증이 심해서 물건을 놓고 오**기 일쑤예요**.
Yumi suffers from forgetfulness, so she is apt to forget to bring things.

2.2.4.10 *–기 전 'before'*

In this pattern, the –기 is followed by the noun 전 (前) 'before'. Tense cannot be marked on the verb.

–기 전 may then be rounded off in three different ways: (1) by adding the particle of location 에 (refer to 3.2.4.1), (2) by adding the possessive particle 의 (refer to 3.2.3) or (3) by using the copula:

1. –기 전에
2. –기 전의
3. –기 전이에요

The first pattern (–기 전에) translates as 'before doing'. It links two actions or states, with the first occurring chronologically before the second:

자**기 전에** 이를 닦아요.
Before going to bed I brush my teeth.

학교에 가**기 전에** 은행에 들렀어요.
Before going to school I dropped by the bank.

잊어버리**기 전에** 지금 주세요.
Give it to me now before you forget.

The second pattern (–기 전의) translated as 'of before . . .' and is always followed directly by a noun:

해가 지기 **전의** 주변 풍경을 찍었어요.
I took a photo of the surroundings before the sun set.

시험을 치르기 **전의** 긴장이 풀렸어요.
The nervousness of before taking the exam lifted.

The third pattern (–기 전 followed by the copula) translates as 'it is/was before . . .':

미나가 태어나**기 전이었어요**.
It was before Mina was born.

실업이라는 개념이 사회 문제로 떠오르**기 전이었어요**.
It was before the concept of unemployment appeared as a social problem.

Finally, note that 전 may also appear after regular nouns:

점심 **전에** 회의가 끝날 예정이에요.
The meeting is scheduled to finish before lunch.

결혼 **전에** 유학을 갔어요.
I went to study abroad before marriage.

2.2.4.11 *–기 짝이 없–* 'very'

This pattern, which is formed by following the nominalized expression with –짝이 없– literally meaning 'there is no parallel/pair', has an emphatic meaning that commonly translates as 'very', 'so', 'terribly' or 'dreadfully':

미안하**기 짝이 없어요**. *I'm dreadfully sorry.*

바다가 아름답**기 짝이 없었어요**. *The sea is awfully beautiful.*

인호는 25살 되었어도 아직유치하**기 짝이 없어요**.
Inho is 25, but he's so childish.

후끈한 온실처럼 무덥**기 짝이 없었어요**.
It's terribly humid, like a sweltering greenhouse.

2.2.4.12 *–기나 하– 'just'*

The pattern –기나 하– combines –기 with the particle (이)나 (refer to 3.3.5.2), here in the meaning of 'just'. Tense markers do not appear with this pattern.

–기나 하– is used to mark a possible course of action that, although not first choice in an ideal world, is perhaps the best available to the person who has to perform it or represents a basic level that may be expected. As in the following examples, the pattern frequently attaches to the auxiliary verb pattern –(아/어) 보– 'try doing' (refer to 5.1.8).

한번 먹어 보**기나 해**.
Just try eating it once [it might not be that bad].

한 번 만나 보**기나 하세요**.
Just try meeting him once [and he/she might not be that bad].

미나는 우리한테 밥 한번 사 주**기나** 했어?
Has Mina ever just bought us a meal?

바이올린을 만져 보**기나** 했어요?
Have you ever just touched a violin?

–기나 하– can also be used in angry or sarcastic expressions meaning 'why don't you just . . .'.

빨리 먹**기나** 해!
Why don't you just eat up [and stop bugging me, etc.]?

빨리 사**기나** 해라.
Why don't you just go ahead and buy it [and stop dawdling].

2.2.4.13 *–기는 'no way'*

The pattern –기는 is a combination of –기 with the topic particle 는. –기는 may be abbreviated to –긴. In honorific speech, this should be followed by –요.

–기는 is used similar to English expressions 'No way!' or 'What do you mean?' when the speaker wants to reject an observation made by the interlocutor. To do this, the speaker repeats the verb from the previous sentence and adds this ending:

A: 유미가 정말 예쁘지요? *Yumi is really pretty, isn't she?*

B: 예쁘<u>**기는**</u>요. 미나가 훨씬 나아요. *No way. Mina is much better.*

A: 인호가 바보인가 봐. *Inho seems to be an idiot.*

B: 바보이<u>**긴**</u>. 얼마나 똑똑한데. *No way. He is so clever.*

A: 어디 가? *Where are you going?*

B: 가<u>**긴**</u>. 내가 어디를 가.
There's no way I'm going anywhere? Where would I have to go?

Frequently, –기는 appears in response to a compliment. By rejecting the compliment, the speaker appears humble:

A: 한국말 너무 잘하시네요. *You speak Korean so well.*

B: 잘 하<u>**기는**</u>요. 아직 서투른걸요.
Not really. My Korean is still really clumsy.

A: 와! 테니스를 잘 치네! *Wow! You play tennis so well.*

B: 잘 하<u>**긴**</u>. 배운 지 얼마나 안 됐어.
Not really. I haven't been learning long.

2.2.4.14 *–기는 하–* 'indeed'

–기는 하– combines –기 with the topic particle 는 (refer to 3.3.2.1) followed by the verb 하–. Tense markers do not appear before –기.

This pattern has an emphatic feeling and is used when the speaker realizes, accepts or concedes that a piece of information (often provided by the interlocutor) is indeed correct.

걷는 게 빠르<u>**기는 하네요**</u>!
(You were right), walking is indeed faster.

물론 돈이 없으면 힘들<u>**기는 해요**</u>.
Of course, if you don't have money, it is indeed tough.

인호가 착하<u>**기는 해요**</u>. *Inho is certainly nice.*

In addition to conceding that the information is indeed correct, in some contexts the pattern implies that the information is of limited significance. For example, the final example may imply, according to context, that Inho is *just* nice and not particularly talented, good looking, suitable, etc. Due to this feeling conveyed by this construction –기는 하– is frequently followed by verbal connectives that can express contrast, namely –지만 (refer to 7.2.1) and –는데 (refer to 7.3.12):

한글을 읽**기는 하지만** 말하기가 너무 어려워요.
I do read Korean, but speaking is too difficult.

그 여자는 예쁘**긴 하지만** 마음씨가 나빠요.
She does have a pretty face, but she's not a nice person.

Aside from using the verb 하–, the same meaning can also be conveyed by repeating the original verb. This is particularly common when the main verb is short and when the speaker wants to be particularly emphatic:

입어 보니까 **예쁘긴 예뻐요**!
Now that I've tried it on, it sure is pretty.

한글을 읽**기는 읽지만** 발음은 너무 못해요.
He can indeed read Hangul, but his pronunciation is terrible.

우리 딸은 잘 먹**기는 먹는데** 12개월인데도 9킬로 밖에 안 돼요.
Our daughter certainly eats well but she's 12 months and only weighs 9kg.

2.2.4.15 –기(는)커녕 'far from'

This pattern is a combination of –기 and the particle (은/는)커녕 (refer to 3.3.3.10), with the 는 element being optional in casual speech. Tense markers do not appear with this pattern.

–기는커녕 takes on meanings such as 'far from . . . ing':

즐겁**기는커녕** 아주 불쾌해요.
Far from being joyful, I feel very unpleasant.

주말에 쉬**기는커녕** 정신없이 일했어요.
Far from resting over the weekend, I worked hard.

칭찬을 듣**기는커녕** 꾸지람만 들을 거예요.
In place of hearing praise, he/she will hear only reproach.

2.2.4.16 –기도 하– 'also'

The pattern –기도 하– combines –기 with the particle 도 'also, even' (refer to 3.3.3.6). Tense markers do not appear with this pattern.

The pattern links two states of affairs. Although both states of affairs are true, the first one is primary or most frequent, and the second one is of secondary importance, salience or frequency:

귀가 간지러워요. 가끔 아프**기도 해**요.
My ear is itchy. And it hurts a bit too.

어머니는 시장에서 새우젓과 고사리 장사를 했어요. 그리고 은행 옆에서 지갑을 늘어놓고 팔**기도 했**어요.
Mother sold salt-pickled shrimps and dried bracken shoots at the market. And, at other times, she would also sell wallets on a stall next to the bank.

커피를 주로 마시지만 녹차를 마시**기도 해**요.
Although I normally drink coffee, I also drink green tea.

주로 지하철을 이용했지만 비가 올 때는 가끔 택시를 타**기도 했**어요.
Normally, we used the subway, but when it rained, we sometimes took a taxi.

–기도 하– often occurs twice in a sentence, linked by the verbal connective –고 'and' (refer to 7.3.1). This shows a kind of tandem agreement between noun phrases meaning 'both . . . and . . .' (or 'neither . . . nor . . .' in negative sentences). In these cases, both options are of equal or similar importance, frequency or salience:

한국음식은 맵**기도** 하고 짜**기도** 해요.
Korean food is both hot and salty.

학생 같**기도** 하고 깡패 같**기도** 해요.
He both looks like a student and looks like a gangster.

그 식당은 싸**기도** 하고 맛있**기도** 해서 인기가 많아요.
That restaurant is both cheap and delicious, so it is popular.

In another and rather different usage, the pattern –기도 하– may simply serve as an expression of emphasis, roughly equivalent to English expressions such as 'really', 'certainly', 'surely' or 'indeed'. Note that this usage of –기도 하– tends to go together with emphatic sentence-final endings such as the exclamatory –네 (refer to 9.5), the plain style –(ㄴ/는)다 (refer to 6.1.4) or the assertive –아/어라 (refer to 6.1.4):

저 산은 참 크**기도** 하네요!	*That mountain is certainly big!*
오늘은 참 춥**기도** 하다!	*It sure is freezing today!*

얼래? 예쁘**기도 해**라!
My, my, what have we here? Aren't you a pretty one!

2.2.4.17 –기만 하– 'only'

This pattern combines the nominal form with the particle 만 (refer to 3.3.3.1) meaning 'only' and the verb 하–.

When the construction occurs with a processive verb, the meaning is 'he/she only . . .' or 'he/she does nothing but . . .':

아기가 울**기만 해요**.	*The baby does nothing but cry.*
대학생 때 놀**기만 했어요**.	*When I was a student, I did nothing but 'play'.*
그냥 읽**기만 해**!	*Just read it!*

When the construction occurs with a descriptive verb, it depicts the continuation of a state (with the state often being undesirable or resistant to any attempts to change it).

하루 종일 힘들**기만 했어요**.	*I had a tough time all day long.*
아직 모든 게 낯설**기만 해요**.	*Everything still feels unfamiliar.*

2.2.4.18 –기로 하– 'decide to . . .'

In this pattern, the plain nominal form –기 is marked with the instrumental particle (으)로 (refer to 3.2.5.1) and followed by the verb 하–. The whole pattern -기로 하– usually translates as 'decide to' or 'choose to'. Note that this pattern is restricted to processive verb stems in the plain nominal form.

> 오늘 저녁에 미나를 만나**기로 했어요**.
> *I decided to meet Mina this evening.*

> 오늘은 집에 있**기로 했어요**.
> *I decided to stay home today.*

> 회사를 그만두**기로 했어요**.
> *I made up my mind to quit my job at the company.*

The nominal form may be negative (refer to 4.2), translating as 'decide not to do':

> 여름에 미국에 안 가**기로 했어요**.
> *I decided not to go to America in the summer.*

> 술을 마시지 않**기로 했어요**.
> *I made up my mind not to drink.*

The verb 하– in this pattern can be replaced by other verbs that express ways of choosing or deciding, including 결정하– 'decide', 결심하–/작정하– 'resolve', 약속하– 'promise', 선택하– and the idiomatic 마음을 먹– 'make up one's mind':

> 담배를 끊**기로 작정했어요**.
> *I have set my mind on quitting cigarettes.*

> 죽을 때까지 그 이야기를 하지 않**기로 약속했어요**.
> *I promised not to talk about that until the day I die.*

> 주식에 투자하**기로 마음 먹었어요**.
> *I made up my mind to invest in stocks.*

2.2.4.19 *–기로 되– 'be supposed to . . .'*

This pattern is closely related to –기로 하– (refer to 2.2.4.18) both in formation and in meaning. The structural difference is that 하– is replaced by 되– 'become'. This shift connotes a change from active to passive meaning (for wider discussion, see 'passives with 되-', refer to 4.4.1.2). The decision being talked about is thus one that is out of the speaker's control, in other words, something that has been decided by someone else or that is being imposed on the speaker. The pattern –기로 되– then translates as 'be decided that someone does', 'be supposed to', 'be expected to do', 'be scheduled to'.

Compare the difference in meaning between the sentences on the left using –기로 하– and those on the right using –기로 되–:

–기로 하 –	**–기로 되–**
다 같이 가**기로** 했어요 *We decided to go all together.*	다 같이 가**기로** 되었어요. *It's been decided that we're all going together.*
서류는 내일 보내**기로** 했어요. *We have decided to send the documents tomorrow.*	서류는 내일 보내**기로** 되었어요. *It's been decided to send the documents tomorrow.*

As can be seen in the following example, in present tense –기로 되– most commonly occurs in the –아/어 있– form (refer to 4.3.3.2), which expresses a present state (i.e., the state of 'being supposed to do something').

서류는 내일 보내**기로** 되어 있어요.
We are supposed to send the documents tomorrow.

서울 역 앞에서 만나**기로** 되어 있어요.
We are supposed to meet in front of Seoul station.

미나는 내일 병원에 입원하**기로** 되어 있어요.
Mina is scheduled to go into hospital tomorrow.

2.2.4.20 *–기를/길 바라–* 'hope'

In this pattern, –기 is followed by the object particle 를 and the verb 바라– hope to create the expression 'I hope . . .'. The combination of –기 and 를 is frequently shortened to –길.

그 사람이 대통령으로 당선되**기를 바랍니다**.
I hope that he'll be elected as president.

The object particle is frequently omitted in casual speech, simplifying the form to –기 바라–:

더 친해지**기 바라**. *I hope we become closer.*

However, even in casual speech, 를 is not omitted when the nominalized phrase it is attaching to is focussed or emphasized by the speaker (refer to 3.3.2 for more discussion of 를):

나는 잘 **살기를 바라**지 않는다. 그보다 네가 훌륭한 사람이 되**기를 바란**다.
I don't want us to live well [i.e., become rich]. I just want you to become a more upstanding person.

바라– can be replaced with similar verbs of desire expectation or longing such as 원하– 'desire, want', 기대하– 'expect', 기원하– 'wish' and 고대하– 'await eagerly'. Note that with the final three verbs, 를 is rarely omitted.

미나가 미국으로 가**길 원했어요**.
Mina wanted to go to America.

부모님은 내가 선생님이 되**기를 기대하셨어요**.
My parents expected me to be a teacher.

세계 소프트웨어 시장에서 대한민국 소프트웨어의 브랜드 가치가 더욱 **높아지길 고대한다**.
We eagerly await the brand equity of Korean software to continue to rise in the global software market.

This pattern – particularly with the verb 바라–is commonly employed in formulaic expressions that are used to express goodwill towards the hearer. Such expressions are typically employed as closings to e-mails and letters or in greeting cards.

늘 건강하시고 행복하게 사시**기를 바랍니다**!
I hope you always live healthily and happily! (= Take care of yourself and all the best!)

축복이 가득한 한 해가 되**기를 기원합니다**.
I wish you a new year full of blessings.

–기를 바라– also appears in formal requests (particularly on signs or public announcements) such as the following that you may hear on public transport. In these formal requests, it is more natural to drop 를:

내리실 때 조심하시**기 바랍니다**.
Please mind your step when you get off.

내리실 때는 두고 내리는 물건이 없는지 다시 한 번 살펴보시**기 바랍니다**.
Please make sure you have all your belongings with you when you get off.

2.2.4.21 –기에 'upon', 'because'

In this pattern, –기 appears immediately followed by the particle of location 에 (refer to 3.2.4.1). This pattern cannot appear with past or future tense marking and is most commonly encountered in written Korean. In spoken Korean, it can be replaced by the clausal connective –길래 (although this is more restricted in meaning – refer to 7.1.10) or other causal connectives (refer to 7.1).

–기에 expresses causation, with similar English equivalents being 'upon . . .', 'with . . .', 'because . . .'. The second clause typically depicts an action (often performed by the speaker himself) and the first clause provides a reason for that action (typically an event outside the speaker's control):

그 사람이 길을 묻**기에** 내가 가르쳐 주었어요.
Upon asking, I showed him/her the way to go.

비가 오**기에** 밖에 나가지 않았어요.
With it raining, [I] didn't go out.

친구가 온**다기에** 나는 집에서 기다리기로 했어요.
Hearing that my friend was coming, I decided to wait at home.

As can be seen in the final example, –기에 may occur after the quotative ending –ㄴ다 (refer to 10.2.1) when the first part of the sentence constitutes reported speech (in this instance, my friend saying that he was coming).

2.2.4.22 –기에 따라 'depending on'

This construction combines the –기 nominal form with 따라, meaning 'according to' or 'depending on'. It can only occur with processive verbs:

그 사람은 보**기에 따라** 달리 보여요.
He looks different depending on how you look at him.

치료하**기에 따라** 흉터가 생기지 않는 경우가 있다.
Depending on the type of treatment, there are cases where no scar is left.

This construction may appear after nouns in addition to nominal forms:

쇼핑 습관은 성별**에 따라** 달라요.
Shopping habits differ according to sex.

2.2.5 *Nominal form –음*

The nominal form –음 operates in the same way as –기 to convert a verb into a noun form. This form is more common in writing or formal speech and is frequently substituted by –(으)ㄴ/는 것 (refer to 8.2.2) in more casual speech. When attaching to a verb stem that ends with a vowel, the form is abbreviated to –ㅁ.

	Base	–음
consonant base	믿– *believe*	믿음 *belief*
vowel base	소중하– *be precious*	소중함 *preciousness*
irregular: ㅂ/ㅜ verbs	밉– *be detestable*	미움 *detestableness*
irregular: ㄷ/ㄹ verbs	깨닫– *realize*	깨달음 *realization*
irregular: ㅅ/ㅇ verbs	짓– *build, write*	지음 *building, writing*

In addition to the plain base, nominalizers with –음 may also be formed on past bases, future bases with –겠– and honorific bases with –시–. As shall be discussed below, –음 appears with past bases at a particularly high frequency.

Past base	Future base	Honorific base	
갔**음**	가겠음	가**심**	*going*
했**음**	하겠음	하**심**	*doing*

Although both –음 and –기 possess the same function of nominalization, the effect that they have on the verb are quite distinct. On the one hand, –기 simply makes a verb behave like a noun – the resultant nominalized form still retains its verb-like meaning and refers to the act of doing something. For example, when –기 is added to 믿– 'believe' the resultant form 믿기 means 'the act of believing'. On the other hand, when –음 is added the noun may lose its verb-like properties and cease to refer to an act. Instead, it may refer to a more abstract concept. 믿음, for example, translates as 'belief' rather than 'the act of believing'. The following are some other examples that show this contrast between –기 and –음:

Verb		*With –기*	*With –음*
믿– *believe*	→	믿기 *(the act of) believing*	믿음 *belief*
살– *live*	→	살기 *(the act of) living*	삶 *life*
알– *know*	→	알기 *(the act of) knowing*	앎 *knowledge*
죽– *die*	→	죽기 *(the act of) dying*	죽음 *death*

Whereas –기 designates the existence (or non-existence) of events, processes and states of affairs that are situated in time (i.e., that would have a given start and end point), –음 is usually employed when what is being talked about is an abstract 'truth' (or non-truth) that exists outside of space and time and is not physically 'real'. –음 thus often occurs with descriptive verbs; the addition of –음 turns the descriptive verb into an abstract nominalized form as in the following:

Descriptive verb			*Abstract nominalized form*	
소중하–	*be precious*	→	소중**함**	*importance, preciousness*
맑–	*be clear*	→	맑**음**	*clarity*
아름답–	*be beautiful*	→	아름다움	*beauty*

Alternatively, –음 can also be used when talking about a past truth (or non-truth) – about something that is asserted to have happened (or to have not happened). –음 thus also frequently occurs with processive verbs in the past tense:

Processive verb		*Past nominalized form*	
가–	→	갔**음**	*having gone*
졸업하–	→	졸업했**음**	*having graduated*

The verbs that commonly after a noun phrase constructed with –음 tend to be of a certain kind and quite different from those used with –기. They commonly include those that denote 'knowing/recalling/finding out (a certain truth or non-truth)', 'believing (a certain truth or non-truth)', '(a certain truth or non-truth) being (in)visible/(un)clear', etc. Here is a list of verbs that frequently occur after –음:

알–	*know/realize*	생각하–	*think*	느끼–	*feel*
깨닫–	*realize*	밝히–	*bring to light*	믿–	*believe*
잊–	*forget*	뚜렷하–	*is clear*	틀림없–	*be true*
상기하–	*recall*	자랑하–	*boast*	인정하–	*admit*
부인하–	*deny*	분명하–	*be clear*	증명하–	*prove*

Here are some examples using these verbs:

그 말을 굳게 믿었**음**이 분명해요.
It was clear that he/she strongly believed those words.

음악을 들으니 나이 먹었**음**을 깨닫네요.
I realize that I am getting old when I hear that music.

불법행위를 저질렀**음**을 인정했어요.
He/she admitted committing criminal acts.

법을 어기지 않았**음**을 증명했어요.
I proved that I had not broken the law.

–음 has one further specific use that is not shared by other nominal forms. It is used in abbreviated sentences in public signs, publications and notes, such as the following:

인공색소 없**음**	*No artificial colours.*
아르바이트 구**함**	*Part-time worker wanted.*
10시에 유미에게 전화 왔**음**	*Phone call from Yumi at 10.*
내일 일찍 오겠**음**	*Will come early tomorrow.*

This usage extends to the use of 드림 (from 드리–, object honorific verb 'give') and 올림 (from 올리– 'offer, present') in letter closings when addressing elders and non-intimates/strangers:

김민수 올**림**/드**림** *Yours sincerely, Kim Minsu*

2.2.6 Using –(으)ㄴ/는 것 to create nominal forms

Even though Korean has specialized nominal forms, speakers of Korean frequently use another means of turning a verb phrase into a noun, particularly in casual spoken language. This works by using the modifier form (refer to Chapter 8 for full description), followed by the dependent/bound noun 것 (refer to 2.1.2.1), which here literally means 'act, fact'. The pattern thus literally means 'the act of doing . . .' or 'the fact that one does . . .':

For processive verbs in the present tense, the form is –는 것:

비가 오**는 것**	*the fact that it's raining*
신문을 읽**는 것**	*the fact that he's reading the newspaper*

For processive verbs in the past tense or for all descriptive verbs (regardless of tense), the form is –(으)ㄴ 것:

비가 **온 것**	*the fact that it rained*
돈이 많**은 것**	*the fact that one has lots of money*

The pattern –(으)ㄴ/는 것 represents the most natural choice (even in formal speech or writing) when talking about seeing or hearing something or talking about being aware (or not being aware) of an ongoing fact:

비가 오**는 것**을 봤어요. *I saw it raining.*

한국말로 이야기하**는 것**을 들었어요.
I heard them speaking in Korean.

애기가 자**는 것**을 몰랐어요.
I didn't know that the child was sleeping.

Otherwise, particularly in casual spoken language, –(으)ㄴ/는 것 can replace –기 or –음 in the functions described previously in this chapter (refer to 2.2.3, 2.2.5). Note however that this does not include specific sentence patterns with –기 (refer to 2.2.4).

Here are some examples of –(으)ㄴ/는 것 replacing –기 or –음 with no alteration in meaning:

–기/–음	*–(으)ㄴ/는 것*
피아노 치**기**가 좋아요. *I like to play the piano.*	피아노 치**는 것**이 좋아요. *I like to play the piano.*
가르치**기**가 쉬워요. *Teaching is easy.*	가르치**는 것**이 쉬워요. *Teaching is easy.*
오**기**를 기다리고 있어요. *We are waiting for him/her to come.*	오**는 것**을 기다리고 있어요. *We are waiting for him/her to come.*
거짓말했**음**을 인정했어요. *I admitted I had lied.*	거짓말**한 것**을 인정했어요. *I admitted I had lied.*

However, there are some instances in which –(으)ㄴ/는 것 provides a different interpretation than the use of –기 (particularly when sentence subjects are dropped). The interpretation of sentences with –(으)ㄴ/는 것 tend to be more focussed on the position of the individual speaker; expressions with –기 express more general truths or things that are not seen from the speaker's viewpoint:

–기	*–(으)ㄴ/는 것*
오징어가 먹**기**가 좋아요. *The squid is good/easy to eat.*	오징어 먹**는 것**이 좋아요. *Eating squid is good/I like eating squid.*
여기서 술 마시**기**가 좋아요. *Here is good for drinking alcohol.*	여기서 술 마시**는 것**이 좋아요. *I like drinking alcohol here.*

2.3 Pronouns

Overview

Pronouns are words that can be used in place of nouns, typically either to avoid repetition or redundancy or when we are unsure of the exact name or identity of the person or thing in question.

Pronouns for talking about people ('personal pronouns') are typically divided into first person pronouns (such as 'I', 'we' in English), second-person pronouns ('you') and third-person pronouns ('he', 'she', 'they'). There are also demonstrative pronouns ('this', 'that', etc.), reflexive pronouns ('myself', 'yourself', 'himself', 'herself', etc.) and interrogative pronouns ('what', 'where', 'who', etc.).

Although these categories apply well to European languages, the following description will show that they do not always apply so well to Korean. In fact, rather than belonging to a separate grammatical category, Korean pronouns may be better described just as being the same as normal nouns. The reason why we treat them as a separate category here is for the convenience of readers and because the choice of these forms can be particularly tricky (and thus requires full explanation).

It should be pointed out before we begin that Korean uses fewer pronouns than English. The reason for this is that, when you repeatedly refer to the same person or thing, there is no strict requirement that you have to use a pronoun. Firstly, as Korean is a language in which elements that are obvious from context can be dropped, you may not need to repeat any reference at all. Secondly, even if you do repeat reference to the person or thing, repeating the person's name or the name of the object is usually more acceptable than it is in English.

However, when you do need to use a pronoun, choosing which pronoun to use can be very difficult to decide. This is because Korean has a long list of pronoun forms and the choice of them tends to rely on your social relationship to the person you are conversing with.

2.3.1 *Personal pronouns*

2.3.1.1 *First-person pronouns*

Korean has two distinct pronoun forms for the first person: the plain 나 'I' (plural: 우리 'we') and the humble (self-lowering) form

저 'I' (plural: 저희 'we'). When you are talking to intimates and children in non-honorific speech styles (refer to 6.1), you should use the plain forms. When you are talking to people older or superior to you in honorific speech styles, you should use the humble forms.

Note that both of the pronouns for 'I' have different forms when they occur before the subject particle 가 (refer to 3.2.1).

나	+	가	=	내가
저	+	가	=	제가

Any pronoun can be made possessive by adding the possessive particle 의 (refer to 3.2.3). When this 의 combines with 나 and 저, the resulting form can be contracted. By coincidence, this contracted form is the same as that which occurs when these pronouns precede 가.

나의	→	내
저의	→	제

2.3.1.2 *Second-person pronouns*

For the second person, there are a number of non-honorific pronoun forms: 너 (plural: 너희(들)), 자네 (plural: 자네들), 당신 (plural: 당신들) and 자기 (plural: 자기들). These forms all have very specific and limited applications: Korean does NOT have a universal 'you' that can be applied politely in all interactions.

너 is an intimate pronoun that can be used towards close friends of the same or younger age and towards children. It commonly occurs with either the 'intimate' or the 'plain' speech style (refer to 6.1.3, 6.1.4):

너는 뭐 하냐? *[PLAIN]*   *What are you doing?*

When 너 comes before the subject particle 가 (refer to 3.2.1), it has the alternative form 네 (네가). In addition, the possessive formed by combining 너 with the possessive particle 의 –너의– is also commonly abbreviated to 네. Since many younger speakers pronounce the vowels ㅔ and ㅐ the same, 네 'you, yours', thus becomes homophonous with 내 'my, mine'. To avoid this confusion, many younger speakers pronounce (and even write) 네 as 니:

Original form	*Contracted form*	*Pronunciation*
너 + 가	네가	니가
너 + 의	네	니

자네 is a pronoun that is used non-reciprocally by older adults (of at least 30 years of age) towards younger adults, or reciprocally within groups of older friends. It most commonly occurs with the 'familiar' speech style (refer to 6.1.5). The usage of this pronoun and register of speech is becoming more unusual in modern Korean society, at least in spoken language:

이 일은 **자네**가 하게. *[FAMILIAR]* *You do this job.*

당신 (當身) is sometime mistakenly taken to be the closest form to the English 'you'. However, its usage is in actual fact extremely restricted and great caution should be exercised. In modern Korean, it is most frequently used between couples, particularly when those couples are older than forty. Otherwise, this pronoun sometimes gets used as a deliberate way of being disrespectful and rude to someone when involved in an argument or confrontation:

당신이 뭔데 이래라 저래라 하는 거야! [INTIMATE]
Who do you think you are ordering me to do this and do that?

자기 (自己) represents a new, second-person pronoun that is most frequently used between young unmarried couples. Originally, this form was a reflexive pronoun (refer to 2.3.3). It is only relatively recently (within the last 50 years) that it has also started to be used as a second-person pronoun:

자기 지금 뭐 해? *What are you doing now?*

In addition to these forms, there are several other expressions that may be used in a similar way to pronouns. An elderly person may be respectfully addressed as **어르신**:

어르신 어디 편찮으세요? *Are you feeling unwell?*

Elder speakers may address an adult stranger as **댁**:

댁은 어디에 가세요? *Where are you going?*

When addressing someone of similar age and you are unsure how else to call him or her, you may say **그쪽**, literally meaning 'that side':

그쪽은요? *How about you?*

In song lyrics or poetry, you may encounter the rather antiquated **그대**:

나의 곁에 **그대** 없는 세상 있을 수도 없겠죠.
There cannot be a world where you are not by my side.

When using automated machines or internet sites, you may see the form **귀하** (貴下) as a way of addressing 'you'. This form was originally an honorific word for 'to' used when addressing envelopes to an elder or senior.

귀하의 비밀번호는 최소한 8 개 문자를 포함해야 합니다.
Your PIN number must consist of at least eight characters.

As these descriptions suggest, there are many circumstances in Korean where it is not appropriate to apply any second-person pronoun at all. This particularly applies to interactions with elders, status superiors and non-intimates when you are using the 'polite' and 'formal' speech styles (refer to 6.1.1, 6.1.2). So, if it is not possible to use any pronoun, what should you do? The first strategy is to retain the addressee's name or otherwise a title or kinship term (refer to 6.3). When you are unsure what term of address would be appropriate, using 선생님 (which literally means 'teacher') represents a safe choice. The second strategy is just to avoid saying anything at all – it is perfectly possible to form a Korean sentence with the subject and/or object dropped when it is obvious from context who you are talking about.

2.3.1.3 *Third-person pronouns*

Technically speaking, Korean has no proper third-person pronouns at all. Instead, Korean uses expressions that translate as 'that person', 'that woman', 'that thing', etc. Where appropriate, the word for 'that' (그) can be replaced by 'this' (이) or 'that . . . over there' (저), as discussed in more detail below.

When referring to a human third-person referent, the most generic form is 그 사람 'that person'. 그이 can also be used with similar meaning. However, it should be noted that these terms are non-honorific. When referring to an elder or status superior, you should replace 사람 with the honorific 분 (refer to 6.2.3). You could also refer to someone honorifically by using an honorific title such as 선생님 'teacher' – 그 선생님 'that teacher'. It should also be pointed out that 그 사람 and 그 분 may be understood by default to mean 'he' rather than 'she'. When it is necessary to clarify the sex of the person you are talking about, use 그 남자 'that man' (그 남자분 to be honorific) or 그 여자 (그 여자분 to be honorific).

그 사람은 너무 잘난 척 해요.	*He/she is too much of a show off.*
그 분은 갑자기 찾아오셨어요.	*He/she suddenly came to visit me.*
그 남자는 어떻게 되었나요?	*What on earth became of him?*
그 여자분은 제 선배님이세요.	*That woman is my university senior.*

There are a few other variants that you will frequently hear in spoken Korean, which tend to be used in non-honorific contexts. The term **그 애** (shortened in speech to 걔; plural 걔네들), literally meaning 'that child', is used not only to refer to children, but also by younger speakers to talk about those of the same or younger age. Similarly, you may refer casually to someone of the same or younger age as **그 친구**. Although this literally means 'that friend', it does not necessarily connote any intimacy in this usage. One's own son or someone extremely close may also be referred to as 그 **녀석** 'that guy/chap/boy'.

걔는 숨쉬는 것도 거짓이에요.
When he/she does as much as breathe, it is a lie.

걔네들은 왜 그러는 거냐?
Why do those guys carry on like that?

그 친구는 좋은 학생이에요.
He/she is a good student.

그 녀석 또 싸웠구나!
He has been fighting again!

In written Korean – particularly in novels translated from English – you may see the forms 그 and 그녀 as equivalents to 'he' and 'she', which are abbreviations of 그이 and 그여자, respectively. It should be noted, however, that these are literary devices that were devised to facilitate the translation of pronouns from European languages. They are not used in speech and rarely used in general writing.

Finally, a quick comment should be made on the choice of 이 'this', 그 'that', 저 'that over there' when referring to third persons. This three-way distinction between three demonstrative expressions (refer to 2.3.2), 이, 그 and 저, is different to the two-way distinction in English between 'this' and 'that'. 이 is equivalent to English 'this' and literally marks that the third-person entity is situated in proximity to the speaker. Both 그 and 저 correspond to English 'that', but whereas 그 marks proximity to the hearer, 저 marks that the entity is in a place 'over there' which is physically distant to both the speaker and the hearer. When talking about an entity not present at the speech event, 그 is generally used rather than 저.

이	*'this'*	situated near speaker
그	*'that'*	situated near hearer (or not present)
저	*'that . . . over there'*	situated far from speaker and hearer

When referring to a person who is present at the speech event, the most common form is 이 (i.e., 이 사람, 이 분, 얘, etc.) for the simple reason that present persons are generally physically located close to the speaker. The 저 form (i.e., 저 사람, 저 분, 쟤, etc.) is used for a person who is present, but located far from the speaker. However, research has shown that speakers may also sometimes use 저 to refer to people standing or sitting right next to them (refer to Oh 2010). In such cases, rather than marking physical location, use of 저 marks that the person in question is located in a different category regarding the topic of conversation. For example, Oh's (2010) research features a husband using the sentence 저 사람이 추워서 'that person over there is cold' to refer to his wife during a discussion about whether to turn off the air-conditioning. Here, the use of 저 signals that the wife is in the group of people within the room who are feeling too cold, whereas the husband is not.

The 그 form (i.e., 그 사람, 그 분, 걔, etc.) is rarely used for referring to people present at the speech event since it is unusual in a speech event for a person to be located far from the speaker and near the hearer. Instead, this form is used as the typical way for referring to a non-present person. However, the 이 form (i.e., 이 사람, 이 분, 얘, etc.) can also be used to give more prominence. For example, when retelling a story, Korean speakers may use the 이 form when referring to the main character, but the 그 form for others (refer to Oh 2007).

2.3.2 Demonstrative pronouns

Demonstrative pronouns for non-personal objects are formed by combining the demonstrative expression 이 ('this'), 그 ('that'), 저 ('that over there'), followed by bound nouns 것 ('thing'), 때 ('time'), or 곳 ('place'). As described in the previous section (2.3.1), the choice between 이, 그, 저 relates to how near the entity is to the speaker and hearer.

		Thing	*Time*	*Place*	*Usage*
		–것	-때	-곳	
this	이	이것	이때	이곳	near speaker
that	그	그것	그때	그곳	near hearer
that over there	저	저것	접때	저곳	not near speaker or hearer

Note that 것 may be abbreviated to 거 (and to 게, 걸 and 건 when it occurs with the subject, object and topic particles respectfully – refer to Chapter 3)

Here are some examples:

이게 한국 음식이에요.
This is Korean food.

그때는 달라요.
That [time, occasion] is different.

이곳은 미국 속의 작은 서울이에요.
This is a 'little Seoul' within America.

2.3.3 *Reflexives and reciprocals*

Korean has five reflexive pronouns: 자기, 자신, 저/지, 당신 and 자체. The first four of these are used for people, the fifth is used for objects.

자기 is most often used in the third person (although it can also appear in the second person).

> 처음으로 **자기**의 옷을 직접 샀어요.
> *He/she bought him/herself clothes for the first time.*

> 그 여자는 **자기**가 미인인 줄 알아요
> *She thinks that she herself is beautiful.*

자신 (自身) can be used in the first, second or third person and can also appear alongside 자기 ('자기 자신') for special emphasis, as in the third example:

> **자신**만 생각하지 맙시다. *Let's not just think of ourselves.*

> **자기 자신**에게 거짓말을 해요. *He/she is lying to him/herself.*

저 is a colloquial equivalent of 자기. It is often pronounced (and even written) as '지':

> 유미는 **지**가 필요할 때만 연락하는 거야.
> *Yumi only contacts me when she needs something for herself.*

> 왜 **지** 생각만 하는 거야?
> *Why does he/she only think of him/herself?*

Note that when you are referring to someone who you need to talk about in honorifics, 자기, 자신 and 저 should not be used. Traditionally, **당신** may be used in this function, although this is becoming rarer in modern Korean (and is only commonly applied when referring to one's parents, grandparents or teachers):

> 할아버지는 **당신**이 100살까지 사실 것이라고 하셨어요.
> *Grandfather said that he will live to be 100.*

Rather than using 당신, most Korean speakers prefer to avoid reflexive pronouns when using honorifics. In other words, they just delete the pronoun completely or repeat the original form of address.

When talking about inanimate objects, the Korean equivalent of 'itself' is **자체** (自體):

방법 **자체**가 문제예요	*The method itself is the problem.*
그 **자체**의 무게로 쓰러졌어요.	*It fell of its own weight.*

Korean also has one reciprocal pronoun: 서로, which means 'each other' or 'one another'. For added emphasis, 서로 can be duplicated to form 서로서로:

유미와 미나는 **서로** 싫어해요.
Yumi and Mina hate each other.

서로서로 도와주는 친구들이에요.
We are friends who help each other.

2.3.4 Interrogative pronouns

Korean interrogative pronouns (and other question words) are as follows:

누구	*who*	어디	*where*	언제	*when*
무엇 [뭐]	*what*	왜	*why*	얼마	*how much*
어떻게	*how*	어느	*which*	어떤	*what kind of*
무슨	*what kind of, what*	웬	*what/why on earth*	몇	*how many, what*

Here are examples of these in sentences:

유미 남자 친구가 **누구**예요?	*Who is Yumi's boyfriend?*
지금 **어디**에 가세요?	*Where are you going now?*
언제 오셨어요?	*When did you come?*
뭐 드시겠어요?	*What would you like to eat?*
왜 한국말을 배우세요?	*Why do you learn Korean?*
맥주가 **얼마**예요?	*How much is the beer?*
한국어를 **어떻게** 배우셨어요?	*How did you learn Korean?*

어느 나라에서 오셨어요?	*Which country are you from?*
어떤 음식을 좋아하세요?	*What kind of food do you like?*
무슨 영화를 보셨어요?	*What film did you see?*

너 **웬** 말이 이렇게 많아?
Why on earth are you talking so much?

한국어를 공부한 지 **몇** 년 됐어요?
How many years have you studied Korean?

As you can see in these examples, these question pronouns are sometimes followed by particles (refer to Chapter 3) in the same way that other nouns are. In the case of 누구 'who', note that when this question pronoun combines with the subject particle 가 (refer to 3.2.1), it contracts to 누가:

누가 그런 말을 했어요? *Who said that?*

It should be noted that, in addition to be used in questions, Korean question pronouns can be used in statements as indefinite pronouns. In such cases, rather than meaning 'who', 'when', 'where', etc., they instead take on the meaning of 'someone', 'somewhere', 'sometime', etc. Here are some examples:

누가 왔어요.
Someone has come.

어디 가서 이야기하자.
Let's go somewhere and talk about it.

언제 한번 저녁이나 함께 합시다.
Let's have dinner together sometime.

무엇 좀 먹었으면 좋겠어요.
I would like to eat something.

Some question words can take different forms when they are used as indefinite pronouns:

누구 who	누군가 someone
어디 where	어딘가 somewhere
언제 when	언젠가 sometime

뭐 what 뭔가 something

왠 what/why on earth 왠가 for some reason

2.4 Numbers and counting

Overview

Korean is not content with having just one number system but has two separate systems: Pure-Korean numerals and Sino-Korean numerals. Each of these has distinct and separate usages. Korean numbers do not tend to occur alone but appear in combination with 'counters' – words that specify the kind of item being counted.

2.4.1 *Pure Korean and Sino-Korean numbers*

Korean has two parallel sets of numbers. There is one of native origin, often called pure Korean numerals, and another one of Chinese origin, usually called Sino-Korean numerals. As will be explained in more detail below (refer to 2.4.2), the uses of these two sets of numbers are usually quite distinct.

As you will see in the lists below, Sino-Korean numbers are more straightforward than their pure Korean counterparts. Once you have learned 1 to 10 in Sino-Korean, all other numbers up to 99 can be formed just by combining these three elements. For example, 20 is literally 'two-ten', 30 is 'three-ten', etc. In the Pure Korean system, however, there are separate words for 20, 30, etc. Note that some of the pure Korean numbers have different forms that are used before counters (refer to 2.4.2).

	Pure Korean numerals	*Sino-Korean numerals*
1	하나 [한 before counter]	일
2	둘 [두 before counter]	이
3	셋 [세 before counter]	삼
4	넷 [네 before counter]	사
5	다섯	오

6	여섯	육
7	일곱	칠
8	여덟	팔
9	아홉	구
10	열	십
11	열하나 [열한 before counter]	십일
20	스물 [스무 before counter]	이십
30	서른	삼십
40	마흔	사십
50	쉰	오십
60	예순	육십
70	일흔	칠십
80	여든	팔십
90	아흔	구십
100	(온)	백; 일백
200		이백
1,000	(즈믄)	천; 일천
10,000		만; 일만
100,000		십만
1,000,000		백만
10,000,000		천만
100,000,000		억; 일억
1,000,000,000		십억

As can be seen, the Sino-Korean system is more developed for the expression of high numbers than the pure Korean system. Indeed, even though the pure Korean system does have words for 100 and 1,000, these are only found in older texts and never appear in modern Korean. Thus, in the present-day language, the pure Korean system can only be used for counting up to 99. For this reason, even when counting things that normally occur with the pure Korean system (refer to 2.4.2), speakers must switch to the Sino-Korean set for quantities of 100 or larger. The other possible alternative is to mix the two systems. For example, when saying the number 121, a speaker may say 100 in the Sino-Korean system and 21 in the pure Korean (i.e., 백 스물 하나). In spoken language, the point where speakers switch from the pure Korean system to the Sino-Korean often happens much sooner than 100. Indeed, you may frequently hear speakers 'switch' to the Sino-Korean system for quantities of 30 or above, particularly for round numbers.

The two Korean numerals differ in the way ordinals (i.e., 'first', 'second', 'third', etc.) are formed. The native ordinals are formed with the suffix –째, as in 둘째 'second' and 셋째 'third'. The exception is 하나 'one' because the ordinal 'first' is the special form 첫째. From the ten units on, however, 한 is used instead of 첫–, and 두 is used for 'two' instead of 둘– as in 열한(번)째 'eleventh', 열두(번)째 'twelfth', 스물한(번)째 'twenty-first', and 스물두(번)째 'twenty-second'. In contrast with this native system, the Sino-Korean ordinals are expressed by attaching the prefix 제– to the basic numerals, as in 제일 'first', 제이 'second', 제십삼 'thirteenth'.

2.4.2 *Which system to use*

The pure Korean numbers are used in the following situations:

1 to count real tangible things such as potatoes, cars, cups of coffee, books, fish and people
2 to express someone's age with the counter 살 (see below) (Sino-Korean is also possible here with the counter 세)
3 to say the hour (o'clock)
4 to count hours, months (also possible in Sino-Korean) and sometimes years (although the Sino-Korean system is more commonly used for the last of these) (refer to 2.4.4)

The Sino-Korean numbers are used in the following situations:

1 to talk about figures, sums and prices
2 to say the minute and the second (and for counting minutes and seconds)

3 to say the date
4 to count weeks, months, years and days (although all of these *can* be done in pure Korean and, for counting days, there are occasions when pure Korean numbers need to be used)

As noted above, Korean numbers often appear, not on their own, but followed by a counter word that marks what is being counted. The table below summarizes the most common counters used in Korean, but does not include counters used for naming and counting periods of time. These are dealt with separately below (refer to 2.4.4).

Unit being counted	*Counter*	*Number system*	*Example*
objects	개	Pure Korean numbers	사과 한 개 *one apple*
cups	잔		커피 두 잔 *two cups of coffee*
paper; tickets	장		종이 세 장 *three sheets of paper*
books	권		책 네 권 *four books*
boxes; cases	상자		사과 다섯 상자 *five boxes of apples*
bags	봉지		과자 한 봉지 *one bag of snack food*
bottles	병		맥주 두 병 *two bottles of beer*
vehicles; appliances; machines	대		자동차 세 대 *three cars* 냉장고 네 대 *four refrigerators* 기계 세 대 *three machines*
buildings	채		집 한 채 *one house*
animals	마리		고양이 한 마리 *one cat* 생선 한 마리 *one fish (to eat)*
people	사람		고객 한 사람 *one customer*
	명		일본 사람 한 명 *one Japanese person*
	분*		선생님 한 분 *one teacher*
years of age	살		스무 살 *twenty years old*
times	번		두 번 *two times; twice*
kinds	가지		세 가지 *three kinds*

floors	층	Sino-Korean numbers	3 (삼) 층 *the third floor*
portions	인분		불고기 3 (삼) 인분 *three portions of pulgogi*
won	원		10,000 (만) 원 *ten thousand won*
dollars	불		10 (십) 불 *ten dollars*
pounds	파운드		100 (백) 파운드 *one hundred pounds*
metres	미터		1000 (천) 미터 *a thousand metres*

*honorific form (refer to 6.2.3)

As the list above shows, the counter 분 can mean either 'people' or 'minutes' depending on context. However, the ambiguity is also solved by the fact that the two counters go with different number systems:

2.4.3 *Sentence patterns with numbers*

The examples shown in the previous table all follow the basic sentence pattern of noun-numeral-counter. Although this is the most common sentence pattern that occurs in number constructions, it is by no means the only one. There are actually four different sentence patterns that can occur with numerals:

1 Noun-Numeral:
학생 다섯이 숙제를 안 했어요.
Five students didn't do their homework.

2 Noun-Numeral-Counter:
학생 다섯 명이 숙제를 안 했어요.
Five students didn't do their homework.

3 Numeral-Noun:
다섯 학생이 숙제를 안 했어요.
Five students didn't do their homework.

4 Numeral-Counter-Possessive Particle-Noun:
다섯 명의 학생이 숙제를 안 했어요.
Five students didn't do their homework.

The usage and conditions for selecting each of the four patterns shown above are slightly different. As the most widely used pattern in modern Korean, pattern (2) is used with no special restrictions. The use of pattern (1) is more restricted. It is a natural number construction for counting people, but can also be used with many countable nouns in informal or colloquial situation: 커피 둘 'two coffees', 빵 하나 'one bread', etc. Pattern (3) was used extensively in Middle Korean, but now its use has diminished. Pattern (4) is mostly a written rather than a colloquial usage.

When you want to form a question that in English would translate as 'how many . . .?' or 'how much . . .?', use the question word 몇 and combine it with the counter word for the item in question. The following is an abbreviated list of the resulting expressions:

Item	*Question expression*	*Example*
objects	개	사과 **몇 개** 먹었어요? *How many apples did you eat?*
cups	잔	소주 **몇 잔** 마셨어요? *How many glasses of soju did you drink?*
paper; tickets	장	기차 표 **몇 장** 샀어요? *How many train tickets did you buy?*
books	권	책 **몇 권** 읽었어요? *How many books did you read?*
animals	마리	고양이 **몇 마리** 있어요? *How many cats are there?*
people	명	학생 **몇 명** 왔어요? *How many students came?*
times	번	한국에 **몇 번** 갔어요? *How many times have you been to Korea?*
floors	층	사무실은 **몇 층**에 있어요? *What floor is the office on?*
metres	미터	수영장은 **몇 미터**예요? *How many metres is the swimming pool?*

When asking the date, you can ask what literally means 'what month, what day' it is. Note that the expression for 'what day' is the one-word 며칠 (*not* '몇 일'). Contrary to the common assumption that 며칠 is composed of 몇+일, this word developed historically from the unrelated '며츨' in Middle Korean. This explains what, on the face of it, appears to be an unusual spelling.

몇 월 며칠이에요?
What is the date?

몇 월 며칠에 입국하셨어요?
On what date did you enter the country?

며칠 can also be used for asking about periods of time (i.e., 'how many days . . .'):

며칠(동안) 서울에 머무르셨어요?
How many days did you stay in Seoul?

When asking 'how many . . .' questions, the particle –(이)나 (refer to 3.3.5.2) is frequently heard following the counter. Addition of this particle gives a feeling of approximation (similar to using 'about' in English) and thus works to make the question sound softer:

부작용은 **몇 년이나** 갈까요?
How long will the side effects last?

하루에 커피를 **몇 잔이나** 드시나요?
How many cups of coffee do you drink in a day?

2.4.4 Counting and naming periods of time

The occasion when the selection of numeric systems becomes most complicated and where both systems are often used together is in the expression of time.

2.4.4.1 Years

When referring to a certain year, the Sino-Korean numbers are used with the counter for years 년:

2003(이천삼)년	*the year 2003*
몇 년 생이세요?	*What year were you born in?*
85(팔십오)년 생이에요.	*I was born in 1985.*

When counting years, either the Sino-Korean numbers with 년 or the Pure-Korean numbers with 해 can be used. Although both have identical meaning, the Sino-Korean system is more commonly heard these days:

몇 해	or	몇 년	*how many years?*
한 해		일 년	*one year*
두 해		이 년	*two years*
세 해		삼 년	*three years*

2.4.4.2 *Months*

To express the names of the months, use the Sino-Korean numbers in combination with 월'month'. Note that 유월 'June' and 시월 'October' are irregular forms.

일월	*January*	이월	*February*
삼월	*March*	사월	*April*
오월	*May*	유월	*June*
칠월	*July*	팔월	*August*
구월	*September*	시월	*October*
십일월	*November*	십이월	*December*

For counting years and months, both number systems can be used, but with different counters. The Sino-Korean system appears with 개월 and the pure Korean numbers are accompanied with 달– both means of expression are commonly heard in spoken Korean. With the Pure-Korean system note that, for three and four, 세 and 네 may be replaced by 석 and 넉, particularly in the speech of older generations.

몇 달	or	몇 개월	*how many months*
한 달		일 개월	*one month*

두 달	or	이 개월	*two months*
세/석 달		삼 개월	*three months*
네/넉 달		사 개월	*four months*

2.4.4.3 Weeks

Korean has two expressions that correspond to 'week' –주간 and 주일– which can both appear either with the Pure Korean or Sino-Korean numerals. However, the most common way to count weeks is to abbreviate 주일 to 주 and use Sino-Korean numbers:

몇 주	*how many weeks*		
일 주	*one week*	이 주	*two weeks*
삼 주	*three weeks*	사 주	*four weeks*

2.4.4.4 Days

When expressing the day of the month, the Sino-Korean system is used in combination with the 일 followed optionally by 날 in colloquial Korean:

오 일(날) *the fifth of the month*

Without the addition of 날, this pattern can also be used to count a duration of days:

삼십 일 *thirty days*

Although this pattern is used exclusively for counting periods of 30 days or more, other systems exist for smaller numbers.

First, for periods under twenty days, there is a special set of words that can be used instead. The special words for '1 day' and '2 days' listed below remain the most common ways to express these periods in Korean. However, although one may sometimes hear the expressions for 3, 4 and 10 days, most of the other expressions are fairly rare in the speech of younger Koreans, who prefer instead to use Sino-Korean numbers with 일.

하루	*1 day*	이틀	*2 days*
사흘	*3 days*	나흘	*4 days*
닷새	*5 days*	엿새	*6 days*
이레	*7 days*	여드레	*8 days*
아흐레	*9 days*	열흘	*10 days*
열하루	*11 days*	열 이틀	*12 days*
열사흘	*13 days*	열 나흘	*14 days*
열닷새	*15 days*	열 엿새	*16 days*
열이레	*17 days*	열 여드레	*18 days*
열아흐레	*19 days*		

In addition, it is also possible to express a date by combining the Pure-Korean numbers with 날. Some speakers, particularly those of older generations, use this to count from 21–29 days. However, from 30 days, this means of expression is never used:

스무날	*20 days*	스무하루	*21 days*
스무이틀	*22 days*	스무사흘	*23 days*

2.4.4.5 *Telling the time*

To tell the time in Korean,use the pure Korean numerals followed by 시 which is equivalent to 'o'clock':

한 시 *one o'clock* 여섯 시 *six o'clock* 열두 시 *twelve o'clock*

To say 'half past', put '반' 'and a half' after this expression:

한 시 반 *1:30* 세 시 반 *3:30* 열 한 시 반 *11:30*

A specific number of minutes after the hour is expressed by Sino-Korean numbers with 분 'minute' after the expression:

한 시 이십분	*1:20*	여섯 시 십오 분	*6:15*
열 한 시 오십오 분	*11:55*		

To express the number of minutes before the hour, use the same expression but add 전 'before' at the end:

한 시 십 분 전
10 minutes to one [one o'clock 10 minutes before]

다섯 시 십오 분 전
quarter to five [five o'clock 15 minutes before]

For 'am' and 'pm', you use 오전 'am' and 오후 'pm' at the beginning of the expression:

오전 세 시 *three am* 오후 네 시 *four pm*

In spoken language, 아침 'in the morning' or 새벽 'in the early morning, in the small hours, at dawn' are typically used in case of 오전 'am'. Although 오후 'pm' is used in spoken language, it is only generally applied to mean 'in the afternoon'. 낮 may also be used to refer to the afternoon. To say 'in the evening' or 'at night', 저녁 and 밤 are used instead.

새벽 세 시 *three o'clock in the morning*
아침 일곱 시 *seven o'clock in the morning*
낮 한 시 *one o'clock in the afternoon*
오후 네 시 *four o'clock in the afternoon*
저녁 일곱 시 *seven o'clock in the evening*
밤 아홉 시 반 *half past nine in the evening*

To say 'exactly such-and-such a time', you put 정각 after the time expression:

한시 반 정각(에) *(at) exactly 1:30*

The word 시 means 'hour' only in the sense of a point in time, an 'o'clock'. For length or duration of time, 시간 'hour' is used (시간 also means 'time' in general):

여섯 시간 일했어요. *I worked [for] six hours.*
몇 시간 일했어요? *How many hours did you work?*

2.4.4.6 *Telling the date*

Dates are given in Korean by giving the year first (followed by the counter 년), then the month (월) and finally the day (일).

2019(이천십구)년 12(십이)월 10(십)일 *10th December 2019*

Chapter 3

Particles

Overview

This chapter looks at a special category of words in Korean: particles (조사), which are also in some contexts referred to as 'postpositions'. These particles attach to the end of nouns (and sometimes other kinds of word) to signal their grammatical function or to add extra meaning.

Two kinds of particles are identified and discussed in turn: case particles (격조사) and special particles (보조사 or 특수조사). Case particles are used to express the syntactic role of the noun or noun phrase to which they are attached. Special particles are used only to add to the meaning – for example, they are used for emphasis and focus.

3.1 Defining particles

Korean particles indicate or provide further information regarding the grammatical function of words in a sentence. The use of particles in Korean contrasts with their absence in English where word order rather than any grammatical marker tells speakers of English how words relate to each other in a sentence. In the following English sentence, for example, we know that Mia is the subject of the sentence because 'Mia' comes before the verb, and that the 'snake' is the object of the sentence because 'a snake' comes after the verb. The sentence can only be taken to mean that it was *Mia* who ate *the snake* (and not *the snake* that ate *Mia*):

Mia ate a snake.

In Korean, identifying the grammatical role of words simply through word order is complicated by the fact that word order is relatively flexible (see 1.1.2.1). Speakers thus rely primarily on particles rather than word order to interpret the grammatical function of different words. To be sure, Korean has a common word order for simple sentences that is subject–object–verb (see 1.1.2.1). However, with appropriate use of particles, the same meaning can be achieved by putting the object before the subject. Thus, even though the following two sentences have different word orders, due to use of particles, the following two sentences can both only be interpreted as meaning that it was *Mia* who ate *the snake* (and not *the snake* that ate *Mia*):

미아가	뱀을	먹었어요.
Mia-**subject**	snake-**object**	ate

Mia ate the snake.

뱀을	미아가	먹었어요.
snake-**object**	Mia-**subject**	ate

Mia ate the snake.

'Subject' and 'object' are just two of the grammatical roles (or 'cases') that particles can signal. Particles are also used to mark possession (like ' . . .'s' or 'of' in English), location (like English 'in', 'at', 'to', 'from', etc.), means or method (like 'by' in English) and a host of other meanings such as 'and', 'only', 'even', 'every', 'about', 'like', etc.

Korean particles can be divided into two categories: case particles, which are used to express the grammatical role of the noun or noun phrase to which they attach; and special particles, which are used to express extra additional meanings. The following sections discuss these two sets of particles in turn.

3.2 Case particles

Case particles mark the syntactic function of nouns appearing in the sentence. This section looks at seven kinds of case particles: subject, object, possessive, movement/location, instrumental, comitative and vocative.

3.2.1 The subject particle 이/가

The subject particle is one of several 'two-shape' particles; in other words, it has two different forms depending on whether it attaches to a noun that ends in a consonant or a noun that ends in a vowel. 이 is the form that occurs after a consonant and 가 after a vowel. When talking about an elder, status superior, etc. who needs to be referred to using honorifics, an alternative subject particle should (or at least can) be used: 께서 (see 6.2.3).

The words 나 'I (plain)', 저 'I (humble)' 너 'you' and 누구 'who?' have altered shapes before this particle. These are as follows:

나 → 내가

저 → 제가

너 → 네가 (frequently pronounced as [니가] in colloquial speech)

누구 → 누가

이/가 is mainly used to mark what can be considered to be the grammatical subject of the sentence.

마리<u>가</u> 맥주를 마셨어요.	*Mari drank beer.*
키위<u>가</u> 너무 비싸요.	*The kiwis are too expensive.*
한국에 온 지 1년<u>이</u> 되었어요.	*One year has passed since I came to Korea.*

There are, however, many situations in which grammatical subjects appear without 이/가. This first of all occurs when 이/가 is replaced by other particles with which it cannot (or does not usually) occur, including 만 'only' (refer to 3.3.3.1), 도 'also' (refer to 3.3.3.6) and, most notably the topic particle 은/는 (refer to 3.3.2.1). In colloquial speech, subject nouns often appear with no particle at all. The question of choosing between 이/가 and 은/는 or dropping any particle altogether will be explored in more depth in the section on 은/는(refer to 3.3.2.1).

Another complication is that there are a number of expressions in Korean where the element that is marked with the subject particle would not necessarily be considered the subject in English or other languages. Firstly, 이/가 appears with the verb 되– 'become', in sentences such as the following:

의사**가** 되고 싶어요.	*I want to become a doctor.*

Furthermore, the subject particle (and not the object particle) is used when talking about someone (not) having something (with the verbs 있– and 없–), someone having many of something (많–) and someone needing something (필요하–). These constructions literally mean 'for me, . . . exists/doesn't exist', 'for me, . . . are plentiful' and 'for me, . . . is necessary' and hence the subject marker is correct. The first noun is typically marked either by the topic marker (refer to 3.3.2.1), or the locative 에게/한테(refer to 3.2.4.4), but see discussions below.

저는 자전거**가** 있어요.	*I have a bicycle. – lit., 'for me, a bicycle(subject) exists'*
저는 오토바이**가** 없어요.	*I don't have a bicycle. – lit., 'for me, a motorbike(subject) doesn't exist'*
유미는 신발**이** 많아요.	*Yumi has many shoes. – lit., 'for Yumi, many shoes(subject) exist'*
민호는 시간**이** 필요해요.	*Minho needs time. – lit., 'for Minho, time(subject) is needed'*

Similarly, in place of sentences such as 'I like . . .' or 'I hate . . .', Korean frequently uses constructions that translate directly as 'for me, . . . is good' or 'for me, . . . is hateful'. Such constructions result in similar patterns of particle use as above (and in phrases quite distinct to anything found in English):

저는 유미**가** 좋아요.
I like Yumi. – lit., 'for me, Yumi(subject) is good'

저는 뱀**이** 싫어요.
I hate snakes. – lit., 'for me, snakes(subject) are hateful'

미아는 대한민국**이** 너무 자랑스러웠어요.
Mia was so proud of Korea. – lit., 'for Mia, Korea(subject) was so proud'

As noted, in the above examples, the first noun is most commonly marked by the topic particle (refer to 3.3.2.1), or the locative

에게/한테 (refer to 3.2.4.4). However, with a slightly different nuance, the topic particle can be replaced by the subject particle resulting in a clause with two apparent subjects. Use of the subject particle works to place more focus on the first noun (resulting in the translations below 'it is . . . who/that . . .') (refer to 3.3.2.1):

유미가 신발**이** 많아요.	*It is Yumi who has many shoes.*
제가 뱀**이** 싫어요.	*It is I who hates snakes.*

A second circumstance in which these apparent 'double-subject' sentences occur is with possessive constructions. Here, the first noun could also be marked with the possessive particle 의 (see 3.2.3). Use of the subject particle instead brings the first noun into more focus and results in translations such as 'it is . . . who/that . . .':

유미가 동생**이** 예뻐요.	*It is Yumi whose younger sister is pretty.*
민수가 눈**이** 커요.	*It is Minsu whose eyes are big.*

Whether both of the nouns in these kinds of sentences actually constitute grammatical subjects per se is a complex argument that is still being debated by Korean linguists!

3.2.2 The object particle 을/를

The object particle is a two-shape particle: 을 is used after a consonant and 를 is used after a vowel. In colloquial speech, after a vowel, 를 is often abbreviated to just –ㄹ, especially in common expressions like 날 'me', and 이걸 'this thing'. Also, in colloquial speech, 을/를 may frequently be dropped when the status of the noun in question as sentence object is obvious from context. This tends to particularly occur with common noun + verb combinations such as 밥 먹어요 'eat rice'.

In most cases, nouns marked by 을/를 correspond directly to the concept of 'object' in English. In colloquial speech, given the fact that 을/를 can be omitted if the noun's 'object-hood' is clear, inclusion of 을/를 can work to place extra emphasis on the noun in question:

소파에 앉아 텔레비전**을** 봤어요.
I sat on the sofa and watched television.

아기가 잠을 잘 자요.
The baby sleeps (lit., 'sleeps a sleep)' well.

아저씨가 트로트 음악을 좋아해요.
The man likes 'trot' music.

Although the object will most generically appear after the subject, the use of grammatical marking on both means that the word order can change without altering the meaning in any way. Thanks to the use of particles, the following two sentences can both only be interpreted as meaning 'mother sees baby' (and never 'baby sees mother'):

어머니가 애기를 봐요. *Mother sees baby.*

애기를 어머니가 봐요. *Mother sees baby.*

As previously noted, in spoken Korean, either subject or object particle may be dropped. If only one particle drops, there is still no problem to interpret the sentence: 어머니가 애기 봐요 and 어머니 애기를 봐요 can only mean 'mother sees baby'. If both particles are omitted, the sentence could become ambiguous. However, without any marking, the noun phrases in the sentence would usually be interpreted as subject-object order: 어머니 애기 봐요 normally means 'mother sees baby'.

Let us now examine some complications regarding the use of 을/를, including some usages in which it marks a noun that does not appear to be the actual object as such. As well as marking the sentence object, 을/를 can also appear with locative nouns where we would more commonly expect to see 에 'to/in/at' (3.2.4.1) in the first two examples and 에서 'from' (refer to 3.2.4.3) in the last two:

마리가 병원을 혼자 갔어요.
Mari went to the hospital alone.

수요일마다 요리 학원을 다녀요.
I attend cookery school every Wednesday.

백화점을 나와서 시장으로 갔어요.
After leaving the department store, I went to the market.

해가 지자 산**을** 내려왔어요.
When the sun set, we came down from the mountain.

In the sentences above, using 을/를 in place of 에 or 에서 does not result in any important shift in meaning. However, when 을/를 replaces 에서 in its 'dynamic location' function (refer to 3.2.4.3), an important change may take place. In the following examples, whereas 에서 merely depicts that the activity happened in the given place, 을/를 signals that the subject of the sentence performed the activity right across the given place from start to finish. With regards to this, some linguists adopt the concepts of 'partial affectedness' and 'total affectedness': 에서 indicates 'partial affectedness' and을/를 indicates 'total affectedness'.

에서	***을/를***
민호가 운동장**에서** 뛰었어요. *Minho went running **at** the playing field.*	민호가 운동장**을** 뛰었어요. *Minho ran **right round** the playing field.*
누나가 강**에서** 헤엄쳤어요. *Older sister swam **in** the river.*	누나가 강**을** 헤엄쳐 건넜어요. *Older sister swam **across** the river.*

One further use of 을/를 worth mentioning is before expressions ending in –(으)로 (refer to 3.2.5.1). These include . . . 을/를 목적으로 'with the purpose/intention of . . .', . . . 을/를 기준으로 'according to the basis/standard of . . .', . . . 을/를 대상으로 'aimed at . . .', . . . 을/를 끝으로 'ending with . . .' and . . . 을/를 토대로 'based on'. These expressions are generally formal and/or bookish.

이 분**을** 끝으로 더 이상 받지 않겠습니다.
Ending with this person, we're not going to accept any more.

재일동포와 결혼**을** 목적으로 일본에 입국하려고 합니다.
I'm going to enter Japan with the intention of marrying a Japanese Korean.

성적**을** 기준으로 학생들을 평가하지 마세요.
Don't measure students by their grades

As a final point, similar to the way that 이/가 can appear twice in one clause (refer to 3.2.1), this can also happen with 을/를.

In informal speech, 을/를 can be used where we would normally expect the possessive 의 (refer to 3.2.3) on the first noun in sentences such as the following:

의	**을/를**
개가 민수**의** 다리를 물었어요.	개가 민수**를** 다리**를** 물었어요.
The dog bit Minsu's leg.	*The dog bit Minsu in the leg.*
미아가 유미**의** 옷을 잡았어요.	미아가 유미**를** 옷**을** 잡았어요.
Mia grabbed Yumi's clothes.	*Mia grabbed Yumi by her clothes.*

As can be appreciated in the different English translations, by marking both nouns with the object marker, the sentences in the second column emphasize that the action of the dog and of Mia effected Minsu and Yumi respectively more directly. Such double use of the object marker can only be employed when the second noun is something like a body part or piece of clothing that is in a relationship of inalienable possession or contiguity with the first noun (refer to Yeon 2003).

'Double object' constructions may also appear in colloquial speech in sentences such as the following, where the first noun would more normally be marked with 에게/한테 'to (a person or animal)'. Such usage should be understood as casual usage that does not result in any shift in meaning:

민수가 개**를** 밥**을** 먹였어요. *Minsu fed the dog.*

3.2.3 The possessive particle 의

This one-shape particle is most commonly pronounced as [에], although you might occasionally hear [의] in careful speech.

When 의 attaches to the pronouns 나 'I (plain)', 저 'I (humble)' and 너 'you', the resulting construction is frequently abbreviated as follows:

Pronoun	*Full possessive form*	*Abbreviated possessive form*
나	나의	내
저	저의	제
너	너의	네

In its most basic usage, 의 operates similar to '. . .'s' or 'of . . .' in English to indicate possession or alternatively that the noun in front modifies, describes, or limits the meaning of the second one. The following examples illustrate the simple possessive meaning of 의 (that translates as '. . .'s') in written-style sentences:

선생님**<u>의</u>** 강아지 이름은 도진이라고 한다.
The teacher's puppy is called 'Tojin'.

남자친구**<u>의</u>** 소지품을 돌려주었다.
She gave back her boyfriend's personal effects.

'올케'라는 말은 오빠나 남동생**<u>의</u>** 부인에게 부르는 말이다.
'Olk'e' means your older brother or younger brother's wife.

The above examples are all from written Korean, where this particle is most commonly used. In the following spoken examples, 의 would most commonly be dropped:

민호**<u>(의)</u>** 책이에요? *Is this Minho's book?*

어느 분**<u>(의)</u>** 잡지예요?
Whose [which esteemed person's] magazine is it?

유미**<u>(의)</u>** 연필이에요, 미나**<u>(의)</u>** 연필이에요?
Is it Yumi's pencil, or is it Mina's?

There may be times when the inclusion of 의 is preferred since, without it ambiguity may occur or an alternative meaning may be produced:

with <u>의</u>	*without* <u>의</u>
민호**<u>의</u>** 형이 부지런해요.	민호 형이 부지런해요.
Minho's older brother is hardworking.	*Older brother Minho is hardworking.*

의 also occurs in various noun-noun combinations, where English would typically use 'of'. Again, the inclusion of 의 in these combinations will be more strictly applied in writing.

예술**<u>의</u>** 아름다움	꽃**<u>의</u>** 향기
the beauty of art	*the scent of flowers*

대통령**의** 미국 방문
the president's trip to America

아파트**의** 주인
the apartment's owner

축하**의** 잔치
a party of celebration (= a celebratory party)

스승**의** 날
teacher's day

최선**의** 선택
the choice of the best (= the best choice)

사랑**의** 감정
the feeling of love

100 킬로**의** 몸무게
a body weight of 100 kilos

순금**의** 보석
jewellery of pure gold

내 월급**의** 두 배
two times (that of) my salary

행운**의** 여신
the goddess of luck

One important difference between English and Korean possessives is that the Korean possessive must always be followed by another noun. Therefore, Korean cannot form sentences such as the English 'this is John's', or 'this is mine'. To communicate the same meaning, Korean can make use of the unspecific bound/dependent noun 것 'the thing, the one', which can be abbreviated to 거 in casual speech (refer to 2.1.2.1). As in the second and third examples below from spoken language, 의 may be frequently omitted in this function as well.

내가 빌린 자전거는 내 친구**의** 것이다.
The bike that I borrowed is my friend's.

그 이메일 주소는 민수 씨 **거**예요.
That e-mail address is Minsu's.

이 건 **내 거**야!
This is mine!

의 also appear after other particles such as 에 'to/in/at', 에서 'in/at', 과/와 'and/with' and (으)로부터 'from'. The reason for this is that phrases ending in 에서, 과/와 and (으)로부터 cannot directly modify a noun. Therefore, although you can say 'we spent a day in Paris', you cannot say 'the day in Paris . . .' without the addition of 의 (giving a phrase that literally means 'the day of in Paris . . .'):

파리**에서** 하루를 보냈다.
We spent a day in Paris.

파리**에서의** 하루는 길었다.
The day that we spent in Paris was long.

친구**와의** 약속.	*A promise with a friend.*
바다**로부터의** 선물.	*A present from the sea.*
유럽**에서의** 한국학.	*Korean studies in Europe.*
서양**과의** 첫 만남.	*The first meeting with the West.*

3.2.4 Particles of movement and location

Particles covered in this section mark location in/at a certain place or otherwise movement towards/away from a given location/person.

3.2.4.1 에 'to/in/at'

에 is a one-shape particle that has two distinct main usages that we will consider in turn: usage as a particle of movement, and usage as a particle of location.

As a particle of movement, 에 is used like 'to' (or 'at' and 'in') in English to express movement towards a destination or goal. Note that, in this usage (and generally speaking in this usage only), 에 can be dropped in colloquial speech.

미나가 싱가포르**에** 갔어요.	*Mina went to Singapore.*
민수가 공부하러 도서관**에** 왔어요.	*Minsu came to the library to study.*
우리 오빠는 대학**에** 입학했어요.	*My brother entered university.*
어디**에** 가요?	*Where are you going?*

This usage extends to talking about putting something 'in' a certain place, adding something to something, or writing or otherwise recording something somewhere, etc. In this usage, 에 may sometimes be substituted for 에다(가) (refer to 3.2.4.2).

돈을 주머니**에** 넣었어요.	*I put the money in my pocket.*
한지**에** 이름을 썼어요.	*I wrote my name on Korean paper.*
하드**에** 파일을 저장했어요.	*I saved the file onto the hard drive.*

봉투**에** 우표를 붙였어요. *I stuck a stamp on the envelope.*

마당**에** 사과 나무를 심었어요. *I planted an apple tree in the yard.*

에 is also used when talking about giving, sending, reporting, etc. something 'to' a non-animate entity (such as a place, institution, etc.). When the referent is human (or animal), 에게 or 한테 (refer to 3.2.4.4) is used instead.

민호 선물을 민호의 집**에** 보냈어요.
I sent Minho's present to his house.

조사 결과를 회사**에** 보고했어요.
I reported the survey results to the office.

아이를 유치원**에** 맡겨 놓고 출근해요.
I entrust my children to a kindergarten and go to work.

We now move on to consider use of 에 as a marker of location. In this usage, 에 operates like 'in' or 'at' in English when talking about someone/something being somewhere in a static state. Note, however, that not 에 but 에서 is used when talking about someone/something performing a dynamic action in a certain place, as discussed below (refer to 3.2.4.3).

우리는 교실**에** 있어요. *We're in the classroom.*

민호가 학교**에** 없어요. *Minho's not at school.*

유리는 바닥**에** 앉았고 유미는 소파**에** 누웠어요.
Yuri sat on the floor and Yumi lay on the sofa.

이모는 캐나다**에** 살아요. *My (maternal) aunt lives in Canada.*

Note that 살– 'lives' may appear with 에 as in the last example, but may also appear with the 'dynamic' marker 에서 (refer to 3.2.4.3).

에 is also the particle that is used to locate something in time. When you want to say 'at' six o'clock, 'on' Sunday, 'in' May, 'in 2019', etc., use 에:

6시**에** 일어나요. *I get up at six o'clock.*

월요일**에** 쉬어요. *On Monday(s) I take it easy.*

아침**에** 우유를 사요. *In the morning I buy milk.*

2013년 6월**에** 한국에 처음 갔어요. *I first went to Korea in June 2013.*

Let us now consider a few more marginal uses of 에. Firstly, 에 can be used after a noun that constitutes the cause of a certain state or condition. In this usage, 에 can often be replaced by –(으로) (refer to 3.2.5.1) or 때문에 (refer to 2.2.4.2):

바람**에** 꽃이 다 떨어졌어요.
The flowers were all knocked over by the wind.

비**에** 옷이 젖었어요.
My clothes got soaked by the rain.

칼**에** 손을 베었어요.
I cut my finger on the knife.

그 여자 고운 미소**에** 내 마음이 녹아요.
My heart melts at her beautiful smile.

Secondly, 에 can be used in expressions such as 'A is (not) matched/ appropriate/ close/comparable, etc. 'to' B' when B is inanimate (에게/한테 (refer to 3.2.4.4) is used for people/animals):

벽지는 이 방**에** 어울리지 않아요.
This wallpaper does not match the room.

옛날의 정치는 현실**에** 맞지 않아요.
Old-fashioned politics do not match the reality.

기차가 아무리 빨라져도 비행기**에** 비할 수 없어요.
No matter how fast trains become, they can't be compared to airplanes.

Thirdly, 에 is used like 'for' in English in expressions of quantity and price as follows:

사과는 다섯 개**에** 4000원이에요.
*The apples are [selling at] five **for** 4000 won.*

배는 천 원**에** 두 개예요.
*The pears are 1000 won **for** four.*

과자는 한 사람**<u>에</u>** 한 개씩이에요.
*The snacks are one **<u>for</u>** each person.*

Fourthly, 에 can be used to say that something is 'in addition to' or 'on top of' something else:

민수는 잘생긴 얼굴**<u>에</u>** 키가 커요.
Minsu has a handsome face and, on top of that, is tall.

짜장면**<u>에</u>** 탕수육을 시켰어요.
I ordered black bean noodles and, on top of that, sweet and sour pork.

Finally, 에 forms an integral part of a large number of common expressions including . . . 에 관하여 'regarding . . .', . . . 에 대해서 'about . . .', . . . 에 의하면 'according to . . .' and . . . 에 따라 'in accordance with':

여수 투어**<u>에 관하여</u>** 문의 드립니다.
I would like to make inquiries regarding the tour to Yeosu.

아직 한국 역사**<u>에 대해서</u>** 모르는 게 정말 많아요
There are still many things I don't know about Korean history.

통계**<u>에 의하면</u>** 미국 내에 700,000명의 의사가 있습니다.
According to the statistics, there are 700,000 doctors in the US.

연령**<u>에 따라</u>** 술에 취하는 정도가 다르다.
The effects of alcohol differ with age.

3.2.4.2 *에다(가) 'in/on'*

In colloquial speech, the particle 에 is sometimes replaced by 에다(가) when talking about actions that, generally speaking, involve placing something 'in' or 'on' something else (or doing something 'in' or 'on' something else):

책상 위**<u>에다</u>** 놓아 주세요.	*Please put it on top of the desk for me.*
사진은 홈피**<u>에다가</u>** 올렸습니다.	*I uploaded the photo onto my homepage.*

큰 냄비**<u>에다가</u>** 삶으세요.	*Boil it in a large saucepan.*
얼굴**<u>에다</u>** 발라 봤어요.	*I tried rubbing it (the cream, etc.) on my face.*
어깨**<u>에다</u>** 문신을 했어요.	*I had a tattoo on my shoulder.*
이 종이**<u>에다가</u>** 쓰세요.	*Write it on this paper.*

소주**<u>에다가</u>** 고추 가루를 타 먹으면 감기가 나아질 거예요.
If you mix chilli powder into soju and drink it, your cold will get better.

에다(가) can also replace 에 when the meaning is 'in addition to' or 'on top of':

라면**<u>에다가</u>** 김밥이 어울릴까요?
In addition to ramen, would kimbap go well?

유미는 예쁜 얼굴**<u>에다가</u>** 성격까지 좋아요.
On top of having a pretty face, Yumi even has a good personality.

When this form combines with the question word 어디 'where', you might hear the contracted form 어디다 or the colloquial 어따:

<u>어디다</u> 놓을까요?
Where shall I put it?

돈이 생겼는데 **<u>어따</u>** 써야 될까요?
I've come into some money; where should I spend it?

3.2.4.3 *에서 'from/in/at'*

에서 is a one shape which, in colloquial speech, is liable to be abbreviated to 서, especially in the expression '어디서' 'from/at where'. 에서 has two distinct main usages that we will look at in turn: usage as a particle of movement and usage as a particle of location.

As a particle of movement, 에서 is used like 'from' in English to mark a departure point or a source:

영국**<u>에서</u>** 왔습니다.
I came from the UK (i.e., I come from the UK).

회사**에서** 가면 한 시간 걸려요.
If you go from the office, it takes one hour.

서울**에서** 출발했어요.
I departed from Seoul.

The place of departure may at times be more metaphorical:

민수가 아이**에서** 청소년으로 성장했어요.
Minsu grew from a child to an adolescent.

질투심**에서** 때렸어요.
I hit him/her out of jealousy.

우리 입장**에서** 보면 많이 부족해요.
If we look at it from our position, it is insufficient.

This usage extends to instances where the speaker is talking about 'from' one place or time 'to' another. The second noun is commonly marked with 까지 (refer to 3.3.3.5). In this function, 부터 (refer to 3.3.3.4) could be used following 에서 as indicated in brackets. 부터 could also simply replace 에서.

유미가 머리**에서(부터)** 발끝까지 예뻐요.
Yumi is pretty from head to toe.

서울**에서(부터)** 부산까지 네 시간 걸려요.
It takes four hours from Seoul to Busan.

한 시**에서(부터)** 두 시까지 점심 시간이에요.
Lunch time is from one to two o'clock.

Furthermore, this pattern with 에서 is used for talking about extracting or taking something out of or from somewhere:

주머니**에서** 사탕을 꺼냈어요.
I took some sweets out of my pocket.

앨범**에서** 누나 사진 한 장을 뺐어요.
I took a photo of older sister out of the album.

인터넷**에서** 베꼈어요.
I copied it from the Internet.

에서 is also used when talking about 'receiving' something 'from' a non-animate place or institution. For a human (or animal), 에게서/한테서 (see 3.2.4.6) is used instead.

회사**에서** 전화가 왔어요.
I received a phone call from the office.

학교**에서** 장학금을 받았어요.
I received a scholarship from the school.

이 책**에서** 많은 영향을 받았어요.
I received a lot of influence from this book.

We now move on to look at 에서 as a marker of location. In this usage, 에서 operates like 'in' or 'at' in English when talking about someone or something performing a dynamic action in a certain place. This contrasts with the use of 에 (see 3.2.4.1), which can only be used when talking about someone or something statically being, sitting, lying, living etc. in a given place. Compare the following:

에	*에서*
미나가 학교**에** 있어요. *Mina is at school.*	미나가 학교**에서** 공부해요. *Mina is studying at school.*
유미가 소파**에** 누웠어요. *Yumi lay on the sofa.*	유미가 소파**에서** 잤어요 *Yumi slept on the sofa.*
거리**에** 사람들이 많아요. *On the street, there are many people.*	거리**에서** 사람들이 춤을 춰요. *On the street, people are dancing.*

With some verbs both 에 or 에서 may be possible, but with subtly different nuances:

에	*에서*
민수가 부산**에** 살아요. *Minsu lives in Busan.*	민수가 부산**에서** 살아요. *Minsu lives in Busan.*
학생들이 술집**에** 모였어요. *The students gathered at the pub.*	학생들이 술집**에서** 모였어요. *The students gathered at the pub.*
런던에 집을 샀어요. *[I] bought a house in London.*	런던에서 집을 샀어요. *[I] bought a house in London.*

In the above, use of 에서 instead of 에 places emphasis on the active qualities of the verbs to 'live', 'gather' and 'buy'. With the first example, in addition to 'Minsu lives in Busan', the sentence could perhaps in certain contexts be taken to imply that Busan is the place where he does his business or makes a living. In the final example, it is implied that the speaker actually engages in the activity of purchasing the house.

The 'location' provided with 에서 may also be something less tangible such as an atmosphere or situation:

좋은 분위기**에서** 회의가 진행되었어요.
The meeting took place in a good atmosphere.

이 상황**에서** 공부하기가 쉽지 않아요.
It's not easy to study in these circumstances.

에서 may also sometimes mark nouns that would be subjects in corresponding English sentences. This most commonly occurs when discussing the services provided, the decisions made, etc. of a company or other institution, meaning that it is still marking the 'source' of the action.

이 비용은 회사**에서** 부담합니다.
The company will take on the expenses.

이 법은 나라**에서** 정했어요.
The nation decided the law.

Note that some of the functions of 에서 can be covered alternatively by (으)로부터 (refer to 3.2.4.8).

3.2.4.4 *에게/한테 'to'*

에게/한테 are both one-shape particles that have identical usages, with 한테 being somewhat more colloquial. Two other colloquial particles that have similar functions are 더러 (see 3.2.4.5) and 보고 (see 3.2.4.6). Note that the honorific 께 should (or at least can) be used in place of 에게/한테 when the preceding noun is a person who needs to be talked about using honorifics (refer to 6.2.2.2).

In their most basic use, 에게 and 한테 are used when talking about giving, sending, or otherwise conveying something towards a person (or possibly animal):

미나가 민수**에게** 선물을 주었어요. *Mina gave a present to Minsu.*

유미가 미라**한테** 노래를 가르쳤어요. *Yumi taught a song to Mira.*

친구**한테** 물어봤어요. *I asked ('to') a friend.*

닭**에게** 모이를 주었어요. *I gave feed to the chickens.*

에게/한테 are also used when talking about moving towards someone:

미나가 유미**에게** 다가왔어요. *Mina came up to Yumi.*

에게/한테 can also be used in place of the subject particle 이/가 (refer to 3.2.1) or the topic particle 은/는 (refer to 3.3.2.1) in constructions containing the verbs of existence 있– 'exist', 없– 'doesn't exist' or otherwise verbs such as 남– 'be left', 많– 'be many' 적– 'be few' 생기– 'happen':

민호**에게** 그만한 돈이 없어요.
Minho doesn't have that kind of money.

교수님이 빌려 주신 책은 수미**에게** 있어요.
The book that the professor lent out is with Sumi.

형**에게** 급한 문제가 생긴 것 같아요.
Older brother seems to have an urgent problem.

In constructions such as the above, 에게/한테 more commonly replaces the subject or topic particle when the second noun phrase is something specific and concrete rather than something general. For example, in the second sentence we are talking about a specific book rather than just 'a book' or books in general. Indeed, in this sentence 에게 cannot be replaced by 이/가.

Moving onto some more marginal uses of 에게/한테, these particles are used in expressions such as 'A is (not) matched/appropriate/close/comparable, etc. "to" B' when B is a human or animal (에 is used for inanimate nouns):

이 치마는 유미**에게** 어울리지 않아요.
This skirt does not suit Yumi.

아빠의 모자는 너**에게** 너무 커!
Dad's hat is too big for you!

에게/한테 is also used when talking about being caught, discovered, deceived, etc. 'by' someone:

도둑이 경찰**에게** 잡혔어요.	*The thief was caught by the police.*
유미가 민수**에게** 속았어요.	*Yumi was deceived by Minsu.*
개**에게** 물렸어요.	*I was bitten by a dog.*

Another use of 에게/한테 occurs when talking about making somebody do something. This pattern is looked at in more detail under discussions of causatives (refer to 4.4.2). In such sentences, 에게/한테 may be replaced by (으)로 하여금 (refer to 3.2.4.7).

엄마가 아이**에게** 숙제를 하게 했어요.
Mother made the child do his/her homework.

엄마가 아이**에게** 물을 마시게 했어요.
Mother made the child drink water.

As a final note, both 에게 and 한테 are commonly used in place of 에게서 and 한테서 (particularly in casual colloquial speech) when talking about receiving something 'from' a human or animal. These usages are covered under discussions of 에게서/한테서 (refer to 3.2.4.7).

3.2.4.5 *더러* 'to'

더러 has the same meaning as 에게 and 한테, but unlike 에게 and 한테, 더러 never occurs when talking about animals. You may hear Korean speakers use the object particle before 더러 (as in 날더러 'to me' and 널더러 'to you'), although this is not standard.

The usage of 더러 is more restricted than 에게 and 한테. It is used almost exclusively with reported speech patterns, in other words when talking about ordering, saying or asking things to other people (refer to Chapter 10). Unlike 에게 and 한테, it is not commonly used when talking about giving or sending something to someone. Here are some representative examples;

동생**더러** 한국에 올 때 사오라 해야겠어요.
I'd better ask my younger sister to buy it for me next time she comes to Korea.

대체 누가 너**더러** 개새끼래?
Who was it who called you a son of a bitch?

엄마가 나**더러** 빨리 집에 오래.
Mom told me to come home quickly.

자세한 것은 수미**더러** 물어봐라.
For the details, try asking Sumi.

As shown in the above examples, it is only used when the noun it attaches to is the speaker him/herself or another person of equal or lower status. It is not used for people of higher status. As in the second and third examples, it often occurs when the speaker is talking about something that was said in a negative or unwelcome tone.

3.2.4.6 *보고 'to'*

보고 is used in an almost identical fashion to 더러 (refer to 3.2.4.5). Although the two can be used interchangeably in spoken language, 더러 tends to be used more in quoted commands, whereas 보고 is used more in quoted statements and questions.

나**보고** 예쁘다는 사람은 엄마뿐이야.
Only mum tells me I'm pretty.

판매자분이 언니**보고** 어디 사시냐고 했더니 인천에 산다고 말했죠.
The vendor asked sister where she lived and she replied that she lived in Incheon.

한국 사람들은 다들 저**보고** 결혼 빨리 했다고 그래요.
Korean people always tell me that I got married quickly.

3.2.4.7 *에게서/한테서 'from'*

Whereas 에게/한테 (refer to 3.2.4.4) are used for talking about conveying something 'to' someone, the addition of 서 and the resultant 에게서 and 한테서 take on the opposite meaning: receiving something 'from' a human or animal entity. Confusingly, however, it should be noted that, especially in casual speech, 서 is frequently dropped. This results in the same forms being used for 'to' and 'from'. The following could therefore mean 'to Minho' or 'from Minho':

민호**에게** *to/from Minho*

The addition of a verb (and/or a context), however, always works to eliminate any ambiguity:

민호**에게** 선물을 주었어요. *I gave a present to Minho.*

민호**에게** 선물을 받았어요. *I received a present from Minho.*

Here are some further example sentences showing the use of 에게서 and 한테서:

나한테 어머니**한테서** 편지가 왔어요.
A letter came from my mother to me.

한국인 친구**한테서** 욕을 많이 배웠어요.
I learned a lot of swear words from my Korean friend.

직장 선배**에게서** 충고를 들었어요.
I received advice from a senior at work.

3.2.4.8 *(으)로부터 'from'*

(으)로부터 is a particle with two forms or shapes: 로 is used after a noun that ends in a vowel OR the consonant ㄹ; 으로 is used after all other consonants:

After vowels	*After* /ㄹ/	*After other consonants*
바다**로부터**	마을**로부터**	산**으로부터**
from the sea	*from villages*	*from mountains*

This particle can be used in place of 에서 (with no change in meaning) when talking about movement away 'from' a non-human or non-animal entity. Although identical in meaning to 에서, the feeling is more formal. Indeed, this particle only tends to occur in writing and formal speech.

산**으로부터** 시원한 바람이 불어왔다.
A cool breeze came from the mountains.

언니**로부터** 영향을 많이 받았다.
I received a lot of influence from my big sister.

그 병은 미국**으로부터** 전염되었다.
That disease spread from America.

가구를 애완견**으로부터** 보호할 수 있어요.
You can protect your furniture from your pet dog.

3.2.4.9 *Particle phrase (으)로 하여금 'letting/making (someone do something)'*

The particle phrase expression (으)로 하여금 is composed of the instrumental particle (으)로 (refer to 3.2.5.1) and the adverb 하여금, meaning 'letting', 'making' or 'forcing'. (으)로 하여금 may be used in place of the particle 에게/한테 (refer to 3.2.4.4) when talking about allowing or forcing somebody to do something. This pattern commonly occurs with causative sentences (refer to 4.4.2) and can more frequently be observed in formal speech or writing.

학생들**로 하여금** 공부를 하게 했어요.
He/she made the students study.

그 직업은 민수**로 하여금** 언론계로 나서게 했다.
The job gave Minsu a start in journalism.

그 전쟁이 인호**로 하여금** 평화주의자가 되게 했다.
The war made Inho into a pacifist.

3.2.5 *Instrumental particles*

Instrumental particles are used to mark the 'instrument' (tool, means, method, etc.) by which a task is performed. The principal instrumental particle in Korean is (으)로. We deal with this first, before considering the related particles (으)로서 and (으)로써 and the related particle phrase (으)로 인해(서).

3.2.5.1 *(으)로 'by/with/as'*

(으)로 is a particle with two forms or shapes: 로 is used after a noun that ends is a vowel OR the consonant ㄹ; 으로 is used after all other consonants:

After vowels	*After /ㄹ/*	*After other consonants*
종이**로**	연필**로**	책**으로**
with paper	*with a pencil*	*with a book*

The particle (으)로 is used to mark the 'instrument' by which a task is performed. The 'instrument' may be a tool (e.g., write 'with' a pencil) or a means or method (e.g., go 'by' plane; speak 'in' English):

연필**로** 편지를 썼어요.	*I wrote a letter with a pencil.*
젓가락**으로** 김치를 먹었어요.	*I ate kimchi with chopsticks.*
비행기**로** 갑시다.	*Let's go by plane.*
영어**로** 말했어요.	*I spoke in English.*

수영할 때 입**으로** 숨을 쉬어야 해요.
When you swim, you have to breathe with your mouth.

김 선수는 피나는 노력**으로** 금메달을 땄어요.
Athlete Kim won the gold medal by hard graft.

It is also used when talking about the material or ingredients by which something is made or composed:

김치는 배추**로** 만들어요.	*Kimchi is made from Chinese cabbage.*
나무**로** 지은 집이에요.	*It's a house made of wood.*

(으)로 can be used similar to 'as' or 'for' in English when expressing the function or capacity in which something is being used for. This extends to discussions of the capacity in which a human referent is performing a certain function:

이 방을 교실**로** 써요.	*They use this room as a classroom.*
학생**으로** 한국에 있어요.	*He is in Korea as a student.*

민수가 유미를 애인**으로** 생각해요.
Minsu thinks of Yumi as his girlfriend.

(으)로 can also be applied after adnominal forms with –적 (refer to 11.2.1.2, 11.3.2.2).

정열적**으로** 공부해요. *He/she studies passionately.*

법률적**으로** 복잡해요. *It is legally complicated.*

Another use of (으)로 is when talking about exchanging something 'for' something else:

비싼 것을 싼 것**으로** 바꿨어요.
I exchanged an expensive one for a cheap one.

Similarly, (으)로 is also used when discussing a change from one state 'into' another (which may include breaking something into two or more pieces):

큰 바퀴벌레**로** 변했어요.
He/she turned into a big cockroach.

어린 꼬마가 멋진 총각**으로** 성장했어요.
The little boy grew up into a handsome man.

바지를 여러 갈래**로** 찢었어요.
I tore the trousers into several pieces.

One more use of (으)로 is for expressing the reason for a resultant state or action. This most commonly occurs with names of illnesses, types of accidents, weather conditions, etc. that bring about a negative consequence. Note that in these situations –(으)로 인해(서) can be used (refer to 3.2.5.4). 때문에 (refer to 2.1.2.13) also has a similar usage.

폐병**으로** 죽었어요. *He died of tuberculosis.*

교통사고**로** 죽었어요. *He died because of a traffic accident.*

갑자기 내린 눈**으로** 교통이 마비되었어요.
Due to the sudden snowfall, the transport system has become paralyzed.

Finally, (으)로 can be used in place of 에 when talking about going/coming 'to' a place.

시간이 되면 우리 집**으로** 오세요.
If you have time, come over to our house.

민수가 호주**로** 이민을 갔어요
Minsu emigrated to Australia.

어디**로** 가세요?
Where are you heading?

In these examples, the use of (으)로 places more emphasis on the 'path' or process of getting to the place in question, whereas 에 places more emphasis on the final goal or destination. Therefore, whereas 어디로 가세요? in the final example can be translated as 'where are you heading?' (in addition to 'where are you going?'), 어디에 가요? should be translated simply as 'where are you going?'

Although in expressions such as the above both (으)로 and 에 can be used, after expressions ending in 쪽 'way, direction, side' (refer to 2.1.2.23), only (으)로 is used. This is because these expressions by their nature focus on the process of 'going right' or 'coming this way' rather than a specific end point.

오른쪽**으로** 가세요. *Go to the right.*

이쪽**으로** 오세요. *Come this way.*

3.2.5.2 *(으)로서 'as'*

(으)로서 can be used in place of (으)로 (refer to 3.2.5.1) when referring to the capacity in which someone (or something) is performing a certain function. Although simple (으)로 can be used for the same purpose, the addition of 서 adds a sense of emphasis or weight and is thus particularly useful when solemnly discussing the duties placed on someone (or on an institution) performing in a certain capacity:

저는 우리 회사 사장**<u>으로서</u>** 모든 책임을 감당하겠습니다.
As president of this company, I will take full responsibility.

투명하고 공정한 은행**<u>으로서</u>** 최선을 다하겠습니다.
As a transparent and impartial bank, we pledge to do our best.

이건 널 사랑하는 사람**<u>으로서</u>** 하는 충고야.
This is advice as someone who loves you.

3.2.5.3 *(으)로써 'by means of'*

(으)로써 can be used in place of (으)로 (refer to 3.2.5.1) when referring to the instrument (tool, means, method, etc.) by which a task is performed or the materials/ingredients by which something is made or composed. Note, however, that unlike (으)로, (으)로써 is not used when expressing means of transportation. The addition of 써 works to provide emphasis or a sense of formality. The resultant expressions tend to sound somewhat bookish:

술**<u>로써</u>** 기분을 달랬다.
She soothed her feelings with alcohol.

냉면은 메밀**로써** 만들어지는데 밀면은 밀가루**<u>로써</u>** 만들어진다.
Naengmyŏn noodles are made from buckwheat, but milmyŏn noodles are made from wheat flour.

그는 자신의 힘과 노력**<u>으로써</u>** 많은 어려움을 극복해 냈다.
With force and effort, he managed to overcome many difficulties.

In writing, (으)로써 is used with nominalized clauses with –음 (refer to 2.2.5) to create the expression 음으로써:

친환경 차량을 보급함**<u>으로써</u>** 환경에 공헌한다.
We contribute to the environment by producing environmentally friendly cars.

모든 소녀들은 교육받음**<u>으로써</u>** 자신의 삶을 충만하고 생산적으로 살 권리가 있다.
All girls have the right to live full and productive lives by receiving education.

3.2.5.4 *Particle phrase (으)로 인해(서) 'due to'*

(으)로 인해서 marks the noun that it is attached to as being the cause for a subsequent result, which is expressed in the following clause:

폭풍**으로 인해(서)** 비행기가 한 시간 지연되었다.
The plane was delayed one hour due to heavy rain.

많은 사람들이 재정문제**로 인해(서)** 스트레스를 받는 것으로 알고 있다.
I am aware that many people are receiving stress due to financial problems.

Note that this same meaning can actually be achieved just by using (으)로 on its own (refer to 3.2.5.1) and that 때문에 (refer to 2.1.2.13) also has a similar usage. (으)로 인해서 can be interchangeable with/abbreviated to (으)로 해서 in colloquial speech.

3.2.6 *Comitative particles*

Comitative particles are grammatical markers that are used to attach two nouns together, similar to 'and' or 'with' in English. This section covers three such markers: 과/와, 하고 and (이)랑.

3.2.6.1 *과/와 'and/with'*

과/와 is a two-shape particle which is 과 after consonants and 와 after vowels. You may notice that, unlike other two-shape particles, it is the form that starts with a consonant (i.e., 과) that follows consonants and the form that starts with a vowel (i.e., 와) that follows vowels. 과/와 is mostly used in formal writing and scripted or careful speech; otherwise 하고 or (이)랑 are used instead (see 3.2.6.2, 3.2.6.3)

과/와 operates like 'and' in English to link two or more nouns:

형**과** 누나와 같이 소풍을 갔다.
I went on an outing with older brother and older sister.

우리는 삶에서 많은 어려움**과** 위험도 만나게 된다.
In life we get to meet lots of difficulties and dangers.

매년 그 여자에게 꽃**과** 초콜릿을 보냈다.
He sent her flowers and chocolates every year.

과/와 can also be used like 'with' in English when discussing the people (or possibly animals) with which you perform the activity in question. In this usage, 과/와 is often followed by 같이 (or 함께) 'together':

주말을 애인**과** (같이) 보냈다.
I spent the weekend with my boy/girlfriend.

유미가 애완견**과** (같이) 산다.
Yumi lives with her pet dog.

It is also possible to use 과/와 (함께) to mean 'together with':

유미는 부모님**과 (함께)** 살고 있다.
Yumi lives together with her parents.

담배**와 (함께)** 술은 건강에 해롭다.
Together with cigarettes, alcohol is harmful to your health.

Similar expressions are also possible by using 과/와 with 같이 (or 마찬가지로 'the same'). However, the nuance is somewhat different. Whereas 과/와 함께 merely adds one item onto an item of similar status, 과/와 같이/마찬가지 makes a comparison between the two which may be quite metaphorical.

다른 회사**와 마찬가지로** 영리를 추구하는 기업이다.
Just like any other company, we are a business that pursues profits.

미나가 영화 배우**와 같이** 예쁘게 생겼다.
Mina is pretty looking, just like a movie star.

In addition to this, 과/와 are used with other expressions of comparison and contrast such as . . . 과/와 비교하– 'compared with', . . . 과/와 비슷하– 'similar to', . . . 와/과 같– 'the same as', . . . 과/와 다르– 'different to', etc.:

한국의 해군력은 주변국**과** 비교하면 어떤가?
How does Korean naval strength fare if we compare it to neighbouring countries?

일본 기후가 한국**과** 비슷하다.
Japan's climate is similar to Korea's.

여자는 남자**와** 확실히 다르다.
Women are certainly different from men.

와/과 can be followed by other particles including –도 (refer to 3.3.3.6) to give the meaning 'and also' or 'also with' –만 (refer to 3.3.3.1) to give the meaning 'and only' or 'only with' and the topic particle –는 (refer to 3.3.2.1) which usually provides a sense of contrast:

유미가 미나**와도** 잘 싸운다.
Yumi fights a lot with Mina too.

공기밥 하나를 주문해서 김치**와만** 먹었다.
I ordered a bowl of rice and ate it only with kimchi.

그 배우가 KBS**와는** 인터뷰 안 한다.
That actor does not do interviews with KBS (implication: he does interviews with other channels).

3.2.6.2 하고 'and/with'

하고 is a one-shape particle that takes on the same basic functions as 과/와 (refer to 3.2.6.1). However, whereas 과/와 is the set form in formal writing or structure speech, 하고 is the most commonly used form in everyday speech.

Just like 과/와, 하고 operates like 'and' in English to link two or more nouns:

민수**하고** 인호는 시험에 떨어졌어요.	*Minsu and Inho failed the exam.*
맥주**하고** 마른 오징어를 주세요.	*Give me beer and dried squid.*

Also like 과/와, 하고 can be used like 'with' in English when discussing the people (or possibly animals) with which you perform the activity in question. In this usage, 하고 is often followed by 같이 (or 함께) 'together':

언니**하고** (같이) 목욕탕에 갔어요.
I went to the sauna with my older sister.

애완견**<u>하고</u>** (같이) 가까운 산을 다녀 왔어요.
I went to a nearby mountain nearby with my pet dog.

Also like 와/과, 하고 is used with expressions of comparison and contrast:

민수**<u>하고</u>** 비교하면 인호가 솔직한 편이에요.
Compared to Minsu, Inho is quite honest.

미나 성격은 유미**<u>하고</u>** 비슷해요.
Mina's personality is similar to Yumi's.

형은 모든 면에서 나**<u>하고</u>** 달라요.
Older brother is different to me in all respects.

하고 can be followed by other particles including –도 (refer to 3.3.3.6), –만 (refer to 3.3.3.1) and –는 (refer to 3.3.2.1):

미나는 유미**<u>하고도</u>** 연락해요.
Mina keeps in touch with Yumi too.

유미**<u>하고만</u>** 사이가 좋아요.
I only have a good relationship with Yumi

촌놈이라 서울 사람**<u>하고는</u>** 안 맞더라고요.
As a country bumpkin, I don't get along with Seoul folk. (implication: I get on well with other people)

3.2.6.3 *(이)랑 'and/with'*

(이)랑 is a two-shape particle that takes on the form 이랑 after consonants and 랑 after vowels. It has the same basic functions as 과/와 (refer to 3.2.6.1) and 하고 (refer to 3.2.6.2). Like 하고, it is more of a spoken form than a written form. Indeed, it tends to sound more casual and colloquial even than 하고 and should be avoided in more formal or polite speech.

Just like 과/와 and 하고, (이)랑 operates like 'and' in English to link two or more nouns:

백김치**<u>랑</u>** 총각김치가 있어요.
There is white kimchi and radish kimchi.

찜질방에서 미아**랑** 인호를 봤어.
I saw Mia and Inho at the sauna.

Also like 과/와 and 하고, (이)랑 can be used like 'with' in English when discussing the people (or possibly animals) with which you perform the activity in question. In this usage, (이)랑 is often followed by 같이 (or 함께) 'together':

친구**랑** (같이) 영화를 보러 갔어요.
I went to watch a movie with my friend.

애완견**이랑** (같이) 자는 게 더러워?
Is it dirty to sleep with your pet dog?

Also like 와/과 and 하고, (이)랑 is used with expressions of comparison and contrast:

미나는 언니**랑** 키가 비슷해.
Mina's height is similar to older sister's.

민수 형은 인호 형**이랑** 완전히 달라.
Older brother Minsu is completely different to older brother Inho.

(이)랑 can be followed by other particles including –도 (refer to 3.3.3.6), –만 (refer to 3.3.3.1) and –는 (refer to 3.3.2.1):

결혼한 친구**랑도** 친구 할 수 있지.
You can still be friends with a friend who is married.

요즈음 인호가 여자친구**랑만** 놀아.
These days Inho only hangs out with his girlfriend.

엄마**랑은** 말이 안 통해.
With my mother, we don't understand each other.

3.2.7 Vocative particle 아/야

'Vocatives' refer to forms (typically names or other forms of address) that are used to identify and attract the attention of the person being addressed. When a name/address form appears as a vocative, it exists outside of the grammatical structure of the sentence and can often be considered optional. For example, in the English sentence 'John, what are you doing?', the vocative 'John' appears outside of the grammar of the sentence (this is proven by the fact that, even if it is deleted, the sentence is still grammatical). 'You' on the other hand is a non-vocative form (and must be maintained for the English sentence to be grammatical).

In Korean, when names appear as vocative, they may be marked with the particle 아/야, with 아 appearing after a consonant and 야 after a vowel. This form tends to only occur with Korean (or Korean-sounding) names:

유진**아**, 너 지금 뭐 하니? *Yujin, what are you doing?*

유미**야**, 너 어디 가는 거냐? *Yumi, where are you going?*

As in the examples above, this form can only be used in non-honorific speech (refer to 6.1) when addressing intimates of similar/younger age or children. In other situations, 아/야 cannot be used and another form of address has to be maintained (refer to 6.3). Note that, even in non-honorific speech use of 아/야 is optional to a certain extent. Indeed, 아/야 could be omitted in both of the examples above, although the resulting sentences would sound colder, less friendly. etc.

아/야 may also appear with kinship terms (when the relationship in question is close enough to use non-honorific language), particularly in female speech. It may also appear with some other intimate or condescending forms of address or playful uses of derogatory expressions.

언니**야**, 지금 시간 있어?
Elder sister, do you have time now?

엄마**야**, 보고 싶어!
Mum, I miss you!

학생들**아**, 이리 와 봐!
Students, come over here!

바보**야**, 왜 울어?
Hey you fool, why are you crying?

이것**아**, 무슨 그런 터무니없는 소리를 해?
Hey you (lit. 'this thing'), why are you talking such rubbish?

Of most importance, remember that this form can only be used when the name appears as a vocative, i.e., outside of the grammatical structure of the sentence. It cannot be used in sentences such as the following:

유미는 뭐 하는 거야?	*What are you (=Yumi) doing?*
유미 생각은 어때요?	*What are your (=Yumi's) thoughts?*

3.3 Special particles

Rather than marking grammatical roles as such, special particles add extra meaning (or otherwise emphasize or put focus on) the nouns to which they attach. The current section covers six groups of particles: plural, topic/focus, extent, frequency, approximation/optionality and comparison.

3.3.1 *Plural particle 들*

Addition of the one-shape particle 들 works like the addition of –s in English to mark a noun as plural. However, whereas –s in English is obligatory in plural contexts, this is not the case with 들, which is frequently dropped. This point can be illustrated by comparing English movie titles with their Korean translations:

Original English title	*Korean translation*
The Searcher**s**	수색자
Transformer**s**	트랜스포머
Lord of the Ring**s**	반지의 제왕
3 Idiot**s**	세 얼간이

Several patterns can be identified regarding where 들 is used and when it is not. First, with expressions of number, 들 cannot normally occur with non-human nouns (i.e., in expressions such as 'three dogs' or 'four apples'). It can optionally be used with human nouns, although it is more common to not use it:

사람(들) 다섯 명 왔어요. *Five people came.*

학생(들) 열 명을 가르쳐요. *I teach ten students.*

Next, with non-numerical expressions that connote plurality such as 많아요 'are many' 들 can optionally be used for both human and non-human nouns.

사람(들)이 많아요. *There are many people.*

건물(들)이 많아요. *There are many buildings.*

들 is required when the speaker is talking about a specified entity which is plural. This means that when the noun in questions is preceded by a demonstrative such as 이 'this', 그 'that' or 저 'that . . . over there' which all express specificity, 들 must be retained:

그 사람들이 과연 최선을 다했을까요?
Do you think those people really did their best?

이번 여름에는 저 책들은 꼭 읽어봐야죠.
I've really got to read those books this summer.

In other expressions that imply that you are talking about something specific, 들 should also be maintained:

여기 산들이 참 아름답다.
The mountains here are beautiful.

'우리 좋은 놈들 아닙니다'
'We are not good guys' (from the poster for the movie Nice Guys)

Secondly, without 들, the 'default' understanding of many nouns will be singular and 들 must be retained in order to produce a clear plural meaning. Sentences such as the following would normally need 들 in order to be understood as plural. Notably, as in the above these kinds of sentences tend to be about specific entities:

친구들하고 밤새도록 수다를 떨었어요.
I stayed up all night chattering with my friends.

우리 마당에 은행 나무**들**이 있어요.
There are gingko trees in our yard.

Plural marking in Korean also differs from English in that whereas English – s simply specifies that there is two or more of the entity in question, 들 provides a feeling of mass quantity. An online image search for '학생들' will turn up pictures of large groups of students assembled *en masse*, whereas 'students' will give you pictures of both small and large groups of students.

Finally, note that 들 differs from the plural markers in many languages in that it can attach to other parts of the sentence other than the noun. Such uses of 들 typically indicate that the utterance is being addressed to multiple hearers and creates a similar feeling to adding 'everyone' or 'guys' to the end of an English sentence:

어서**들** 오세요.	*Welcome, everyone!*
많이**들** 먹어.	*Eat up, guys.*
빨리**들** 결정하세요.	*Make your minds up quickly, everyone.*
즐기면서**들** 하세요.	*Have a good time doing it, guys.*

In this usage, 들 can even be placed even at the end of a sentence:

어서 오세요**들**.	*Welcome, everyone!*
빨리 결정하세요**들**.	*Make your minds up quickly, everyone.*

들 may also appear in this way when the 'multiple' entities are not the hearers, but the people (or things) being talked about (as in B's reply below, where the use of '들' indicates that two or more friends are in the library).

A: 친구들이 어디에 있어요?	B: 도서관에**들** 있어요.
Where are your friends?	*They're all in the library.*

3.3.2 Particles of topic and focus

Particles of topic and focus work to emphasize or de-emphasize the nouns to which they are attached. The following particles are covered under this section: 은/는 (the topic particle), (이)야 ('if it's . . .') and (이)야말로 ('indeed').

3.3.2.1 *Topic particle 은/는*

The topic particle is a two-shape particle that is 은 after consonants and 는 after vowels. In casual conversation, 는 sometimes abbreviates to ㄴ especially with some common expressions such as 난 'I' and 이건 'this thing'.

은/는 may follow other particles including 에 (refer to 3.2.4.1), 에서 (refer to 3.2.4.3), 에게/한테 (refer to 3.2.4.4), 에게서/한테서 (refer to 3.2.4.7) and (으)로 (refer to 3.2.5.1). However, it cannot occur with the subject particle 이/가 (refer to 3.2.1) or the object particle 을/를 (refer to 3.2.2) – if 은/는 is used to mark the subject or object it must replace rather than occur alongside these particles.

In the following discussions of this particle, we first look at the underlying function of 은/는 to 'topicalize' the word or phrase to which it attaches. We then consider some specific situations in which a word or phrase needs to be 'topicalized'.

Any noun phrase or postpositional phrase can be 'topicalized' by the addition of the topic particle. However, the constituent that most commonly gets marked with the topic particle is the subject of the sentence:

> 아이들**은** 엄마한테 선물을 주었어요.
> *The children gave a gift to mother.*

Because 은/는 most frequently occurs after the grammatical subject of the sentence, knowing when to use 은/는 and when to use 이/가 is an important problem for learners of Korean. This question will be dealt with in the discussions below.

We now look at some examples showing the topic particle attaching to other constituents in the sentence. As can be seen in the following examples, this often (but not always – see below) results in the topicalized element moving to the start of the sentence. As can be seen in the following examples, by marking a certain constituent with 은/는, it takes on the status of being the main thing that is (already) being talked about – the (pre-)established 'topic' of the conversation. The rest of the sentence then provides 'comment' (i.e., further information that may not be known to the hearer) regarding the already established 'topic'.

> 선물**은** 아이들이 엄마한테 주었어요. (Topic = Direct Object)
> *As for the present, the children gave it to mother.*

엄마에게는 아이들이 선물을 주었어요. (Topic = Indirect Object)
To the mother, the children gave the present.

엄마한테서는 아이들이 선물을 받았어요. (Topic = Source)
From mother, the children received the present.

어제는 유미가 바빴어요. (Topic = Time)
Yesterday, Yumi was busy.

학교에서는 선생님이 영어를 가르치세요. (Topic = Location)
At school, the teacher teaches English.

So, the basic rule of thumb for using 은/는 is that it should appear after something that is the pre-established topic of conversation. For something to be a pre-established topic, it must have been mentioned before. Thus, when choosing whether to mark the subject of the sentence with the subject particle 이/가 or the topic particle 은/는, a deciding factor is often whether the person, object, etc. has already been mentioned in the discourse. When a new person or object first emerges in the discourse, it is frequently (but not always, see discussions below) marked with 이/가 to show that it constitutes 'new information'; when it is mentioned again as a pre-established topic, it is marked with 은/는:

유미 씨가 왔어요. 유미 씨는 맥주를 사 가지고 왔어요.
Yumi (new information) has come. She (old information) has bought beer.

A: 유미 씨가 왔어요.
Yumi (new information) has come.

B: 그래요? 유미 씨는 내일 올 줄 알았는데 . . .
Really? I thought Yumi (old information) was coming tomorrow.

Similarly, when a speaker repeats another sentence constituent (rather than the subject), this also gets marked with the topic particle:

A: 내일 뭐 해?
What are you doing tomorrow?

B: 내일은 놀이공원에 가.
Tomorrow, I'm going to the amusement park.

In the example above, 는 provides a nuance similar to the English, 'well, if we are talking about tomorrow'. This nuance can be created by moving any constituent of the sentence to the start and marking it with 은/는. In these kinds of sentences, 은/는 plays the role of 'stage setting' – the topic sets the state for what the sentence is going to be about and the rest of the sentence fills the state with further information, questions, etc.:

부산에서**는**, 뭐 했어요?
Speaking of Pusan – what did you do there?

고려대학교에**는**, 교환학생들이 많아요.
Speaking of Korea University, there are many exchange students.

Note that in many of the example above, the word marked with 은/는 could easily be deleted in natural conversation. In fact, it is common for the topic marker to occur after the part of the sentence that could be most easily left out if you wanted to make your sentence shorter. In line with this, 은/는 often occurs after words that are not old information as such, but are 'given' or obvious and which could be dropped (remember that Korean is a language where what it obvious can often just be left out – refer to 1.1.4). For this reason, 은/는 often appears after 'I' when it is obvious that you are talking about yourself:

저**는** 아르헨티나 사람입니다. *I am Argentinian.*

As an extension of this, 은/는 rather than 이/가 tends to appear with subjects included in statements of universally acknowledged fact or common sense, or with generic nouns ('men in general'; 'women in general'):

지구**는** 둥글어요. *The earth is round.*
여름**은** 더워요. *Summer is hot.*
여자**는** 남자의 미래다. *Woman is the Future of Man (movie title)*

It should be stressed that 은/는 cannot appear after new information being brought up for the first time. This is especially the case when the 'new' word or phrase in question constitutes the answer to a question sentence containing a question word such as 무엇,

누구, 어디, etc. In the following sentences, 은/는 CANNOT usually follow any of the underlined words:

A: 냉장고에 뭐가 있어요?
What is there in the fridge?

B: **김치하고 계란이** 있어요.
There is kimchi and eggs.

A: 누가 하시겠어요?
Who is going to do it?

B: **제가** 할게요.
I will do it.

A: 어디에서 만났어요?
Where did you meet?

B: **지하철역에서** 만났어요.
We met at the underground station.

In addition to the 'old/given' versus 'new information' rule, one further rule seems to govern the use of 은/는. This particle can also be used for marking up a contrast between two parallel statements (one of which may be implied rather than explicitly stated). When marking up a contrast, the noun marked by 은/는 does not always need to be moved to the start of the sentence and 은/는 is pronounced with more emphasis and higher pitch.

First of all, we see this 'contrast' function being applied when the speaker marks up a shift from one 'topic' he/she was talking about to a new 'topic' that he/she wants to bring up:

A: 소주**가** 있어요?
Do you have soju?

B: 아니요, 없어요.
No, we don't.

A: 그럼, 맥주**는** 있어요?
Then how about beer, do you have that?

In a dialogue such as the above, even though 'beer' is being mentioned for the first time in the final sentence, it is marked with 은/는 to show a contrast with the other alcoholic drink – soju – mentioned before.

Contrast can also be marked up between two topics appearing in the same sentence through repetition of 은/는:

형**은** 의사고 누나**는** 선생입니다.
Older brother is a doctor and older sister is a teacher.

남자<u>는</u> 멍청하고 여자<u>는</u> 미쳤다.
Men are Stupid and Women are Crazy (book title)

영화<u>는</u> 많이 안 보지만 드라마<u>는</u> 자주 봐요.
I don't watch many films, but I often watch dramas.

내일<u>은</u> 시간이 없지만 내일모레<u>는</u> 시간이 있어요.
I don't have time tomorrow, but I have time the day after tomorrow.

Frequently, the comparison is made, not with something that is explicitly stated, but by means of implication. For example, in the following dialogue the answer of the waitress in B may be taken to implicate that there are other alcoholic beverages available. The sense that something else is being implicated is also increased by the use of the verb ending –는데 (refer to 7.3.12):

A: 맥주 있어요?
Do you have beer?

B: 맥주<u>는</u> 없는데요.
We don't have ***beer****.*

Similarly, the following sentences may (depending on context) result in implications such as those given in brackets:

동생<u>은</u> 안 갔어요.
Younger brother didn't go [but the rest of the family did].

언니<u>는</u> 예뻐요.
Your older sister is pretty [but you're not].

토요일에<u>는</u> 시간이 없어요.
I don't have time on Sunday [but another time may be possible].

간호사에게<u>는</u> 인사 못 했어요.
I didn't manage to say hello to the nurse [but I did to the doctor].

It is quite possible that the 'contrastive' function and the 'old/given information' function of 은/는 may both appear in the same sentence:

나<u>는</u> 영어<u>는</u> 배웠어요.
I (old information) learned English (contrastive – I did not learn another language).

친구**는** 방에**는** 없어요.
My friend (old information) is not in the room (contrastive – he is somewhere else).

In addition to the more common functions of 은/는 described above, this particle may also at times be applied to add emphasis to a certain part of the sentence. In this use, 은/는 may appear attached to some clausal connectives such as –(으)니까 (refer to 7.1.6) and –다(가) (refer to 7.3.11):

비가 오니까**는** 우산을 가지고 가야지.
*You have to take an umbrella **because** it's raining.*

유미가 코트를 입다가**는** 벗었어요.
*Yumi put on her coat **then** took it off again.*

As discussed above, choosing between 은/는 and 이/가 marks a distinction between old information or contrast (은/는) and new or important information (이/가). However, it should be noted that a third option is available to Korean speakers: to use no particle at all. The sentence, 'your sister is pretty', for example, could thus be rendered according to any of the three following versions:

1. 이/가 언니가 예뻐요
2. 은/는 언니는 예뻐요
3. no particle 언니 예뻐요

If the speaker uses 이/가, it sounds like the speaker is answering the question, 'who is pretty?' or emphasizing that the sister is the (only) pretty one. With 은/는, at least when pronounced with high pitch, it could sound like the speaker is contrasting the pretty sister with someone else who is not so good looking, possibly the hearer. By dropping the particle in the third sentence, these meanings can be avoided, meaning that this rendition of the sentence might be the most appropriate version.

Similarly, let's imagine a situation where two people are waiting for the bus. One speaker sees that the bus is coming and announces '버스 온다!'. Here using no particle is the best option since 'bus' is not the important information (rather, it is the fact that it is coming that is important), and neither is bus the established topic of conversation or being contrasted with a different mode of transportation.

3.3.2.2 *(이)야 'if it's . . .'*

(이)야 is a two-shape particle: 이야 follows consonants and 야 follows vowels. (이)야 places emphasis on the noun to which it attaches and gives the meaning that the state of affairs being presented is necessarily and unquestionably the case. This can first of all simply take on the meaning of 'if it's . . .' or 'if it were'

라면이**야** 내가 제일 잘 끓여. *If it's ramen, I can cook it the best!*

말이**야** 쉽지. *If it's talk, it's easy. (= Talk is cheap).*

When used in conversation, in addition to emphasizing the noun to which it attaches, (이)야 often connotes an expectation that the speaker is going to offer some kind of contrast with the item in question or disagree with the interlocutor regarding its status:

A: 민호는 돈이 많아.
Minho has a lot of money.

B: 돈이**야** 많지. 하지만 행복하지는 않아.
Of course he has a lot of money. But he's not happy.

A: 유리는 일본말 실력이 대단하네.
Yuri has a great command of Japanese.

B: 대단하긴 뭐가 대단해? 그 정도**야** 쉽지.
What's so great about it? That level is easy.

A: 민호가 정말 잘생겼어.
Minho is so good looking.

B: 잘 생기기**야** 잘생겼지. 근데 너한테 너무 과분해.
Well of course he's good looking. But he's out of your league.

As is shown in the final example, (이)야 can attach to nominalized forms with –기 (2.2.3).

3.3.2.3 *(이)야말로 'indeed'*

(이)야말로 is a two-shape particle: 이야말로 follows consonants and 야말로 follows vowels. (이)야말로 takes on meanings such as 'indeed', 'really', or 'exactly':

서울**이야말로** 아름다운 도시예요.
Seoul is indeed a beautiful city.

부모**야말로** 가장 좋은 의사예요.
It is indeed parents who are the best doctors.

이제**야말로** 손흥민이 부상을 조심할 때입니다.
This is exactly the time when [soccer player] Son Heung-min has to be beware of injuries.

A: 앞으로 잘 부탁드립니다.
I ask you to please show me kindness (overlook my mistakes, etc.) [set greeting expression]

B: 아니에요, 저**야말로** 잘 부탁드립니다.
Don't mention it. It is I who should ask for your kindness.

3.3.3 Particles of extent

Particles treated in this section work to define the extent to which a state of affairs applies.

3.3.3.1 만 *'only'*

만 is a one-shape particle with the basic meaning of 'only'. It can occur after various other particles including as follows:

에 (refer to 3.2.4.1)	→	에만	*only to, at/in*
에서 (refer to 3.2.4.3)	→	에서만	*only from, at/in*
에게/한테 (refer to 3.2.4.4)	→	에게/한테만	*only to (someone)*
에게서/한테서 (refer to 3.2.4.7)	→	에게서/한테서만	*only from (someone)*
(으)로 (refer to 3.2.5.1)	→	(으)로만	*only by means of*

만 can also occur followed by the subject, object and topic particles. However, more commonly, these will just drop:

이/가 (refer to 3.2.1)	→	만이	*only (subject)*
을/를 (refer to 3.2.2)	→	만을	*only (subject)*
은/는 (refer to 3.3.2.1)	→	만은	*only (topic)*

Let us now look at some examples of 만 functioning as 'only' to restrict the meaning of the noun to no more than what is specified:

짜장면**만** 있어요. *We only have black bean noodles.*

우체국에**만** 가요. *I'm going only to the post office.*

한국말로**만** 하십시오. *Speak only in Korean.*

죽을 때까지 너**만**을 사랑할게. *I will love only you until I die.*

When 만 is used in sentences with numerical expressions, rather than strictly taking the meaning of 'only', 만 can be understood to limit the amount to what is specified, meaning no more, no less or exactly [the number specified]:

한 병**만** 주세요. *Give me just one bottle.*

두 시간**만** 공부했어요. *I studied for two hours but not longer.*

만 can also be used after the nominalizing suffix –기 (refer to 2.2.3):

무사히 돌아오기**만**을 바라요.
I only hope that he/she returns safely.

부동산 가격이 내려가기**만**을 기다려요.
I'm only waiting for the price of real estate to fall.

A nominalized phrase can be followed by the verb 하– 'does' to create the expression –기만 하- (refer to 2.2.4.17).

Furthermore, 만 can attach after various verbal endings. For example, 만 can attach after the –야 verb ending (refer to 7.5.7) to intensify the meaning of 'only if':

군대에 가야**만** 이해할 수 있어요.
You can only understand if you go to the army.

보충제는 반드시 먹어야**만** 해요?
Will it only do if you eat supplements? (= Do you have to eat supplements?)

만 can also attach after –고 in the Korean progressive tense pattern –고 있– (refer to 4.3.3.2):

듣고**만** 있었어요. *I was just listening.*

3.3.3.2 뿐 'only'

When applied as a particle, the one-shape 뿐 has two usage patterns.

Firstly, it can be used followed by the copula to mean 'it is only . . .'. Sentences such as the following have an emphatic effect:

이 세상에서 내가 사랑하는 사람은 너**뿐**이야.
It is only you that I love out of all the people in the world.

내가 필요한 건 시간**뿐**이에요.
The only thing I need is time.

왜 항상 욕**뿐**이야?
Why is it always nothing but cussing?

The pattern may also appear with the negative copula to mean 'it is not only/just'. 뿐 may be followed by 만 (refer to 3.3.3.1) for added emphasis.

가고 싶은 사람은 너**뿐만**이 아니야.
It's not just you who wants to go.

그건 한국**뿐만** 아니야. 월남에도 마찬가지야.
That's not just Korea. It's exactly the same in Vietnam.

The second usage of 뿐 builds on this use with the negative copula. But instead of ending the sentence, the negative copula takes the form 아니라 and is followed by a second clause. The sentence as a whole thus means 'not just . . . but . . . as well'. For emphasis, 뿐 may be followed by 만 (refer to 3.3.3.1).

한국어**뿐만** 아니라 일본어도 알아요.
I don't just know Korean, but Japanese as well.

한국**뿐만** 아니라 해외에서도 인기 폭발이에요.
This is not just a craze in Korea, but abroad as well.

3.3.3.3 밖에 'except for'

Etymologically, the expression 밖에 is not strictly a particle. However, in essence, it operates like a particle in that it adds meaning to the noun that it follows. It also makes sense to consider 밖에 at this juncture as it represents another way (in addition to 만, refer to 3.3.3.1) to express the meaning 'only'.

밖에 originates from the word 밖 'outside' and the particle 에 'in/at', thus meaning literally 'on the outside; in the area outside'. Indeed, the expression frequently operates in this original function:

집 **밖에** 나무를 심었어요. *I planted a tree outside of my house.*

However, by extension, 밖에 also metaphorically comes to mean 'outside of' or 'except for' or 'only'. It thus restricts the scope of the noun phrase preceding it to no more than what is specified. In this usage, it operates like a particle and should be written without spacing from the preceding noun:

나무**밖에** 없어요.
There is nothing outside of/except for a tree. (= There is only a tree).

Although the function of 밖에 largely corresponds to that of 만, there are two crucial differences. Firstly, 밖에 must always appear with a negative verb (which is not the case for 만). Compare the following sentences:

밖에	*만*
연필**밖에** 없어요. *I have nothing but a pencil.*	연필**만** 있어요. *I only have a pencil.*
어제 밤 영화관에 저**밖에** 안 갔어요. *No one but me went to the movies last night.*	어제 밤 영화관에 저**만** 갔어요. *Only I went to the movies last night.*
고기**밖에** 못 먹었어요. *I could eat nothing except for meat.*	고기**만** 먹었어요. *I could only eat meat.*

Apart from this important grammatical difference, 밖에 also differs in nuance from 만. Compared to 만, 밖에 has a stronger negative bias – it indicates that the item, people, amount etc. in question is somehow less or inferior to what it should normally be. With the inherent negative meaning of the following sentences, 밖에 is much more natural than 만:

유미는 자기**밖에** 몰라요.
Yumi doesn't care about anything except herself (implies – she should care more for others).

한국말 중에는 욕**밖에** 몰라요.
In Korean, I only know swear words (implies – it would be more normal if I knew other things as well).

The difference between 밖에 and 만 is felt most keenly with numerical expressions. With 만, the expression often has no negative connotation at all and simply applies that the quantity in question is 'no more', 'no less' or 'exactly' the number specified. However, with 밖에, the negative connotation is very strong.

하루에 두 시간**밖에** 안 자요. *I only sleep two hours per day.*
10,000원**밖에** 없어요. *I only have 10,000 won.*

3.3.3.4 부터 'from'

The one-shape particle 부터 has the basic meaning of 'from' and most commonly occurs with time expressions or with numbers that form part of a natural numerical sequence (such as page numbers, question numbers, prices etc.):

2 시**부터** 일해요.
I work from 2 o'clock.

그 영화는 4월 1일**부터** 개봉돼요.
The movie will open on April 1st.

그 남자는 처음**부터** 이유 없이 싫었어요.
I hated him from the start for no reason.

60 쪽**부터** 읽었어요
I read from page 60.

가격은 100,000원**부터**입니다.
The price is from 100,000 won.

부터 may also occur with objects or more abstract notions, typically when these either have a natural order or when the speaker is attempting to impose an order on them:

무슨 말**부터** 하는 게 좋을까요?
Where should I start (from)? (lit. 'from which words should I say?')

한국어 공부할 때 단어**부터** 외워야 하나요?
When you study Korean, do you have to begin from memorizing vocabulary?

When the point of departure is a location rather than a time or number, 에서 is more commonly applied (refer to 3.2.4.3). In addition, 에서 may also combine with 부터 to form 에서부터, which in turn can be abbreviated to 서부터.

미국**에서부터** 기름값이 올랐어요.
The price of oil went up starting with the US.

어디**서부터** 시작해야 할지 모르겠어요.
I don't know where to start.

3.3.3.5 *까지 'up until'*

The one-shape particle 까지 has the opposite meaning of 부터 (refer to 3.3.3.4). With time and numerical expressions, it translates as meaning 'to', 'until' or 'by':

6 시**까지** 일해요.
I work until 6 o'clock.

14 일**까지** 리포트를 제출해 주세요.
Please hand in your essays by the 14th.

우리는 끝**까지** 싸우겠습니다.
We will fight until the end.

밤늦게**까지** 공부했어요.
We studied until late into the night.

Unlike 부터 (refer to 3.3.3.4), 까지 is also commonly used when talking about going up to or reaching a certain place:

집**까지** 30분쯤 걸려요.
It takes about 30 minutes to reach home.

지하철역**까지** 데려다 줄게요.
I'll take you up to the underground station.

부터 frequently occurs in the same sentence as 까지 (or 에서 with places) to express 'from . . . to/until . . .':

두 시**부터** 네 시**까지** 사무실에서 공부해요.
I studied in the office from two until four.

처음**부터** 끝**까지** 엉터리였어요.
It was rubbish from beginning to end!

서울역**에서** 강남**까지** 30분쯤 걸려요.
It takes about 30 minutes from Seoul station to Gangnam.

In addition to the basic meaning of 'to/until/by', 까지 by extension can mean 'even (as far as)' or 'and even' to express a situation beyond the normal bounds of expectation:

병원에 가서 엑스레이 찍고 MRI**까지** 전부 찍었어요
At the hospital, I had an x-ray and even an MRA scan done.

그 사람을 위해서 목숨**까지** 걸 필요는 없어요.
You don't have to go as far as risking your life for that person.

In this use, 까지 is similar to 조차 (refer to 3.3.3.7), 마저 (refer to 3.3.3.8) and certain uses of 도 (refer to 3.3.3.6). However, unlike these other particles, the meaning of 'even' conveyed by 까지 is not necessarily negative (as can be seen in the first two examples above). One more difference is that when the particle appears in positions besides that of subject, it is natural to use 까지 in affirmative constructions and 조차 in negative constructions. For this reason, 까지 is more natural in the first example below and 조차 in the second.

그는 도박으로 집**까지** 날렸어요.
Through gambling he even lost the house.

그는 이웃과 인사**조차** 안 해요.
He doesn't even greet the neighbours.

3.3.3.6 도 'also', 'even'

The one-shape particle 도 may follow other particles including the following:

에 (refer to 3.2.4.1)	→	에도	*also/even to, at/in*
에서 (refer to 3.2.4.3)	→	에서도	*also/even from, at/in*
에게/한테 (refer to 3.2.4.4)	→	에게/한테도	*also/even to [someone]*
에게서/한테서 (refer to 3.2.4.7)	→	에게서/한테서도	*also/even from [someone]*
(으)로 (refer to 3.2.5.1)	→	(으)로도	*also/even by means of*

However, 도 cannot occur with the subject particle 이/가 (refer to 3.2.1) or the object particle 을/를 (refer to 3.2.2) – if 도 is used to mark the subject or object it must replace rather than occur alongside these particles.

도 can be said to have two basic meanings. Firstly, it can take on the meaning of 'too', 'also', 'as well'. Secondly it can mean 'even' (in the sense of 'I don't *even* have 100 won').

Let's first of all look at some examples of 도 appearing in the meaning of 'too', 'also', 'as well'. As can be seen in the final example, 도 may also appear with verbs – the verb in question is nominalized using –기 and the sentence is rounded off with the verb 하– (2.2.4.15).

A: 사과를 사자. *Let's buy apples.*

B: 바나나**도** 사자. *Let's buy bananas too*

A: 저는 냉면을 시킬게요. *I'll order iced noodles.*

B: 저**도**요. *Me too.*

이것은 한국제품이에요. 저것**도** 한국제품이에요.
This is a Korean product. That is a Korean product too.

어제 포장마차에서 술을 마셨어요. 노래방에서**도** 마셨고요.
Yesterday I drank alcohol at the drinking stall. And I drank at karaoke too.

오늘 인호하고 영화를 보고 저녁**도** 먹었어요.
Today I saw a movie with Inho and ate dinner too.

공부하기**도** 해요.
I'm studying too.

As can be seen in the examples above, whereas corresponding English words such as 'too' and 'as well' tend to occur at the end of the sentence, the Korean 도 must always attach to the thing which is being stated in addition.

도 is also used in negative sentences, where English would use 'either' instead:

이것은 수입품이 아니에요. 저것**도** 수입품이 아니에요.
This isn't an import. That isn't an import either.

시간이 없어서 우체국에 못 갔어요. 은행에**도** 못 갔고요.
I was out of time, so I couldn't go to the post office. I couldn't go to the bank either.

In its 'too', 'also', 'as well' function, 도 often occurs twice in a sentence. This shows a kind of tandem agreement between noun phrases meaning 'both . . . and . . .' (or 'neither . . . nor . . .' in negative sentences):

아침에**도** 밤에**도** 일해요.
I work both in the morning and at night.

인호는 친구**도** 적**도** 아니에요.
Inho is neither a friend nor an enemy.

도 may also appear twice in a sentence with two clauses (which are typically linked with –고, refer to 7.3.1) in the meaning of 'both . . . and . . . too' (or 'neither . . . nor . . . either' in negative sentences):

학생**도** 있고 직장인**도** 있어요.
There are both students and there are workers too.

그 술집은 술 값**도** 싸고 분위기**도** 좋아요.
At that pub, the price is both cheap and the atmosphere is good too.

It is also possible to form sentences such as the above by nominalizing two verbs (descriptive or possessive) using –기 and rounding off each clause with the verb 하– 'do' (2.2.4.15).

Let us now look at 도 in its second usage where it takes on the meaning of 'even'. This meaning arises when the noun to which 도 attaches is somehow unlikely, or an extreme case. For instance, in the first example, not even having 1000 won (a relatively small sum of money, roughly equivalent to 1 US dollar) is an extreme case presented by the speaker as evidence that he/she really does not have any money at all. In this usage 도 can be replaced or used in combination with the more emphatic 조차 (refer to 3.3.3.7).

1000원**도** 없어요.
I don't even have 1000 won.

세 살 먹은 아이**도** 알아요.
Even a three-year-old child knows that.

화장실에 갈 시간**도** 없이 바빠요.
I'm so busy that I don't even have time to go to the bathroom.

어제 오빠가 올 줄은 꿈에**도** 몰랐어요.
I never thought even in my dreams that older brother would come yesterday.

독도에 가게 될 줄은 상상**도** 못 했어요.
I never even imagined that I would go to Dokdo.

With the inclusion of 도, the following negative sentences take on the meaning 'I haven't/don't even . . . (yet)':

세수**도** 안 했어요. *I haven't even had a wash [yet].*
시작**도** 안 했어요. *I haven't even started [yet].*

To form similar constructions with long negation (refer to 4.2.2), 도 attaches after –지:

보지**도** 못 했어요. *I haven't even seen it.*
집에 가지**도** 못 했어요. *I haven't even been home.*

도 also frequently attaches to the word for 'still'/'yet' –아직– forming 아직도 'even still', 'not even yet':

민수가 아직**도** 놀고 있어요.
Minsu is still playing/hanging out/taking time out.

그 여자를 아직**도** 못 잊었어요.
I still haven't forgotten her.

도 frequently co-occurs with 아무 to create expressions such as the following:

아무도	아무것도	아무데도
no one at all	*nothing at all*	*nowhere at all*

3.3.3.7 조차 'even'

조차 is a one-shape particle, the meaning of which is similar to 'even' in English. The nuance is much stronger than 도 (refer to 3.3.3.6) but not as strong as 마저 (refer to 3.3.3.8). In other words, this particle indicates that the state or action of the noun in question is very low, or even bottom, on the scale of expectation. The following sentence, for example, implies that Minho is one of the least likely, if not *the* least likely, of all people to miss out on a party:

민호**조차** 파티에 안 왔어요.
Even Minho did not come to the party.

아침도 굶고 점심**조차** 못 먹었어요.
I skipped breakfast and could not eat even lunch.

조차 can optionally be followed by 도 (refer to 3.3.3.6) to intensify the feeling of expectations not being met:

여자 친구**조차도** 내 말을 안 믿었어요.
Even my girlfriend did not believe what I said.

For further emphasis, the expression can be preceded by 심지어:

심지어 미국**조차도** 반대하지 않아요.
Even the USA of all countries is not against it.

조차 represents the most natural choice (rather than 도, 마저 or 까지) when talking about not even being able to do, write, remember, etc. the most basic things:

그 여자 이름**조차도** 몰라요.
I don't even know her name.

한글**조차** 쓸 줄 몰라요.
He/she does not even know how to write Hangul.

3.3.3.8 마저 'even'

마저 is a one-shape particle with the same basic usage as 조차 (refer to 3.3.3.7) and the same basic meaning of 'even'. However, the difference between 마저 and 조차 is that 마저 marks the state or action associated with the noun in question as being an extreme, even outlandish possibility, or the final possible item remaining.

차 사고로 부인하고 아들**마저** 잃었어요.
Due to the car accident, he lost his wife and even his son.

너**마저** 나를 떠나가면 어떻게 살아?
If even you were to leave me, how should I go on living?

빚 때문에 집을 팔고 차**마저** 팔았어요.
Because of the debt, we sold the house and even the car.

그는 심지어 건강**마저** 잃었다.
What is worse, he lost even his health.

Note that 마저 may at times also appear as an independent word:

그것도 **마저** 먹어라. *Eat the rest of it as well.*

하던 얘기 **마저** 끝낼게요. *I'll finish my sentence.*

3.3.3.9 치고/치고는 'with exception', 'pretty . . . for a . . .'

치고 and 치고는 have their origins in the verb 치–, which here means 'count', 'include' or 'consider'. The particles are used when talking about whether we 'consider' something to be typical or atypical of a category that evoked. However, the two variants have opposing meanings: 치고 communicates that the category applies 'without exception', whereas 치고는 marks an exception to the rule.

치고 is used to indicate that a characteristic of noun is true in all cases. It is normally followed by a double negative construction to emphasize that the rule applies 'without exception':

술 좋아하는 사람 **치고** 악한 사람 없어요.
People who drink alcohol, without exception, are never bad people.

한국사람 **치고** 김치 안 먹는 사람은 아마 없을 거예요.
Among Korean people, without exception, there is no one who does not eat kimchi.

부부 **치고** 부부싸움 안하는 사람이 어디 있어요?
Among married people, without exception, are there really any couples who don't quarrel?

On the other hand 치고는 is used to indicate that the preceding noun is an exception to the general rule. It can be followed by –(으)ㄴ/는 편이다 'to tend to be'. The overall nuance is similar to the English 'pretty . . . for a . . .':

외국 사람 **치고는** 한국말을 잘 하는 편이에요.
She speaks Korean pretty well for a foreigner.

농구 선수 **치고는** 키가 작네요.
He's pretty short for a basketball player.

초등학생 **치고는** 비만인 편이에요.
That kid's pretty obese for a primary school student.

3.3.3.10 *(은/는)커녕 'far from'*

The special particle (은/는)커녕 may attach either to a noun or to a verb nominalized by –기 (refer to 2.2.3). 커녕 is most commonly preceded by 은/는–은 after a consonant and 는 after a vowel; however, 은/는 may be dropped in colloquial speech.

(은/는)커녕 takes on meanings such as 'anything but', 'far from', 'on the contrary', 'let alone', 'to say nothing of'. It most often appears in the pattern 'A는커녕 B도/조차/마저 . . . (negative verb)' meaning, 'far from A, not even B'.

일등은**커녕** 이등**도** 못하겠어요.
Far from first place, he/she won't even achieve second place.

택시는**커녕** 버스를 타고 다닐 돈**조차** 없어요.
I don't even have enough money to get around by bus, let alone a taxi.

뛰기는**커녕** 걷지**도** 못하겠어요.
Far from running, he cannot even walk.

하루 종일 국수는**커녕** 물 한 모금**마저** 못 마셨어요.
I haven't even had a sip of water all day, to say nothing of a bowl of noodles.

(은/는) 커녕 can be replaced (with little change in meaning) by the expression '말할 것도 없고' 'without saying anything of'. However, this expression combines with nouns rather than the nominalizer –기 (refer to 2.2.3).

택시는 **말할 것도 없고** 버스 타고 다닐 돈**도** 없어요.
I don't even have enough money to get around by bus, let alone a taxi.

To express the meaning 'to say nothing of' in a positive sense, the word 물론 'of course, needless to say' is used in place of the particle 조차.

10,000원은 **물론** 100,000원도 빌려 줄 수 있어요.
I'll lend you 100,000 won, to say nothing of 10,000 won.

3.3.4 Particles of frequency

Particles in this section express frequency and/or regularity.

3.3.4.1 마다 'every'

마다 is a one-shape particle that does not change form depending on whether it follows a consonant or vowel. The particle has the basic meaning of 'every' or 'each':

아침**마다** 신문을 사요.
I buy a paper every morning.

일요일**마다** 서점들이 문을 닫아요.
Every Sunday the bookstores close.

부산행 고속버스는 10 분**마다** 출발해요.
Buses to Busan depart every 10 minutes.

사람**마다** 성격이 달라요.
Each person has a different personality.

In the following expressions, the nouns 밤 'night' and 날 'day' are repeated, the first occurrence followed by –이면 (the copula + the conditional –면, refer to 7.5.1) and the second by 마다. The resulting expression emphasizes the meaning of constant repetition and has a similar ring to English expressions such as 'night after night' or 'each and every day'. Although these expressions most commonly occur with 밤 'night', '날' 'day' and other time expressions, they may also sometimes occur with other nouns such as 사람 'person'.

밤**이면** 밤**마다** 악몽을 꾸어요.
Night after night, I have nightmares.

날**이면** 날**마다** 오는 게 아니에요.
This is not the kind of thing that happens every day.

날이면 날마다 can be most frequently heard in the set idiomatic expression above.

3.3.4.2 씩 *'apiece'*

씩 is a one-shape particle that does not change form depending on whether it is preceded by a noun or a consonant. 씩 marks regularity or equal distribution. Although this is something that is not always made explicit in English, the most similar word is 'apiece' (as in 'two biscuits apiece'). Note in the following examples how 씩 attaches after the word denoting the thing that is being evenly distributed (books, 10,000 won, etc.):

학생들한테 책 한 권**씩** 주었어요.
I gave the students one book apiece.

아이들한테 과자 한 봉투**씩** 주었어요.
I gave the kids one bag of snacks apiece.

소주를 두 병**씩** 마셨어요.
We drank two bottles of soju each.

The usage of 씩 as a marker of even distribution covers the use of 'per' (or 'a/an') in English in expressions such as 'eight hours per/a night', 'one bottle per/a day', etc.:

밤마다 여덟 시간**씩** 자요. *I sleep 8 hours a night.*

소주를 매일 한 병**씩** 마시면 알코올중독이라 볼 수 있나요?
If you drink one bottle of soju a day, can you see it as alcoholism?

3.3.5 Particles of approximation and optionality

Particles in this section are used to express that the noun in question is only approximate or an option.

3.3.5.1 쯤 'about'

쯤 is a one-shape particle that does not change form depending on whether it is preceded by a vowel or a consonant. 쯤 means 'about', 'approximately' or 'around' and most commonly occurs with time and/or numerical expressions:

어젯밤 20 명**쯤** 왔어요.
About twenty people came last night.

12 시**쯤**에 잤어요.
I slept at about 12 o'clock

작년 여름**쯤**에 그 남자를 처음 만났어요.
I first met him around summer last year.

30대 후반**쯤** 돼 보이는 부부가 왔어요.
A couple came that looked like they were in around their late 30s.

In such sentences, 쯤 often co-occurs with the expression 한 (also meaning 'about' or 'approximately').

> **한** 두 시**쯤** 우리 집에 와요.
> *He comes to our house at about two o'clock.*

The particle 쯤 is also sometimes applied in other expressions of approximation that are not time-related or numerical, such as in 쯤 돼 보이– 'look more or less like . . .':

> 선생님**쯤** 돼 보이는 분이 계셨어요.
> *There was someone who looked more or less like a school teacher.*

3.3.5.2 *(이)나 ('about', 'or', 'just')*

(이)나 is a two-shape particle. It appears as 이나 when following a consonant and as 나 when following a vowel. This particle has four distinct usages that we look at it turn: (1) to create expressions of approximation or generalization, (2) to communicate that a quantity is greater than expected (3) to mark something as a second-best choice and (4) to express choice (or indifference to choice).

In its first usage as a marker of approximation or generalization, (이)나 works in the same way as 쯤 (refer to 3.3.5.1) to express the meaning of 'about', 'approximately' or 'around'. However, this meaning is only usually available when another word of approximation (such as 한 'about', 'approximately') is included or when the sentence is a question such as 'about how many . . .?':

몇 시간**이나** 걸려요?	*About how many hours does it take?*
몇 개**나** 살까요?	*About how many should we buy?*
한 1000명**이나** 왔어요.	*About 1000 people came.*

Another way in which (이)나 becomes involved in the marking of generalization is when it attaches to question words. In such cases, the question words lose their interrogative meaning and generalized words such as 'anyone', 'anywhere', etc. are created:

누구	*who?*	누구**나**	*anyone; everyone*
무엇	*what?*	무엇**이나**	*anything; everything*
언제	*when?*	언제**나**	*any time; all the time; always*

어디	*where?*	어디**나**	*anywhere; everywhere*
어디서	*where?*	어디서**나**	*[happening] anywhere; everywhere*
어느것	*which . . . ?*	어느것**이나**	*anything; either [thing]*

A similar meaning can be obtained by combining –나 with the word 아무, which by itself means 'anyone, anybody', and in front of another noun means 'any, any old':

아무**나**	*anyone*
아무것**이나**	*anything*
아무 때**나**	*any time*
아무 데**나**	*any place*
아무 데서**나**	*[happening at] any place*
아무 책**이나**	*any book [at all]*

In its second function, (이)나 is used to communicate that a quantity is greater than expected or more than is necessary (similar to English 'as much as'). In this function, (이)나 can be thought of as the opposite of 밖에 (refer to 3.3.3.3), which expressed that the quantity is not as much as what is required or is normally the case. The following examples compare these two markers:

(이)나	*밖에*
학생 열명**이나** 왔어요. *As many as ten students came.*	학생 열명**밖에** 안 왔어요. *Only ten students came.*
50,000원**이나** 있어요. *I have as much as 50,000 won.*	50,000원**밖에** 없어요. *I only have 50,000 won.*
소주 두 병**이나** 마셨어요. *I drank as many as two bottle of soju.*	소주 두 병**밖에** 못 마셨어요. *I could only drink two bottles of soju*

In its third function, (이)나 marks the noun it follows as a possible option, but one that is not necessarily first choice. In suggestions or invitations, this usually just works to weaken what the speaker is proposing and leave more options open for the hearer to opt out or propose another plan. This usually translates into English as 'or something', etc.:

영화**나** 볼까요?
Shall we see a movie or something?

차**나** 마실까요?
Shall we drink some tea or something?

심심하면 남자 친구랑 데이트**나** 하지.
If you're bored, why don't you just go on date with your boyfriend or something?

In other examples, what is being marked by (이)나 is more obviously a second choice rather than what would normally be preferred. This normally translates into English as 'just':

하이트가 없으면 카스**나** 사자.
If there's no 'Hite' (beer), let's just buy 'Cass'

밥이 없으면 빵**이나** 먹지.
If there's no rice, let's just eat bread.

With this meaning of 'just', (이)나 can also be used in angry or sarcastic expressions meaning 'why don't you just . . .'. As can be seen in the third example, in this function (이)나 can also attach to the nominalizing form –기 (refer to 2.2.3):

네 일**이나** 신경 써!
Why don't you just worry about your own affairs! (= Mind your own business!)

쓸데없는 소리하지 말고 네 일**이나** 해!
Stop talking nonsense and just get on with your work!

빨리 먹기**나** 해!
Why don't you just eat up! [and stop bugging me, etc.].

In its fourth function, (이)나 is used to express choice between two nouns in a similar way to 'or' in English.

지하철**이나** 버스를 타고 가세요. *Take the underground or a bus.*

미국**이나** 유럽에도 절이 있고 불교신자가 있어요.
Even in the US or Europe there are temples and Buddhists.

When –이나 is attached to both nouns, it signals that the speaker is indifferent and that either choice is acceptable:

산**이나** 바다**나** 다 좋아요.
Either the mountains or the sea would be good.

커피**나** 차**나** 아무거나 주세요.
Just give me anything – coffee or tea.

3.3.6 Particles of comparison and contrast

Particles covered in this section are used to express degree of similarity or difference between two or more nouns.

3.3.6.1 처럼 'like'

처럼 is a one-shape particle that operates in the same way as 'like' in English to say that 'something/ someone is 'like' (i.e., the same as or similar to) something/someone else':

인호는 나**처럼** 정치학을 전공해요.
Inho majors in Political Science like me.

누나가 영화배우**처럼** 예뻐요.
Older sister is pretty like a movie actor.

유미는 가수**처럼** 노래를 불러요.
Yumi sings like a pop singer.

In examples such as the above, 처럼 can be substituted for 같이 with no perceptible change in meaning (refer to 3.3.6.2).

처럼 may also occur following –(으)ㄴ/는 것(refer to 2.2.6), thus linking two clauses:

아까 말한 것**처럼** 지금 경기도 지역에 살아요.
As I just said, I live in the Gyeongi area.

인호는 마치 모든 것을 아는 것**처럼** 말해요.
Inho speaks like he knows everything.

외국에서 살아도 한국에서 사는 것**<u>처럼</u>** 문자 주고 받을 수 있어요.
Even if you live abroad, you can receive and send text messages just like you live in Korea.

Similar sentences to the above can be created by using the patterns –듯이 (refer to 7.8.1) or –다시피 (refer to 7.8.2).

3.3.6.2 *같이 'like'*

Although the one-shape 같이 can function as a particle, it can also appear as an independent word – an adverb meaning 'together'. This adverb is derived from the verb 같– meaning 'is the same'.

같이 operates in the same way as 'like' in English (and as 처럼, refer to 3.3.6.1) to say that 'something/someone is 'like' (i.e., the same as or similar to) something/ someone else'.

미나 얼굴은 조각**<u>같이</u>** 아름다워요.
Mina's face is beautiful like a statue.

그 남자는 저를 어린애**<u>같이</u>** 취급해요.
He treats me like [I were] a little child.

밤인데도 대낮**<u>같이</u>** 밝아요.
Even though it's night, it's as bright as day.

Although this usage of 같이 is identical to 처럼 (refer to 3.3.6.1), by reverting to the original verb 같– some additional patterns of usage can be evoked. 같– can be applied as a verb to mean 'something/someone is like something/someone else'. The noun should be followed by 와/과 'and' (refer to 3.2.6.1), although this is dropped in casual speech:

미나 얼굴은 조각(과) **<u>같아요</u>**. *Mina's face is like a statue.*

This (와/과) 같– can take other verb endings including conditionals (as in the first sentence) and modifying endings (as in the second):

저 **<u>같으면</u>** 이런 사람과 친구 안 해요.
If you were like me (i.e., if I were you), I would not be friends with that kind of person.

저 **같은** 초보자들도 책을 보면 이해가 갈까요?
Would novices like me be able to understand by looking at a book?

3.3.6.3 *만큼 'as . . . as'*

만큼 is a one-shape particle that is used to express that two things are equal or have reached the same extent. This commonly translates into English as 'as . . . as':

우리 형**만큼** 키가 컸어요.
I have become as tall as my older brother.

오늘은 어제**만큼** 덥지 않아요.
As for today, [it] is not as hot as yesterday.

기대**만큼** 점수가 안 나왔어요.
The score didn't come out to the extent of [my] expectation.

만큼 can also be preceded by a modifier clause (refer to Chapter 8):

고민하고 노력한 **만큼** 결과가 나쁘지 않게 나온 것 같아요.
The result doesn't seem too bad compared with the worry and effort.

3.3.6.4 *보다 'more than'*

보다 is a one-shape particle used in comparative sentences to mean 'more than' or 'rather than'. Rather than attaching to the noun which is 'superior', 'more', 'preferred', 'greater', etc., it attaches to the noun to which this object, person etc. is being compared. Observe the following sentence pattern:

러시아는	한국**보다**	커요.
Russia	*Korea-보다*	*big*

Russia is bigger than Korea.

여름이 겨울**보다** 좋아요.
Summer is nicer than winter.

오늘은 어제**보다** 시간이 많이 있어요.
I have more time today than yesterday.

사진**보다** 실물이 예뻐요.
She is prettier in person than in photographs.

꽃**보다** 초콜릿이 낫지 않을까요?
Wouldn't chocolates be better rather than flowers?

The word 더 'more' can optionally be included in the sentence:

작년**보다** 단풍 색깔이 **더** 예뻐요.
The colour of the maples is prettier than last year.

To produce the opposite meaning – i.e., that 'A is LESS . . . than B', insert 덜 'less' instead:

수입쇠고기가 작년**보다 덜** 팔려요.
Imported beef is selling less than last year.

To intensify the meaning, you can insert 훨씬 'by far' (which is sometimes abbreviated to 훨 colloquial speech), 한층 'still more' or 엄청 'exceedingly' (colloquial):

고속버스**보다** 기차가 **훨씬** 빨라요.
The train is way faster than the express bus.

7월**보다** 8월이 **한층 더** 더워져요.
It gets even hotter in August than in July.

백화점**보다** 시장이 **엄청** 싸요.
The market is exceedingly cheaper than the department store.

Extra emphasis can also be created when 보다 is followed by the particle 도 (refer to 3.3.3.6) or the particle 은/는 (refer to 3.3.2.1):

홍차**보다도** 커피가 먹고 싶어요.
I'd rather have coffee (even more) than tea.

산**보다도** 높고 바다**보다도** 깊어요.
It is taller even than the mountains and deeper even than the sea.

A further construction can be created by preceding 보다 with a modifier clause and 것 (refer to 8.2.2) to create a construction meaning 'rather than . . .'. The particle phrase may be followed by 오히려 'rather, preferably'.

오늘은 버스를 기다리는 것**보다** (오히려) 뛰어 가는 것이 빨랐어요.
Today it was faster to run there than waiting for the bus.

백 번 듣는 것**보다** 한번 보는 것이 좋아요.
It's better to see a thing once (rather) than hear it a hundred times.

그 사람은 내가 생각했던 것**보다** 키가 컸어요.
He was taller than I thought he would be.

한국어는 예상했던 것**보다** 어려워요.
Korean is more difficult than I expected.

Note that in the final two constructions '생각했던 것보다' 'more than I thought' and '예상했던 것보다' 'more than I expected' can be abbreviated to '생각보다' and '예상보다'.

3.3.6.5 *따라 'unusually'*

The particle 따라 attaches to time expressions such as 오늘 'today', 그날 'that day' and 올해 'this year' to express that the state of affairs being talked about applies exclusively to the quoted period of time and is different to the normal state of affairs. When translated into English this is usually rendered as 'unusually' or with expressions such as 'today of all days'.

오늘**따라** 날씨가 쌀쌀하네요.
The weather is unusually chilly today.

어제**따라** 남편이 일찍 들어왔어요.
Yesterday my husband came home unusually early.

그 날**따라** 못 오신 분들이 많았어요.
On that day, unusually, many people didn't come.

3.3.6.6 대로 *'in accordance with'*

대로 is a particle meaning 'in accordance with' or 'in conformity with':

선생님 말씀**대로** 하겠습니다.
I'll do as you ('teacher') say.

마음**대로** 하세요.
Do as you wish.

그냥 편하게 제 느낌**대로** 썼어요.
I just wrote in a carefree way, following my feelings.

대로 can be used as a bound noun preceded by a modifier clauses, as discussed elsewhere in this book (refer to 8.2.19). It also forms an integral part of the word 그대로, formed from the demonstrative 그 'that' and 대로 and meaning 'as it is' or 'the same as it has ever been':

현실을 있는 **그대로** 받아들여요
Accept the reality as it is.

너는 **그대로**야.
You look the same as ever. (= You haven't changed a bit).

그냥 **그대로** 있어야 해
You have to stay as you are.

Chapter 4

Verbs

4.1 Characteristics of Korean verbs

Overview

Korean is a language in which a vast number of grammatical functions are achieved by attaching different endings to verbs. Thus, it is of particular importance to understand the underlying qualities of Korean verbs and how they are formed. This section introduces the basic types of Korean verbs, their underlying forms and how you can attach different endings to them.

4.1.1 *Types of verbs: processive and descriptive*

Korean has two main categories of verbs: processive verbs and descriptive verbs. Processive verbs correspond to verbs in languages such as English – words that are used to describe an action or a process such as 먹어요'eat', 마셔요'drink' and 가요 'go'.

Descriptive verbs, however, are different to anything found in English. Their meanings correspond to English adjectives. However, unlike English adjectives, they do not need to occur with a copula such as 'be'. They are freestanding. The Korean word 예뻐요, therefore, means 'be pretty', 추워요 means 'be cold', 시끄러워요 means 'be noisy' and so forth. Descriptive verbs behave in many ways exactly the same as processive verbs and take many of the same endings, etc. English adjectives, on the other hand, behave similar to nouns (note the grammatical similarity of sentences such as 'she is busy' and 'she is a doctor').

However, there are some important differences between the characteristics of processive verbs and descriptive verbs:

1 Processive and descriptive verbs behave differently in the 'plain' speech style (refer to 6.2.4), and other sentence patterns that incorporate it such as reported speech constructions (refer to Chapter 10). Most crucially, in statements, the ending for processive verbs is –ㄴ/는다, whereas in descriptive verbs it is –다.
2 Unlike processive verbs, descriptive verbs cannot occur with the present dynamic modifier –는 (refer to 8.1.2) and other sentence patterns that incorporate it.
3 Whereas processive verbs can freely appear in imperative sentences, descriptive verbs prescriptively cannot. Sentences such as 바쁘세요 'be busy' or 차가워라 'be cold' cannot be used as imperatives. However, note that some speakers may use descriptive verbs that imply some sort of behaviour with imperatives such as 조용하세요 'be quiet', 건강하세요 'be healthy' and 행복하세요 'be happy', although this usage may not be considered standard.
4 Descriptive verbs are also restricted in appearing in hortative sentences (i.e., sentences that mean 'let's . . .'). You cannot say sentences such as 예쁘자 'let's be pretty' in Korean. However, note again that in actual language usage speakers tend to break this rule by using hortative sentences with descriptive verbs that have behavioural properties such as 행복하자 'let's be happy' or 조용하자 'let's be quiet'.

There is a small set of verbs that can be either processive or descriptive depending on the context in which they are used:

1 낫– has two different meanings: 'is better' and 'gets better' or 'recovers'. In the first usage, it is descriptive, in the second it is processive. This can be seen by the way that in the first usage it takes the –다 plain speech style ending and in the second usage it takes –는다:

물 한 잔이 약보다 **낫다**.
A glass of water is better than medicine.

생활습관을 바꾸면 병이 **낫는다**.
If you change your lifestyle, your illness will get better.

2 크– has two different meanings: 'is big' and 'gets bigger' or 'grows'. In the first usage, it is descriptive, in the second it is processive:

와! 집이 참 **크다**! *Wow, the house is nice and big!*

와! 아이가 참 잘 **큰다**! *Wow, the kid is growing nicely!*

3 Although typically considered a descriptive verb, 늦다 'be late' may sometimes be used as a processive verb when talking about the late behaviour of a human, or the late running of a train, etc.:

영수가 너무 늦**는다** *Yongsu is running late.*

기차가 너무 늦**는다**. *The train is running late.*

시간이 너무 늦**다**. *The time is too late.*

4 있– has two different meanings: 'exist' and 'stay'. In the first usage, it is descriptive, in the second it is processive:

냉장고에 오렌지 주스가 **있다**. *There is juice in the fridge.*

저녁 7시 이후에는 항상 집에 **있는다**. *I am always at home at seven in the evening.*

However, note that 있– in both usage can take the present dynamic modifier –는 (refer to 8.1.2):

냉장고에 있**는** 오렌지 주스 *The juice that is in the fridge*

집에 있**는** 사람 *A person who is at home*

계시–, the honorific equivalent of 있– is also descriptive when it means 'exist' and 'processive' when it means 'stay':

할아버지가 안 **계시다**. *I don't have a grandfather.*

할아버지가 안 **계신다**. *Grandfather is not here.*

Note however that 없–, the negative equivalent of 있–, behaves like a descriptive verb.

남동생이 **없다**. *I don't have a younger brother.*

or *Younger brother is not here.*

However, like 있–, 없– can take the present dynamic modifier –는 (refer to 8.1.2):

없<u>는</u> 남동생	*the younger brother I don't have*
	or *the younger brother who is not here*

5 The negative auxiliary verb 않– can behave like a processive or a descriptive verb depending on whether what proceeds it is a processive verb (as in the first example) or a descriptive verb (as in the second example):

유미 씨는 계란을 먹지 <u>**않는다**</u>.	*Yumi doesn't eat eggs.*
유미 씨는 게으르지 <u>**않다**</u>.	*Yumi isn't lazy.*

6 When the support verb 하– combines with nouns to form processive verbs such as 공부하– and 운동하– (refer to 4.1.2), it will naturally behave according to the processive verb patterns. However, remember that descriptive verbs that end in –하– such as 피곤하– or 깨끗하– will behave according to the descriptive verb patterns.

4.1.2 *Types of verbs: 하– verbs*

Korean has a set of processive verbs that are formed by combining a noun with the support verb 하–. Here are some common examples:

Original noun	*Verb*
공부 *studying*	공부하– *to study*
생각 *thought*	생각하– *to think*
시작 *the start*	시작하– *to start*
운동 *exercise*	운동하– *to exercise*
준비 *preparation*	준비하– *to prepare*
청소 *cleaning*	청소하– *to tidy up*

As in the examples above, this pattern most commonly occurs with Sino-Korean nouns (i.e., nouns that are combinations of Chinese characters or whose origins are Chinese words). However, it may also occur with words loaned from other languages, typically English, including 드라이브하– 'go for a drive' and 쇼핑하– 'go shopping'.

Processive verbs with 하– are normally written as one word. However, the original noun and 하– may at times be written as separate verbs with the object particle (refer to 3.2.2) or alternatively the topic particle (refer to 3.3.2.1) written after the noun:

공부를 했어요.	*I've studied.*
준비는 했어요.	*I've done the preparation.*

In addition, when you want to use short negation with 안 or 못 (refer to 4.2.1), this element always has to come between the noun and 하–:

운동을 안 했어요.	*I didn't exercise.*
운동을 못 했어요.	*I couldn't exercise.*

When you want to insert an adverb (such as 많이 'many, much', 빨리 'quickly' and 즐겁게 'pleasantly'), these elements may come either before the whole verb or between the noun and 하– (the latter is considered more natural):

많이/즐겁게 운동(을) 했어요.	*I exercised a lot/happily.*
운동을 많이/즐겁게 했어요.	*I exercised a lot/happily.*

In addition to these processive verbs formed by the addition of 하–, note that Korean also has a set of descriptive verbs that end in 하–. With these verbs, more caution is required as the part preceding 하– is not always an independent noun that can be written separately (such as 참하- 'nice and pretty' or 깨끗하– 'is clean'). When this is the case, these descriptive verbs ALWAYS have to occur with 하– as one word.

Also, it should be noted that in addition to 하–, Korean has a number of other 'support verbs' that can follow a noun to change it into a verb phrase. The most common of these other support verbs are listed below. It should be noted that these other support verbs generally have a specific meaning and are much more restricted in their usage than 하–.

Support verb	Examples
가– *go*	여행(을) 가– *go travelling,* 출장(을) 가– *go on a business trip*
*당하– *suffer*	강간(을) 당하– *be raped,* 협박(을) 당하– *be threatened*
*되– *become, be*	기대되– *be expected,* 걱정되– *be worried*
*받– *receive*	간섭(을) 받– *be interfered with,* 사랑(을) 받– *be loved*
***드리– *do (for/to superior)*	인사 드리– *greet (a superior)* 전화 드리– *phone (a superior)*
**시키– *make*	공부(를) 시키– *make someone study,* 주의(를) 시키– *make someone pay attention*
오– come	이민오– *immigrate,* 구경오– *come sight seeing*
*입– *suffer*	피해(를) 입– *suffer loss,* 상처(를) 입– *suffer injury*

* These support verbs are discussed in more detail in the section on passives (refer to 4.4.1)
** This support verb is discussed in more detail in the section on causatives (refer to 4.4.2.4)
*** This support verb is discussed in more detail in the section on object honorifics (refer to 6.2.2)

4.1.3 Types of verbs: negative verbs

Korean has two special verbs that have inherent negative meanings and that are quite different to anything found in English: 없– 'not exist, not stay, not have', etc. –and 모르– 'not know'. These verbs are the negative counterparts of 있– and 알– respectively.

Negative sentence	*Positive sentence*
유미가 일본어를 **몰라요**.	미나가 중국어를 **알아요**.
Yumi doesn't know Japanese.	*Mina doesn't know Chinese*

교실에 컴퓨터가 **없어요**.	교실에 화분이 **있어요**.
There is no computer in the classroom.	*There is a pot plant in the classroom.*

Since Korean has these negative verbs, it is not usually possible to use the positive verbs 있– 'exist, have' and 알– 'know' with 'short negation' patterns with 안 and 못 (refer to 4.2.1). It is however possible to use these verbs with 'long negation' (refer to 4.2.2).

4.1.4 Types of verbs: the copula (equational verb)

The copula is a special verb-like form which is used similar to the English verb 'be' (am, are, is) in 'equational sentences' – sentences of the pattern 'A is B' (such as 'this is a pen', 'I am a vegetarian', etc.). The base form (refer to 4.1.5) of the copula is –이–. In the 'polite' (refer to 6.1.1) style, it is rendered as –이에요:

저는 영국 사람**이에요**.	*I am British.*
소주는 한국 술**이에요**.	*Soju is Korean alcohol.*

One peculiarity of the copula is that the –이– base itself can in most circumstances be dropped when the preceding noun ends in a vowel. When this happens, the verb ending appears to attach directly to the preceding noun:

여자**다**.	*She is a woman.*	plain speech style (refer to 6.1.4)
여자**니까**.	*Because she is a woman.*	–니까 *connective ending (refer to 7.1.6)*
여자**네요**!	*Boy, she is a woman!*	–네 *sentence ending (refer to 9.5)*

One time when this cannot always happen is with the 'formal' speech style (refer to 6.1.2). Here, the –이– only tends to drop with some very common nouns such as 거 'thing, fact', 저 'I' and 어디 'where'.

그 건 제 **겁니다**.	*That one's mine.*
접니다.	*It's me.*
고향이 **어딥니까**?	*Where is your home town?*

With the 'polite' speech style, the form after a vowel is –예요. This is typically pronounced –에요, although you may hear the full pronunciation of –예요 in careful speech:

이 것은 일본 잡지**예요**. *This is a Japanese magazine.*

이 책은 누구 거**예요**? *Whose book is this?*

Unlike other verbs, –이– always has to be preceded by a noun and can never appear on its own. As can be seen in the examples above, in writing, there should be no space between the noun and –이–.

The negative form of the copula is 아니– (아니에요 in the 'polite' style). Unlike –이–, 아니– is an independent word that may appear on its own and has to be written spaced. The subject particle (refer to 3.2.1) or the topic particle (refer to 3.3.1) may appear after any preceding noun.

그 사람은 한국 사람(이) **아니에요**. *He/she is not Korean.*

이 것은 제 책(이) **아니에요**. *This is not my book.*

그 분은 교수(가) **아니에요.** *He/she is not a professor.*

A: 회사원이에요?
Are you an office worker?

B: **아니에요**. 공무원이에요.
I'm not. I'm a civil servant.

'아니에요' also represents a very simple and humble way to reject a compliment or to reply to thanks and apology (similar to 'It's nothing') in English:

A: 한국말 잘하시네요!
Wow, you speak Korean really well!

B: **아니에요**. 아직 많이 부족합니다.
Not really. I'm still very lacking.

A: 도와주셔서 고맙습니다.
Thanks for your help.

B: **아니에요**.
It's nothing.

Note that the copula and negative copula have the variant forms –이라– and –아니라– that occur with certain verb endings such as –(아/어)서 and –(아/어)도:

휴일**이라서** 그런지 사람이 없어요.
Because it is a holiday, there are not many people.

한국 사람**이라도** 김치를 잘 안 먹어요.
Even though I am Korean, I don't eat much kimchi.

4.1.5 Verb bases

Korean verbs are composed of bases onto which different endings are attached. The way that Korean verbs will behave depends primarily on whether they end in a vowel or in a consonant, and is also influenced by which verb appears in the base. There are also some groups of irregular verbs that you need to watch out for, as they will behave differently when other endings are attached.

Type of verb	*Example verb base*	
consonant base (ㅏ/ㅗ in base)	받–	*receive*
consonant base (other vowel in base)	먹–	*eat*
vowel base ending in ㅏ	가–	*go*
vowel base ending in ㅐ	보내–	*send*
vowel base ending in ㅗ	오–	*come*
vowel base ending in ㅜ	주–	*give*
vowel base ending in ㅣ	마시–	*drink*
vowel base ending in ㅡ	쓰–	*write*
irregular: ㅂ/ㅜ verbs	굽–	*broil*
irregular: ㄷ/ㄹ verbs	듣–	*listen*
irregular: ㅅ/ㅇ verbs	짓–	*build*
irregular: ㄹ doubling	부르–	*sing*
irregular: ㄹ dropping	놀–	*play*
irregular: ㅎ dropping	하얗–	*be white*

We now list the some of the most common irregular verbs that belong to the categories given above

ㄷ/ㄹ verbs

걷– *walk* 듣– *listen* 묻– *ask*

ㅅ/ㅇ verbs

낫– *be/get better* 짓– *build*

ㄹ doubling

다르– *be different* 모르– *not know* 부르– *sing; be full* 빠르– *be fast*

오르– *rise, go up*

ㄹ dropping

걸– *make (phone call)*	놀– *play, have fun*	들– *lift, hold*	멀– *be far*
물– *bite*	살– *live*	알– *know*	열– *open*
말– *desist*	팔– *sell*	풀– *undo, solve*	

ㅂ/ㅜ verbs

가깝– *be near*	가볍– *be light*	고맙– *be thankful*
굽– *broil*	눕– *lie down*	맵– *be spicy*
무겁– *be heavy*	쉽– *be easy*	어렵– *be difficult*
즐겁– *be enjoyable*	춥– *be cold*	덥– *be warm*

ㅎ dropping

그렇– *be like that*	노랗– *be yellow*	빨갛– *be red*
어떻– *be a certain way*	이렇– *be like this*	저렇– *be like that*
파랗– *be blue*	하얗– *be white*	

4.1.6 The infinitive form

In order to conjugate Korean verbs, in addition to knowing the base form, it is also useful to know what is called the infinitive form (note that the 'infinitive' form of Korean verbs is quite different to the concept in European languages).

The basic rule for adding the infinitive is to add either –아 or –어 to the base. –아 is added when the verb base contains the vowels ㅏ or ㅗ; –어 is added in all other cases. Note however, the following irregularities:

1 Vowel bases ending in ㅏ, ㅐ and ㅓ: nothing is added (the infinitive is the same as the base). Note however that ㅔ does not follow this pattern and that 어 needs to be added (e.g., 세어 'count', 메어 'carry')
2 Optionally, vowel bases ending in ㅗ: ㅗ may combine with the –아 ending to form –ㅘ. This is more common in casual speech and writing.
3 Optionally, vowel bases ending in ㅜ: ㅜ may combine with the –어 ending to form –ㅝ. This is more common in casual speech and writing. Note that the verb 푸– 'scoop' has the unusual infinitive form 퍼.
4 Vowel bases ending in ㅣ: ㅣ combines with the –어 ending to form –여
5 Vowel bases ending in ㅡ: the final ㅡ drops and then –어 is added
6 Irregular ㅂ/ㅜ verbs: the final ㅂ changes to ㅜ (or ㅗ for verbs containing ㅏ in the base). This ㅜ then combines with the –어 (or 아) ending to form –ㅝ (or ㅘ).
7 Irregular ㄷ/ㄹ verbs: ㄷ is replaced by ㄹ, then –어 is added
8 Irregular ㅅ/ㅇ verbs: ㅅ drops and then –아/어 is added
9 Irregular ㄹ doubling verbs: the ㄹ from the final syllable doubles so that it is also included at the end of the first syllable, then the final ㅡ drops and –어 or 아 is added.
10 Irregular ㄹ dropping verbs: the ㄹ is NOT dropped (as it is with some '2-shape' endings – see below). –아/어– is added in the same way as a regular verb.
11 Irregular ㅎ dropping verbs: the ㅎ drops and the remaining 아/어 or 야 combines with the infinitive ending to become 애 or 얘 respectively.

Check out examples of these in the table below:

Type of verb	*Base*	*Infinitive*	
consonant base (ㅏ/ㅗ in base)	받–	받아	*receive*
consonant base (other vowel)	먹–	먹어	*eat*
vowel base ending in ㅏ	가–	가	*go*
vowel base ending in ㅐ	보내–	보내	*send*
vowel base ending in ㅗ	오–	와	*come*

vowel base ending in ㅜ	주–	줘	*give*
vowel base ending in ㅣ	마시–	마셔	*drink*
vowel base ending in ㅡ	쓰–	써	*write*
irregular: ㅂ/ㅜ verbs	굽–	구워	*broil*
	곱–	고와	*beautiful*
irregular: ㄷ/ㄹ verbs	듣–	들어	*listen*
irregular: ㅅ/ㅇ verbs	짓–	지어	*build*
irregular: ㄹ doubling	부르–	불러	*sing*
	모르–	몰라	*not know*
irregular: ㄹ dropping	놀–	놀아	*play*
irregular: ㅎ dropping	그렇–	그래	*be like that*
	하얗–	하얘	*be white*

The infinitive form is important to know for two reasons:

1 On its own, the bare infinitive is the same as the present tense of the 'intimate' speech style (refer to 6.1.3).
2 The infinitive form is an important building block for attaching different verb endings, as shall be discussed below (refer to 4.1.8).

If you have trouble forming the infinitive form from the base, it may actually be easier just to think of the 'intimate' speech style (refer 6.1.3) ending as this will be the same. Alternatively, think of the 'polite' speech style (refer 6.1.1) and if you drop the –요 off the end, you will be left with the infinitive.

4.1.7 The dictionary form

When you look for verbs in the dictionary, you will not find the base form or the infinitive form but what is known as the 'dictionary form'. The dictionary form is constructed by adding –다 to the base.

Type of verb	*Base*	*Dictionary form*	
consonant base (ㅏ/ㅗ in base)	받–	받다	*receive*
consonant base (other vowel)	먹–	먹다	*eat*
vowel base ending in ㅏ	가–	가다	*go*
vowel base ending in ㅐ	보내–	보내다	*send*
vowel base ending in ㅗ	오–	오다	*come*
vowel base ending in ㅜ	주–	주다	*give*
vowel base ending in ㅣ	마시–	마시다	*drink*
vowel base ending in ㅡ	쓰–	쓰다	*write*
irregular: ㅂ/ㅜ verbs	굽–	굽다	*broil*
irregular: ㄷ/ㄹ verbs	듣–	듣다	*listen*
irregular: ㅅ/ㅇ verbs	짓–	짓다	*build*
irregular: 르 doubling	부르–	부르다	*sing*
irregular: ㄹ dropping	놀–	놀다	*play*
irregular: ㅎ dropping	하얗–	하얗다	*be white*

Note that the dictionary form is only used for listing verbs in the dictionary, or for citing verbs (for example, in descriptions of Korean grammar).

4.1.8 Attaching verb endings

Through the addition of verb endings, a variety of different functions and meanings can be achieved including tenses, negatives and honorifics. When these endings attach to the verb, there are three main types of endings that attach to verbs in three separate ways (see below for two some exceptions):

1 One-shape endings which attach in a regular fashion to the base and which always have the same form. Examples include –고 'and' (refer to 7.3.1) –지만 'but' (refer to 7.2.1), and the dictionary form –다.

2 Two-shape endings which attach to the base but change form depending on whether they attach to a consonant base or a vowel base. When they attach to a consonant base, the ending has a form beginning in '—'. When they attach to a vowel base, this '—' is not needed. Examples include the honorific –(으)시– (refer to 6.2.1.1), the causal ending –(으)니까 (refer to 7.1.6), and the future tense –(으)ㄹ 거– (refer to 4.3.2.2). For discussions of one special case (–ㅂ니다/습니다), see below.
3 Endings which incorporate the infinitive form. Examples include the 'polite' speech style –(아/어)요 (refer to 6.1.1), the causal connective (아/어)서 (refer to 7.1.1) and the past tense –았/었– (refer to 4.3.1.1).

The following table demonstrates these three usages using –고 'and' as an example of a one-shape ending, the causal ending –(으)니까 as an example of a two-shape ending and the 'polite' speech style –아/어요 as an example of an ending incorporating the infinitive form.

Type of verb	*Base*	*1-Shape*	*2-Shape*	*Infin.*
		[-고]	*[–(으)니까]*	*[–아/어요]*
consonant base (ㅏ/ㅗ)	받– (*receive*)	받고	받으니까	받아요
consonant base (other)	먹– (*eat*)	먹고	먹으니까	먹어요
vowel base ending in ㅏ	가– (*sleep*)	가고	가니까	가요
vowel base ending in ㅐ	보내– (*send*)	보내고	보내니까	보내요
vowel base ending in ㅗ	오– (*come*)	오고	오니까	와요
vowel base ending in ㅜ	주– (*give*)	주고	주니까	줘요
vowel base ending in ㅣ	마시– (*drink*)	마시고	마시니까	마셔요
vowel base ending in ㅡ	쓰– (*write*)	쓰고	쓰니까	써요
irregular: ㅂ/ㅜ verbs	굽– (*broil*)	굽고	구우니까	구워요
irregular: ㄷ/ㄹ verbs	듣– (*listen*)	듣고	들으니까	들어요
irregular: ㅅ/ㅇ verbs	짓– (*build*)	짓고	지으니까	지어요
irregular: ㄹ doubling	부르– (*sing*)	부르고	부르니까	불러요
irregular: ㄹ dropping	놀– (*play*)	놀고	노니까	놀아요
irregular: ㅎ dropping	하얗– (*be white*)	하얗고	하야니까	하얘요

Note in the above table the following behaviours of irregular verbs with two-shape patterns:

1 irregular ㅂ/ㅜ verbs: ㅂ drops and ㅜ (or ㅗ) is added. This is then followed by the ending without the addition of '—':
2 irregular: ㄷ/ㄹ verbs: ㄷ is replaced by ㄹ and then followed by the ending with the extra '—'.
3 irregular: ㅅ/ㅇ verbs: ㅅ drops, but note that the ending with the extra '—' is used.
4 irregular: ㄹ dropping. With the majority of endings, including –(으)니까 shown in the table, ㄹ is dropped. However, when the verb ending attached starts with 'ㄹ' (for example, –(으)러, used when talking about 'going somewhere to do something', refer to 7.7.2) or ㅁ (for example, –(으)면 'if', refer to 7.5.1) the ㄹ is retained and the ending attaches directly to the base without the addition of '—':

놀러	*(go to) play*	놀면	*(go to) play*
팔러	*(go to) sell*	팔면	*(go to) sell*
열러	*(go to) open*	열면	*(go to) open*

5 irregular: ㅎ dropping. The ㅎ drops and the ending is added without the addition of '—':

There are two other variant two-shape patterns that behave a little different from the others. The first is the formal speech style (both in its statement form –ㅂ니다/습니다 and its question form –ㅂ니까/습니까, refer to 6.1.2). The –ㅂ니다 and –ㅂ니까 endings follow vowels and with these, irregular verbs behave as they would with any other two-shape ending. However, when the –습니다 and –습니까 endings occur after consonants, irregular verbs behave as they more generally would with one-shape endings, producing forms such as the following:

irregular: ㅂ/ㅜ verbs	굽– *(broil)*	굽습니다
irregular: ㄷ/ㄹ verbs	듣– *(listen)*	듣습니다
irregular: ㅅ/ㅇ verbs	낫– *(get better)*	낫습니다

The second is the plain style statement ending (refer to 6.1.4). When occurring with present tense processive verbs, this ending is -ㄴ다 with a vowel base (e.g., 간다 'goes'). However, the form after a consonant base is –는다 (e.g., 먹는다 'eats') rather than a form beginning with '—', as is more typical with two-shape patterns.

4.2 Negatives

Overview

Korean has two main ways to make a statement or question negative: (1) short negation using 안 and 못 and (2) long negation using –지 않– and –지 못하–. In addition to this, commands and proposals are made negative through using the form –지 말–. This sub-chapter considers these patterns in turn and then examines certain expressions that must always contain negative verbs.

4.2.1 *Short negatives with 안 and 못*

To put a verb into the short negative form, you place before it one of the two negative words 안 and 못. These two negative words have quite distinct meanings. 안 is a more neutral negative word that simply means 'does not' or 'is not', although it can in some contexts imply that the speaker is agentively choosing not to perform an action. 못, on the other hand has the meaning of 'cannot' and implies lack of ability. 못 may signal that the speaker is unable to perform the action, even if she/he wants to. Note that due to the fact that it signals lack of ability, 못 cannot appear with descriptive verbs, at least in the short negation pattern (but see long negation refer to 4.2.2).

With their distinct nuances, the choice between 안 and 못 can produce quite different meanings:

안	못
한국어를 **안** 배웠어요. *I didn't learn Korean.*	한국어를 **못** 배웠어요. *I couldn't learn Korean [maybe I wanted to, but I did not have the opportunity, money, ability, etc.].*
술을 **안** 마셔요. *I don't drink alcohol.*	술을 **못** 마셔요. *I can't drink alcohol [maybe I am allergic to it, on medication, forbidden on religious grounds, etc.]*

As in the above examples, 못 'cannot' tends to imply that a situation is outside the speaker's control. With 안, on the other hand, the sentences could mean that the speaker deliberately chooses not to perform the actions noted. Because of this, only 안 (and not 못) can appear with expressions of deliberateness such as 일부러 ('deliberately'), 의도적으로 ('intentionally'):

수업에 **일부러 안** 갔어요.
I deliberately did not go to class.

남편과 이혼하고 **의도적으로 안** 만났어요.
After divorcing my husband, I deliberately did not meet him.

With verbal constructions formed from a Sino-Korean noun and the support verb 하– (refer to 4.1.2), 안 and 못 must always come between the Sino-Korean noun and 하–:

집안 청소(를) **안** 해요. *I don't clean the house.*

숙제(를) **못** 했어요. *I could not do the homework.*

The copula can only be made negative through short negation with 안. Note that the resultant form is written as one word: 아니– (refer to 4.1.4):

미국 사람 **아닙니다**. *I'm not American.*

내 잘못 **아니야**. *It's not my fault.*

4.2.2 Long negatives with –지 않– and –지 못하–

Long negatives are formed by attaching –지 to the verb base and following this with the negative elements 않– or 못하–. This can then be followed by tense markers (refer to 4.3), speech styles (refer to 6.1) and other verb endings. The –지 ending attaches to the verb base according to the normal patterns of one-shape endings (refer to 4.1.8)

Generally speaking, –지 않– and –지 못하– can be considered as having equivalent meanings to the short negation patterns with 안 and 못 respectively:

–지 않–	–지 못하–
잠을 자**지 않았어요**.	잠을 자**지 못했어요**.
I didn't sleep.	*I couldn't sleep.*

결혼하**<u>지 않았군요</u>**! So you're not married!

결혼하**<u>지 못했군요</u>**. So you couldn't get married!

However, one difference is that although the short pattern with 못 cannot appear with descriptive verbs, the corresponding long pattern with –지 못하– can. Resulting constructions express a strong negative meaning and often hint at the speaker's dissatisfaction that certain qualities are missing:

아들은 똑똑하**<u>지 못해요</u>**.
The son isn't bright at all.

키가 작고, 얼굴이 별로 예쁘**<u>지 못해요</u>**.
She's short and her face is not at all pretty.

물이 깨끗하**<u>지 못해요</u>**.
The water is not at all clean.

One further difference is that long negation allows for the addition of particles (subject, object and topic) after –지. This works to place additional emphasis on the verb in question:

써 보지<u>는</u> 않았지만 괜찮을 것 같아요.
*I haven't actually **tried** using it, but it seems okay.*

음식은 제 입맛에는 맞지<u>를</u> 않았어요.
*The food did not **suit** my palate.*

슬리퍼가 예쁘긴 한데 부드럽지<u>가</u> 못하네요.
*The slippers are pretty, but they're not at all **soft**.*

Apart from these differences –지 않– and –지 못하– can generally be used interchangeably with 안 and 못 respectively. However, whereas the short form is more direct and colloquial, the long form is less direct and more formal and bookish. In addition, with some long descriptive verbs (three or more syllables) short negation sounds clumsy and long negation is preferred:

아름답지 않아요	more common than	안 아름다워요	*not beautiful*
깨끗하지 않아요	more common than	안 깨끗해요	*not clean*
부족하지 않아요	more common than	안 부족해요	*not insufficient*

Also, only long negation tends to be used with descriptive verbs and adverbial forms derived through –답–, –스럽–, –롭– (refer to 11.3.2.3). and –적– (refer to 11.3.2.4). Short negatives here would sound very awkward:

남자답지 않아요	*not man-like*
자유롭지 않아요	*not natural*
사랑스럽지 않아요	*not loveable*
엽기적이지 않아요	*not bizarre*

Finally, the lexically negative verbs 없– 'not exist' and 모르– 'not know' (refer to 4.1.3) are only compatible with long negation. The same largely applies to their positive counterparts 있– 'exist' and 알– 'know', although the latter may occasionally occur with 안 in specific contexts (particularly with –아/어 주– refer to 5.1.12).

가능성이 **없지는 않아요**.
It's not that there is no possibility.

네 마음을 **모르지 않아**.
It's not that I don't know your true feelings.

관심이 **있지 않아요**.
I'm not that interested.

수영하는 방법을 잘 **알지 못해요**.
I don't really know the techniques of swimming.

4.2.3 Negative commands and proposals with –지 말–

Although both short negation (refer to 4.2.1) and long negation with 않– or 못하– (refer to 4.2.2) can be used with statements and questions, neither can be applied in commands and proposals. Instead, these sentence types are made negative by using a long negation pattern with the auxiliary verb 말– 'desist'. As can be seen in the following examples, 말– is an ㄹ dropping irregular verb:

듣지 마십시오!	[FORMAL; subject honorifics]
듣지 마세요!	[POLITE; subject honorifics]

듣지 말아요! [POLITE]
듣지 말아! [INTIMATE]
Don't listen!

듣지 맙시다 [FORMAL]
듣지 말자 [PLAIN]
Let's not listen.

Note that the form of 말– in 'polite' and 'intimate' style commands is frequently abbreviated to 마요 and 마 respectively in colloquial speech:

신경 쓰지 마요	[POLITE]	*Don't concern yourself with it.*
걱정하지 마	[INTIMATE]	*Don't worry about it.*

With a small set of common verbs formed with the support verb 하–, the '하지' element may be omitted in casual speech:

걱정/염려 마	*Don't worry about it.*
연락 마	*Don't contact me!*
접근 마	*Don't approach me!*

Although the principal use of 말– is with commands and proposals, there are other sentence patterns that can also incorporate this form of negation:

아직 할까 **말**까 생각 중이에요. (refer to 5.4.3)
I'm still thinking about whether to do it or not.

먹지 **말**아야겠어요. (refer to 7.5.7)
I shouldn't eat it.

사든지 **말**든지 상관없어요. (refer to 7.4.2)
It doesn't matter whether you buy it or not.

내가 가거나 **말**거나 상관하지 마세요. (refer to 7.4.1)
Whether I go or not, it has nothing to do with you.

공부하나 **마**나 시험 결과는 똑 같아요. (refer to 7.2.3)
My test results are the same whether I study or not.

In addition, 말– may frequently be followed by the additional connective –고 (refer to 7.3.1) to form the pattern –지 말고, meaning 'instead of . . . do . . .':

기다리**지 말고** 지금 당장 시작합시다.
Instead of waiting, let's start right now.

복사기는 사**지 말고** 빌려 쓰세요.
Instead of buying a printer, rent one.

At times, '말고' may appear not after a verb but after a noun. In such cases, '말고' operates as a pseudo-particle to mean 'rather than' or 'except for':

커피 **말고** 홍차 주세요.
Give me tea rather than coffee.

결혼 **말고** 연애만 하고 싶어요.
Rather than getting married, I just want to date.

한국어 **말고** 다른 외국어도 할 줄 아세요?
Except for Korean, do you know any other foreign languages?

4.2.4 Expressions that require negative verbs

Korean contains a large number of expressions that can only be used with verbs in a negative form (or verbs that have a negative meaning) – these are sometimes referred to in formal linguistics as 'negative polarity items'

그리/그다지 *that (much)*	**그리** 예쁘지는 않아요. *She's not that pretty.*
다시는 *never again*	**다시는** 늦지 않겠습니다. *I will never be late again.*
도무지 *at all; simply*	이 창문은 **도무지** 안 닫혀요. *This window simply will not close.*
도저히 *at all; simply*	이것으로는 **도저히** 안 되겠어요. *This simply will not do.*

밖에 (refer to 3.3.3.3) *except for; besides*	30 분**밖에** 못 잤어요. *I did not sleep except for 30 minutes.*
별로 *particularly*	**별로** 춥지 않아요. *It's not particularly cold.*
전혀 *at all*	공포는 **전혀** 못 느꼈어요. *I did not feel any horror at all.*
절대 *absolutely*	**절대** 믿지 마세요. *Don't even think of believing that.*
조금도 *not at all*	**조금도** 염려하지 마세요. *Don't worry about it at all.*
좀처럼 *seldom*	이 지방은 **좀처럼** 눈이 안 와요. *It seldom snows in this region.*
통 *at all*	요즈음 민수가 **통** 오지 않아요. *These days Minsu does not come at all.*

4.3 Tense

Overview

This section describes how to form past and future tenses and talk about progressive actions and continuous states. In addition to the simple past tense, we look at what is known as the 'past-past or discontinuous past tense' and the 'observed or perceived past tense'. Under 'future tense', we look at two different forms, –겠– and –(으)ㄹ 거, and provide a brief overview of other forms with future-related meanings covered elsewhere in the book. We then give some rules of thumb for choosing the most appropriate future expression. The section on progressives describes and contrasts two patterns: –고 있– and –아/어 있–.

4.3.1 *Past tenses*

Korean has three past tense forms that we look at in turn: the simple past tense with –았/었–, the past-past or discontinuous past tense with –았었/었었– and the observed or perceived past tense with –더–.

4.3.1.1 Simple past –았/었–

The past tense –았/었– is formed by combining the infinitive form of the verb (refer to 4.1.6) with 'ㅆ' to produce a 'past base'. The choice of –았– or –었– (or whether 'ㅆ' on its own is sufficient) depends on the same rules for conjugating the infinitive form.

	Base	*Infinitive*	*Past base*
consonant base	받– *receive*	받아	받았–
vowel base	가– *go*	가	갔–

To this past base, a speech style and other endings can be added:

갔습니다	*went ('formal' style)*
갔어요	*went ('polite' style)*
갔어	*went ('intimate' style)*
갔다	*went ('plain' style)*

To make honorific forms, add –(으)셨– in place of the present tense honorific marker –(으)시–. –(으)셨– is a combination of –(으)시– followed by –었– and attaches to the verb in the same way as –(으)시–. This creates an honorific past base:

	Base	*Honorific*	*Honorific past*
consonant base	받– *receive*	받으시–	받으셨–
vowel base	가– *go*	가시–	가셨–

To this honorific past base, other endings can be added in the normal way:

가셨습니다	*went (honorific, 'formal' style)*
가셨어요	*went (honorific, 'polite' style)*
가셨어	*went (honorific, 'intimate' style)*
가셨다	*went (honorific, 'plain' style)*

The past tense form is generally applied in the same way as English to talk about events and states that took place prior to the time of speaking. However, it is worth noting here that there are a group of verbs in Korean for which the past tense form can also express a present state. In English, these forms usually translate either into the present progressive tense, present perfect tense or a present tense adjective. In these cases, –았/었– expresses not the past, but a situation that now exists as a result of something that has happened or changed before the present time.

신랑이 너무 **늙었어요**.
The bridegroom is too old (lit. 'has aged')

신부가 어머니를 **닮았어요**.
The bride takes after her father (lit. 'has taken after')

사장님이 오늘도 빨간 와이셔츠를 **입으셨어요**.
The boss is wearing a red shirt today, too. (lit. 'has put on')

민수가 **결혼했어요**.
Minsu is married (lit. 'has got married')

미나가 독일에 **갔어요**.
Mina has gone to Germany (lit. 'went to Germany')

할아버지가 **오셨어요**.
Grandfather has come (lit. 'came')

유미가 돈을 많이 **모았어요**.
Yumi has made a lot of money (lit. 'made')

4.3.1.2 *Past-past or discontinuous past –았/었었–*

The 'past-past or discontinuous past' tense involves attaching the past tense marker twice onto the same verb to give the form –았/었었–. On the first syllable, the choice of –았– or –었– (or whether 'ㅆ' on its own is sufficient) works identically to the simple past tense –았/었– (refer to 4.3.1.2), which in turn depends on the same rules for conjugating the infinitive form (refer to 4.1.6).

The usage of past-past or discontinuous past has three functions. First, it can be used to mark 'reverse order': the event listed second actually occurred before the event mentioned first:

> 오늘 아침에 눈이 오는 것을 **봤다**. 서울에 오기 전에는 제주도에 살아서 눈을 많이 못 **봤었다**.
> *This morning I saw that it was snowing. Before I came to Seoul, I lived in Cheju Island, so I had not seen much snow.*

Second, it can show that the action has been completed and is disconnected, as it were, from the present. For instance, whereas the simple past sentence 오빠가 왔어요 'older brother has come' means that older brother came *and is still here*, the past-past or discontinuous past sentence 오빠가 왔었어요 'older brother came' implies that he came *but has now left again*. This distinction applies to the set of verbs mentioned in the previous section that in simple past form tend to connote a meaning that is relevant to the present. Here are some further examples:

동생이 베트남에 **갔어요**. *Younger brother has gone to Vietnam [and is there now].*	동생이 베트남에 **갔었어요.** *Younger brother went to Vietnam [and has returned].*
오빠가 돈을 많이 **모았어요**. *Older brother has made a lot of money [and still has it now].*	오빠가 돈을 많이 **모았었어요.** *Older brother made a lot of money [and has spent it all].*
결혼**했어요**. *I am married [and am married now].*	결혼**했었어요**. *I was married [but am now divorced].*
전화 **왔어요**. *You have a phone call [and the person is still on the line].*	전화 **왔었어요**. *You had a phone call [while you were away].*

Thirdly, the past-past or discontinuous past may be used just to express that the state of affairs being discussed appears remote and removed from the present. Frequently, the implication is that the state of affairs has changed and no longer applies:

> 일본어를 **전공했었어요**.
> *I used to specialize in Japanese [but now specialize in something else].*

어렸을 때는 아주 **약했었어요**.
I used to be very weak when I was young [but am stronger now].

옛날에는 교회를 **다녔었어요**.
In the past, I used to attend church [but don't now].

영화를 예전에 한 번 **봤었어요**.
I saw that movie once a long time ago [but it feels very disconnected from the present].

4.3.1.3 *Observed or perceived past tense –더*

Korean has a set of 'observed' or 'perceived' verb endings that are used mainly for talking about the past. These endings are used in place of or in addition to the past tense when the speaker wants to communicate that he has sensory **evidence** for what he is talking about. This sensory evidence usually comes either from something that he has seen or heard. Statements with evidential verb endings can be translated as 'it has been observed that . . .', 'I have sensory evidence to the fact that . . .' or simply 'I saw/noticed/realized/felt/heard . . .'. Questions with observed verb endings mean 'has it been observed . . .?', 'does someone have sensory evidence to the effect that . . .?' or 'have you seen/noticed/realized/felt/heard . . .?'

The basic form of this observed tense is –더–. It primarily occurs in the plain speech style (refer to 6.1.4), where it is followed by the ending –라 in statements and –냐 in questions.

	Base	*Observed (plain style)*	
		Statement	*Question*
consonant base	받– *receive*	받더라	받더냐?
vowel base	가– *go*	가더라	가더냐?

The question form in the plain speech style may also appear as –디 (as in 받디?, 가디? and 굽디?).

The 'observed' tense can also occur with honorific bases (refer to 6.2.1.1), past bases (refer to 4.3.1.1) and future bases with –겠– (refer to 4.3.2.1) (although the use of the 'future' base is generally used to produce an inferential meaning rather than to mark future time per se):

Present	*Honorific*	*Past* –았/었–	*Future* –겠–
가더라	가시더라	갔더라	갔겠더라

The past base with –더– does not usually occur with descriptive verbs. With processive verbs, it indicates that the action in question had been completed at or before the time of observation or perception. Compare the following:

–더–	–았/었– + –더–
눈이 오**더라**.	눈이 왔**더라**.
[I saw that] it was snowing.	*[I saw that] it had snowed.*
유미가 학교에 가더**라**.	유미가 학교에 갔**더라**.
[I saw] Yumi going to school.	*[I noticed that] Yumi had already gone to school.*

–더– can be followed by the 'polite' speech style ending, and the resultant form is –데요 (–더– + –어요). However, this form is not frequently used perhaps because the ' –더– ' is not salient in this merged form. Instead, speakers find other ways to use –더– in its original form and still use the polite speech style. One way to do this is to follow –더– with the –ㄴ데 ending (refer to 7.3.12) in statements or by –ㄴ가 (refer to 9.3) in questions to give the composite forms –던데요 and –던가요.

Verb base	–데요	–던데요	–던가요?
받– *receive*	받데요	받던데요	받던가요?

In the 'formal' style, the observed past tense looks quite different. Instead of 더, the form is '디' (a contracted form of –더– followed by the historical hearer honorific 이; refer to 6.1.2). This '디' occurs in the same place as the '니' part of the normal statement and question forms. Put simply, –(습)**니**다 and –(습)**니**까 change to –(습)**디**다 and –(습)**디**까 respectfully:

	Base	Observed (formal style)	
		Statement	*Question*
consonant base	받– *receive*	받습디다	받습디까?
vowel base	가– *go*	갑디다	갑디까?

As noted above, the observed or perceived past tense is used when the speaker wants to indicate that he/she has sensory evidence (typically, seen or heard) of what he/she is reporting. Here are examples:

옆에서 지켜보니까 누구보다도 더 열심히 공부하**더라**.
Now that I've seen him/her from close quarters, [I noticed that] he/she studies harder than anyone.

우리 딸들이 그 영화를 너무 재미있게 보**던데요**.
[I saw that] our daughters really enjoyed that movie.

A: 교수님은 계세요?
Is the professor here?

B: 도서관에 계시**던데요**.
[I saw that] he was in the library.

야당후보가 대통령이 되겠**던데요**.
[I recall that] it seemed probable that the opposition party candidate would become president.

요즘 날씨 무지 춥**더**라.
[I've felt that] the weather is really cold these days.

호주는 12월에 덥습**디**다.
[I recall that] Australia was hot in December

그 환자가 꼭 죽겠**던데요**.
[From what I observed], that patient is going to die for sure.

An important restriction on the use of this tense is that it cannot usually occur with a first-person subject. This is because this tense is used to indicate something that the speaker has observed from a remote standpoint and one is not usually able to do this with one's own actions. However, one exception to this is when the speaker is reporting an action that he/she carried out in a dream or without conscious awareness or when the speaker reports observing his/her actions from the outside, as it were (similar to English 'I found myself . . .'). In such cases, the use of the observed tense places the speaker in a separate, objective position, from which he/she has, in a sense, observed him/herself.

어제 꿈 속에서 내가 비키니를 입었**더라**.
In my dream last night, I found myself wearing a bikini.

지 말로는 술을 끊었다는데 믿지는 못 하겠**더라**.
According to him/her, he/she has given up alcohol, but I find myself unable to believe it.

Another exception is when the sentence includes a verb expressing feelings or reactions. In such cases, the rule is reversed: the observed tense can only be used when the speaker is expressing his/her own feelings or reactions. The reason why the observed tense cannot be used to describe the feelings of a third person is because such feelings cannot normally be observed from a removed position.

나는 그 영화가 너무 무섭**더**라.
I found that movie so scary.

세상에서 우리 엄마 김치가 제일 맛있**더**라.
I find my mom's kimchi the most delicious in the world.

그 여배우는 실제로 보니 정말 예쁘**더**라.
Seeing that actress in the flesh, I found her pretty.

그걸 생각하니까 막 화가 나**더**라.
Upon having that thought, I found myself getting angry.

As in the final two examples above, when the speaker provides information regarding how he/she formed this feeling, this is given in the –(으)니 (refer to 7.1.7) or –(으)니까 (refer to 7.1.6) pattern.

The –더라 ending of the evidential marker in the 'plain' style is frequently suffixed by another ending –고 to form –더라고. This, in turn, can be changed into the 'polite' style with the addition of –요: –더라고요. This –고 has its origins in reported speech (refer to Chapter 10) and therefore can add nuances similar to the English 'let me tell you that I found . . .' or 'I'm telling you that I found . . .' With these nuances, the use of –더라고 adds authority to what the speaker is saying and marks the content of the utterances as something that the hearer needs to know. Since utterances with 더라고 are always informative for the hearer, they cannot occur in soliloquy (i.e., when you are talking to yourself): this restriction is not shared by –더라.

태국 날씨가 덥**더라고**.
I found the Thailand weather to be hot.

그 식당 음식이 맛있**더라고**.
[I found that] the food at that restaurant is delicious.

예쁜 옷을 많이 입으니까 정말 기분 좋아지**더라고**요.
On wearing a lot of pretty clothes, I found that my mood really improved.

4.3.2 Future tenses

Korean has two 'future tense' markers: (1) –겠– and (2) –(으)ㄹ 거–. After describing these two constructions, we present other forms with future-related meanings (4.3.2.3) and summarize the use of future-related expressions (4.3.2.4).

4.3.2.1 –겠–

In terms of grammatical formation, the closest thing Korean has to a future tense marker is the one-shape –겠–. Adding this creates a 'future base':

	Base	*Future base (–겠–)*
consonant base	받– *receive*	받겠–
vowel base	가– *go*	가겠–

This base then has to be suffixed with other endings including, at the very least, a speech style ending:

가겠습니다 *will go ('formal' style)*
가겠어요 *will go ('polite' style)*

가겠어 *will go ('intimate' style)*

가겠다 *will go ('plain' style)*

To make honorific future forms, you simply add –겠– to the honorific base:

	Base	*Honorific*	*Future honorific*
consonant base	받– *receive*	받으시–	받으시겠–
vowel base	가– *go*	가시–	가시겠–

Although most grammars of Korean refer to –겠– as a 'future' marker, this form actually has a variety of different usages that only infrequently seem to correspond to 'future tense'. Let us consider meanings that seem to correspond to 'future' first, before looking at other applications of –겠–.

The first kind of expression in which –겠– appears to express 'future' is in formal announcements. Typically occurring with the formal speech style, such announcements tell a large or general audience about forthcoming proceedings or information regarding what will happen later:

잠시 후 기차가 출발하**겠**습니다.
The train will depart shortly.

대통령께서 입장하시**겠**습니다.
The president will now make his entrance.

내일은 흐리고 비 또는 눈이 오**겠**습니다.
Tomorrow will be cloudy with rain or snow.

The second occurrence of –겠– that appears to be 'future' is when the speaker expresses a promise, offers to perform a task or expresses an intention made either at or just before the time of speaking. In such expressions, using –겠– makes the speaker's intention sound definitive, solemn and binding.

커피숍 앞에서 기다리**겠**습니다.
I'll wait for you in from of the coffee shop.

내일 다시 찾아오**겠**습니다.
I will call again tomorrow.

내일까지 하**겠**습니다.
I [promise I] will do it by tomorrow.

아버지, 내년까지 결혼하**겠**습니다.
Father, [I swear] I will get married by next year.

Similar meanings can be communicated with the sentence ending –(으)ㄹ게 (refer to 9.9).

Thirdly, –겠– is used in conjunction with the negative 못 (refer to 4.2.1) when the speaker is expressing something that he/she is unwilling or unable to do in the near future:

아 눈물이 나서 말을 못 하**겠**어요.
I'm crying so much that I simply can't speak.

숨이 차서 더 이상 못 가**겠**어요.
I'm out of breath, so I simply can't go any further.

왠지 그 여자한테는 고백 못 하**겠**어요.
For some reason, I can't confess my feelings to her.

Now let us look at some meaning of –겠– that do not appear to correspond so well to the concept of 'future'.

Firstly, –겠– appears with formal offers and requests that correspond to the English 'would you (like) . . .?':

음료수 뭘 드시**겠**습니까? *What would you like to drink?*

여기 앉으시**겠**어요? *Would you like to sit here?*

크리스마스와 새해를 저희 집에서 보내시**겠**어요?
Would you like to spend Christmas and New Year at our house?

근무시간이 어떻게 되는지 알려주시**겠**어요?
Would you be so kind as to tell me the working hours?

Secondly, –겠– frequently occurs with inferential expressions that correspond broadly to the English, 'I'll bet'. In this usage, the subject of the sentence is normally in the second or third person (you,he, she, it, they):

와! 고구마가 너무 맛있**겠**다!
Wow! Those sweet potatoes look really delicious.

정말 골치가 아프시**겠**어요.
That must be a real headache.

미화가 집에 있**겠**어요.
I'll bet Mi-hwa is at home.

열심히 노력하시는 아드님이 자랑스러우시**겠**어요.
You must be so proud of your hard working son.

The future marker –겠– can also be added to the past base when the inference being made regards a state of affairs from the past:

동생이 부산에 벌써 도착했**겠**어요.
Little brother must already have arrived in Busan.

아버지는 지금쯤 비행기를 타셨**겠**어요.
Father must be on the plane by now.

갑자기 밥솥이 터졌으니 얼마나 당황했**겠**어요.
How shocked you must have been when the rice cooker suddenly blew up.

내가 CF모델 될 줄 상상이나 했**겠**어요?
Would I ever even have imagined that I would become a TV commercial model?

Finally, –겠– frequently occurs with the verbs of knowing (알겠어요) and not knowing (모르겠어요) when stating whether you are aware or unaware of something. In such expressions, Korean speakers frequently prefer to use –겠– for the added tentativeness that it connotes. 모르겠어요 is like the English 'I wouldn't know'.

4.3.2.2 –(으)ㄹ 거–

Although the form –겠– is often thought of as a future marker, a much more common way to mark future tense in Korean is to add –(으)ㄹ 거–, which behaves as a two-shape ending. This –(으)ㄹ 거– form is composed of the future modifier –(으)ㄹ (refer to 8.1.1) followed by the noun 것 'thing, fact', which is typically (but not always) shortened to 거. To complete the sentence, this '거' then has to be followed by the copula form to produce a construction that literally means 'it is a future thing that . . .'. Since

'거' ends in a vowel, the copula form that follows will drop the ' –이– ' base part. In the four most common speech styles, this results in the following forms:

갈 겁니다	*will go ('formal' style)*
갈 거예요	*will go ('polite' style)*
갈 거야	*will go ('intimate' style)*
갈 거다	*will go ('plain' style)*

–(으)ㄹ 거– is used to mark a 'probable future'. In other words, it is used when talking about things that you might do in the future or things that might happen in the future. It is generally NOT used to talk about definite plans, particularly in the near future. Here are some examples of –(으)ㄹ 거– used to talk about things you will probably do in the future:

내일 집 청소를 **할 거예요**.
I will [probably] clean the house tomorrow [but don't have a definite plan].

내년에 차를 **살 거예요**.
I will [probably] buy a car next year [but don't have a definite plan].

내일 태원하고 점심을 **먹을 거예요**.
I will [probably] have lunch with Taewon tomorrow [but don't have a definite appointment].

Here are some examples of –(으)ㄹ 거– used to make predictions about things that will probably happen in the future:

내일은 비가 **올 거에요**.	*It will [probably] rain tomorrow.*
밤에 **추울 거에요**.	*It will [probably] be cold at night.*

In addition to marking probable futures, –(으)ㄹ 거– can also sometimes be used to make inferences about present situations. This is particularly the case when it occurs with the copula:

분명히 여자친구가 한국인**일 거예요**.
Clearly, his girlfriend must be Korean.

그것이 유미의 집이 **아닐 거예요**.
That surely wouldn't be Yumi's house.

태원은 부산에서 살고 **<u>있을 거예요</u>**.

Taewon is probably living in Pusan.

틀림없이 다 거짓말**<u>일 거예요</u>**.

Without doubt, it must all be lies.

In this inferential usage, the ending –(으)ㄹ 거– can also be added to the past base to mean 'probably . . .', 'must have . . .':

단순한 실수가 **<u>아니었을 거예요</u>**.

It couldn't have been just a simple mistake.

한국으로 **<u>떠났을 거예요</u>**.

He/she must have departed for Korea.

영화가 지금 **<u>끝났을 거예요</u>**.

The movie must be over by now.

한국에 10년 넘게 **<u>살았을 거예요</u>**.

He/she must have lived in Korea for more than ten years.

4.3.2.3 *Other forms with future-related meanings*

In addition to –겠– and –(으)ㄹ 거–, Korean has a number of other grammatical items that although not generally considered future tense markers, possess future-related meanings. The following forms, presented here with brief examples and cross-references, are covered elsewhere in the book:

–(으)ㄹ게 promises, volunteering	내가 할게요. *I'll do it.*	(9.9)
–(으)려고 하– intentions	일찍 가려고 해요. *I intend to go early.*	(7.7.2)
–(으)ㄹ까 하– 'think of doing'	도서관에 갈까 해요. *I'm thinking of going to the library.*	(5.4.3)
–(으)ㄹ텐데 'I'm afraid'	내일 추울 텐데요. *I'm afraid it will be cold tomorrow.*	(9.11)
–기로 하– 'decide to'	오늘 집에 있기로 했어요. *I decided to stay home today.*	(2.2.4.18)

4.3.2.4 *Summary of Korean futures*

This section provides a practical summary regarding which future form is most suitable across a variety of different situations. Observations should be taken as a general guide rather than rigid rules – there is a degree of flexibility in the use of all Korean future constructions and usage frequently overlaps.

1. Talking about a definite plan you have for the future

As you may have noticed, none of the forms discussed over the last few pages are specifically used when talking about a definite concrete plan for the near future. In actual fact, definite future plans are often expressed with no future marking at all but in the present simple tense. If you are going to Korea next month, the plan is set in stone and you have already bought your ticket, etc., the most natural way to express it is as follows:

다음 달에 한국에 **가요**.
I am going to Korea next month (lit. 'I go to Korea next month').

2. Talking about an intention formed before the time of speaking

When talking about an intention that does not yet form a definite plan per se, then –(으)려고 하– (refer to 7.7.2) and –기로 하– (refer to 2.2.4.18) can be used. You may also use –(으)ㄹ 거– in this function.

3. Talking about things you might or will probably do in the future

When talking about things you might or will probably do but don't have a set-in-stone plan, –(으)ㄹ 거– is the most common ending. To make things sound even more tentative, –(으)ㄹ까 하– (refer to 5.4.3) can be used.

4. Making a promise

Both –겠– and –(으)ㄹ게 (refer to 9.9) may be used for this function. However, –겠– sounds more deferential and makes your promise sound more binding.

5. Volunteering to do something

If you want to put your hand up and say 'I'll do it', –(으)ㄹ게 (refer to 9.9) is the most common construction. –겠– is also possible if extra deference or solemnity is required.

6. Making a prediction about the future

When predicting the future (e.g., 'it will rain tomorrow'), –(으)ㄹ 거 or–겠– may be used:

비가 오겠어요. *It will rain tomorrow.*
비가 올 거야.

There is a difference between these sentences, however. Use of –겠– in the first sentence indicates deductive reasoning on the part of the speaker: he/she has made this prediction based on evidence (dark clouds, people carrying umbrellas, etc.). The second sentence with –(으)ㄹ 거 sounds simply like the speaker's own presumption.

4.3.3 Continuous tense

Korean has two forms that correspond to continuous tense. The –아/어 있– form is used for talking about continuous states; –고 있– is used primarily for talking about continuous actions.

4.3.3.1 Continuous states with –아/어 있–

The –아/어 있– pattern is formed by using the infinitive form (refer to 4.1.6) of the verb and then following this with 있–. The pattern is typically used with non-transitive processive verbs (i.e., that do not take an object), although there are a few exceptions such as 향하– 'face, aim at', 피하– 'avoid'. Verbs also are typically ones that connote some kind of end point. Possible non-transitive verbs include those formed by making a verb passive (refer to 4.4.1).

The construction has to be followed by a speech style ending and may also be followed by the past tense, future tense and other verb endings. To make the expression honorific, 계시– (refer to 4.4.1.2) is used in place of 있–:

유미가 앉아 있어요.	*Yumi is sitting down.*	[present, 'polite' style]
유미가 앉아 있었어요.	*Yumi was sitting down.*	[past, 'polite' style]
유미가 앉아 있겠어요.	*Yumi must be sitting down.*	[future –겠–, 'polite']
선생님은 앉아 계세요.	*Teacher is sitting down.*	[present, honorific, 'polite' style]

The pattern is used to depict that the person or entity being talked about has moved or been put into a certain place, position or state and that this place, position or state is being maintained. The pattern can most commonly be heard with verbs of body position (sitting, standing, etc.), verbs of being closed or open, verbs that depict that something is included, installed, etc. and also verbs of motion (go. come, etc.).

그냥 피곤해서 **누워 있어요**.
I'm tired, so I'm just lying down.

창문이 **열려 있는** 것 같아요.
It seems like the window is open.

감시 카메라가 많이 **설치돼 있어요**.
Many CCTV cameras are installed.

서비스는 **포함돼 있어요**?
Is service included?

형과 누나가 다 미국에 **가 있어요**.
Older brother and older sister have both gone to America.

나는 지금 일본에 **와 있어요**.
I have now come to Japan.

Note how sentences with 가– 'go' or 오– 'come' translate into English as 'has come' or 'has gone'.

One point to note about this pattern is that it can be used in imperatives, particularly when the speaker is telling the hearer to go to a certain place or adopt a certain position and then stay there:

닥치고 가만히 **앉아 있어라**.
Just shut up and stay sitting down quietly.

방에 **가 있어라**.
Go to your room and stay there.

4.3.3.2 *Continuous actions with –고 있–*

The –고 있– pattern is formed by attaching the one-shape ending –고 to a processive verb base and then 있–. The construction is followed by a speech style ending and may also be followed by the past tense, future tense and other verb endings. To make the expression honorific, 계시– (refer to 6.2.1.2) is used in place of 있–. The main verb may also be made honorific, particularly in cases where the verb in question has a separate honorific form (refer to 6.2.1.2).

유미가 자고 있어요.	*Yumi is sleeping.*	[present, 'polite' style]
유미가 자고 있었어요.	*Yumi was sleeping.*	[past, 'polite' style]
유미가 자고 있겠어요.	*Yumi must be sleeping.*	[future –겠–, 'polite']
선생님은 주무시고 계세요.	*Teacher is sleeping.*	[present, honorific, 'polite' style]

This form is used essentially in the same way as 'be . . . ing' in English to talk about an ongoing, continuous activity.

미나가 지금 저녁 식사를 **준비하고 있어요**.
Mina is preparing dinner now.

민수가 고장 난 텔레비전을 **고치고 있어요**.
Minsu is repairing the broken television.

미나가 맥주를 **마시고 있었어요**.
Mina was drinking beer.

민지는 일하고 있지만 미화는 **놀고 있어요**.
Min-ji is working, but Mi-hwa is playing.

지금 북한에도 눈이 **오고 있겠네요**.
It must be snowing now in North Korea as well.

There are two possibilities for making negative expressions with –고 있–. Firstly, you can use the long negation pattern –지 않– (refer to 4.2.2) at the end of the expression:

그 친구를 **만나고 있지 않아요**. *I'm not meeting that friend.*

Secondly, you can use the long negation pattern on the main verb:

그 친구를 **만나지 않고 있어요**. *I'm getting along without meeting that friend.*

The second pattern has a slightly different nuance to the first. It implies that the subject is getting along or managing to get by without doing the action in question.

Although the form –고 있– may seem quite similar to the English progressive tense, there are several important differences between the Korean form and its English counterpart.

Firstly, whereas in English progressive tense is obligatory when talking about an activity that is going on now, the Korean progressive is usually optional and used only for emphasis. For example, in most circumstances, if someone asks you on the telephone what you are doing now, both of the following answers are possible (note how, in English, the equivalent of the first sentence would not normally be suitable):

밥을 먹어요. *I eat my meal.*

밥을 먹**고 있어요**. *I'm eating my meal.*

Although both sentences above are possible, the interpretation may be slightly different. Whereas the second sentence emphasizes that I am in the middle of eating my meal, the first sentence could also be interpreted as meaning that I am about to eat my meal (but have not actually started yet).

It should be noted, however, that the use of –고 있– is not always optional, particularly in the past tense. With a certain set of verbs that depict an activity with an end point, use of the simple past tense denotes that this end point has been reached (and therefore cannot have a continuous interpretation). If you want to say that the activity was ongoing and incomplete, you will have to use –고 있–:

Past simple	–고 있–
지갑을 찾**았어요**.	지갑을 찾**고 있었어요**.
I found my wallet.	*I was looking for my wallet.*

Secondly, whereas in English the progressive tense can have a future reading, this is not the case in Korean. In English, if you say 'I am going now' this often actually means that you are about to set off but are not actually on your way yet. However, in Korean, the equivalent progressive construction (지금 가고 있어요) can only be interpreted as meaning that you have left your point of departure and are in the process of going.

Thirdly, the Korean progressive can appear with a set of verbs that rarely take the progressive in English. This leads to the creation of constructions such as 알고 있어요 'I am knowing', 모르고 있어요 'I am not knowing', 사랑하고 있어요 'I am loving/I am in love', 믿고 있어요 'I am believing', 원하고 있어요 'I am wanting', 기억하고 있어요 'I am remembering' and 느끼고 있어요 ('I am feeling'). Although the English equivalents of these sentences generally sound odd or have restricted usage, these expressions are extremely common in Korean. They are used to emphasize that the knowing, believing, feeling, etc. constitutes a progressive or a temporary state of affairs. The phrase 알고 있어요 is particularly common and is often used to mean 'I already know (so you didn't need to tell me)'.

Fourthly, unlike in English, the Korean progressive can occur in imperatives (particularly in non-honorific speech styles). In such usages, the English equivalent would generally be expressed with 'keep' or 'stay' rather than the progressive:

> 여기서 기다리**고 있어**.
> *Stay waiting here.*

> 시장에 갔다 올 테니깐 공부하**고 있어라**.
> *I'm going to the market, so keep on studying.*

Fifthly, with verbs of 'wearing', the progressive results in ambiguity between two possible meanings. The following sentence could mean either that 민수 is 'putting' on the trousers or is 'wearing' them:

민수가 하얀 바지를 입**고 있어요**.
Minsu is putting on/wearing white trousers.

The meaning is usually clarified by context:

민수가 방에서 하얀 바지를 입**고 있어요**.
Minsu is putting on white trousers in his room.

민수가 하얀 바지를 멋있게 입**고 있어요**.
Minsu is stylishly wearing white trousers.

Sixth and finally, unlike in English this pattern cannot be used when talking about standing, sitting or lying somewhere. –아/어 있– (refer to 4.3.3.1) is used instead.

4.4 Derived verbs: passives, causatives and others

Overview

Korean has various processes for forming passive and causative verbal constructions. Passive sentences are constructions in which the 'patient' (or recipient) of the action of the verb is promoted to subject (for example, '*the apple* was eaten (by John)'). In active sentences (for example, 'John ate *the apple*'), the 'patient' (or recipient) appears as the sentence object. The use of a passive sentence normally results from the speaker's desire to place more focus on the recipient of the action and to de-emphasize (or even omit) the person or entity that is actually performing the action in question.

Causative sentences are constructions that depict an agent causing, forcing or simply allowing a patient to perform an action (for example; 'he made me eat the apple', 'he let me eat the apple').

In addition to passives and causatives, the current chapter also looks at ways that Korean used related means to transform descriptive verbs into processive verbs.

4.4.1 Passives

Korean has four different ways of making a sentence passive: (1) to derive a passive form by the addition of a verbal suffix

–이–/–기–/–히–/–리–, (2) to use 되– as a support verb, (3) to use other support verbs with inherent passive meanings and (4) to apply the pattern –아/어 지–.

4.4.1.1 Derived passive verbs –이–/–기–/–히–/–리–

For a limited number of verbs, a separate passive verb form can be derived by the addition of a verb ending. This ending has four possible shapes: –이–, –기–, –히– and –리–. The addition of this ending results in the creation of a new, separate passive verb that can be found listed in the dictionary as an independent word.

The choice of whether –이–, –기–, –히– or –리– is used depends in general on certain sound patterns:

1. –이– occurs after /ㄲ/ or a vowel (including when there is a silent ㅎ in the written script, such as in 놓이다 [노이다])
2. –기– occurs after the continuant consonant ㄴ, ㅁ, or ㅅ.
3. –히– occurs after the stop consonant ㄱ, ㅂ and ㄷ.
4. –리– occurs after another ㄹ.

The following is a list of the most common verbs that can be made passive in this way:

Basic verb		*Derived verb*	
잡–	*catch*	잡히–	*be/get caught*
걸–	*hang it*	걸리–	*it hangs, be/get hanged*
먹–	*eat*	먹히–	*be/get eaten, be/get swallowed up*
놓–	*put*	놓이–	*be/get put*
밟–	*step on*	밟히–	*be/get stepped on*
보–	*see, look at*	보이–	*be visible, can be seen*
닫–	*close it*	닫히–	*it closes, get closed*
듣–	*listen to, hear*	들리–	*be heard, be audible*
열–	*open it*	열리–	*it opens, get opened*
쌓–	*pile, heap it*	쌓이–	*accumulate; get piled*

싸–	*wrap it*	싸이–	*be wrapped, enveloped*
팔–	*sell it*	팔리–	*it sells (well), get sold*
집–	*pick it up*	집히–	*get picked up, 'picks up'*
씹–	*chew it*	씹히–	*it 'chews', get chewed*
끊–	*snap it, cut it off*	끊기–	*get cut off*
담–	*put it in a vessel*	담기–	*it fills, be put in (a vessel)*
잠그–	*immerse it, steep it*	잠기–	*it sinks, submerges*
잠그–	*lock it, fasten it*	잠기–	*it locks, get fastened*
묻–	*stick to it, stain it*	묻히–	*get smeared, stained*
묻–	*bury it, conceal it*	묻히–	*get buried, concealed*
덮–	*cover it*	덮히–	*get covered*
뽑–	*select it, extract it*	뽑히–	*get picked, extracted, selected*
쓰–	*write it*	쓰이–	*it 'writes', get written*
섞–	*mix it*	섞이–	*get mixed; it mingles, blends*
뜨–	*open (eyes, ears)*	뜨이–	*(eyes, ears) open, be opened, awake*
물–	*bite it*	물리–	*get bitten*
밀–	*push it*	밀리–	*get pushed; back up, accumulate*
풀–	*solve it; resolve it*	풀리–	*get resolved, solved, cleared away*
쫓–	*chase it*	쫓기–	*get chased*
벗-	*take off*	벗기-	*get taken off*
빼앗–	*snatch it away*	빼앗기–	*get snatched away*
안–	*hug it, embrace it*	안기–	*get embraced*

These passive forms are primarily used in sentences in which the recipient of the action of the verb is made the focus of the sentence (rather than the person or entity performing the action):

이 교재는 요즘 잘 안 **쓰여요**.
This textbook is not used much these days.

침실에서도 라디오가 **들려요**?
The radio can be heard all the way from your bedroom?

어제 밤에 우리 학교에 들어왔던 도둑놈이 **잡혔대요**.
They say the thief that broke into our school last night was caught.

표가 다 **팔려서**, 못 갔어요.
The tickets were all sold out, so we couldn't go.

방금 지하철에서 내리면서 발을 **밟혔어요**.
Somebody stepped on my foot as I was getting off the subway.

When the person or entity performing the action is included, this is marked with 에게/한테 (refer to 3.2.4.4) (for people and animals) and 에 (refer to 3.2.4.1) (for inanimate entities), which normally translates as 'by' (or 'with'):

안개**에 싸여서** 바다가 잘 안 보이는데요!
It's covered with fog so you can't see the sea very well!

애기가 어머니 품**에 안겨서** 자고 있어요.
The baby is sleeping embraced in its mother's bosom.

우리 동생은 개**한테 물렸어요**.
My little brother was bitten by a dog.

However, there are some cases in which using 에게 or 에 in this function may result in ambiguity. For example, with the verb 팔리– 'get sold', 에게 in the following example would normally be interpreted as meaning 'to' rather than 'by':

외국인**에게 팔렸어요**. *It was sold to a foreigner.*

Thus, with these kinds of verbs, a different construction 에 의해 must be used to produce the meaning 'by':

외국인**에 의해 팔렸어요**. *It was sold by a foreigner.*

In addition to the usages noted above, the passive forms are also used to indicate that something happens spontaneously or out of one's control:

창문이 **<u>열렸어요</u>**.
The window opened [of its own accord].

이 문은 자동적으로 **<u>잠겨요</u>**.
This door locks automatically.

전화가 고장 났나 봐요. 자주 **<u>끊겨요</u>**.
The telephone seems to be broken. It keeps cutting out.

이 불고기는 너무 질겨서 잘 안 **<u>씹혀요</u>**.
This pulgogi is so tough it doesn't chew (= it can't be chewed) easily.

The passive form can also occur with the –아/어 있– construction (refer to 4.3.3.1), which signals a resultant continuing state:

문이 **<u>열려 있어요</u>**.	*The door is open.*
산 위에 눈이 **<u>쌓여 있어요</u>**.	*There's snow piled up on the mountain.*
책상 위에 **<u>놓여 있어요</u>**.	*It is (placed) on top of the desk.*

4.4.1.2 *Passives with 되–*

For 하– verbs (refer to 4.1.2), a passive can be formed by replacing 하– with 되– 'become'. Here is a list of some common examples of these constructions:

Active verb with 하–		*Passive with 되–*	
기대하–	*expect*	기대되–	*be expected*
걱정하–	*worry*	걱정되–	*be worried*
공개하–	*make public*	공개되–	*be made public*
사용하–	*use*	사용되–	*be used*
선출하–	*elect*	선출되–	*be elected*
완성하–	*complete*	완성되–	*be completed*
왜곡하–	*distort*	왜곡되–	*be distorted*
이해하–	*understand*	이해되–	*be understood*
해결하–	*solve*	해결되–	*be solved*

Here are some examples of these in passive sentences

김 선생이 시장으로 **선출되었어요**.	*Mr. Kim was elected mayor.*
새 건물이 **완성되었어요**.	*A new building was completed.*
그 내용이 일반에게 **공개되었어요**.	*The content was made public.*

As with the passive verbs analysed above (refer to 4.4.1.1), passive constructions with 되– can also be used with expressions of spontaneity or to convey that something is occurring outside the speaker's control:

살짝 **긴장되네**. *I'm getting a tad nervous.*

방에서 **공부가 잘 안 되면** 도서관에 가야 해요.
If you can't study (lit. 'if studying doesn't go well') in your room, you have to go to the library.

그 영화가 가장 **기대되네요**.
That film is the one that people are looking forward to.

아무리 용서를 하려고 해도 **용서가 안 돼요**.
No matter how much I want to forgive him, I simply can't.

4.4.1.3 *Passives with other support verbs*

Passive-like constructions can also be constructed using a number of verbs with inherently passive meanings: 입– and 받–.

The first of these, 당하–, literally means 'suffer', 'undergo'. This verb can be used with Sino-Korean nouns (and occasionally other nouns) that have inherent negative meanings. Common constructions include those in the following list

Active		*Passive with 당하–*	
강간하–	*rape*	강간당하–	*be raped*
공격하–	*attack*	공격당하–	*be attacked*
거절하–	*rejection*	거절당하–	*be rejected*
무시하–	*ignore, look down on*	무시당하–	*be ignored, be looked down on*

고소하–	*sue*	고소당하–	*be sued*
침략하–	*invade*	침략당하–	*be invaded*
부상하–	*wound*	부상당하–	*be wounded*
왕따시키–	*bully*	왕따당하–	*be bullied*
사기치–	*swindle*	사기당하–	*be swindled*
암살하–	*assassinate*	암살당하–	*be assassinated*
협박하–	*threaten*	협박당하–	*be threatened*

Here are some examples of these constructions in sentences:

제가 미국에서 입국을 **거절당했어요**.
I was refused entry to the USA.

인터넷에서 물건을 사다가 **사기당했어요**.
I got swindled when I was buying goods on the Internet.

제가 중학교 다닐 때, **왕따당했었어요**.
I got bullied when I was at middle school.

조선은 일본한테 **침략당했어요**.
Choson was invaded by Japan.

The second of these verbs, 받– 'get', 'receive', may occur with nouns that are either negative or positive. Although some negative nouns such as 협박 'threat' may occur with either 당하– or 받–, only the former is used for more extremely negative nouns such as 강간 'rape' and 암살 'assassination'.

Active		*Passive with 받–*	
협박하–	*threaten*	협박받–	*be threatened*
간섭하–	*interfere*	간섭받–	*be interfered with*
비난하–	*criticize*	비난받–	*be criticized*
처벌하–	*punish*	처벌받–	*be punished*
주목하–	*pay attention to*	주목받–	*receive attention*
칭찬하–	*praise*	칭찬받–	*be praised*
존경하–	*respect*	존경받–	*be respected*

Here are some examples of these constructions in sentences:

정말 많은 **칭찬을 받았어요**. *I received really a lot of praise.*

그 영화는 개봉되기도 전에 굉장히 많은 **주목을 받았어요**.
That film was receiving a lot of attention even before it was released.

The third of these verbs, 입–, literally meaning 'wear', 'suffer' or just 'receive', appears with a more limited set of nouns.

Active		*Passive with 입–*	
상처(를) 주–	*inflict an injury*	상처(를) 입–	*suffer an injury; be hurt*
피해(를) 주–	*inflict a loss*	피해(를) 입–	*suffer a loss*
은혜(를) 주–	*give benefits, grace, blessings, favour*	은혜(를) 입–	*receive benefits, grace, blessings, favour*

Here are some examples of these constructions in sentences:

지진에 많은 사람들이 **피해를 입었어요**.
Many people suffered damage through the earthquake.

예전에는 제가 사장님의 **은혜를 입었어요**.
In the past, I received the favours of the boss.

그 말 때문에 **상처를 입은** 사람들이 많아요.
Many people have been hurt by those words.

As a final note, it should be pointed out that two more verbs –맞– 'get struck' and 속– 'get deceived' have inherently passive meanings (at least in the absence of any suffix or auxiliary).

김 선생이 유탄에 **맞았어요**.
Mr. Kim got struck by a stray bullet.

나한테 **속았지**?
You've been deceived by me, haven't you? (= I tricked you, didn't I?)

4.4.1.4 *Passives with –아/어 지–*

This pattern combines the infinitive form of the verb (refer to 4.1.6) with the auxiliary verb –지–. Although the pattern may occur both with descriptive and processive verbs, in the former case, the use of –아/어 지– actually transforms the descriptive verb into a processive verb – a process that is discussed separately below (refer to 4.4.3.1).

In the case of processive verbs, the effect of adding –아/어 지– varies according to whether it attaches to an 'intransitive' verb (i.e., a verb that does not take an object), or a 'transitive' verb (a verb that takes an object).

When –아/어 지– attaches to an intransitive verb, it does not create a 'passive' sentence as we would normally understand it. Rather, it expresses potentiality – that something is possible. This potentiality often goes contrary to the speaker's expectation (refer to Yeon 2003), as in the following examples:

Without –지–	*With 지–*
트럭이 빙판 위로 지나갔어요.	트럭이 빙판 위로 **지나가졌어요**.
The truck went over the ice.	*The truck was able to go over the ice.*
요즘 바빠서 극장에 잘 안 가요.	요즘 바빠서 극장에 잘 안 **가져요**.
Because I'm busy these days, I don't go to the theatre often.	*Because I'm busy these days, I am not able to go to the theatre often.*

When –아/어 지– attaches to a transitive verb (i.e., a verb that takes an object), a typical passive construction is created. As in the following active-passive contrasts, the object of the active sentence becomes the subject of the passive sentence:

Active	*Passive*
민호가 나무로 집을 만들었어요.	집이 나무로 **만들어졌어요**.
Minho built a house out of wood.	*The house was made of wood.*
유미가 쓰레기를 길에 버렸어요.	쓰레기가 길에 **버려졌어요**.
Yumi dumped rubbish on the street.	*Rubbish was dumped on the street.*
사람들이 강물을 막았어요.	강물이 **막아졌어요**.
People blocked the river water.	*The river water was blocked.*

In addition to transitive verbs that take one object, –지– can also attach to verbs that take two objects (i.e., a direct and an indirect object) – 'ditransitive' verbs, as they are known:

Ditransitive active verb	*Passive verb*
밝히– *make clear*	밝혀지– *become clear*
알리– *inform*	알려지– *be known*
주– *give*	주어지– *be given*

The ditransitive verbs 밝히–, and 알리– are verbs derived by the morphological process of causativization (refer to 4.4.2.1). Here are some examples of these passives in sentences:

이제 사장님의 본래 의도는 충분히 **밝혀졌어요**.
Now, the boss's original intention has become sufficiently clear.

그 가수가 해외에도 많이 **알려졌어요**.
That singer has become well none abroad as well.

많은 문제가 우리에게 **주어졌다**.
Many problems were given to us.

4.4.2 Causatives

Causatives are sentences that depict an agent causing, forcing or simply just allowing or permitting a patient to perform an action. Korean causatives thus cover a wide range of possible English meanings including 'he/she made me . . .', 'he/she caused me to . . .' and 'he/she let me . . .'.

Causativization is a process diametrically opposite to the process of passivization that we looked at in the previous section (refer to 4.4.1). Passivization is 'intransitivizing'; in other words it eliminates the propensity for a verb to have an object. For example, whereas the first active sentence below requires an object ('fish'), the second does not:

<u>민호</u>가 <u>고기</u>를 잡았어요.	***Minho*** *caught a* ***fish***.
<u>고기</u>가 잡혔어요.	*The* ***fish*** *got caught.*

Causativization, on the other hand, is transitivizing or ditransitivizing; in other words, it changes a verb that does not need an object into a verb that needs an object. Or, it changes a verb that only needs one object into a verb that needs two objects. For example, the first sentence below requires no object, but the second requires an object (fish).

고기가 죽었어요.	*The **fish** died.*
민호가 **고기**를 죽였어요.	***Minho** killed a **fish**.*

In other cases, whereas the first active sentence below requires only one object ('fish'), the second requires two ('fish' and 'Minho'):

민호가 **고기**를 잡았어요.	***Minho** caught a **fish**.*
유미가 **민호**에게 **고기**를 잡게 했어요.	***Yumi** made **Minho** catch a **fish**.*

Korean causative verbs are often ambiguous regarding whether the causation takes place by force or coercion (A *makes* B do something) or otherwise simply by permission (A *lets* B do something). This can usually be clarified by the context.

Korean has four ways to form causative constructions which are discussed in turn below.

4.4.2.1 Derived causative verbs

For a limited number of verbs, a separate causative verb form can be derived by the addition of a verb ending. This ending has seven possible shapes: –이–, –기–, –히–, –리– and –우–, –구–, –추–. For verbs that take the first four shapes, the causative form is often the same as the derived passive form (refer to 4.4.1.1). However, note that some are different such as 먹이– 'cause to eat' versus 먹히– 'is eaten'. Also, note that some of these causative verbs (such as 죽이– 'cause to die; kill') do not have derived passive counterparts.

Here is a list of some of the most common causative verbs along with the basic verbs from which they derive. Note that two of these verbs have irregular causative forms: 없– becomes 없애– and 끝나– becomes 끝내–.

Basic verb		Derived verb	
알–	know	알리–	let [someone] know, inform
앉–	sit	앉히–	seat [someone]
잡–	catch	잡히–	have [something] caught; have [someone] catch
좁–	be narrow	좁히–	make [it] narrow, narrow [it]
죽–	dies	죽이–	kill
없–	be lacking	없애–	eliminate; get rid of
입–	get dressed	입히–	dress [someone]
			make [someone] get dressed
감–	bathe, wash	감기–	have [someone] bathe or wash
걷–	walk	걸리–	have [someone] walk
깨–	wake up	깨우–	wake [someone] up
끝나–	[something] stops	끝내–	stop [someone], finish [someone]
굶–	starve	굶기–	allow/make [someone] to go hungry
굽–	be bent	굽히–	bend [something]
마르–	get dry	말리–	dry [something], makes [something] dry
먹–	eat	먹이–	feed, let/make [someone] eat
날–	[something] flies	날리–	fly [something]; have [something] fly
남–	remain, be left	남기–	leave [something] [remaining behind]
넓–	be wide, broad	넓히–	widen, broaden [something]

놀–	play; have fun; relax;	놀리–	let [someone] play; make fun [of]
	take [time] off		[someone]; give [someone] [time] off;
높–	be high	높이–	raise [up), elevate
늦–	be late; be loose	늦추–	postpone; loose
오르–	rise, ascend	올리–	raise, lift; present, give
빗–	comb [one's hair]	빗기–	comb [someone else's hair]
벗–	get undressed,	벗기–	undress [someone else],
	take off clothes		take off [someone else's clothes]
보–	see, look at	보이–	show, let [someone] see
살–	live	살리–	make let live; save, revive
서–	stand; [a car] stops	세우–	erect it; stop [a car]
신–	put on [shoes, socks]	신기–	put on [someone else's shoes, socks]
			make [someone] put on [shoes, socks]
덥–	be hot, warm	덥히–	heat [something], warm [something] up
타–	[something] burns	태우–	burn [something]
타–	ride [a horse, bicycle, etc.]	태우–	give a ride [to somebody], pick up [someone]
	take [a bus, train, etc.]		[a bus, etc.] carry [someone]
돌–	[something] turns	돌리–	turn [something], make/let [something]
			go around; pass [something] around
돋–	sprout/come out	돋구–	stimulate, whet

As noted above, making a verb causative changes the transitivity of the verb (i.e., the number of objects that it takes). For some verbs, this increases from zero to one:

집이 **넓어요**. *The house is 'wide' (= big).*	→	집을 **넓혔어요**. *I 'widened' (= extended) the house.*

For others, it increases from one to two. In these cases, the indirect object (here, the child), is marked with 에게/한테 (refer to 3.2.4.4):

아이가 양말을 **신었어요**. *The child put on his/her socks.*	→	아이에게 양말을 **신겼어요**. *I put on the child's socks for him/her.* *I made the child put on his/her socks.*

Here are further examples of some of these derived verbs in sentences:

손님을 식탁의 상석에 **앉혔어요**.
We sat the guest at the head of the table.

잉어탕을 만드는 방법을 **알려** 주세요.
Please inform (= tell) me how to make carp stew.

음식을 **남기지** 마세요.	*Don't leave any food.*
젖은 옷을 **말렸어요**.	*I dried the wet clothes.*
말씀 **높이세요**.	*Elevate your speech a bit. (= Use honorifics.)*
말씀 **낮추세요**.	*Lower your speech. (= Drop the honorifics.)*

세관원은 남자의 옷을 **벗기고** 몸을 수색했어요.
The customs officer stripped the man and searched him.

학생을 **놀리고** 싶지 않아서 숙제를 많이 주었어요.
I didn't want to give the students time off, so I gave them a lot of homework.

의사들은 그 환자를 **살리려고** 모든 노력을 다했어요.
The doctors tried everything they could to save that patient.

살인을 저지르고 나서 모든 증거를 **<u>없앴어요</u>**.
After committing the murder, he got rid of all the evidence.

개가 배탈이 나서 **<u>굶겨야</u>** 했어요.
The dog had a stomach ache, so we had to keep it off its food.

As noted above, in many cases the derived causative form is the same as the derived passive form. In such cases, whether the meaning is passive or causative can only be established in context:

Passive	*Causative*
남산이 나에게 **<u>보여요</u>**. *Namsan mountain is visible to me.*	어머니가 아이에게 그림책을 **<u>보였어요</u>**. *The mother is showing the picture book to the baby.*
아기가 어머니에게 **<u>업혔어요</u>**. *The baby was put on its mother's back.*	어머니가 유미에게 아기를 **<u>업혔어요</u>**. *The mother put the baby on Yumi's back.*
유미가 민호에게 **<u>안겼어요</u>**. *Yumi was embraced by Minho.*	유미가 민호에게 꽃다발을 **<u>안겼어요</u>**. *Yumi put the bouquet in Minho's arms.*

4.4.2.2 *Causatives with –게 하–*

The second way to form a causative construction is to add the adverbative form –게 (also used for forming adverbs – refer to 11.2.1.2) and follow this with the verb 하–. This pattern can be applied to any verb, including those that can also be made causative through derived means (refer to 4.4.2.1):

As with derived causatives, –게 하– increases the transitivity of the verb (i.e., the number of objects that it takes):

No object		*One object*
아이가 자요. *The child sleeps.*	→	어머니가 **<u>아이</u>**를 자게 해요. *Mother made the child sleep.*

One object		*Two objects*
아이가 **<u>책</u>**을 읽어요. *The child read the book.*	→	어머니가 **<u>아이</u>**에게 **<u>책</u>**을 읽게 해요. *Mother made/let the child read the book.*

Like derived causatives, the –게 하– construction can be ambiguous regarding whether the causation took place through coercion (A *makes B do* something) or permission (A *lets* B do something). However, the –게 하– construction has a more specific meaning of causation than the derived forms and thus cannot take on certain specific simple transitive meanings of the derived causative verbs, leading to some contrasting readings as in the examples below:

Derived causative	*–게 하–*
어머니가 아이에게 옷을 **입혔어요**. *Mother dressed the child.*	어머니가 아이에게 옷을 **입게 했어요**. *Mother made the child put on clothes.*
어머니가 아이에게 신발을 **신겼어요**. *Mother put the shoes on the child.*	어머니가 아이에게 신발을 **신게 했어요**. *Mother made the child put on shoes.*
어머니가 아이에게 밥을 **먹였어요**. *Mother fed the child.*	어머니가 아이에게 밥을 **먹게 했어요**. *Mother made the child eat.*
어머니가 아이에게 책을 **보였어요**. *Mother showed the book to the child.*	어머니가 아이에게 책을 **보게 했어요**. *Mother made the child look at the book.*
어머니가 아이를 **눕혔어요**. *Mother laid the child down.*	어머니가 아이를 **눕게 했어요**. *Mother made the child lie down.*
어머니가 아이를 **앉혔어요**. *Mother sat the child down.*	어머니가 아이를 **앉게 했어요**. *Mother made the child sit down.*
어머니가 아이를 **죽였어요**. *Mother killed the child.*	어머니가 아이를 **죽게 했어요**. *Mother made the child die.*

In addition, idiomatic usages that thrive with certain derived causatives tend not to be available for –게 하–. For example, the following usages of the derived transitive 죽이 – 'kill' cannot be achieved through –게 하–:

오늘 날씨 정말 **죽인다**.
It's 'killer' (= awesome) weather today.

이 **<u>죽일</u>** 놈아!
Damn you wretch!

목소리/숨/감정/발소리를 **<u>죽이고</u>** . . .
. . . with a subdued voice/bated breath/feelings suppressed/muffled footsteps

Here are further examples of the –게 하– construction in full sentences:

시험 앞두고 아이를 못 **<u>놀게 해야 해요</u>**.
Before an exam, you can't let the children play.

<u>기다리시게 해서</u> 죄송합니다.
I'm sorry to have kept you waiting.

아이들을 일찍 **<u>자게 했어요</u>**.
I made the children go to bed early.

라디오를 좀 **<u>작게 하세요</u>**
Turn the radio down a little.

4.4.2.3 *Causatives with –도록 하–*

The causative form –게 하– (refer to 4.4.2.2) can be replaced with the alternative pattern –도록 하–. Using –도록 하– makes the causation sound softer or less direct. Here are some examples:

교수님께서 학생들한테 교실을 청소하**<u>도록</u>** 하셨어요.
The professor made the students clean the classroom.

유미는 나를 쉬**<u>도록</u>** 했어요.
Yumi let me take a rest.

고향에서 온 친구를 우리 집에서 머물**<u>도록</u>** 했어요.
I let my friend from my home town sleep at our house.

아이들을 일찍 자**<u>도록</u>** 해야 해요.
You have to make the children go to bed early.

–도록 하– (and –도록 on its own) have several other functions that are described elsewhere (refer to 7.6.3).

4.4.2.4 *Causatives with 시키–*

For 하– verbs (refer to 4.1.2), causatives can also be formed by substituting the support verb 하– for the verb 시키–. When used as a main verb, 시키– has the original meaning of 'order (food, etc.)'.

인수는 비빔밥을 시키고 민수는 갈비탕을 시켰어요.
In-su ordered pibimbap and Minsu ordered kalbitang.

When used as a support verb, it takes on the meaning of 'cause' or 'make'. Unlike derived causatives or –게 하–, causatives with 시키– do not usually connote permission (A *lets* B do something), but only deliberate coercion. As in the first example below, the noun preceding 시키– may optionally be followed by the object particle:

학생들한테 공부(를) **시켰어요**.
I made the students study a lot.

구두닦이에게 구두를 수선 **시켰어요**.
I had my shoes mended by a shoeshine boy.

그 놈이 내 딸을 임신 **시켰어요**.
That wretch got my daughter pregnant.

동생에게 방 청소를 **시켰어요**.
I made my younger brother/sister clean the room.

피곤하니까 말(을) **시키지 마**!
I'm tired, so stop making me talk. (=Stop trying to talk to me, stop asking me things.)

4.4.3 Transforming descriptive verbs into processive verbs

Korean has two processes for transforming descriptive verbs into processive verbs: (1) adding the auxiliary –지– and (2) adding the auxiliary –하–. Both of these forms attach to the infinitive form of the verb (refer to 4.1.6).

4.4.3.1 *Forming processive verbs with –지–*

The addition of the auxiliary verb –지– turns a descriptive verb into a processive verb adding the meaning of 'becoming' or 'getting':

Descriptive verbs		*Processive verbs*	
덥–	*be warm*	더워지–	*become warm*
높–	*be high*	높아지–	*become high*
좋–	*be good*	좋아지–	*get better*
예쁘–	*be pretty*	예뻐지–	*get prettier*
용감하–	*be brave*	용감해지–	*become brave*

Here are some examples of these forms in sentences:

올 여름에는 치마가 더 **짧아진다**.
This summer, skirts are getting even shorter.

눈이 많이 내리고 **추워졌어요**.
It's snowed a lot and it's become colder.

그 친구가 안 본 사이에 **예뻐졌어요**.
In the time that I didn't see her, my friend got prettier.

요즘 건강이 **좋아졌어요**.
Recently my health got better.

In addition to changing descriptive verbs into processive verbs, –지– can also be used to form passives on processive verbs, as discussed previously in this chapter (refer to 4.4.1.4).

4.4.3.2 *Forming processive verbs with –하–*

Certain descriptive verbs that are cognitive or emotive in nature and that denote psychological states can be changed into processive (action) verbs with the addition of –하–:

Descriptive verbs		*Processive verbs*	
좋–	*be good*	좋아하–	*like*
싫–	*be disliked*	싫어하–	*hate*
부럽–	*be jealous*	부러워하–	*envy*
고맙–	*be thankful*	고마워하–	*be thankful for*
(–고) 싶–	*want*	(–고) 싶어하–	*[somebody else] wants* (refer to 5.3.4)
기쁘–	*be glad*	기뻐하–	*[somebody else] is glad*
슬프–	*be sad*	슬퍼하–	*[somebody else] is sad*

The addition of –하– has two distinct functions. Firstly, for verbs such as the first four, –하– turns an inner feeling (i.e., being jealous) into an active expression of this feeling (i.e., envying something). When talking about yourself or your immediate interlocutor (i.e., the person you are talking to), both the descriptive verb and the processive verb may be used. Despite the different English translations given above, note that 좋– 'be good' and 싫– 'be disliked' in particular are often used to express (at least by extension) the meanings of the corresponding processive verbs: 'like' and 'hate'. Note that whereas the descriptive verb takes the subject particle (refer to 3.2.1), the processive verb takes an object particle (refer to 3.2.2):

Descriptive verb	*Processive verb*
저는 닭고기가 **좋아요**. *For me, chicken is good.* *(= I like chicken).*	저는 닭고기를 **좋아해요**. *I like chicken.*
저는 커피가 **싫어요**. *For me, coffee is disliked.* *(= I dislike coffee).*	저는 커피를 **싫어해요**. *I dislike coffee.*
저는 언니가 **부러워요**. *I am jealous of my older sister.*	저는 언니를 **부러워해요**. *I envy my older sister.*

Although in some cases 좋아요/좋아해요 (and 싫어요/싫어해요) may be fairly interchangeable (at least in the first- and second-person), it is important to point out cases in which only one of the two may be appropriate. Firstly, although 좋아요 'is good' may be used by extension to mean 'likes', the reverse does not apply. In other words, 좋아해요 'likes' cannot be used to mean 'is good'. More importantly, whereas 좋아요 is used for talking about more temporary feelings of liking something (i.e., 'I like this particular chicken that I am eating now'), 좋아해요 is used when discussing your general likes and preferences (i.e., 'I like chicken in general').

The second function of these processive verbs is for talking about the psychological states of other people (who are not you and your immediate interlocutor). When talking about other people, the descriptive verb cannot normally be used and the constructions with –하– have to be used instead. We thus get contrasts between first/second-person sentences and third-person sentences as shown below:

First/second person	*Third person*
저는 한국에 가고 **싶어요**. *I want to go to Korea.*	마이클은 한국에 가고 **싶어해요**. *Michael wants to go to Korea.*
너무 **부럽지요**? *You're so jealous, aren't you?*	유미가 너무 **부러워하겠지요**? *Yumi must be really jealous, right?*
저는 **슬퍼요**. *I am sad.*	어머니가 **슬퍼하셨어요**. *Mother was sad.*

Chapter 5

Auxiliary (support) verbs

Overview

'Auxiliaries' are additional verbs or support verbs that are used supplementary to the main verb and which 'help' or 'support' it by supplying extra information regarding the way that the speaker views the event being talked about.

Korean auxiliary verbs always occur after the main verb and can be classified according to the form of the verb they follow. The majority of auxiliaries occur after the –(아/어) 'infinitive' ending (refer to 5.1). Other auxiliaries occur after –다 (refer to 5.2), –고 (refer to 5.3), –ㄹ까 (refer to 5.4), –나/ㄴ가 (refer to 5.5), –게 (refer to 5.6) and –(어/아)야 (refer to 5.7)

The meanings of constructions containing auxiliary verbs are often connected to the original meaning of the verb in question. For example, 가– (originally meaning 'go') depicts an action or state progressing *away from* the current place/time, whereas 오– (originally meaning 'come') depicts an action or state progressing *towards* the current place/time. However, note that such connections are not always as transparent.

5.1 Auxiliary verbs with –(아/어)

This set of constructions attach after the infinitive form of the verb (refer to 4.1.6):

5.1.1 –(아/어) 가– (ongoing activity 'away')

This construction employs 가– (that as a main verb means 'go') as an auxiliary verb to communicate that the action or state in question involves movement away from the speaker or person being talked about. Rather than physical movement, the construction normally depicts temporal movement; in other words, an ongoing process progressing away from the present (or other given time) and into the future (or, less commonly, the past). With processive verbs, –아/어 가– can usually be translated as 'keep on', 'go on', 'continue (doing)'. In the case of descriptive verbs the nuance of –어 가– is better captured by 'get (to be)' or 'grow – er (and – er)'.

미국 경제가 망해 **간다**.
The American economy continues to go downhill.

꽃이 다 피어 **가요**.
The flowers have almost reached the state of fully blooming.

벌써 사랑이 식어 **가나요**? *Is our love already cooling off?*

모든 고생을 다 겪어 **가며** 아이들을 키웠어요.
I brought up my children undergoing all sorts of hardships.

늘어 **가는** 인구문제는 중국의 골치거리다.
A problem of continuously increasing population is a nuisance to China.

부모님이 늙어 **가는** 모습을 보니 슬퍼요.
I am sad to see my parents getting old.

5.1.2 –(아/어) 오– (ongoing activity 'towards')

Whereas the use of 가– ('go') as an auxiliary verb depicts movement away (from the speaker, person being talked about, present time, etc.) (refer to 5.1.1), use of 오– (originally meaning 'come') depicts movement in the opposite direction. Put simply, this form is applied when talking about a process that has continued over a period of time up to the present, or over a period of time leading up to another given reference time. In translating –(아/어) 오– with processive verbs such renderings as 'has kept on . . .', 'has (always or continuously) . . .', 'has been . . .' will be useful. In the case of descriptive verbs, the usual translation will be 'getting . . .' or 'growing – er (and – er)':

배가 고파 **오네요**! *I'm getting hungry.*

남편과 함께 17년 동안 식육점을 운영해 **왔어요.**
She has run a butcher's shop with her husband for 17 years.

그 문제를 해결하기 위해 많은 노력을 해 **왔습니다**.
We have continued to exert much effort in order to solve these problems.

살아 **온** 세월보다 살아갈 세월이 더 많아요.
The time I will [continue to] live [in the future] is more than the time I have lived [so far].

점심시간이 가까워 **오**니까 빨리 끝냅시다.
Since lunch time is getting close, let's finish quickly.

5.1.3 –(아/어) 내– (finish, achieve)

When used as a main verb, 내– means 'submit', 'present', 'despatch', 'put forth', 'pay' or 'draw out'. What all of these meanings have in common is that they involve a movement that creates a final state that is 'presented', 'despatched', etc. from the movement in question and that is typically final, climactic and represents successfully reaching a given end point.

When applied as an auxiliary verb, 내– retains this meaning of following a process through to the end and reaching a final conclusion or goal derived from the action in question. It depicts the act of doing something through to the end, 'going all the way' or simply completing a process properly and thoroughly. The final goal or conclusion is often reached despite certain difficult circumstances, dangers or hardships.

우리 해 **냈다**!
We did it! (newspaper headline after Korean football team qualify for World Cup semi-final)

통증이 심했지만 견뎌 **냈어요/** 참아 **냈어요**.
The pain was severe, but I managed to bear it.

어려운 책을 끝까지 읽어 **냈어요**.
I read this difficult book right through to the end.

결국 시계를 찾아 **냈어요**.
Finally, I found my watch.

김 교수님은 많은 제자들을 길러 **내셨어요**.
Professor Kim managed to train many graduate students.

의사들은 암의 원인을 밝혀 **내기** 위해 열심히 연구한다.
Doctors are hard at work trying to establish the factors causing cancer.

5.1.4 –(아/어) 놓– (do all the way)

When used as a main verb, 놓– means 'set free', 'let go', 'lay down', 'place' or 'put'. By extension from this meaning of 'placing' and 'releasing', when used as an auxiliary verb, the resulting construction –(아/어) 놓– means 'do something and leave it in that state'.

This construction can first of all be used simply to specifically mark that an activity is completed. As can be seen in the following comparison, an action marked with –(아/어) 놓– is generally understood as being completed or finished, which is not necessarily the case when the construction is not applied:

without –(아/어) 놓–	*with –(아/어) 놓–*
개가 신발을 물어뜯었어요	개가 신발을 물어뜯어 **놓았어요**.
The dog has chewed my shoes.	*The dog has [completely] chewed up my shoes.*

The second sentence here implies that the shoes are totally chewed up and therefore probably unusable.

The pattern –(아/어) 놓– is frequently followed by the additional connective –고 (refer to 7.3.1). The resulting construction states that the first action has been completed, so that the speaker can move on to the second. In such cases, the first action is usually something more odious, burdensome or duty-bound, whereas the second is something more enjoyable. In English, this translates with expressions such as 'get something done (and)':

숙제를 하고 저녁을 먹었어요.	숙제를 해 **놓고** 저녁을 먹었어요.
I did my homework and ate dinner.	*I got my homework done and then ate dinner.*

방을 깨끗이 정리해 **놓고** 놀러 나가.
Get your room tidied and then go out to play.

차를 고쳐 **놓고** 맥주를 마셨어요.
I got the car repaired and then drank a beer.

결혼을 해 **놓고** 유학을 갔어요.
I got myself married and then went overseas to study.

The construction can also be used to stress that the state reached by completing the action is (or should be) maintained:

창문 좀 열어 **놓으세요**.
Please leave the window open.

외출할 때 난방을 꺼 **놓으세요**.
Turn (lit. leave) off the heating when you leave the room.

As an extension of this meaning, the construction is frequently applied when talking about performing an action now in order to be ready for later events or processes:

값이 오르기 전에 미리 사 **놓으면** 좋겠어요.
I hope I should buy some [and keep it] before the prices go up.

밥을 많이 먹어 **놓아서** 배고프지 않아요.
As I ate a lot before, I am not hungry.

5.1.5 –(아/어) 두– (do for future reference)

The verb 두– as a main verb means 'put', 'place', 'deposit', 'store away' or 'leave aside'. The core meaning is in some ways similar to 놓– (refer to 5.1.4); however, there are two key differences. First, whereas 놓– denotes 'releasing' something from the sphere (of interest or influence) of the speaker, 두– specifically connotes putting something in a place that is still within the speaker's field (refer to Lee 1993). Second, 두– implies some kind of time span for the action: when we deposit or store something away, it is usually for an extended period of time.

Due to these specific semantic differences between 놓– and 두–, when used as auxiliary verbs, whereas –(아/어) 놓– may simply denote performing an action in order to complete it or get it out of the way,

–(아/어)두– specifically expresses that the action is performed for future use or advantage, typically by or on behalf of the speaker

with –(아/어) 놓–	*with –(아/어) 두–*
문을 열어 **놓았어요**. *I left the door open (for no specific purpose).*	문을 열어 **두었어요**. *I left the door open [for specific personal future use, e.g., to take something out through the door].*
서류를 준비해 **놓았어요**. *I finished preparing the documents [and got it out of the way].*	서류를 준비해 **두었어요**. *I finished preparing the documents [and so I have them for my future personal use].*

Here are some further examples:

젊었을 때 공부를 해 **두어야 돼요**.
Study [for the future] while you are still young.

한국 사람들은 김치를 가을에 만들어 **두었다가** 겨울 동안 계속 먹어요.
Koreans make kimchi in the fall, and eat it throughout the winter.

내 말을 잘 들어 **두어라**.
Pay attention to what I am going to say [for future use].

그 일은 민수한테 맡겨 **두세요**. *Leave that work for Minsu.*

5.1.6 –(아/어) 대– (do repeatedly)

As a main verb, 대– has the meaning of 'holding something so that it is in contact with something else' (e.g., holding a cup to one's lips). It can also mean 'supply' or 'provide'. When used as auxiliary verbs, these meanings are retained to some extent: –(아/어) 대– is used to depict the continuous or repetitive occurrence of an action (we can think of this as continuous occurrences of an action being brought into contact with each other (refer to Lee 1993)., or a continuous line of supply). The repetition depicted is typically to an extreme extent and is viewed negatively:

아이가 계속해서 울어 **대서** 너무 시끄러워요.
The child just keeps on crying and crying – it's so noisy.

학생들이 너무 떠들어 **대서** 수업을 할 수 없었어요.
Students kept making noise, so I couldn't teach the lesson.

유미는 계속해서 거짓말을 해 **댔어요**.
Yumi just kept on telling lies.

아이는 사탕을 달라고 졸라 **댔어요**.
The children kept pestering me to give them sweets.

그들은 서로 잘못이 없다고 우겨 **댔다**.
They kept insisting that they had done nothing wrong.

그는 쉬지 않고 계속 먹어 **댄다**.
He kept on eating, without stopping.

5.1.7 –(아/어) 버리– (do completely for regret or relief)

The verb 버리–, as a main verb, means 'throw away', 'dump', 'cast aside', 'get rid of', 'abandon' or 'leave behind'. These meanings are retained to some extent when 버리– is used as an auxiliary verb in the –(아/어) 버리– construction. This pattern is used when talking about finishing a process through to the end so that it is, metaphorically, 'disposed of'. The pattern is rather similar in meaning and usage to –(아/어) 치우– (refer to 5.1.13) and –고 말– (refer to 5.3.2). These similarities are covered in the respective sections on these two constructions later in this chapter.

At times, the completion or 'disposal' of the activity in question may be to the regret of the speaker:

유미가 일찍 가 **버렸어요**. *[To my regret] Yumi just left early.*

아이스크림이 다 녹아 **버렸어요**. *All of the ice-cream melted.*

공항에 늦게 도착하는 바람에 비행기를 놓쳐 **버렸어요**.
Arriving late at the airport, I missed my plane.

With some verbs that by nature involve a high degree of regret, –(아/어) 버리– may occur particularly frequently. This particularly applies to 잊– 'forget' and 잃– 'lose', which combine with –(아/어)

버리– at will, with the subsequent construction frequently being written as one word: 잊어버리– and 잃어버리– (and indeed appearing in the dictionary as one word).

> **잊어버리지** 않도록 수첩에 적어 놓으세요.
> *Please write it down in your planner so that you don't forget.*

> 교통카드를 **잃어버리는** 바람에 환승 할인은 받지 못했어요.
> *Since I lost my travel card, I could not get a discount when I changed buses.*

These 'regretful' occurrences include times when the speaker recklessly performs an action, often contrary to his/her plan (or quicker than he/she thought possible) or even without being fully conscious of what he/she was doing:

> 그 동안 모은 돈은 다 하루 만에 써 **버렸어요**.
> *I spent [and wasted] all of the money I had saved in just one day.*

> 한 시간 만에 그 많은 술을 마셔 **버렸어요**.
> *We drank all of that alcohol in just one hour.*

In addition to completion or 'disposal' that is regretful, –(아/어) 버리– is also used when talking about an activity performed to the relief of the speaker (or the person being talked about). Here, completing the action to the end (often as quickly as possible or with minimum investment) takes a psychological weight off the mind of the speaker (or the person being talked about):

> 귀찮아서 개를 팔아 **버렸어요**.
> *I sold my dog, which had been a nuisance to me.*

> 그 남자가 보낸 편지는 다 찢어 **버렸어요**.
> *I ripped up all the letters he sent me.*

> 그 기억을 싹 지워 **버리고** 싶었어요.
> *I wanted just to get rid of those memories.*

5.1.8 –(아/어) 보– (try doing)

When 보– is used as a main verb, it means 'look' or 'see'. Applied as an auxiliary verb, the meaning becomes more abstract: it means 'try [doing something] to see if you can do it' <u>or</u> 'sample something to see what it is like'. What this meaning of 'trying' shares with the original meaning of 보– is the sense of exploration, of seeing (or of experiencing something through another sense) and then establishing its possibility or its character.

In the first set of examples below, –(아/어) 보– means 'try or attempt something to see if you can do it'

> 깁스를 풀고 걸어 **<u>봤어요</u>**.
> *After taking off the plaster cast, I tried to walk.*

> 한국말로 설명해 **<u>봤는데</u>** 설명할 수 없었어요.
> *I attempted explaining in Korean, but I couldn't.*

Although –(아/어) 보– can be used in this way, it more commonly means 'try something to sample it and see what it is like', as in the next set of examples. This includes some common combinations such as 먹어 보– 'try (eating/drinking)' or 'taste (something)' and 입어 보– 'try on'. In this meaning, –(아/어) 보– frequently co-occurs with 한 번, which literally means 'just once'.

> 이거 먹어 **<u>봐</u>**. 아주 맛있어.
> *Try [eating or drinking] this. It's really delicious.*

> 손님, 이거 한번 입어 **<u>보세요</u>**.
> *Customer, why don't you quickly try this on?*

> 그 여자를 한 번 만나 **<u>볼까요</u>**?
> *Shall I try meeting that girl [just once, to see what she is like].*

In order to express the opinions formed by having sampled the action in question, –(아/어) 보– can be followed by –니까 (refer to 7.1.6) or –니 (refer to 7.1.7). The second clause then is frequently rounded off by –더 (refer to 4.3.1.3):

> 알탕을 먹어 **<u>보니까</u>** 국물이 시원하**<u>더</u>**라고요.
> *I tried alt'ang and the broth was spicy and refreshing.*

> 그 여자를 만나 **<u>보니까</u>** 성격이 이상하**<u>더</u>**라.
> *I met that girl and I found her personality to be strange.*

In addition to simply trying something to see what it is like, you might try something to find out or establish a specific state of affairs. Note that in such expressions in English, 'try' can normally be omitted:

우체국에 가 **<u>봤지만</u>** 편지는 없었어요.
I tried going (= went) to the post office [to see if there was any letter], but there wasn't one.

강남 가는 버스를 어디서 타는지 물어**<u>봤어요</u>**.
I tried asking (= asked) where I could take a bus to Gangnam.

Note that the verb 묻– 'ask', due to its intrinsic exploratory meaning, frequently occurs with the –(아/어) 보– construction (as in the final example above). In fact, it can be found in the dictionary as a single word.

With the meaning of 'sampling', –(아/어) 보– is often used when asking and answering questions about whether you have ever done something:

산낙지를 먹어 **<u>봤어요</u>**? *Have you ever eaten live octopus?*

강릉에 가 **<u>봤어요</u>**? *Have you ever been to Gangneung?*

In this meaning, –(아/어) 보– may also occur in combination with the pattern –ㄴ 적/일(이) 있– (refer to 8.2.29), which more strictly specifies the meaning of 'have you ever':

안동 소주를 마셔 **<u>본</u>** 적이 있어요?
Have you ever drunk Andong soju?

한국 소설을 읽어 **<u>본</u>** 일이 있어요?
Have you ever read a Korean novel?

The –(아/어) 보– construction is also used to make utterances less direct by softening the speaker's assertion. In imperatives, telling someone to 'try reading' or 'try eating' is naturally softer and more polite than simply telling them to 'read' or 'eat'. Indeed, the force of imperatives with –(아/어) 보– is perhaps similar to the English 'why don't you . . .?' or 'could/would you . . .?':

그늘에 잠시 앉아 **<u>보세요</u>**.
Why don't you sit in the shade for a moment?

이 제품 꼭 한 번 써 **<u>보세요</u>**.
Why don't you give this product a go (just once)?

–(아/어) 보– is also used to soften speaker's assertion in greeting expressions and promises with –겠–:

먼저 가 **보겠습니다**. *I will try going first. (set greeting used when leaving).*

한 번 해 **보겠습니다**. *I will give it a go.*

5.1.9 –(아/어) 보이– (seem)

As a main verb, 보이– means 'be visible' or 'show'. When applied as an auxiliary verb, this meaning of 'visibility' extends to making an inference or prediction based on sensory (usually visual) evidence. Only used with descriptive verbs, this pattern typically translates as 'look . . .' or 'seem . . .':

그것이 제일 맛있어 **보여요**. *That looks to be the most delicious.*

안색이 안 좋아 **보여요**.
You don't look well. (lit. 'Your face colour doesn't look good.')

인호는 착해 **보이지만** 실제로 그렇지 않아요.
Inho looks nice and kind, but really he's not.

유미 씨는 30 살이 넘었는데도 아직 대학생같이 젊어 **보여요**.
Yumi has passed 30, but she still looks young, like a university student.

Note that in place of –아/어 보이–, –게 보이– (refer to 5.6.2) may be used with no large difference in meaning.

5.1.10 –(아/어) 빠지– (lapse into a negative state)

When applied as a main verb, 빠지– means 'fall' or 'lapse into'. By extension, when used as an auxiliary, it denotes deterioration in the state of affairs under discussion. The main verb in this pattern is usually a descriptive verb, and also tends to carry a negative implication.

요즘 교수들은 생각이 낡아 **빠졌어요**.
The way that professors think these days has become so old-fashioned.

민호는 게을러 **빠져서** 성공하기 어려울 거에요.
Minho has got so lazy that there is no way he'll succeed.

김치가 시어 **빠져서** 먹을 수가 없네요.
The kimchi has turned all sour and I cannot eat it.

썩어 **빠진** 정치는 바꾸어야 해요.
We have to change politics, which has become rotten to the core.

내 늙어 **빠진** 얼굴이 뭐가 예뻐?
What do you think is pretty about my old withered face?

5.1.11 –(아/어) 쌓– (do repeatedly)

As a main verb, 쌓– originally means 'pile up', 'heap up' or 'put in a pile/heap'. When applied as an auxiliary verb, this meaning of 'stacking things up' translates into doing an activity repeatedly and/or continuously, to an extent that is irritable or irksome to the speaker:

아이가 울어 **쌓아요**. *The child just keeps on crying.*

개가 짖어 **쌓아요**. *The dog keeps on barking.*

굶은 사람처럼 먹어 **쌓더니** 배탈이 났어요.
After eating and eating like someone who was starving, he/she got a stomach ache.

The usage of –아/어쌓– is essentially the same as –아/어 대– (refer to 5.1.6). However, the image that they conjure up is quite different. Whereas –아/어쌓– depicts repetition as a process of piling things up one on top of another, –아/어 대– expresses repetition as the linking up of actions one after another (refer to Lee 1993).

5.1.12 –(아/어) 주– (perform a favour)

The verb 주– as a main verb originally means 'give'. When applied as an auxiliary verb in the –아/어 주– construction, this meaning of 'giving' becomes more abstract in that what is given is an action rather than things. Put more simply, this expression is used when talking about doing something (such as a favour) for the benefit of someone else. These are known in linguistics as benefactive constructions. As can be seen in the first two examples, the person benefiting from the action can be marked with the particle 에게/한테 'to' (when the beneficiary actually receives something tangible from the action, such as money), or 을 위해 'for (the sake of)' (when the beneficiary receives a favour, but no actual tangible benefit):

유미는 인호**에게** 돈을 빌려 **주었어요**. *Yumi lent money to Inho.*

손님들은 안주인**을 위해** 음식을 다 맛있게 먹어 **주었어요**.
The guests ate hungrily all the food for [the sake of] the hostess.

볼펜으로 써 **주세요**. *Please write it for me with a pen.*

내 친구를 소개 해 **줄게요**. *I'll introduce my friend to you.*

유미 씨는 우리 아이를 좀 봐 **주고** 있어요.
Yumi is looking [after] our child for us.

Particularly when sentence subjects and/or objects are dropped, the inclusion/exclusion of –아/어 주– can result in sentences taking on quite different interpretations:

without –(아/어) 주–	*with –(아/어) 주–*
유미한테 돈을 빌렸어요. *I borrowed some money from Yumi.*	유미한테 돈을 빌려 **주었어요**. *I lent Yumi some money.*
약을 사세요. *Buy some medicine.*	약을 사 **주세요**. *Buy me some medicine.*
말해! *Speak out!/Say it!*	말해 **줘**! *Tell me!*

When the beneficiary of the action is higher in status than the speaker (and, in instances in which the person being talked about is not the hearer, also higher than the hearer), 주– should be replaced by its honorific counterpart 드리– (refer to 6.2.2.1). The particle –에게/–한테 will also be substituted for –께 (refer to 6.2.2.2):

할아버님**께** 선물을 보내 **드렸어요**. *I sent grandfather a present.*

사진을 보여 **드릴게요**. *I'll show you the photos.*

그 친구는 책 한 권을 나**한테** 사 **줬고**, 어머니**께** 꽃을 사 **드렸어요**.
My friend bought a book for me and bought some flowers for my mother.

Since –아/어 주– implies 'benefit' for the recipient of the action, its usage can take on certain politeness functions. For example, when thanking someone for coming, the following expression is standard as it implies that your coming was to my benefit (and the expression thus shows deference to the hearer and humbles the self):

와 **주셔서** 감사합니다. *Thanks for coming.*

5.1.13 –(아/어) 치우– (do rashly)

When applied as a main verb, 치우– has the meaning of 'remove' or 'clean up'. As an auxiliary verb, this meaning of 'clean up' extends to expressing doing something completely (often in one go, or in the twinkling of an eye). The action often comes about subconsciously to the speaker, or through his/her own rash actions. Alternatively, the speaker may perform the action quickly just to purposefully get it out of the way

밥 한 그릇을 눈 깜짝할 사이에 먹어 **치웠어요**.
He ate up a bowl of rice in the twinkling of an eye.

남동생이 그 많은 숙제를 단숨에 해 **치우고** 놀러 나갔어요.
My younger brother finished all that homework in one go and went out to play.

인호는 노름에 빠져서 집까지 팔아 **치웠어요**.
Inho got indulged in gambling and even had to sell off his house.

The meaning of this pattern is similar to –아/어 버리– (refer to 5.1.7). However, –아/어 치우– has stronger nuances than –아/어 버리– in that the action is performed at lightning speed and is totally completed (without any 'leftovers', etc.). Also, the frequency of –아/어 치우– is much lower than –아/어 버리–. It is not particularly productive in that it only commonly occurs with a small selection of verbs (such as 하– 'do', 먹– 'eat', 팔– 'sell' 갈– 'change' and 집– 'pick up').

5.2 Auxiliary verbs with –다

This set of constructions embellishes either the base or the infinitive form of the verb (refer to 4.1.6) with –다 and then follows this with an auxiliary verb. As a verb ending –다 also appears in the construction –다(가) (refer to 7.3.11), which indicates the interruption of one action and transition to a new and superseding action. In auxiliary constructions with –다 this meaning is somewhat retained in that the action depicted is somehow stopped or interrupted.

5.2.1 –다 말– (stop after)

This pattern combines –다 with the negative verb 말– 'desist' (refer to 4.2.3), with the resulting construction depicting that an action was ceased before being properly completed:

그 드라마는 일부만 조금 보**다 말**았어요.
I stopped after watching only a little of that drama.

아침은 몇 술 먹**다 말**았잖아요.
She stopped eating breakfast after only a few spoonfuls.

내가 말을 하**다 말**았네.
I didn't finish speaking.

너무 달아서 마시**다 말**았어요.
It was too sweet, so I couldn't drink it all.

5.2.2 –다 보– (after trying doing)

This pattern attaches –다 to the base of the verb and then follows this with 보–. –다 보– is essentially comparable in meaning to the –아/어 보– pattern discussed previously in this chapter. (refer to 5.1.8). However, with the addition of –다, the meaning shifts from simply 'try' to a more remote 'after having tried'. The construction is then followed by –니까 (refer to 6.1.6) or –니 (refer to 6.1.7) and then the speaker's feelings or discoveries after having tried the activity in question:

노트북으로 게임을 하다 **보니까** 뜨거워졌어요.
After trying playing games on my laptop, it became hot.

한국어를 공부하다 **보니까** 자신감이 생겼어요.
After having studied Korean, I've gained in confidence.

이래저래 마시다 **보니까** 술이 늘어 버렸어요.
After trying drinking this and that, I've ended up being able to drink a lot more.

살다 **보니까** 힘든 일이 참 많아요.
After having lived a bit, there are a lot of tough things to overcome.

5.2.3 –(아/어)다 주– (run an errand)

This pattern attaches –다 to the infinitive form of the verb and then follows this with 주–. This pattern is comparable in meaning to the –아/어 주– pattern discussed previously (refer to 5.1.12). Like –아/어 주–, it is used when talking about doing something (such as a favour) for the benefit of someone else. The difference is that, with the inclusion of '다', the favour involves some kind of shift in space, in other words going somewhere else in order to perform the favour, such as when asking someone to run an errand. Compare the following:

–(아/어) 주–	*–(아/어)다 주–*
맥주를 사 줘. *Buy me a beer. (said at the bar or shop)*	맥주를 사**다** 줘. *Go and buy me a beer [from the shops, etc.].*
책을 빌려 줘. *Lend me your book.*	책을 빌려**다** 줘. *Go and borrow a book for me [from the library].*
컵을 씻어 줘. *Wash this cup for me [in the sink right here].*	컵을 씻어**다** 줘. *Go [to the kitchen] and wash this cup for me.*

As with –아/어 주–, 주– will be replaced by the honorific 드리– when the person benefitting from the favour is a status superior:

선생님, 집까지 모셔다 **드릴게요**.
Teacher, I will accompany you up to your house.

제가 과자 사다 **드릴게요**. *I will buy the snacks.*

5.3 Auxiliary verbs with –고

This set of constructions attach the one-shape ending –고 to the verb base and then follow this with an auxiliary verb.

5.3.1 –고 나– (after finishing)

When applied as a main verb, 나– means 'come out' or 'break out'. As an extension to this meaning, the –고 나– construction is used to indicate that the speaker (or person being talked about) has completed and 'emerged', so to speak, from performing the action of the main verb and is now free to perform another action or simply to reap the benefits of the action that has been completed. –고 나– thus typically translates as 'after finishing/completing' or 'after you have'.

An important point to note is that –고 나– rarely completes a sentence. Rather, a connective ending or modifier gets attached to –고 나– and another clause follows. When this second part of the sentence depicts the action that is carried out after the first action was finished/completed, the connective ending used is typically –어서 (refer to 7.1.1):

숙제를 끝내고 **나서** 친구들이랑 놀았어요.
After finishing my homework, I hung out with my friends.

왕이 죽고 **나서** 나라가 발전했어요.
The nation developed after the king died.

To give a similar meaning, the modifier patter –은/ㄴ 다음에, 뒤에, 후에 (refer to 8.2.7) can be used with –고 나– :

집 청소를 하고 **난** 뒤에 저녁을 준비했어요.
After finishing the cleaning, I prepared dinner.

여자친구랑 헤어지고 **난** 후에 너무 우울했어요.
After breaking up with my girlfriend, I was so depressed.

When the second action (or state) comes about on condition of the first action being completed, the conditional connective –(으)면 (refer to 7.5.1) is used:

하룻밤 자고 **나면** 다 나아질 거예요.
If you sleep a good night's sleep, you will become better.

운동을 하고 **나면** 그 결과 몸이 튼튼해져요.
If you exercise, your body will become stronger.

When the second part of the sentence expresses something that was discovered (or a state which came about, perhaps unexpectedly) on completion of the first action, –니까 (refer to 7.1.6) is used:

그 로션을 몸에 바르고 **나니까** 피부가 촉촉하고 부드러워요.
After applying that lotion on my body, my skin feels moist and soft.

저녁을 먹고 **나니까** 또 잠이 오네요.
After eating dinner, I feel sleepy again.

It should be noted that the expression of completion expressed by –고 나– contains none of the connotations of performing the first action in a complete manner, or quickly, recklessly, etc. as expressed by –어 버리– (refer to 5.1.7) or –어 치우– (refer to 5.1.13). –고 나– is most similar in meaning to –은/ㄴ다음에, 뒤에, 후에, which is discussed in the chapter on modifiers (refer to Chapter 8).

5.3.2 –고 말– (end up)

As a main verb, 말– means 'cease', 'leave off', 'stop', although it only infrequently occurs by itself. When used in an auxiliary construction, the meaning of 'ceasing' transitions to a meaning similar to English expressions such as 'end up doing' or 'wind up doing' or simply 'finally', 'at last' or 'in the end'.

안 가고 싶었지만,친구들이 다 가게 되어서 나도 가고 **말았어요**.
I didn't want to go, but it turned out that all my friends were going and so I wound up going too.

미국이 드디어 이라크를 공격하고 **말았어요**.
The US finally attacked Iraq.

화장지가 없어서 종이를 쓰고 **말았어요**.
I had no toilet tissue, and so ended up using paper.

드디어 싸움이 벌어지고 **말았어요**.
Eventually there was a fight after all.

To emphasize the nuance of 'winds up' or 'ends up', –야 can be added after –고, to make –고야 말–:

결국, 밤 새고야 **말았어요**.
In the end, we wound up staying up all night.

–고 말– is similar in meaning and usage to –(아/어) 버리– (refer to 5.1.7). However, one important difference is that –고 말– is not used when expressing relief or happiness to have finished something. Therefore, –고 말– cannot replace –(아/어) 버리– in sentences such as 어려운 숙제를 다 해 버렸어요 'I finished all of the difficult homework.', or 남은 음식을 다 먹어 버렸어요. 'I've eaten up all the leftovers'.

5.3.3 –고 보– (do and then realize)

This construction is similar to –(아/어) 보– 'try doing' (refer to 5.1.8) discussed previously. Unlike –(아/어) 보– which has more universal application, –고 보– is limited to talking about trying something 'first' or 'for the time being' and then seeing how things pan out from there:

공짜 술이니 우선 마시고 **보자**.
Since this is free drink, let's just try the stuff first.

여하튼 일단 아침부터 먹고 **봅시다**.
Anyway, let's just start by eating breakfast.

무슨 일인지 모르지만 먼저 설명부터 듣고 **보지요**.
I don't know what's up, but let's try listening to the explanation first.

–고 보– is often followed by a connective ending and then another clause. The most common endings are –니까 (refer to 6.1.6) or –니 (refer to 6.1.7), forming the construction –고 보니(까)–. The construction combines the sense of 'trying' conveyed by –고 보– and the sense of 'discovery' expressed by –니 to mean 'now that I've given . . . a go, I've found that . . .':

사정을 듣고 **보니** 불쌍하군요.
Now that I've heard the circumstances, I realize it is pitiful.

결혼하고 **보니** 생각했던 남편이 아니네요.
Now that I've gone and got married, my husband isn't the man I thought he was.

Although –고 보– most commonly occurs with processive verbs, it may also appear with descriptive verbs, but with a distinctly different meaning. With descriptive verbs, it indicates that the speaker, if only momentarily, considers the contents expressed by the verb as extremely important or as an expected or 'given' state of affairs. In these constructions, –고 보– is followed either by –(아/어)야 되/하– 'must/have to' (refer to 7.5.7.1) or, with a similar nuance, –ㄹ 일이– :

도서관은 조용하고 **봐**야 돼요. *A library has to be quiet.*

여자는 예쁘고 **볼**일이에요. *Women really ought to be pretty.*

5.3.4 –고 싶– (want to do)

Unlike other auxiliary verbs, 싶– is not used as a main verb and is fairly opaque in meaning in contemporary Korean. Its original meaning was 'to think to oneself' (refer to Kim 2010) and it is used in expressions of desire and inference.

The pattern –고 싶– expresses your want, wish or desire to do something. It can only be used in the first and second person (i.e., when talking about yourself and the person you are talking to):

한국에 가고 **싶어요**. *I want to go to Korea.*

어머니를 보고 **싶어요**.
I want to see my mother. (= I miss my mother).

저는 유명한 가수가 되고 **싶어요**.
I want to become a famous singer.

그 신발은 홈쇼핑에서 봤는데 꼭 갖고 **싶더라고요**.
I saw those shoes on home shopping and I really want to get them.

파티에 가고 **싶었는데** 아파서 못 갔어요.
I wanted to go to the party, but I couldn't because I was ill.

When talking about a third person (i.e., someone who is not yourself or the person you are talking to), 싶– is substituted by 싶어하–. This is part of a wider process by which descriptive verbs (싶– behaves as a descriptive verb) change into processive verbs when talking about the emotions or desires of others (refer to 4.4.3.2):

Talking about self or hearer	*Talking about other person*
편지를 쓰고 **싶어요**.	편지를 쓰고 **싶어해요**.
I/you/we want to write a letter.	*He/she/they want(s) to write a letter.*
한국에 가고 **싶어요**.	한국에 가고 **싶어해요**.
I/you/we would like to go to Korea.	*He/she/they would like to go to Korea*

In modifier constructions (refer to Chapter 8), –고 싶– sometimes appears in the contracted form –고픈 (rather than the full form –고 싶은 or –고 싶어하는), although this usage is not considered standard.

하고픈 말이 있습니다. *I have something I'd like to say.*

5.4 Auxiliary verbs with –(으)ㄹ까

These patterns use –(으)ㄹ까 as their base. As a sentence ending, –(으)ㄹ까 is used for tentative suggestions (similar to 'shall I/we . . .?') or conjectures (refer to 9.10). When it is followed by auxiliary verbs, it takes on a range of other meanings, typically involving conjecture or otherwise tentative future plans.

5.4.1 –(으)ㄹ까 보– (think it might)

This pattern follows –(으)ㄹ까 with the verb 보– 'look', 'see'. However, unlike in other support verb patterns using 보– (refer to 5.1.8, 5.2.1, 5.3.3), this particular pattern does not contain any sense of 'seeing', 'exploring' or 'trying'. Rather, it has two separate specific usages that we shall consider in turn.

Firstly, it is used when the speaker expresses a worry about a possible future negative turn of events. This may then be followed by a second clause that expresses what the speaker is doing in order to prepare for this possibility or simply by an expression of the worry itself. In many ways this pattern works similar to the English 'in case':

화요일에 눈이 올까 **봐** 걱정이에요.
I'm worried in case it snows on Tuesday.

비가 올까 **봐** 우산을 가지고 나왔어요.
I brought an umbrella in case it rains.

틀릴까 **봐** 아무 말도 안 했어요.
I didn't say anything in case I was wrong.

정거장을 놓칠까 **봐** 잠을 안 자요.
I never sleep [on the bus] in case I miss my stop.

Secondly, this same pattern is used when the speaker is talking about something that he/she is thinking about doing in the future. This typically translates as 'I think I will' and is similar in nuance and usage to –ㄹ까 하– discussed below.

대학교를 졸업하고 한국에 갈까 **봐요**.
I think I'll go to Korea after I graduate university.

내일 오래간만에 푹 쉴까 **봐요**.
Tomorrow, I think I'll take a long overdue rest.

5.4.2 –(으)ㄹ까 싶– (afraid it might)

This pattern combines –(으)ㄹ까 with the auxiliary verb 싶–, which may express desire or inference. In this pattern, it is used in the second meaning.

Firstly, the pattern is used to express conjecture usually with a negative nuance similar to the English 'I'm afraid . . .':

오후에 비가 올까 **싶어요**.
I'm afraid it might rain in the afternoon.

신발이 좀 클까 **싶어요**.
I'm afraid those shoes are going to be a bit too big.

Secondly, it is used when the speaker is reporting his or her own thoughts in an indirect, tentative or objective manner. In these cases, the verb must always be in the negative. This usage is essentially equivalent to that of –나/–(으)ㄴ가 싶– (refer to 5.5.2)

가장 필요한 것은 자신감이 아닐까 **싶어요**.
I think the thing we need the most would be confidence.

이것은 가족 단위로 봐도 좋은 영화가 아닐까 **싶습니다**.
I think this would be a good movie even for families.

혼자 고민하니까 머리가 아파서 글로 쓰면 조금 낫지 않을까 **싶어서** 글을 올립니다.
My head aches from worrying about this problem alone, so I am writing this thinking that by doing so may make things better.

Thirdly, this pattern can be used when the speaker is talking about something that he/she is thinking about doing in the future in a similar way to –ㄹ까 하– (or –ㄹ까 보–) described elsewhere in this section:

내일 그랜드 호텔 수영장에나 한번 가 볼까 **싶어요**.
I think I might go to the Grand Hotel swimming pool tomorrow.

그냥 다른 여자를 만날까 **싶어요**.
I think I might just meet another woman.

5.4.3 –(으)ㄹ까 하– (think of doing)

This pattern combines –(으)ㄹ까 with the auxiliary verb 하– 'do'. This 하– may then take a speech style ending to round off the sentence or be followed by another ending, such as a connective (refer to Chapter 7). The construction is most commonly used when the speaker is thinking over a proposed course of action and translates as '(I am) thinking of (doing so-and-so)':

테니스를 칠까 **해요**. *I'm thinking of playing tennis.*

유학 갈까 **했었는데** 생각을 바꿨어요.
I had been thinking of going overseas to study, but I changed my mind.

On occasions, 하– may be replaced with verbs of thinking such as 생각하– 'think', 망설이– 'hesitate', 걱정하– 'worry', 고민하– 'agonize over':

콘택트렌즈는 불편해서 라식 수술을 받을까 **생각하고 있어요**.
Because contact lenses are uncomfortable, I am thinking of having laser eye surgery.

무슨 옷을 골라 입을까 **망설이고 있어요**.
He/she is hesitating over which clothes to put on.

When two different courses of action are being considered, these are listed in succession and –(으)ㄹ까 is repeated:

하숙집에 갈까 원룸을 얻을까 생각중입니다/**걱정입니다**.
I'm thinking/worrying about whether to go to a homestay or get a studio flat.

When the speaker is thinking about whether he/she should carry out the proposed course of action or not, the negative verb 말– 'desist' (refer to 4.2.3) is used as the second verb, creating the construction–(으)ㄹ까 말까 (하–) :

학교에 갈까 말까 **생각 중이에요**.
I'm debating whether or not to go to school.

취직을 할까 말까 **고민하고 있어요**.
I'm agonizing over whether or not to get employed.

In addition to being used when the speaker is talking about plans of action that he/she is considering, this pattern can also be applied when the speaker is reporting conjectures that he/she has made about something that happened in the past:

가끔씩 결혼 안 했더라면 어땠을까 **생각해 봐요**.
I sometimes think about what it would have been like if I hadn't got married.

아들을 잃은 부모의 마음이 얼마나 아팠을까 **생각했어요**.
I thought about how much pain the parents who lost their son must have suffered.

5.5 Auxiliary verbs with –나/–(으)ㄴ가

This set of constructions build on the verb ending –나/–(으)ㄴ가 (refer to 9.3). –(으)ㄴ가 is used for present tense descriptive verbs and the copula (and, by extension with the future –ㄹ 거, as this ends with the copula); –나 is used elsewhere (including for descriptive verbs and the copula in past tense or with the future form –겠–).

In its original use, –나/–(으)ㄴ가 is applied for constructing tentative questions. When it is followed by an auxiliary verb, patterns that express conjecture are created.

5.5.1 –나/–(으)ㄴ가 보– (look like)

This pattern follows –나/–(으)ㄴ가 with the verb 보– 'look' or 'see'. The one-shape –나 is used for processive verbs, whereas the two-shape –(으)ㄴ가 occurs with descriptive verbs.

The construction conveys a conjecture made on the back of what the speaker has seen (or heard, or perceived in any other way), typically translating as 'it looks like'.

밖에 비가 많이 오나 **봐요**.	*It looks like it's raining a lot outside.*
유미는 다리가 아픈가 **봐요**.	*Yumi seems to have hurt her leg.*
바보인가 **봐요**.	*He/she seems to be a fool.*
선생님은 오늘 안 오셨나 **봐요**.	*It looks like teacher hasn't come today.*

As this construction involves a conjecture made on the back of sensory evidence, it is not usually used with first-person subjects. However, when the speaker is talking about him/herself as if from an external viewpoint, you may hear sentences such as the following:

제가 너무 기대를 했나 **봐요**.	*It looks like I expected too much.*
내가 머리가 좋은가 **봐요**.	*It looks like I am really clever.*

5.5.2 –나/–(으)ㄴ가 싶– (think it might)

The principal usage of this pattern occurs when the speaker is reporting his or her own thoughts in an indirect, tentative or objective manner. In these cases, the verb must always be in the negative. This usage is essentially equivalent to –(으)ㄹ까 싶– (refer to 5.4.2)

그냥 삼겹살 하셔도 상관없지 않나 **싶어요**.
I don't think it will matter even if you just cook samgyŏpsal.

사실대로 말하는 것은 거짓말을 하는 것보다는 좋지 않나 **싶더라고요**.
I think it would be better to speak honestly rather than tell a lie.

설득력이 부족하지 않나 **<u>싶습니다</u>**.
I think it might be lacking in conviction.

In addition, the pattern can be used when the speaker reminisces about the past, typically when reporting regret.

왜 그렇게 고민했나 **<u>싶더라고요</u>**. *I wonder now why I worried so much.*

내가 왜 안 갔나 **<u>싶더라고요</u>**. *I wonder why I didn't go.*

5.6 Auxiliary verbs with –게

5.6.1 –게 되– (turn out so that)

This expression combines the adverbative form –게 (refer to 11.2.1.2) with the auxiliary verb 되–, meaning 'become' or 'come about'. This pattern is used to express a final result that comes about from a change in state, opinion or plan that often goes contrary to the speaker's original expectations or is outside of the speaker's control. This commonly translates into English as 'it turned out that', 'things worked out in such a way that' or 'I came to understand/realize/believe/etc. that':

재미있게 **<u>됐어요</u>**.
It turned out to be interesting.

벌써 나뭇잎이 누렇게 **<u>됐어요</u>**.
The tree leaves have already turned yellow.

못 가게 **<u>됐어요</u>**.
It's turned out that I can't go.

그 사람의 입장을 이해하게 **<u>됐어요</u>**.
I have to understand that person's position.

내일부터 도서관에서 일하게 **<u>됐어요</u>**.
I'm to begin working at the library tomorrow.

회사 일로 한국에 오게 **<u>됐어요</u>**.
I have to come to Korea on company business.

Since –게 되– at times depicts that the way things turned out was outside the speaker's control, the pattern takes on certain politeness functions. Firstly, it can be used when the speaker wants to make clear that the action he/she took was unavoidable. As in the following examples, this is a particularly useful strategy when apologizing:

자꾸 전화 드리게 **돼서** 죄송합니다.
I would like to apologize for having to phone you so often.

오늘 약속을 어기게 **된** 것 심히 죄송합니다.
I am sorry for breaking off our engagement today.

In addition, the speaker may use this pattern to sound humble. By expressing the result as something outside of his/her control, he/she cannot be taken to be bragging or taking credit for it:

과장으로 승진하게 **됐어요**.
It turns out that I've been promoted to department head.

국가 대표팀 선수로 뽑히게 **됐어요**.
I have been chosen for the national [sports] team.

5.6.2 –게 보이– (seem)

Featuring the support verb 보이– 'be visible, show', this pattern is essentially identical in meaning to the –아/어 보이– pattern described previously in this chapter (refer to 5.1.9). Like –아/어 보이–, –게 보이– is used solely with descriptive verbs to express an inference or prediction based on sensory evidence – almost always visual evidence.

카레라이스가 맛있게 **보여요**.
The curry-rice looks delicious.

미어캣 눈빛이 너무 슬프게 **보여요**.
Meerkats' eyes look so sad.

운명이 너무 안타깝게 **보여요**.
His/her fate seems to be pitiful.

입어 보니까 예쁘고 날씬하게 **보여요**.
Trying it on, it looks so pretty and slim.

5.7 Auxiliary verb with –(아/어)야

5.7.1 *–(아/어)야 되–/하– (must, have to)*

This pattern combines the –(아/어)야 (refer to 7.5.7) meaning 'only if' with the auxiliary verb 되– 'becomes' or 하– 'does'. This expresses obligation and most typically translates into English as 'have to' or 'must'. This pattern is explained in more detail in Chapter 7 (refer to 7.5.7.1).

Chapter 6

Honorifics

Overview

One of the most salient features of the Korean language is the intricate system of honorifics. This system is so pervasive that it is impossible to speak a single sentence without calculating your relative social status and/or degree of familiarity with the person/people you are talking to (and talking about!) and deciding on the appropriate 'level' of honorification.

To be sure, speakers of all languages change the way they speak depending on their relationship with the hearer (and on the formality of the setting). In English, for example, although an immigration officer may ask you the formal 'What is the purpose of your visit?', it would sound strange to hear friends talking to each other in this way when they bump into each other in the supermarket! Similarly, although you might address your teacher or a customer as 'Sir', it would sound sarcastic to talk to your friend in this way.

However, the systematic way in which the grammar of each and every sentence in Korean can be changed to reflect social relationships goes far beyond anything found in European languages. When using this system, you always have to make two separate calculations:

1 *You have to calculate your relationship with the person you are talking to.* Verbs have different endings attached to them determined by the social relationship between the speakers; this is called ***hearer honorifics*** (or ***speech styles***) and is dealt with in section 6.1.

2 *You have to calculate your relationship with the person you are talking* ***about.***
Verbs and other parts of speech add endings or apply special lexical forms to show respect to the person being referred to (often the same person as the person you are talking to, but by no means always). These forms are never used by the speaker to refer to himself or herself. These are called ***referent honorifics*** and are covered in section 6.2

Finally, section 6.3 covers the use of terms of address, which is intrinsically linked to the use of honorifics.

6.1 Speech styles (hearer honorifics)

Speech styles are expressed through a system of verb endings that are attached to every single sentence-final verb. Most researchers recognize six different styles, as summarized in the table below. The English names shown here for the styles are those that are most commonly used in linguistics. However, the descriptions contained in them have limitations; for instance the 'polite' style is only actually 'polite' when used in an appropriate context.

English name of style	*Korean name*	*Statement*	*Question*	*Command*	*Proposal*
'formal' style	합쇼체	-(스)ㅂ니다	-(스)ㅂ니까	-(으)십시오	-(으)십시다
'polite' style	해요체	-아/어/요			
'semiformal' style	하오체	-오/소		-오	-ㅂ시다
'familiar' style	하게체	-네	-나/-는가	-게	-세
'intimate' style'	해체	-아/어			
'plain' style	해라체	-다	-(느)냐	-(어)라/-(으)라	-자

All of these speech styles have quite distinct patterns of use will be described in detail below. However, for general purposes, the styles can be divided into three groups:

1 The 'formal' and the 'polite' are 'honorific styles' that can be used for addressing superiors and/or strangers/non-intimates. These form a register of language known in layman terms as 존댓말 'respect speech'.
2 The 'semiformal' and the 'familiar' are 'authoritative styles' that can be used by older adults towards younger adults or their peers. These can sound rather power-laden in modern Korean – the use of both these styles is on the wane.
3 The 'intimate' and the 'plain' are 'non-honorific styles' that can be used for addressing intimates of similar or inferior age and/or rank. These form a register of language commonly known as 반말 'half speech'.

Given the restricted usage of the second group, the use of hearer honorifics in contemporary Korean relies primarily on the distinction between 존댓말 'respect speech' and 반말 'half speech'. Not only do these two registers of language use distinctive verb endings, recent research shows that they are also distinct at the non-verbal level. When speakers are using 존댓말 'respect speech' towards status superiors they tend to speak slower, quieter and with lower pitch (refer to Brown et al. 2014). They also use smaller and fewer frequency gestures, stiffer postures and refrain from casual non-verbal behaviour (refer to Brown & Winter 2019).

6.1.1 The polite style

The 'polite' represents the most universal of the Korean speech styles in that it can be used both with superiors and with those of similar or younger age (when intimacy is low). This speech style can be heard in a wide range of daily interactions: storekeepers reciprocate it with customers, strangers use it on the street when asking for and giving directions and non-intimate casual acquaintances reciprocate it with each other. However, it can sound too casual if repeatedly used either in formal settings or in interactions with notable status superiors. On such occasions, use of the 'formal' (refer to 6.1.2) may be preferred. In addition, it may sound too distant for addressing close long-term friends and is over polite for addressing children – here, the 'intimate' style would be more appropriate (refer to 6.1.3).

The polite style comprises the infinitive form of the verb (refer to 4.1.6) followed by –요. The ending is the same regardless of whether you are making a statement, asking a question, making a command or making a proposal. The meaning will be determined both by the speaker's intonation and by the context.

	Base	*Infinitive*	*'Polite'*
consonant base	받– *receive*	받아	받아요
vowel base	가– *go*	가	가요

Although the above can be used as imperatives, orders in the polite style most typically occur with the addition of the subject honorific marker –(으)시– (refer to 6.2.1.1). When –(으)시– combines with the polite style, the resultant form is –(으)세요:

여기 앉**으세요**. *Take a seat here, please.*

잠시만 기다리**세요**. *Wait a moment, please.*

When the polite style attaches after the past tense –았/었– (refer 4.3.1.1) or the future –겠 (refer to 4.3.2.1), it always takes the form 어요:

어떻게 하면 좋을지 몰랐**어요**. *I didn't know what I should do.*

그 건 잘 모르겠**어요**. *I wouldn't really know that.*

The polite style can also occur after other sentence endings (refer to Chapter 9), including –지 (refer to 9.18) and –네 (refer to 9.5). Here, the form is simply –요:

오늘 날씨가 정말 춥네**요**. *Boy, the weather is cold today!*

우리 강아지 너무 귀엽지**요**? *Our puppy is so cute, isn't it?*

Finally, although the 'polite' style is typically thought of as a verb ending, the –요 ending of this style may also appear as a polite particle after nouns or other parts of speech. This first of all occurs when the speaker gives a one-word utterance. In these cases, without the addition of –요, such utterances would generally be taken as non-honorific speech. When the word in question ends in a consonant, the form may be pronounced (and written) as –이요 (as in the final example).

왜**요**?	*Why?*
어디**요**?	*Where?*
누구**요**?	*Who?*
저**요**.	*Me.*
커피**요**.	*Coffee.*
비빔밥**이요**.	*Pibimbap.*

In honorific speech, you may also hear –요 being attached in mid-sentence after the topic marker –는 (refer to 3.3.2.1) or after connective endings, especially –고 (refer to 7.3.1) and –는데 (refer to 7.3.12). This appears to be more common in the speech of females and, when overused, can sound somewhat childish.

제 생각에는**요** 그 말은 핑계예요.
In my opinion, that's an excuse.

현재 부산이고**요** 고향은 안동이에요.
Now I'm in Busan and my home town is Andong.

친구가 왔는데**요** 같이 가도 될까요?
My friend has come, can we go together?

그런데**요**, 그 사람은**요** 학생 같아요.
But, that guy seems to be a student.

6.1.2 The formal style

The 'formal' style is used on its own in settings that demand a high level of formality such as job interviews, formal business meetings, formal speeches and TV news. In such settings, use of the 'polite' would sound too informal.

Otherwise, when speaking honorifically, speakers often mix the 'formal' style with the 'polite' style. In such cases, the mixture of 'formal' versus 'polite' will depend both on the level of formality and on the age-rank relationship between the speakers. In other words, speakers will tend to mix in a higher frequency of the 'formal' when speaking to a status superior and/or in a structured setting. In addition, the 'formal' is often used in first meetings before the ice has been broken and conversation has moved onto more casual topics. In such cases, repeated use of the 'polite' can sound too casual. On the other hand, when talking casually to a non-intimate who is of similar or younger age, the 'formal' will appear at a lower frequency or even not at all. The 'formal' is also thought to sound masculine (whereas repeated use of the 'polite' sounds feminine). In addition to the influence of age-rank and formality, the 'formal' style also tends to occur in the following circumstances:

Firstly, the 'formal' occurs in many set expressions. With these expressions, use of the 'polite' often runs the risk of sounding too informal:

감사**합니다**/고맙**습니다**	*Thank you*
죄송**합니다**	*Sorry*
만나서 반갑**습니다**	*Nice to meet you*
처음 뵙겠**습니다**	*How do you do? (expression used at first meeting)*
잘 먹었**습니다**	*I ate well (expression of thanks used after a meal)*

Secondly, particularly in semi-structured discussions (such as academic debate or TV talk shows), the 'formal' tends to occur with strong expressions of factual information that may be new to the hearer (refer to Strauss & Eun 2005; Brown 2015). The polite, on the other hand, tends to accompany expressions of conjecture or common sense, or when the speaker is trying to 'connect' with the audience. One reason why the polite is used for the latter functions is that these require the use of certain sentence endings that are incompatible with the formal style such as –네 (refer to 9.5) or –지 (refer to 9.18).

To make statements in the formal style, you add the ending –ㅂ니다/습니다 (pronounced [ㅁ니다], [슴니다]) to the base of the verb, –ㅂ니다 when the base ends in a vowel and –습니다 when it ends in a consonant. Although –습니다 is a fixed form in the contemporary language, it is historically formed from a fusion of four elements: the object honorific marker – *sop* – (refer to 6.2.2), the present tense marker – *no* –, the hearer honorific –이, and the statement ending –다 (refer to 6.1.4).

As mentioned previously (refer to 4.1.8), whereas with –ㅂ니다 irregular verbs behave according to as they would with any other two-shape ending, with –습니다 irregular verbs behave as they more generally would with one-shape endings. –ㅂ니다/습니다 may also attach after the honorific marker –시– (refer to 6.2.1.1), the past tense –았/었– (refer to 4.3.1.1), the future –겠– (refer to 4.3.2.1) and also the future –ㄹ 거 (refer to 4.3.2.2):

	Consonant base	*Vowel base*
Present tense	받습니다 *receive*	갑니다 *go*
–시–	받으십니다	가십니다
–았/었–	받았습니다	갔습니다
–겠–	받겠습니다	가겠습니다
–ㄹ 거	받을 겁니다	갈 겁니다

'Formal' style questions are made by replacing the final –다 of the formal statement with –까, in other words by adding an ending that has the shape –습니까 (pronounced [–슴니까]) after consonants and the shape –ㅂ니까 (pronounced [–ㅁ니까]) after vowels as follows:

Consonant base	*Vowel base*
받습니까? *receive*	갑니까? *go*

'Formal' style commands are made by adding the ending –읍시오 to consonant bases and –ㅂ시오 to vowel bases. Note, however, that it is practically unheard of to use this ending without the subject honorific –(으)시– (refer to 4.4.1.1) preceding it – thus making the combined ending –(으)십시오:

Consonant base	*Vowel base*
받으십시오 *receive*	가십시오 *go*

For verbs that have a special subject honorific form (refer to 4.4.1.2) that includes –시– in their base, –(으)ㅂ시오 is added after–시– :

계십시오 *stay!* 주무십시오 *sleep!* 잡수십시오 *eat!*

'Formal' style proposals ('let's . . .') are made by adding the ending –읍시다 to consonant bases and –ㅂ시다 to vowel bases. It is very often used with the subject honorific –(으)시– (refer to 6.2.1.1) preceding it – thus making the combined ending –(으)십시다. Irregular verbs behave according to the normal patterns associated with the addition of two-shape endings (refer to 4.1.8).

Consonant base		*Vowel base*	
받읍시다/받으십시다	*receive*	갑시다/가십시다	*go*

6.1.3 *The intimate style –* Panmal *style*

The 'intimate' style – often referred to as 반말 *panmal* (literally, half-speech) is used as the principal non-honorific style when addressing intimates of similar or younger age. It can also be used by adults towards children (regardless of intimacy) and, in some situations, when addressing a non-intimate adult of notably younger age or notably lower rank. Although this style is frequently used in contemporary Korean, a high degree of caution is required. When misused towards a stranger, non-intimate or someone of higher age or status, it can signal a high degree of disrespect. The 'intimate' style is frequently mixed in speech with the plain style, as discussed below (refer to 6.1.4).

To form the 'intimate' style, simply remove the final –요 ending from the 'polite' style (refer to 6.1.1) (see below for a few exceptions). In the present tense, this means that the 'intimate' style is the same form as the infinitive (refer to 4.1.6). Given that the 'polite' and the 'intimate' are, respectively, the most commonly occurring 'honorific' and 'non-honorific' styles, it is this addition or omission of –요 that most commonly marks the boundary between 존댓말 'respect speech' and 반말 'half speech' and to which Korean speakers are extremely sensitive. Here is a list of examples showing this alternation from the 'polite' to the 'intimate':

	'Polite'	'Intimate'	
consonant base	받아요	받아	*receive*
vowel base	가요	가	*go*

The rule of just subtracting –요 from the 'polite' style to form the 'intimate' also works with the past tense –았/었– (refer to 4.3.1.1) and the future –겠– (refer to 4.3.2.1):

	'Polite'	'Intimate'	
–았/었–	받았어요	받았어	*receive*
–겠–	받겠어요	받겠어	

However, note that the 'intimate' form is slightly different from the 'polite minus –요' format in the following patterns:

1. After the referent honorific –(으)시– (refer to 6.2.1.1):

'Polite'	'Intimate'
받으세요	받으**셔** *receive*

2. After the copula –이 (and the negative copula 아니–) (refer to 4.1.4):

   –이에요   –이**야**

   아니에요   –아니**야**

3. With future expressions with –ㄹ 거– (refer to 4.3.2.2)

   받을 거예요   받을 거**야**

With sentence endings (refer to Chapter 9) including –지 (refer to 9.18) and 네 (refer to 9.5), the 'polite minus –요' rule works, with the result that nothing is added at all:

이 음악을 들어 봤지?
You've heard this music, haven't you?

어라! 홈쇼핑이 TV보다 재미있네!
Boy, home shopping sure is more interesting than TV!

6.1.4 *The plain style*

The plain style has two distinct usages. Firstly, it is used when writing to a general audience (newspapers, textbooks, written announcements, etc.), or when there is no specific individual addressee (diary, personal essay, etc.). In such cases, it works as a matter-of-fact and neutral style. Secondly, it is used in 'non-honorific' speech when addressing intimates of similar or younger age, usually mixed with the 'intimate' style.

Although the 'intimate' and the 'plain' are often mixed in colloquial speech, their usages are not identical. Firstly, the 'plain' style is often felt to be 'lower' than the 'intimate' particularly in questions and orders. Thus, repeated use of the 'plain' tends to be more appropriate in cases where the speaker is considerably older than the hearer (such as a father addressing his son). The 'plain' may also be applied when the speaker intentionally wants his/her speech to sound 'colder'. For instance, in Korean TV dramas you may hear Korean parents using this form when they disapprove of their children's behaviour.

Secondly, the statement form of the 'plain' style (–다) tends to occur with information that the speaker has recently and suddenly realized, particularly when this information is mostly relevant to the hearer. Consider the following examples:

1. Two friends are preparing to go swimming in the sea. The friend who tests the temperature of the water first may shout the following exclamation to the other friend thus not only expressing his/her own surprise, but also warning the other friend that the water is freezing cold!

   차갑**다**! *It's cold!*

2. Two friends are waiting for a bus that is taking ages to come. When one friend finally sees the bus arriving, he/she may exclaim as follows:

   버스 온**다**! *The bus is coming!*

3. Two friends are looking for a wallet that one of the friends has lost. When one friend finally finds the wallet, he/she may exclaim as follows:

   찾았**다**! *I've found it!*

Thirdly, the statement form of the 'plain' style (–다) may occur in more general exclamations, even when what is being exclaimed about is not so noteworthy to the hearer. Indeed, these exclamations with –다 often have the status of soliloquy; in other words, they are uttered as if the speaker is speaking to him/herself. As such utterances are not aimed directly at the hearer, you may hear them even in a situation where the speaker is talking predominantly in honorific speech styles!

와! 찌개가 너무 맛있**다**!	*Wow, the stew tastes great!*
경치가 죽인**다**!	*This is killer [=great] scenery!*
야, 기분 좋**다**!	*Ah! I feel good!*

Fourthly, the 'plain' style is often used when the speaker is boasting. Such utterances tend to be accompanied by a sing-song intonation

나 유럽에 간**다**!	*I'm going to Europe!*
그 남자한테 선물을 받았**다**!	*I got a present from that guy!*
나 다음달에 결혼한**다**!	*I'm getting married next month.*

Fifth and finally, the plain style often occurs when the speaker is delivering a common saying or quotation:

아는 게 힘이**다**.	*Knowledge is power.*
작은 고추가 맵**다**.	*Small peppers are hot. (= Small people are tough).*
인생은 짧고 예술은 길**다**.	*Art is long, life is short.*

As well as being an important style to learn in its own right, the 'plain' is also important because it forms the basis for quotations or 'reported speech' (refer to Chapter 10).

The plain style is technically the most difficult style to form as there are different endings for statements, questions, proposals and commands and also separate forms for descriptive and processive verbs:

Plain style statements

Statements in the 'plain style' have different endings depending on whether the verb is descriptive or processive. For descriptive verbs, add –다 to the base as in the examples below. This creates a form that is identical to the dictionary form (refer to 4.1.7).

	Base	*'Plain' statement*
consonant base	작– *be small*	작다
vowel base	싸– *be cheap*	싸다

As for processive verbs, these are made into 'plain' style statements by an ending which has the shape –ㄴ다 when attached to vowel bases and –는다 when attached to consonant bases:

	Base	*'Plain' statement*
consonant base	받– *receive*	받는다
vowel base	가– *go*	간다

With the past tense –았/었– (refer to 4.3.1.1) and the future –겠– (refer to 4.3.2.1), simply –다 is added to all verbs irrespective of whether they are descriptive or processive:

	Descriptive	*Processive*
–았/었–	작았다	받았다
–겠–	싸겠다	받겠다

However, with the honorific –(으)시– (refer to 6.2.1.1), whereas –다 is used with descriptive verbs, –ㄴ다 is used with processive verbs:

Descriptive		*Processive*	
작으시다	small	받으신다	receive
빠르시다	fast	부르신다	call, sing

The Plain Style statement form of the copula (refer to 4.1.4) is –이다. The past form (refer to 4.3.1.1) is –이었다 and the future with –겠– is –이겠다 (refer to 4.3.2.1). The negative form is 아니다.

결혼한 부부에게 임신은 커다란 기쁨이<u>**다**</u>.
Pregnancy is a great joy to married couples.

난 이제 부자<u>**다**</u>.
I am a rich man now.

어제는 내 여자 친구 생일이었<u>**다**</u>.
Yesterday was my girlfriend's birthday.

마음이 넓고 참 좋은 사람이겠<u>**다**</u>.
He/she's a broad-minded warm person.

사람은 짐승이 아니<u>**다**</u>.
People are not animals.

As noted previously (refer to 4.1.1), there are a small number of verbs that may be either processive or descriptive. With these verbs, particular care is needed when applying the plain style, as your choice of the descriptive ending –다 or the processive ending –ㄴ다/– 는다 will affect the way the sentence is interpreted.

Plain style questions

There are three ways to form questions in the plain style: (1) adding –(으)냐 or –느냐 and (2) adding –니 and (3) adding –(으)ㄴ가/–는가

(a) –(으)냐 or –느냐

The choice between –(으)냐 and –느냐 depends on whether the verb is descriptive or processive. Descriptive verbs take the two-shape ending –(으)냐, with –으냐 following a consonant and –냐 following a vowel. However, note that –(으)냐 typically shortens to –냐 in colloquial speech

	Base	*'Plain' question*	
		Full	*Contracted*
consonant base	작– *be small*	작으냐	작냐
vowel base	싸– *be cheap*	싸냐	(same)

Processive verbs originally use the one-shape ending –느냐. This ending is however frequently shortened simply to –냐 in colloquial speech.

	Base	'Plain' question	
		Full	Contracted
consonant base	받– *receive*	받느냐	받냐
vowel base	가– *go*	가느냐	가냐

With the past tense –았/었– (refer to 4.3.1.1) and the future –겠– (refer to 4.3.2.1), –느냐 is attached to ALL verbs. However, this is also frequently abbreviated to –냐 in colloquial language.

		Processive	Descriptive
–았/었–	Full form	받았느냐	작았느냐
	Abbreviated	받았냐	작았냐
–겠–	Full form	받겠느냐	작겠느냐
	Abbreviated	받겠냐	작겠냐

The copula form is –이냐 and 아니냐 in the negative.

This plain style ending is widely used in colloquial speech (at least in the contracted variants given above), but sounds rather condescending and argumentative. It is most commonly used when the speaker is higher in status or age than the hearer and is sometimes used when the speaker is negatively predisposed in some way towards the information being asked for, as in the following examples (refer to Lee 1991).

너 지금 뭐 하**냐**? *What on earth are you doing now?*

숙제 다 했**냐**? *Have you done all your homework?*

돈 갚으러 왔**냐**? *Have you come to pay the money back?*

(b) –니

–니 is also a form frequently heard in colloquial speech. Although it does not share the occasional negative predisposition of –느냐/–(으)냐,

its usage presupposes that the interlocutors are either highly intimate or that the speaker is older than the hearer. Indeed, this form is perhaps most commonly heard being used by adults addressing children.

	Base	*'Plain' question*
consonant base	받– *receive*	받니?
vowel base	가– *go*	가니?

The same –니 form may also attach after the honorific marker –(으)시– (refer to 6.2.1.1), past tense –았/었– (refer to 4.3.1.1), future with –겠– (refer to 4.3.2.1) and future with –ㄹ 거– (refer to 4.3.2.2). The copula form is –이니 and 아니니 in the negative.

Although the –느냐/–(으)냐 and –니 endings are used in colloquial speech, in writing these are replaced by the familiar style question ending –(으)ㄴ가/–는가 (refer to 6.1.5).

Plain style proposals

Plain style proposals are formed by adding the one-shape ending –자. This ending is very common in colloquial speech; indeed, it tends to accompany all non-honorific proposals.

	Base	*'Plain' proposal*
consonant base	받– *receive*	받자
vowel base	가– *go*	가자

Plain style commands

Plain style commands have three possible forms: (1) –(으)라, (2) –아/어라 and (3) –거/너라.

(a) –(으)라

This is the original form of the 'plain' style command, but is rarely used in spoken language in contemporary Korean. –(으)라 works as a two-shape ending with –으라 attaching after a consonant and –라 after a vowel.

	Base	*'Plain' command*
consonant base	받– *receive*	받으라
vowel base	가– *go*	가라

Negative commands with –지 말– are rendered as –지 말라 (although this is often pronounced as –지 마라):

보지 말라 *don't look*

In contemporary Korean, the –(으)라 form is most frequently seen in written rather than spoken language. For example, in a textbook or exam you might see an instruction such as the following:

다음 글을 우리말로 번역하**라**.
Translate the following passage into 'our language' (i.e., Korean).

Or on a poster at an anti-American rally, you may see something like this:

미군을 추방하**라**! *Throw out the American Army!*

When –(으)라 does occur in speech, it is often with expressions of generic truths:

항상 진리를 찾**으라**. *Always seek the truth!*

그대 앞날에 축복이 있**으라**. *Blessings are ahead of you!*

Note that it is –(으)라 rather than –아/어라 that is used to form commands in indirect quotations in spoken as well as written language (refer to Chapter 10).

(b) –아/어라

In spoken language, instead of the –(으)라 form, you will more often hear the –라 ending attached to the infinitive form of the verb (refer to 4.1.6) to form –아/어라:

	Base	*'Plain' command*
consonant base	받– *receive*	받아라
vowel base	가– *go*	가라

Negative commands with –지 말 – are rendered as –지 말아라. This, in turn, is frequently abbreviated to –지 마라:

Full form	*Abbreviated*	
보지 말아라	보지 마라	*Don't look*

Contrary to previous observations that commands are restricted in their appearance with descriptive verbs (refer to 4.1.1), note that –아/어라 may occasionally occur with descriptive verbs that have no behavioural qualities. However, in these cases –아/어라 is not functioning as a command but as an exclamatory ending. Exclamations appearing with –아/어라 tend to be strong in nature.

아이구! 예뻐**라**! *My, my! How pretty!*

와! 너무 맛있**어라**! *Wow! Boy, this tastes good!*

(c) –거/너라

The verbs 가– 'go' and 오– 'come' have irregular variants in plain style commands that may be used instead of the regular –아/어라. These endings are –거라 and –너라 respectively:

Base	*Irregular*	*Regular*
가– *go*	가거라	가라
오– *come*	오너라	와라

These forms are more frequently used in colloquial language and by older speakers. You may hear some speakers attach –거라 to other verbs beyond 가– 'go' (e.g. 자거라 'sleep', 먹거라 'eat', 앉거라 'sit', 있거라 'stay'), although this is considered nonstandard.

6.1.5 Familiar style

The familiar style is formed by adding –네 for statements, –게 for commands, –세 for proposals, and –(으)ㄴ가/–는가 for questions.

The statement form –네, the command form –게 and the proposal form work –세 all work as one-shape endings:

이 일은 **자네**가 하**게**. *You take this job.*

어제 **자네** 아버님을 만났**네**. *I met your father yesterday.*

어서 빨리 가**세**. *Let's go quickly.*

–네, –게 and –세 are not widely used in contemporary South Korea, although you may occasionally hear them being used by older speakers. These forms are most typically used by older male speakers to non-reciprocally address younger male adults (although they may also occasionally appear in interactions featuring female speakers, and/or in reciprocal contexts). In these usages, they may occur with the second-person pronoun 자네 'you' (refer to 2.3.1.2), as in the examples above. Using these forms typically index that the speaker is in a position of authority, but also that he/she is treating the younger party with a degree of reserve or respect. It tends to sound less condescending than non-reciprocal use of intimate or plain styles.

The question form –(으)ㄴ가/–는가 enjoys more widespread usage, since it is often used in formal writing. Take the following magazine headlines, for instance:

'아이폰 XS·XR' 너무 비**싼가**?
Is the I-Phone XS·XR too expensive?

나는 어디에서, 어떻게 왔**는가**?
Where did I come from and how?

The two-shape –(으)ㄴ가 is used for descriptive verbs:

	Base	*'Plain' question*
consonant base	작– *be small*	작은가?
vowel base	싸– *be cheap*	싼가?

The one-shape –는가 is used for processive verbs, and also for past tense forms of all verbs:

	Base	*'Plain' question*
consonant base	받– *receive*	받는가?
vowel base	가– *go*	가는가?

The copula form is –인가 and 아닌가 in the negative.

6.1.6 *Semi-formal style*

Statements in the semi-formal style is formed by adding -오 when the base has no final consonant and -소 in cases where it does. -소 is also used after the past tense –았/었– (refer to 4.3.1.1) and the future –겠– (refer to 4.3.2.1):

여기서 뭐하**오**?	*What are you doing here?*
혹시 밥 먹**소**?	*Are you eating, by any chance?*
날 두고 어딜 갔**소**?	*Where did you go without me?*
당신은 안 가겠**소**?	*Aren't you going?*

Commands are formed with –(으)시오:

그만 쉬도록 하**시오**	*Take a break.*

Like the 'familiar' style, the 'semi-formal' style can be used by older adults towards those of equal or lower status. However, the 'semi-formal' involves a higher degree of reserve than the 'familiar'. Traditionally, this style was used by a husband towards his wife in combination with the pronoun 당신 'you' (refer to 2.3.1.2). However, this kind of usage has declined in modern South Korea and only a minority of the population seem to have retained this style.

6.2 Referent honorifics

The previous section discussed the use of speech styles – forms that are used to express your social relationship with the people you are talking TO. This section now looks at referent honorifics, which mark the relationship with the people you are talking ABOUT, in other words, who appear in the sentence either as the grammatical subject or the grammatical object. The person you are talking ABOUT is sometimes the same as the person you are talking TO as in the examples below:

선생님, 어디 가**십니까**?	*Esteemed teacher, where are you going?*
손님, 여기 앉**으십시오**.	*Esteemed customer, please take a seat here.*

In the above, the teacher and the customer are both the (implied) grammatical subjects of the sentences. Thus, the speaker combines use of the 'formal' speech style (refer to 6.1.2) with the referent honorific –(으)시 – (refer to 6.2.1.1) to form –(으)십니까? and –(으)십시오 respectively. This combination of endings shows respect to the teacher and the customer respectively both as the person being talked TO and the person being talked ABOUT.

However, the person being talked ABOUT is, of course, often totally different from the person being talked TO:

> 동생, 할아버지**께서** 오**신다.**
> *Younger brother, esteemed grandfather is coming.*

In the above, the person being talked ABOUT is grandfather, who is shown respect through the use of the referent honorific –(으)시– and the case marker 께서 (refer to 6.2.1.3). However, since the hearer is 'younger brother', the speaker uses the non-honorific 'plain' speech style (refer to 6.1.4).

The current section looks at forms that are used to show respect towards someone appearing as the subject of the sentence (refer to 6.2.1) and as the object (refer to 6.2.2) and then looks at honorific nouns (refer to 6.2.3). In the final subsection, we look at how the different parts of the Korean honorifics system fit together (refer to 6.2.4).

6.2.1 Subject honorifics

Subject honorifics express deference towards the grammatical subject of the sentence. The most common way to do this is to add the 'subject honorific marker' –(으)시– to the verb base. In addition to this, there are a few lexical substitutions that will be explained below.

6.2.1.1 The subject honorific marker –(으)시–

Most verbs can be made 'honorific' and express respect to the person appearing as the grammatical subject of the sentence simply by adding the two-shape ending –(으)시– to the verb base. This creates a 'honorific base':

	Base	*Honorific base*
consonant base	받– *receive*	받으시–
vowel base	가– *go*	가시–

To this honorific base, a speech style and other endings can be added. As in the second line, the combination of the subject honorific marker and the polite speech style is –(으)세요 (although it is occasionally written and pronounced as –(으)셔요).

가십니다	*go (subject honorific; "formal" style)*
가세요 (←가셔요)	*go (subject honorific; "polite" style)*
가셔	*go (subject honorific; "intimate" style)*
가신다	*go (subject honorific; "plain" style)*

–(으)시– should be used under the following circumstances. First, it should be included when you are referring to a third person who is older than you or superior to you in social standing, particularly teachers, professors, superiors at work, parents and grandparents. Compare its inclusion in the first example when referring to 'grandfather' and its absence in the second example to 'younger sibling':

할아버지는 부지런하**세요**.	*Grandfather is industrious.*
동생이 부지런해요.	*Younger sibling is industrious.*

Secondly, it should be used when asking a question to someone of superior social standing, an adult stranger or a non-intimate (unless you know they are considerably younger than you) when the question is inquiring about the actions, thoughts, etc. of the hearer ('what are you doing?', 'what do you think?', etc.):

선생님, 어디 가**세요**?	*Teacher, where are you going?*
할아버지, 어떻게 생각하**세요**?	*Grandfather, what do you think?*

Thirdly, it should be used in commands. Here, use of –(으)시– is particularly common and may appear even when there is no gap in age or social status:

선생님, 여기 앉**으세요**.	*Teacher, take a seat here.*
할아버지, 우리 집으로 오**세요**.	*Grandfather, come to our house.*

Although –(으)시– is originally a 'subject' honorific form, it can sometimes appear in cases where the 'subjecthood' of the person being honoured is questionable. This tends to occur when referring to an esteemed person's body parts, ailments, clothes and possessions. In the following examples, although –(으)시– is used to show respect to 할아버지 'grandfather', it is arguable whether 'grandfather' is the true 'subject' of any of these sentences. Indeed, it could be claimed that 수염 'whiskers', 종기 'boil' and 방 'room' are the subjects of the sentences:

할아버지께서 수염이 많**으세요**.
Grandfather has many whiskers.

할아버지께서 손에 종기가 나**셨어요**.
Grandfather has had a boil appear on his hand.

할아버지는 방이 크**세요**.
Grandfather's room is big.

6.2.1.2 *Verbs with special subject honorific forms*

For a small set of verbs that describe situations involving the human body, just adding –(으)시– is not enough. For these verbs, the verb base itself has to be substituted for a special honorific verb base. These verb bases all contain –(으)시– as an integral part:

Non-honorific base	*Honorific base*
자– *sleep*	주무시–
있– *stay*	계시–
먹– *eat*	잡수시–, (드시–)
마시- *drink*	드시- (잡수시-)
죽– *die*	돌아가시–
아프– *be ill*	편찮으시–
말하– *speak*	말씀하시–

A few extra notes are required regarding the forms for 'stay', 'eat', and 'be sick':

1 계시– only replaces 있– when the intended meaning is 'somebody stays'. 있– can also be used in possessive constructions to mean 'somebody has'. In these constructions, 있– is not replaced

but is suffixed with –(으)시– to form the honorific base 있으시–. Consider the following examples:

할아버지는 서울에 **계세요**. *Grandfather is (= stays) in Seoul.*

할아버지는 돈이 **있으세요**. *Grandfather has (= possesses) money.*

2 In addition to using 잡수시– as an honorific form for eat, speakers also frequently substitute 먹– 'eat' for the euphemistic 들– 'take'. As an ㄹ dropping irregular verb, this becomes 드시– as an honorific base. Speakers may also use the expression 식사하– 'have a meal', which becomes 식사하시–.
3 As well as 편찮으시– 'be ill', it is also possible to make the plain verb 아프– honorific by adding –(으)시: 아프시–. However, the usages of these two forms are distinct. Generally speaking, 편찮으시– is more formal and more honorific, and 아프시– is less formal and less honorific. In addition, it could be said that whereas 편찮으시– is used for discussing illness or pain affecting the body in general ('be ill', 'be in pain'), 아프시– is only used for talking about ailment in a particular body part ('. . . hurts'):

할아버지는 오늘 **편찮으세요**. *Grandfather is ill today.*

할아버지는 머리가 **아프세요**. *Grandfather's head hurts.*

These honorific verbs occur in some common greetings and set expressions:

안녕히 **계세요**. *Goodbye (lit. 'stay in peace'].*

안녕히 **주무세요**. *Good night.*

맛있게 **드세요**. *Enjoy your meal.*

6.2.1.3 *Subject honorific particle 께서*

When expressing subject honorification, as well as marking deference on the verb, the subject particle 이/가 (refer to 3.2.1) can also be replaced by the honorific particle 께서:

할아버지**께서** 자동차가 없으세요?
Doesn't your grandfather have a car?

동생**이** 자동차가 없어요?
Doesn't your younger brother have a car?

께서 can also be followed by the topic particle 는 (note that this does not apply to 이/가):

아버님**께서는** 무엇을 하세요?   *What does your father do?*

Although, in theory, 께서 should always be applied in sentences such as the above, in everyday speech its inclusion is frequently overlooked. One may often hear teachers, grandparents, etc. talked about without any use of 께서; indeed, in informal conversation overuse of 께서 may sound like 'overdone' honorification (refer to Lee & Ramsey 2000). However, in formal speech and writing, it should always be included.

Furthermore, although we may expect that 께서 would appear with honorific terms of address and kinship terms that include –님 (refer to 6.3.2) (and not to appear with plain terms), in ordinary conversation such rules of co-occurrence are only loosely followed. In the following, although the first sentence may be the most 'correct', all of the following four combinations may be heard in the sentence 'father helped me':

아버**님께서** 도와주셨어요.	–님 + 께서
아버지**께서** 도와주셨어요.	께서
아버**님이** 도와주셨어요.	–님
아버지**가** 도와주셨어요.	–

6.2.2 *Object honorifics*

Object honorification is the expression of deference toward the person affected by the action of the verb. In older stages of Korean (in particular, Middle Korean), the verbal suffix – *sop* – was used in this function; it formed an opposing pair with the subject honorific marker, –시–. However, this form has now been lost and, in modern Korean, object honorification can only be expressed through lexical substitutions.

6.2.2.1 *Verbs with special object honorific forms*

The following verbs have special object honorific forms:

Non-honorific base	*Honorific base*
주– *give*	드리–
묻– *ask*	여쭙–

Non-honorific base	*Honorific base*
보– *see*	뵙–
데리– *accompany*	모시–
말하– *speak*	말씀드리–

Examples of these verbs in usage can be found in the following section below (refer to 6.2.2.2).

Although this seems to be a very limited set of forms, the object honorific form 드리– has a wider application than simply meaning 'give'. Firstly, it also replaces 주– as an auxiliary verb in benefactive constructions (refer to 5.1.12). Secondly, it can replace the support verb 하– in 하– verbs (refer to 4.1.2):

Non-honorific		*Object honorific*	
전화하–	*call*	전화 드리–	*call [sb esteemed]*
연락하–	*contact*	연락 드리–	*contact [sb esteemed]*
부탁하–	*requests*	부탁 드리–	*request [to sb esteemed]*
인사하–	*greets*	인사 드리–	*greet [sb esteemed]*
축하하–	*congratulates*	축하 드리–	*congratulate [sb esteemed]*

6.2.2.2 *Object honorific particle 께*

When talking about giving something to, asking, speaking to, contacting, congratulating, etc., a person who needs to be respected, the locative particle 에게 or 한테 (refer to 3.2.4.4) is replaced by the honorific 께. Here are some examples of object honorifics showing 께 and/or the object honorific verbs introduced in the previous section:

이 책을 선생님**께** **드렸어요**.
I gave this book to my teacher.

그런 일은 할아버지**께** **여쭈어** 보세요.
Ask grandfather things like that.

오늘 도서관에서 선생님을 **뵈었어요**.
I saw the teacher in the library today.

부모님을 **<u>모시고</u>** 갔어요.	*I took my parents.*
사장님**<u>께</u>** **<u>말씀</u>** **<u>드렸어요</u>**.	*I told the boss.*
할머니**<u>께</u>** 전화 **<u>드렸어요</u>**.	*I phoned my grandmother.*
할아버지**<u>께</u>** 인사 **<u>드렸어요</u>**.	*I greeted grandfather.*

6.2.3 *Honorific nouns*

Some Korean nouns also have special honorific forms:

Non-honorific	*Honorific*
집 *house, home*	댁
나이 *age*	연세, 춘추*
밥 *cooked rice, meal*	진지
술 *alcohol*	약주
병 *illness*	병환
생일 *birthday*	생신
이름 *name*	성함, 존함**
말 *speech, word*	말씀
사람 *person*	분

*old-fashioned form, ** highly formal form

Whereas the non-honorific forms are used to talk about the house, age, meal, birthday, etc. of someone of similar or subordinate status, the honorific terms are used to talk about the house, age, meal, birthday, etc. of someone esteemed.

When these forms are applied in combination with the honorific verbs and particles introduced earlier in this chapter, some basic expressions can be rendered with totally separate lexical sets depending on who you are talking about. In the following examples, whereas the plain 이 (subject marker), 밥 'meal' and 먹– 'eat' are used for talking about the younger sister, the honorific 께서 (subject marker), 진지 'meal' and 잡수시– 'eat' are used for talking about grandfather:

할아버지**<u>께서</u>** **<u>진지</u>**를 **<u>잡수십</u>**니다.
Grandfather is eating his meal.

여동생이 밥을 먹어요.
Younger sister is eating her meal.

In addition to the nouns listed above, some titles and kinship terms also have a separate honorific form. These are commonly formed by adding the honorific suffix –님 (refer to 6.3.2, 6.3.3).

6.2.4 Putting the honorifics system together

This section and the previous one have introduced speech styles and different kinds of referent honorifics. We now look at how these different elements work together as an integrated system and provide more information about the contexts where referent honorifics are needed.

When the hearer and referent(s) **are different people,** speech styles and referent honorifics should be understood as totally independent systems. If you need to signal respect to both the person you are talking to **and** the person you are talking about, you will use honorific speech styles **and** referent honorifics:

선생님, 할아버지**께서** 뭐 하**십니까**?
Teacher, what does your grandfather do?

Similarly, if you do not need to signal respect either to the listener **or** to the hearer then non-honorific speech styles can be used **and** referent honorifics can be omitted:

민호야, 동생이 뭐 하**니**? *Minho, what does your little brother do?*

However, if you need to signal respect **only** to the hearer, you will have to use an honorific speech style **but** drop the referent honorifics:

선생님, 민호 뭐 해**요**? *Professor, what does Minho do?*

And finally, when you **only** need to show respect to the sentence referent, then you will use referent honorifics **but** opt for a non-honorific speech style:

민호야, 할아버지 뭐 하**시니**? *Minho, what does your grandfather do?*

In these cases where the referent and the hearer are different people, referent honorifics are most commonly used when talking about people who are considered to be of notably high status. This commonly includes your parents, grandparents, teachers, professors, bosses and others of high occupational rank and elderly people.

When the hearer and referent(s) are the same person, hearer and referent honorifics work together to express respect to the hearer/referent. In such cases, it is most common for referent honorifics to occur with honorific speech styles (and for referent honorifics to be omitted with non-honorific speech styles), as in these example:

사장님, 어디 **가세요**?
[subject honorifics; polite speech style] *Boss, where are you going?*

민지야, 어디 가?
[no subject honorifics; intimate speech style] *Minji, where are you going?*

However, this is not always the case. Although the social factor that exercises most influence over both styles is relative social status (age, rank, etc.), the choice of speech styles displays more connection to the level of intimacy. Thus, in cases when you are talking to (and about) someone who is of equal or inferior social status but with whom you are not intimate, it may be appropriate to use honorific speech styles (to signal the lack of intimacy) but drop the referent honorifics (to signal that you are of equal or superior social standing):

민호 씨, 어디 가**요**? *Minho, where are you going?*

The opposite pattern of using non-honorific speech styles but referent honorifics is less common. However, this may sometimes be heard by a daughter towards her mother, for example, with the non-honorific style signalling intimacy, but the referent honorific signalling respect for age difference (although this would not normally be considered 'standard'):

엄마, 어디 가셔? *Mum, where are you going?*

Regarding the use of honorifics when the hearer and referent are the same entity, it should be noted that there are commonly two circumstance in which this becomes the case. Firstly, the hearer and referent are identical in personal questions which would include 'you' in the English translation:

어디 가**세요**? *Where are you going?*

어떻게 생각하**십니까**? *What do you think?*

In such cases, referent honorifics are generally included when addressing all status superiors as well as strangers and many non-intimates.

The second common case where the hearer and the referent are the same person is imperatives; in other words, when you are telling someone what to do:

이쪽으로 오**세요**. *Come this way please.*

전화번호를 가르쳐 주**세요**. *Please tell me your [[?]] telephone number.*

In imperatives, as long as you are using honorific speech styles, referent honorifics are most commonly included. In other words, even if you are talking to a non-intimate of similar or younger age who you normally address in honorific speech styles but without referent honorifics, you may include them when commanding them to do something. The reason for this seems to be that telling someone what to do is always rather sensitive so speakers want to sound as polite as possible.

6.3 Terms of address

Overview

This sub-chapter provides a thorough overview of the forms that Koreans use to call and refer to each other. The system of address terms in Korean is quite complex, and works in integration with the honorifics system to mark factors such as social status and intimacy.

Korean terms of address are complicated by the fact that the situations in which you can just call someone by their name are extremely limited. As a general rule of thumb, it is only possible to call someone by their name if they are the same age or younger than you. Otherwise, the name will be replaced by (or supplemented by) a title or kinship term. In this chapter, the use of names, titles and kinship terms are described in turn, before the way to address someone politely is summarized in the final section:

6.3.1 Names

Korean names usually consist of three syllables. The first syllable is the surname (the most common Korean surnames being 김 Kim, 이 Lee and 박 Pak), and this is usually followed by a two-syllable given name; for example, 김대중, 노무현, 김일성, 이승만, 박정희. There are odd exceptions. Sometimes the given name will only contain one syllable, for example, 김구, 허웅. Sometimes the given name contains three syllable or more, although this is not common, for example, 김세레나, 박새미나. There are some surnames which have two syllables: for example, 황보, 독고, 선우.

In Korean, the surname (when it is used) always comes first, the opposite of the English order. Therefore, 연재훈's surname is 연, and his given name is 재훈. The following table shows some common Korean surnames:

김	이	박	최	장	남	홍	허	서	배	조
노	정	전	임	오	강	안	한	심	윤	송

Korean names rarely occur in isolation but followed by another element. First of all the title-word 씨 may be used after both full names and given names (however, it does not generally occur after surnames):

Full name + 씨: 김민수 씨 Given name + 씨 민수 씨

Full name + 씨 is a generic way to call the name of an unknown person for identification purposes. For example, when you are in a crowded waiting room at a doctor's surgery, this is the form of address that will be used to tell you that it is your turn to go in and see the doctor, although you may also hear 님 used instead (refer to 6.3.2). Full name + 씨 may also be used in the workplace between colleagues.

Given name + 씨 is a non-intimate form of address that can be used towards acquaintances of similar age. Note that you cannot refer to yourself as '. . . 씨'.

When you are addressing an intimate of similar or younger age or a child, you do not need to use 씨. However, when you are calling someone's given name as a vocative, you can attach the vocative particle, which is 아 after a consonant and 야 after a vowel (refer to 3.2.7). This only occurs in combination with non-honorific speech styles (refer to 6.1) and only tends to occur with Korean (or Korean-sounding) names:

유진**아**, 점심 먹었어?	*Yujin, have you eaten lunch?*
유미**야**, 너 지금 시간 있니?	*Yumi, do you have time now?*

In addition, when a given name ending in a consonant appears without the addition of 씨, 아 or another title (refer to 6.3.2) or kinship term (refer to 6.3.3), it usually appears with the suffix 이, which adds an extra layer of intimacy. This also only tends to occur with Korean (or Korean-sounding) names:

유진**이**, 그게 무슨 말이야?	*Yujin, what do you mean?*
유진**이가** 간다고 했어요.	*Yujin said she is going.*
효진**이를** 만났어요.	*I met Hyojin*
영민**이는** 그렇지 않아요.	*Yŏngmin is not like that.*

As can be seen in the final three examples above, 이 frequently appears followed by particles (refer to Chapter 3). The combination '이가' (i.e., 이 and the subject particle 가 (refer 3.2.1)) is particularly common and represents the most common way to mark a 'bare' given name appearing as a sentence subject.

6.3.2 Titles

Although, as discussed in the previous section, name + 씨 represents the most generic way to call someone's name in Korean, this can only generally be used towards acquaintances of similar age. When you are addressing someone older than or superior to you, you will have to use another title or a kinship term.

When addressing an elder or superior, perhaps the most common term of address is 선생님. This title literally means 'esteemed teacher' and is primarily used towards one's own teachers and others of the teaching profession. It is also the prototypical way to address medical doctors. However, it can be used towards adults in general as a respectful form of address and may be considered the closest to referring to someone as 'Mr . . .' or 'Sir'. 선생님 is most polite on its own without an accompanying name. However, it is also possible to use it AFTER a surname or a full name:

김인호 선생님	*Mr. Inho Kim*
김 선생님	*Mr. Kim*

선생님 cannot be used to talk about yourself – you cannot introduce yourself as '. . . 선생님'. The reason for this is because –님 is an honorific suffix that pays respect to the person you are talking about (and there is no need to pay respect to yourself).

There are scores of other address terms that are used in Korean society. Like 선생님, these are usually composed of a first part such as 선생 that refers to a position, occupation or societal role and this honorific particle –님. By including –님, the term of address becomes suitable for addressing superiors. On the other hand, by dropping –님, the term becomes appropriate for addressing an equal or inferior. Here are some terms of address in common use in the Korean workplace:

Non-honorific title		*Honorific title*	
회장	*company president*	회장님	*esteemed company president*
사장	*company manager*	사장님	*esteemed company manager*
차장	*deputy manager*	차장님	*esteemed deputy manager*
과장	*department head*	과장님	*esteemed department head*
실장	*section chief*	실장님	*esteemed section chief*
대리	*deputy section chief*	대리님	*esteemed deputy section chief*

You may also sometimes hear Koreans use the English address terms 'Mr' (e.g., 미스터 강), 'Mrs' (e.g., 미세스 정) and 'Miss' (e.g., 미스 김). However, unlike in English these are not particularly respectful terms and cannot be used towards a status superior. Indeed, 미스 in particular is probably most frequently used by businessmen towards their (female) secretaries or by doctors, etc. towards their (female) reception staff. Adolescents and young adults may also be addressed by their name suffixed by 군 (for males) or 양 for females.

6.3.3 *Kinship terms*

Due at least in part to the complex hierarchical nature of Korean family relationships, Korean has a list of highly distinctive and extensive kinship terms. The Korean kinship terms are often more specific than in European languages and make extra distinctions based on male/female, older/younger and paternal/maternal.

Korean kinship terms can be divided two groups. The first group has two kinship term sets depending on the gender of the speaker (or person being talked about). For example, whereas a man refers to his father-in-law as 장인, a woman refers to her father in law as 시아버지:

	A male's	*A female's*
Father-in-law	장인(어른)	시아버지
Mother-in-law	장모	시어머니
Spouse	아내 / 부인	남편
Brothers/Sisters	형제 (brothers)	자매 (sisters)
Older brother	형	오빠
Older sister	누나	언니

As can be seen in the above, there are two words that are equivalent to the English 'wife'. However, the usage of these words is not identical. Whereas 부인 is an honorific term that can only be used respectfully to refer to another man's wife, 아내 is a plain term that can be used to refer to one's own wife. It is also possible to refer to your own wife as '집사람' (lit. 'home-person') or '와이프' (from the English 'wife').

The second group of kinship terms can be used by both genders.

Grandparents	조부모
Paternal grandfather	할아버지
Maternal grandfather	외할아버지
Paternal grandmother	할머니
Maternal grandmother	외할머니

Parents	부모
Father	아버지
Mother	어머니
'Dad'	아빠
'Mom'	엄마
Son	아들
Daughter	딸
Grandchild(ren)	손주
Grandson	손자
Granddaughter	손녀(딸)
Younger sibling	동생
Younger brother	남동생
Younger sister	여동생
Paternal uncle	큰아버지 *(an older brother of one's father)*
	작은아버지 *or* 숙부 *(a married younger brother of one's father)*
	삼촌 *(an unmarried younger brother of one's father)*
	고모부 *(the husband of the sister of one's father)*
Paternal aunt	고모 *(both older or younger sister of one's father)*
	큰어머니 *(the wife of an older brother of one's father)*
	작은어머니 *or* 숙모 *(the wife of a married younger brother of one's father)*
Maternal uncle	외삼촌 *(both older and younger brother of one's mother, regardless of their marital status)*
	이모부 *(the husband of a sister of one's mother).*

Maternal aunt	이모 *(both older or younger sister of one's mother)*
	외숙모 *(the wife of both older and younger brother of one's mother)*
Son-in-law	사위
Daughter-in-law	며느리
Cousin	사촌

Some kinship terms can be made 'honorific' through the addition of –님 (refer to 6.3.2). The following list shows the most common occurrences of this alternation; note that the forms marked with an asterisk show some degree of irregularity between the honorific and non-honorific form. For some kinship terms, including notably 언니 'older sister (of a woman)' and 조카 'niece/nephew', there is no commonly used honorific form.

	Non-honorific	*Honorific*
grandparents	조부모	조부모님
grandfather	할아버지	할아버님*
grandmother	할머니	할머님*
parents	부모	부모님
father	아버지	아버님**
mother	어머니	어머님**
older sister (of a man)	누나	누님*
older brother (of a man)	형	형님
older brother (of a woman)	오빠	오라버님*
younger sibling	동생	아우님*
daughter	딸	따님*
son	아들	아드님*

** = These forms are more commonly used as address terms for parents-in-law (or someone else's parents) rather than your own parents.

The use of honorific kinship terms is less regular than the use of honorific titles discussed previously. '부모님' is the most commonly used of these terms and represents the universal way to refer to either your own parents or those of other people. The other honorific kinship terms are generally only used in formal settings. The honorific terms for 'daughter' and 'son' (따님 and 아드님) are used for referring to the children of status superiors.

In the family, a strict hierarchy is respected whereby younger family members never address older family members by their first name but by a title. This applies to siblings: a man will always address his older brother as 형 and his older sister as 누나 and a woman will use 오빠 and 언니 respectively. Even twins born minutes apart will use this system, with the 'younger' twin calling his sibling 'older brother/sister'.

In addition to being used within the family, many of these terms can be used 'fictively'; in other words, they can be applied to relationships outside the family that have similar age dimensions to the corresponding family relationships. For example, the terms for 'older brother/sister' can be used towards intimates of marginally superior age. In addition, 할머니 'grandmother' and 할아버지 'grandfather' are frequently heard being used as generic ways for addressing elderly people.

Korean also applies something that is called teknonymy. This is basically a way of referring to someone in relation to their children, in other words, calling someone something that translated as 'so-and-so's mother' or 'so-and-so's dad' (commonly using the name of the eldest child):

민수 어머니	*Minsu's mother*
민수 아버지	*Minsu's father*
민수 엄마	*Minsu's mom*
민수 아빠	*Minsu's dad*

These expressions are first of all used within the extended family, although only towards those of younger age. Interestingly, the latter two expressions are also frequently used as terms of address between married people with children. In addition, it is possible to use these towards casual acquaintances (as long as they are not older than you), particularly when you are a teacher, neighbour, etc. who knows the child.

6.3.4 How to address someone

The way you address someone in Korean will depend on your relative social status with that person and also on the degree of intimacy. This section provides you with some basic rules of thumb that you should follow.

Addressing intimates of similar age

When addressing a friend the same age or younger than you, just using their first name is fine. This can be suffixed by the intimate vocative particle, which is –아 after a consonant (e.g., 영민아) and –야 after a vowel (e.g., 민수야) (refer to 3.2.7). Alternatively, for names that end in a consonant, you can also use the suffix –이 (e.g., 영민이) (refer to 6.3.1). Using these suffixes makes the address sound warmer and closer, but make sure you are intimate enough to use these.

Addressing intimates of older age

When you are addressing an intimate who is one or more years older than you, it is not usually appropriate to apply their name. Instead, you should use the appropriate word for 'older brother/sister' (refer to 6.3.3). However, note that these terms are only appropriate for fairly marginal age differences, perhaps up to ten years. After this point, you will probably have to retain a title used for addressing an age-rank superior (refer to 6.3.2).

Addressing elders and notable superiors

When someone is around ten or more years older than you – or if they are a status superior in your workplace or your teacher/professor – you should always address them by an appropriate title. If you are unsure which title to use, you can apply 선생님 (lit. 'teacher') as a generic respectful form of address. These titles should be applied no matter how 'intimate' the relationship may become.

Addressing non-intimates and strangers

For non-intimates and strangers, the basic rule of thumb is to maintain titles wherever possible, particularly towards those older than you. When the person is of similar or younger age, it may be appropriate to use their full or first name in combination with –씨 (refer to 6.3.2).

In encounters with strangers where you do not know their name and are unsure of their relative social position, the application of generic titles is a good strategy. For male blue collar workers of marriageable age or above, 아저씨 (lit. 'uncle') may be used. For women, the equivalent is 아주머니/아줌마 (although be careful not to use this towards younger women). Elderly strangers may be addressed as 할아버지 'grandfather' and 할머니 'grandmother'. Those of university age and below are frequently hailed as 학생 'student'. Outside of this, as previously noted, the use of 선생님 'teacher' represents a good form of universal respectful address.

Addressing notable subordinates and children

Children are addressed using their first names. These can be suffixed by –아/야 or –이 (refer to 6.3.1).

Unless you are intimate, preserving a degree of respect in the way you address notable subordinates is a good idea. Otherwise, your speech can easily sound high-handed. For subordinates within the office, a non-honorific title is appropriate (refer to 6.3.2). For more casual acquaintances, name + 씨 usually suffices.

For addressing an intimate who is younger than you, apply the strategies mentioned above for addressing intimates of similar age.

Chapter 7

Clausal connectives

Overview

This chapter looks at different ways of linking two or more clauses together to form longer sentences by adding connective endings to the verb in the first clause.

The chapter classifies these verbal connectives into eight groups according to their primary function: causal, contrastive, additional/sequential, optional, conditional, causative, intentive and comparison. It should however be noted that many verbal connectives have other usages that go beyond their primary function; thus, these categories should be applied only as a basic guide.

One way in which connective endings tend to differ concerns whether they can be preceded by the past tense –았/었– and/or future tense with –겠–. Whereas some endings are compatible with these tense markers, others are not. We point out these restrictions where they exist.

7.1 Causal connectives

Causal connectives mark a cause and a result. The cause is expressed in the first clause; the result is expressed in the second. These constructions most typically translate into English as '. . . , so . . .' or 'because . . . , . . .'.

OTHER CAUSAL CONSTRUCTIONS

Apart from the causal connectives described in this chapter, other constructions that express cause and effect treated elsewhere in this book are as follows:

1. –기에 (refer to 2.2.4.21)
2. –기 때문에 (refer to 2.2.4.2)
3. –는 바람에 (refer to 8.2.23)
4. –는 통에 (refer to 8.2.39)

7.1.1 –(아/어)서

The ending –(아/어)서 is formed on the infinitive form of the verb (refer to 4.1.6). Note that the –(아/어)서 form of the copula has two variants: –이라서 is more common and considered 'standard', but you may also encounter –이어서.

One important restriction on the use of –(아/어)서 is that tense markers are not usually used before it, and their appearance is not considered standard. It is sufficient to mark tense on the verb at the end of the sentence. Thus, in constructions such as the following, tense is not needed on the first verb:

아**파서** 못 갔어요 *I was ill, so I couldn't go.*

However, it appears that tense marking with –(아/어)서 is starting to appear in casual Korean speech. With the future tense marker –겠–, you may hear sentences such as 너무 아프**겠어서** 연고를 발라 줬어요 'It looked like it hurt so much that I put on some ointment for him/her'. Nevertheless, the standard sentence would be 너무 아플 것 같아서 연고를 발라 줬어요 'It looked like it hurt so much that I put on some ointment for him/her'. You might hear also hear sentences with past tense –았/었– such as 너무 아**팠어서** 나중에 멍이 들지 않을까 하는 생각까지 들었다 'It hurt so I thought that I might get a bruise later'. However, the use of past tense in such sentences will sound awkward to many.

–(아/어)서 can however be preceded by the honorific marker –(으)시– (refer to 6.2.1.1) to form –(으)셔서:

아프**셔서** 못 가셨어요. *He/she was ill, so he/she couldn't go.*

Although classified as a causal connective here, –(아/어)서 can express sequence as well as cause. In sentences containing –(아/어)서, the first clause provides an action or situation in which the event or circumstances in the second clause then comes to pass. The second clause is therefore either consequential (cause and result) to or merely sequential to the first clause. It is useful to consider these consequential and sequential usages separately.

As a **consequential marker**, –(아/어)서 expresses that the event or state in the second clause follows as a natural result of what is expressed in the first clause. The causation should be predictable and fairly undisputable according to common knowledge (refer to Lukoff & Nam 1982; Sohn 1992).

The expression thus conveys natural consequence rather than something the individual speaker is trying to claim based on his/her own opinion. When the speaker wishes to express his/her own individual reason (or assert his/her own explanation for why something took place), –(으)니까 should be used instead (refer to 7.1.6). Here are some examples of common-sense causation with –(아/어)서:

돈이 없**어서** 가지 못해요.	*I didn't have any money, so I couldn't go.*
늦**어서** 택시를 타고 갔어요.	*It was late, so I took a taxi.*
물가가 비**싸서** 살기가 힘들어요.	*Prices are expensive, so life is hard.*

There are two further specific usages of –(아/어)서 that occur as an extension of this consequential meaning.

Firstly, –(아/어)서 frequently occurs with 좋아요 'good' in the second clause of the sentence. Such sentences literally mean '[so-and-so happens], so it's good', but a better English translation would be 'I'm glad (that) . . .' or 'It's a good thing (that) . . .' For example:

새 바지를 **사서** 좋아요.	*I'm glad I bought new trousers.*
수진 씨가 **와서** 좋아요.	*I'm glad Sujin came.*

Secondly, –(아/어)서 occurs with expressions of thanks and apology. Such sentences literally mean '. . ., so thank you' or '. . ., so sorry' but can be more naturally translated as 'Thank you for . . .' 'I'm sorry (that) . . .'. Consider the following examples:

도와 주**셔서** 감사합니다. *Thank you for helping (me).*

늦**어서** 죄송합니다. *Sorry for being late.*

As a **sequential marker**, –(아/어)서 denotes that the second clause takes place in a state or in a position created by the first clause. The events in the two clauses have to be tightly linked, and must be expressed in the chronological order in which they occurred. One common case in which this usage occurs is when verbs of direction (such as 가– 'go' and 오– 'come') appear in the first clause and the activity performed at the location reached is included in the second. Such constructions translate into English as 'go somewhere to do something'. Consider the following examples:

포장마차에 **가서** 소주를 마셨어요.
I went to the drinking stall and drank some soju.

학교에 **와서** 공부를 했어요.
I came to school and studied.

저 신호등을 **지나서** 내려 주세요.
Please drop me off after (passing) the traffic lights.

In this sequential use, other verbs may appear with –(아/어)서. First of all, when you are talking about standing, sitting, lying, getting up, etc. and then doing something in that position, –(아/어)서 is the correct connective to use:

유미가 **앉아서** 커피를 마셨어요. *Yumi sat down and drank coffee. [i.e., Yumi drank coffee sitting down].*

민수가 **누워서** 책을 읽었어요. *Minsu lay down and read a book. [i.e., Minsu read a book lying down].*

학생들이 **서서** 애국가를 불렀어요. *The students stood up and sang the national anthem.*

아침에 **일어나서** 세수했어요. *I got up in the morning and had a wash.*

In addition, when talking about procuring or creating an item and then doing something with that item, –(아/어)서 can be used as in the following examples.

만년필 하나 **사서** 선생님께 드렸어요.
I bought a fountain pen and gave it to the teacher.

라면을 끓**여서** 먹었어요.
I cooked some noodles and ate them.

서류를 작성**해서** 보냈어요
I filled out the documents and sent them

키보드를 고**쳐서** 썼어요
I fixed the keyboard and used it.

Here are some further examples of constructions where –(아/어)서 takes on a sequential meaning:

친구를 만**나서** 소주를 마셨어요.	*I met a friend and drank coffee.*
결혼**해서** 아기를 낳았어요.	*I got married and had a baby.*
돈을 모**아서** 집을 샀어요.	*I made some money and bought a house.*

As a final point, – (아/어)서 can also be used as a sentence ender when the second clause is omitted or has previously been expressed. In such circumstances, – 요 should be attached to the end in order to form the 'polite' (refer to 6.1.1) speech style. Otherwise, the sentence will be interpreted as the 'intimate' style (refer to 6.1.3):

A: 왜 파티에 안 갔어?	*Why didn't you go to the party?*
B: 돈이 없**어서**.	*Because I don't have money.*

너무 배고파요. 점심을 못 먹**어서요**.
I'm so hungry. Because I didn't eat lunch.

7.1.2 –아/어

– 아/어 is most frequently treated as an abbreviated and slightly more bookish version of – (아/어)서 (refer to 7.1.1). Although this generally holds true, there are at least two circumstances in which – (아/어)서 cannot be shortened to – 아/어: (1) after the copula (refer to 4.1.4) and (2) when used at the end of a sentence

In addition, when 아/어 attaches to an honorific base (refer to 6.2.1.1), the full form –(으)시어 must be retained. This cannot be contracted to –셔 as is typically the case when followed by –(아/어)서: –(으)셔서:

와 주**<u>시어</u>** 감사합니다. (Full form used with –아/어) [<u>NOT</u> '주셔']
Thank you for coming.

와 주**<u>셔서</u>** 감사합니다. (Contracted form used with –아/어서)
Thank you for coming.

Similarly, with the verb 하–, the full form 하여 tends be used. This is not normally shortened to '해' as it typically applied in other contexts (including when –(아/어)서 is used).

열심히 공부하**<u>여</u>** 변호사가 됐어요. (<u>NOT</u> normally '공부해')
I studied hard and became a lawyer.

7.1.3 –아/어서인지

This is a variant form of the causal construction -아/어서 (refer to 7.1.1). With the addition of -인지, the causation is presented in a more sceptical way and the reason given is presented as only one possible explanation. This typically translates as 'perhaps it's because' or 'perhaps that is why'.

프랑스 전통음식 중에도 피와 내장만으로 만든 순대나 떡과 비슷한 음식이 있**<u>어서인지</u>** 프랑스사람들이 더 많이 찾는다.
Among French traditional food, there are dishes with blood and intestines like sundae *(Korean blood sausage) and also dishes that are similar to rice cakes so perhaps that is why French people seek out Korean food more.*

날씨가 계속 쌀쌀 해**<u>서인지</u>** 커피가 자꾸 땡긴다.
Perhaps it's because the weather continues to be chilly that I keep on wanting to drink coffee.

7.1.4 –아/어서(는) 안 되–

This pattern literally means 'when something happens, it will not do'. In other words, the pattern expresses that something must not happen or that you must not do something.

The pattern is similar in function to the more –(으)면 안 되– (refer to 7.5.1.5), which has the same function of expressing prohibition.

아침에 일어나자마자 해**선 안 될** 10가지 행동
10 things you must not do straight after you get up in the morning

결혼은 중요한 일이니까 쉽게 결정해**서는 안 돼**요.
Marriage is an important matter, so you must not decide too readily.

초코렛은 강아지가 먹**어서는** 절대 **안 돼요**.
The puppy must not eat chocolate.

7.1.5 –(아/어) 가지고

This ending combines the infinitive form of the main verb with the verb 가지–. This is then rounded off with the –고 ending (refer to 7.3.1).

In its original usage, the verb 가지– means 'have', 'hold', 'carry', 'possess' and frequently occurs with the continuous tense (refer to 4.3.3.2) as in the following example:

유미 씨는 사진기를 늘 **가지고** 있어요.
Yumi is always carrying a camera.

The '가지고' form can also behave like a particle to mean 'with' or 'by means of':

고양이가 쥐를 **가지고** 놀아요.
The cat is playing with a mouse.

그 사람 **가지고** 놀리지 마세요.
Don't make fun of ('with') him.

한 달에 50만원 **가지고** 어떻게 살아요?
How can you live on ('with') 500,000 won a month?

Furthermore, 가지– can be followed by 가– 'go' and 오– 'come' to form the compounds 가지고 가– 'take (something somewhere)' and 가지고 오– 'bring (something somewhere)':

저는 내복이랑 겨울잠바를 **가지고** 갔어요.
I took thermal underwear and a winter jacket with me.

We now turn our attention specifically to the pattern –(아/어) 가지고. This pattern can first of all occur followed by 가– 'go' and 오– 'come' as in the example above. With the addition of an extra verb, this pattern is used when talking about creating or procuring an item and then taking or bringing it somewhere.

김밥을 만들**어 가지고** 올게요.
I'll make some kimbap *and bring it along.*

아이스크림을 **사 가지고** 갔어요.
He/she bought some ice cream and took it along with him/her.

However, when the pattern is followed by verbs other than 가–/오– or their compounds, it takes on a quite different meaning. Basically, the meaning is parallel to that of –(아/어)서 (refer to 7.1.1), but the feeling is more colloquial. In the colloquial speech of younger speakers, –(아/어) 가지고 appears to replacing –(아/어)서 in many cases. In the same way as –(아/어)서, the first clause provides an action or situation in which the event or circumstances in the second clause then comes to pass. The second clause is therefore either consequential to or merely sequential to the first clause.

In consequential constructions, the contents of the second clause take place as a natural consequence of the contents of the first clause:

술에 취해 **가지고** 고생했어요.
I got drunk, so I had hard time.

우유를 쏟아 **가지고** 옷이 다 젖었어요.
I spilled the milk, so my clothes got completely wet.

Similar to –(아/어)서, in sequential constructions, the contents of the second clause take place not only after that of the first clause but, more importantly, in a state created by the event mentioned in the first clause. Most typically, the first clause refers to the creation, procurement or change in state of an object and the second clause refers to how this newly created/procured/changed item is then put to use:

돈을 모아 **가지고** 전세계 여행했어요.
I made some money and then used it to travel the world.

물고기를 잡아 **가지고** 찌개를 끓였어요.
I caught a fish and made a stew with it.

한국어를 공부해 **가지고** 한국 회사에 취직했어요.
I studied Korean and then used it to get employed at a Korean company.

7.1.6 –(으)니까

This causal construction is formed by adding the two-shape ending (refer to 4.1.8) –(으)니까 to the verb stem: –으니까 after consonants, –니까 after vowels. Unlike –(아/어)서 (refer to 7.1.1), –(으)니까 may be preceded by tense markers to form –었으니까 (past tense) and –겠으니까 (future tense), although this tends to occur only when it appears in the 'causation' function and not in the 'discovery' function (see below):

하**니까**	*does, so (present)*	먹**으니까**	*eats, so (present)*
했**으니까**	*did, so . . . (past)*	먹었**으니까**	*ate, so (past)*
하겠**으니까**	*will do, so . . . (future)*	먹겠**으니까**	*will eat, so . . . (future)*

However, the future forms listed above are rare in modern Korean. More commonly, in place of –겠– (refer to 4.3.2.1), the –을 거– future form (refer to 4.3.2.2) is used instead to form –을거니까:

할 거니까	*will do, so . . . (future)*	먹**을 거니까**	*will eat, so . . . (future)*

Another alternative for the future tense is to use the form –(으)ㄹ테니까 (refer to 7.1.8).

After the –(으)니까 ending, it is possible to attach the topic particle 은/는 (refer to 3.3.2.1), which is most commonly written and pronounced abbreviated to –(으)니깐. Again, this is something that is not possible with –(아/어)서 (refer to 7.1.1).

밖에 추우**니깐** 옷을 따뜻하게 입고 가세요.
Since the weather is cold, dress warmly.

Looking at the usage of this form, just like –(아/어)서 (refer to 7.1.1), –(으)니까 also has two distinct usages. In addition to 'causation', –(으)니까 can also be used to mark 'discovery'. These two usages are explored in turn.

As a 'causation' connective, –(으)니까 is used to express a reason for a particular state or action. The reason is expressed in the first clause and the state or action that the reason pertains to is stated in the second clause. Unlike –(아/어)서 which marks natural consequence, –(으)니까 is used to express a subjective reason that is dependent on the speaker's own judgment or justification (refer to Lukoff & Nam 1982; Sohn 1992). Compare the following two sentences:

물가가 비싸**서** 살기가 힘들어요.
Prices are expensive, so life is hard. ('Life is hard as a natural consequence of prices being expenses.')

물가가 비싸**니까** 살기가 힘들어요.
Prices are expensive, so life is hard. ('In my opinion, the reason why life is hard is because prices are expensive.')

Due to the fact that –(아/어)서 marks natural consequence and –(으)니까 marks subjective reasoning, –(아/어)서 represents the more natural choice in sentences that express a causation that is based on shared common human knowledge regarding the world around us:

싱가포르는 적도에서 가까**워서** 날씨가 일 년 내내 더워요.
Singapore is close to the equator, so [naturally] the weather is hot all year round

The above sentence could be expressed with –(으)니까, but it would sound more like the speaker's own personal argument.

When you are expressing something seems to go against common sense, –(으)니까 is the better choice:

눈이 오**니까** 포근한 느낌이 들어요. *It's snowing, so it feels warm.*

돈이 많**으니까** 걱정이 많아요.
I have a lot of money, so I have many worries.

유미는 딸만 셋을 낳았**으니까** 이번에는 아들을 낳을 거야.
Since Yumi has already born three daughters, this time she will have a son.

In addition, when you are making an inference based on conjecture and circumstantial evidence, –(으)니까 is the more natural choice:

민호가 잘생겼**으니까** 여자 친구가 있을 것 같아요.
Minho is good looking, so he probably has a girlfriend.

The most important distinguishing usage that makes the use of –(으)니까 quite different to –(아/어)서 is that only –(으)니까 can be used when the second clause of the sentence contains anything other than a simple statement (or possibly question) – i.e., a command, proposal, suggestion, invitation or request. As the justification for such speech acts is always based on the speaker's subjective reasoning, only –(으)니까 is appropriate:

COMMAND: 늦었**으니까** 빨리 가라.
It's late, so go quickly.

PROPOSAL: 시간이 없**으니까** 빨리 가자.
We don't have time, so let's go quickly.

SUGGESTION: 추우**니까** 안으로 들어가십시다.
It's cold, so let's go inside.

INVITATION: 날씨가 좋**으니까** 공원에 같이 갈까요?
The weather's good, so shall we go to the park together.

REQUEST: 사장님이 지금 안 계시**니까** 다시 전화해 주세요.
The boss isn't here at the moment, so please phone back later.

Another big difference is that –(으)니까 cannot replace –(아/어)서 in politeness-related expressions (만나서 반갑습니다 'Nice to meet you', 초대해 주셔서 감사합니다 'Thanks for inviting me', 늦어서 죄송합니다 'Sorry I'm late'). Likewise, –(으)니까 is not used when giving reasons or excuses for your wrongdoings. Here too –(아/어)서 is preferred, seemingly since you want excuses to sound like natural, unavoidable reasons rather than something you are trying to actively argue for:

차가 많이 막**혀서** 늦었어요.
I'm late because there was a lot of traffic.

We now look at the 'discovery' function of –(으)니까. In this function, the first clause contains an action that brings about a realization that is expressed in the second clause. Here, –(으)니까 cannot be thought of as expressing causation per se, but rather it takes on a sequential meaning and most commonly translates into English as 'when'. This function first of all occurs with verbs of motion (the speaker goes to or enters a place to find something there):

집에 가**니까** 친구가 와 있었어요.
When I went home, [I found that] my friend was there.

교실에 들어가**니까** 학생들이 있었어요.
When I entered the classroom, [I found that] the students were there.

전화를 하**니까**, 받지 않았어요.
When I telephoned, they didn't answer.

In addition, this usage occurs when the speaker does or tries something for the first time and either makes a discovery or forms an opinion. Such sentences frequently feature the –아/어 보– (refer to 5.1.8) or –다 보– (refer to 5.2.1) patterns in the first clause.

그 책을 읽**어 보니까** 재미있더라고요.
Having read that book, I found it interesting.

일본 음식을 먹어 보**니까** 싱거웠어요.
Having tried [eating] Japanese food, I found it bland.

서로 이야기를 하다 보**니까** 같은 대학교 동창이었어요.
After having had the chance to talk to him, I found we are alumni from the same university.

As a final point, –(으)니까 can also be used as a sentence ender when the second clause is omitted or has previously been expressed. In such circumstances, –요 should be attached to the end in order to form the 'polite' speech style (refer to 6.1.1). Otherwise, the sentence will be interpreted as the intimate style (refer to 6.1.2):

A: 왜 이렇게 서두르세요? — *Why are you in such a hurry?*

B: 시간이 없으**니까**요. — *Because I don't have time.*

내가 할게. 내가 시간이 있으**니까**.
I'll do it. Because I have time.

7.1.7 –(으)니

– (으)니 is most frequently treated as an abbreviated and slightly more bookish version of –(으)니까 (refer to 7.1.6). Although this explanation generally holds, there are a few key differences that are worth listing:

1 Unlike – (으)니까, –(으)니 cannot occur in sentence-final position.
2 Unlike –(으)니까, –(으)니 cannot be followed by the topic marker –는
3 – (으)니 tends to be more frequently used in the 'discovery' function rather than the 'causation function'.

In very formal and polite writing addressed to a specific audience, the rather antiquated honorific marker –(사)오- may be added to make the form –(사)오니. This tends to feature in written texts addressed to (potential) customers or users of a product or service:

교환, 반품이 불가능할 수 있**사오니**, 각 상품의 상품 상세정보를 꼭 참조하십시오.
Since exchanges and returns are not possible, please make sure you refer to the detailed information about each product.

쾌적한 환경을 위해 금연을 실시하**오니** 꼭 지켜 주시기 바랍니다.
Since we implement a no-smoking policy for a better environment, please make sure you follow it.

7.1.8 –(으)ㄹ테니까

This is a combination of –(으)ㄹ터 which expresses the speaker's intention and the sequential ending of copula –이니까 described in (refer to 7.1.6)

–(으)ㄹ테니까 has two distinct usages. In the first usage, the speaker expresses his/her only own volitional action in the first clause, which provides the condition for the hearer performing another action in the second. Put simply, the speaker says 'since I am going to do A, you can do B':

술은 내가 살 **테니까** 너는 안주 좀 사 와.
Since I am going to buy the alcohol, you can buy some appetizers.

내가 집을 볼 **테니까** 다녀오세요.
I'll be watching the house, so you go out [on your errands].

좋은 사람 소개해 드릴 **테니까** 만나 보시겠어요?
I am going to introduce you to somebody nice, so will you meet him/her?

In the second usage, the first clause provides a strong future prediction based on the opinion of the speaker. The second clause then provides a suggestion or piece of advice based on the preceding prediction. In other words, the speaker is saying 'since A is going to happen, you should do B' or 'since A is going to happen, let's do B', etc.:

내일 비가 올 **테니까** 오늘 가세요.
Since its going to rain tomorrow, go today.

반드시 성공할 **테니까** 걱정하지 마세요.
Since you're definitely going to succeed, don't worry.

With this second usage, it is also possible that the first clause may appear in past tense. In such usages, the first clause is not a future prediction but an inference about a past action or event:

어제 힘들었을 **테니까** 오늘은 쉬세요.
Since you must have had a tough day yesterday, take a rest today.

With both uses of –(으)ㄹ테니까, the ending can be shortened to –(으)ㄹ테니 without any notable change in meaning.

7.1.9 –(으)므로

The causal connective –(으)므로 is composed of the nominalizing ending –음 (refer to 2.2.5) and the instrumental particle –으로 (refer to 3.2.5.1). This connective represents a formal register of speech and is normally restricted to formal written language.

–(으)므로 can be used to express a wide range of causal meanings, including common-sense causations and personal subjective reasonings. A few examples are shown below:

교통 신호를 무시하였**<u>으므로</u>** 벌금을 물었다.
I was fined because [I] disregarded a traffic signal.

춘향은 정절이 높았**<u>으므로</u>** 후세 여성의 거울이 되었다.
Since Chunhyang was so virtuous, she became a mirror for womanhood in later ages.

이 물건은 수입품이**<u>므로</u>** 세금이 붙는다.
This item attracts tax because it is imported goods.

Unlike –(으)니까 (refer to 7.1.6), –(으)므로 should not normally be used with commands, proposals, suggestions, invitations or requests.

7.1.10 –길래

The one-shape causal connective –길래 is a spoken form used with any verb, and indicates cause or reason. In –길래 constructions, the first clause contains someone else's action or otherwise, an external situation and/or something outside of the speaker's control. The second clause contains the speaker's (or other focal actor's) responsive action to that:

배가 몹시 아프**<u>길래</u>** 병원에 갔어요.
I had a terrible stomach-ache, so I went to the hospital.

그 책이 싸**<u>길래</u>** 한 권 샀어요.
That book was cheap, so I bought one.

학생이 숙제를 마쳤**<u>길래</u>** 집에 가라고 했어요.
Because the student had finished his homework, I told him to go home.

In addition, when used in questions, –길래 is applied to ask a reason behind a certain action or event. In this case, the pattern –길래 is always preceded directly by a question word. It is used to set up a question about something surprising, puzzling or amazing to the speaker. One way to get at the flavour of this ending in English is with 'just . . .' or by attaching '-ever' to the question word. Here are some examples.

유미 씨는 어디 갔**<u>길래</u>** 이렇게 안 보여요?
Wherever has Yumi gone, that she should be so conspicuously absent?

다른 컴퓨터하고 뭐가 다르**길래** 이렇게 비싸요?
Just what makes it so different from other computers, that it should be so expensive?

야, 네가 뭐**길래** 나한테 이래라, 저래라 명령하니?
Hey, just who do you think you are, ordering me to do this, and do that?

무슨 일이 있었**길래** 이렇게 술을 마시고 들어왔어?
Just what on earth happened, for you to come home drunk like this?

어제 몇 시간 잤**길래** 그렇게 하품을 해?
Just how many hours did you sleep yesterday that you are yawning like that?

요즘 뭘 하**길래** 숙제를 못 해요?
What are you doing these days that you can't do your homework?

In all examples above, –길래 is interchangeable with the expression –기에 (refer to 2.2.4.21). However, the use of –길래 and the use of –기에 are not totally identical. Whereas –기에 is a bookish connective, –길래 has traditionally been treated as its colloquial counterpart. But in truth, –기에 actually has a less restrictive meaning than –길래. In statements with –길래 the first clause should contain an external consequence and the second clause should always contain the speaker's (or other focal actor's) own responsive action, but this is not a requirement for –기에 (refer to Ahn 2002). Due to this, whereas –기에 can be used in all of the following examples, –길래 is not permissible in the first sentence below, sounds awkward in the second, but works fine in the third. Whereas the second clause in sentence 3 contains the speaker's responsive action, sentence 1 contains a state (loudness) and 2 a natural effect of that state (being unable to study), both of which are generally incompatible with –길래.

1. 아이들이 떠들**기에** 방이 시끄러웠어요. [–**길래** *not* possible]
   Because the children were making a clamour, the room was noisy.

2. 아이들이 떠들**기에** 내가 공부할 수 없었어요. [–**길래** sounds awkward]
   Because the children were making a clamour, I could not study.

3. 아이들이 떠들**길래**/**기에** 내가 아이들을 혼내 주었어요. [both possible]
   Because the children were making a clamour, I gave them a scolding.

Finally, in the following sentence as well 길래 is not possible. Although on this occasion the second clause does contain a responsive action, the first clause contains the speaker's own internal state, over which he has some degree of control. The first clause needs to include an external or uncontrollable situation in order for –길래 to be used.

나는 그 여자를 사랑하**기에** 떠납니다. [–**길래** *not* possible]
'Because I love her, I'm leaving'.

7.1.11 –느라고

The one-shape ending –느라고 attaches only to processive verb stems and the subject of the two clauses is always the same. It cannot be followed by commands or propositions.

With –느라고, the first clause contains an ongoing continuous action. The second clause then expresses a negative or unexpected consequence of this action, which may occur even after the ongoing action has stopped or while it is still ongoing. Typical translations include 'what with . . . ing', 'on account of the process of . . . ing' or 'because of . . . ing'.

요즘 시험 공부 하**느라고** 아주 바빠요.
What with studying for exams, I'm very busy.

점심 먹**느라고** 늦었어요.
What with eating lunch and all I was late.

어제 밤에 공부하**느라고** 늦게 잤어요.
What with studying last night, I went to bed late.

골라서 사**느라고** 시간이 많이 걸렸어요.
It took a long time to find the right thing.

하루종일 뭐 하**느라고** 청소도 못 했어요?
What did you do all day that you couldn't do the cleaning?

자동차를 고치**느라고** 이번 달 월급을 다 썼어요.
What with repairing the car and everything, I spent all my salary.

7.1.12 –(으)랴

The two-shaped ending –(으)랴 is used in the same way as –느라고 (refer to 7.1.11) to list continuous actions that lead to a negative consequence. The difference with –느라고 is that –(으)랴 is used not just once but two or more times in the same sentence for listing multiple reasons for the state of affairs:

공부하**랴** 알바하**랴** 정신이 없다.
I'm losing my mind studying and doing my part time job.

낮에는 회사에 다니**랴** 밤에는 집안일하**랴** 고생이 많다.
He's having a really hard time going to the office during the day and doing the housework at night.

7.1.13 –더니 and –(았/었)더니

–더니 is a combination of the observed past tense marker –더 (refer to 4.3.1.3) and the ending –(으)니 (refer to 7.1.7). Although it can be said to basically combine the basic meanings of the two, the end result also has its own specific functions.

Generally speaking, –더니 is used when a speaker recalls past events and then describes a resultant consequence or discovery. The translation would be 'seeing as . . .', 'since . . .' or 'when . . .'. The subject is usually second or third person.

너무 많이 먹**더니** 배가 아픈 것 같아요.
As he ate too much, I observed, he seems to have stomachache.

열심히 일하**더니** 사장이 되었어요.
Since she worked hard, I observed, she became president of the company.

한국말을 열심히 공부하**더니** 지금은 한국말을 유창하게 말해요.
Since he studied Korean hard, I observed, he now speaks it fluently.

In another but similar usage, this pattern recollects the contents of the preceding clause as something directly experienced, and relates this to the contents of the following clause, which are the result of changes over the course of time.

눈이 오**더니** 따뜻해졌어요.
[I saw] it was snowing and now it's turned warmer.

바람이 불**더니** 비가 오네요.
[I saw] first the wind, and now the rain.

이곳에 학교가 많**더니**, 지금은 유흥업소로 꽉 찼군요.
[I saw] there used to be many schools here, but now it is filled with entertainment shops.

어제는 선생님의 기분이 좋으시**더니**, 오늘은 안 좋아 보이시는군요.
Yesterday [I saw] he was in a good mood, but today he looks down.

–더니 can also appear following the past tense marker (refer to 4.3.1.1) to form –었더니. However, the usage and meaning of –었더니 are quite different from when –더니 appears on its own. The main difference is that whereas –더니 appears with the second or third person, –었더니 only takes a first person subject. The first clause contains an event and the second clause expresses a direct consequence (usually with a different grammatical subject) that the speaker experienced as a result of this event. The usage is similar to the 'discovery' function of –(으)니까 (refer to 7.1.6).

어젯밤에 늦게까지 공부**했더니** 피곤해요.
Because I studied until late last night, I feel tired.

술을 너무 많이 마**셨더니** 머리가 아파요.
I drank too much, so I've got a headache.

한참 쉬**었더니** 몸이 가뿐해 졌어요.
I've had a bit of rest so now I feel refreshed.

학교에 **갔더니** 아무도 없었어요.
When I went to the school, nobody was there.

내가 춤을 추**었더니** 모두 웃었어요.
I danced, then everybody laughed.

7.1.14 –(으)ㄹ라

This two-shape connective ending is similar in meaning to the auxiliary verb pattern –(으)ㄹ까 보– (refer to 5.4.1). The first clause contains a worry that the speaker has about a possible future event. The second clause contains something that should be done to prepare for this possible eventuality. Note however that, unlike the less restricted –(으)ㄹ까 보–, the use of –(으)ㄹ라 is limited mainly to cases where a speaker is giving advice either to a close friend or someone younger.

다**칠라** 조심해라.
You're going to hurt yourself – watch out!

학교에 늦**을라** 빨리 일어나라.
Get up quickly or you'll be late for school.

감기 걸**릴라** 목도리 해라.
Put on a scarf or you are going to catch cold.

Note that this pattern may appear as a sentence ender without a second clause. In such cases, the advice has either been previously mentioned or otherwise implied.

서둘러라. 늦**을라**.	*Hurry up. You're going to be late*
빨리 가봐. 벌써 떠났**을라**.	*Go quickly. He's already gone.*

7.2 Contrastive connectives

Contrastive connectives mark a contrast between two different or contradictory states or events.

7.2.1 –지만

The most common ways to mark contrast in Korean are with –(으)ㄴ/는데 (refer to 7.3.12) or –지만. –지만 is a one-shape ending that attaches to the verb base. –지만 can be preceded both by the past tense marker –았/었– and by the future tense marker –겠– :

하지만	*does, but . . . (present)*	먹**지만**	*eats, but . . . (present)*
했지만	*did, but . . . (past)*	먹었**지만**	*ate, but . . . (past)*
하겠지만	*will do, but . . . (future)*	먹겠**지만**	*will eat, but . . . (future)*

This ending marks a strong opposition between two contrasting or contradictory states of affairs. This overriding meaning of 'contrast' or 'contradiction' can be broken down into three distinct applications that we deal with in turn.

Firstly, when the subject of both clauses is different, a contrast is described between two people, things, or states of affairs. To emphasize the strong contrast, both subjects are marked with the topic particle (refer to 3.3.2.1).

딸은 똑똑하**지만** 아들은 똑똑하지 않아요.
The daughter is bright, but the son is not bright.

나이는 많**지만** 마음은 아직 젊어요.
I am old, but my heart is still young.

성 차이는 인정하**지만** 성차별은 싫어요.
I recognize gender differences, but I don't like gender discrimination.

In the second usage, the speaker recognizes the existence of a certain state of affairs in the first clause, but then presents a contradictory truth in the second clause that is seen as being of more significance. Here, the subject of the two clauses is often the same.

김치를 먹을 수 있**지만** 별로 좋아하지 않아요.
I can eat kimchi, but I don't like it much.

오늘 춥**지만**, 시장에 가야 해요.
Today is cold, but I have to go to the market.

단기적으로 효과가 있겠**지만**, 장기적인 부작용이 클 수 있어요.
In the short term it would be effective, but the long-term side effects can be big.

With this second usage, to emphasize the idea that the information in the first clause *is* true but of limited significance, the verb may be nominalized by –기 (refer to 2.2.3), suffixed by the topic particle –는 (refer to 3.3.2.1) and followed by the verb 하– 'do' in the –지만 form (–기는 하지만). The result is more similar to the English 'even though' rather than simply 'but':

민호를 좋아하긴 하**지만** 결혼 상대로 생각하지 않아요.
Even though I like Minho, I do not think of him as a prospective husband.

Thirdly, like the English 'but', –지만 is used in expressions such as 'excuse me but' and 'sorry but':

실례(하)**지만** 성함이 어떻게 되세요?
Excuse me, but what's your name?

죄송하**지만** 질문하나 해도 될까요?
Sorry, but can I ask a question?

7.2.2 –(으)나

The contrastive ending –(으)나 is a two-shape ending, with –으나 being used after consonants and –나 after vowels. It has several usages, some of which overlap the usage of –지만 discussed previously (refer to 7.2.1).

First of all, –(으)나 can be applied exactly like –지만 to express a contrast between two different people, objects or states of affairs:

값은 좀 비싸**나** 음식 맛은 좋아요.
It's a bit expensive, but the taste is good.

Also, –(으)나 can be applied exactly like –지만 when the speaker recognizes the existence of a certain state of affairs in the first clause, but then presents a contradictory truth in the second clause that is seen as being of more significance.

어제 술집에 갔**으나** 술은 마시지 않았어요.
I went to a bar yesterday, but I didn't drink any alcohol.

In these usages that overlap with –지만, –(으)나 is somewhat more common in written language.

–(으)나 also has some additional usages that are quite distinct to –지만. First of all, –(으)나 can be used twice in the same sentence attached to two predicates of contrasting meaning to give the reading 'whether . . . or . . .'. The implication of the pattern is that the state of affairs given in the final clause comes about regardless of the two choices given in the first part of the sentence. In this usage, –(으)나 functions in a similar way to –거나 (refer to 7.4.1) or –든지 (refer to 7.4.2).

그 사람은 자**나** 깨**나** 술만 마셔요.
Whether awake or sleep, he always drinks.

앉**으나** 서**나** 허리가 아파요.
Whether I sit or stand, my back hurts.

좋**으나** 싫**으나** 해야 해요.
You must do it whether you like it or not.

To create the meaning 'whether . . . or not', use the verb 말– 'desist' for the second verb (refer to 4.2.3). This contracts to –마 to create the pattern –나 마나, which is dealt with separately in the following subsection (refer to 7.2.3).

Furthermore, when –(으)나 is used after clauses containing question words such as 무엇 'what', 어디 'where', 누구 'who', 언제 'when' and 어떻게 'how', the implication is that what is expressed in this clause is of no consequence. Such constructions usually translate into English as 'whoever . . .', 'whatever . . .', 'wherever . . .', etc. Here are some examples:

> 내가 어디 가**나** 상관하지 마.
> *Wherever I go, just mind your own business.*

> 뭘 먹**으나** 살이 안 쪄요.
> *Whatever I eat, I don't put on weight.*

Finally, –(으)나 sometimes occurs in modifying constructions linking two identical descriptive verbs. In such usage, the meaning of –(으)나 has nothing to do with contrast – it merely works to add emphasis to the adjective in the same way as adding 'very', 'really' or using a superlative.

> 크**나** 큰 죄인이 되고 말았어요.
> *He/she ended up becoming a really big criminal.*

> 작**으나** 작은 피해도 없게 하는 것이 행정의 원칙이다.
> *The principle of administration is to avoid even the smallest damages.*

> 기**나** 긴 세월동안 기다렸어요.
> *I waited a really long time (many years).*

7.2.3 –(으)나 마나

– (으)나 마나 is combination of the –(으)나 form described in the previous section (refer to 7.2.2) and the verb 말 'desist' (refer to 4.2.3), also in the –(으)나 form. The meaning created is 'whether . . . or not' and the pattern is used when either of two options or possibilities ultimately have no influence on the final result.

> 학생들을 혼내주**나 마나**, 마찬가지예요.
> *It's all the same whether or not you give students a hard time.*

시험을 보**나 마나**, 그 학생은 떨어질 거예요.
The student probably will fail whether he takes the exam or not.

그런 회의는 하**나 마나**예요.
It won't do any good whether or not we hold such a conference.

가보**나 마나** 없을 거예요.
Whether you go or not, she's not going to be there.

7.2.4 –(으)되

–(으)되 is a peculiar two-shape contrastive connective that is used primarily in formal writing. The behaviour of this ending is peculiar in that the –으되 variant is only used after the verbs 있– 'exist' and 없– as well as the past and future tense markers –았/었– and –겠–. Otherwise, –되 is used is used even for verb bases ending in a consonant (e.g., 먹되 'eat').

–(으)되can be used in the same way as –지만 to mark a contrast between two states of affairs:

제 발표는 한국어로 하**되** 영어로 된 요약문을 준비하겠습니다.
My presentation will be in Korean, but I will prepare a summary in English.

음식은 자주 먹**되** 적게 먹는 것이 좋아요.
Eating regularly, but eating small amounts is good.

기간은 짧았으**되** 많은 것을 배웠습니다.
The time was short, but I have learned a lot.

그 선수는 재능은 있으**되** 재능을 살리지 못한다.
That athlete has talent, but he can't apply it.

7.2.5 –(아/어)도

The verbal connective –(아/어)도 is formed on the infinitive form of the verb and may on occasion be preceded by past tense –았/었– or the future marker –겠–. However, more commonly, tense is only marked on the second clause. The copula may appear in two forms when combined with –(아/어)도: 이어도 or, more commonly in colloquial speech, –이라도. The latter is considered to be standard Korean. In addition to taking on the main functions of –(아/어)도 that are described below, –이라도 can function almost like a particle to mean 'even' or 'at least':

하루에 반 시간씩**이라도** 어휘를 외워야 돼요.
You should memorize vocabulary even if it's only for half an hour a day.

다른 것이 없으니까, 이것**이라도** 좋아요.
This one will be all right, since you haven't got any others.

저는 못 가겠어요. 유진 씨**라도** 갔다 오세요.
As I won't be able to go, at least you go [without me], Yujin.

Besides these special usages with the copula, the usage of –(아/어)도 is similar to the second function of –지만 (refer to 7.2.1) and –(으)나 (refer to 7.2.2) described in the previous two sections. In other words, the speaker recognizes the existence of a certain state of affairs in the first clause, but then presents a contradictory truth in the second clause that is seen as being of more significance. However, the feeling created by –(아/어)도 is stronger or more emphatic than that of –지만 and –(으)나. Rather than 'but' or 'though', the feeling conveyed is more similar to the English 'even though'.

돈이 많지 않**아도**, 늘 물건을 사요.
Even though I haven't much money, I'm always buying things.

포장마차가 멀**어도** 자주 가요.
Even though the drinking tent is far away, I go there often.

바람은 불**어도** 춥지 않아요.
Even though it's windy, it's not cold.

비가 주룩주룩 와서 우산을 들고 나**가도** 젖어요.
As it's streaming down with rain, you get wet even if you take an umbrella.

Since this pattern can also be used to discuss future or hypothetical situations, its usage also stretches to cover the English 'even if':

내일 눈이 **와도** 갈 거예요.
Even if it snows tomorrow, I'll go.

공부하지 않**아도** 시험을 잘 치를 수 있어요.
Even if you don't study, you can do well on the exam.

Some further special usages of –(아/어)도 that do not correspond directly to the meaning of 'contrast' are dealt with separately in the subsections below.

7.2.5.1 –(아/어)도 *in permissive constructions*

– (아/어)도 is commonly employed in sentences where the speaker asks for or gives permission. Most typically, the second clause contains the verb 되– which literally means 'become', but here can be understood better as 'work', 'be okay', 'be alright', etc. The construction as a whole thus literally means 'does it work (for you)/is it okay/is it alright even if I . . .'. Commonly, this translates into English as 'is it alright/ok if . . .' or simply 'can I . . .'.

> 오늘 밤에 집에 늦게 돌아**와도 돼**?
> *Is it alright if I come home late tonight?*

> 여기서 사진을 찍**어도 돼요**?
> *Can I take photographs here?*

> 이 바지를 한번 입어 봐**도 돼요**?
> *Can I try it on these trousers?*

In place of 되–, you can also use 좋– 'be good' or 괜찮– 'be okay':

> 오늘 새 옷을 입**어도** 좋아요?
> *May I wear my new clothes today?*

> 내일 조금 늦게 **와도** 괜찮아요?
> *Is it ok if I come slightly late tomorrow?*

The ending –겠– may also be used on the final verb. This functions like 'would' in English ('would it be alright . . .') to make the request for permission more tentative and therefore polite:

> 전화를 사용**해도** 되겠어요?
> *Would it be alright if I used the phone?*

The same construction can be used in statements of permission as well as just requests for permission. To refuse permission, use the expression –(으)면 안 되– (refer to 7.5.1.5).

7.2.5.2 Don't have to . . . *with* –지 않아도

To say 'have to . . .' in Korean, you use the construction –(아/어)야 되/하– (refer to 7.5.7.1). However, the negative equivalent – 'don't have to' – is formed using a negative permissive construction –지 않아도 되–/좋–/괜찮–, which literally translates as 'even if you don't do it, it's okay'. This normally combines long negation (refer to 4.2.2) with the –아/어도 construction. Here are some examples of this pattern:

내일은 야근하지 **않아도** 돼요.
You don't have to work nights tomorrow.

이 책을 보지 않**아도** 괜찮아요.
You don't need to read this book.

병원비 내지 않**아도** 돼요.
You don't have to pay the hospital fees.

As well as forming this construction using long negation, it is also possible to convey the same meaning using short negation with 안 (refer to 4.2.1):

학교에 안 **가도** 좋아요.
You don't have to go to school.

수술 안 해**도** 되겠어요.
You don't have to have an operation.

오늘 은행에 가**도** 좋고 안 가**도** 좋아요.
It doesn't matter whether I go to the bank today or not.

7.2.5.3 *Idiomatic –(아/어)도 expressions*

There are a few idiomatic expressions with –(아/어)도 that are used as adverbs. These take on a special maximum-minimum meaning:

늦어도	*at the latest (even though it's late)*
적어도	*at least (even though it's few or small)*
많아도	*at (the) most (even though it's a lot)*

일러도	*at the earliest (from 이르- 'be early')*
커도	*at the largest*
빨라도	*at the fastest*
멀어도	*at the farthest*
가까워도	*at the nearest*

Here are some examples of these in sentences:

적어도 한 달에 한 번씩은 시스템과 데이터를 백업하세요
You should back up your system and data at least once a month.

자동차는 **빨라도** 한 시간에 팔십 마일밖에 못 가요.
At the fastest, your car won't do over eighty miles an hour.

늦어도 10시까지는 집에 돌아가야 해요.
We have to return home by 10 o'clock at the latest.

It should be noted that these same verbs may also occur in normal (i.e., non-idiomatic) constructions with –(아/어)도 to take on the more typical meaning of 'even though/if'. It is only when they are used as adverbs that they adopt the special idiomatic meanings described above.

7.2.6 –더라도

– 더라도 is a one-shape ending that may be preceded by the past tense marker (refer to 4.3.1.1). This construction creates a similar meaning of concession to –(아/어)도 (refer to 7.2.5). However, the concessive meaning is somewhat stronger with the contents of the two clauses often lying in powerful (or even poignant) contradiction to each other. Furthermore, rather than accepting the state of affairs presented in the first clause as 'fact', the speaker implies that it is perhaps just hypothetical (or, that even if it were true, it is of no consequence whatsoever). Suitable translations in English include 'no matter how . . .', 'however many . . .', etc.

피곤하**더라도** 네 일은 제대로 해라.
No matter how tired you are, do your work properly.

아무리 가난하**더라도** 결코 좌절하지 말아라.
However poor you may be, never lose hope!

몇 번을 물어 보**더라도** 내 대답은 마찬가지예요.
However many times you may ask, my answer will be the same.

For added emphasis, the construction frequently occurs preceded by the quotative (refer to 10.2). This adds the flavour of English expressions such as 'even supposing that' or 'even if we grant that':

그 사람이 살인자라(고) 하**더라도** 나는 그 사람을 사랑한다.
Even if we grant that he is a murderer, I still love him.

아무리 이메일이 편하다고 하**더라도** 이메일에는 보내는 사람의 마음이 담겨 있지 않은 것 같아요.
No matter how convenient we grant that e-mails are, they don't seem to contain the emotions of the people sending them.

7.2.7 –고도

The one-shape connective ending –고도 is an amalgamation of the additional connective –고 (refer to 7.3.1) and the particle –도 (refer to 3.3.3.6). Here, –고 takes on a sequential meaning of 'after' or 'then' and –도 has the meaning of 'even'. Thus, as a whole, the construction means 'even after'. –고도 cannot be preceded by tense markers.

공짜로 영화 보**고도** 후회했어요.
Even after watching the movie for free, I regretted doing so.

결혼하**고도** 일을 계속하고 싶어요.
Even after I get married, I want to continue working.

포도주를 두 잔 마시**고도** 잠이 안 왔어요.
Even after drinking two glasses of wine, I couldn't sleep.

밤에 라면을 먹**고도** 얼굴이 안 부었어요.
Even after eating ramen at night, my face did not go puffy.

7.2.8 –(아/어)서라도

The verbal ending –아/어서라도 is a combination of the causal connective –(아/어)서 (refer to 7.1.1), the variant form of the copula –라– (refer to 4.1.4) and the particle –도 'even' (refer to 3.3.3.6). The pattern gives what is usually a hypothetical action in the first clause that the speaker (or person in question) would be prepared to carry out in order to achieve the result in the second clause. The pattern typically translates as 'even if it means'.

책 살 돈이 없으면 빌**려서라도** 읽어야 해요.
If I don't have any money to buy books, I would and read them even if it means borrowing them.

카드 빚 내**서라도** 꼭 사고 싶어요.
I want to buy it even if it means getting into debt on my credit card.

몸을 팔**아서라도** 자식들을 먹이고 교육시켜야 해요.
Even if it means selling your own body, you have to feed and educate your kids.

거짓말을 해**서라도** 성공해야 해요.
You have to succeed, even if it means lying.

7.2.9 –(으)ㄴ들

The ending –(으)ㄴ들 is constructed on the state-result modifier ending –(으)ㄴ(refer to 8.1.3) followed by '들'. Similar in meaning to –(아/어/)도 (refer to 7.2.5), this connective concedes or acknowledges the contents of the first clause but then implies that the conclusion reached in the following clause comes about regardless of the preceding clause. Examples are as follows:

시험에 떨어지고 나서 후회**한들** 무슨 소용이 있어요?
What's use of regretting after failing exams?

아무리 부자**인들** 어떻게 그렇게 화려하게 살 수 있을까요?
Even though he is a rich man how can he live so extravagantly?

힘이 약하다 **한들** 너보다야 약하겠느냐?
I may be weak, but I am sure I'm no weaker than you.

7.2.10 –(으)ㄹ지라도

The two-shape ending –(으)ㄹ지라도 also possesses a concessive meaning, very similar to that of –(아/어)도 (refer to 7.2.5). It can be attached to a past tense base to form –(었/았)을지라도. It typically translates as 'even if':

비판을 받**을지라도** 할 말은 해야 해요.
Even if we are criticized, we have to say what we have to say.

내가 뇌물은 받**았을지라도** 편의를 봐주지는 않았어요.
Even if I received a bribe, I did not make any accommodations.

아무리 가난**할지라도** 남의 것을 훔치면 안 돼요.
Even if you are poor, you mustn't steal other people's things.

아무리 바**쁠지라도** 부모님 생신을 잊어서는 안 돼요.
Even if you are busy, you must not forget your parents' birthdays.

시험이 끝**났을지라도** 결석하지 마세요.
Even if you have finished your exams, don't be absent.

7.2.11 –(으)ㄹ지언정

The two-shape ending –(으)ㄹ지언정 is another variation on constructions expressing concession and is similar in meaning to –(아/어)도 (refer to 7.2.5).

굶어 죽**을지언정** 그 친구 도움은 받고 싶지 않아요.
Even if we have to starve, I don't want to accept that friend's house.

나이는 어**릴지언정** 생각하는 것은 어른스러워요.
Even though he/she is young, his way of thinking is like an adult.

이번에 금메달은 놓쳤**을지언정** 좋은 경험을 해서 다행이에요.
Even though we missed out on the gold medal this time, it was a good experience for us.

7.2.12 –(으)ㄹ망정

The two-shape ending –(으)ㄹ망정 is another concessive construction similar in meaning to –(아/어/)도:

은혜는 못 갚**을망정** 배반을 하면 안 돼요.
Even if you can't replay the favour, you should not turn against me.

고맙다고는 못 **할망정** 왜 화를 내요?
Even if you can't say sorry, why are you getting angry?

아무리 비가 많이 **올망정** 안 갈 수가 없어요.
Even if it rains a lot, not going is not an option.

7.2.13 –거늘

This one-shape concessive construction is used when the preceding clause contains a natural or obvious fact or a general truth, and the speaker inserts his/her (often reproachful) opinion in the following clause. In other words, this pattern is used to spotlight the speaker's argumentative attitude in light of an obvious or general truth in the preceding clause.

사람에게는 다 부모가 있**거늘** 나만 부모가 없다.
While all others have parents, I alone have no parents.

남편은 아내를 사랑해야 하**거늘**, 그 부부는 항상 싸우기만 한다.
A husband ought to love his wife, but that couple always fight each other.

인생은 빈손으로 왔다가 빈손으로 가는 것이**거늘** 너무 욕심을 부릴 필요가 없지요.
Life is like coming empty-handed and leaving it empty-handed, and there is no need for being so greedy.

7.2.14 –느니

This one-shape ending, which attaches only to processive verbs, expresses that the contents of the second clause are better than or preferable to those of the first clause. The second clause can also be accompanied by adverbs like 차라리 'preferably', 'rather (than)'. One can add the comparative particle 보다 (refer to 3.3.6.4) to this pattern with no change in meaning.

선생님께 부탁드리**느니** 내가 스스로 하는 게 낫겠어요.
It would be better for me to do it rather than asking the teacher to do it.

이렇게 사**느니**보다 (차라리) 죽는 게 편하겠어요.
I would rather die than live like this.

천국의 종이 되**느니** 차라리 지옥의 왕이 되겠어요.
I'd rather be a king in hell than a slave in heaven.

Another pattern with this ending juxtaposes two contradictory clauses, each ending in –느니. These two clauses in –느니 are rounded off with a final clause which summarizes the gist of the dispute or issue.

두 사람이 가**느니** 안 가**느니** 다투고 있습니다.
The two people are having a quarrel about whether or not to go.

관광지로는 경주가 좋다**느니** 설악산이 좋다**느니** 하면서 말이 많아요.
There is a big debate over which is better as a tourist destination, Gyeongju or Seoraksan.

7.2.15 –(아/어) 봤자

This construction is built on the –아/어 보– auxiliary verb pattern (refer to 5.1.8), which has the meaning of 'trying'. Here, it is followed by the past tense marker (refer to 4.3.1.1) and the ending –자. The construction links a first clause, the contents of which the speaker considers to be futile or a waste of time, effort, etc. to even try. This futility is then expressed in the second clause, most frequently with expressions such as 소용없–. Resulting sentences thus take on the meaning 'it is no use trying . . .':

울**어 봤자** 무슨 소용이 있겠어?
What's the use in crying?

민호에게 말**해 봤자** 아무 소용 없어요.
There's no use talking to Minho.

비싼 멀티비타민 먹**어 봤자** 건강에 아무 효과 없어요.
Even if you eat expensive vitamins, they are not effective for your health.

질투**해 봤자** 달라지는 게 뭐가 있어?
What difference is getting jealous going to make?

7.3 Additional and sequential connectives

Additional and sequential connectives list two or more actions or events that are either parallel and exist side by side or otherwise are chronological and follow on from each other.

7.3.1 –고

The one-shape –고 is the most common and universal additional/ sequential ending. It may be preceded by past tense (refer to 4.3.1.1) and the future –겠– (refer to 4.3.2.1). It can also occur after a quotative form (refer to Chapter 10) as –다고. –고 operates like 'and' in English to link two clauses. The two clauses may be parallel actions or truths or otherwise take place in succession. Let us look at these two usages in turn.

The first use of –고 is to list parallel actions or states.

민수 씨는 한국 사람이**고**, 마이클 씨는 호주 사람이에요
Minsu is Korean and Michael is Australian

나한테는 책을 주었**고**, 어머니한테는 꽃을 드렸어요.
He/she gave me a book and also gave my mother some flowers.

유미는 은행에 있**고** 미나는 우체국에 있어요.
Yumi is at the bank and Mina is at the post office.

저녁에 약속 있다**고** 바로 퇴근했어요.
Saying she had plans in the evening, she finished work straight away.

The second use of –고 is to list actions in their chronological sequence. In this usage, –고 would translate into English as 'and then'.

저녁에는 책을 읽**고** 자요.
In the evenings, I read books and then go to sleep.

저녁에는 몇 시간쯤 공부하**고** 자요?
How long do you study at night before you go to bed?

화장하**고** 머리를 빗어요.
I do my makeup and [after that] comb my hair.

숙제를 하**고** 놀아라.
Do your homework and then play.

It should be noted that past tense marking (refer to 4.3.1.1) works differently across these two basic usage patterns. For listing past tense actions without wanting to specify a sequence, the past tense marker is included. In contrast, for the chronological 'and then' meaning, past tense marking needs to be omitted. The inclusion or exclusion of past tense marking can therefore change the meaning of sentences that are otherwise identical:

미나한테 책을 주었**고**, 유미에게 꽃을 주었어요.
I gave a book to Mina and gave flowers to Yumi.

미나한테 책을 주**고**, 유미에게 꽃을 주었어요.
I gave a book to Mina and then gave flowers to Yumi.

In addition to these two basic meanings, –고 can also be used when the first clause creates a state in which the action in the second clause takes place. This results in turns of expression quite different from English:

옷을 입**고** 자요.
I put on my clothes and sleep – i.e., 'I sleep with my clothes on'

버스를 타**고** 가요.
I take the bus and go – i.e., 'I travel by bus'

유미가 아이를 업**고** 뛰었어요.
Yumi gave her child a piggyback and ran – i.e., 'Yumi ran with her child on her back'

서로 껴안**고** 울었어요
They held each other and cried – i.e., 'They cried holding each other'

신문을 깔**고** 앉았어요
I spread out a newspaper and sat on it – i.e., 'I sat on a spread-out newspaper'

Negatives can be formed with the –고 construction in several ways. Firstly, you can simply add 안 or 못 before the verb to form short negation (refer to 4.2.1):

옷을 **안** 사고 . . . *doesn't buy clothes and . . . (= without buying clothes)*

Secondly, a long negative can be formed with –지 않고 or –지 못하고 (refer to 4.2.2):

돈을 많이 벌지 **못하고**
can't earn much money and . . . (= without earning much money)

In these negative forms, the expression translates as 'instead of . . . ing', 'rather than . . . ing', 'without . . . ing':

술 안 마시**고** 노래방에서 노래하는 것이 힘들어요.
It's hard to sing at karaoke without having drunk alcohol.

점심은 사 먹지 말**고** 만들어 먹자.
Let's make lunch rather than buying it.

PC방 가지 말**고** 집에서 게임을 즐겨라.
Enjoy playing [computer] games at home rather than going to the Internet cafe.

If the final verb is a command or proposition, another kind of negative construction is used: –지 followed by auxiliary 말– 'desist' (refer to 4.2.3):

자지 **말고**, 일어나라!
Don't sleep, get up.

이 기회를 놓치지 **말고**, 지금 신청하세요.
Don't miss this chance; apply now.

남에게 폐 끼치지 **말고** 잘 살자.
Let's live happily without being bothersome to others.

The resulting '말고' construction can also be applied after nouns (in a similar way to a particle) to mean 'rather than' or 'except for', as previously discussed (refer to 4.2.3).

명동**말고** 홍대로 가자.
Let's go to Hongdae rather than Myeongdong.

전화**말고** 이메일로 연락주세요.
Contact me via e-mail rather than phone.

Finally, –고 can also be used as a sentence ender when the second clause is omitted or has previously been expressed. –고 gives the feeling that the utterance is adding additional information to what has already been said. In such circumstances, –요 should be attached to the end in order to form the 'polite' speech style (refer to 6.1.1). Otherwise, the sentence may be interpreted as the 'intimate' style (refer to 6.1.3):

집이 아담하**고** 좋아요. 깨끗하**고**요.
The house is cosy and nice. It's clean, too.

A: 유미가 예쁘지?
Yumi is pretty, isn't she?
B: 어, 옷도 잘 입**고**.
Yeah, and she dresses well too.

어디 가? 옷을 예쁘게 입**고**.
Where are you going? Dressed prettily like this.

This use of 고 is also frequently heard in questions. In such instances, the feeling conveyed is that the question is being tagged onto what has previously been said. If –요 is attached to the end it becomes the 'polite' speech style (refer to 6.1.1). Otherwise, the sentence may be interpreted as the 'intimate' style (refer to 6.1.3):

점심은 먹었**고(요)**? *And you've had lunch, as well?*

부모님은 안녕하시**고(요)**? *And your parents are well, too?*

With a falling rather than a rising intonation, these questions can take on special rhetorical functions. The speaker either points out a difference between the hearer's previous words and current actions (as in the first example) or says 'if you do that, whatever am I supposed to do?' (as in the second):

안 간다고 할 때는 언제**고**?
I thought you said you weren't going?

네가 안 가면 난 어떻게 하**고**?
If you don't go, whatever am I supposed to do?

7.3.2 –고서

Usage of –고서 is comparable to the sequential usage of –고 (refer to 7.3.1). Application of –고서 in preference to simple –고

emphasizes the fact that the two events are in a chronological relationship, with the second event occurring necessarily after the first event. The second event may also to some extent take place as a result of the first event or in a state created by it:

유미가 손을 씻**고서** 밥을 먹었어요.
Yumi washed her hands and ate her meal.

미나가 민수에게 화를 내**고서** 후회했어요.
Mina got angry at Minsu and then regretted it.

– 고서 can also be used when the first clause creates an ongoing state in which the event expressed in the second clause takes place:

회사를 그만두**고서** 놀고 있어요.
After quitting the company, I'm taking a break.

자동차를 몰**고서** 고향에 갔어요.
I drove the car and went to my home town – i.e., 'I travelled to my home town by car'.

In addition to this main function, –고서 can at times express contrastive sequencing – something similar to the English 'even after . . .':

점심을 먹**고서** 안 먹었다고 했어요.
Even after eating lunch, he said that he hadn't eaten.

뇌물을 받**고서** 모르는 척 했어요.
Even after receiving bribe, he/she pretended not to know about it.

7.3.3 –고는

– 고는 is composed of the –고 connective ending (refer to 7.3.1), followed by the topic marker 은/는 (refer to 3.3.2.1). The pattern is used similar to 고서 (refer to 7.3.2) to link an ongoing circumstance in the first clause, with an event in the second clause:

나는 누구에게도 빚지**고는** 못 산다.
I can't live being in debt to someone.

술의 힘을 빌리지 않**고는** 나의 진심을 말할 용기가 나지 않았어요.
Without the help of alcohol, I don't have the courage to speak my mind.

–고는 also appears followed by the verb 하- (refer to 4.1.2) to form the special expression –고는 하–, which is frequently abbreviated into –곤 하–. This construction is used for depicting a habitual action. The marking of tense occurs at the end of 하– and never before –고. Depending on the tense marking, the form can be used for talking about habitual actions in the past, present or future.

그 거울은 꼭 이렇게 대답**하곤 했**다.'왕비님도 아름답지만 숲 속에 사는 백설 공주님이 가장 아름다워요.'
The mirror would reply like this:'You are beautiful, but Snow White who lives in the forest is the most beautiful of all'.

그림 그리다가 소파에서 잠들**곤 해**.
After painting a picture, I sometimes fall asleep on the sofa.

시골에 가서 살면 일찍이 자**곤 하**겠지요.
I suppose you will make a habit of going to bed early when you go to the countryside.

7.3.4 –고 나–

This construction, which means 'after having (done something)' or 'after having finished/completed doing something' or 'after being through with . . .' is covered in the auxiliary verbs chapter (refer to 5.3.1).

7.3.5 –답시고/랍시고

This form sees -고 preceded by –답시 (or -랍시 when used with the copula), which is built on the indirect quoative pattern –(ㄴ/ –는)다 (refer to 10.2). The form is used when the speaker quotes a previous statement in the first clause, typically which he/she goes on to belittle or ridicule in some way. The construction implies that the quoted phrase is ridiculous, laughable, humorous or pompous and the sentence itself tends to sound sarcastic. Although the usage of –답시고 is similar to –다고 (see 7.3.1), the latter lacks this sarcastic feeling.

너는 밥 먹**는답시고** 핸드폰만 보나?
I thought you said you were going to eat, so why are you just looking at your phone?

너도 다른 여자들처럼 다이어트 한**답시고** 단식하는 거 아니야?
Like other women, I hope you're not saying you're going on a diet and then just starving yourself?

빠른 길로 간**답시고** 이 도로로 왔는데 지옥이 따로 없구다.
If you said you wanted to go by a fast route, then going by this road is just like hell.

언니는 예쁘**답시고** 남자들에게 건방지게 군다.
While saying that she is pretty, my older sister behaves arrogantly towards men.

선배**랍시고** 도와주는 일 없이 잔소리만 하고 다닌다.
Saying he's my senior, he goes around nagging me without ever being any help.

7.3.6 –거니와

This one-shape ending links two parallel statements, which are generally closely connected to the same content matter. The second clause typically adds further information or support for the claim made in the first clause. In examples such as the following, –거니와 can typically be substituted by –고 (refer to 7.3.1), which has a far higher frequency.

유미는 얼굴도 예쁘**거니와** 마음씨도 좋아요.
Yumi has a pretty face and also a warm heart.

머리도 아프**거니와** 속이 터져요.
My head hurts and my stomach is going to explode.

민호는 노름도 안 하**거니와** 술 담배도 안 해요.
Minho doesn't gamble and he doesn't drink or smoke.

그 식당은 더럽**거니와** 불친절해요.
That restaurant is dirty and the staff are unkind.

The –거니와 construction may also occur with expressions such as 다시 말하– or 거듭 강조하–, with the meaning of 'reiterate', 'emphasize', etc. Here, –거니와 can be replaced with the higher frequency –(으)ㄴ/는데 (refer to 7.3.12) with little change in meaning.

다시 말하**거니와** 이번 대선은 혁명이었습니다.
To reiterate, this presidential election was revolutionary.

거듭 강조하**거니와** 내일은 절대로 늦으시면 안 됩니다.
To emphasize one more time, you simply cannot be late tomorrow.

7.3.7 –(으)면서

The ending –(으)면서 is a two-shape ending that cannot be preceded by tense markers. This form functions to link two consecutive actions that are being performed at the same time. This typically translates into English as 'while':

나는 아침 먹**으면서** 신문을 읽어요.
I read the paper while I eat breakfast.

음악을 들**으면서** 고향을 생각했어요.
I was thinking of home while listening to music.

기차를 타고 오**면서** 공부를 했어요.
I studied while I was coming on the train.

This expression also frequently occurs with descriptive verbs while listing complementary features that pertain to the same person, object, etc.:

그 기차는 빠르**면서** 좋아요. *The train is fast and nice, too.*
중국 음식은 싸**면서** 맛이 좋아요. *Chinese food is cheap and delicious*

The one important difference between this expression and the English 'while' is that the subject of two clauses are typically the same. When you are talking about two different actions being performed simultaneously by two different people, the better construction to use is the modifier pattern –(으)ㄴ 동안 (refer to 8.2.12) instead.

By addition of the particle 도 (refer to 3.3.3.6) to form –(으)면서도, the meaning is altered to 'even while'. In this usage, this ending can be preceded by tense makers:

오빠는 늘 놀았**으면서도** 시험에 합격했어요.
My brother, even while he always played, passed an exam.

민수는 돈이 많**<u>으면서도</u>** 잘 쓰지 않아요.
Minsu, even while having a lot of money, doesn't spend much.

This composite pattern is similar in meaning to –(아/어)도 (refer to 7.2.5). However there are two important differences. Firstly, although with –(아/어)도 the subject of both clauses may be different, with –(으)면서도 they are typically the same. Secondly, with –(으)면서도, the two clauses tend to contain actions that are ongoing in nature.

7.3.8 –(으)면서부터

This is a combination of the connective ending -(으)면서 'while' (refer to 7.3.7) and the particle 부터 'from (a time/place)' (refer to 3.3.3.4). It produces the meaning 'ever since':

열 살이 넘**<u>으면서부터</u>**는 밥도 짓고, 빨래도 하고, 집안 청소와 바느질까지도 하였다.
Ever since she turned 11 she did the cooking, washed the clothes, cleaned the house, and did the sewing.

운동을 시작하**<u>면서부터</u>** 몸이 가벼워졌다.
Ever since I started exercising, my body has felt lighter.

7.3.9 –(으)며

The ending –(으)며 is a two-shape ending that may be preceded by past tense (refer to 4.3.1.1) and the future –겠– (refer to 4.3.2.1). –(으)며 is often taken as being a bookish form of –(으)면서 (refer to 7.3.7) and rarely occurs in spoken language. Certainly, –(으)며 can replace –(으)면서 when describing two simultaneous actions:

아침 식사를 하**<u>며</u>** 책을 봤다.
I read a book while I ate breakfast.

강의를 들**<u>으며</u>** 중요한 내용을 적었다.
I took notes while listening to the lecture.

When describing simultaneous actions, –(으)며 is restricted in the same way as –(으)면서 to situations in which the same person is performing two simultaneous actions. However, the use of –(으)며

in formal writing is more widespread than the use of –(으)면서 in colloquial speech and the function is broader. –(으)며 is frequently used simply like 'and' to list complementary features or actions. Here, usage is most similar to that of –고 (refer to 7.3.1):

학교에는 수영장이 없**으며** 운동장도 없다.
At school, there is no swimming pool or sports field.

가을은 선선하**며** 여름은 덥다.
It's cool in autumn and it's hot in summer.

대부분은 회사원이**며** 일부는 대학생이다.
The majorities are office workers and the minorities are university students.

As can be seen in the examples above, in this second usage the subjects of the two clauses may be the same or different.

7.3.10 –자(마자)

The pattern –자(마자) is a one-shape ending that cannot be preceded by tense markers. It most frequently occurs with processive verbs. The '마자' element may drop in some situations, as discussed below.

With the –자(마자) pattern, the event stated in the second clause occurs instantaneously after the event in the first clause is completed, identical to the use of 'as soon as' in English:

내가 정거장에 오자**마자** 기차가 떠났어요.
The train left as soon as I got to the station.

눕자**마자** 잠이 들었어요.
I fell asleep as soon as I lay down.

오빠가 탄 비행기가 떠나**자마자** 눈물이 났어요.
Tears came to my eyes as soon as the plane took off with my big brother aboard it.

그 소설 책을 읽기 시작하**자마자** 불이 꺼졌어요.
The light went off as soon as I started reading the novel.

The '마자' element may be dropped, which results in a change of meaning: the immediacy of the expression is lost. Rather than strictly meaning 'as soon as', the nuance is often closer to 'when' or 'upon (doing)'. In the expression below, for instance, the reminiscing is not something that necessarily took place instantaneously as the speaker heard the song and thus the omission of –마자 is preferable:

그 노래를 듣**자** 옛날 생각이 났지요.
Upon hearing that song I was reminded of the days gone by.

여름이 되**자** 선풍기가 잘 팔려요.
Now it is summer, electric fans are selling well.

Note that when the second clause contains a command, proposal, suggestion, invitation or request, '마자' must always be included:

집에 도착하**자마자** 밥을 먹자.
Let's eat lunch as soon as we arrive home.

회사를 나서**자마자** 택시를 타라.
Grab a taxi as soon as you get out of the office.

졸업하**자마자** 결혼할까요?
Shall we get married as soon as we graduate?

7.3.11 –다(가)

The ending –다(가) is a one-shape ending that occurs most frequently with processive verbs and which may be preceded by past tense marking. Although the full form of this ending is –다(가), there are some usage patterns in which this shortens to –다, as we shall see below. –다(가) has the underlying meaning of 'transition'. The construction as a whole depicts transition from one action performed in the first clause to a new action or state taking place in the second.

Without past tense marking on the first clause, –다(가) indicates the interruption of one action and transition to a new and superseding action.

한 시간 동안 울**다가** 잤어요.
I cried for an hour and then fell asleep.

하늘이 맑**다가** 갑자기 흐려졌어요.
The sky was clear and then clouded over.

좀 더 놀**다가** 가.
Hang out with me a bit more and then go. (=Stay a bit longer.)

With verbs that have a natural end point or goal (such as come (somewhere), go (somewhere), make (something), prepare (something)), the use of –다(가) indicates that the first action is still in progress and not yet completed when the second action takes place. This leads to translations in English such as 'while (doing)' or 'in the course of doing', 'on the way (to doing)', or even 'was doing, but':

시장에 가**다가** 우체국에 들렀어요.
I stopped in at the post office on the way to the market.

홈페이지 만들**다가** 포기했어요.
I gave up in the course of making a homepage.

아저씨가 수박을 팔**다가** 다 못 팔았어요.
The man was selling watermelons, but didn't sell them all.

준비를 하시**다가** 질문이 있으시면 언제든지 전화하세요.
If, in the course of preparing, you should have any questions, call me any time.

Included in this usage are descriptions of unplanned events, particularly accidents. The first clause expresses what the person was doing when the accident took place and the second clause provides the specifics of the mishap.

뛰어 가**다가** 넘어졌어요.
I fell down while I was running.

야채를 썰**다가** 손가락을 베었어요.
I cut my finger while I was chopping vegetables.

스키를 타**다가** 다리를 다쳤어요.
I hurt my leg while I was skiing.

When past tense marking is added to –다(가), the resulting –었다가 undergoes an important change in meaning. Instead of being ongoing or unfinished, the addition of –었– marks the first action as completed. The completed action then transitions into a superseding action expressed in the second clause. Compare the meanings of the two sentences below, the first without past tense marking and the second with it added:

시장에 가**다가** 우체국에 들렀어요.
I stopped in at the post office on the way to the market (i.e., while I was going to the market).

시장에 갔**다가** 우체국에 들렀어요.
I went to the market [first], and then dropped by the post office.

In many cases, the content of the second clause is an unexpected consequence that comes about after the completion of the first action:

소주를 마셨**다가** 필름이 끊겨버렸어요.
I drank soju and then passed out.

말참견을 했**다가** 야단 맞았어요.
I made an uncalled-for remark and was scolded for it.

With the past tense marker, the two verbs frequently depict reversible actions such as buy-sell, put on-take off, etc.:

새 컴퓨터를 샀**다가** 팔았어요.
I bought a new computer but then sold it [again)].

양말을 신었**다가** 벗었어요.
I put on socks and then took them off [again].

This use of reversible actions occurs most frequently with the verbs 가– 'go' and 오– 'come' and other similar verbs of motion. In Korean, to emphasize that you are going somewhere and coming back, it is common to express this with 갔다 오– 'go and come (back)':

대사관에 갔**다** 왔어요.
I've been to the embassy. (= I went to the embassy and then came back.)

서점에 갔**다** 올게요.
I'll go to the bookstore and then come back.

Sentences similar to the final example above are frequently applied in leave taking, with the final verb taking future tense either with –ㄹ게 (refer to 9.9) or, for an extra level of deference –겠– (refer to 4.3.2.1) typically followed by the 'formal' speech style (refer to 4.3.4). In fact, such expressions work even without specifying where you are actually going:

갔**다** 올게요.	[CASUAL-POLITE]	*I'm off [and I'll be back].*
갔**다** 오겠습니다.	[FORMAL]	*I'm off [and I'll be back].*

With reversible actions –다(가) can be included after each action and the sentence can then be rounded off by the verbs 하– 'do' or 그러– 'be like that', depicting a repeated back and forth pattern of action.

저 할머니는 연세가 많으셔서 정신이 왔**다** 갔**다** 해요.
That granny is old, so sometimes she's with it, and sometimes she's not.

이 하나가 늘 아팠**다** 괜찮았**다** 해요.
One of my teeth is always aching off and on.

불을 자꾸 켰**다가** 껐**다가** 하지 마세요.
Stop turning the lights on and off!

아이들이 일어났**다** 앉았**다** 해요.
The children keep standing up and sitting down repeatedly.

– 다(가) can also be preceded by the intentive marker –(으)려 (refer to 7.7.2). The resulting construction depicts an intention that was either disrupted or was subsequently changed to another plan:

공원에 가려**다가** 비가 와서 못 갔어요.
I was going to go the park, but it rained so I didn't go.

전화하려**다가** 이메일을 썼어요.
I was going to phone, but I e-mailed [instead].

Also, –다(가) frequently follows the pattern –ㄹ까 하– 'thinking of' (refer to 5.4.3). The resultant construction expresses that the speaker was thinking of performing a certain action but then changed his/her mind.

김치찌개를 먹을까 하**다가** 된장찌개를 먹었어요.
I was thinking of eating kimchi stew, but ate soybean paste stew [instead].

유미를 만날까 하**다가** 만나지 않았어요.
I was thinking of meeting Yumi, but [in the end] I didn't meet her.

We now turn to consider another pattern of usage with –다(가): use after the infinitive form rather than the verb stem and with '가' normally dropped. This pattern marks a transition to a new action that is a logical continuation from an already completed action. One common occurrence of this usage is with the support (auxiliary) verb 주– (originally meaning 'give'). This pattern is used when talking about going somewhere to do something (such as a favour) for the benefit of someone else and is discussed in more detail in the chapter on auxiliary (support) verbs (refer to 5.1.12).

손예진 씨의 싸인 좀 얻어**다** 주세요.	*Can you get me Son Yejin's autograph?*
물 좀 갖**다** 주세요.	*Go and get me some water.*

This usage also commonly occurs with the verb 보– 'to see'. As discussed in the chapter on auxiliary (support) verbs (refer to 5.1.8), this pattern is frequently used when talking about the feelings experienced or discoveries made upon doing something. However, it can also be used in the following expressions that translate as 'look . . . wards':

내려**다** 봐요	*look downwards*
올려**다** 봐요	*look upwards*
돌아**다** 봐요	*look backwards, turn around and look*
내**다** 봐요	*look out(wards)*

7.3.12 –(으)ㄴ/는데

The connective ending –(으)ㄴ/는데 is one of the most frequently used connectives in Korean and has a host of interrelated usages that could correspond to most or even all of the different connective patterns dealt with in this chapter. Its inclusion under 'additional' connectives is for purposes of convenience – 'addition' is just one of several meanings that –는데 can take on.

For processive verbs, –는데 is added to the base; for descriptive verbs –(으)ㄴ 데 is used instead. When the past marker –았/었– (refer to 4.3.1.1) or the future –겠– (refer to 4.3.2.1) is included, –는데 is always used irrespective of what kind of verb it is attaching to. For future tense, in addition to –겠는데 (i.e., –겠– + –는데), it is also possible to use –(으)ㄹ 건데 (a fusion of –(으)ㄹ 거– (refer to 4.3.2.2) and –ㄴ데). For the existential verbs 있– 'exists' and 없– 'does not exist', the –는데 form is used, giving the forms 있는데 and 없는데.

The underlying usage of –(으)ㄴ/는데 can be summarized as follows. The first clause provides background information that the speaker then elaborates on or uses as a basis for what he/she states in the second clause. The contents of this second clause may either be simply additional to what is stated in the first clause or it may be consequential or even contradictory to it (however, it must always be logically related). Thus, when translated into English, –(으)ㄴ/는데 constructions can be rendered using connective terms as diverse as 'and', 'so' and 'but'. Confusing as this may sound, the use of –(으)ㄴ/는데 can be quite easily understood if we examine some specific usages in turn.

One common time when –(으)ㄴ/는데 occurs in conversation is when the speaker needs to provide background information to the hearer regarding the main business that he wants to talk about. Although the important information is included in the second clause, the first clause provides background information that is useful to the hearer in understanding the situation. In the first example below, for instance, the important information that the speaker wishes to convey is that he has come to see the professor. However, he first uses the –(으)ㄴ/는데 clause to provide some background information (in this case, identifying who he is):

저는 한국 학생**인데**, 김민수 교수님을 뵈러 왔어요.
I'm a Korean student and I've come to see Professor Kim Minsu.

나 내일 서울에 가**는데**, 뭐 부탁할 것 없냐?
I'm going to Seoul tomorrow; do you need anything?

이 차는 외제차**인데** 좀 비싸요.
This is a foreign car; it's rather expensive.

12 시가 넘었**는데** 유미가 아직도 안 왔어요.
It's past 12 o'clock and Yumi still hasn't come.

In sentences such as the last two above, the background information provided in the first clause often gives rise to certain inferences on the part of the hearer. To be more specific, the first clause in the third sentence implies that foreign cars are likely to be expensive and the first clause in the fourth sentence implies that 12 o'clock is very late and that Yumi really ought to have come by now.

One specific context in which the speaker may need to provide this kind of background information is when he/she wants to make it clear to the hearer how he/she has come by the information he/she is stating or claiming in the second clause:

제가 직접 확인했**는데** 가격이 올라갔더라고요.
I checked myself – and the price has gone up.

일기예보를 봤**는데** 내일 비가 온대요.
I saw the forecast – they say it's going to rain tomorrow.

Background information is also required when performing commands, proposals, suggestions, invitations and requests. When telling or suggesting to someone that they do something, for example, the speaker often needs to provide a bit of background information to justify the command, suggestion, etc. This information can be conveyed in the –(으)ㄴ/는데 clause:

8시가 되었**는데** 빨리 학교에 가라. [COMMAND]
It's 8 o'clock; go to school quickly.

답답**한데** 밖으로 가자. [PROPOSAL]
It's stuffy in here; let's go outside.

힘드시겠**는데** 좀 쉬고 가세요. [SUGGESTION]
You must be exhausted; have a rest and then go.

시내에 가**는데** 같이 갈까요? [INVITATION]
I'm going into town; would you like to go with me?

여기가 시끄러**운데** 좀 더 크게 말씀해 주십시오. [REQUEST]
It's noisy here; please speak a bit louder.

With some constructions of this kind, some similarity can be noted between the use of –(으)ㄴ/는데 and that of the causal connective –(으)니까 (refer to 7.1.6). However, the connotations of using one or the other are quite different. As can be seen in the English translations in the below, whereas with –(으)ㄴ/는데 the first clause is just framed as relevant background information, with –니까 the clause becomes a direct reason for the speech act performed in the second clause:

날씨가 좋**은데** 공원에 갈까요?
The weather's nice; how about going to the park?

날씨가 좋**으니까** 공원에 갈까요?
The weather's nice, ***so*** *how about going to the park?*

What initially appears to be a somewhat separate usage of –(으)ㄴ/는데 is to link two clauses that express contrastive meanings. Here, the usage appears to be most similar to contrastive connectives such as –지만 (refer to 7.2.1). However, the feeling of contrast is not as forceful as that provoked by –지만. Rather, than wanting to provide a direct contrast between the contents of the two clauses, the speaker is merely evoking the first state of affairs as relevant background information which happens to be in contrast to the main state or event expressed in the second clause:

어제는 날씨가 좋았**는데** 오늘은 비가 와요.
The weather was good yesterday, but it's raining today.

많이 먹었**는데** 아직도 배가 고파요.
I ate a lot, but I'm still hungry.

겨울이 왔**는데** 김장을 아직 안 했어요.
Autumn has come, but I haven't made the winter kimchi yet.

This contrastive meaning of –(으)ㄴ/는데 is also available when the speaker questions whether the hearer is really doing something given the background information stated in the first clause:

눈이 오**는데** 가니?
It's snowing; are you [still] going?

속이 좋지 않**은데** 술을 마시니?
You have a stomachache and you're drinking alcohol?

'도' can be added to form –(으)ㄴ/는데도. Similar to in the –(아/어)도 construction, (refer to 7.2.5) –(으)ㄴ/는데도 has a similar meaning to 'although', 'even though' or 'in spite'. In other words, the addition of '도' makes the meaning one of concession or opposition rather than of mere contrast.

> 비가 오**는데도** 찾아와 주셔서 고맙습니다.
> *Thank you for coming to see me in spite of the rain.*

> 영문과를 졸업했**는데도** 영어 못해요.
> *Even though he graduated from an English Department, he can't speak English.*

This usage can be taken as an abbreviation of the expression '. . . –(으)ㄴ/는데도 불구하고' 'disregarding the circumstance that . . .':

> 추**운데도 (불구하고)** 나가서 놀고 싶어요?
> *You want to go out and play in spite of the cold?*

> 열심히 공부했**는데도 (불구하고)** 시험에 떨어졌어요.
> *I failed the exam even though I studied hard.*

In addition to occurring as a connective ending, –(으)ㄴ/는데 frequently appears as a sentence ender as well. To make such an ending compatible with the 'polite' speech style –요 is tacked on the end: –(으)ㄴ/는데요. In such cases, the omission of the second clause generally communicates that the speaker could elaborate if asked to, has more to say on the topic, or is leaving it to the hearer to draw their own conclusions.

One specific situation in which –(으)ㄴ/는데 may appear in sentence-final position is when providing a polite but negative response to a question, typically one that is misguided (refer to King & Yeon 2002):

A: 일본 사람이세요?
Are you Japanese?

B: 아닌데요. 중국 사람**인데요**.
I'm afraid not – I'm Chinese. [Why? Are you looking for a Japanese person?]

A: 김 과장님 계세요?
Is section chief Kim here?

B: 지금 안 계시**는데요**.
I'm afraid not [but would you like me to elaborate?]

Another extension of this circumstantial meaning of –(으)ㄴ/는데 is exclamations. Such usages usually give rise to certain inferences on the part of the hearer. Examples of possible inferences from the following examples are given in brackets:

눈이 많이 왔**는데요**!
My, we've had a lot of snow! [we might have to stay home today]

오늘은 날이 참 추**운데요**!
My, what a cold day it is! [we'll have to take the baby back in]

맛이 좋**은데요**!
My, it tastes great! [and you were telling me it doesn't look good]

그 소문 들어 본 일이 없**는데요**!
I've never heard that rumour before! [are you sure?]

At times –(으)ㄴ/는데 may operate in a mode somewhere between a sentence connector and a sentence ender. Applying a special suspensive intonation, the speaker pauses after the first clause and hesitates before continuing. The function of –(으)ㄴ/는데 here is to signal to the hearer that the speaker still hasn't finished, warning him/her not to jump in yet (refer to King & Yeon 2002). When speaking politely, –요 may either be included or omitted in this usage:

오늘은 대단히 바**쁜데** . . . 다음에 가는 게 더 낫지 않을까요?
I'm very busy today . . . wouldn't it be better to go next time?

내일 비가 온다**는데** . . . 그래도 오시나요?
They say it's going to rain tomorrow . . . despite this, are you going to come?

장을 보러 가**는데**(요) . . . 뭐 사다 드릴까요?
I'm going grocery-shopping . . . do you want me to get anything for you?

7.3.13 –(으)ㄹ 텐데

This two-shape ending is a combination of –(으)ㄹ 터, which expresses inference and sometimes futurity, similar to –(으)ㄹ 거– (refer to 4.3.2.2), and the copula –이 plus the ending –(으)ㄴ/는데 (refer to 7.3.12). The expression basically follows the same usage patterns as –(으)ㄴ/는데, with the addition of –(으)ㄹ 터 providing the sense that the contents of the first clause is a conjecture rather than a fact.

바쁘**실 텐데** 신경써 주셔서 고맙습니다.
I guess you must be busy, so thanks for taking the time.

아**플 텐데** 잘 참으시네요.
It must hurt a lot, but you are putting up with it well.

분명 혼자 갔**을 텐데** 사진은 누가 찍어 주었어요?
I'm sure you went alone, so who took the photo?

다른 책도 많았**을 텐데** 왜 하필 이 책을 선택했을까요?
There must have been many other books, so why on earth did he/she choose this one?

Note that some speakers will use –(으)ㄹ건데 instead of –(으)ㄹ텐데.

7.4 Optional connectives

Optional connectives are used to list two or more choices or possibilities.

7.4.1 –거나

– 거나 is a one-shape ending that may be preceded by past and future tense markers. In its most basic usage, this ending is used to list two or more alternative actions or states and can be translated as '(either . . .) or' in English.

주말엔 등산을 가**거나** 골프를 쳐요.
On the weekends I either go hiking or play golf.

이메일을 쓰**거나** 전화를 하세요.
Write me an e-mail or give me a call.

내가 없을 때 손님이 찾아오**거나** 전화가 오면 적어 두세요.
If any guest calls or drops by while I'm out, please make a note of it.

It is also possible to attach –거나 to both verbs and then to follow the final verb with 하– 'do':

내일 영화를 보**거나** 노래방에 가**거나** 하자.
Tomorrow let's either watch a film or go to karaoke.

깊**거나** 물살이 세**거나** 하면 차라리 배를 타세요.
Get on the boat if the water is deep or the current is strong.

In addition, this pattern can be used with a pair of verbs of opposite meaning (attaching to both verbs, and often followed by –간에) to bring about the meaning 'whether . . . or . . .'. The implication is that the choice between these two or more predicates is irrelevant or of no consequence, and that, rather, the content of the following clause is what is truly important. In this case, the –거나 can be shortened to –건.

날씨야 춥**거나** (춥**건**) 덥**거나** (덥**건**) 간에 예정 시간에 떠나자.
Whether the weather is hot or cold, let's leave at the regular time.

내가 결혼을 하**거나** (하**건**) 이혼을 하**거나** (하**건**) 너하고는 상관 없는 일이다.
Whether I get married or I get divorced, it's nothing to do with you.

To create the meaning 'whether . . . or not', use the verb 말– 'desist' for the second verb (refer to 4.2.3):

그 선생님은 학생들이 듣**거나** (듣**건**) 말**거나** (말**건**) 혼자만 얘기하세요.
Whether the students listen or not, that teachers just goes on talking on his own.

Finally, –거나 (again followed optionally by –간에) is used after clauses containing question words such as 무엇 'what', 어디 'where', 누구 'who', 언제 'when' and 어떻게 'how' to imply that what is expressed in this clause is of no consequence. Such constructions usually translate into English as 'whoever . . .', 'whatever . . .', 'wherever . . .', etc.:

내가 누구를 만나**거나** 간에 상관하지 마라!
Whoever I meet, it's no concern of yours!

민수가 어디 가**거나** 간에 인기가 많아요.
Wherever Minsu goes, he is popular.

7.4.2 –든지

–든지 is a one-shape ending that has the same basic functions as –거나 (refer to 7.4.1). Note that –든지 is easily confused with –던지 (even by Korean native speakers!), but this is actually a totally separate pattern, which is a combination of observed past –더 plus –ㄴ지 in oblique question (refer to 7.4.4)

Just like –거나, in its most basic function, –든지 operates to link two possibilities. In this usage, it will generally translate as 'or' in English:

> 이번 여름에 미국에 가**든지** 캐나다에 갈 거예요.
> *This summer, we are going to go to America or go to Canada.*

> 한국 음식은 보통 맵**든지** 짜요.
> *Korean food is usually spicy or salty.*

Again in a similar way to –거나 (refer to 7.4.1), this pattern can be used with a pair of verbs of opposite meaning (attaching to both verbs), to bring about the meaning 'whether . . . or . . .': In this case, the ending –지 can be optionally omitted, which is not the case in the first usage.

> 자동차가 비싸**든지** 싸**든지** 오늘은 사야 해요.
> *Whether it is expensive or cheap, we have to buy the car today*

> 싫**든** 좋**든** 설날이니까 고향에 가야 해요.
> *Whether you like it or not, because it is lunar New Year, you have to go to your home town.*

To create the meaning 'whether . . . or not', insert 안 before the second verb or use the verb 말– 'desist' instead (refer to 4.2.3):

> 비가 오**든** 안 오**든** 예정대로 갈 거예요.
> *Whether it rains or not, we are going to go as planned.*

> 오**든지** 말**든지** 마음대로 하세요.
> *Whether you come or not, it's up to you.*

Next, and again just like –거나 (refer to 7.4.1), –든지 is used after clauses containing question words such as 무엇 'what', 어디 'where', 누구 'who', 언제 'when' and 어떻게 'how':

> 내가 누구를 만나**든지** 상관하지 마.
> *Whoever I meet, just mind your own business.*

뭘 먹**든지** 잘 씹어서 먹어.
Whatever you eat, just make sure you chew it well.

Finally, –든지 has one additional function. Especially in non-honorific speech or in the 'polite' style (refer to 6.1.1), –든지 can sometimes appear as a sentence-final ending. Sentences ending in –든지 offer advice to the hearer, with this ending framing the advice as just one possible alternative that the hearer may choose from. This translates into English as 'you could just . . .'.

피곤하면 그냥 먼저 자**든지**.
If you're tired, you could just go to bed first.

텔레비전을 고칠 수 없으면 그냥 버리**든지**요.
If you can't fix the television, you could just throw it away.

가든지 말**든지**. *Go or don't go (I don't care)*

7.4.3 –든가

Usage of the form –든가 basically replicates that of –든지 described in the previous section. It means 'whether . . . or . . . (not)':

뭘 사**든가** 상관 없어.
It doesn't matter what you buy.

따라오**든가 말든가** 니들 마음대로 해!
Whether you come or not, just do as you please!

As with –든지, –든가 can also be used in sentence-final position when giving advice:

그렇게 아프면 약을 먹**든가**.
If it hurts that much, just take some medicine.

그 사진도 가져 가고 싶으면 가져 가**든가**.
If you want to have that photo too, then just take it.

Note that just as Korean speakers tend to confuse –든지 with –던지, they also confuse –든가 with –던가, which is a combination of observed past –더 plus the question ending –(으)ㄴ가/–는가 (refer to 6.1.5).

7.4.4 –(으)ㄴ/는지 in oblique questions

The oblique question ending –(으)ㄴ/는지 is an ending with separate patterns for processive and descriptive verbs. For processive verbs, simply add the one-shape –는지; for descriptive verbs, add the two-shape –(으)ㄴ지 instead. When the past marker –았/었– or the future –겠– (refer to 4.3.2.1) is included, –는지 is always used irrespective of what kind of verb it is attaching to. For future tense, in addition to –겠는지 (i.e., –겠– + –는지) it is also possible to use –(으)ㄹ 건지 (a fusion of –(으)ㄹ 거– (refer to 4.3.2.2) and –ㄴ지):

	Processive		*Descriptive*	
present	먹는지	*eat*	예쁜지	*be pretty*
past	먹었는지		예뻤는지	
– 겠–	먹겠는지		예쁘겠는지	
– (으)ㄹ 거	먹을 건지		예쁠 건지	

The –(으)ㄴ/는지 pattern is used for forming what is known as 'oblique questions'. These are question-like elements that are then embedded within a larger sentence. The larger sentence is rounded off with a cognitive verb such as 알– 'know', 모르– 'don't know', 기억하– 'remember', 생각나– 'recall', 잊– 'forget' or 궁금하– 'wonder' or otherwise with a verb of telling or asking such as 가르치– 'tell' or 묻– 'ask'. Note that in English, the oblique question element is a complement clause introduced by a question word: 'whether', 'where', 'who', 'which', etc.

유미가 공부하**는지**	*whether Yumi is studying*
누가 가**는지**	*who is going*
어디가 아**픈지**	*where it hurts*
어느 아이가 제일 똑똑**한지**	*which child is the brightest*
뭐가 **뭔지**	*what is what*

This is how the example oblique questions above could be embedded into longer sentences:

지금 유미가 공부하**는지** 알아요?
Do you know whether Yumi is studying now?

누가 가**는**지 궁금하네요.
I wonder who is going.

어디가 아**픈지** 물어 보세요.
Ask where it hurts.

어느 아이가 제일 똑똑**한지** 기억해요
I remember which child is the brightest.

뭐가 **뭔지** 모르겠습니다.
I don't know what is what.

When an oblique question is given with verbs of asking, the sentence essentially means the same as a quoted question (refer to 10.2.2):

–(으)ㄴ/는지	*Quoted question*
시간이 있**는지** 물었어요. *I asked if he/she had time.*	시간이 있(느)냐고 물었어요. *I asked if he/she had time.*
언제 가**는지** 물어 보자. *Let's ask him/her when he/she is going.*	언제 가(느)냐고 물어 보자. *Let's ask him/her when he/she is going.*

At times, oblique question ending with –(으)ㄴ/는지 may appear two or more times in the same sentence. This translates as 'whether . . . or . . .' or 'whether . . . or not':

이게 술**인지** 물**인지** 모르겠어요.
I don't know whether this is water or alcohol.

비가 오**는지** 안 오**는지** 한번 내다 보세요.
Take a look to see whether it's raining or not.

열심히 일하**는지** 안 하**는지**가 문제예요.
The question is whether he/she is working hard or not.

Oblique questions can also be used as complete sentences as a way to ask an indirect question. This kind of question tends to occur in formal speech followed by the politeness marker –요

and is commonly used in television interviews (as in the first example) and in formal greeting expressions (second and third examples):

부인과 결혼하시겠다는 결심을 언제 하셨**<u>는지</u>**요?
When did you resolve to marry your wife?

교수님 그 동안 건강하셨**<u>는지</u>**요?
Professor, have you been in good health during that time?

즐거운 추석 보내셨**<u>는지</u>**요?
Have you had a nice Chusŏk?

7.4.5 –(으)ㄹ지 in oblique questions

The oblique question ending –(으)ㄹ지 is a two-shape ending that uses the same form for processive and descriptive verbs. It may occur with the past tense marker –았/었– but not with future tense:

The use of –(으)ㄹ지 is essentially the same as –(으)ㄴ/는지(refer to 7.4.4): it works to embed an oblique question within a sentence. However, unlike –(으)ㄴ/는지, –(으)ㄹ지 contains a feeling of conjecture. In other words, the contents of the question are not a fact that can be verified, but merely a guess, opinion or subjective viewpoint.

그 사람이 어떤 음식을 좋아**<u>할지</u>** 전혀 모르겠어요.
I have no idea what kind of food he would like.

과연 유미가 뭐라고 했**<u>을지</u>** 궁금해요.
I wonder what Yumi might have said.

네가 나라면 어떻게 했**<u>을지</u>** 말해 봐.
Tell me what you would have done if you had been me.

In the same way as –(으)ㄴ/는지, –(으)ㄹ지 may also appear twice in the same sentence to present two possible alternatives:

저 여자가 한국 사람**<u>일지</u>** 아**<u>닐지</u>** 어떻게 알아요?
How can you tell if that woman might be Korean or not?

One particular usage of –(으)ㄹ지 occurs when the pattern is followed by the particle –도 'also, even' (refer to 3.3.3.6) and then the verb 모르– 'doesn't know'. Literally meaning, 'I don't know whether', the pattern is used idiomatically to express a possibility in a similar way to how English speakers may apply a word such as 'might':

시장에서는 비**쌀지도** 모르겠어요.
It might be expensive at the market.

난 어쩌면 결혼 **할지도** 몰라요.
I might perhaps get married.

너무 긴장돼서 쓰**러질지도** 몰라요.
Because I'm so nervous, I might collapse.

월급 올려달라고 하면 해고**할지도** 몰라요.
If I ask for a pay raise, I might get fired.

–(으)ㄹ지 may also be used sentence finally, followed by –요 in the polite speech style. Sentences such as these are typically used when the speaker is in a state of doubt over an issue or course of action.

어떻게 하면 좋**을지**요?	*What might be the best thing to do?*
선생님이 어디 가**셨을지**?	*Where might teacher have gone?*

7.4.6 –(었/았)던지 in oblique questions

Past tense oblique questions can also be formed by inserting the observed/perceived past tense –더 (refer to 4.3.1.3) to make the construction –(었/았)던지. The '었/았' can be included or not depending on the context. When it is included, it provides a viewpoint whereby the speaker is looking backwards from a point in the past (similar to 'had gone', 'had done', etc. in English):

어디까지 **갔던지** 기억이 안 나요.
I don't remember how far we had gone.

Without '었/았', the sentence refers just to an ongoing, continuous situation in the past:

그 사람이 얼마나 열심히 일하**던지** 물어봤어요.
I asked how hard we worked.

7.4.7 –(으)ㄹ락 말락 (하–)

In this pattern, the two-shape ending –(으)ㄹ락 attaches to the main verb. This is then followed by the negative verb 말– 'desist' (refer to 4.2.3) and a repetition of the same –(으)ㄹ락 ending. This can then be followed by another clause or, frequently, just by the verb 하–. The pattern expresses incompletion – that something is on the verge of happening or is almost happening but ultimately has failed to come to fruition.

날씨는 비가 **올락 말락** 하네요.
The weather keeps looking like it's going to rain (without it actually raining yet).

잠이 **들락 말락** 할 때 밖에서 소리가 들려서 깼어요.
Just as I was about to fall asleep, I heard a sound from outside and woke up.

연인들이 **들릴락 말락** 한 작은 소리로 속삭였어요.
The lovers were whispering in a quiet voice that could barely be heard.

그 여배우는 엉덩이가 **보일락 말락** 한 드레스로 이목을 끌었어요.
The actress attracted attention by wearing a dress that almost revealed her behind.

7.5 Conditional connectives

Conditional connectives combine a condition expressed in the first clause that must be satisfied in order for the state of affairs in the second clause to come into effect.

7.5.1 –(으)면

–(으)면 is a two-shape ending; it attaches to consonant bases as –으면 and to vowel bases as –면. It may be preceded by past and future tense markers. As in the following examples, –(으)면 has the basic meaning of 'if':

오늘 오후에 날이 좋**으면** 공원에 가려고 해요.
If it's nice this afternoon, I'm thinking of going to the park.

오늘 시간이 없**으면** 내일 만나요.
If you don't have time today, let's meet tomorrow.

매운 음식을 먹**으면** 배가 아파요.
If I eat spicy food, I get a stomachache.

The use of –(으)면 is not strictly limited to conditional situations as is the case with English 'if'. As well as occurring with situations that are hypothetical, –(으)면 can also occur with situations that are certain to take place. In such examples, –(으)면 tends to translate better as 'when' rather than 'if':

봄이 오**면** 꽃을 보러 나갈 거예요.
When spring comes, I'm going to go out and see the flowers.

그냥 6시 되**면** 퇴근해 버릴까 생각 중이에요.
When it gets to 6 o'clock, I'm thinking of just going home (from work).

In other examples, –(으)면 may translate as 'given that' or 'seeing as':

형**이면** 형답게 행동해야 돼요.
Seeing as you are the older brother, you have to act as such.

날마다 하루에 10분**이면** 쉽게 용돈 벌이는 할 수 있어요.
Given just ten minutes a day, you can earn some extra cash.

With the addition of past-tense marking or past-past marking, the resultant construction –(았/었)었으면 displays some different patterns of usage. Firstly, it can simply be used when talking about a past event or situation. This frequently occurs when the speaker is expressing his/her regret that a certain state of affairs failed to materialize; in such cases, the sentence-final verb is often marked with –(으)ㄹ텐데 (refer to 9.12) or –(으)ㄹ 거– (refer to 4.3.2.2) preceded by past tense marking

조금만 일찍 갔(었)**으면** 만날 수 있었을 텐데/있었을 거예요.
If I had just gone a little earlier, I could have met him/her.

키가 좀 더 컸(었)**으면** 모델이 될 수 있었을 텐데/있었을 거예요.
If I had only been a little taller, I could have become a model

In sentences such as the above, –(았/었)더라면 (refer to 7.5.5) is frequently applied instead.

In addition, –(았/었)으면 can be used when expressing regret that a desired present situation differs from reality. In such cases, –(았/었)더라면 (refer to 7.5.5) cannot be used instead.

한국말을 잘했**<u>으면</u>** 원이 없겠어요.
If I could only speak Korean well, I would have nothing else to wish for.

There are a number of special uses for the conditional that lead to English translations quite different from word-for-word versions of the Korean. These are discussed in the following subsections.

7.5.1.1 –(았/었)으면 좋–

An –(으)면 sentence ending with 좋– 'good' literally means 'if . . . happens, it would be good'. In practice, this is used to express a hope or wish ('I wish . . .'; 'I hope . . .'). In the case of wishes that differ from present reality (or hopes that are somewhat far-fetched), the addition of the past tense marker is common, producing the construction –(았/었)으면 좋–.

As in the following examples, –(았/었)으면 좋– is most commonly followed by the ending –겠– (refer to 4.3.2.1). Otherwise, to provide a tinge of regret, –(으)련만 (refer to 9.14) may be used instead.

어서 방학이 오**<u>면</u>** 좋겠어요.
I hope the vacation will come soon.

얼굴은 좀 더 작았**<u>으면</u>** 좋겠어요.
I wish my face were a little bit smaller.

집이 조금만 더 넓었**<u>으면</u>** 좋으련만.
I wish the house were a little bit bigger.

– (았/었)으면 좋겠– is also employed like the English 'shall' in sentences such as the following:

무슨 가게에 가**<u>면</u>** 좋겠어요? *Which store shall we go to?*
언제 하**<u>면</u>** 좋겠어요? *When shall we do it?*

These sentences can also express mild obligation:

공부를 좀 더 하**<u>면</u>** 좋겠어요. *You should study a little more.*

With the addition of 얼마나 'how', –(았/었)으면 좋겠– comes to mean 'how wonderful it would be if . . .'. In this pattern, in place of –겠–, –(으)ㄹ까 (refer to 9.10) may be used instead.

시간이 많이 있었**으면** 얼마나 좋겠어요.
How wonderful it would be if we had a lot of time!

비가 오지 않았**으면** 얼마나 좋을까요?
How wonderful it would be if it weren't to rain!

7.5.1.2 *–(으)면 고맙겠–*

A conditional verb in –(으)면 followed by the future form 고맙겠어요 means literally 'if you do so-and-so, I would be grateful'. This is a polite way of requesting that someone do something:

일찍 좀 오시**면** 고맙겠어요.
I'd appreciate it if you'd come a little early.

빠른 답변 주시**면** 고맙겠습니다.
I would be grateful for your quick reply [to letter, e-mail, etc.]

연락처를 남겨 놓으시**면** 고맙겠습니다.
I would be grateful if you could leave your contact details.

7.5.1.3 *–(았/었)으면 하–*

–(았/었)으면 하– has a similar flavour to –(으)면 고맙겠– (refer to 7.5.1.2). It is a formal way of asking someone to do something, normally corresponding to English patterns such as 'I should be grateful if . . .':

좀 더 열심히 일해 주셨**으면 합니다**.
I should be grateful if you would work a bit harder.

다시 한 번 써 주셨**으면 해요**.
I should be grateful if you would write it one more time.

7.5.1.4 *–(으)면 되–*

Here –(으)면 is followed by the verb 되–, which literally means 'becomes', but here can be understood better as 'works', 'is okay', 'is alright', etc. The construction as a whole thus literally means 'if you . . ., it is okay/ is alright/ will do'. In practice, the construction is used when talking about satisfying a minimum requirement and commonly translates into English as 'be enough/sufficient'.

얼마**면** 돼요? ~ 이 정도**면** 돼요.
How much will do? ~ This much will do.

시험을 보기 전에 이 책만을 읽**으면** 돼요.
Before you take the exam, it will be sufficient just to read this book.

다른 사람 걱정하지 말고 너만 취직하**면** 돼.
Don't worry about other people – it's enough just if you get a job.

To emphasize the feeling that a minimum requirement is being expressed, sentences with –(으)면 frequently feature the particle만 'only' (refer to 3.3.3.1) on the relevant noun:

라면은 3분만 끓이**면** 됩니다.
Cook the ramen for just three minutes.

The expression is also used when talking and asking the requirements regarding how to do something:

온라인으로 할려면 어떻게 하**면** 되나요?
If I want to do it online, what do I need to do?

7.5.1.5 –(으)면 안 되–

Here, –(으)면 되– (refer to 7.5.1.4) is made negative by the addition of 안 (refer to 4.2.1). The resultant construction thus literally means 'if you . . ., it is NOT okay/ is NOT alright/ will NOT do'. This expression is used when denying someone permission or when telling someone what they should/must not do:

너무 늦게 일어나**면** 안 돼.
You shouldn't get up too late.

늦게까지 테레비젼을 보**면** 안 돼.
You are not allowed to watch TV until late.

약속을 잊거나 어기**면** 안 돼요.
You must not forget or break your promise.

흡연자들을 너무 죄인 취급하**면** 안 돼요.
You should not treat smokers like criminals.

To express the opposite meaning, in other words to grant permission, use the expression –아/어도 되– (refer to 7.2.5.1).

7.5.1.6 –지 않으면 안 되–/안 ... 면 안 되–

In this pattern, a negative is added before the –(으)면 안 되– construction reviewed in the previous section (refer to 7.5.1.5). The negative may be formed either through long negation (refer to 4.2.2) or short negation (refer to 4.2.1). The resultant construction literally means 'if you DON'T . . ., it is NOT okay/ is NOT alright/ will NOT do'. Basically, this is a convoluted way of saying that you have to or must do something.

long negation	*short negation*
공부하지 않**으면** 안돼요.	공부를 안 하**면** 안 돼요.

You ought to study. [= If you don't study, it won't do.]

형의 말을 듣지 않**으면** 안 돼요.	형의 말을 안 들**으면** 안 돼요.

You must do as older brother says. [=You must listen to older brother's words.]

에너지 효율을 높이지 않**으면** 안 된다.	에너지 효율을 안 높**이**면 안 된다.

We have to raise energy efficiency.

The obligation this construction expresses is stronger than the more generic obligation construction –(아/어)야 되/하– (refer to 7.5.7.1) or expressions of hope or wish with –(았/었)으면 좋겠– (refer to 7.5.1.1).

7.5.2 –다면/–라면

This construction sees the conditional form –(으)면 preceded by quotation patterns (refer to 10.2). It thus literally means 'if you say that', 'if it is said that', 'if it is true that' or 'if it is the case that'.

This construction is first of all applied when the speaker quotes a previous statement (typically made by the hearer) in the conditional sentence:

A: 인호가 올 것 같아.
I think Minho is coming.

B: 인호가 **온다면** 왜 전화도 안 했어?
If (you say) he is coming, why hasn't he even phoned?

A: 미나가 결혼한대요
They say that Mina is getting married.

B: 정말이요? 미나가 결혼**한다면** 큰 선물을 준비해야겠네요.
Really? If (it's true that) Mina is getting married, we'll have to prepare a big present for her.

However, the pattern can also be used with other hypothetical conditionals. The use of the quotative gives the sense that what is being expressed in the first half of the sentence is merely being taken as a hypothesis that may not necessarily turn out to be true:

사람에게 한 가지 목표가 있**다면** 그건 사랑일 거예요
If it is true that humans only have one goal, then that (goal) must be love.

북한이 핵무기가 있**다면** 일본에 큰 위협이 돼요.
If (it is true that) North Korea has nuclear missiles, it is a big threat to Japan.

In some circumstances, the speaker's choice of –다면/–라면 over the simple –(으)면 may signal that the speaker doubts the truth of a certain state of affairs. Compare the following:

–(으)면	*–다면/–라면*
미나가 오**면** 이 일을 할 수 있어요.	미나가 온**다면** 이 일을 할 수 있어요.
If/when Mina comes, we can do this job.	*If Mina really comes, we can do this job.*

7.5.3 –(으)려면

This ending contains –(으)려 (refer to 7.7.1), which expresses intention, followed by the conditional –(으)면. The pattern translates as 'if you intend to' or 'if you want to':

불어를 배우**려면** 프랑스에 가야 돼요.
If you want to learn French, you have to go to France.

살을 빼**려면** 녹차를 마셔라.
If you want lose weight, drink green tea.

여행 비용을 아끼**려면** 찜질방에서 자라.
If you want to save on travel expenses, sleep at the sauna.

Note that this ending can become pronounced with an extra 'ㄹ' as –(으)ㄹ려면 in colloquial speech and may even be written as such.

7.5.4 –다(가) 보면

This pattern combines the auxiliary verb pattern –다 보– 'after trying doing' (refer to 5.2.1) with the conditional –(으)면. The meaning is basically: 'if you do something for a while, then . . .' or 'if one does something over a period of time [and then steps back to reflect on it] . . .'. Here are some examples:

쭉 가**다 보면** 오른 쪽에 있어요.
If you carry on straight [for a while], it's on the right.

자꾸 만**나다 보면** 알게 될 거예요.
If you meet him frequently, you'll come to realize it.

사업을 하**다가 보면** 그럴 때가 다 있어요.
If you try doing business for a while, there are plenty of times like that.

여러 번 듣**다 보면** 무슨 소리인지 들을 수 있을 거예요.
If you listen to it several times, you'll be able to make out what they're saying.

7.5.5 –(았/었)더라면

This pattern is formed by combining the conditional ending –(으)면 onto the observed past tense –더라– (refer to 4.3.1.3). This is always preceded by a verb in past tense.

The pattern is used exclusively for talking about past events that are hypothetical or did not come into being. Although this may also be communicated simply by using a past tense conditional (refer to 4.3.1.1), the application of –았/었더라면 places more emphasis on the speaker's feeling of regret. The second clause usually contains the ending –을 텐데 (refer to 9.12) or –(으)ㄹ 거– (refer to 4.3.2.2) preceded by past tense.

자동차를 타고 왔**더라면**, 시간이 좀 더 있었을 거예요.
If we had taken a cab [here], we would have had a little more time.

오늘 오후에 비가 왔**더라면**, 공원에 가지 말라고 했을 텐데.
If it had rained this afternoon, I would have told them not to go to the park.

지금 알고 있는 걸 그때도 알았**더라면** 대학교에서 공부를 열심히 했을텐데요.
If I had known then what I know now, I would have studied harder at university.

7.5.6 –거든

The conditional ending –거든 is similar in meaning to –(으)면 (refer to 7.5.1). However, the usage of –거든 is different to –(으)면 in that the second clause is usually a command, proposition, or promise.

돈이 모자라**거든** 나한테 말 해.
If you don't have enough money, tell me.

힘들**거든** 쉬었다 하세요.
If it is hard, rest a little and then do it.

옷이 안 맞**거든** 언제든지 바꾸러 오세요.
If the clothes don't fit, come and change them any time.

After –거든, the second clause may also contain a future proposition or conjecture, typically featuring –(으)ㄹ까요?, –겠– or –(으)ㄹ거에요:

비가 그치**거든** 걸어 갈까요?
When it stops raining, shall we walk there?

돈이 생기**거든** 여행을 할 거예요.
When we get some money, we will go travelling.

아이들이 대학교에 가**거든** 이사를 하겠어요
When the kids enter university, I guess we'll move.

In addition to having a more restrictive usage than –(으)면 (refer to 7.5.1), –거든 also includes a higher degree of certainty than –(으)면 that the contents of the first clause will actually take place. Thus, in sentences such as the final example above, the speaker is actually fairly confident that his kids will go to university.

– 거든 can also appear as a sentence-final ending. Since in such cases the usage and meaning is quite distinct, this is discussed separately in the 'sentence endings' chapter (refer to 9.2).

7.5.7 –(아/어)야

The verbal connective –(아/어)야 is formed on the infinitive form of the verb. This connective is most commonly heard when it forms the basis for the modal expression –아/어야 되–/하– 'must do, have to do'. This expression is dealt with separately below (refer to 7.5.7.1).

Otherwise, –(아/어)야 creates a necessary condition similar to 'only if' in English. This form indicates that the action stated in the first clause is necessary for the action in the second clause to be realized.

공부를 열심히 해**야** 합격할 수 있어요.
You can pass the exam only if you study hard.

먹어 봐**야** 맛을 알지요.
You have to try it to know what it tastes like.

자리에 앉아**야** 뒷사람이 볼 수 있어요.
You have to sit down for the people [behind] to see.

아이를 길러 봐**야** 부모의 은혜를 알아요.
You have to raise a child to know your debt to your parents.

The particle 만 'only' (refer to 3.3.3.1) can be added after –(아/어)야 to strengthen the meaning that the course of action being put forward is the only way to achieve the goal in question.

주민등록증이 있어**야만** 투표할 수 있습니다.
You may vote only if you have an ID card.

–(아/어)야 may sometimes appear followed by 얼마나 'how (much)' and the same verb repeated. In these cases, the expression connotes that the speaker accepts the truth in question, but still questions the extent to which it may really be the case. This is similar to 'even if we grant that it is [adjective], how [adjective] can it really be?':

힘들어**야** 얼마나 힘들겠어.
Even granted that it is hard, how hard can it really be?

비싸**야** 얼마나 비싸겠어요.
Even granted that it is cheap, how cheap can it really be?

7.5.7.1 –(아/어)야 되/하–

This pattern combines the –(아/어)야 (refer to 7.5.7) meaning 'only if' and then the auxiliary verb 되– 'becomes' or 하– 'does'. Literally, this expression means 'only if you do . . ., will it do'. In practice, this expresses obligation and most typically translates into English as 'have to' or 'must'.

내일까지 숙제를 내**야 돼**요.
I have to hand in my homework by tomorrow.

책임을 져**야 돼**요.
You have to take responsibility

늦어서 자동차를 타고 가**야 돼**요.
It's late, so I'll have to go by car.

사장님이 그 회의에 참여하셔**야 해**요.
The company president has to participate in that meeting.

Although in many situations, the verbs 되– 'becomes' or 하– 'does' alternate quite freely, there is a potential meaning distinction. Namely, whereas –(아/어)야 되– refers to necessity, –(아/어)야 하– refers to obligation. For this reason, –(아/어)야 되– works better in the following example:

이번 경기는 이겨**야 된**다. *We have to win this game.*

Here, winning the game can be considered as something that is necessary or important, but it is not an obligation as such.

When this construction is applied to a verb in the past tense, it translates as 'should have done'. This normally indicates obligations that one has failed to meet, or paths of behaviour that would have been better than that actually taken:

어젯밤에 숙제를 했**어야 됐**지만, 손님이 와서 못했어요.
I should have done my homework last night, but a guest came, so I couldn't.

진작 말을 했**어야 했**어.
You had to say something earlier.

In spoken language some constructions that combine –아/어야 되/하– with other verb endings can be contracted. Namely, when –아/어야 되/하– is followed by the ending –지 (refer to 9.18) indicating shared knowledge or with –겠– (refer to 4.3.2.1) expressing future tense or conjecture, the '되/하' element can be dropped and the resulting construction can be written as one word:

Full form		*Contracted form*
가야 하지요	>	가야지요
가야 하겠어요	>	가야겠어요

Here are some examples of these in sentences:

빨리 가**야겠어**요.	*I'll have to hurry along.*
내일 다시 와 봐**야겠어**요.	*Guess I'll have to come again tomorrow.*
담배를 끊**어야지**요.	*I have to stop smoking, you know.*
말은 조심**해야지**.	*You have to watch what you say, you know.*

7.5.8 –(아/어)서야

–(아/어)서야 is a combination of the causal connective –(아/어)서 (refer to 7.1.1) with the –야 ending from –(아/어)야 (refer to 7.5.7). Combing the sequential meaning of –(아/어)서 with the meaning of 'only' provided by –야, this ending means "only upon . . .' or 'only after':

나이가 들**어서야** 부모님의 말씀을 이해하게 되었어요.
Only after becoming older have I come to understand the words of my parents.

밤이 늦**어서야** 비로소 민호가 돌아왔어요.
Only after the night had become late did Minho come back. (=Minho didn't come back until late at night.)

20세기에 들어**와서야** 대학 교육이 시작되었어요.
Only when the 20th century came did University education start.

7.5.9 –(으)면 . . . –(으)ㄹ수록

This pattern is formed by repeating the same verb twice in succession. The first occurrence of the verb is followed by conditional ending –(으)면 (refer to 7.5.1); the second occurrence is followed by the ending –(으)ㄹ수록. The first occurrence of the verb (i.e., the occurrence with –(으)면) can usually be dropped, particularly in set expressions (see below).

This pattern is used in expressions with similar structure to English expressions such as 'the bigger the better' or 'the more the merrier':

크**면** **클수록** 좋아요.
The bigger the better.

그 이야기는 들**으면** 들**을수록** 재미있어요.
The more I hear that story, the more interesting it is.

돈은 많**으면** 많**을수록** 쓰는 것이에요.
The more money you have, the more you spend.

그 자동차는 보**면** **볼수록** 사고 싶어요.
The more I look at that car, the more I want to buy it.

Two set expressions that occur with this pattern are '나이를 먹을수록' 'as you get old' and '시간이 갈수록' 'as time goes by'. With these set expressions, the first verb is more commonly dropped.

시간이 **갈수록** 영국이 좋아져요.
As time goes by, I come to like England.

나이를 **먹을수록** 뚱뚱해져요.
The older I get, the fatter I get.

In the '시간이 갈수록' 'as time goes by' expression above, 시간 'time' may also be dropped without any change in meaning. '갈

수록' also frequently appears preceded by other nouns to express something going by or continuing:

공부가 **갈수록** 어려워져요.
The more we study, the more difficult it gets.

아프가니스탄의 상황이 **갈수록** 위험해지고 있다.
The more the Afghanistan situation goes on, the more dangerous it gets.

7.6 Causative connectives

Causative connectives link an action in the first clause that causes, forces, makes or permits the state of affairs in the second clause to take place. One additional expression of similar meaning, –(으)ㄹ 정도로 is dealt with elsewhere under modifier clauses (refer to 8.2.30).

7.6.1 –게

This ending –게, which is a one-shape ending that cannot be preceded by tense markers, is dealt with elsewhere under discussions of adverbs (refer to 11.2.1.2). When preceded by a descriptive verb, the resultant construction forms adverbs such as 맛있게 'deliciously', 재미있게 'interestingly' and 예쁘게 'prettily':

유미가 예쁘**게** 웃었어요. *Yumi smiled prettily.*

However, when –게 attaches to processive verbs, the resultant construction takes on quite a different meaning: 'so that' or 'in a manner that':

모두가 듣**게** 큰 소리로 말했어요.
I spoke in a loud voice so that everyone could hear.

목이 터지**게** 노래를 불렀어요.
I sang so that my throat exploded. (= I sang until I was hoarse.)

부모님께서 편안히 계시**게** 우리들이 신경을 써야 해요.
We have to take pains so that our parents are comfortable.

In casual speech, the clause containing –게 may sometimes be postponed until the end of the sentences:

큰 글씨로 쓰세요, 모두가 잘 보**게**.
Write in large letters, so everyone can see.

In addition, in final sentence position, –게 can adopt some additional functions. First, it is used in a similar way to the ending –(으)려고 (refer to 7.7.1) when inquiring about the intentions of the hearer. Although –게 and –(으)려고 are similar in meaning when used for this function, whereas –게 emphasizes the end point (i.e completion of the intended action), –(으)려고 emphasizes the formation of the intention itself and the projection towards the stated goal.

그 돈을 다 어디에 쓰**게**?
How are you intending to spend all that money?

왜 벌써 코트를 입으세요? 집에 가시**게요**?
Why are you putting on your coat already? Are you intending to go home?

Secondly, the ending is used at the end of conditional question sentences (refer to 7.5). In such conditionals, satisfying the condition stated in the first clause would naturally lead to the content of the second clause taking place. However, in reality, failure or inability to satisfy the condition has led to the second state of events failing to take place. In such circumstances, –게 communicates a feeling of sarcasm:

내가 테니스를 그렇게 잘 쳤으면 테니스 선수가 되었**게**?
If I had played tennis that well, would I have become a tennis player?

미나가 마음에 드는 사람이 있으면 벌써 결혼했**게**?
If Mina had someone she liked, would she have got married already?

7.6.2 –게끔

This ending combines –게 (refer to 7.6.1) with the intensifier –끔. The addition of –끔 adds extra emphasis to the need for the hearer (or person being referred to) to take utmost care to perform the action in the first clause as specified in order for the contents of the second clause to take place:

부모님이 안심하**게끔** 잘 말씀 드렸어요.
I explained everything to my parents well so that they would feel at ease.

뒷일이 없**게끔** 잘 처리하세요.
Manage the matter carefully so there will be no trouble later.

다시 고장나는 일이 없**게끔** 잘 고쳐 주세요.
Please repair it perfectly so that it will not be broken again.

7.6.3 –도록

The one-shape connective –도록 cannot be preceded by tense markers. It has three different usages.

Firstly, in its most basic usage it is similar to –게 (refer to 7.6.1), –게끔 (refer to 7.6.2) and –정도로 (refer 7.2.25) in expressing the meaning 'so as to', 'so that', 'in a manner that', etc. The causative force of –도록 tends to be weaker than –게.

잊어 버리지 않**도록** 복습을 많이 하세요.
Please revise a lot so that you won't forget [what you have studied].

방청객이 들을 수 있**도록** 일부러 크게 말했어요.
I intentionally spoke in a loud voice so that the audience could hear me.

앞으로 늦지 않**도록** 노력하겠습니다.
I will try not be late in the future.

Secondly, it is used with expressions related with time to show that an action continued 'until' a certain time. It is particularly used when this certain time is late or continues until longer than what may more often be the case.

어젯밤 늦**도록** 공부했어요.	*I studied until late last night.*
해가 뜨**도록** 잤어요.	*I slept until sunrise.*
밤새**도록** 이야기했어요	*We stayed up all night talking.*

Finally, –도록 can be followed by the verb –하 'does' to form the expression –도록 하–. This expression is first of all used to mean something similar to 'make sure' in orders ('make sure you . . .'), proposals ('let's make sure we . . .') and promises ('I will make sure I . . .'):

음주를 삼가(하)**도록 하세요**.
Make sure you avoid alcohol.

택시에서 내릴 때 개인소지품 잘 챙기**도록 합시다**.
Let's make sure we take all our personal belongings when we get out of taxis.

앞으로 조심하**도록 하겠습니다**.
I will make sure I am more careful in future.

– 도록 하– can also be used in causatives (refer to 4.4.2.3).

7.7 Intentive connectives

Intentive connectives express an intention in the first clause that is made possible by performing the action stated in the second clause of the sentence. Please refer to Chapter 4 for more discussion of ways to express future intentions (refer to 4.3.2).

7.7.1 –(으)러

–(으)러 is a two-shape ending that only occurs with processive verbs and which cannot be preceded by tense marking. In the first clause, the speaker states an action that he (or the referent of the sentence) intends to perform. The second clause states where the speaker (or the referent of the sentence) went/came to perform the said action. As such, the second clause can only contain 가– 'go', 오– 'come', 다니– 'attend, go to regularly' or compound verbs derived from them:

역으로 친구를 만나**러** 갔어요.
He's gone to the station to meet a friend.

점심 먹**으러** 식당에 가요.
I'm going to the cafeteria to eat lunch.

놀**러** 오세요.
Come over to 'play'. (=Have fun, hang out, relax.)

편지를 쓰**러** 위층으로 올라갔어요.
He's gone upstairs to write a letter.

Note that –(으)러 cannot be used when you are talking about doing something else apart from going or coming in order to perform an action. If you want to use other verbs, you will have to use another intentive connective: –(으)려고 (refer to 7.7.2) or –기 위하– (refer to 2.2.4.7).

7.7.2 –(으)려고

This intentive ending is a two-shape ending, with –(으)려고 attaching to verb stems that end in a consonant and –려고 attaching to vowels. One of the most common occurrences of –(으)려고 is with 하– 'does' (or optionally 그러–) in the second clause to create –(으)려(고) 하: an expression of future intention dealt with at the end of this section.

Let us examine first the other uses of –(으)려고 as a verbal connective. In the first clause, the speaker states an action that he (or the referent of the sentence) intends/intended or desires/desired to perform. The second clause states an action that the speaker (or the referent of the sentence) is undertaking in order to perform the said action. Unlike –(으)러 (refer to 7.7.1), this second clause may contain any processive verb

저는 한국에 가**려고** 지금 한국말을 공부하고 있어요.
I'm learning Korean, with the intention of going to Korea.

택시를 잡**으려고** 40분 기다렸어요.
I waited 40 minutes to get a taxi.

여섯 시에 일어나**려고** 일찍 잤어요.
I went to bed early intending to get up at 6.

In colloquial speech, the clause containing –(으)려고 may often be postponed to the end of the sentence (or may appear on its own):

운동 기구를 왜 샀어요? 살을 빼**려고**?
Why did you buy the exercise equipment? To lose weight?

In final sentence position, –(으)려고 may take on one further function in casual speech. It is used to express extreme doubt on the part of the speaker that the content of the sentence is possible in reality (similar to English 'Could . . . really?'). The clause frequently contains the adverb 설마 that intensifies the expression of disbelief:

설마 혼자서 삼겹살 10인분이나 먹**으려고**?
Could someone really eat ten portions of pork belly on their own?

설마 동생이 언니보다 키가 크**려고**?
Could the little sister really be taller than the older sister?

In place of the –고 part of –(으)려고, it is also possible to include other connective endings. Firstly, when expressing a past intention that was then abandoned or not followed to completion, the transitional marker –다(가) can be attached (refer to 7.3.11):

혼자 가**려다가** 친구하고 같이 갔어요.
I was going to go alone, but I went together with my friend.

양주를 마시**려다가** 너무 비싸서 소주를 마셨어요.
I was going to drink whisky, but it was so expensive that I drank soju.

When the first clause contains a hypothetical situation, –(으)려 can be followed by the conditional endings –(으)면 (refer to 7.5.1) or –거든 (refer to 7.5.6). The resultant construction means 'if you intend to' and is discussed elsewhere (refer to 7.5.3):

The form –으려 can also occur followed by the suppositional expression –나 보– (refer to 5.5.1) to express conjecture about a future situation:

내일 비가 **오려나 봐요**. *It looks like it's going to rain tomorrow.*

– 으려 can be followed by the causal connectives –(으)니 (refer to 7.1.7) and –(으)니까 (refer to 7.1.6). This expresses causation based on something that is going to occur in the future:

내일 파티를 하**려니까** 와인을 가지고 오세요.
Since it is going to have a party tomorrow, bring wine with you.

Note that –으려 can become pronounced with an extra 'ㄹ' as –(으)ㄹ려 in colloquial speech and may even be written as such.

When –(으)려고is followed by the verb 하–, this creates a construction for expressing future intention. Note that 하– may be replaced by 그러– 'do like that', or just dropped entirely:

내일 도서관에 가려고 해요. with '하– '

내일 도서관에 가려고 그래요. with '그러– '

내일 도서관에 가려고.	without '하– '; 'intimate' style
내일 도서관에 가려고요.	without '하– '; 'polite' style
	I'm going to the library tomorrow

Another way to contract –(으)려고 하– is to omit the '고': –(으)려 하–. In the 'formal' speech style, this can be further abbreviated to –(으)렵니다:

내일 도서관에 가려 해요.	contracted form; 'polite' style
내일 도서관에 가렵니다.	further abbreviated form; 'formal' speech style

– (으)려고 하– expresses an intention formed before the time of speaking. Although the intention may not necessarily be a solid plan, it constitutes something that the speaker has already had in mind.

주식에 투자하**려고 해요**.
I intend to invest in stocks.

애인과 단둘이 여행을 가**려 해요**.
I plan to go travelling just with my boy/girlfriend.

내년에도 한국어 공부를 계속하**려고 합니다**.
I intend to continue my Korean language studies next year, too.

A: 숙제 했어? *Have you done your homework?*	B: 아직 안 했어요. 지금 하**려고요**. *Not yet. I'm going to it now.*

In addition to speaker intentions, –(으)려고 하– may be used to indicate that an event is about to happen. In such cases, –(으)려고 하– indicates immediacy. Frequently, it gives the feeling that the preparatory stages for the event starting are already underway, and that the commencement of the event is certain and cannot be stopped:

기차가 떠나**려고 해**요.
The train is about to depart.

사람들이 건물로 들어가**려고 해**요.
The people are about to enter the building.

When the expression is followed by the past tense, it conveys an intention that the speaker held in the past but either abandoned or did not follow through to completion:

내가 바로 그 이야기를 하**려고 그랬어요**.
I was just going to talk about that.

팥빙수를 만들어 먹**으려고 했어요**.
I was going to make p'atpingsu and eat it.

결혼 안 하**려고 했어요**.
I wasn't planning to get married.

This is frequently followed by a verbal connective such as –지만 (refer to 7.2.1) or –(으)ㄴ/는데 (refer to 7.3.12) and an explanation of why the intention was not fulfilled and/or a description of what the speaker ended up doing instead:

저녁을 먹**으려고 그랬지만** 시간이 없어서 못 먹었어요.
I was about to eat my dinner but I couldn't because there was no time.

결혼식에 가**려고 했는데** 아파서 못 갔어요.
I was going to go to the wedding but I was ill so I couldn't.

Note that –(으)려고 하– can become pronounced with an extra 'ㄹ' as –(으)ㄹ려고 하– in colloquial speech and may even be written as such. Refer to 4.3.2.4 for discussion of how –(으)려고 하– compares with that of other forms with future-related meanings.

7.7.3 –고자

– 고자 is a one-shape connective ending that has the same basic function as the more common –(으)려고 (refer to 7.7.2). It is used to link an action in the first clause that the speaker is carrying out in order to achieve a goal stated in the second clause. In comparison to –(으)려(고), –고자 occurs more frequently in formal speech or writing.

김 사장님을 만나 뵙**고자** 여기까지 왔습니다.
I've come all this way to meet president Kim.

몇 가지 여쭙**고자** 이렇게 메일을 드립니다.
I'm writing this e-mail in order to ask you a few things.

새로운 모습으로 다시 거듭나**고자** 열심히 노력하고 있습니다.
I'm trying hard to turn over a new leaf.

– 고자 frequently occurs simply with 하– 'do' in the second clause to create a sentence expressing future intention: 'I intend to . . .'. The resulting construction is basically a more formal version of –(으)려고 하– (refer to 7.7.2).

이번 발표에서는 그 개념을 간단히 설명하**고자** 합니다.
In this presentation, I intend to briefly explain that concept.

이 자리를 빌려서 저의 입장을 말씀드리**고자** 합니다.
I intend to take advantage of this opportunity to explain our position.

7.8 Comparison connectives

In what we call 'comparison' connectives, a comparison is made between two states of affairs. Frequently, whereas the contents of the second clause are factual, the contents of the first clause are figurative or hypothetical.

7.8.1 –듯이

This connective ending takes on the meaning of 'as if' or 'just as'. It is used firstly when comparing one thing to another in a figurative way:

땀을 비 오**듯이** 흘려요.
Sweat is dripping as if it were raining.

구름은 춤을 추**듯이** 움직였어요.
The clouds moved just like they were dancing.

나의 자유가 소중하**듯이** 남의 자유도 똑같이 소중해요.
Just as my own freedom is precious, so is the freedom of other people.

The construction is also frequently used in expressions such as 'as you know', 'as I just said' or 'as you see'.

다 잘 **아시듯이** 다음 대회는 부산에서 열릴 예정입니다.
As you all know, the next convention is planned to be held in Busan.

아까 말씀 **드렸듯이** 학교마다 다 다릅니다.
As I just said, it is different in every school.

In these example, –듯이 can be replaced by –다시피 (refer to 7.8.2).

7.8.2 –다시피

This one-shape ending –다시피 is similar in meaning to –듯이 (refer to 7.8.1); in other words, it normally translates as '(just) as'. However, the usage is much more restricted. –다시피 is generally only used with verbs that are connected to perception, such as 알– 'know', 보– 'see', 듣– 'hear', 느끼– 'feel' and 짐작하– 'guess':

아시**다시피** 내일 공식 기자회견 갖을 겁니다.
As you know, we will have an official press conference tomorrow.

보시**다시피** 구형보다 훨씬 더 세련되었습니다.
As you can see, it is much more stylish than the old model.

들으셨**다시피** 회의가 내일 9시부터 시작됩니다.
As you have heard, the meeting starts tomorrow from 9 o'clock.

여러분들이 이미 느끼시**다시피** 새해에는 많은 변화가 예상됩니다.
As you may already have sensed, the New Year is expected to bring many changes.

This construction is similar, in meaning, to using –(으)ㄴ/는 것 (refer to 2.2.6) followed by the particle 처럼 (refer to 3.3.6.1), which is a more common choice in casual speech:

내가 아까 **말한 것처럼** 나도 처음에는 안 믿었어요.
As I just said, even I didn't believe it as first.

Although –다시피 is most commonly used with verbs of perception, it may occasionally occur with other verbs. On these occasions, the sentence takes on a figurative meaning:

소리를 지르며 날**다시피** 뛰었어요.
Screaming loudly, he ran as if he was flying.

거의 싸우**<u>다시피</u>** 소리치는 목소리로 노래를 불렀어요.
He/she sang in a screeching voice as if he/she was fighting.

Figurative uses of –다시피 may at times be followed simply by 하–. In such instances, the whole sentence or clause takes on the meaning 'it is as if . . .' or ' . . . practically . . .'.

유미 씨는 도서관에서 살**<u>다시피</u>** 하네요.
Yumi practically lives in the library.

요즘은 날마다 비가 오**<u>다시피</u>** 하네요.
These days, it is as if it rains every day.

Chapter 8

Modifiers

Overview

Modifiers refer to words or phrases that are used to 'modify' (i.e., elaborate, describe, clarify, identify, delimit) a noun or noun-like phrase. In English, modifiers typically include the use of adjectives before the noun (**pink** sweater, **pretty** girl) or relative clauses that follow the noun (the sweater **that I wore yesterday**, the girl **who bought me lunch**). In Korean since adjectives also operate as verbs ('descriptive verbs'), the process of forming modifiers follows just one pattern. Verbs – both descriptive and processive – are placed before the noun and are put into a special modifier form.

The current chapter describes the formation of various modifier forms and then analyses sentence patterns in which they appear as an integral part.

8.1 Modifying forms

Korean has four basic modifying forms which differ in terms of tense:

1. the future/prospective modifier –(으)ㄹ
2. the present dynamic modifier –는
3. the state/result modifier –(으)ㄴ
4. the continuous past modifier –던

It is also possible to combine the future/prospective modifier and the continuous past modifier with the past tense marker 았/었 to create two more possibilities:

5. the discontinuous past modifier –(았/었)던
6. the prospective past modifier –(았/었)을

Except for the dynamic modifier –는, all of these forms can occur either with descriptive or processive verbs:

	Form	Descriptive verb	Processive verbs
1.	–(으)ㄹ	쌀 것 *thing that will be cheap*	먹을 것 *thing I will eat/thing to eat*
2.	–는	–	먹는 것 *thing I am eating*
3.	–(으)ㄴ	싼 것 *cheap thing*	먹은 것 *thing I have eaten*
4.	–던	싸던 것 thing *that was cheap*	먹던 것 *thing I was eating*
5.	–(았/었)던	쌌던 것 *thing that used to be cheap*	먹었던 것 *thing I ate before/ thing I used to eat*
6.	–(았/었)을	쌌을 것 *thing that would have been cheap*	먹었을 것 *thing that I would have eaten*

Over the sections below, the structure and usage of these forms are described in turn. Then, in sections 8.1.7 we look briefly at cases where modifiers occur in combination with the intentive –(으)려.

8.1.1 *The future/prospective modifier –(으)ㄹ*

The future/prospective modifier is a two-shape verb ending, with –을 attaching to verb bases that end in a consonant and –ㄹ attaching to those that end in a vowel. Although this form can attach to descriptive verbs, this usually only occurs in certain specific constructions (refer to 8.2)

Future/prospective modifiers are used when the contents of a modifying expression depicts a state of affairs that will take place in the future (i.e., when talking about something that **will be** worn, read, hot, far, etc.):

내가 **심을** 꽃
the flowers that I'm going to plant

공부를 할 학교
the school where you are going to study at

졸업할 날
the day we'll graduate

영어를 **가르칠** 사람
a person who is going to teach English
(or a person whom (I) am going to teach English to)

Here are some examples of these in full sentences:

내가 **심을** 꽃은 여름이 되면 필 거예요.
The flowers that I'm going to plant will bloom in the summer.

공부할 학교는 바로 이곳이에요.
The school where you are going to study at is this place right here.

졸업할 날이 가까워지네요!
The day we'll graduate is getting closer!

영어를 **가르칠** 사람은 한국 사람이에요.
The person who is going to teach English is Korean.
(or – The person whom [I] am going to teach English to is Korean.)

When followed by 사람 'person' or 분 'person (honorific)', the future modifier construction may also translate as 'people who want to' or 'people who plan to':

저녁에 커피 **드실** 분은 여기 오세요.
People who are planning to drink coffee this evening, please come this way.

In some contexts, the prospective modifier can also translate as '. . . to . . .' ('thing to eat', 'person to meet', etc.):

<u>**먹을**</u> 것이 없어요.
We haven't got anything to eat.

<u>**만날**</u> 사람이 있어요.
I have someone to meet.

아파트 <u>**임대하실**</u> 분을 찾습니다.
[We are] Looking for someone to rent an apartment.

8.1.2 The present dynamic modifier –는

The one-shape ending –는 is used to denote a dynamic ongoing action and thus cannot appear with descriptive verbs or the copula. It connotes an action that is in progress, ongoing, currently taking place, or happening habitually (something that is (being) worn, read, etc.).

<u>**먹는**</u> 사람	*the person who is eating*
잘 <u>**팔리는**</u> 자동차	*the car which is selling well*
남자가 <u>**하는**</u> 말	*what the man says*
가족들이 <u>**다니는**</u> 교회	*the church that my family attend*

Here are some examples of these in sentences:

밥을 빨리 <u>**먹는**</u> 사람을 싫어해요.
I hate people who eat quickly.

최근에 가장 잘 <u>**팔리는**</u> 자동차 차종은 무엇인가요?
Which make of car do you reckon is selling the best these days?

그 남자가 <u>**하는**</u> 말을 믿지 말고 하는 행동을 보세요.
Instead of listening to what that man says, take a look at the behaviour he does.

가족들이 <u>**다니는**</u> 교회에 가고 싶어요.
I want to go to the church that my family attend.

Although –는 cannot occur with descriptive verbs, it can occur with the existential verbs 있– 'exist' and 없– 'not exist'. Note that 있는 and 없는 are frequently used in cases where no such expression is required in English or when English uses 'with' or 'without' instead:

해변가 바로 **옆에 있는** **식당에서 점심을 먹었어요.**
We ate lunch at a restaurant [which is] right next to the coast.

승용차 **없는** 서울 거리는 어떤 모습이었을까요?
What would the Seoul streets have looked like without any private cars?

This usage extends to the following descriptive verb constructions that include 있–/없– as an integral part:

–있다	**–없다**	
맛있는	맛없는	*tasty/not tasty*
재미있는	재미없는	*interesting, fun/boring*
멋있는	멋없는	*stylish/not stylish*

8.1.3 The state/result modifier –(으)ㄴ

The state/result modifier is a two-shape verb ending, with –은 attaching to verb bases that end in a consonant and –ㄴ attaching to those that end in a vowel. The –(으)ㄴ modifier depicts a state or a result that still has present consequences. From this underlying meaning, the meaning and usage of –(으)ㄴ is quite distinct depending on whether it occurs with descriptive verbs (or the copula) or with processive verbs.

With descriptive verbs (or the copula), it connotes a present or ongoing state:

넓은 집	*house which is wide (= large)/a large house*
어려운 한국어 문법	*difficult Korean grammar*
은행원**인** 김유미	*the Kim Yumi who is a banker*
비법 **아닌** 비법	*a secret which is not a secret*

Here are some examples of these in full sentences:

넓은 집으로 이사를 가고 싶어요.
I want to move to a large house.

어려운 한국어 문법을 어떻게 다 배울 수 있을까요?
How can I ever learn all this difficult Korean grammar?

은행원**인** 김유미 씨가 찾아오셨어요.
The Kim Yumi who is a banker has come.

저의 비법 **아닌** 비법을 공개해 봅니다.
We are going to make public the secret which is not a secret.

With processive action verbs, on the other hand, –(으)ㄴ connotes an action that has taken place in the past. This past action often has relevance to a current state of affairs. This is particularly the case for verbs that, when used in the past tense, tend to communicate a present state (refer to 4.3.1.1), such as in the following examples. 결혼한 사람 thus means 'a person who has got married' (and is therefore married now) rather than simply 'a person who got married (sometime in the past)':

결혼한 사람	*a person who has got married (= a married person)*
수영복을 **입은** 여자	*a woman who has put on a swimming costume (= a woman who is wearing a swimming costume)*
잘 **익은** 고기	*meat that has been well-done (= well-done meat)*
썩은 이	*a tooth that has decayed (= a decayed tooth)*

Here are examples of these in sentences:

일찍 **결혼한** 사람과 늦게 **결혼한** 사람 중 어느 쪽이 더 후회하기 쉬워요?
Between a person who got married early and a person who got married late, which is more likely to regret it?

수영복을 **입은** 여자들이 많았어요.
There were many women wearing swimming costumes.

잘 **익은** 고기를 **구운** 김치와 함께 맛있게 먹었어요.
I ate delicious meat that was well-done with fried kimchi.

<u>**썩은**</u> 이 때문에 밤에 진통제를 많이 먹었어요.
I took a lot of painkillers at night because of my decayed tooth.

With other verbs as well, the meaning of –(으)ㄴ tends to have present significance. 먹은 고기 more commonly means 'the meat I have eaten (and is still in my stomach!)' rather than simply 'the meat I ate (at some time in the past)'. Likewise, 먹은 사람 more commonly means 'the person who has eaten (and is therefore not hungry now)' rather than simply 'the person who ate (at some time in the past)'.

<u>**먹은**</u> 사람	*person who has eaten (or who ate)*
<u>**쓴**</u> 편지	*the letter which I have written (or I wrote)*
<u>**죽은**</u> 사람	*a person who has died (or who died); a dead person*
<u>**배운**</u> 것	*thing that I have learned (or that I learned)*

Here are examples of these in sentences:

지금 점심을 <u>**먹은**</u> 사람도 있겠지만 저는 아직 못 먹었어요.
There must be many people who have eaten lunch by now, but I haven't yet.

손으로 글을 <u>**쓴**</u> 편지를 받는 것은 참 즐거운 일이에요.
It is really nice to receive a letter that has been written by hand.

<u>**죽은**</u> 사람이 <u>**산**</u> 사람과 소통할 수 있어요?
Can a dead person communicate with the living?

아이가 생긴 후 <u>**배운**</u> 것이 많았어요.
There are many things I have learned since I had a child.

Note, however, –(으)ㄴ may also appear in cases where the state of affairs has no clear relevance to the present. Here, –(으)ㄴ simply marks a completed action in the past:

여기는 우리 아버지가 다니<u>**신**</u> 학교에요.
This is the school that my father attended.

However, sentences such as the above are more commonly expressed using the discontinuous past modifier –(았/었)던 (refer to 8.1.5), which would make the modifier clause '아버지가 다니셨던 학교' in this case.

8.1.4 The continuous past modifier –던

The one-shape –던 can occur with both processive and descriptive verbs.

With processive verbs, it connotes an action or a state that was previously taking place and that was progressive in nature rather than finished or completed. This most typically translates in English into 'which has been' or 'which was being'.

신문을 **읽던** 사람
The person who was reading a newspaper

오랫동안 만나고 **싶던** 사람
A person who I had wanted to meet for a long time

어제 **마시던** 술
The alcohol we were drinking yesterday [but didn't finish]

살던 집
The house where we were living/where we used to live

Here are some more examples of these in sentences:

신문을 **읽던** 사람은 큰 소리로 웃었어요.
The person who was reading a newspaper laughed in a loud voice.

오랫동안 만나고 **싶던** 사람이 오늘 왔어요.
Someone I've been wanting to see for a long time has come today.

어제 **마시던** 술이 좀 남았어요.
There is some of the booze left which we were drinking yesterday.

여기는 한국 처음 왔을 때 **살던** 집이에요.
This is the house where we lived when we first came to Korea.

When used with descriptive verbs, –던 indicates a situation that continued for a period of time but has now changed:

유명하던 가수
The singer who used to be famous

춥던 날씨
The weather that had been cold

백만장자**이던** 김 사장
President Kim who used to be a millionaire

앓던 이
The tooth that was hurting

Here are some more examples of these in sentences:

유명하던 가수가 지금은 늙었어요.
The singer who used to be famous is old now.

어제까지도 **춥던** 날씨가 따뜻해졌어요.
The weather that had been cold until yesterday became warm.

몇 년 전까지도 백만장자**이던** 김 사장이 거지가 됐어요.
Mr. Kim who was a millionaire until just few years ago became a beggar.

앓던 이를 뽑았어요.
I had the tooth pulled that had been hurting me.

8.1.5 The discontinuous past modifier –(았/었)던

– (았/었)던, which combines the past tense marker with the continuous past modifier –던, depicts an action or a past state that is completed, that no longer applies or that is simply felt to be remote.

With descriptive verbs (or the copula), it connotes a previous state that used to be the case in the distant past or a state that has now been altered:

옛날에 **유명했던** 경기 고등학교	*Kyonggi High School, which used to be famous in prior days*
학생**이었던** 시절	*the days when I was a student*
길었던 머리	*hair that had been long*
맛있었던 짜장면 집	*a black bean noodle restaurant that had been tasty*

Here are some more examples of these in sentences:

옛날에 **유명했던** 경기 고등학교가 이 자리에 있었어요.
Kyonggi High School, which used to be famous in prior days, used to be on this spot.

학생**이었던** 시절을 생각하고 있었어요.
I was thinking of the days when I was a student.

길었던 머리를 자르고 찍은 사진이에요.
This is a photo I took after cutting my hair which had been long.

맛있었던 짜장면 집은 다 어디로 사라졌나요?
Where have all the tasty black bean noodle restaurants disappeared to?

With processive action verbs, –(았/었)던 can take on two different meanings. Firstly, with verbs which when used in the past tense tend to communicate a present state (refer to 4.3.1.1), –(았/었)던 can be used to denote a past state that no longer applies:

결혼했던 사람	*a person who was married [but not anymore)*
신었던 하이힐	*the shoes that I wore [but then took off)*
끊었던 담배	*the cigarettes that I had given up [but have now gone back to)*
죽었던 예수	*Jesus, who had been dead [but was then resurrected]*

Here are examples of these in sentences:

전 사실 한 번 **결혼했던** 사람이고 혼자 살고 있어요.
Actually, I am someone who used to be married and now live alone.

어제 **신었던** 하이힐을 또 신었어요.
I put on the high heels again that I had worn yesterday.

끊었던 담배를 다시 피워요.
I have now gone back to smoking the cigarettes that I had given up.

죽었던 예수가 3일 째 아침에 부활했다.
Jesus, who had been dead, was resurrected on the morning of the third day.

Secondly, use of –(았/었)던 can simply imply that the action in question represents a remote past. If the main verb is in the past tense, the modifier clause with –(았/었)던 usually implies that the action in this clause took place before that in the main clause. Here are some examples

어제 **<u>왔던</u>** 사람이 또 왔어요.
That person who came yesterday is here again.

그 사람이 옛날에 파티에 가서 **<u>만났던</u>** 사람 아니에요?
Isn't that the person we met at that party a long time ago?

귀신을 쫓기 위해 조상들이 **<u>먹었던</u>** 음식은 무엇이 있나요?
What food was there that our ancestors ate to drive out spirits?

인류가 처음으로 **<u>마셨던</u>** 술이 포도주였어요.
The alcohol that the human race first drank was wine.

8.1.6 The prospective past modifier –(았/었)을

–(았/었)을 combines the past tense marker with the prospective modifier –을. Use is limited to certain modifying expressions, notably modifier + 것 (refer to 8.2.2), modifier + 것 같– (refer to 8.2.3), –(으)ㄹ 때 (refer to 8.2.17), –(으)ㄹ 뻔하– (refer to 8.2.25) and –(으)ㄹ줄 알– /모르– (refer to 8.2.31).

8.1.7 Intentive –(으)려 with modifiers

The intentive element –(으)려 (refer to 7.7.2) may occur with the present dynamic modifier –는 (refer to 8.1.2) to express an intention in the present, and with the continuous past modifier –던 to expresses a past intention. The resulting constructions tend to occur only with processive verbs:

– 려는 먹으려는 것
thing I'm intending to eat/thing I'm about to eat

– 려던 먹으려던 것
thing I was intending to eat/thing I was about to eat

Here are some examples, the first two with –려는 and the remaining three with –려던:

한국에 가**<u>려는</u>** 사람을 알아요.
I know someone who is intenting to go to Korea.

그 버스를 **<u>타려는</u>** 사람이 너무 많네요.
There are too many people who want to get on that bus.

<u>하려던 말</u>을 잊었어요.
I forgot what I was going to say.

그래서 **<u>뉴욕으로 가려던 사람</u>**은 보스턴으로 가게 되었어요.
The person who was intending to go to New York ended up going to Boston.

마네킹 흉내로 **<u>경찰을 속이려던 도둑이</u>** 결국 체포되었다.
A thief who was trying to give police the slip by pretending he was a mannequin was arrested.

8.2 Sentence patterns with modifier clauses

Korean contains a number of common sentence patterns that use modifying forms as essential building blocks.

8.2.1 –는 가운데 'in the middle of'

This construction combines the dynamic modifier -는 with the noun **<u>가운데</u>** 'middle, centre'. It is used in written language when describing an event that occurred (often suddenly or unexpectedly) in the middle of or amid another longer, ongoing process.

경기 침체에 대한 우려가 커지**<u>는 가운데</u>** 주가가 곤두박질쳤다.
Stocks dropped sharply amid growing concern about economic stagnation.

모든 가족들이 지켜보**<u>는 가운데</u>** 눈을 감았다.
She closed her eyes with her family watching over her. (= She passed away surrounded by her family.)

8.2.2 modifier + 것 'the fact that'

This pattern combines any modifier form with the bound noun 것 'thing', 'fact' (which is frequently abbreviated to 거) (refer to 2.1.2.1):

비가 오**<u>는 것</u>**	*the fact that it's raining*
신문을 읽**<u>는 것</u>**	*the fact that he's reading the newspaper*

The pattern is widely used in the same way as a nominal construction to change a verb phrase into a noun phrase. This noun phrase then becomes a constituent of a matrix sentence:

피아노 치**는 것**이 좋아요. *I like to play the piano*

비가 오**는 것**을 보고 있어요. *I'm watching it rain.*

This usage is discussed in more detail elsewhere (refer to 2.2.6).

The pattern –는 것 may also be followed by the verb 어떠– 'how about' in expressions of suggestion or advice. The pattern translates as 'how about . . .?' or 'why don't you try . . .?'

담배는 끊으시**는 것이 어때요**?
Why don't you try giving up smoking?

영화를 보러 가**는 것이 어때요**?
How about going to watch a movie?

Furthermore, the pattern frequently appears followed by the copula to produce an expression that literally means 'it is the fact that'. This expression is primarily used in equational sentences, when stating that a noun A 'equates to' a noun B (with the second noun being a nominalized verbal expression using modifier + 것).

대중목욕탕이 가지고 있는 장점은 사우나 시설이 있**는 것이다**.
The main advantage that public bathhouses possess is the fact that they have a sauna.

정말 원하는 것은 모두가 안 싸우고 행복하게 사**는 것이에요**.
What I really want is for everyone not to fight and to live happily.

This usage extends to the pattern '. . . 아니라 . . . –는 것이– ' meaning 'A is not B but C':

언어를 배우는 것은 언어뿐만 아니라 문화까지 배우**는 것이에요**.
Learning a language is not just learning a language but also learning culture.

자신의 행복은 다른 사람이 만드는 것이 아니라 내가 만드**는 것이다.**
My own happiness is not something that is made by other people, but something I make myself.

Besides sentences such as the above, –는 것 plus the copula frequently occurs in sentences where it adds nothing to the factual meaning. In these cases, it has the function of explaining or clarifying what could otherwise be puzzling.

> 따라서 미국의 경기 침체가 동아시아 국가 전반으로 파급 되**었던 것이다**.
> *Thus, it was the case that the US financial stagnation spread to whole of the East Asian countries.*

> 쉽게 말하자면 온라인 커뮤니티를 이용하는 마케팅은 크게 성공**한 것이다**.
> *To put things in simple terms, it is a fact that marketing which has taken advantage of online communities has been a big success.*

In formal speech or writing (as in the above), as well as clarifying the meaning, it also makes the claims of the speaker or writer sound more like an objective fact rather than a subjective claim (similar to the addition of 'it is the case that . . .' or 'it is a fact that . . .' in English). Notice that, as in the examples above, it frequently appears with expressions of reiteration such as 따라서 'thus', 즉 'that is to say' and 쉽게 말하자면 'put simply':

In more colloquial language, use of this pattern has an emphatic function. In expressions such as the following, modifier + 것 emphasizes that the speaker has performed or is performing the action in question.

A: 숙제 했어? *Have you done your homework?*	B: 지금 하**는 거야**. *I'm **doing** it now.*
A: 어제 형 **만났어**? *Did you meet older brother yesterday?*	B: 오늘 만**나는 거야**. *I'm **meeting** him today.*

Usage in informal language extends to questions that have an incredulous edge similar in nuance to 'what on earth . . .?' or 'what do you think . . .?' in English.

> 뭐 하**는 거야**? 시끄러워.
> *What do you think you're doing? It's noisy.*

> 이 시간에 어디 가**는 거야**?
> *Where on earth are you going at this time?*

8.2.3 modifier + 것 같– 'it seems that'

This expression combines a verb in any of the six modifier forms, the bound noun 것 'thing', 'fact' (refer to 2.1.2.1) and the verb 같– 'is the same, is similar, is like'. Put together, the expression means 'it seems that . . .' or 'it looks/sounds like . . .'.

future/prospective modifier	비가 올 것 같아요	*it seems like it will rain*
present dynamic modifier	비가 오는 것 같아요	*it seems like it is raining*
state/result modifier	비가 온 것 같아요	*it seems like it has rained*
continuous past modifier	비가 오던 것 같아요	*it seems like it was raining*
discontinuous past modifier	비가 왔던 것 같아요	*it seems like it had rained*
prospective past modifier	비가 왔을 것 같아요	*it seems like it would have rained*

This pattern is extremely popular in spoken Korean. In addition to being used in the original meaning of 'it seems like . . .', it is also used when speakers of English would say 'I think . . .'. Some speakers will use it just to sound vague in situations where there is absolutely no doubt or question of seeming or appearing. For example, while coughing and sniffling, a speakers may say '감기 걸린 것 같아요' 'I (seem to) have caught a cold' (refer to King & Yeon 2002).

그 영화가 재미있**을 것 같아요**.
It seems that the movie will be interesting.

건망증이 심해지**는 것 같아요**.
My forgetfulness seems to be getting worse.

오늘은 기분이 **좋은 것 같아요**.
Today he/she seems to be in a good mood.

저는 불오징어가 더 맛있**던 것 같아요**.
For me, the bulgogi with squid seemed to taste better.

유미가 그때부터 아프기 시작**했던 것 같아요**.
It seems that Yumi had started to be ill from that time.

좀 더 연습할 시간을 주셨으면 좋**았을 것 같아요**.
I think it would have been better if you had given us more time to practice.

In addition to being preceded by modifying constructions, it should be noted that 같– can occur following nouns as well:

여름 **같아요**.	*It feels like summer.*
그 소녀는 천사 **같아요**.	*That girl is like an angel.*

8.2.4 –(으)ㄹ 겸 'with the combined purpose of'

This pattern is applied when listing two or more joint purposes for performing a single action. The first action appears with the connective –고 'and' (refer to 7.3.1) and the second appears with the prospective modifier followed by 겸 (refer to 2.1.2.2). This pattern can only appear with processive verbs.

바람도 쐬고 친구도 만**날 겸** 부산에 갔어요.
I went to Busan to enjoy the breeze and see my friends, too.

칵테일도 마시고 좋은 음악도 들**을 겸** 재즈 바에 갔어요.
We went to a jazz bar to drink cocktails and listen to nice music.

This pattern also appears in an extended form as ' –(으)ㄹ 겸 . . . (으)ㄹ 겸 (해서)':

손자도 **볼 겸 딸도 만날 겸 해서** 왔어요.
I've come to see my daughter and see my grandson at the same time.

구경도 **할 겸 기분전환도 할 겸 해서** 여행을 떠나려고 해요.
I am planning to go on a trip so as to combine some sightseeing with a change of pace.

8.2.5 –(으)ㄹ 계획이– 'plan to'

This pattern employs the prospective modifier followed by the noun 계획 (計劃) ('plan') and the copula (refer to 4.1.4). It is used to talk about future plans and intentions.

일주일에 두 번씩 만나서 공부**할 계획이에요**.
I plan to meet him/her twice a week and study.

시월 달에 대사님이 우리 학교를 방문**할 계획입니다**.
The ambassador is planning to visit our school in October.

내년에 일본에 갈 때, 가족을 데리고 **갈 계획이에요**.
Next year when I go to Japan, I plan to take my family.

In addition to 계획 'plan', similar constructions can be made with the following nouns: 예정 'plan, intention', 생각 'thought, idea', 작정 'decision, intention' 셈 'calculation', 'plan', and 마음 'heart/mind':

언제쯤 떠**날 예정**이에요?
When do you plan to leave?

졸업한 후에 동양에서 일**할 생각이에요**.
I plan to work in the Far East after graduating.

한국말을 열심히 배**울 작정이에요**.
I plan to study Korean very hard.

내일부터 일에 치중**할 마음이에요**.
I intend to concentrate on my work from tomorrow.

앞으로 어떻게 **할 셈이에요**?
What are you planning to do from now on?

8.2.6 –(으)ㄴ|는 김에 'while you're at it', 'seeing as'

This pattern is composed of the present dynamic modifier –는 or the state/result modifier -(으)ㄴ, the bound noun 김 (refer to 2.1.2.4) and the particle 에 (refer to 3.2.4.1). It expresses the meaning 'seeing as . . .' or 'while . . .':

시내에 나**온 김에** 술이나 마시지요.
Seeing as we've [already] come downtown, what about having a drink?

한국에 가**는 김에** 열흘 정도 머무를 생각이에요.
Seeing as I have to go to Korea, I'm thinking of staying ten days.

A: 시장에 잠깐 갔다 올게요. *I'm just off to the market briefly.*

B: 가는 **김에** 과일 좀 사 와요. *While you're at it, buy some fruit.*

–(으)ㄴ/는 김에 is frequently preceded by the adverb 이왕, which we can translate as anyway, anyhow:

이왕 전화한 김에 하나만 물어보자.
While I've got you on the line anyway, let me ask you a question.

8.2.7 –는|던 길(에) 'on the way to'

This expression combines the word 길 'road' or 'street' with a modifying clause either containing the present dynamic modifier –는 or occasionally the continuous past modifier –던. With the present dynamic modifier –는, the pattern means 'to be on the way to/from . . .':

우체국에 가**는 길이에요**. *I'm on my way to the post office.*

기차역에 가**는 길에** 이 편지를 부쳐 주실래요?
Would you mind posting this letter for me on your way to the train station?

교회에서 돌아오**는 길에** 유미를 만났어요.
I met Yumi on my way back from church.

In the past tense, –는 길에 can be replaced with –던 길에 with little change in meaning:

집에 가**던 길에** 담배 하나 살까 하고 뒷주머니 지갑을 찾는데 없더라고요.
On the way home, it occurred to me to buy some cigarettes, but when I looked in my pocket for my wallet, I realized it wasn't there.

공항에 나가**던 길에** 교통사고를 당했어요.
On the way out to the airport, I had a traffic accident.

8.2.8 –(으)ㄴ 나머지 'as a result'

This pattern combines the state/result modifier with the word 나머지, which literally means 'the rest' or 'the remainder'. The resulting construction expresses causation: the content of the second clause takes place 'as a result of' or 'from an excess' of the situation presented in the first clause:

나는 피곤**한 나머지** 집에 오자마자 침대에 털썩 드러누웠어요.
I was so tired that as soon as I got home I plopped myself down on the bed.

다리를 **<u>다친 나머지</u>** 도망가지 못했어요.
My leg was hurting so much that I could not run away.

8.2.9 –(으)ㄴ 다음/뒤/후에 'after'

This pattern combines the state/result modifier on a processive verb with any of three expressions that mean 'after': 다음에, 뒤에 or 후에 (後–). The expression links two activities, the second occurring chronologically after the first:

영화가 끝**<u>난 후에</u>** 술 마시러 술집에 갔어요.
After the movie finished, we went to a bar to drink.

음악을 다 들**<u>은 뒤에</u>** 신문을 읽었어요.
After listening to the music, I read the newspaper.

점심을 먹**<u>은 다음에</u>** 도서관에 갔어요.
After I ate lunch, I went to the library.

Note that the pattern with the opposite meaning, –기 전에 'before . . .', is formed on a nominalized form rather than a modifier (refer to 2.2.4.10).

8.2.10 –는/–(으)ㄴ 대로 'in accordance with'

In this pattern, the present dynamic or state/result modifier is followed by the bound noun 대로 (refer to 2.1.2.5). This results in two main patterns of usage.

Firstly, the pattern is used similarly to English expressions such as 'in accordance with', 'in conformity with' or simply 'as':

느**<u>낀 대로</u>** 이야기 해 보세요.
Speak as you feel.

그 사람이 하고 싶**<u>은 대로</u>** 하게 했어요.
I let him do as he liked.

교수님께서 말씀하**<u>신 대로</u>** 했어요.
I did as the professor told me.

Secondly, the pattern is used in a similar way to –자 마자 (refer to 7.3.10) to express the meaning 'as soon as':

알아보**는 대로** 저한테 이야기해 주세요.
Tell me as soon as you find out.

수업 시간이 끝나**는 대로** 곧 돌아오세요.
Come right home as soon as school is over.

기회가 닿**는 대로** 찾아뵙겠습니다.
I will visit you as soon as an opportunity arises.

Note that 대로 can also be used directly after nouns, as discussed previously in this book (refer to 2.1.2.5).

8.2.11 –는 데 'in the matter of'

This construction combines the present dynamic modifier with the noun 데 'place'. As noted earlier (refer to 2.1.2.7), 데 may appear with modifying constructions to give the literal meaning of 'a place where':

사람 없**는 데**로 가자.
Let's go to a place where there are no people.

However, sentences with the present dynamic modifier and 데 are not limited to this literal meaning. They can also be used to me 'in the matter of', 'in the process of' or simply 'when':

한국어를 배우**는 데** 가장 어려운 것은 뭐예요?
When learning Korean, what is the most difficult thing?

고속버스는 기차로 연결되지 않는 목적지까지 가**는 데** 편리한 교통수단입니다.
Express buses are a convenient form of transportation when you are going somewhere that does not have train connections.

8.2.12 –는 동안/사이에 'while'

This expression typically applies the present dynamic modifier followed by 동안 'during' (refer to 2.1.2.8), or 사이 'interval'. Unlike one other pattern that translates as 'while . . .' –(으)면서 (refer to 7.3.7), these patterns typically include different subjects in each of the two clauses. Whereas 동안 is used for longer ongoing activities, 사이 normally occurs with an activity that occupies a shorter time interval:

공부하**는 동안에** 도둑이 들어왔어요.
While I was studying, a burglar came in.

남들이 노**는 동안에** 우리는 일했어요.
While others were playing, we worked.

아버지께서 목욕하시**는 사이에** 손님이 왔어요.
While my father was bathing, a guest came.

엄마가 안 보**는 사이에** 형이 남동생을 때렸어요.
While mum wasn't watching, older brother hit younger brother.

Occasionally 동안 or 사이에 may occur after the state/result modifier –(으)ㄴ. This happens with processive verbs that when used in the –(으)ㄴ form connote a present resultant state. It is particularly common with the verbs 가– 'go' and 오– 'come' (and compound verbs based on these):

학교에 **간 사이에** 친구가 집에 왔어요.
While we were away at school, my friend came to my house.

사장님이 나**간 사이에** 아무 일도 안 했어요.
While the boss was out, I didn't do anything.

연예인이 모자를 잠시 벗**은 사이에** 사진 기자가 사진을 찍었어요.
While the celebrity took off his/her hat for a moment, the photographer took a picture.

자리를 비**운 동안에** 중요한 전화를 놓쳤어요.
While I was away from my post, I missed an important telephone call.

It should be pointed out that 동안 and 사이 can also be used directly after nouns:

3 일 **동안** 기다렸어요. *I waited for three days.*

쉬는 시간 **사이에** 호빵을 하나씩 나누어 먹었어요.
During break time, we shared and ate ho-ppang.

8.2.13 –(으)ㄹ|-는|-(으)ㄴ 둥 *'may or may not'*

This pattern combines the prospective, present dynamic or state/result modifiers with the bound noun 둥 (refer to 2.1.2.9). The pattern appears twice in the same sentence to show an alternation or vague choice between one of two or more contradictory but equally likely state of affairs. The second is usually followed by the negative 말– 'desist' (refer to 4.2.3).

일을 하**는 둥 마는 둥** 게으름을 피우고 있어요.
He is being lazy – you can't tell if he is working or not.

말을 **할 둥 말 둥** 하다가 입을 다물고 말았어요.
He was on the verge of saying something, but ended up keeping his mouth shut.

눈이 **올 둥 말 둥** 하네요. *It may snow or may not.*

얼굴을 **본 둥 만 둥**하고 그냥 지나갔어요.
I just saw glanced at her face absentmindedly and passed by.

8.2.14 –(으)ㄹ|-는|-(으)ㄴ 듯 *'just like'*

Here, a modifier is followed by the bound noun 듯 (refer to 2.1.2.10) and then by another clause. The construction takes on the meaning of 'as if' or 'just like':

집은 아무도 없**는 듯** 조용했어요.
The house is quiet, as if no one is there.

오랜 친구를 만**난 듯** 반가웠어요.
I was happy like I was meeting a long lost friend.

배가 터**질 듯** 많이 먹었어요.
I ate like my stomach would explode.

The pattern may at times occur twice (on the second occasion with a negative verbal expression) to express uncertainty:

생각이 **날 듯 말 듯** 하네요.
It's on the tip of my tongue.

화장을 **한 듯 안 한 듯** 예뻤어요.
She was pretty, hard to tell whether she was wearing make-up or not.

A similar meaning can be conveyed by combining a modifier pattern and 것 (refer to 8.2.2) with the particle 처럼 (refer to 3.3.6.1), 과/와 같이 or 과/와 비슷하게.

'듯' also forms an integral part of the patterns –(으)ㄹ|–는|–(으)ㄴ 듯하–/듯 싶– (refer to 8.2.15) and –듯이 (refer to 7.8.1) described elsewhere.

8.2.15 –(으)ㄹ|–는|–(으)ㄴ 듯하–/듯 싶– 'seem like'

In this pattern, a modifying form is followed by 듯하– or 듯싶–. The pattern is used when the speaker is making a conjecture about a present, past or future state of affairs and is similar in meaning to the 것 같– (refer to 8.2.3) pattern or –(으)ㄹ|–는|–(으)ㄴ 모양이– (refer to 8.2.21).

민호에게 안 좋은 일이 있**는 듯해요**.
It sounds like something is up with Minho.

모든 파일이 삭제**된 듯해요**.
It looks like all of the files have been erased.

이 문제에 대해서 아무것도 모르시**는 듯 싶습니다**.
It seems like you don't know anything about this problem.

착각하**신 듯 싶습니다**.
It appears that you have misunderstood.

8.2.16 –(으)ㄹ 따름이– 'only'

Here, the prospective modifiers –(으)ㄹ combines with 따름 'only' and the copula –이–. The resulting expression, which means 'I only . . .' or "we can only . . .', is similar in meaning to the more common –(으)ㄹ 뿐 (refer to 8.2.26). However, the usage tends to be restricted to formal language, and typically to ritualized expressions of apologies and thanks:

일을 잘못하여 변명할 여지도 없고 그저 죄송**할 따름입니다**.
I know what we did wrong and since there is no room for excuses, we can only apologize.

아무리 감사드려도 모자라다고 생각하지만 늘 그저 항상 감사드**릴 따름입니다**.
I'm sure that no matter how thankful I am it's not enough, so I can only continue to always be thankful.

그저 해야 할 일을 **했을 따름입**니다.
I only did what I had to do.

8.2.17 –(으)ㄹ 때 'when'

This pattern combines the prospective modifier form with the bound noun 때 (refer to 2.1.2.12), which means 'when':

밥을 먹**을 때** 소리 내지 마라. *Don't make a sound when you eat.*

저는 기분이 나**쁠 때** 노래방에 가서 목이 터지도록 노래를 불러요.
When I'm in a bad mood, I go to karaoke and sing until I am hoarse.

어렸**을 때** 제 꿈은 만화가가 되는 거였어요.
When I was young, my dream was to become a cartoonist.

집에 도착했**을 때** 아무도 없었어요.
When I arrived home, there was no one there.

The expression can also be followed by 마다 to mean 'every time when . . .' or 'whenever':

시간이 있**을 때마다** 틈틈이 할 수 있어요.
You can do it little by little whenever you have time.

그 뉴스를 **볼 때마다** 눈물이 나요
Every time I see that news, tears come to my eyes.

때 can sometimes be replaced by 적 with no alteration in meaning:

어렸**을 적에** 한국을 떠났어요. *I left Korea when I was young.*

Finally, note that 때 can also be used following nouns, as discussed elsewhere (refer to 2.1.2.12). This includes expressions such as those below which would require the verb 'be' in English:

학생 **때**	*when I was a student*
다섯 살 **때**	*when I was 5*
시험 **때**	*when we have exams*
크리스마스 **때**	*when it is Christmas/at Christmas*
장마 **때**	*when it is the monsoon season/in the monsoon season*

8.2.18 –(으)ㄹ 리 없– 'no way that'

This pattern combines the prospective or past prospective modifier with the bound noun 리 (refer to 2.1.2.14) and the negative existential verb 없–. The resultant pattern takes on the meaning 'there is no way that' or 'it is not possible that':

천만에! 그런 짓을 했**을 리 없어**.
God forbid! There's no way that he/she would have behaved like that.

한국 사람**일 리 없어요**.
There's no way that he/she could be Korean.

그 사실은 단 한 명도 부정**할 리 없어요**.
It's impossible that even one person could deny that fact.

없– may on occasion be substituted for verbs or expressions with similar negative meanings:

네가 그것을 **모를 리 만무하다**.
It's utterly impossible that you could not know that.

In questions, in other words when you are asking 'is there any way that . . .?', 있– is used in place of 없–:

핸드폰이 **터질 리가 있어**?
Is it really possible that a mobile phone could get a signal (here)?

해결책이 **<u>없을 리가 있어</u>**?
Could it really be that there is no solution? (= There must be a solution.)

8.2.19 –는/ –(으)ㄴ 마당에 'in the situation where'

This construction combines the present dynamic modifier or the state/result modifier with the word 마당. The first clause talks of a situation, often negative, against which the action depicted in the second cause takes place.

헤어지**<u>는 마당에</u>** 하고 싶은 말은 없어요?
In this moment when we saying goodbye, do you have anything to say?

모두 떠나**<u>는 마당에</u>** 나 혼자 남아 있을 수는 없었다.
In the situation where everyone is leaving, I could not stay on my own.

에티오피아에선 굶어 죽**<u>는 마당에</u>** 유럽에서는 수 천톤에 이르는 싱싱한 오렌지를 바다에 내다 버리고 있다.
In the situation where people in Ethiopia are starving to death, in Europe thousands of tons of fresh oranges are being dumped in the sea.

8.2.20 –(으)ㄹ 만하– 'worth'

This pattern combines the prospective modifier with 만하–. The expression takes on the meaning 'worth':

그 영화는 한 번쯤 **<u>볼 만해요</u>**. *That movie is worth seeing once.*

인생은 **<u>살아 볼 만해요</u>**. *Life is worth living.*

<u>믿을 만한</u> 여자니까 뭐든지 얘기하세요.
She is trustworthy so you can tell her anything.

그 여자의 용감한 행동은 **<u>칭찬할 만해요</u>**.
That woman's brave deeds are worth praising.

8.2.21 –(으)ㄹ/–는/–(으)ㄴ 모양이– 'seem like'

This pattern combines a modifying form with the Sino-Korean noun 모양 (模樣), which literally means 'shape' or 'form', followed by the copula (refer to 4.1.4). It is used when the speaker is making a conjecture and is similar in meaning to the 것 같– (refer to 8.2.3) pattern or –(으)ㄹ/– 는/–(으)ㄴ듯하– (refer to 8.2.15).

비가 **올 모양이다**. *It looks like it's going to rain.*

그 선생님이 잘 가르치시**는 모양이에요**.
It seems like that teacher teaches well.

집집마다 잔치가 벌어지**는 모양이에요**.
It sounds like they are having a party at each and every house.

이제 온 걸 보니 어제 늦게까지 술을 마**신 모양이지요**.
Seeing he/she arriving now, it seems like he/she must have been drinking until late last night.

8.2.22 –(으)ㄹ 바에(는/야) 'rather . . . than'

This construction combines the prospective modifier, the bound noun 바 (refer to 2.1.2.16), the particle 에 (refer to 3.2.4.1), and optionally the particle 는 (refer to 3.3.2.1) or 야 (refer to 3.3.2.2). The expression connects two clauses, each expressing two possible courses of action. The speaker rejects the course of action expressed in the first clause and opts for the one in the second clause. Although the choice in the second clause would not be the speaker's first choice of action, at least it is preferable to the choice in the first clause.

군대 **갈 바에(는/야)** 차라리 죽고 싶어요.
I would rather die than go to the army.

좋아하지 않는 여자를 **만날 바에(는/야)** 그냥 혼자서 크리스마스를 보내는 것이 더 좋네요.
Rather than meeting a woman who I don't particularly like, I would rather spend Christmas alone.

재수**할 바에(는/야)** 나 일찍 돈을 벌러 다닐 거예요.
Rather than retaking my last year at high school, I would rather go out and earn some money.

확실히 36살에 결혼**할 바에(는/야)** 23살에 하는 게 낫지요.
It's certainly better to marry at 23 than at 36.

8.2.23 –(으)ㄴ/–는 바람에 'because of'

This pattern combines the present dynamic or state/result modifier form with the expression 바람에 'as a result'. The expression depicts a reason or cause in the first clause with a result or effect in the second clause. The contents of the first clause is generally an unexpected event. The contents of the second clause is usually an adverse or negative consequence of this, although positive consequences area also possible (see final example):

눈이 **오는 바람에** 교통이 막혔어요.
Because it was snowing, the traffic was jammed.

날씨가 **추운 바람에** 감기에 걸렸어요.
Because the weather was cold, I caught a cold.

아이들이 **떠드는 바람에** 조금도 잘 수 없었어요.
I could not sleep at all because the children made a noise.

술에 **만취한 바람에** 술값을 다 냈어요.
In his drunken state, he paid for all the alcohol.

시험이 쉽게 **나오는 바람에** 합격했어요.
Because we were given an easy exam, I passed it.

Note that unlike the comparative expression –기 때문에 (refer to 2.2.4.2), –은/는 바람에 cannot be followed simply by the copula.

8.2.24 –(으)ㄴ/–는 반면(에) 'but on the other hand'

This pattern combines a modifying form with the Sino-Korean noun 반면 (反面), literally meaning 'other side', followed optionally by the particle 에. The construction takes on the meaning 'but on the other hand' or 'but at the same time' and is used to directly juxtapose two contrasting states of affairs. The expression is most commonly encountered in writing or formal speech.

이 약은 약효가 빠**른 반면** 부작용이 있어요.
The effects of this medicine are swift; but at the same time, it has some side effects.

수출은 증가하**는 반면** 수입은 감소하고 있다.
Exports are increasing; but on the other hand, imports are decreasing.

한국 사람들이 대체로 영어를 읽고 쓰기는 잘 하**는 반면에** 듣고 말하기 부분은 매우 약하다.
Koreans generally read and write English well; but on the other hand, are weak when it comes to speaking and listening.

Note that 반면에 may also appear at the start of a sentence preceded optionally by 그 'that':

피씨(PC)는 갈수록 가격 경쟁이 심해진다. **그 반면에** 맥(Mac)은 경쟁이 거의 없는 상태이기 때문에 가격을 내릴 이유가 없다.
As time goes by, competition for PCs is getting stronger. But on the other hand, since the 'Mac' is in the position of having virtually no competition, there is no reason for the price to fall.

8.2.25 –(으)ㄹ 뻔하– 'nearly'

This pattern, which combines the prospective modifier with the verb 뻔하–, means 'almost does', 'barely escapes doing', or 'is on the verge of'. The pattern most often occurs in the past, with the implication that the thing that was almost done or did not happen, was avoided at the last minute. This pattern often goes with the adverb 하마터면 'nearly', 'almost'.

아이가 물에 빠져 **죽을 뻔했어요**.
The child nearly drowned.

그 사람은 부자가 **될 뻔했어요**.
He just missed being a rich man.

그 여자는 **하마터면** 강에 **빠질 뻔했어요**.
She nearly fell into the river.

하마터면 자동차하고 **부딪칠 뻔했어요**.
I nearly collided with the car.

Although this pattern commonly translates as 'nearly' or 'almost', it cannot be used in place of all English expressions that employ these words. Specifically, the use of –(으)ㄹ 뻔하– is limited to talking about events that 'nearly' or 'almost' occurred, but were averted at the last minute. It *cannot* be used when talking about a process that has started but has 'nearly' or 'almost' been finished or to say that 'nearly' or 'almost' all of a certain thing are or behave in a certain way. Here, 거의 다 'almost all' is used instead:

거의 다 먹었어요.
I've almost eaten everything. (= I've almost finished eating.)

드디어 **거의 다** 왔어요.
At last we have nearly come the full way. (= We're nearly there.)

그 감독 영화는 **거의 다** 재미있어요.
That director's films are almost all interesting.

8.2.26 –(으)ㄹ 뿐 'only'

This expression combines the prospective modifier –(으)ㄹ with the bound noun 뿐 (refer to 2.1.2.17) 'only'. Note that this '뿐' can also be applied after nouns as a particle (refer to 3.3.3.2).

The pattern can then be completed in four possible ways. Firstly, –(으)ㄹ 뿐 can appear followed just by the copula to mean 'only', 'just' or 'it is only':

그저 내 할 일을 **할 뿐**이에요.	*I merely did only what I had to do.*
일년에 한두 번 만**날 뿐**이에요.	*I only meet him/her once or twice a year.*
통계만을 믿**을 뿐**이에요.	*It is only statistics that I believe.*

The pattern may also appear with the negative copula to mean 'it is not only/just'. In this usage, 뿐 may be followed by 만 (refer to 3.3.3.1) for added emphasis:

눈이 많이 왔**을 뿐만** 아니었어요.
It wasn't just that it snowed a lot.

어부들은 바람에 의존**할 뿐만** 아니었다.
The fishermen did not rely only on the wind.

The second usage of 뿐 builds on this use with the negative copula. But instead of ending the sentence, the negative copula takes the form 아니라 and is followed by a second clause, meaning 'not just . . . but . . . as well'. For extra emphasis, 뿐 may be followed by 만 (refer to 3.3.3.1) to form 뿐만 아니라.

공부를 잘**할 뿐만 아니라** 마음씨도 좋아요.
He/she does not only study hard, but is kind-hearted as well.

단순히 노래만 잘 **할 뿐만 아니라** 그 복잡한 감정처리는 정말 탁월해요
He/she does not just simply sing well, but he/she expresses complex emotions outstandingly.

그 정치인은 무능**할 뿐만** 아니라 부패해요.
That politician is not just untalented, but is corrupt as well.

Thirdly, 뿐 may also be followed by '더러'. The resulting sentence pattern '뿐더러' operates exactly the same as 뿐만 아니라, the only difference being is that it feels somewhat more colloquial.

한국어를 **할 뿐더러** 일본어도 해요.
He/she not only speaks Korean, but Japanese as well.

깎아 줄 뿐더러 가끔 덤도 줘요.
They not only give discounts but also throw in a bit more as well.

Fourth and finally, 뿐 may on occasion be followed by another clause. The extra clause specifies the element missing by the restricted nature of the clause featuring 뿐.

그저 앞을 **바라볼 뿐**, 별다른 대꾸를 하지 않았다.
He just stared straight ahead, without any other response.

조금의 기스만 **났을 뿐** 아무 이상이 없습니다.
It just had a little scratch, without any real problem.

8.2.27 –(으)ㄹ 수 있–/없– 'can /cannot'

This pattern combines the prospective modifier –(으)ㄹ with the bound noun 수 (refer to 2.1.2.18), meaning 'case', 'circumstance'; 'way', 'means' and the existential verbs 있– 'exist' or 없– 'not exist'. 수 may be followed by the subject or topic particle.

With 있– 'exist', the pattern translates as 'can'; with 없– 'not exist', the pattern translates as 'cannot'. This meaning of 'can' and 'cannot' takes on a number of different usages. Firstly, it can be used for talking about general abilities (being able to, knowing how to do something). However, it should be noted that, for this usage, the pattern –(으)ㄹ 줄 알– /모르– (refer to 8.2.31) is more commonly used. In addition, for 'cannot', short negation with 못 (refer to 4.2.1) is also more common.

한글을 **쓸 수 있어요**. *I can write Korean.*

수영은 **할 수 있는데** 테니스는 못 쳐요.
I can swim, but I can't play tennis.

김치를 잘 담**글 수 있어요**. *I can make kimchi well.*

Secondly, –(으)ㄹ 수 있– /없– is used when talking about an ability that is situated in time (as in the first two examples below) or under certain conditions or restrictions (as in the remaining two examples):

오늘은 약속이 있어서 **갈 수 없어요**.
I cannot go today because I have other plans.

월요일까지 제출**할 수 있을까요**?
Will you be able to hand it in by Monday?

돈이 없어서 **갈 수 없어요**.
I can't go, as I have no money.

왼손으로 테니스를 **칠 수 있어요**?
Can you play tennis with your left hand?

Thirdly, the negative pattern –(으)ㄹ 수 없– can be used for expressing prohibition: 'you are not allowed to . . .'. However, this meaning is more typically expressed with –(으)면 안 되– (refer to 7.5.1.5).

미술관에서 사진을 찍**을 수 없습니다**.
You cannot take photos in the gallery.

이곳에서는 주차**할 수 없습니다**. *You cannot park here.*

Fourthly, the pattern can be used when discussing a possibility:

다음 주 눈이 **올 수가 있대요**.
They say that it could snow next week.

물이 **뜨거울 수 있으니** 조심하시기 바랍니다.
As the water may be hot, please be careful.

A: **그럴 수가 있어**? *Can that be possible?*
B: 말도 안 돼. **그럴 수가 없어**. *No way! That can't be so.*

In this usage, to express the given possibility as being only one of two or more eventualities, 수 is followed by the particle 도 'also', 'even' (refer to 3.3.3.6) This gives the meaning 'can also':

영국 여름 날씨가 **따뜻할 수도 있어요**.
The British summer weather can be warm as well

2013이면 북극 여름 빙산이 **사라질 수도 있어요**.
The summer polar icecap could even disappear by 2013.

Fifth and finally, to express a lack of choice or an eventuality outside one's control, the negative pattern –(으)ㄹ 수 없– can be followed by 밖에 'except for'. The resulting construction means 'can/could do/be nothing but . . .':

처음이라서 **힘들 수밖에 없어요**.
Because it's the first time, it can't be anything but hard.

길이 막히면 좀 **늦을 수 밖에 없어요**.
If there is a traffic jam, you cannot be anything else but late.

결국 야당이 **동의할 수밖에 없었어요**.
In the end, the opposition party could do nothing else but agree.

8.2.28 -(으)ㄴ/는 이상(에(는)) 'since'; 'unless'

This pattern combines a modifying form with the Sino-Korean noun 이상(以上), which literally means 'more than' and 'above', followed optionally by the particles 에 (refer to 3.2.4.1) and 는 (refer to 3.3.2.1). The pattern takes on quite different meanings depending on whether it appears with a positive or a negative verb.

When the verb is positive, the pattern takes on the meaning of 'since . . . has already happened, we have no choice but to . . .':

약속**한 이상(에는)** 지켜야 해요.
Since I have made a promise, I have to keep it.

여기까지 **온 이상**, 이제 돌이킬 수 없어요.
Since we have come this far, we can't go back.

우리도 결혼**한 이상** 아기를 갖고 싶은 마음을 갖게 되었어요.
Now that we are married, we have come to want a baby.

이미 계약을 **한 이상** 어쩔 수 없어요.
Since we have already made a contract, there is nothing that can be done.

When the verb is negative, the pattern states a sole condition in the first clause that would have to be met in order for the contents of the second clause to come into being. This generally translates into English as 'unless'

아주 늦지 않**은 이상** 꼭 아침을 먹고 나가요.
Unless I am very late, I always eat breakfast.

저 같으면 미치지 않**은 이상** 결혼 안 하겠어요.
If I were you, unless I was crazy, I would not get married.

수술했다고 말하**지 않는 이상** 수술했는지 알 수 없어요.
Unless he/she tells you about the operation, you would never know.

엄청나게 노력을 안 하**는 이상** 한국 사람처럼 말하는 것은 거의 불가능해요.
Unless you put in a great deal of effort, it is almost impossible to speak just like a Korean.

8.2.29 –(으)ㄴ/–는 일/적이 있–/없– 'ever/never'

This sentence pattern combines the present dynamic modifier –는 or the state/result modifier –(으)ㄴ with the words 일 and 적 (both meaning event, act, experience) and the existential verb 있– 'exist' or 없– 'not exist'.

With the state/result modifier –(으)ㄴ, the pattern is used to talk about whether you have ever had the experience in question. It is frequently preceded by –아/어 보– (refer to 5.1.8) with the literal meaning of 'try', as can be seen in the examples below. In this usage, 적 is more common than 일, although both may be used.

한국에 가 **본 적이 있어요**?	*Have you ever gone/been to Korea?*
막걸리를 마셔 **본 적이 있어요**.	*I have tried makkŏli.*
닭발을 먹어 **본 일이 없어요**.	*I have never eaten chicken feet.*

With the dynamic modifier –는, the pattern is used to talk about whether you ever do something or experience something in your daily life. In this usage, it is 일 that is more common that, although 적 may also be used.

극장에 가**는 일이 있어요**?	*Do you ever go to the theatre?*
나중에 후회하**는 일이 있어요**.	*I sometimes regret things later.*
포기하**는 일이 없어요**.	*I never give up.*

8.2.30 –(으)ㄹ 정도로 'to the extent that'

This pattern combines the prospective modifier with the Sino-Korean noun 정도 (程度) 'extent' and the instrumental particle –로. It is used for expressing the extent to which a state of affairs applies and commonly translates in English in constructions such as 'so . . . that' (e.g., 'so short that' or 'so much that'):

동생은 엉덩이가 보**일 정도로** 짧은 치마를 입고 있었어요.
My younger sister was wearing a skirt so short that you could almost see her bottom.

우리 사장님은 매일 아침 5시에 일어**날 정도로** 부지런하세요.
Our company president is so hard-working that he gets up every morning at 5 o'clock.

배꼽이 빠**질 정도로** 재미있게 웃었어요.
We laughed so much our belly-buttons almost fell out. [idiomatic expression]

Note that a similar meaning can be expressed with the pattern –도록 (refer to 7.6.3).

8.2.31 –(으)ㄹ|–는|–(으)ㄴ 줄 알– /모르– 'think/know'

This pattern combines a modifier with the bound noun 줄 (refer to 2.1.2.20), followed by the verbs 알– 'know' or 모르– 'not know'. The resulting pattern has three distinct usages.

Firstly, with 알– 'know', the pattern is used when talking about something that one presumed or thought, but now realize to be incorrect or when talking about the inaccurate presumptions of others:

Prospective: 못 오**실 줄** 알았어요.
I thought you wouldn't be able to come.

Past prospective: 한국 팀은 졌**을 줄** 알았어요.
I thought the Korean team would have lost.

Present dynamic: 자**는 줄** 알았어요.
I thought you were sleeping.

State/result: 그 사람이 한국에 **간 줄** 알았어요.
I thought he had gone to Korea.

내가 바보**인 줄** 알아?
Do you think I'm stupid?

In addition to talking about presumptions that one later realized to be incorrect, the pattern can also appear when talking about knowledge that one believes to be true but chooses to ignore:

당근이 몸에 좋**은 줄** 알지만 먹기 싫어요.
I know that carrots are good for health, but I don't like eating them.

열심히 공부해야 **하는 줄** 알았지만 최선을 다하지 못했어요.
I knew I had to study hard, by I was unable to try my hardest.

This usage extends to the expression '그럴 줄 알았어', which is the Korean equivalent of 'I knew it'.

Secondly, with 모르– 'not know', the pattern is used when talking about something that you were not aware of, but have now realized to be the case:

Prospective:	**들킬 줄** 몰랐어요. *I didn't realize that we would get found out.*
Present dynamic:	수다 떨면서 먹느라고 시간 **가는 줄** 몰랐어요. *Busy chatting and eating, I didn't notice the time passing.*
State/result:	독감에 **걸린 줄** 몰랐어요. *I didn't know that I had caught the flu.*
	그 사람은 자식이 **귀한 줄** 몰라요. *He doesn't know how precious children are.*

Thirdly, when used in the present tense with the prospective modifier, the pattern can be used for discussing having knowledge of a skill ('know how to' or 'don't know how to'):

한국 음식을 **만들 줄** 아세요?	*Do you know how to make Korean food?*
스키를 **탈 줄** 알아요.	*I know how to ski.*
저는 운전을 **할 줄** 몰라요.	*I don't know how to drive.*

In this usage, the pattern is similar in meaning to –(으)ㄹ 수 있–/없– (refer to 8.2.27). However, whereas strictly speaking –(으)ㄹ 줄 알/모르– refers to 'knowing how to do something', –(으)ㄹ 수 있–/없– refers to 'being able to do something'. A person may know how to do something, but not currently be able to do it, as demonstrated in the following example:

피아노를 **칠 줄** 알지만 오늘은 팔이 아파서 칠 수가 없어요.
I know how to play the piano, but I'm not able to play it today since I hurt my arm.

8.2.32 –는 중에/도중에 'in the middle of . . .'

The present dynamic modifier followed by the bound nouns 중 (中) or 도중 (途中), both meaning 'middle' (refer to 2.1.2.21), communicate that one was in the middle of doing one action when a second action took place:

아기가 머리를 감기**는 중에** 잠들었어요.
While I was in the middle of washing the baby's hair, the baby fell asleep.

수업을 하**는 도중에** 전화가 왔어요.
While I was teaching, I got a phone call.

Note that 중에/도중에 may appear preceded simply by a noun, as discussed elsewhere (refer to 2.1.2.21).

8.2.33 –는 중– 'be in the middle of'

This pattern combines the prospective modifier with 중 as in the previous pattern (refer 7.2.27). However, on this occasion, 중 is followed by the copula and the pattern as a whole means 'in the middle of . . . ing' or 'I am . . . ing'. The usage is fairly similar to the continuous tense with –고 있– (refer to 4.3.3.2).

지금 점심을 먹**는 중이에요**.	*I'm in the middle of eating lunch.*
생각하**는 중이에요**.	*I'm thinking about it.*
살까 말까 망설이**는 중이에요**.	*I'm wavering about whether to buy it or not.*
읽어 보려고 노력하**는 중입니다**.	*I'm trying to read it.*

With sentences such as the last example that contain –(으)려고 (refer to 7.7.2) in the meaning of 'trying', this can be shortened to '려는 중":

쿠키를 만들**려는 중이에요**. *I'm trying to make cookies.*

To emphasize the meaning of continuity, –는 중– may appear preceded by –고 있– (refer to 4.3.3.2):

자료를 모으**고 있는 중이에요**.
I'm in the middle of collecting data.

옷을 다리**고 있는 중이에요**.
I'm in the middle of doing the ironing.

– 는 중 may also be followed by the particle 에 (refer to 3.2.4.1) and then a brand new clause. In such cases, the first clause presents a continuos action and the second clause presents another action or circumstance that occurred 'while' the first action was in progress:

밥을 먹**는 중에** 전화가 왔어요.
A phone call came while I was eating.

다이어트 하**는 중에** 가장 힘든일이 뭐예요?
What is the hardest thing while you are dieting?

Note that 중 may appear preceded simply by a noun, as discussed elsewhere (refer to 2.1.2.21).

8.2.34 –(으)ㄹ 즈음(에) 'when'

This pattern combines a prospective modifier form with the word 즈음 'time, occasion'. This commonly translates into English as 'when . . .' and is similar in usage to the more common expression -(으)ㄹ 때 (refer to 8.2.17).

큰 누님이 결혼**할 즈음에** 난 대학생이 되었다.
When my eldest sister got married, I was just entering university.

아이에게 거의 다가**갈 즈음** 아이는 겁먹은 얼굴로 땅을 보고 있었다.
When he got near to the girl, she was looking at the ground with a frightened face.

8.2.35 *–(으)ㄴ 지 'since'*

This construction is built on the state/result modifier –(으)ㄴ, which is followed by 지 (refer to 2.1.2.22). This is then followed by a time expression and then either the copula –이– or, more commonly, with one of the following verbs: 되– 'become' or 넘– 'exceed'. The expression as a whole translates as 'it is (has been/has been more than) a certain period of time since':

대통령이 취임**한 지** 1년이다.
It's a year since the president took office.

한국에 **온 지** 2 년이 됐어요.
It's been 2 years since I came to Korea.

부산에 가 **본 지** 참 오래됐어요.
It's a very long time since I've been to Busan.

중국말 해 **본 지**가 벌써 십 년이 넘었어요.
It's been more than ten years now since I've tried talking Chinese.

As can be seen in the final example, 지 can be followed by the subject particle (refer to 3.2.1) and also by the topic particle (refer 3.3.2.1). When occurring with 되– and 넘–, the time expression itself may appear with the subject particle (as in the second and fourth examples above).

Notice that a negative modifier clause in this construction actually refers to the same situation as if the clause were affirmative; the situation is just viewed differently:

인호를 만**난 지**가 한 달이 됐어요.
It's been one month since I met Inho. (= I haven't met Inho for one month.)

인호를 못 만**난 지** 한 달이 됐어요.
It's been one month that I haven't met Inho. (= I haven't met Inho for one month.)

8.2.36 *–(으)려던 참이– 'just about to'*

This pattern sees a processive verb followed by the continuous past intentive modifier, the bound noun 참 and the copula. The expression is used when talking about something you are 'just about to' do:

그 말을 하**려던 참이**었어요. *I was just about to say that.*

이제 막 저녁 먹으러 가**려던 참이**에요.
We are just about to go and have dinner.

이제 저녁 먹**으려던 참인**데, 안 먹었으면 와서 앉아.
We are just about to eat, so if you haven't eaten yet come and take a seat.

8.2.37 –(으)ㄴ 채(로) 'as it is'

This pattern combines a processive verb in the state/result modifier form with the bound noun 채 (refer to 2.1.2.24), which can be optionally followed by the instrumental particle –(으)로 (refer to 3.2.5.1). The pattern expresses that the person being talked about performed the action in the second part of the sentence in the state created by the contents of the first part of the sentence. This state is typically not the normal state in which the action in question is performed or goes contrary to expectation. In addition to translations such as 'just as it is' and 'as it stands' it may frequently be rendered in English in constructions including 'with/without'.

신발도 신지 않**은 채** 달려나갔어요.
I dashed out without even putting my shoes on.

인사도 못 **한 채** 왔어요.
I came without even having said goodbye.

안경을 **쓴 채** 목욕탕에 들어갔어요.
I went in to the sauna with my glasses on.

산 채 묻었어요.
They buried him alive.

불을 **켠 채** 자요.
He sleeps with the light on.

구두를 신**은 채** 들어오면 안 돼요.
You mustn't enter the room with your shoes on.

8.2.38 –는 척하– 'pretend'

Here, a modifying form is followed by the expression 척하–, which has the meaning of 'pretend':

아는 친구였지만 모르**는 척했어요**.
He/she was someone I knew, but I pretended I didn't.

이해하**는 척하**지 마!
Don't pretend you understand.

버스에서 **자는 척**하면서 할머니에게 자리를 양보 안 했어요.
Pretending to be asleep, I didn't give up my seat on the bus to a grandmother.

예쁜 척해 봤자 아무 소용 없어요.
There's no point pretending to be pretty.

The pattern may also be used when talking about someone putting on airs (or, frequently, when telling them not to act in that way):

잘난 척하지 마라.	*Don't be so stuck up.*
똑똑한 척하지 마.	*Don't be a smart aleck.*
착한 척하지 마세요.	*Stop being so nice.*

In addition to 'pretence', the pattern may express making (or not making) a sign (that you have heard, seen something, etc.):

그는 내 말을 들**은 척**도 안 했어요.
He acted like he didn't even hear me.

여자 친구하고 같이 있는 거 같아서 아**는 척** 못 했어요.
As you seemed to be with your girlfriend, I couldn't show that I knew you.

On occasions the '하' part of the construction may be dropped and replaced by other phrases:

모르는 척 슬쩍 지나쳤어요.
I passed by pretending not to know him/her.

잘난 척 그만 해라. *Stop being so stuck up.*

Note that '척' may be replaced by '체' with no perceptible change in meaning:

길에서 나를 못 **본 체했어요**.
He/she pretended not to see me on the street.

8.2.39 –는/–(으)ㄴ 탓 'due to'

This construction combines a present dynamic or state/result modifier with the word 탓 'reason' (also meaning 'fault', 'blame'). Somewhat similar to 바람에 (refer to 8.2.23), it expresses a reason in the first clause that leads to a consequence in the second, which is typically negative. The expression is rather bookish and is rarely heard in casual speech.

남편이 상습적으로 바람을 피우**는 탓에** 이혼을 할 수 밖에 없었다.
Due to her husband habitually having affairs, she had no choice but to divorce.

일을 많이 **한 탓**에 머리색이 희끗희끗해졌다.
Due to working so much, his hair became speckled with grey.

This pattern can be followed by the copula to mean 'the reason why . . . is . . .':

책이 안 팔리는 이유는 재미가 없**는 탓**이에요.
The reason why the book did not sell is because it is boring.

Note that 탓 followed by the copula may be preceded by a noun instead of a modifier construction in sentences such as 기차를 놓친 것은 네 탓이다 'missing the train is your fault'.

8.2.40 –(으)ㄴ/–는 통에 'in the commotion'

This pattern consists of the present dynamic or state/result modifier followed by 통에 'as a consequence'. Similar to –는 바람에 (refer to 8.2.23), it is used when talking about a causation process that is outside of the speaker's deliberate control. However, whereas –는 바람에 is preferred when cause in the first clause is a sudden incident leading to result in the second clause, –는 통에 is more suitable when talking about somebody putting you in a state of confusion owing to which an adverse or negative consequence came about:

남편이 너무 서두르는 **통에** 열쇠를 집에다가 두고 왔어요.
In the commotion of my husband being in such a hurry, we left the keys at home.

사람들이 너무 떠드는 **통에** 정신을 차릴 수가 없었어요.
In the commotion of people making such an uproar, I was unable to pull myself together.

아기가 밤새 우는 **통에** 한잠도 못 잤어요.
In the commotion of the baby crying all night long, we couldn't sleep a wink.

Note that 통에 can also be used after nouns:

전쟁 **통에** 사람이 많이 죽었다.
Many people died in the ravages of war.

난리 **통에** 온 가족이 뿔뿔이 흩어졌어요.
In all the troubles, the whole family became scattered.

8.2.41 –(으)ㄴ|는 한– *'as much as'*

In this pattern, a modifying form is followed by the Sino-Korean noun 한 (限), which literally means 'limits', 'bounds' or 'end'. The pattern translates as 'as much as' or 'as long as'. It appears most frequently with the descriptive verb 가능하– 'be possible' in the construction '가능한 한' meaning 'as . . . as possible' or with expressions of similar meaning:

가능**한 한** 빨리 팩스로 보내 주세요.
Please send it to me by fax as soon as possible.

힘이 닿**는 한** 계속 노력하겠습니다.
I will keep trying to the best of my ability.

체력이 되**는 한** 나에게 은퇴는 없습니다.
As long as I am physically healthy, I won't think about retiring.

제가 아**는 한** 동경에서 제일 맛있는 횟집이에요.
As far as I know, it is the most delicious raw fish restaurant in Tokyo.

Chapter 9

Sentence endings

Overview

This chapter examines verb endings that operate as sentence endings. These endings are used to round off a sentence and do not need to be followed by any other element.

When left in their bare form, all of these sentence endings will be interpreted as being the non-honorific 'intimate' speech style (refer 6.1.3). To make the sentence 'honorific' (and suitable for use when addressing superiors, elders, non-intimates and strangers), –요 (the polite speech style ending, refer to 6.1.1) should be added. These sentence endings cannot occur with any other style, such as the 'formal' (refer to 6.1.2) and the 'plain' (refer to 6.1.4).

OTHER SENTENCE ENDINGS IN THIS BOOK

Many other patterns covered elsewhere in this book may occur at the end of sentences, including nominative patterns such as –기나 하– (refer to 2.2.4.12) or –기는 (refer to 2.2.4.13) and quotation patterns such as –단다 (refer to 10.3.2) or –단 말이– (refer to 10.4.6).

However, two things make the patterns in this chapter different from those covered elsewhere. Firstly and most importantly, endings covered in this chapter can generally only occur at the end of sentences and never elsewhere. Secondly, unlike the vast majority of endings covered elsewhere, the endings we look at in this chapter can end a sentence without the addition of another element (although –요 will be required to make the sentence 'polite').

Note that a number of the causal connectives covered in Chapter 7 may also at times work as sentence enders without the addition of another element, including the following:

1. –(아/어)서 (refer to 7.1.1)
2. –(으)니까 (refer to 7.1.6)
3. –(으)르라 (refer to 7.1.14)
4. –고 (refer to 7.3.1)
5. –(으)ㄴ/는데 (refer to 7.3.12)
6. –(으)ㄹ텐데 (refer to 7.3.13)
7. –거든 (refer to 7.5.6)

In the cases of –(으)ㄹ텐데 and –거든, these endings have quite separate functions when they occur at the end rather than the middle of the sentence. For this reason, we provide separate sections for them in this chapter. For the other endings in the list above, use of them in sentence-final position is covered under the main entry in Chapter 7.

9.1 –고말고 'of course'

–고말고 originates from the additional one-shape connective pattern –고 (refer to 7.3.1), followed by the negative verb 말 –'desist', followed again by the –고 pattern. The form is used, normally in an affirmative response to a question, to emphasize that the statement is true, natural or a 'given'.

A: 박 사장님을 잘 아세요?
Do you know president Pak?

B: 알**고말고**요. 아주 가까운 사이에요.
Of course I know him. We are very close.

A: 이 책은 다 보고 나서 꼭 돌려줘.
You have to give this book back to me when you have looked at it.

B: 돌려주**고말고**. 걱정하지 마!
Of course I will give it back. Don't worry.

A: 음식이 다 맛있지요?
The food is all delicious, isn't it?

B: 맛있**고말고**요. 이 식당이 비싸잖아요.
Of course it is. This restaurant is expensive, you know.

Instead of repeating the main verb, the speaker may also use the verb 그렇– 'do like that':

A: 경치가 정말 아름답군요! *The view is really beautiful!*

B: 그렇**고말고**요. *Of course it is!*

– 고말고 may be replaced with –다마다 (refer to 9.6) with little difference in meaning.

9.2 –거든 'it's because', 'you see'

– 거든 is a one-shape ending that may occur preceded by the past tense marker (refer to 4.3.1.1) and by –겠– (refer to 4.3.2.1).

In its most basic usage, –거든 is applied when adding an explanation for something you said in the previous sentence. Typical translations are 'because' or 'you see'.

나는 노래방에 안 가요. 노래를 싫어하**거든**요.
I don't go to the noraebang. I don't like singing, you see.

오늘 학교에 안 가요. 공휴일이**거든**요.
I don't go to school today. It's a holiday, you see.

그럼 잘됐네요. 약속을 취소하려고 전화했**거든**요.
It has turned out well, then. I was just ringing up to cancel the appointment, you see.

At times, the second sentence, rather than giving a reason per se, may simply explain to the hearer where the speaker has gleaned the information (as in the first example below), or clarify that something is correct according to the speaker's own experience (as in the second example).

오늘 비가 올 거야. 난 어제 일기예보를 봤**거든**.
It's going to rain today. I saw the weather forecast yesterday, you see.

우리 나라의 경우 보도 자료를 보면 마약성 진통제를 너무 적게 쓰는 게 문제가 되기도 합니다. 많이 안 쓰**거든**요.
Medical doctor: In our country's case, according to the reported information, using clinical painkillers too rarely actually becomes a problem. We don't use a lot [according to my own experience], you see.

However, sentences with –거든 often occur when you have no preceding sentence that needs to be explained or clarified. In such cases, the speaker is providing justification for his actions, or possibly referring to something that he/she has said some time in the past. As in the following examples, these sentences may be used to rebuke the assumptions implied by the other speaker:

A: 왜 먹어 보지도 않고 맛없다고 그러는 거야?
Why are you saying it doesn't taste good when you haven't even tried it?

B: 난 원래 이런 음식 싫**거든**.
I've always hated this kind of food, you see.

A: 설거지 안 해?
You're not going to wash the dishes.

B: 난 어제 했**거든**. 오늘 네가 해.
I did it yesterday, you know. You do it today.

A: 조깅 같이 하지.
Why don't you go jogging with me?

B: 됐어. 난 오늘 운동 벌써 했**거든**.
Forget it. I've already exercised today.

– 거든 can also appear as a connective ending, as discussed elsewhere (refer to 7.5.6).

9.3 –나?/ –(으)ㄴ가? dubitative questions

This pattern has two distinct forms: –나 and –(으)ㄴ가. The choice of pattern will depend on whether you are dealing with a descriptive or a processive verb and on the inclusion/exclusion of tense markers.

The two-shape –(으)ㄴ가 is used predominantly with descriptive verbs and the copula. It does not normally appear with tense markers:

작은 고추가 매**운가**요? *Are small chillies hot?*

옷이 너무 **작은**가? *Are these clothes too small?*

책**인가**요? *Is it a book?*

Occasionally, you may also hear speakers using –(으)ㄴ가 with processive verbs, although this is considered nonstandard. In this case, the form becomes –는가.

먹**는가**요? *Is he/she eating?*

학교 가**는가**? *Is he/she going to school?*

–나 is the more common choice for processive verbs. This ending behaves as a one-shape pattern:

음악 즐겨 듣**나**요? *Do you enjoy listening to music?*

You may also hear speakers use –나 with descriptive verbs too, which again is considered nonstandard:

옷이 너무 작**나**? *Are these clothes too small?*

– 나 is used with the past tense –았/었– (refer to 4.3.1.1) and the future –겠– (refer to 4.3.2.1). In such cases, it occurs with either processive or descriptive verbs:

먹었나?	*ate?*	예뻤나?	*will eat?*
먹겠나?	*will eat?*	예쁘겠나?	*will be pretty?*

Note however that futures with –ㄹ 거– (refer to 4.1.4) appear not with –나 but with –(으)ㄴ가. The reason for this is that this form is based on the copula.

먹을 **건가**? *will eat?*

Although 있– and 없– behave like processive verbs and therefore take –나, with the honorific 계시–, you may hear either –나 or –ㄴ가 (the latter is more common):

사장님께서는 계시**나**요? *Is the president here?*

사장님께서는 계**신가**요? *Is the president here?*

This ending is used when asking a question in order to make the speaker's attitude sound more uncertain. This first of all works to make the question softer (and therefore generally politer), something like adding 'I wonder' to the end of a question in English:

저 기억나시**나**요?	*Do you remember me, by any chance?*
유미가 지금 있**나**요?	*Is Yumi there now, I wonder?*
몇 시에 올 **건가**요?	*I wonder what time he/she will come.*

In addition to polite questions, the form may also occur when the speaker is ruminating about a puzzling question that has been bugging him or her. These types of questions may be addressed directly to the hearer, or they might be soliloquy (i.e., spoken as if talking to oneself):

기사에 등장하는 사람 이름을 가명으로 할 때 어떻게 이름을 짓**나**요?
When they give someone a false name in a newspaper article, I wonder how they make those up?

내 안경 어디다 두었**나**? *Where did I put my glasses, I wonder?*

9.4 –(는)군, –(는)구나, –(는)구려, –(는)구만/구먼 exclamations

This sentence ender has four possible variants which are, in general order of frequency, –(는)군, –(는)구나, –(는)구만/구먼, and –(는)구려. These endings can all be followed by –요, except for –(는)구나 and –(는)구려. They all share the same basic function of marking exclamations, although there are some small differences in nuance (see below).

The '는' element is required for processive verbs in the present tense and may attach either to the verb stem or after the honorific –시– (refer to 6.2.1.1):

가**는군**요!	*You're going! (non-honorific)*
가시**는군**요!	*You're going! (honorific)*

When the verb is descriptive, '는' is not required:

예쁘**군**요!	*She's pretty! (non-honorific)*
예쁘시**군**요!	*She's pretty! (honorific)*

–(는)군 and the other variants can also appear after the past tense marker (refer to 4.3.1.1) and after –겠– (refer to 4.3.2.1):

힘들었**군**요! *You had a hard time!*

맛있겠**군**요! *It must be delicious!*

This ending is applied when the speaker becomes aware of something for the first time (by seeing, hearing about it, etc.) and wishes to express a spontaneous emotional reaction or exclamation to it, usually including a degree of surprise. In English, this is often done with an exclamation such as 'ah', 'my', 'gosh', etc. or just by using a dramatic intonation:

김유미 씨이시**군**요! 반갑습니다!	*Ah, so you're Kim Yumi! Pleased to meet you!*
왔**구나**!	*Wow, you're here!*
여기 살기가 정말 좋**군**요.	*My, living here is really good!*
한국말을 참 잘하시**는군**요.	*Boy, you sure speak Korean well!*
비가 왔**구면**!	*Oh, so it's rained!*
그 여자가 정말 아름답**구만**.	*Boy, she sure is pretty.*
겨울이라 그런지 정말 춥구려.	*Maybe because its winter, it sure is cold!*

Although –(는)군, –(는)구나 and –(는)구려 most commonly occurs with information that is perceived at around the time of speaking, –구만/구면 may occasionally occur when narrating a past event and conveying a perception made at that time:

어제 술집에 갔는데 오래간만에 그 친구를 봤**구만/면**!
I went to the pub last night and, oh, I saw that friend for the first time in ages!

Although the four variants –(는)군, –(는)구나, –(는)구려 and –(는)구만/구면 all share the same basic function, some small differences exist. Many speakers (particularly younger speakers and/or female speakers) will use –(는)군요 (with the –요 ending) when speaking honorifically, but otherwise use –(는)구나 in non-honorific language. To many, –(는)군 in non-honorific language sounds like the speech of elder males, or else like written speech or soliloquy.

Furthermore, the usage of –(는)구만/구먼 extends to some situations where neither –(는)군 or –(는)구나 would be possible. Namely, it can be used when rebuking the other speaker:

A: 아, 맛없네. *This doesn't taste good.*

B: 뭐가 맛있기만 하**구만**. *Why not? It tastes fine to me!*

A: 민수가 오늘부터 일찍 일어난다고 했어요.
Minsu said he is going to get up early from today.

B: 일찍은 무슨? 아직도 자**는구만**!
Early? He's still sleeping!

In addition to the patterns covered so far, the '군' element can also be added directly after the observed/perceived past tense –더 (refer to 4.3.1.3) to form –더군. This –더군 is used when the speaker is reminiscing about something that happened in the past, typically which involved perceiving something for the first time:

성당문을 열고 안으로 들어가 보려고 했더니 문이 잠겨 있**더군요**.
I intended to open the door of the Catholic church and go inside, but then I realized that it was locked.

중년 커플이 일어서더니 바다 속으로 막 달려가**더군**.
[I saw that] the middle-aged couple got up and suddenly ran into the sea.

9.5 –네 evidential exclamations

–네 operates as a one-shape ending which may occur preceded by the past tense marker –았/었– (refer to 4.3.1.1) and by –겠– (refer to 4.3.2.1). The –네 ending is similar in usage and meaning to –(는)군 (refer to 9.4). In other words, this ending is applied when the speaker wishes to express a spontaneous emotional reaction or exclamation, usually including a degree of surprise.

이 커피가 진하**네**요! *My, this coffee sure is strong!*

아이구, 실수를 했**네**요! *Oh dear, I've really committed a blunder.*

설탕 사야 되겠**네**요! *Oh dear, we'll have to buy some more sugar.*

한국말 잘하시**네**요! *My, you sure speak Korean well!*

Although this basic usage is similar to –(는)군, two subtle differences can be pointed out. Firstly, whereas with –(는)군 the contents of the sentence may be an exclamation based on an initial conjecture on the part of the speaker, with –네, the exclamation represents a conclusion that the speaker has arrived at after some degree of consideration. If a doctor were to utter the following two sentences, the first with –(는)군 may just be an initial observation based on the symptoms described by the patient. The second –네 would be more likely to occur after the blood pressure had been tested and the fact of the matter had been ascertained:

고혈압이**군**요.	*Ah, you must have high blood pressure.*
고혈압이**네**요.	*Ah, it turns out you have high blood pressure.*

The second difference is that –네 tends to be used more when the information goes against the expectation of the speaker. In the following, the second sentence with –네 more explicitly states that the speaker did not expect that the hearer would have met 'that guy' (perhaps because she had said before that she did not like him, etc.):

어제 그 남자를 만났**군**!	*Ah, so you met that guy yesterday!*
어제 그 남자를 만났**네**!	*Ah, so you did meet that guy yesterday [after all]!*

9.6 –다마다 'of course'

This pattern is used the same way as –고말고 in an affirmative response to a question, to emphasize that the statement is true, natural or a 'given':

A: 기억하세요?	*Do you remember?*
B: 기억하**다마다**요.	*Of course I remember!*

A: 같이 가시겠어요?	*Would you like to go together?*
B: 당연하지. 가**다마다**요.	*Of course I would!*

9.7 –담/람 disapproval

–담 is a colloquial verb ending, which may also appear in the 'polite' style as –담요. –람 is used after the copula.

–담 is used primarily with question words and occurs when the speaker is expressing a strong emotional reactions at something newly perceived. In many cases, this strong reaction amounts to disapproval about the state of affairs under discussion. Resulting sentences generally translate using 'what on earth . . .?', 'who the hell . . .?' and so forth:

누가 이렇게 했**담**?
Who on earth did this?

이 많은 술을 어떻게 다 마신**담**?
How on earth are we going to drink so much booze?

뭐가 그렇게 우습**담**?
What on earth do you think is so funny?

약속을 잘 지키는 애가 웬일**이람**?
She usually keeps her promises, so what on earth is going on?

On occasion, –담 can also be used with strong reactions of a positive nature:

커피가 어쩜 이렇게 예쁘게 생겼**담**?
How can coffee look this pretty?

무슨 과일이 이리 맛있**담**?
What kind of fruit could be this yummy?

Especially in this positive usage, –다니 (refer to 10.4.1) can be used in a similar way.

9.8 –(으)ㄹ걸 presumptions, regrets

–(으)ㄹ걸 is a two-shape ending that has its origins in the combination of –(으)ㄹ 거 (refer to 4.3.2.2) with the object particle 을/를.

The pattern is used first of all when the speaker expresses a presumption, guess or conjecture. The content of this inference is typically contrary to the beliefs or expectations of the hearer. –(으)ㄹ걸 is used by the speaker as a soft and indirect means to disagree with the interlocutor.

A: 민수가 지금 고등학생이지요?
Minsu is a high school student, isn't he?

B: 글쎄. 아직 중학생**일걸**요.
I'm not sure. I reckon he's still a middle school student.

A: 그 여자가 민호 여자 친구인가 보다.
That woman must be Minho's girlfriend.

B: 아**닐걸**. 민호 여자 친구는 훨씬 예**쁠걸**.
I don't think so. Minho's girlfriend must be much prettier.

In addition to presumptions that go against the beliefs of the hearer per se, –(으)ㄹ걸 may also appear when the speaker simply wants to make the conjecture sound tentative:

미아는 어렸을 때도 예뻤**을걸**요.
Mia must have been pretty when she was young as well.

예전에 이곳이 극장이었**을걸**.
I reckon this was a theatre in the past.

The second usage of –(으)ㄹ걸 is for talking, with a sense of regret, about things that the speaker him/herself failed to do, chose not to do or was unable to do in the past. Such sentences typically translate as 'should have . . .' or 'would have'. Since such expressions always connote a past state of affairs, the past tense marker –았/었– tends only to be used with verbs whose past form expresses a present state (refer to 4.3.1.1):

그 돈을 그냥 받을**걸**.
We should have just taken the money

맛있어 보인다! 나도 그걸로 시킬**걸**.
That looks tasty. I should have ordered that too!

그 옷은 진작에 나왔으면 봄에 더 자주 입었**을걸**
If those clothes had come out earlier, I would have worn them more often in spring.

Note that, rather than ending a sentence, –(으)ㄹ걸 (in both the 'inference' function and the 'regret' function) may at times be followed by a quoting verb (refer to 10.2.6).

오래 볼 수 없<u>**을걸**</u> 하고 생각하니 너무 슬퍼졌어요.
I became sad thinking I might not see him/her for a long time.

저도 코트 입<u>**을걸**</u> 후회하고 있어요.
I am regretting not wearing a coat.

In the 'regret function', –(으)ㄹ걸 may also be followed by 그렇– 'do like that' without any vast change in meaning from the original form.

사랑한다고 말<u>**할걸**</u> 그랬지.
I should have told him/her I loved him/her.

차라리 아들 결혼식 때 축의금을 받<u>**을걸**</u> 그랬어요.
At our son's wedding, we should just have accepted monetary gifts.

차라리 다른데 <u>**갈걸**</u> 그랬어요.
We should have just gone somewhere else.

9.9 –(으)ㄹ게 promise-like futures

The form –(으)ㄹ게 is a two-shape ending, with –을게 following a consonant and –ㄹ게 following a vowel. It can be changed into the 'polite' style with the addition of –요: –(으)ㄹ게요.

–(으)ㄹ게 is used only with processive verbs and almost entirely for the first person (I, we). It is used when the speaker is spontaneously promising or volunteering to perform an action in the immediate future. The action tends to be within the direct control of the speaker and is usually of relevance or benefit to the hearer.

A: 잠시만 기다려 줘. 화장실에 갔다 <u>**올게**</u>.
Wait a minute. I'll just pop into the bathroom.

B: 그래. 여기서 기다리고 있<u>**을게**</u>.
Sure. I'll be waiting here.

A: 너무 덥다!
It's so hot!

B: 그렇지. 내가 창문을 열어 <u>**줄게**</u>.
Right. I'll open the window for you.

A: 내가 먼저 **<u>갈게</u>**요.
I'll be on my way.

B: 그래요. 내일 전화**<u>할게</u>**요.
Ok. I'll phone you tomorrow.

A: 뭐 먹을래요?
What do you want to eat?

B: 난 비빔밥을 먹**<u>을게</u>**요.
I'll eat pibimbap.

–겠– (refer to 4.3.2.1) may also be used in a similar way to –(으)ㄹ게 when expressing promises and spontaneous intentions. The difference is that –겠–, particularly when used with the 'formal' speech style (refer to 6.1.2), tends to sound more deferential and solemn. For this reason, –겠– is more appropriate when speaking to elders and status superiors, particularly in leave-taking expressions (such as '먼저 가겠습니다' 'I'll be going first' or '다녀 오겠습니다' 'I'll go and come back'), or when trying to make your promise sound more sincere and binding. However, due to its solemn feel, –겠– is not generally used when expressing your intention to perform small and menial tasks (even when speaking to elders).

9.10 –(으)ㄹ까? suggestions, tentative questions

–(으)ㄹ까 operates as a two-shape ending: –ㄹ까 attaches after a consonant and –을까 after a vowel.

The basic underlying meaning of –(으)ㄹ까 is that the speaker is pondering about something. When the sentence is not addressed to any hearer (i.e., when the speaker is talking to him/herself), then this equates merely to self-pondering. The subject tends to be third person, but may be first person as in the final example:

왜 나를 그렇게 싫어**<u>할까</u>**?	*Why does he hate me that much?*
과연 그렇게 **<u>될까</u>**?	*Could that really happen?*
어제 왜 술을 그렇게 마셨**<u>을까</u>**?	*Why did we drink so much alcohol last night?*

When directed to a hearer, the sentence now asks for the hearer's opinion on the matter on which the speaker is pondering. In these cases, the subject of the sentence is most typically third person (i.e., with he, she, it, etc.). Typical translations include 'I wonder if . . .' or 'Do you reckon/suppose . . .?':

내일 추**울까**요?
Do you suppose it will be cold tomorrow?

지금 가면 너무 늦**을까**?
If I go now, I wonder if it will be too late?

비행 중, 승무원은 어디서 **쉴까**요?
During a flight, where do you reckon the flight attendants rest?

서울에서 강릉까지 버스로 얼마나 걸**릴까**요?
How long do you reckon it will take to go from Seoul to Gangneung by bus?

벌써 왔**을까**요?
Do you suppose he/she's already come?

그림 속 여인은 과연 자신의 미소만큼 행복했**을까**요?
Do you reckon the woman in the picture was really as happy as her smile suggests?

Short negation and long negation patterns are used (refer to 4.2):

평발이면 군대 안 **갈까**요?
I wonder if you don't have to go to military service if you are flat footed.

유미는 왜 혼인신고를 하지 않았**을까**요?
Why do you reckon Yumi didn't register her marriage?

When –(으)ㄹ까 occurs in the first person ('I') and depicts a future action involving the speaker, the sentence translates into a tentative offer to perform the action. This translates into English as 'Shall I . . .':

제가 문을 닫**을까**요? *Shall I close the door?*
내가 언제 한번 들**를까**요? *Shall I drop by sometime?*
이 서류는 어디다 놓**을까**요? *Where shall I put these documents?*

This usage as 'Shall I . . .' frequently features the verb 주– 'give' (and its object honorific counterpart 드리–) either as a main verb or as an auxiliary verb (refer to 5.1.12). This results in sentences where the speaker is offering to give something to the hearer or to do something for him/her.

소주 **줄까**? *Shall I get you some soju?*

사진을 보여 **줄까**? *Shall I show you the photos?*

제가 도와드**릴까요**? *Shall I help you?*

Sentences such as these also appear in service industry talk, where the waiter/waitress, sales assistant, etc. is asking the customer what he/she would like:

맥주는 몇 병 드**릴까요**? *How many bottles of beer can I get you?*

맵게 해 드**릴까요**? *Would you like it (made) spicy?*

When the future action involves both the speaker and the hearer, –(으)ㄹ까 translates as 'shall we . . .'. This is used when making informal suggestions. Note that these sentences do not normally take honorifics and are thus not normally used to address an elder or superior.

춤 **출까요**? *Shall we dance?*

맥주 한 잔 마시러 **갈까요**? *Shall we go for a beer?*

주말에 우리 영화나 한번 **볼까요**? *Shall we watch a movie or something on the weekend?*

With the 'Shall I' or 'Shall we" constructions, a negative can be expressed by using the pattern –지 말– 'desist' (refer to 4.2.3):

살 빼지 **말까**? *Shall I not lose weight?*

이 문제는 더 이상 이야기하지 **말까요**?
Shall we not talk about this problem anymore?

To offer two possible alternatives, simply repeat the whole sentence pattern:

소주 **줄까**? 맥주 **줄까**? *Shall I get you some soju? Or some beer?*

Of the two alternatives, one may be positive and the other may be negative. Such constructions translate as 'shall we . . . or not'.

소주 **줄까**? 주지 **말까**? *Shall I get you some soju or not?*

–(으)ㄹ까 can also be followed by a number of support verbs to form constructions with quite different meanings (refer to 5.4).

9.11 –(으)ㄹ래 'feel like (doing)'

This construction is a two-shape verb ending: –ㄹ래 is used after a vowel and –을래 after a consonant. It appears only with processive verbs and cannot be preceded by tense markers.

–(으)ㄹ래 can be used in the first person (i.e., 'I', 'we') or the second person (i.e., 'you') to express a desire, wish, preference, mild intention or inclination. This generally translates as 'want (to do something)', 'feel like (doing something)' and so forth.

A: 뭐 먹**을래**? *What do you want to eat?*

B: 난 비빔밥을 먹**을래**. *I want to eat pibimpap.*

A: 춤 **출래**? *Would you like to dance?*

B: 싫어. 안 **출래**. *I don't want to. I'd rather not.*

너 나랑 사**귈래**? *Do you want to be my girl/boyfriend?*

너희끼리 갔다 와. 우리는 여기 있**을래**.
You guys go. We'd rather just stay here.

This form is generally informal and colloquial. However, it can at times be heard with the honorific –시–, including in polite offers such as the following:

따뜻한 차 한 잔 드**실래**요? *Would you like a nice warm cup of tea?*

여기 앉으**실래**요? *Would you like to take a seat here?*

9.12 –(으)ㄹ텐데 'I'm afraid'

This pattern is primarily a connective ending and was discussed previously in the verbal connectives chapter (refer to 7.3.13). However, when it appears in sentence-final position it takes on some quite different meanings, which is why we discuss it again here.

Firstly, the pattern is used for making predictions, typically about the future. These predictions tend to be negative in content (and may translate into English as 'I'm afraid . . .'):

내일 날씨가 추**울 텐데**요.	*I'm afraid it will be cold tomorrow.*
금요일은 너무 바**쁠 텐데**요.	*I'm afraid Friday is going to be too busy.*
엄청 무거**울 텐데**.	*I'm afraid it will be very heavy.*

For a prediction that refers to the past, –았/었– (refer to 4.3.1.1) is added:

쉬운 일이 아니었**을 텐데**.	*That couldn't have been easy.*
상처가 많았**을 텐데**.	*You must have hurt a lot.*

Secondly, the pattern is used for hypothetical sentences. These may be about the present or future, but are more often about the past, with –(으)ㄹ 텐데 adding a sense of regret. The clause ending in –았/었을 텐데 is commonly preceded by a conditional clause with –(으)면 (refer to 7.5.1):

내가 민호 씨의 주소를 알았었다면 엽서를 한 장 보냈**을 텐데**.
If I had known Minho's address, I would have sent him a postcard.

사운드가 좋은 극장에서 봤으면 괜찮았**을 텐데**.
[The film] would have been ok if we had watched it at a theatre with decent sound.

파티에 갈 수 있었더라면 좋았**을 텐데**.
It would have been good if I had been able to go to the party.
(= I wish I had been able to go to the party.)

In sentences such as the above, –(으)ㄹ 텐데 may be replaced by –(으)ㄹ 거– (refer to 4.3.2.2) with little change in meaning. In some cases, –(으)련마는/(으)련만 (refer to 9.14) may also be possible.

9.13 –(으)랴 'could . . . really?'

This form is incompatible with the polite –요 ending and thus only occurs when addressing intimates and/or status inferiors. It is used to express a doubt that something could be the case:

부모님의 은혜를 어찌 잊을 수 있**으랴**.
Could she really forget the love of her parents?

설마 여름에 눈이 오**랴**.
Could it really snow in summer?

It occurs in certain proverbs and set expressions, here shown with their idiomatic English equivalents:

아니 땐 굴뚝에 연기 나**랴**. *Where there's smoke there's fire.*

첫술에 배부르**랴**. *Rome wasn't built in a day*

You may also hear it used when the speaker is asking the hearer about his/her intentions, although this usage is somewhat outmoded:

내가 대신 말해 주**랴**?
Do you want me to say it for you?

이런 힘든 일을 이 나이에 내가 하**랴**?
Do you really want me to do this hard work, at my age?

9.14 –(으)련마는/ –(으)련만 'should, must'

The two-shape ending –(으)련마는 (and its more common abbreviated version –(으)련만) is used when the speaker is making a conjecture. The conjecture normally pertains to the expected state of affairs – as to how something really should be! It is similar in meaning to certain usages of –(으)ㄹ 거– (refer to 4.3.2.2) or –겠– (refer to 4.3.2.1).

하숙 생활을 하면 가끔 집 생각이 나**련만**.
I suppose if you live in a boarding house, you must sometimes think of home.

대학생이면 애인도 있**으련만**.
If you are a university student, you really should have a boy/girlfriend.

약을 그 정도 먹었으니 나**으련만**.
If you have taken that much medicine, you should have got better.

Sentences such as the above may then be followed by another clause that contradicts the expectation:

하숙 생활을 하면 가끔 집 생각이 나**련만** 너는 왜 안 나?
I suppose if you live in a boarding house you must sometimes think of home – but why is it that you don't?

대학생이면 애인도 있**으련만** 너는 없다고?
If you are a university student, you really should have a boy/girlfriend – but you are telling me you don't?

약을 그 정도 먹었으니 나**으련만** 아직도 아프니?
If you have taken that much medicine, you should have got better – but are you still ill?

Similar to –(으)ㄹ 텐데 (refer to 9.12), –(으)련마는 may also appear in hypothetical sentences, typically including the conditional –(으)면 (refer to 7.5.1). In such constructions, –(으)련마는 most frequently appears with the descriptive verb 좋 – 'is good' to produce sentences meaning 'wouldn't it be good if' or 'I wish/hope . . .':

모든 일이 소원대로 되었으면 좋**으련만**.
I hope everything goes as you wish.

나도 그렇게 좀 한가했으면 좋**으련만**.
I wish I too was not so busy.

약을 그 정도 먹었으니 나으면 좋**으련만**.
You have taken that much medicine, so I wish you would have got better.

9.15 –(으)렴/–(으)려무나 granting permission; orders

–(으)렴 and –(으)려무나 attach only to processive verbs and are used when granting permission, giving orders or making suggestions. These forms never take the 'polite' –요 ending and are therefore only appropriate for use towards intimates and/or status subordinates. These endings have a soft and friendly feel.

그 일이 그렇게 하고 싶으면 한번 해 보**렴**.
If you want to do it like that, then just go ahead and give it a try.

좀 쉬었다 가**렴**.
Have a rest before you go.

올해는 공부 좀 열심히 하**려무나**.
You really should study hard this year.

이제 그만 가서 자**려무나**.
Why don't you go and sleep now?

9.16 –(으)마 promise-like futures

This two-shape ending is used when the speaker is expressing a promise and/or a decision made at or just before the time of speaking. Essentially, this is identical to the use of –ㄹ게 (refer to 9.9) and certain usages of –겠– (refer to 4.3.2.2). The difference is that –(으)마 is only used by older (or superior) speakers addressing younger (or subordinate) interlocutors. –(으)마 never appears followed by the 'polite' –요 ending (refer to 6.1.1) and is therefore intrinsically non-honorific.

한국에 오면 맛있는 거 많이 사 주**마**.
If you come to Korea, I'll buy you a lot of delicious things to eat.

지금 입맛이 없어. 나중에 먹**으마**.
I don't have any appetite now. I'll eat later.

지옥의 문 앞에서 기다리**마**!
I'll be waiting for you at the gates of hell!

책 잘 읽**으마**. 고맙다.
I'll enjoy reading this book. Thanks.

9.17 –잖아 'you know'

This one-shape ending originates from an abbreviation of the long negation question pattern –지 않– (refer to 4.2.2). It may occur with the past tense and future tenses (with either –겠– or –ㄹ 거).

–잖아 is used when the speaker provides information that he/she believes the interlocutor to already be aware of and thus seek his/her confirmation and/or agreement. Essentially, this is similar to some uses of –지 (refer to 9.18). However, –잖아 is much more emphatic than –지 and contains a stronger expectation that the hearer is aware of (or really should be aware of) the information being conveyed. The feeling is best translated into English with expressions such as '(don't) you know' or 'can't you see':

A: 이 음식이 왜 이렇게 맛없을까요?
Why do you suppose this food is so tasteless?

B: 영국 음식이**잖아**요!
But it's British food, you know.

A: 그 여자 마음에 안 들어?
You don't like that girl?

B: 응. 못생겼**잖아**.
She's ugly, can't you see.

괜찮아, 다음에 더 잘 하면 되**잖아**!
It's okay. If you do well next time, you'll be fine, you know.

As this expression supposes that the hearer is aware of the information being conveyed, it often occurs with common sayings or expressions of general truths

무소식이 희소식이**잖아**요.
No news is good news, of course.

결혼은 해도 후회, 안 해도 후회라는 말이 있**잖아**요.
They say that, with marriage, whether you do it or not, you live to regret it, you know.

When said with an aggressive or exasperated tone, the pattern indicates that the speaker is annoyed by the interlocutor. This might first of all take place when the interlocutor has forgotten or appears to be unaware of something that he/she really should know.

A: 빨리 와!
Hurry up!

B: 내 다리가 아프**잖아**!
My leg's hurting, you know!

A: 숙제 안 해?
You're not going to do my homework?

B: 난 벌써 했**잖아**!
I've already done it, don't you know.

This may also happen when the speaker feels that he/she is being incessantly pestered by the interlocutor:

건드리지 말라 그랬**잖아**!
Didn't I tell you not to bug me!

가기 싫다고 했는데 왜 자꾸 가라는 거야? 싫다**잖아**!
I told you I didn't want to go, so why do you keep telling me to go? I said, I didn't want to!

Finally, this usage may occur when the speaker is asked a stupid question to which the answer is too obvious.

A: 왜 결혼했어?
Why did you get married?

B: 사랑하**잖아**!
It's because I love him/her, stupid!

A: 우리 한국말 시험 언제 해?
When do we have our Korean exam?

B: 너 진짜 몰라? 내일이**잖아**!
You really don't know? It's tomorrow, stupid.

9.18 –지 tag questions

The one-shape ending –지 may be preceded by tense markers. When it is followed by the polite ending –요, the combination is sometimes pronounced and even written (in casual writing) as –죠.

When a speaker uses –지, the underlying meaning is that the speaker is confident that the content of his utterance is true, right or plausible and that he/she expects the hearer to agree with him/her. In practice, this results in a number of different usages depending on the context and intonation.

First, when the sentence is said with a rising intonation, the speaker is usually inviting the confirmation of the hearer. The meaning is therefore similar to a tag-question ('don't you', 'isn't it', 'didn't he', 'can't she', etc. in English, 'innit' in some urban dialects of British English, 'n'est pas' in French):

그 책은 정말 재미있**지요**?	*That book's interesting, isn't it?*
어제 많이 힘들었**지**?	*You had a hard time yesterday, didn't you?*
한국 사람이시**지**요?	*You're Korean, aren't you?*
내일 우리 집에 올 거**지**?	*You're going to come to our house tomorrow, aren't you?*

Second, when the sentence is said with a falling intonation, the speaker expresses that the listener should know or be aware of the content of the remark. English translations like 'as you might expect', 'as you know', 'of course' may convey this tone. Unlike in the examples above, the speaker is not asking for the hearer's confirmation and is taking the truth of his/her utterance as a given.

한국은 여름에 날씨가 덥**지**요.
Korea is hot in summer, as you know.

유미가 어제 아팠**지**요.
Yumi was ill yesterday, you know.

누구나 실수하**지**.
Everyone makes mistakes, you know.

선생님이시니까 항상 점심 값을 내시**지**요.
As he/she is the teacher, he/she always treats us to lunch, as you may expect.

This usage may also be applied in response to a yes/no question to emphasize 'of course I have done what you are asking':

A: 설거지했어?
Have you washed the dishes?

B: 그럼, 했**지**.
Of course, I've done it

This usage also commonly appears in stock expressions that include the meaning of 'of course' in their semantics:

물론이**지**요. *Of course.*

당연하**지**요. *That goes without saying.*

This includes the expression –기 마련이– (refer to 2.2.4.3):

누구나 실수하기 마련이**지**요.
Of course, it's to be expected that anyone can make a mistake.

Thirdly, –지 can appear in sentences with a first person subject (i.e., 'I') when the speaker is making an offer to the hearer or is volunteering to do something. In such cases, addition of –지 makes the sentence sound softer and friendlier:

제가 써 드리**지**요. *Let me write it for you.*

제가 (돈을) 내**지**요! *I'll pay! (or: Let me pay!)*

Fourth, –지 can also be used in imperative sentences, with the underlying meaning 'I am telling you what to do and I expect you to comply with my request'. However, in practice these kinds of commands are generally convey a tone of friendly urging (rather than the normal feeling of demanding that imperatives may often convey). Common translations include 'how about' or 'why don't you':

한 잔 더 하**지**. *How about another drink?*

마음대로 하**지**. *Just do what you like.*

커피 한 잔 드시**지**요. *How would you like a cup of coffee?*

These imperative sentences with honorifics and –지 are often used in proposals that include the participation of the speaker as well, where English would use 'let's . . .'. Although Korean also has a proposal type ending –ㅂ시다 'let's . . .', this ending is not normally used towards status superiors. Instead, it is politer to use –지 together with honorific marker –시– :

가까운 산에 등산이나 같이 가시**지**요.
Let's go hiking together at a nearby mountain.

다음 주에 점심이나 같이 하시**지**요.
Let's have lunch together sometime next week.

Fifth, when –지 is used in question sentences that contain a question word (얼마 'how much', 몇 'how many', 누구 'who' etc.), it acts to make the question sound softer and/or more friendly:

저거 얼마**지**요? *How much is it?*

지금 몇 시**지**요? *What time is it?*

Finally, –지 frequently combines with the –(아/어)야 ending (refer to 7.5.7.1), which expresses obligation or necessity, to make the form –야지. The literal meaning of the whole construction is something like 'you have to do. . ., don't you know'. The form is used when expressing obligations or necessities that the speaker believes the listener should be aware of and agree with. It is frequently used by parents when reminding children of the rules:

다른 친구와도 어울려 지내**야지**. *You should mix with other kids.*

엄마 말을 잘 들어**야지**. *You should listen to what Mum is saying.*

When used in the past tense, it can refer to what should have been done:

진작 말을 했어**야지**. *You should have said something before.*

Chapter 10

Quotations

Overview

'Quotations' (also known as 'reported speech') are used when repeating or relaying what someone else said (or, at times, when reiterating your own words, reporting things that are commonly said or believed, reporting the thoughts of yourself/others, etc.).

There are two ways to report what someone has said: a direct quotation, which gives the exact words spoken, and an indirect quotation, which gives the words in a changed style. In Korean, the second of these methods is particularly complex in that different verb endings are required depending on whether the phrase that was said was a simple statement, a question, a command or a proposal. In addition, in colloquial speech, a variety of abbreviated reduced quotation forms are used, each with their specific discourse functions.

10.1 Direct quotations

Direct quotes are used when you want to relay the actual words or thoughts in their original form. To do this, simply say or write the original phrase in its entirety, follow this with 라고 or 하고 and then round-off the sentence with a reporting verb (such as 말하– 'say', 묻– 'ask', etc.). As is the case with other quotation patterns, 하– 'do' (or 그렇– 'do like that' in casual speech) is frequently used in place of a specific reporting verb.

Actual words	*Reported in direct quotations*
'내일까지 숙제를 하세요' *'Do your homework by tomorrow'.*	선생님은 '내일까지 숙제를 하세요' **라고말씀하셨어요**. *The teacher said 'Do your homework by tomorrow'.*
'날씨가 너무 좋다' *'The weather's so good'.*	민호가 '날씨가 너무 좋다' **라고 했어요**. *Minho said 'The weather's so good'.*

Here are some further examples:

신문기자가 '영국에 왜 오셨습니까?' **하고 물었어요**.
The newspaper reporter asked, 'Why did you come to the UK?'

그 때 인호가 '갑시다' **라고 했어요**.
At that moment, Inho said, 'let's go'.

'건강을 챙겨야지' 하**고 생각하기** 시작했어요.
I started thinking, 'I have to look after my health'.

'혼자 가지 말고 같이 가자' 그러더라고. '야, 그러자. 같이 가자' 그랬지.
She said, 'don't go alone, let's go together'. I said, 'okay, let's go together'.

Note in the final example the use of the observed/perceived past tense marker –더라(고) (refer to 4.3.1.3) in the reporting verb 그러더라고 in the first sentence. Since observed/perceived past tense is usually used for reporting the actions of a third person as perceived by the speaker, we can tell that this sentence refers to the words of another person ('she'), even though this is not specifically mentioned. Also note that 라고/하고 is dropped in this example, which sometimes happens, particularly with the verb 그렇– 'do like that'.

When reporting noises that are expressed through onomatopoeic words, note that only –하고 (and not –라고) is used:

첫 수탉이 '꼬끼오!' **하고 목청을 뽑았다**.
The first cock cried, 'Cock-a-doodle-do!'

10.2 Indirect quotations

Indirect quotations are also used when reporting what someone said. But instead of keeping the quotation in its original form (and with quotation marks), you alter the phrase and incorporate it directly into the structure of the sentence (without quotation marks). To take an example from English, a **direct** quotation such as:

Tom said, 'I am going home'.

can alternatively be expressed as an **indirect** quotation as follows:

Tom said he was going home.

Korean expresses indirect quotation by attaching the verb ending –고 onto the end of the 'plain' style (refer to 6.1.4) and then following this with a 'quoting verb':

간다**고**	말했어요
goes-plain style-고	said
He said he was going.	

As well as 'quoting verbs' with specific meanings such as 말하– 'say' and 물어 보– 'ask', you can also just use the generic verbs 하– 'do' and 그렇– 'do like that'. A complete list of 'quoting verbs' is provided later in this chapter (refer to 10.2.6).

As indirect quotations use the 'plain' speech style (refer to 6.1.4) as an integral building block, it is important to have a good grasp of the plain speech style before reading.

10.2.1 Quoted statements

Statements can be quoted indirectly by attaching the plain speech style statement ending –(ㄴ/–는)다 to the phrase being quoted, following this immediately with –고 and then using a reporting verb. As with other quotation patterns, 하– 'do' (or 그렇– 'do like that') is frequently used in place of a specific reporting verb. The resulting pattern thus looks like this: –(ㄴ/–는)다고 하–. Note that the –고 sometimes drops, particularly if the reporting verb is 그렇–.

Actual words	*Reported in indirect quotations*
'집에 가요'.	민호는 집에 **간다(고) 했어요**.
'I'm going home'.	*Minho said he's going home.*

'유미가 예뻐요'.	민호는 유미가 **예쁘다(고) 했어요**.
'Yumi is pretty'.	*Minho said that Yumi is pretty.*
'날씨가 안 좋아요'.	민호는 날씨가 **안 좋다(고) 그랬어요**.
'The weather's not good'.	*Minho said that the weather isn't good.*

As in the above examples, the person doing the 'saying' normally comes at the start of the sentence. However, when the quotation is very long, it is sometimes easier to put it between –고 and the reporting verb:

오늘 날이 좋아서 산에 **간다고** 민호가 **말했어요**.
Minho said that we go to the mountain since the weather's so nice today.

As in the example '민호는 유미가 예쁘다고 했어요', when the subject of the quoted part is different to the subject of the 'saying part', the former (i.e., Yumi) is marked with the subject particle and the latter (i.e., Minho) is typically marked with the topic particle (or otherwise, also with the subject particle).

Although quoted statements normally follow the plain style statement ending, there is one important exception; the copula –이– (and its negative counterpart 아니–) (refer to 4.1.4). Although in the plain style the copula is –이다 (and 아니다 in the negative), in reported speech it becomes –이라 (and 아니라).

Actual words	*Reported in indirect quotations*
남편은 한국 사람이에요.	남편은 한국 사람**이라고 했어요**.
'My husband is Korean'.	*She said that her husband is Korean.*
비싼 것 아니에요.	비싼 것 **아니라고 했어요**.
'It's not an expensive one'.	*He said it isn't an expensive one.*

Since the plain speech style can occur after the past tense marker, future expressions with –겠– and the honorific marker, phrases involving all of these forms can be reported in the same way:

past tense:	집을 **샀다고 했어요**. *He/she said he had bought a house.*
future with –겠– :	내일 **오겠다고 했어요**. *He/she said he/she will come tomorrow.*

honorific: 아버님은 오늘 못 **<u>가신다고 하셨어요</u>**.
Father said he would can't come today.

Quotes for future time can also be reported using the –(으)ㄹ 거– pattern (refer to 4.3.2.2). Since this pattern is built on the copula, this becomes –거라고 in reported speech (or –것이라고 in its full form).

오늘 저녁에 늦게 **<u>올 거라고 했어요</u>**.
He/she said he/she would come late tonight

In addition to reporting something that somebody said, you can also report something that you have heard with the verb 듣– 'hear':

그 사람이 한국말 공부를 잘 **<u>한다고 들었어요</u>**.
I heard he was studying Korean hard.

Here are some further examples:

공원에서 산책하고 싶**<u>다고 했어요</u>**.
He/she said he/she'd like to take a walk in the park.

전화하시겠**<u>다고 그랬어요</u>**?
Did you say you were going to make a telephone call?

제가 내일 찾아뵙겠**<u>다고 전해 주세요</u>**.
Please tell him/her that I will go and visit him/her tomorrow.

Quoted statements are also used when you are reporting what something is called. This can include introducing your own name, where the form –(이)라고 합니다 represents a polite ritualized way of introducing yourself:

안녕하십니까? 런던 대학교 한국학과 3학년에 재학 중인 김 한나**<u>라고 합니다</u>**.
Hello. I'm called Hannah Kim and I'm a third year student in the Korean Studies department at London University.

10.2.2 Quoted questions

For quoted questions, use the –느냐 question form of the plain speech style in the case of processive verbs, and the –(으)냐 question form in the case of descriptive verbs and then follow this with

–고 and a verb of reporting. In colloquial speech, the '느' and '으' elements are frequently deleted giving a colloquial one-shape question form –냐. Note, however, that –느냐 or –(으)냐 is still regarded as standard in written Korean.

Actual words	*Reported in indirect quotations*
'밥을 먹어요?'	밥을 먹**(느)냐고 했어요**.
'Are you eating?'	*I asked if they were eating.*
'유미가 어디 있어요?'	민호는 저에게 유미가 어디 있**(느)냐고 물었어요**.
'Where is Yumi?'	*Minho asked me where Yumi was.*
'날씨가 좋아요?'	민호가 저한테 날씨가 좋**(으)냐고 물었어요**.
'Is the weather nice?'	*Minho asked me if the weather was nice.*

As with other patterns of indirect reported speech, –느냐고 하– can occur after the past tense marker, future expressions with –겠– and the honorific marker:

past tense:	언제 왔**(느)냐고 물었어요**. *He/she asked me when I had come.*
future with –겠– :	내일 가시겠**(느)냐고 했어요**. *He/she asked if I would come tomorrow*
honorific:	여동생은 아버님께서 시간이 되시**(느)냐고 물었어요**. *Younger sister asked if father had time.*

To report the question and subsequent answer (or reaction) within the same sentence, –더니 (refer to 10.1.9) is attached to the reporting verb:

제가 여자 친구에게 사랑하**냐고 물어봤더니** 모른다고 대답했어요.
I asked my girlfriend if she loved me and she answered that she didn't know.

유미에게 몇 살이**냐고 물어봤더니**, 갑자기 화를 냈어요.
When I asked Yumi how old she was, she suddenly got angry.

Here are more examples:

의사한테 병이 오래가겠**느냐고 물어 보세요**.
Ask the doctor if the illness will last long.

선생이 나한테 왜 좀 일찍 가지 못했**느냐고 말했어요**.
The teacher asked me why I couldn't go there a little earlier.

사회자가 연예인에게 어떻게 그렇게 예쁘**냐고 계속 질문했어요**.
The host kept asking the celebrity how it could be that she was so pretty.

10.2.3 Quoted proposals

Proposals can be quoted by attaching –고 하– to the 'plain' style proposal ending –자:

Actual words	*Reported in indirect quotations*
'갑시다!'	가**자고 했어요**.
'Let's go'.	*He/she suggested we go.*
'영화를 같이 보자!'	민호는 영화를 같이 보**자고 했어요**.
'Let's watch the film together'.	*Minho suggested watching the film together.*

Since proposals cannot occur in the past or future, –았/었– (past tense marker) and –겠– (future tense marker) never appear in this construction.

Here are more examples of quoted proposals.

민호는 인호에게 사업을 같이 **하자고 했어요**.
Minho suggested to Inho that they go into business together.

퇴근 길에 포장마차에 가서 소주 한 잔 **하자고 했어요**.
He/she suggested that we go to the drinking stall for a drink of soju on the way home.

노래방에 **들르자고**, 노래 한번 **부르자고 졸랐었어요**.
He/she pestered me by suggesting that we go to karaoke and that we sing a song.

여자 친구에게 **결혼하자고 했는데** 여자친구는 장난인 줄 알았어요
I suggested to my girlfriend that we get married, but she thought I was joking.

10.2.4 Quoted commands

Commands can be quoted by adding –고 and a verb of reporting to the –(으)라 command form of the plain speech style. Note that –(으)라 is used and not the colloquial variant –아/어라 (refer to 6.1.4).

Actual words	*Reported in indirect quotations*
빨리 먹어!	빨리 **먹으라고 했어요**.
'Eat up quickly!'	*He/she told me to eat quickly.*
여기서 내리세요.	운전기사가 저에게 여기서 **내리라고 했어요**.
'Get off here'.	*The driver told me to get off here.*

As in the final example, the person towards whom the command is directed is marked with the particle 에게/한테 (refer to 3.2.4.4). You might also hear –더러 (refer to 3.2.4.5) being used in place of these, although this usage is generally restricted to those of equal or lower status. When the person receiving the command is an elder or notable superior, the honorific particle –께 should be used instead:

할아버지**께** 편히 **쉬시라고 했어요**.
I told grandfather to rest comfortably.

As commands cannot take future and past tense, this pattern does not occur with the tense markers –았/었– and –겠–. However, as shown in the above example, it may appear with the honorific marker –시–.

Here are some further examples:

어머니는 나더러 오늘 아침 일찍 **일어나라고 했어요**.
Mother told me to get up early this morning.

선생님께서는 영어를 하지 말고 한국말을 **하라고 하셨어요**.
The teacher told us to speak Korean instead of English.

내가 운동화 **신으라고 했잖아**? 엄마가 말할 때 들었어야지.
I told you to wear your sneakers, didn't I? You have to listen to your mother when she's speaking.

Note that commands featuring 주– 'give' (as a main verb or an auxiliary verb) undergo special transformations (refer to 10.2.5).

10.2.5 The verb 주– in quoted commands

Special care is needed when dealing with the verb 주– 'give', in indirect quoted commands, both when it appears as a main verb and as an auxiliary verb in the construction –아/어 주– (refer to 5.1.12) (which is used when talking about performing an action for the benefit of someone else).

In quoted commands, 주– is frequently replaced by 달라–. However, for this to take place, an important condition has to be met: the person making the command must be the same as the person who stands to benefit from the action being commanded.

Actual words	*Reported in indirect quotations*
'그 책을 주세요' *'Please give me that book'.*	그 책을 **달라고 했어요**. *He/she told me to give him/her that book.*
'김치찌개 하나 주세요'. *'One kimchi stew, please'.*	김치찌개 하나 **달라고 했어요**. *I asked the waiter to give me one kimchi stew.*
'내일 까지 전화해 주세요'. *'Give me a call by tomorrow'.*	민호는 내일까지 전화해 **달라고 했어요**. *Minho told me to give him a call by tomorrow.*
'유미야, 점심 사 줘' *'Yumi, [why don't you] buy me lunch'*	민호는 유미에게 점심을 사 **달라고 했어요**. *Minho told [asked, suggested to] Yumi to buy him lunch.*

In cases where the person to whom the command (or request) is being addressed is a notable superior, etc. and would typically be addressed in honorifics, the special form 주십사 should be used instead:

Actual words	*Reported in indirect quotations*
'사장님, 도착하시는 대로 전화해 주십시오'.	사장님께 도착하시는 대로 전화해 **주십사(고) 부탁 드렸어요**.
'Boss, please phone me as soon as you arrive'.	*I requested to the manager that he phoned me as soon as he arrived.*
'교수님, 추천서 좀 써 주십시오'.	교수님께 추천서를 좀 **써 주십사(고) 부탁드렸어요**.
'Professor, please write a reference for me'.	*I requested to the professor that he wrote a reference for me.*

In cases where the person benefiting from the action is a different person to the one making the command, 주– is maintained in the form 주라고:

Actual words	*Reported in indirect quotations*
'인호에게 돈 좀 주세요'.	민호가 인호에게 돈 좀 **주라고 했어요**.
'Give some money to Inho'.	*Minho told me to give some money to Inho.*
'유미야, 수미에게 떡을 갖다 줘라'.	민호는 유미에게 수미한테 떡을 갖다 **주라고 했어요**.
'Yumi, take these rice cakes to Sumi [for me]'.	*Minho told Yumi to take some rice cakes to Sumi.*

10.2.6 Quoting verbs

As we have seen in this section, a variety of verbs can be used in reported speech. The most common verbs you will hear are summarized below (refer to Choo & Kwak 2008):

1. Generic verbs	*Examples*
하– *do*	안 간다고 했어요. *He/she said he/she is not going.*
그렇– *do like that*	누가 농담한다고 그래요? *Who said I'm joking?*

2. Saying-type verbs	*Examples*
경고하– *warn*	그 약은 악영향을 끼친다고 경고했어요. *I warned him that the medicine had adverse effects.*
노래를 하– *repeatedly ask; beg*	돈을 달라고 노래를 했어요. *He/she kept begging me to give him/her money.*
말하– *say*	시간이 없다고 말했어요. *He/she said he/she did not have time.*
맹세하– *swear*	나만을 사랑한다고 맹세하지 않았어? *Didn't you swear to love only me?*
명령하– *order*	빨리 가라고 명령했어요. *He/she told me to go quickly.*
묻– *ask*	화장실이 어디냐고 물어봤어요. *He/she asked where the toilet was.*
부탁하– *request*	도와 달라고 부탁했어요. *He/she asked me to help.*
설명하– *explain*	의사는 관절염에 효과가 있다고 설명했어요. *The doctor explained that it was effective for arthritis.*
우기– *insist*	많이 안 먹었다고 우겼어요. *I insisted that I hadn't eaten a lot.*
재촉하– *push*	빨리 먹으라고 재촉했어요. *He/she pressed me to eat quickly.*
주장하– *claim*	지원 제도를 마련해야 한다고 주장했어요. *He/she claimed that we had to set up a system of support.*
칭찬하– *compliment*	한국말을 잘한다고 칭찬했어요. *I complimented him on speaking Korean well.*

3. Thinking-type verbs	*Examples*
결론 내리– *conclude*	가능성이 매우 적다고 결론 내렸어요 *They concluded that the possibility was very small*
믿– *believe*	사진에 찍히면 영혼을 뺏긴다고 믿어요. *They believe that if you have your photo taken, your soul will be taken away.*
보– *view*	좋은 기회라고 봐야지요. *You have to look on it as a good opportunity.*
생각하– *think*	오래 전부터 참 괜찮은 여자라고 생각했어요. *From a long time ago, I thought she was a good woman.*
예측하– *expect*	올 겨울은 평년보다 따뜻할 거라고 예측하고 있군요. *They are predicting that this winter will be warmer than an average year.*
확신하– *believe, be sure*	연락할 시간이 없었을 거라고 확신해요. *I'm sure [it was the case] that he/she did not have time to contact you.*

4. Hearing verbs	*Examples*
듣– *hear*	그 여배우가 성형 수술을 했다고 들었어요. *I heard that actress has had plastic surgery.*
소문을 듣– *hear a rumour*	요즘 다른 남자를 만난다고 소문을 들었어요. *I heard a rumour that she is meeting another man these days.*

Quotations may also be followed by a clause expressing a means of communication (such as letter, e-mail, etc.):

그 친구에게 너무 **고맙다고 메일을 보냈어요**.
I sent an e-mail saying thank you to my friend.

내가 고등학교 때 연예인한테 **사랑한다고 편지를 보낸** 적이 있어요.
When I was a high school student, I once sent a letter to a celebrity saying that I loved him/her.

내 비서가 오늘 아침 **아프다고 전화했어요**.
This morning, my secretary called in sick.

Quotations may also be followed by longer clauses that represent the actions of the person in question, with the preceding quoted clause expressing the thinking or spoken justification that lies behind the action:

네팔에 자원봉사 하러 **간다고 돈을 모으고 있어요**.
He/she is saving money, saying he/she is going to Nepal to do voluntary work.

제가 회사를 그만두고 **유학 간다고 영어를 공부하고 있어요**.
I quit my job and am now studying English, thinking about going to study overseas.

도대체 어디 뺄 살이 **있으시다고 다이어트를 하시는 거예요**?
Where do you think you have any fat to lose, going on a diet?

10.3 Reduced indirect quotations in reported speech

In colloquial speech, the full quotation forms outlined in the previous section are often reduced to the abbreviated forms. There are two sets of abbreviated forms, which are shown as 'abbreviated form 1' and 'abbreviated form 2' in the following table:

	Full form	*Abbreviated form 1*	*Abbreviated form 2*
statements:	–(ㄴ/는)다고 하–	–(ㄴ/는)다고	–(ㄴ/는)대
copula statements	–이라고 하–	–이라고	–이래
questions:	–느냐/(으)냐고 하–	–냐고	–내
proposals:	–자고 하–	–자고	–재
commands:	–(으)라고 하–	–(으)라고	–(으)래
commands with 주–	달라고 하–	달라고	달래

The discussions below look at the first column of abbreviated forms first and then look at the second. Rather than always acting as direct substitutions for the full forms, these abbreviated forms take on their own specific functions and nuances.

10.3.1 –다고, –냐고, –라고, –자고

This first set of reduced forms simply involves leaving off the verb of reporting at the end. When speaking in non-honorific speech styles (refer to 6.1), the sentence can then simply end. When speaking in honorific speech styles, –요 should be attached to the end.

Actual words	*Reported in indirect quotations*
'내일 안 가요'.	내일 안 **간다고요**.
'I'm not going tomorrow'.	*I said I'm not going tomorrow.*
'민호 씨 거예요'.	민호 씨 거**라고요**.
'It's Minho's'.	*I said it's Minho's.*
'언제 와요?'	언제 **오냐고요**?
'When are you going?'	*I asked when you are going.*
'빨리 마십시다'.	빨리 **마시자고요**.
'Let's drink up quickly'.	*I said let's drink up quickly.*
'내일 일찍 오세요'.	내일 일찍 **오시라고요**.
'Come early tomorrow'.	*I said come early tomorrow.*

These forms tend to place emphasis on the act of saying. The feeling is often similar to how English speakers may use prosodic emphasis (higher pitch, louder voicing and elongation) on reporting verbs such as, '*I said*'.

This form of reported speech is perhaps most commonly heard when the speaker repeats something he/she has previously said when the interlocutor fails to hear or heed his/her words as can be seen below:

A: 토요일에 시간이 없어. *I don't have time on Saturday.*

B: 뭐라고? 잘 안 들려. *What? I can't hear what you are saying.*

A: 토요일에 시간이 **없다고**. *I said I don't have time on Saturday.*

In addition to simply repeating what you said, you may use this strategy to clarify what you mean:

A:	왜 전화했어요?	*Why are you phoning me?*
B:	물어볼 거 있어서요.	*Because I have something to ask.*
A:	지금 새벽 2시인데 왜 **전화했냐고요**.	*I mean, why are you phoning me at 2 am?*

These forms can also be used when the speaker wants to assert his/her authority to make the statement in question. The feeling is a little similar to 'let me tell you', 'I'm telling you' or 'I'll tell you what in English':

배고픈데 짜장면이나 먹**자고**.
I'm hungry, so I tell you what, let's eat black bean noodles.

우리 팀은 아주 잘 했**다고**.
I'm telling you that our team did really well.

This extends to usage with 얼마나 'how (much/many)' when boasting with pride:

우리 나라 선수들은 얼마나 열심히 **싸웠다고**!
How hard our country's players/athletes fought!

우리 아들은 얼마나 **똑똑하다고**! *How clever my son is!*

These reduced forms are also used when you want to check or take issue with something that someone else has said that sounds suspect or surprising:

뭐라고? 그 예쁜 여자랑 **헤어졌다고**? 제 정신이니?
What? You said you broke up with that pretty girl? Are you in your right mind?

이거 다 **마시라고**? 미쳤어?
You're telling me to drink all this? Are you crazy?

결혼했냐고? 그걸 왜 알고 싶니?
Am I married? Why do you want to know that?

These forms are also used to express that you hold a different opinion either to the person you are talking to or to a third person. Here, the quoted form is generally accompanied by a question word (typically 뭐 'what?' or 어디 'where?') and the usage tends to be sarcastic:

그 남자 어디가 그렇게 **멋있다고**.
What do you think is so cool about that guy.

A: 이 음악 너무 마음에 들어. *I really like this music.*

B: 그래? 뭐가 **좋다고**. *Really? What's so great about it.*

10.3.2 –대, –내, –래, –재

This second set of reduced forms involves reducing the full quotation forms of –다고 하–, –냐고 하–, –라고 하– and –자고 하– to –대, –내, –래 and –재 respectively. When speaking in non-honorific speech styles (refer to 6.1), the sentence can then simply end. When speaking in honorific speech styles, –요 should be attached to the end. The past tense marker can also be added to make the forms –댔어, –냈어, –랬어 and –잤어.

Actual words	*Reported in indirect quotations*
'내일 안 가요'. *'I'm not going tomorrow'.*	내일 안 **간대요**. *They say he/she is coming tomorrow.*
'민호 씨 거예요'. *'It's Minho's'.*	민호 씨 거**래요**. *They say it's Minho's.*
'언제 와요?' *'When are you coming?'*	언제 **오내요**. *They are asking when you are coming.*
'빨리 마십시다'. *'Let's drink up quickly'.*	빨리 **마시재요**. *They are suggesting we drink up quickly.*
'내일 일찍 오세요' *'Come early tomorrow'.*	내일 일찍 **오시래요**. *They are telling us we should come early tomorrow.*

Whereas the –다고, –냐고, –라고 and –자고 (refer to 10.3.1) place emphasis on the act of saying, –대, –내, –래 and –재 place focus on the content of what was said. For this reason, they are often used in circumstances where the identity of who actually said the content is not important, in other words for reporting hearsay – things that have been heard (often from an unspecified speaker) or that are generally 'said' and believed. In English, this typically translates as 'they say . . .', 'it is said . . .' or 'I've heard that . . .'. Note that the long form can also be used for this, but less commonly so in colloquial speech.

이 음식은 건강에 **좋대요**. *They say this food is good for health.*

결혼은 안 했지만 여자 친구가 **있대요**.
He's not married but I've heard that he has a girlfriend.

내일은 춥고 비가 많이 **온대요**.
I've heard it's going to be cold and will rain a lot tomorrow.

These reduced forms can also be used in colloquial speech in place of the full forms when reporting what is said by a specific individual:

할아버지께서 오늘 **오신댔어요**.
Grandfather said he is coming today.

사람들은 나한테 왜 결혼을 안 **했냈어요**.
People asked me why I wasn't married.

사랑니 빼려고 하는데 큰 병원으로 **가래요**.
I'm going to have my wisdom tooth pulled out and I was told to go to a big hospital.

남자 친구가 자꾸 진지하게 **결혼하재요**.
My boyfriend keeps seriously proposing that we get married.

With the –래 form for commands, you may hear ' –라셔', a combination of –라 and –시– (refer to 6.2.1.1), when the person whose words are being quoted is a status superior:

엄마가 콜라 많이 먹지 말라고 전해 **달라셔**.
Mum told me to tell you not to drink too much cola.

어머님께서 전화하셨는데, 이번 주말이 제사라고 늦지 말고 **오라셔**.
Mum phoned and she said this weekend we are performing a sacrifice so don't be late.

Although this reduced form of speech is –대, –내, –래 and –재 with the polite and intimate speech styles, these reductions look somewhat different in other speech styles (refer to 6.1). The following chart shows verb endings for each style with the verb 가– 'goes'.

Intimate style	*Polite style*	*Plain style*	*Deferential style*
간대	간대요	간단다	간답니다
가내	가내요	가냔다	가냡니다
가래	가래요	가란다	가랍니다
가재	가재요	가잔다	가잡니다

Note that usage of the plain style –단다 extends beyond the expression of quotations and general sayings. It can also be used for explaining something in an objective matter, as if it is an established truth. This often occurs when adults are explaining things to children, but can also be used between close friends. The nuance is similar to 'the truth is . . .' in English:

애들아, 나는 원래 고기를 안 먹는**단다**.
Children, the truth is that I don't usually eat meat.

나는 영국에서 잘 지낸**단다**. 걱정하지 말아라.
The truth is that I'm doing well in England. Don't worry.

세상에는 나쁜 사람도 많지만 좋은 사람도 많**단다**.
Although there are many bad people in the world, the truth is that there are also many good people.

할아버지는 술을 드시면 노래를 부르신**단다**.
The truth is that when grandfather drinks, he likes to sing.

백두산은 한민족의 영산**이란다**.
The truth is that Mt. Baektu is a sacred mountain for Korean people.

10.4 Special patterns with indirect quotations

This section analyses some common grammatical patterns that incorporate elements (typically –다/냐/자/라) of reported speech in their structure.

10.4.1 –다/냐/자/라니(까)

This structure combines quotation patterns with the causation endings –(으)니까 (refer to 7.1.6) or the abbreviated –(으)니 (refer to 7.1.7).

The pattern can first of all be used to link two clauses when a quoted phrase (in the first clause) is expressed as the reason for a state of affairs (in the second clause):

미나는 예쁘**다니까** 좋아하더라고요.
On telling Mina she was pretty, she really liked it.

여동생이 있**다니까** 다들 소개해 달라고 했어요.
On mentioning that I had a little sister, everyone asked me to introduce them to her.

In addition, generally with the abbreviated form –(으)니, the second clause may contain the response or reaction of the speaker to something that the interlocutor has said or something that he/she has heard from a third party:

남자 친구가 이렇게 잘생겼**다니** 부럽네요.
On hearing that your boyfriend is so good looking, I'm feeling jealous.

재미없을 줄 알았는데 **재미있었다니** 다행이네요.
I thought you weren't going to enjoy it, so I'm relieved to hear you had a good time.

The form may appear both with –(으)니까 and –(으)니 at the end of a sentence. When the longer form –(으)니까 is used, this has the function of repeating, clarifying or reiterating something previously said. Although this can also be done by using the first abbreviated quotation pattern, (refer to 10.3.1) using –다/냐/자/라니까 makes the utterance sound more emphatic and often shows the speakers frustration or anger that the interlocutor is not listening to him/her:

앉아! 앉으라고! 앉**으라니까**! 왜 말을 안 들어?
Sit down! Sit down! I told you to sit down! Why don't you listen to me?

가기 싫은 게 아니라 바쁘**다니까**.
It's not that I don't want to go. I told you that I'm busy.

왜 대답 안 해? 관심 없**냐니까**.
Why aren't you answering? I asked you if you are not interested.

뭐 해? 빨리 가**자니까**.
What are you doing? Let's get going quickly.

With the shorter form –(으)니, the structure may be used when asking the interlocutor about what another person said, or to confirm or clarify what he/she has said:

마이클은 한국음식이 맛있**다니**?
Did Michael say that Korean food tasted good?

미나가 누구랑 같이 간**다니**?
Who did Mina say she was going with?

미나가 결혼식이 일요일**이라니**?
Did Mina say that the wedding was on Sunday?

– 다니/ –라니 can also be used at the end of a sentence with strong expressions of disbelief:

여기서 이렇게 만나**다니**!
Fancy meeting you here!

어쩜 바다색이 이렇게도 예쁘**다니**!
How could the colour of the sea be so pretty?

생일이 오늘**이라니**!
I can't believe your birthday is today!

This final usage of –다니/ –라니 is rather similar to some usages of –담/ –람 (refer to 9.7).

10.4.2 –다면/ –라면

This structure combines quotation patterns with the conditional –(으)면 ending and is discussed elsewhere (refer to 7.5.1).

10.4.3 –다/라면서

This pattern combines reported speech with the –(으)면서 ending (refer to 7.3.7), which is originally used like 'while' in English to depict two actions carried out at the same time and by the same person. –다/라면서 may also appear in the contracted form –다/라며.

Note also that –다며 is frequently pronounced or even written as '–다매' or '–대매' in colloquial language, although neither of these forms are considered standard.

This pattern can be used both at the end of a sentence and followed by another clause. When used at the end of a sentence, it expresses that the speaker wants to confirm information that he/she has heard from somewhere else:

딸을 **낳으셨다면서요**?
I heard you had a daughter, right?

요즘 한국 가을 날씨가 **좋다면서요**?
I heard that the Korean autumn weather is good these days, right?

어제 많이 **아팠다면서**?
I heard you were really ill yesterday, right?

When followed by a clause, the second clause depicts an action that accompanies the words of the speaker reported in the first clause:

민호는 유미에게 잘못이 **있다면서** 먼저 사과하지 않겠대요.
Saying that Yumi was to blame, Minho will not apologize first.

민호는 **미안하다면서** 유미에게 선물을 주었어요.
Saying sorry, Minho gave Yumi a present.

10.4.4 –다/라는데

This pattern combines reported speech with the ending –(으)ㄴ/는데 (refer to 7.3.12). This pattern is used when the speaker quotes either something that he/she has heard or otherwise a popular saying and/or common knowledge in the first clause, and then makes a command, proposal, invitation, request, etc. based on this in the second:

내일 날씨가 **좋다는데** 공원에 놀러 갑시다.
They say the weather is good tomorrow; let's go to the park.

부인과 딸들 분가시키고 혼자 **사신다는데** 건강 조심하세요.
I heard you are living apart from your wife and daughter; please take care of your health.

시작이 **<u>반이라는데</u>** 빨리 시작하자.
They say that 'starting is half the battle'; let's start.

At times, the construction may appear without a second clause. In such cases, by ending the sentence with –다는데, the speaker expects the hearer to infer for him/herself what is being commanded, proposed, etc. For example, the first sentence below may imply that since it is going to rain, we should just stay home. And the second clause may imply that since the film is boring, we should watch a different one or go and do something else instead.

내일 비가 **<u>온다는데</u>**. *They say it's going to rain tomorrow.*

그 영화가 **<u>재미없다는데</u>**. *I heard that the film is boring.*

In order to express or emphasize contrast between the quoted information given in the first clause and the contents of the second clause –도 can be added to the end of the construction to give –라/다는데도:

돈이 **<u>없다는데도</u>** 친구가 계속 점심 사 달래요.
Even though I said I don't have any money, my friend keeps asking me to buy him/her lunch.

10.4.5 –(이)라는

This construction involves the copula –이–, the quotation element '라' and the present dynamic modifying form –는 (refer to 8.1.2). It is a contraction of '. . . 이라고 하는 . . . 'a(n) . . . called . . .' (as in "a man called Bill")', but this longer form is only rarely heard.

김유미**<u>라는</u>** 배우를 만났어요.
I met an actress called Kim Yumi.

아르바이트**<u>라는</u>** 말은 원래 독일말이에요.
The word 'arbeit' is originally German.

강릉**<u>이라는</u>** 도시는 강원도에 있어요?
Is the city called Gangneung in Gangwondo?

In colloquial speech, –(이)라는 is often contracted even further to –(이)란:

어제 김유미**란** 사람이 찾아왔어요.
Somebody called Kim Yumi came to visit you yesterday.

경희대에서 홍릉 가는 길에 두부사랑**이란** 식당이 있어요.
By Kyunghee University, on the road towards Hongneung, there is a restaurant called 'Tofu Love'.

10.4.6 –단/냔/잔/란 말이–

This expression combines a quotative with the present dynamic modifying form –는 (refer to 8.1.2). This is contracted to –단/냔/잔/란 and followed by the word 말 'words, speech, what is said' and the copula. Put together, it translates as 'I mean . . .', 'Do you mean . . .', 'What I mean is . . .' or 'I'm telling you . . .', etc. It is used when the speaker wants to specify or amplify exactly what he/she means or to clarify what the speaker has said. Some usages can be similar to –다고 (refer to 10.3.1) or –다니(까) (refer to 10.4.1):

가겠다고 **약속했단 말이에요**.
What I mean is that I've promised to go.

그렇게 만나 보지도 못하고 **갔단 말이야**?
You mean you left without even meeting him/her?

도대체 뭐 하러 여기를 **왔냔 말이야**?
What I mean is what on earth did you come here for?

우리 **헤어지잔 말이야**?
Are you trying to say that we should break up?

The pattern can be made honorific by replacing the plain '말' with the honorific '말씀' (refer to 6.2.3):

몇 천 명을 군대에 보내고도 아직도 **부족하단 말씀입니까**?
Do you mean that even if we send a few more thousands into the army then it won't be enough?

그렇게 하기가 **곤란하단 말씀입니다**.
I mean that will be a bit difficult.

Chapter 11

Other word classes

Overview

This chapter looks at two remaining word classes not yet covered in this book adnouns, and adverbs. We will also look at prefixes and suffixes in this chapter.

11.1 Adnouns

Just as an adverb (refer to 11.2) functions to modify a following verb, adnouns are forms that work to modify a following noun. They are bound forms that cannot be used independently.

The word 'adnoun' is not normally used in descriptions of English grammar – in English there is no single set of words that directly corresponds. Korean adnouns most commonly correspond to English adjectives, or else to demonstratives ('this', 'that' etc.). However, Korean adnouns are very different from typical Korean adjectives. As described elsewhere (refer to 4.1.1), Korean adjectives typically function the same as verbs, indeed, in this book we refer to them as 'descriptive verbs'. However, adnouns that are descriptive in meaning have none of the properties of Korean verbs. Unlike verbs, they cannot take different endings, have one 'frozen' form and always have to be followed directly by a noun. Here are the most common Korean adnouns:

다른	*other*	딴	*other*	여느	*ordinary, usual*
웬	*a certain, some*	각	*each*	별	*different, special*
모든	*all*	온	*all*	갖은	*assorted*
온갖	*all sorts*	전	*all*	새	*new*
헌	*old*	옛	*ancient*	순	*pure*
맨	*the very*	날	*raw*		

다른 과목을 들으세요?
Are you taking any other subjects?

나는 완전히 **딴** 세상에서 자랐어요.
I grew up in a completely different world.

올해는 **여느** 해와 달라요.
This year is different from ordinary years.

웬 낯선 사람이 문 밖에 있어요.
Some unknown man is outside the door.

각 환자마다 45분씩 배당돼요.
Each patient is allotted 45 minutes.

별말씀 다 하십니다.
Don't mention it (lit. 'you are saying all these special things').

모든 호텔이 이미 다 예약이 됐어요.
All of the hotels are already booked up.

그 선수는 **온** 국민의 사랑을 받았어요.
That athlete received the love of the whole nation.

갖은 고생을 겪었어요.
I suffered all kinds of hardships.

온갖 수단과 방법을 다 썼어요
I tried every kind of means and method.

그 날은 **전** 생애에서 제일 행복한 날이었어요.
That was the happiest day of my whole life.

새 차를 샀어요. *I bought a new car.*

헌 옷을 입었어요. *I wore old clothes.*

옛 친구를 만났어요. *I met an old friend.*

아름다운 **순** 우리말 단어들이 많아요.
There are many beautiful pure Korean words.

왜 **맨** 앞에 앉으세요?
Why do you sit at the very front?

날 계란을 먹으면 정말 노래를 잘하나요?
Can you really sing well if you eat raw eggs?

In addition to descriptive adnouns, there are also demonstrative adnouns. Note that Korean has two words that correspond to 'that'. The first (그) is used to refer to something in the immediate vicinity of the hearer. The second (저) is used to index something that is far from the hearer (and also far from the speaker).

이 *this* 그 *that* 저 *that (over there)*

이 모자는 제 거예요.	*This hat is mine.*
그 바지는 잘 어울려요.	*Those trousers really suit you well.*
저 사람은 제 친구예요.	*That person over there is my friend.*

What is different from English demonstratives is that while English demonstratives can be used independently, as in 'I like this', the Korean demonstrative adnouns must be followed by a noun. To say a sentence such as 'I like this', the demonstrative adnoun has to be followed by the dependent noun 것 'thing' (refer to 2.1.2.1). The sentence would thus literally translate as 'I like this thing':

이것	(or 이거 in colloquial language)	*this (thing)*
그것	(or 이거 in colloquial language)	*that (thing)*
저것	(or 이거 in colloquial language)	*that (thing over there)*

When you are referring to a place rather than an object, 곳 'place' is used in place of 것:

이곳	(or 여기 in colloquial language)	*here*
그곳	(or 거기 in colloquial language)	*there*
저곳	(or 저기 in colloquial language)	*over there*

Korean also has adnouns that operate as question words:

어느	*which*
어떤	*what kind of*
무슨	*what (which)*
웬	*what kind of, what on earth, (why)*

Here are examples of these in sentences:

어느 역에서 갈아타요?	*At which station do we have to change?*
어떤 음식을 좋아하세요?	*What kind of food do you like?*
이게 **무슨** 냄새예요?	*What is this smell?*
갑자기 **웬** 일본어를 배우니?	*What's going on with you learning Japanese all of a sudden?*

More information on Korean question words can be found elsewhere (refer to 2.3.4).

11.2 Adverbs

Adverbs are commonly thought of as forms that modify verbs (or verb phrases), including both processive and descriptive verbs. However, certain adverbs may in fact modify any constituent of the sentence (except for nouns) or even entire sentences.

In this section, we look at Korean adverbs according to two different categorizations. In the first section (11.2.1), we describe adverbs according to their grammatical properties. In the second section (11.2.2), we look at adverbs according to their semantics or meanings.

11.2.1 Grammatical classification of adverbs

The current section introduces the major classes of Korean adverbs according to their different grammatical functions.

11.2.1.1 Proper adverbs

Proper adverbs are forms that are not derived from any other word class and function solely as adverbs. Some typical examples are listed here:

늘, 항상, 언제나	*always*
가끔	*sometimes*
이미, 벌써	*already*
바로	*right away*
즉시	*Immediately*
곧	*soon*
먼저	*first, before, in advance*
아주, 매우, 퍽	*very*
더	*more*
덜	*less, not enough*
좀, 조금	*a little*
아마	*probably*
이따금, 종종, (때)때로	*Occasionally*
오래	*for a long time*

Here are examples of some of these in sentences:

물고기는 왜 **항상** 눈을 뜨고 있나요?	*Why do fish always have their eyes open?*
나는 학생들로부터 **가끔** 이메일을 받아요.	*I sometimes receive e-mail from my students.*
벌써 잊어버렸어요?	*Have you already forgotten?*
행복한 소식을 듣고 **바로** 달려왔어요.	*On hearing the happy news, I immediately came running.*
먼저 먹어 봐도 돼요?	*Can I taste it first?*
한 번만 **더** 기회를 주세요.	*Please give me one more chance.*
이 스테이크가 **덜** 익었어요	*The steak is undercooked.*
아마 사실일 거예요.	*It will probably turn out to be true.*
필요한 게 있으면 **즉시** 저를 불러 주세요.	*If you need anything, please don't hesitate to call me [immediately].*
이따금 그 사람이 나를 찾아왔다.	*Sometimes he visited me.*

Some adverbs (such 별로, 전혀, 통, 도저히) are special in that they always have to occur with a negative verb phrase, as discussed elsewhere (refer to 4.2.4).

11.2.1.2 Derived adverbs

Derived adverbs are those formed from other word classes, typically from descriptive verbs.

A limited set of descriptive verbs can be transformed into adverbs by adding the suffix –이 (or –히) to the verb base. The subsequent adverbs tend to represent 'frozen' forms that can be found in the dictionary under separate entries.

–이			
많–	*be many*	많이	*many, much, a lot*
높–	*be high*	높이	*highly*
같–	*be together, be the same*	같이	*alike, altogether*
굳–	*become hard, firm*	굳이	*firmly, obstinately*
바쁘–	*be busy*	바삐	*busily*
빠르–	*be fast*	빨리	*fast*
곱–	*be beautiful*	고이	*beautifully, well*
깨끗하–	*be clean*	깨끗이	*cleanly*

–히			
조용하–	*be quiet*	조용히	*quietly*
부지런하–	*be diligent*	부지런히	*diligently*
쓸쓸하–	*be lonely*	쓸쓸히	*lonely, cheerlessly*
넉넉하–	*be ample, sufficient*	넉넉히	*amply*
무던하–	*be generous*	무던히	*generously*

An even smaller set of adverbs are etymologically derived from verbs (both descriptive and processive) by the derivational suffix –오/우. These adverbs are 'frozen' forms that are listed in dictionaries as separate words. Indeed, for adverbs ending in –오/우, most native speakers are unaware of the original etymology.

넘–	*exceed*	너무	*too much, excessively, so*
잦–	*be frequent*	자주	*often*
돌–	*turns*	도로	*(over) again*
밭–	*to be very close*	바투	*near (by)*

너무 무서워서 말 한 마디도 못 했어요.
I was so scared that I couldn't say a word.

텔레비전은 얼마나 **자주** 보세요?
How often do you watch television?

왔던 길을 **도로** 갔어요.
He/she went back the way he/she had come.

시간이 **바투** 다가왔어요.
The time has come close.

All other descriptive verbs (i.e., those that cannot take the endings –이/–히 or –오/우) can be transformed into adverbial forms by the addition of the one-shape ending –게. Below are some common instances:

늦–	*be late*	늦게	*late*
이렇–	*be like this*	이렇게	*like this, in this way*
그렇–	*be like that*	그렇게	*like that, in that way*
크–	*be big*	크게	*in a big way, out loud*
재미있–	*be interesting fun*	재미있게	*in a fun way, with amusement*
싸–	*be cheap*	싸게	*cheaply*
춥–	*be cold*	춥게	*in a cold way*

늦게 왔어요.
He/she came late.

이렇게 늦으면 어떻게 해요?
If you are late like this, what are we supposed to do?

옷을 **그렇게** 입으면 춥지 않아요?
Aren't you cold if you dress like that?

좀 더 **크게** 말씀해 주세요.
Please speak a little louder.

이 책을 **재미있게** 읽었어요.
I enjoyed reading this book.

그 가게에서 화장품을 **싸게** 팔아요.
They sell cosmetics cheaply at that store.

지난밤에 **춥게** 주무셨지요?
Did you feel cold while sleeping last night?

Note that the form –게 can also attach to processive verbs. In such cases, what is formed is not an adverb but a causative connective meaning 'so that' (refer to 7.6.1). In addition, –게 forms an integral part of the causative construction –게 하– (refer to 4.4.2.2).

Korean also has resources for changing some nouns into adverbs. Firstly, some nouns can be transformed into adverbs by the addition of the instrumental particle (으)로 (refer to 3.2.5.1):

강제	*force*	강제로	*by force*
겉	*outside*	겉으로	*outwardly, on the outside*
날	*day*	날로	*day by day*
속	*inside*	속으로	*inwardly, on the inside*
앞	*front*	앞으로	*going forward, from now on*
진실	*honesty, truth*	진실로	*honestly, truthfully*
진심	*sincerity*	진심으로	*sincerely*

나이 많은 남자와 **강제로** 결혼했어요.
She was forced to marry an older man.

겉으로는 자신 있어 보였어요.
He/she looked confident on the outside.

교통난이 **날로** 심해지는 것 같아요.
The traffic problems seem to get worse day by day.

속으로는 초조했어요.
He/she was anxious on the inside.

앞으로 열심히 할 것을 맹세합니다.
I swear to do my best from now on.

미나 씨는 **진실로** 아름다운 여자에요.
Mina is truly a beautiful woman.

성원에 **진심으로** 감사 드립니다.
We are really thankful for your support.

In addition, some nouns can be made into adverbs by the addition of the suffixes –껏 and –상(上). The first of these means 'to the best of . . .' or 'until . . .' and the second means 'from the viewpoint of . . .' or 'for the sake of . . .':

–껏			
능력	*ability*	능력껏	*to the best of one's ability*
마음	*heart*	마음껏	*to one's heart's content*
성의	*sincerity*	성의껏	*with all one's heart, sincerely*
욕심	*desire, greed*	욕심껏	*as much as one desires*
지금	*now*	지금껏	*until now*

–상(上)			
격식	*formality*	격식상	*for formality's sake*
교육	*education*	교육상	*from the perspective of education*
사정	*circumstances*	사정상	*owing to circumstances*
양심	*conscience*	양심상	*for conscience's sake*
역사	*history*	역사상	*in history*
예의	*courtesy*	예의상	*as a matter of courtesy*
이론	*theory*	이론상	*in theory*
절차	*procedure*	절차상	*for the sake of procedure*
체면	*'face'*	체면상	*to save 'face'*
형식	*form*	형식상	*for form's sake*
편의	*convenience*	편의상	*for convenience*

Here are examples of these in sentences:

저도 제 **능력껏** 도와 드릴께요.
I will also help you to the best of my ability.

마음껏 드시고 가세요.
Please eat as much as you want before you go.

좀 더 **성의껏** 모시겠습니다.
We promise to serve you even better.

욕심껏 먹었어요.
I ate as much as I desired.

지금껏 아무런 효과가 없었어요.
It has not been effective up until now.

교육상 어린이들에게 좋지 않아요.
From the view of education, it is not good for children.

사정상 그런 수단이 용납돼요.
Owing to circumstances, such measures may be warranted.

역사상 유래가 없어요.
It is unparalleled in history.

이론상 태양 위에서 걸을 수 있어요.
In theory, you could walk on the sun.

절차상 격식상 부른 거예요.
I've called you here for the sake of procedure and formality.

체면상 거짓말을 했어요.
I lied to save face.

형식상 몇 가지 질문을 해야 합니다.
I have to ask a few questions for form's sake.

편의상 네 그룹으로 나누었어요.
For convenience, I have divided it into four groups.

Finally, some nouns are also used as adverbs without any change in shape.

Time and place nouns:

오늘	*today*	내일	*tomorrow*	어제	*yesterday*
지금	*now*	여기	*here*	저기	*there*

Discourse nouns:

사실	*in fact*	보통	*usually, normally*	대개	*generally*

오늘 중요한 약속이 있어요.
I have an important appointment today.

지금 해도 돼요?
Can I do it now?

사실 무슨 말인지 모르겠어요.
In fact, I don't know what it means.

보통 아침밥을 안 먹어요.
I don't usually eat breakfast.

주말에 **대개** 외식해요.
I usually eat out on weekends.

11.2.1.3 *Sentence adverbs*

Other adverbs that we have looked at in this section tend to modify specific constituents of the sentence. Sentence adverbs, however, modify the meaning of the whole sentence. Adverbs that belong to this set typically occur at the start (or near the start) of the sentence.

Here are some common examples.

아마(도)	*Perhaps*
제발, 부디*	*Please, I implore you; I beg you, for goodness sake*
반드시	*Without fail*
기어이	*By all means*
물론	*Of course*
당연히	*Naturally*

보통	*Normally*
사실은, 실은	*In fact*
확실히	*Certainly*
혹시	*By any chance*
과연	*Really; Indeed*
만일, 만약	*Hypothetically; Suppose (appears in conditional sentences)*
설마	*On no account; Really*
다행히	*Fortunately*
이왕(이면)	*As long as*
역시	*As expected; As ever*
하마터면	*Almost ('if it had gone a bit more')*

*제발 and 부디 do NOT commonly occur in polite requests in the same way as English 'please' (for example, 'Please, may I have some more coffee').

아마 냉장고에 있을 거예요.
It might perhaps be in the refrigerator.

제발 용서해 주세요.
I implore you to forgive me.

내일은 **반드시** 이기겠습니다.
We will win tomorrow without fail.

기어이 성공할 거예요.
I will succeed by all means.

물론 가겠습니다.
Of course I will go.

당연히 마중 나가요.
Naturally I will be there to meet you.

보통 6시에 퇴근해요.
I normally finish work at 6 o'clock.

저 **사실은** 대학생이 아니에요.
In actual fact, I am not a university student.

확실히 효과가 있었어요.
It certainly was effective.

혹시 제 핸드폰을 봤어요?
Have you seen my mobile, by any chance?

과연 사실일까요?
Could that really be true?

만일 시간이 없으면 내일 봅시다.
If you don't have time, let's meet tomorrow.

설마 그걸 믿는 건 아니겠지?
You don't really believe that?

다행히 비가 그쳤네요.
Luckily it has stopped raining.

이왕 쓰시는 김에 주소도 써 주세요.
As long as you're at it, write your address, too.

역시 또 늦었네요.
As expected, late again!

하마터면 넘어질 뻔했어요.
I nearly fell down.

11.2.1.4 *Conjunctive adverbs*

This set of adverbs mark the relationship between the sentence in which they appear and the one that precedes it.

그리고	*and*
그러나	*but*
그런데 (abbreviated to 근데)	*but, and*
그렇지만	*however, though*
그러니까	*so*
그래서	*so, therefore*
그러면 (abbreviated to 그럼)	*then*
그러므로, 고로, 따라서	*therefore*

그럼에도 불구하고	*nevertheless*
즉	*thus, that is, in other words*
아니면	*otherwise*
혹은	*alternately*
오히려	*rather*
더구나	*moreover*
왜냐하면	*'if you ask why' (way of introducing 'because' sentence)*
심지어	*even worse*
더우기	*furthermore*

As can be seen, the formation of most of these conjunctive adverbs is based on adding a clausal connective (refer to Chapter 7) to the verb 그렇– 'do like that, do in that way'.

11.2.2 Semantic classification of adverbs

This section provides some useful lists of some of common Korean adverbs according to their semantics (i.e., what they mean). The classification below is not designed to be absolute or exhaustive.

11.2.2.1 Time adverbs

The following is a list of common time adverbs that appear in Korean.

Past-time adverbs	
어제	*yesterday*
엊그제	*the day before yesterday*
작년	*last year*

Present-time adverbs	
오늘	*today*
요즈음, 바야흐로	*nowadays*
지금	*now*
이제, 인제	*now (contrastive meaning), from now on*
현재	*at present*
금년, 올해	*this year*

Future-time adverbs	
내일	*tomorrow*
(내일) 모레	*day after tomorrow*
내년	*next year*
장차	*in the future*
앞으로	*from now on*
이따가 [from 있– + 다가 (refer to 7.3.11)]	*after a while, shortly*

Completion	
갓, 막	*just*
금방, 방금	*just now*
아까	*a [little] while ago*
아직(도)	*yet, not yet*
이미, 벌써	*already*

Repetition and Continuity	
한번	*once*
한번도	*not even once*

종종, 곧잘, 흔히, 빈번히	*often*
대개	*usually*
가끔	*occasionally*
때때로	*now and then*
자주	*often*
매년	*every year*
매달, 매월	*every month*
매주	*every week*
매일	*every day*
매번	*every time*
자꾸(만), 재차, 또다시, 거듭, 연신	*repetitively*
잠깐, 잠시	*for a short time*
당분간	*for a while, for the time being*
오래, 오래도록	*for a long time*
내내	*throughout*
계속	*continuously*
줄곧	*constantly*
줄기차게	*incessantly*
늘, 항상, 노상, 항시, 언제나	*always*
길이, 영영, 영구히, 영원히, 마냥	*forever*
밤낮	*day and night*
밤새(도록)	*all night long*
하루 종일	*all day long*
차차	*gradually*

Time-order

미리, 전에, 앞서	*in advance, before*
처음(에)	*to begin with*

먼저	*first of all*
비로소	*initially*
다음	*next*
일찍	*early*
늦게	*late*
마지막으로	*last of all*
드디어, 마침내	*at last*

Other	
새로	*newly*
얼른	*at once*
곧	*soon, immediately*
즉시	*instantly, immediately*

Note that some of these words, in addition to being used as adverbs, can also be used as nouns. In other words, they can appear in sentences as subjects and objects

내일이 추울까요?	*Do you suppose tomorrow [subject] will be cold?*
내년을 기다립시다.	*Let's wait for next year [object].*

11.2.2.2 Degree adverbs

Degree adverbs are used to (de-)intensify a quality that is being described. In general, Korean degree adverbs can be used only with descriptive verbs and not with processive verbs. Therefore, although it is possible to use the degree adverb 아주 'very' in sentences such as '유미가 아주 예뻐요' 'Yumi is very pretty', it is not possible to use 아주 with processive verbs such as '공부해요' 'studies' or '먹어요' 'eats' (the same applies to 'very' in English).

가장, 제일, 최고	*most*
너무	*so, too, overly, to excess*

몹시, 아주, 매우, 무척, 심히, 대단히	*very (much)*
지극히	*extremely*
더욱	*all the more*
참	*really, truly*
꽤	*relatively, fairly well*
훨씬	*by far more, overwhelmingly*
더	*more*
덜	*less*
다	*all*
겨우	*hardly*
조금	*a little*
약간	*slightly*
별로*	*not particularly*
전혀, 조금도*	*totally not*
거의*	*almost*
그리*	*not so much*

*These adverbs always have to appear with a negative phrase (refer to 4.2.4)

11.2.2.3 Manner adverbs

Manner adverbs function to describe the manner in which an action is performed. In direct contrast to degree adverbs (refer to 11.2.2.2), manner adverbs only tend to occur with processive verbs. Therefore, although it is possible to use the manner adverb 잘 'well' in sentences such as '유미가 밥을 잘 먹어요' 'Yumi eats well', it is not possible to use 잘 with descriptive verbs such as '예뻐요' 'is pretty' or '멍청해요' 'is stupid' (the same applies to 'well' in English). Here are a few of the most common examples:

어떻게	*somehow, one way or another*
잘	*well*
함부로	*recklessly*

각각	*each, respectively*
서로	*mutually, together*
마구, 막	*carelessly, at random*
혼자	*alone*
직접(적)	*directly, personally*
간접(적)	*indirectly*
일부러	*on purpose, intentionally*
가만히	*silently*
가까이	*nearly*
달리	*differently*
바로	*just, directly, straightaway*
빨리	*quickly*
천천히	*slowly*
많이	*a lot*
편(안)히	*comfortably*

Although the manner adverb '잘' is described above as meaning 'well', this adverb can actually take on a variety of meanings depending on the context. In addition to meaning 'well' (as in the first three examples below), it can mean 'easily' (as in the fourth), 'exactly' (fifth example), 'safely/in good shape' (sixth example) and 'often/frequently' or 'enjoy' (seventh and eighth examples). The extension to the meaning of 'enjoy' appears to come from the fact that if you do something well or frequently, you probably also enjoy doing it as well. At times, without a supporting context, it may be unclear whether '잘' is being used to mean 'well' or simply 'often' or 'enjoy'.

한국말 정말 **잘**하시네요.	*You speak Korean very well.*
아버님께서는 **잘** 계세요?	*Is your father well?*
다행히 다 **잘**됐어요.	*Luckily, everything turned out well.*
생각이 **잘** 안 나요.	*The thought doesn't come to mind easily. (= I can't remember).*
잘 모르겠어요.	*I'm afraid I don't know exactly*

보내주신 편지 **잘** 받았어요.	*I received the letter you sent me in good shape/safely?*
한국음식을 **잘** 먹어요.	*I eat Korean food often./I enjoy eating Korean food.*
유미는 학교에 **잘** 다녀요?	*Does Yumi go to school regularly? [Is Yumi doing well at school? Does Yumi like going to school?]*

11.2.2.4 *Onomatopoeic/mimetic adverbs*

Korean has a richly developed system of onomatopoeia (words that imitate sounds; in Korean, 의성어) and mimetics (words that imitate movements; in Korean, 의태어). English, of course, also has many onomatopoeic words such as 'ding-dong' and 'splish-splash'. However, English has very few mimetic words, although you can find some isolated examples such as 'helter-skelter'. In English, different types of movement are usually elaborated by using a different verb (for example, in place of a basic verb such as 'walk', you might choose 'stagger', 'scurry', 'waddle' and so forth).

In Korean, onomatopoeic and mimetic words constitute a subclass of adverb. These adverbs may then be followed by a verb that depicts the general action. In the following examples, the general verb '걸었어요' 'walked', is given four different meanings by the addition of different mimetic words

아기가 **아장아장** 걸었어요.
The baby toddled along.

오리처럼 **뒤뚱뒤뚱** 걸었어요
He/she waddled like a duck.

마루 위를 **살금살금** 걸었어요.
I walked on tiptoe on the floor.

부엌으로 **비틀비틀** 걸었어요.
He/she staggered into the kitchen.

Onomatopoeiac and mimetic words may also combine with 하– to form '하– verbs' (refer to 4.1.2) or with other verbs that take on a similar function, namely 대– and 거리–

떡이 **<u>쫄깃쫄깃하네요</u>**!
The rice cake is chewy!

그만 **<u>종알거리고</u>** 숙제해라!
Stop chattering and do your homework.

<u>깨작깨작 대시네</u>!
You're picking at your food!

One common use of onomatopoeic words is for describing the sounds of animals

Animal	*Korean onomatopoeic word*	*English equivalent*
dog	멍멍	*bow-wow*
cat	야옹	*meow*
mouse	찍찍	*squeak*
bird	짹짹	*cheep*
cow	음매	*moo*
pig	꿀꿀	*oink oink*
rooster	꼬끼오	*cock-a-doodle-do*
lion, tiger, etc.	어흥, 으르렁	*growl*

Onomatopoeic and mimetic words can be used for describing a whole range of other sounds and movements. The following is a list of some of the most common onomatopoeic/mimetic words (refer to Choo & Kwak 2008 150–166 for a more complete list). As can be seen, although some of these correspond to English onomatopoeic words, often there is no direct equivalent in English.

바삭바삭 *crunchy*

깜빡(깜빡) *flashing, flickering, with a flash, suddenly*

반짝반짝 *glittering*

폭신폭신 *soft and light*

따르릉 *ring [sound of telephone bell]*

딩동 *ding-dong*

빵빵 *toot, toot*

드르렁(드르렁) *snore*

쿨쿨 *[sleep] deeply*

꿀떡 *gulp*

속닥(속닥) *with a whisper*

중얼(중얼) *with a mumble*

엉엉 *[cry] bitterly*

흑흑 *boo-hoo*

꼬르륵 *with a rumble*

쌩쌩 *[wind blows] hard*

벌벌 *tremblingly*

빙빙 *round and round*

졸졸 *with a murmuring [sound of a stream]*

두근두근 *pit-a-pat (beating of the heart)*

주룩주룩 *streaming down [with rain]*

줄줄 *streaming (sweat, tears, blood, runny nose)*

울퉁불퉁 *bumpily*

펑펑 *[snow, cry] heavily*

끄덕[끄덕] *with a nod*

부슬부슬 *drizzle [with rain]*

뻥긋 *tightly shut [mouth]*

살금살금 *tiptoeing*

우물쭈물 *with hesitation, shilly-shally*

간질간질 *tickling, tingling*

알쏭달쏭 *jumbled, motley*

어질어질 *giddily*

말랑말랑 *soft, tender*

똑똑 *knock, knock*

철컥 *with a click*

Here are some examples of these in sentences:

쿠키가 **바삭바삭**하고 맛있어요.
The cookie is crunchy and delicious.

불빛이 **깜빡** 거리고 있어요.
The light is flashing.

반짝반짝 작은 별 . . .
'Twinkle, twinkle little star . . .'

침대가 **푹신푹신**하네요!
The bed is nice and soft!

시계가 **따르릉** 하고 9시를 알렸어요.
The clock rang as it struck 9 o'clock.

형이 **드르렁드르렁** 코를 골았어요.
Older brother was snoring loudly.

세상 모르고 **쿨쿨** 자고 있어요.
He/she is sleeping deeply, oblivious of everything.

한입에 **꿀떡** 삼켰어요.
He/she swallowed it down in one gulp.

혼잣말로 **중얼**거렸어요.
He/she mumbled to him/herself.

목이 아프도록 **엉엉** 울었어요.
I cried bitterly until my throat hurt.

배에서 **꼬르륵** 소리가 나요.
A rumbling sound is coming from his/her stomach.

나무 사이로 바람이 **쌩쌩** 불었어요.
The wind howled through the trees.

추워서 **벌벌** 떨었어요.
I shivered with cold.

머리가 **빙빙** 도네요!
My head is spinning round and round.

시냇물이 **졸졸** 흐르고 있어요.
The brook is murmuring along.

그 여자를 볼 때마다 가슴이 **두근**거려요.
My heart leaps every time I see that woman.

비가 **주룩주룩** 내리고 있어요
It's streaming down with rain.

땀이 **줄줄** 흘러요.	*I am streaming with sweat.*
길이 너무 **울퉁불퉁**했어요.	*The road was too bumpy.*
눈이 **펑펑** 내렸어요.	*It snowed hard.*
고개를 **끄덕끄덕** 했어요.	*He/she nodded his/her head.*
비가 **부슬부슬** 내리고 있어요.	*It's drizzling with rain.*
입도 **뻥긋** 못 했어요.	*I didn't say a word.*
살금살금 계단을 올라갔어요.	*I tiptoed up the stairs.*
뭐라고 말해야 할지 몰라서 **우물쭈물**하고 있었어요.	*I was shilly-shallying not knowing what to say.*

귀가 **간질간질**하네요!	*My ears are tingling! (usually taken as a sign that someone must be talking about you)*
뭐가 뭔지 **알쏭달쏭**하네요.	*I can't work out what's what.*
머리가 **어질어질**하네요.	*My head is spinning.*
반죽이 **말랑말랑**하네요.	*The dough is so soft.*

누군가가 창문을 **똑똑** 두드리는 소리가 들렸어요.
I heard someone knocking on the window.

문이 **철컥** 닫히는 소리가 들렸어요.
I heard the door shut with a click.

As you may have noticed from the examples given above, Korean onomatopoeia and mimetics are structurally characterized by reduplication. In other words, the same element repeats itself, typically two times. Quite frequently, there may be two or three different versions of the same onomatopoeic word that differ either only in the vowel sound (as in the first set below) or only in alternation between basic, aspirated and tensed consonants (as in the second set). The alternation in vowel or consonant sound results in subtle shifts of meaning

Set 1: Vowel alternation

졸졸/줄줄/질질	*tickling/streaming/dribbling*
간들간들/건들건들	*swaying gently/wobbling*
방글방글/벙글벙글	*[smiling] sweetly/radiantly*
산들산들/선들선들	*[blowing] gently/softly*
찰찰/철철	*brimmingly/overflowingly*
살금살금/슬금슬금	*stealthily and catlike/quietly, furtively*
뱅글뱅글/빙글빙글	*turning round and round/spinning*
생글생글/싱글싱글	*[smiling] affably/gently*
꼬불꼬불/꾸불꾸불	*winding in tight curves/winding back and forth*
쪼글쪼글/쭈글쭈글	*finely wrinkled/crumpled*

소근소근/수근수근	*whispering in a low voice/murmuring*
모락모락/무럭무럭	*puffing/billowing*
보슬보슬/부슬부슬	*[raining] in a light mist/slowly in small drops*
폭신폭신/푹신푹신	*Soft [like a small cushion] / soft [like a big futon]*
퐁당/풍덩	*with a plop/with a dull splash*

Set 2: Consonant alternation	
뱅뱅/뺑뺑	*round and round in large circles/in violent circles*
생긋생긋/쌩긋쌩긋	*[smiling] sweetly/brightly*
숙덕숙덕/쑥덕쑥덕	*[whispering] secretly/slyly*
종알종알/쫑알쫑알	*babbling/rattling on*
부석부석/푸석푸석	*slightly swollen/grossly swollen*
질금질금/찔끔찔끔	*shufflingly/dragging*
겅중겅중/껑충껑충	*jumping lazily/jumping energetically, in great leaps*

In the case of vowel alternation, it is commonly the case that those containing what are sometimes referred to as 'dark vowels' (namely, 어, 에, 여, 예, 우, 워, 위, 유, 웨) connote largeness, heaviness, slowness, dullness and depth. On the other hand, those containing so-called 'bright vowels' (아, 애, 야, 얘, 오, 외, 요, 와, 왜) give a feeling of smallness, lightness, thinness speed and gentleness. As a general rule, whereas those containing the 'dark vowels' are often negative in character, those containing the 'bright vowels' have more positive connotations. Vowels 으 and 이 are generally classified as neutral vowels in this respect.

In the case of consonant alternation, replacing a plain consonant with one that is aspirated or reinforced generally expresses emphasis or greater degree. Using a reinforced consonant sounds strong or intense, while an aspirated consonant connotes violence or harshness.

One other form of alternation that can occur in the creation of onomatopoeic/mimetic words is the addition of different 'extenders' onto an initial 'base'. For example, building on the base '절ㄱ–',

a Korean speaker can form several different mimetic words all with the meaning of 'click':

절걱　절거덕　절겅　절거덩　절그렁

Although the basic meaning is the same, the nuances are subtly different. The use of 'ㄱ' in final position in the first two words gives the feeling of sharpness or abruptness. In contrast, the use of 'ㅇ' in the third, fourth and fifth words connotes a metallic or reverberating quality. The longer two-syllable endings (second, fourth and fifth words) also suggest a more prolonged action (refer to Garrigues 1995).

11.3 Prefixes and suffixes

Prefixes are elements that attach to the front of words to alter their meaning. Suffixes have the same function, but attach at the end of words instead.

11.3.1 *Prefixes*

Korean has a number of prefixes that can attach to the front of nouns and/or verbs and thus create new meanings. In the following tables, the first shows prefixes of Sino-Korean origin and the second shows prefixes of pure Korean origin (refer to Lee & Ramsey 2000; Choo & O'Grady 1996; Choo & Kwak 2010; Ryzhkov 2009). Note that some of the Sino-Korean elements in the first list may appear in other compounds where they cannot be considered to be 'prefixes' as such.

Prefixes of Sino-Korean origin

Prefix	*Examples*	
	Original word	*Derived word*
고(高) *high*	혈압 *blood pressure*	고혈압 *high blood pressure*
	소득 *high income*	고소득 *high income*
남(男)– *male*	동생 *younger sibling*	남동생 *younger brother*

	학생 *student*	남학생 *male student*
다(多)– *multi-*	목적 *purpose*	다목적 *multipurpose*
	문화 *culture*	다목적 *multicultural*
대(大)– *big*	도시 *city*	대도시 *big city*
	가족 *family*	대가족 *big family*
동(同)– *same*	시대 *era*	동시대 *same era*
	업자 *tradesman*	동업자 *business partner*
맹(猛)– *fierce*	공격 *attack*	맹공격 *fierce attack*
	연습 *practice*	맹연습 *rigorous practice*
무(無)– *without*	조건 *condition*	무조건 *unconditional*
	차별 *discrimination*	무차별 *indiscriminate*
반(反)– *anti-*	사회적 *social*	반사회적 *antisocial*
	작용 *reaction*	반작용 *counteraction*
반(半)– *half*	세기*century*	반세기 *half a century*
	자동 *automatic*	반자동 *semi-automatic*
본(本)– *main*	마음 *heart; intention*	본마음 *true intention*
	보기 *example*	본보기 *main example, model*
부(副)– *subsidiary*	사장 *president (of company)*	부사장 *vice president (of company)*
	작용 *effect*	부작용 *side effect*
부/불(不)– *not*	자연 *natural*	부자연 *unnatural*
	균형 *balance*	불균형 *imbalance*
비(非)– *not*	현실 *realistic*	비현실 *unrealistic*
	공식 *formal*	비공식 *informal*
생(生)– *live, living*	방송 *broadcast*	생방송 *live broadcast*
	지옥 *hell*	생지옥 *living hell*
시(媤)– *in-laws (husband's side)*	부모 *parents*	시부모 *husband's parents*
	집 *home*	시집 *husband's family's home*
신(新)– *new*	기록 *record*	신기록 *new record*
	도시 *town, city*	신도시 *new town*

악(惡)– *bad*	영향 *influence*	악영향 *bad influence*
	순환 *cycle*	악순환 *vicious cycle*
양(兩)– *both*	쪽 *side*	양쪽 *both sides*
	팔 *arm*	양팔 *both arms*
여(女)– *female*	직원 *employee*	여직원 *female employee*
	학생 *student*	여학생 *female student*
역(逆)– *counter*	방향 *direction*	역방향 *opposite direction*
	효과*affect*	역효과 *adverse affect*
외(外)– *outside; mother's side*	할머니*grandmother*	외할머니 *maternal grandmother*
	할아버지 *grandfather*	외할아버지 *maternal grandfather*
재(再)– *again*	개발 *development*	재개발 *redevelopment*
	평가 *assessment*	재평가 *reassessment*
저(低)– *low*	혈압 *blood pressure*	저혈압 *low blood pressure*
	소득 *income*	저소득 *low income*
전(前)– *former*	남편 *husband*	전남편 *former husband*
	대통령 *president*	전대통령 *former president*
정(正)– *regular, full*	교수 *professor*	정교수 *full professor*
	회원 *member*	정회원 *regular member*
총(總)– *overall, total*	공격 *attack*	총공격 *full-scale attack*
	선거 *election*	총선거 *general election*
최(最)– *most*	첨단 *cutting edge*	최첨단 *spearhead*
	우선 *priority*	최우선 *highest priority*
현(現)– *present*	대통령 *president*	현대통령 *current president*
	상태 *circumstances*	현상태 *present circumstances*

Prefixes of pure Korean origin

Prefix	*Examples*	
	Original word	*Derived word*
거머– *greedily*	잡–/쥐*grab*	거머잡–/쥐 *grab greedily*

군– *excess*	소리 *sound, words*	군소리 *unnecessary remark*
덧– *additional*	신 *shoes*	덧신 *overshoes*
	이 *tooth*	덧니 *snaggletooth*
되– *again, in reverse*	묻*ask*	되묻 *ask again, ask back*
	씹 *chew*	되씹 *chew over and over*
들이– *hard, profusely*	밀*push*	들이밀 *push hard*
	켜*drink off*	들이켜 *guzzle down*
맏– *eldest*	아들 *son*	맏아들 *eldest son*
	딸 *daughter*	맏딸 *eldest daughter*
맨– *bare*	손 *hand*	맨손 *empty handed*
	발 *foot*	맨발 *barefoot*
빈– *empty*	방 *room*	빈방 *empty room*
	말 *words, language*	빈말 *empty words*
빗– *slanted*	대 *touch*	빗대 *insinuate, allude*
	나가 *go out*	빗나가 *go wide*
수– *male*	개 *dog*	수캐 *dog*
	닭 *chicken*	수탉 *rooster*
암– *female*	개 *dog*	암캐 *bitch (female dog)*
	닭 *chicken*	암탉 *(female) chicken*
엿– *stealthily*	보 *see*	엿보 *spy on*
	듣 *listen*	엿듣 *eavesdrop*
오른– *right*	손 *hand*	오른손 *right hand*
	쪽 *side*	오른쪽 *right side; the right*
외– *only*	아들 *son*	외아들 *only son*
	딸 *daughter*	외딸 *only daughter*
왼– *left*	손 *hand*	왼손 *left hand*
	쪽 *side*	왼쪽 *left side; the left*
짓– *roughly*	누르 *press*	짓누르 *squash*
	밟 *stand on*	짓밟 *trample*
처– *excessively, roughly*	먹 *eat*	처먹 *devour, eat greedily*

	넣 *put, insert*	처넣 *shove in, stuff*
치– *upward*	솟 *soar*	치솟 *rise up suddenly*
	뜨 *open (eyes)*	치뜨 *lift up one's eyes*
풋– *unripe*	고추 *chili*	풋고추 *unripe chili*
	사랑 *love*	풋사랑 *puppy love*
헛– *fruitless*	수고 *effort*	헛수고 *wasted effort*
	소리 *sounds, words*	헛소리 *empty words*
휘– *round-and-round*	날리 *flap in the wind*	휘날리 *flap in the wind*
	젓 *stir*	휘젓 *stir, swing round-and-round*

11.3.2 Suffixes

Unlike prefixes, which simply change the meaning of the word, suffixes in some cases actually change the grammatical category of the words to which they attach. In turn, we look at suffixes that result in the derivation (i.e., creation; transformation) of nouns, adverbs, verbs and adnominal forms.

11.3.2.1 Noun-deriving suffixes

Noun-deriving suffixes may attach either to a verb base or simply to another noun.

We look first at suffixes that attach to a verb base and which result in the derivation of a noun. These processes are discussed in more detail elsewhere (refer to 2.2).

Suffix	*Example*	
	Original verb	*Derived noun*
–이	넓– *be wide*	넓이 *width*
	깊– *be deep*	깊이 *depth*
	놀– *play*	놀이 *game*
–음	웃– *laugh*	웃음 *laughter*

Suffix	Example	
	Original verb	*Derived noun*
	울– *cry*	울음 *crying*
	기쁘– *be happy*	기쁨 *happiness*
–개/– 게	덮– *to cover*	덮개 *a cover*
	지우– *rub out*	지우개 *eraser*
	집– *to pick*	집게 *tweezers*

In the next set, a suffix is added to a noun (or, in some isolated cases, a verb stem or modifier form). This produces a new noun with a different usage. The first list contains suffixes of pure-Korean origin

Suffixes of pure Korean origin

Suffix	Example	
	Original noun	*Derived noun*
–가락 *long slender object*	손 *hand*	손가락 *finger*
	발 *foot*	발가락 *toe*
–감 *material*	옷 *clothes*	옷감 *material (for clothes)*
	신랑 *groom*	신랑감 *good husband material*
–거리 *material, object*	일 *work*	일거리 *piece of work*
	자랑 *pride*	자랑거리 *source of pride*
–꾸러기 *person*	잠 *sleep*	잠꾸러기 *sleepyhead*
	욕심 *greed*	욕심꾸러기 *greedy person*
–꾼 *person*	장사 *trade*	장사꾼 *tradesman*
	술 *alcohol*	술꾼 *(heavy) drinker*
–둥이 *person*	바람 *fickleness*	바람둥이 *womaniser*
	귀염 *affection*	귀염둥이 *child loved by all*
–뱅이 *person*	게으름 *laziness*	게으름뱅이 *lazybones*
	가난 *poverty*	가난뱅이 *poor person*

–보 *person*	잠 *sleep*	잠보 *sleepyhead*
	울– *cry*	울보 *cry baby*
	털 *hair*	털보 *hairy person*
–어치 *worth*	값 *price*	값어치 *monetary value*
	5000 원 *5000 won*	5000 원어치 *5000 won worth*
–이 *person*	멍청하– *be foolish*	멍청이 *fool*
	젊– *be young*	젊은이 *youngster*
–쟁이 *person*	거짓말 *lie*	거짓말쟁이 *liar*
	겁 *fear*	겁쟁이 *coward*
–질 *action*	가위 *scissors*	가위질 *using scissors, cutting*
	도둑 *thief*	도둑질 *thieving*
–짜리 *worth*	50,000 원 *50,000 won*	50,000 원짜리 지폐 *50,000 won banknote*
	10,000 원 *10,000 won*	10,000 원짜리 비빔밥 *pibimbap costing 10,000 won*
–째 *entirely, as it is*	병 *bottle*	병째 *from the bottle*
	껍질 *peel*	껍질째 *peel and all*
–투성이 *covered with*	땀 *sweat*	땀투성이 *covered with sweat*
	거짓말 *a lie*	거짓말투성이 *full of lies*

The next list contains suffixes of Sino-Korean origin. Note that these Sino-Korean elements may appear in other words where they cannot be considered suffixes as such.

Suffixes of Sino-Korean origin

Suffix	*Example*	
	Original noun	*Derived noun*
–가(家) *specialist*	전문 *speciality, expertise*	전문가 *an expert*
	정치 *politics*	정치가 *a politician*
–가(街) *street*	주택 *housing*	주택가 *residential area*
	식당 *restaurant*	식당가 *row of restaurants*

–감(感) *feeling*	거리 *distance*	거리감 *feeling of distance*
	배신 *betrayal*	배신감 *feeling of betrayal*
–객(客) *guest*	여행 *travelling*	여행객 *tourist*
	방문 *visit*	방문객 *visitor*
–경(頃) *around*	아침 7시 *7 in the morning*	아침 7 시경 *about 7 in the morning*
	수요일 *Wednesday*	수요일경 *about Wednesday*
–계(界) *world, circles*	연예 *entertainment, celebrity*	연예계 *the entertainment world*
	영화 *films*	영화계 *the film world*
–과(科) *department*	언어학 *linguistics*	언어학과 *the linguistics department*
	정신 *psychiatry*	정신과 *the department of psychiatry*
–관(官) *an official*	경찰 *the police*	경찰관 *police officer*
	시험*exam*	시험관 *examiner*
–권(券) *ticket, coupon*	상품*gift*	상품권 *gift voucher*
	탑승 *boarding*	탑승권 *boarding pass*
–권(權) *rights, authority*	주도 *leading*	주도권 *leadership*
	소유 *owner*	소유권 *ownership*
–금(金) *money*	기부 *donating*	기부금 *donation*
	계약 *contract*	계약금 *down-payment*
–기(機) *machine*	계산 *calculation*	계산기 *calculator*
	비행 *aviation*	비행기 *airplane*
–기(器) *device*	정수 *pure water*	정수기 *water purifier*
	소화 *extinguishing fire*	소화기 *fire extinguisher*
–력(力) *power*	정신 *psychiatry*	정신력 *mental strength*
	어휘 *vocabulary*	어휘력 *one's vocabulary*
–료(料) *fee*	통화 *talking on the phone*	통화료 *call charge*
	수업 *class*	수업료 *class fee*
–방(房) *room*	노래 *song*	노래방 *karaoke parlour*
	PC(피씨) *personal computer*	PC방 *internet cafe*

–범(犯) *criminal*	살인 *murder*	살인범 *murderer*
	정치 *politics*	정치범 *political offender*
–별(別) *division*	국가 *nation*	국가별 *division based on country*
	색깔 *colour*	색깔별 *division according to colour*
–복(服) *clothes*	임신 *pregnancy*	임신복 *maternity dress*
	수영 *swimming*	수영복 *swimming costume*
–부(部) *section;*	외무 *foreign affairs*	외무부 *Ministry of Foreign Affairs*
ministry	교육 *education*	교육부 *Ministry of Education*
– 비(費) *cost*	생활 *cost of living*	생활비 *cost of living*
	양육 *child-rearing costs*	양육비 *child-rearing costs*
–사(社) *company*	출판 *publishing*	출판사 *publishers*
	신문 *newspaper*	신문사 *newspaper company*
–사(師) *professional*	미용 *beauty*	미용사 *beautician*
	이발 *barbering*	이발사 *barber*
–사(士) *scholar,*	비행 *aviation*	비행사 *aviator*
qualified person	회계 *accounting*	회계사 *accountant*
–생(生) *student; birth*	유학 *studying abroad*	유학생 *overseas student*
	졸업 *graduation*	졸업생 *graduate student*
–서(書) *document*	계약 *contract*	계약서 *contract (document)*
	보고 *reporting*	보고서 *a report*
–석(席) *seat*	운전 *driving*	운전석 *driver's seat*
	방청 *attendance*	방청석 *seats for audience*
–성(性) *nature, quality*	신빙 *credence*	신빙성 *credibility*
	일관 *consistence*	일관성 *consistency*
–세(稅) *tax*	재산 *property*	재산세 *property tax*
	부가 *additional*	부가세 *sales tax*
–세(貰) *rent*	집 *house*	집세 *house rent*
	방 *room*	방세 *room rent*
–소(所) *place*	환전 *foreign exchange*	환전소 *foreign exchange bureau*
	보건 *public health*	보건소 *public health centre*

–수(手) *skilled worker*	운전 *driving*	운전수 *driver*
	소방 *fire-fighting*	소방수 *fire-fighter*
–식(式) *style; ceremony*	한국 *Korea*	한국식 *Korean-style*
	결혼 *marriage*	결혼식 *wedding*
–실(室) *room*	실험 *experiment*	실험실 *laboratory*
	수술 *operation*	수술실 *operating theatre*
–아(兒) *child*	행운 *luck*	행운아 *lucky person*
	문제 *problem*	문제아 *problem child*
–어(語) *language*	한국 *Korea*	한국어 *Korean*
	모국 *motherland*	모국어 *mother tongue*
–원(員) *employee; member*	은행 *bank*	은행원 *bank worker*
	판매 *sales*	판매원 *salesperson*
–원(院) *institution*	고아 *orphan*	고아원 *orphanage*
	양로 *taking care of the elderly*	양로원 *care home*
–용(用) *use*	신사 *gentleman*	신사용 *for [the use of] gentlemen*
	여행 *travel*	여행용 *for [use while] travelling*
–인(人) *person*	현대 *modernity*	현대인 *modern person*
	직장 *job, office, company*	직장인 *company worker*
–자(者) *person*	기술 *skill*	기술자 *technician*
	과학 *science*	과학자 *scientist*
–장(場) *place*	축구 *football*	축구장 *football ground*
	경기 *sports game*	경기장 *stadium*
–지(地) *land*	유적 *remains, ruins*	유적지 *historical site*
	거주 *residence*	거주지 *place of residence*
–치(痴) *fool*	음 *tone*	음치 *person who is tone-deaf*
	길 *street*	길치 *person with no sense of direction*
–초(初) *beginning*	학기 *semester*	학기초 *early in the semester*
	년 *year*	연초 *early in the year*
–탕(湯) *hot water, soup*	대중 *public*	대중탕 *public bathhouse*
	갈비 *ribs*	갈비탕 *beef-rib soup*

–판(版) *edition*	번역 *translation*	번역판 *translated edition*
	한국 *Korea*	한국판 *Korean edition*
–편(便) *side*	우리 *our*	우리편 *our side*
	상대 *counterpart*	상대편 *other side*
–품(品) *goods*	수입 *importing*	수입품 *imported goods*
	중고 *second-hand*	중고품 *second-hand goods*
–학(學) *studies*	언어 *language*	언어학 *linguistics*
	한국 *Korea*	한국학 *Korean studies*
–형(型) *type, model*	혈액 *blood*	혈액형 *blood type*
	2000 년 *the year 2000*	2000 년형 *the 2000 model*
–형(形) *shape, form*	계란 *egg*	계란형 *egg-shaped*
	타원 *oval*	타원형 *oval-shaped*
–화(畫) *picture*	수채 *water colours*	수채화 *a water colour painting*
	풍경 *landscape*	풍경화 *a landscape painting*
–화(化) *–ization*	세계 *world*	세계화 *globalization*
	현대 *modernity*	현대화 *modernization*
–회(會) *meeting*	음악 *music*	음악회 *concert*
	동창 *alumni*	동창회 *alumni association*

11.3.2.2 *Adverb-deriving suffixes*

Adverbs can be derived from verbs by adding the suffixes –이/–히, –오/우 and –게. These processes were described at greater length previously in this chapter (refer to 11.2.1.2). Adverbs can also be derived from some nouns by the addition of the suffixes –껏 and –상 (refer to 11.2.1.2).

11.3.2.3 *Verb-deriving suffixes*

A number of derivation processes take place to create new sets of verbs. As we saw in Chapter 4 (refer to 4.4.1.1), passive verbs can be formed with the addition of –이–/–기–/–히–/–리–. Also as discussed in detail in chapter 4 (refer to 4.4.2.1), causative verbs can be derived by adding the suffixes –이–, –기–, –히–, –리– and –우–, –구–, –추–. A further phenomenon previously discussed in chapter 4 (refer to 4.4.3) is that processive verbs can be formed from descriptive verbs by the addition of –지– or –하–

We now turn our attention to processes by which descriptive verbs are formed by adding suffixes to nouns. Six different suffixes can perform this function –겹–, –답–, –맞–, –스럽–, –롭– and –지–.

Suffix	*Example*	
	Original noun	*Derived descriptive verb*
–겹–	눈물 *tears*	눈물겹– *be touching; bring tears to your eyes*
	힘 *strength*	힘겹– *be strenuous*
	흥 *fun*	흥겹– *be full of fun*
–답–	남자 *man*	남자답– *be manly*
	사람 *person*	사람답– *be humane*
	신사 *gentleman*	신사답– *be gentlemanly*
	어른 *adult*	어른답– *be adult-like*
	학자 *scholar*	학자답– *be scholarly*
–맞–	익살 *humour*	익살맞– *be humorous*
	방정 *rashness*	방정맞– *be rash*
–스럽–	다정 *affection*	다정스럽– *be warm-hearted*
	만족 *satisfaction*	만족스럽– *be satisfactory*
	변덕 *caprice*	변덕스럽– *be capricious*
	부담 *burden*	부담스럽– *be burdensome*
	사랑 *love*	사랑스럽– *be loveable*
	신비 *mystery*	신비스럽– *be mysterious*
	영광 *glory*	영광스럽– *be glorious*
	익살 *humour*	익살스럽– *be humorous*
	의심 *doubt*	의심스럽– *be dubious, suspicious*
	자랑 *boasting*	자랑스럽– *be proud, feels proud of*
	자연 *nature*	자연스럽– *be natural*
	정성 *devotion*	정성스럽– *be devoted*

	조심 *care*	조심스럽– *be careful*
	촌 *the countryside*	촌스럽– *countrified, old-fashioned, untrendy*
–롭–	슬기 *wisdom, sense*	슬기롭– *be wise, sensible*
	신비 *mystery*	신비롭– *be mysterious*
	자유 *freedom*	자유롭– *be free*
	지혜 *wisdom, sagacity*	지혜롭– *be wise, sagacious*
	평화 *peace*	평화롭– *be peaceful*
	향기 *fragrance*	향기롭– *be fragrant*
–지–	값 *price*	값지– *be pricey*
	기름 *oil*	기름지– *be oily, fertile*
	언덕 *hill*	언덕지– *be hilly*

Some descriptive verbs may be formed either by adding –스럽– or simply by using 하–. In the following examples, note that the form with 하– may have a different meaning to the form with –스럽–.

Original noun	*Form with* **하**–	*Form with* –**스럽** –
만족 *satisfaction*	만족하– *satisfied*	만족스럽– *satisfactory*
부담 *burden*	부담하– *burden, shoulder, bear*	부담스럽– *burdensome*
사랑 *love*	사랑하– *love*	사랑스럽– *loveable*
의심 *doubt*	의심하– *doubt*	의심스럽– *dubious*
자랑 *boasting*	자랑하– *boast*	자랑스럽– *proud*
조심 *care*	조심하– *act carefully*	조심스럽– *careful*
창피 *embarrassing*	창피하– *embarrassed*	창피스럽– *embarrassing*

11.3.2.4 *Adnominal suffix –적*

The Sino-Korean suffix –적(的) can be added to nouns to produce adnominal forms

객관 *objectivity*	객관적– *be objective*
공식 *formality*	공식적– *be official, formal*

극단 *extremity*	극단적– *be extreme*
기계 *machine*	기계적– *be mechanical*
개인 *an individual*	개인적– *be personal, individual*
상업 *commerce*	상업적– *be commercial*
세계 *the world*	세계적– *be international*
소극 *passivity, negativity*	소극적– *be passive, negative*
심리 *psychology*	심리적– *be psychological*
역사 *history*	역사적– *be historical*
엽기 *bizarreness*	엽기적– *be bizarre*
일방 *one side*	일방적– *be one-sided*
직선 *a straight line*	직선적– *be straightforward*
주관 *subjectivity*	주관적– *be subjective*
추상 *abstractness*	추상적– *be abstract*
충동 *impulsiveness*	충동적– *be impulsive*
현실 *reality*	현실적– *be realistic*
형식 *form*	형식적– *be for form's sake*

The forms ending in –적– are then completed by the copula to make a descriptive verb or modifier form

유미는 정말 **엽기적이에요**.	*Yumi is really bizarre.*
역사적인 사건이라고 할 수 있어요.	*You could say it is a historical event.*

–적– may also be further derived to form an adverb. In such cases, the copula is not required –으로 can attach directly to –적–:

객관적으로 생각해 보세요.	*Please think objectively.*
형식적으로 검사를 했어요.	*They carried out an inspection for form's sake.*
대통령이 **공식적으로** 사과했어요.	*The president made a formal apology.*

Glossary of linguistic terms

ACTIVE: the opposite of PASSIVE.

ADJECTIVE: a class of word that describes (or modifies, limits, quantifies or specifies). Simple examples in English would include 'tall', 'pretty' and 'arrogant'.

ADNOMINAL (FORM): a word form that MODIFIES a noun or noun phrase.

ADNOUN: bound forms that cannot be used independently and that MODIFY a following noun.

ADVERB: commonly thought of as forms that modify verbs (or verb phrases). However, certain adverbs may in fact modify any constituent of the sentence (except for nouns) or even entire sentences.

ADVERBATIVE (FORM): a form used for creating ADVERBS.

AGENT: a word that identifies the entity that does an action. For example, in the sentence 'John ate the apple', 'John' is the agent.

ARTICLE: a grammatical element that is used to indicate the degree of definiteness. In English, there are two articles the DEFINITE ARTICLE 'the' and the INDEFINITE ARTICLE 'a/an'. Korean does not have articles.

ASPIRATED: a consonant can be described as aspirated when it is pronounced accompanied with a strong puff of air.

AUXILIARY (VERB): additional verbs or support verbs that are used supplementary to the main verb and which 'help' or 'support' it by supplying extra information regarding the way that the speaker views the event being talked about.

(VERB) BASE: the underlying basic part of a verb to which endings can be added.

BOUND NOUN: also known as 'DEPENDENT NOUNS', these are noun forms that cannot occur on their own and that always require an accompanying element.

CASE: the grammatical role of a noun in a phrase, clause, or sentence, such as SUBJECT, OBJECT, INDIRECT OBJECT, etc.

CASE PARTICLES: forms that are used in Korean to express the grammatical role of the noun or noun phrase to which they are attached.

CAUSATIVE: constructions that depict an agent causing, forcing, or simply allowing a patient to perform an action (for example 'he made me eat the apple', 'he let me eat the apple').

CLAUSAL CONNECTIVE: a device used to link two (or more) clauses. In Korean, this is achieved by using verb endings.

CLAUSE: a pair or group of words that consist of, at the bare minimum, a subject and a verb (although, in Korean, the subject may be dropped rather than explicitly included).

COMITATIVE CASE, COMITATIVE PARTICLE: Comitative particles are grammatical markers that are used to attach two nouns together. They work in a similar way to words such as 'and' and 'with'.

COMPLEMENT: a word or phrase that adds to the meaning of a sentence and makes it complete. Without it, the sentence may not be properly formed.

CONSTITUENT: a component part (or grammatical unit) in a sentence. It may be a single word or otherwise a group of words that together serve the same grammatical function.

COPULA: a verb (or verb-like) form with little independent meaning that is used to link the subject of the sentence to another noun phrase (or, in other languages such as English, to an adjective). Korean copula sentences normally work to equate a subject 'A' to another noun-phrase 'B' to give constructions that translate as "A' is 'B".

COUNTER: a word that is used to specify the nature of what is being counted, including English words such as 'loaves' in 'two loaves of bread' and 'cups' in 'three cups of coffee'.

DEFINITE ARTICLE: a grammatical element that indicates definiteness, such as 'the' in English, 'le/la/l'/les' in French or 'der/die/das' in German.

DEPENDENT NOUN: see BOUND NOUN DERIVE, DERIVATIONcreation of new words by adding a PREFIX or SUFFIX.

DESCRIPTIVE VERB: term used in Korean linguistics to refer to verbs that describe (or modify, limit, quantify or specify). The function of Korean descriptive verbs basically corresponds to English ADJECTIVES. However, instead of having to occur with a VERB corresponding to English 'be', they are freestanding in their own right, just like other verbs.

DITRANSITIVE: a verb that take two OBJECTS (i.e., a direct and an indirect object) is described as 'ditransitive'. An example is 'give' in the sentence 'I gave ***John an apple***'.

EQUATIONAL VERB: another term that we use for the Korean COPULA.

FIRST PERSON: 'I' or 'we'.

GENDER: a property of some languages (such as French and German) where every noun is assigned a gender, often with no direct relation to its meaning. Korean does not have gender.

GENITIVE (CASE): also known as the POSSESSIVE (CASE), the genitive is a grammatical element that marks possession (such as the use of 's in English, such as Mike's sandwich).

HEARER HONORIFICS: grammatical or vocabulary items that 'honour' (i.e., show respect) towards the person hearing the sentence, also known in Korean as SPEECH STYLES.

HONORIFICS: grammatical or vocabulary items that 'honour' (i.e., show respect) either to the hearer (in the case of HEARER HONORIFICS) or to the people you are talking about (in the case of REFERENT HONORIFICS).

HORTATIVE: sentences such as 'Let's . . .' in English that work to urge the hearer to follow a course of action. We also refer to these simply as 'proposals'.

HUMBLE FORM: a form that 'lowers' the speaker and places him/her 'below' the hearer or referent (and therefore, by extension, 'raises' and shows respect to the hearer/referent). IMPERATIVE a sentence form used to command or order someone to do something (such as 'Go away!' or 'Come here!')

INDEFINITE ARTICLE: a grammatical element that indicates a lack of definiteness, such as 'a/an' in English, 'un/une/des' in French or 'ein/eine' in German.

INSTRUMENTAL CASE, INSTRUMENTAL PARTICLE: instrumental particles are used to mark the 'instrument' (tool, means, method, etc.) by which a task is performed.

INTERROGATIVE: a question; a sentence that constitutes a question.

INTRANSITIVE: a verb that does not take an object is described as 'intransitive'. Examples in English include 'cough', 'fall' and 'rise'.

KINSHIP TERMS: terms of address used to call or refer to family members, such as 'mother' and 'father'.

LOCATIVE CASE: the grammatical role that represents the location of where an action is taking place. In this book, we include locative particles under 'particles of location'.

LOGOGRAPHIC (WRITING SYSTEM): a writing system where each symbol represents a word or MORPHEME rather than a sound. The best-known example is Chinese characters.

MIMETICS: words that imitate movements, such as 'helter-skelter' in English.

MODIFIER; MODIFY: a word or phrase that adds to the meaning of a following noun, typically by elaborating, describing, clarifying, identifying or delimiting a NOUN or NOUN PHRASE. In English, modifiers typically include the use of adjectives before the noun (***pink*** sweater, ***pretty*** girl, ***tall*** building) or relative clauses that follow the noun (the sweater ***that I wore yesterday***, the girl ***who bought me lunch***, the building ***where I work***). Unlike a complement, a modifier is an optional element. Even if it is omitted, the sentence will still be grammatical.

MORPHEME: the smallest linguistic unit that has meaning. Some words, such as 'touch' may just have one morpheme – you cannot break them into smaller meaningful chunks. However, a word such as 'untouchable' has three morphemes 'un –', 'touch' and '– able'.

NOMINAL FORM: nominal forms are used when you want to talk about the act of doing things (i.e., what is normally expressed by using verbs) as if they were nouns. Put another way, nominal forms are grammatical means for converting verbs into noun forms.

NOUN: a word that is used to name a person, place, thing quality or action. Simple examples in English include 'man', 'apple' and 'perseverance'.

NOUN PHRASE: a phrase where the most important or 'head' word is a noun and which functions as a noun in the sentence. Examples include 'the red apple' ('head' noun = apple), 'the girl with long hair' ('head' noun = girl) and 'the things that you said' ('head' noun = things).

OBJECT: the person or thing that has the action of the verb performed upon it or is affected by the action of the verb. In the sentence, 'Bill ate CAKE', 'cake' is the object of the sentence and 'Bill' is the SUBJECT. Some sentences, such as 'I gave ***John an apple***' may contain two objects. In the example sentence, 'apple' can be referred to as the 'direct object' and John as the 'indirect object'.

OBLIQUE QUESTIONS: question-like elements that are embedded within a larger sentence. An English example would be 'when he will go' in 'I don't know WHEN HE WILL GO'.

ONE-SHAPE: one-shape particles and one-shape verb endings have one uniform form or 'shape' that is used irrespective of whether they follow a consonant or a noun.

ONOMATOPOEIA: words that imitate sounds, such as 'ding-dong' in English.

ORDINAL (NUMBER): 'first', 'second', 'third', etc.

PARTICLES: elements that attach to the end of nouns (and sometimes other kinds of words) to signal their grammatical function or to add extra meaning.

PASSIVE: constructions in which the 'PATIENT' (or recipient) of the action of the verb is promoted to subject (for example, 'the apple was eaten (by John)'). In ACTIVE sentences (for example, 'John ate the apple'), the 'patient' (or recipient) appears as the sentence object.

PATIENT: the entity which is affected by the action of the verb. For example, in 'John ate the apple', 'the apple' is the patient.

PHONEMIC (WRITING SYSTEM): a writing system where each symbol represents a 'phoneme' (a meaningful unit of sound). The Korean script Hangul can be considered a phonemic writing system.

PHONOLOGY; PHONOLOGICAL: speech sounds or, more specifically, the systematic use of sound to encode meaning in language.

PLAIN: a word or form that is not HONORIFIC or not HUMBLE.

POSSESSIVE (CASE) also known as the GENITIVE (CASE), grammatical elements that mark possession (such as the use of 's in English, such as Mike's sandwich).

POSTPOSITION: elements that are equivalent to English PREPOSITIONS such as 'in', 'for' and 'with' but which appear after the noun rather than before it. In Korean, postpositions form a subset of PARTICLES.

PREFIX: elements that attach at the front of a word STEM to alter its meaning. For example, in 'undo', 'un – ' is a prefix.

PREPOSITION: words such as 'in', 'for' and 'with'. See POSTPOSITION.PROCESSIVE VERB: This is a term used in Korean linguistics to refer to verbs that describe an action or process. This basically corresponds to what are simply referred to just as 'verbs' in English and other languages. Korean requires the addition of 'processive' to distinguish 'processive verbs' from 'DESCRIPTIVE VERBS'.

PRONOUN: words (such as he, she, it, they, we, I) that can be used in place of nouns, typically either to avoid repetition or redundancy or when we are unsure of the exact name or identity of the person or thing in question.

PURE KOREAN: A 'pure Korean' word is one that is of Korean origin and not SINO-KOREAN or a word loaned from another language.

REFLEXIVE PRONOUN: a pronoun that is preceded by the noun or pronoun to which it refers within the same clause ('myself', 'yourself', 'himself', 'herself', etc.), although the original noun/ pronoun may be dropped in Korean.

REFERENT: the person or thing being 'referred' to by a noun.

REFERENT HONORIFICS: grammatical or vocabulary items that 'honour' (i.e., show respect) towards the person you are talking about, in other words, who appears as a REFERENT in the sentence. This person may either be the same person as the hearer or somebody else.

RELATIVE CLAUSE: a clause that modifies a noun or noun phrase, for example 'the sweater *that I wore yesterday*', 'the girl *who bought me lunch*', 'the building *where I work*'.

REPORTED SPEECH: quotations, which are used when repeating or relaying what someone else said (or, at times, when reiterating your own words, reporting things that are commonly said or believed, reporting the thoughts of yourself/others, etc.).

SECOND PERSON: 'you'.

SEMANTICS: the meaning of a word/phrase; the study of linguistic meaning.

SINO KOREAN: A 'Sino-Korean' word is one which is formed from Chinese morphemes and which can be written in Chinese characters (although, in contemporary Korean, this only occurs in very formal writing).

STEM: the minimum form of a word to which other elements such as PREFIXES and SUFFIXES can be attached.

SOV: Subject-Object-Verb – the basic word order of Korean.

SPEECH STYLES: see HEARER HONORIFICS.

SUBJECT: the person or thing who is performing the action of the verb (or allotted the attributes given by the verb). In the sentence, 'Bill ate cake', 'Bill' is the subject of the sentence and 'cake' is the OBJECT.

SUFFIX: elements that attach at the end of a word STEM to alter its meaning. For example, in 'untouchable', ' – able' is a suffix.

SUPPORT VERB: This term has two possible meanings (1) the term can refer to a verb with little independent meaning that combines with a noun to change it into a verb (in Korean, this verb is most commonly 하 –) ; (2) the term can also be used to refer to an AUXILIARY VERB.

TEKNONYMY: the practice of addressing or referring to someone in relation to their children, for example, referring to someone not by their own name but as 'Jessica's mother' or 'Sid's father'.

TENSE: the quality for a language to mark the time at which a state or action expressed by a verb took place.

THIRD PERSON: 'He', 'she', 'it'.

TOPIC; TOPIC PARTICLE: In basic terms, a simple sentence is composed of two elements the topic or 'theme' (i.e., what is being talked about) and the comment or 'rheme' (i.e., what the speaker is saying about the topic). Although this topic-comment dichotomy is generally accepted, the meaning of 'topic' in linguistics is difficult to define and a matter of great controversy. In Korean, the topic particle has the basic function of marking something as the (pre-established) topic of conversation.

TRANSITIVE: A verb that takes an object is described as 'transitive'. An example is 'bite' in 'the cat bit me'.

TWO-SHAPE: Two-shape particles and two-shape verb endings have two different forms or 'shapes', one which follows a consonant and one which follows a noun.

VERB: a word that is used to convey an action (eat, sleep, murder) or a state of being (exist, lie).

VERB PHRASE: a phrase that includes a VERB and sometimes other elements to provide information about the SUBJECT of the sentence. In the sentence 'Mary gave Peter a present', for example, 'Mary' is the subject and 'gave Peter a present' is the verb phrase.

VOCATIVE (CASE): grammatical elements that mark the person being addressed by the sentence. In the English sentence, 'Barry, I love you', 'Barry' is a vocative expression (although English does not have grammatical elements that mark vocative case).

VOICED: A consonant is considered 'voiced' when it is pronounced with voice sounds in the vocal cords. In English, for example, g is 'voiced' and k is 'unvoiced'.

WH-QUESTIONS: questions seeking information that in English would contain 'question words' that typically start with wh-, such as 'why', 'when', 'who' and 'where' (note, however, exceptions such as 'how'). Wh-questions contrast with yes-no questions (such as 'Did you read that book?'), where there is no question word and where the answer being sought is 'yes' or 'no' rather than a piece of information.

Related readings and bibliography

The current section lists works that were referred to in the compilation of this book. We begin by listing works that we recommend readers to consult if they require further information about the Korean language. We then list other works that are referenced in this book.

General descriptions of Korean

Lee, Ik-sop & S. Robert Ramsey (2000). *The Korean Language*. Albany, NY SUNY.

Sohn, Ho-Min (1999). *The Korean Language*. Cambridge Cambridge University Press.

Song, Jae Jung (2005). *The Korean Language Structure, Use and Context*. London Routledge.

Descriptions of Korean grammar for linguists

Martin, Samuel (1992). *A Reference Grammar of Korean A Complete Guide to the Grammar and History of the Korean Language*. Rutland, VT Tuttle.

Yeon, Jaehoon (2003). *Korean Grammatical Constructions Their Form and Meaning*. London Saffron Books.

Descriptions of Korean grammar (and other aspects) for language learners

Choo, Miho & Hye-Young Kwak (2008). *Using Korean A Guide to Contemporary Usage*. Cambridge Cambridge University Press.
Kim-Renaud, Young-Key (2008). *Korean An Essential Grammar*. London Routledge.

Lee, Keedong (1993). *A Korean Grammar on Semantic Pragmatic Principles*. Seoul Hankook Munhwasa.

Grammar 'dictionaries' for language learners (written in Korean)

Kungnipkukŏwon [The National Institute of the Korean Language] (2005). *Oegugin-ŭl wiha-n hangukŏ munpŏp 2* [*Korean Grammar for Foreigners 2*]. Seoul Communication Books.

Paek, Pong-ja (1999). *Hangukŏ munpŏp sajŏn* [*Korean Grammar Dictionary*]. Seoul Yonsei University Press.

Grammar-based textbooks and self-study workbooks

Byon, Andrew Sangpil (2008). *Basic Korean A Grammar & Workbook*. New York Routledge.

Byon, Andrew Sangpil (2009). *Intermediate Korean A Grammar & Workbook*. New York Routledge.

King, Ross & Jaehoon Yeon (2002). *Continuing Korean*. Rutland, VT Tuttle.

King, Ross & Jaehoon Yeon (2009). *Elementary Korean (2nd Edition)*. North Clarendon, VT Tuttle.

Korean vocabulary

Choo, Miho & William O'Grady (1996). *Handbook of Korean Vocabulary A Resource for Word Recognition and Comprehension*. Honolulu University of Hawai'i Press.

Korean phonetics, phonology and pronunciation

Choo, Miho & William O'Grady (2003). *The Sounds of Korean A Pronunciation Guide*. Honolulu University of Hawai'i Press.

Korean sociolinguistics

Sohn, Ho-Min (Ed.) (2006). *Korean Language in Culture and Society*. Honolulu University of Hawai'i Press.

Further works referred to in this book

Ahn, Joo-hoh (2002). Hangugŏ kyoyuk-esŏ-ui wonin yŏngyŏlŏmi-e taehayŏ [On Korean Causal Connectives]. Hangugŏ kyoyuk. *Journal of Korean Language Education* 13(2), 159–180.

Brown, Lucien (2015). Revisiting 'polite' – *yo* and 'deferential' – *supnita* speech style shifting in Korean from the viewpoint of indexicality. *Journal of Pragmatics* 79, 43–59.

Brown, Lucien & Bodo Winter (2019). Multimodal indexicality in Korean 'Doing Deference' and 'Performing Intimacy' through nonverbal behavior. *Journal of Politeness Research* 15(1), 25–54.

Brown, Lucien, Bodo Winter, Kaori Idemaru & Sven Grawunder (2014). Phonetics and politeness Perceiving Korean honorific and non-honorific speech through phonetic cues. *Journal of Pragmatics* 66, 45–60.

Garrigues, Stephen (1995). Mimetic parallels in Korean and Japanese. *Studies in Language* 19(2), 359 ff.

Kang, Yoonjung (2014). Voice onset time merger and development of tonal contrast in Seoul Korean stops A corpus study. *Journal of Phonetics* 45, 76–90.

Kim, Minju (2010). The historical development of Korean siph- 'to think' into markers of desire, inference, and similarity. *Journal of Pragmatics* 42(4), 1000–1016.

Lee, Hyo-sang (1991). *Tense, Aspect and Modality A Discourse Pragmatic Analysis of Verbal Affixes in Korean from a*

Typological Perspective. PhD dissertation, University of California at Los Angeles.

Lee, Jung-bok (2004). Intheneys thongsin ene kyengepep-uy thukseng-kwa sayong cenlyak (Characteristics and Strategies of the Korean Honorifics in Internet Communication Language). Enekwahak yenkwu. *The Journal of Linguistic Science* 30, 221–254.

Lukoff, F. & Nam Ki-Shim (1982). Constructions in – nikka and – 6s6 as logical formations. In *The Linguistic Society of Korea, Linguistics in the Morning Calm*. Seoul Hanshin.

Oh, Sun-Young (2007). Overt reference to speaker and recipient in Korean. *Discourse Studies* 9(4), 462–492.

Oh, Sun-Young (2010). Invoking categories through co-present person reference The case of Korean conversation. *Journal of Pragmatics* 42(5), 1219–1242.

Ryzhkov, Andrii (2009). Derivation of expressive verbs in Korean Morpho-stylistic aspects. In *Proceedings of the 6th Korean Studies Graduate Students' Convention in Europe*. Moscow Moscow State University Institute of Asian and African Studies.

Sohn, Sung-ock (1992). Speaker-oriented and event-oriented causals A comparative analysis of – nikka and – ese. *Korean Linguistics* 7, 73–83.

Strauss, Susan & Jong Oh Eun (2005). Indexicality and honorific speech level choice in Korean. *Linguistics* 43(3), 611–651.

Index of grammatical constructions (Korean)

Korean pattern		Function/English equivalent	Section	Page
가/이		subject particle	3.2.1	98
가	[→-나/ㄴ가 보-]	'look like'	5.5.1	250
가	[→-나/ㄴ가 싶-]	'think it might'	5.5.2	250
가	[→-(으)ㄴ가]	dubitative questions	9.3	424
가-	[→-(아/어) 가-]	ongoing activity 'away'	5.1.1	227
가	[→-(으)ㄴ가?]	sentence ending – dubitative interrogative	9.3	424
가지고		'with', 'by means of'	→7.1.5	298
가지고	[→-(아/어) 가지고]	additional connective – 'and'	7.1.5	298
같이		particle of comparison – 'like'	3.3.6.2	159
-개/-게		nominal form	2.2.2	50
거	[→것]	'thing', 'object' or 'affair'	2.1.2.1	39
-거나		optional connective – 'or'	7.4.1	345
-거늘		contrastive connective – 'but', 'while'	7.2.13	323
-거니와		additional connective – 'and'	7.3.6	331
-거든		conditional connective – 'if'	7.5.6	361
-거든		sentence ending – 'it's because', 'you see'	9.2	423
-거라		plain style command	6.1.4	268
건	[→것]	'thing', 'object' or 'affair' (+은/는)	2.1.2.1	39
걸	[→-(으)ㄹ걸	sentence ending – presumptions, regrets	9.8	430
것		'thing', 'object' or 'affair'	2.1.2.1	39
것	[→-(으)ㄴ/는 것]	way of creating nominal forms	2.2.6	72
것	[→modifier+것]	'the fact that'	8.2.2	388

것 같– [→modifier+것 같–]	'it seems that'	8.2.3	391
–게	nominal form deriving ending	2.2.2	50
게 [→것]	'thing', 'object' or 'affair' (+이/가)	2.1.2.1	39
–게	familiar speech style	6.1.5	270
–게	causative connective – 'so that'	7.6.1	366
게 [→–(으)ㄹ게]	promise-like futures	9.9	432
–게	derived adverbs	11.2.1.2	474
–게 되–	'turn out so that'	5.6.1	251
–게/기 마련이–	'be bound to'	2.2.4.3	54
–게 보이–	auxiliary verb – 'seem'	5.6.2	252
–게 하–	causative	4.4.2.2	219
–게끔	causative connective – 'so that'	7.6.2	367
–겠–	future tense	4.3.2.1	193
겸	'...-cum-...'	2.1.2.2	40
겸 [→–(으)ㄹ 겸]	'with the combined purpose of'	8.2.4	392
–겹–	verb-deriving suffixes	11.3.2.3	504
–고	additional connective – 'and'	7.3.1	325
–고는	additional connective – 'and'	7.3.3	329
–고 나–	auxiliary verb – 'after finishing'	5.3.1	242
–고 말–	auxiliary verb – 'end up'	5.3.2	243
–고 보–	'do and then realize'	5.3.3	244
–고 싶–	auxiliary verb – 'want to do'	5.3.4	245
–고야 말–	auxiliary verb – 'end up'	→5.3.2	243
–고 있–	continuous actions	4.3.3.2	202
–고도	contrastive connective – 'even after'	7.2.7	320
–고말고	'of course ...'	9.1	422
–고서	additional connective – 'and'	7.3.2	328
–고자	intentitve connective – 'with the intention of'	7.7.3	373
곳	'place'	2.1.2.3	41
과/와	comitative particle – 'and/with'	3.2.6.1	123
과/와 (함께/같이/마찬가지)	'together with'	→3.2.6.1	124
과/와 같–	'the same as'	→3.2.6.1	124
과/와 다르–	'different to'	→3.2.6.1	124
과/와 비교하–	'compared with'	→3.2.6.1	124
과/와 비슷하–	'similar to'	→3.2.6.1	124
–구–	derived causative verbs	4.4.2.1	215
–구나	sentence ending – exclamations	9.4	426

–구만/구먼	sentence ending – exclamations	9.4	426
–군	sentence ending – exclamations	9.4	426
그것	'that thing' – demonstrative pronoun	→2.3.2	80
그 사람	'that person' – third person pronoun	→2.3.1.3	77
–기	nominal form	2.2.3	50
–기–	derived passive verbs	4.4.1.1	205
–기–	derived causative verbs	4.4.2.1	215
–기 나름이	'depending'	2.2.4.1	52
–기 때문에	'because'	2.2.4.2	53
–기/게 마련이–	'be bound to'	2.2.4.3	54
–기(에) 망정이–	'fortunately ... otherwise'	2.2.4.4	55
–기 시작하–	'start'	2.2.4.5	55
–기 십상이–	'it is easy to'	2.2.4.6	56
–기 위하–	'in order to'	2.2.4.7	56
–기 이를 데 없–/그지 없–	'boundless, endless'	2.2.4.8	57
–기 일쑤이–	'be apt to'	2.2.4.9	58
–기 전	'before'	2.2.4.10	58
–기 짝이 없–	'very'	2.2.4.11	59
–기나 하–	'just'	2.2.4.12	60
–기는	'no way'	2.2.4.13	60
–기는 하–	'indeed'	2.2.4.14	61
–기(는)커녕	'far from'	2.2.4.15	62
–기도 하–	'also'	2.2.4.16	63
–기만 하–	'only'	2.2.4.17	64
–기로 하–	'decide to'	2.2.4.18	64
–기로 되–	'be supposed to'	2.2.4.19	65
–기를/길 바라–	'hope'	2.2.4.20	66
–기에	'upon, because	2.2.4.21	68
–기에 따라–	'depending on	2.2.4.22	69
길(에) [→–는 길(에)]	'on the way to'	8.2.7	394
–길래	causal connective – 'so', 'because'	7.1.10	306
김	('occasion, chance') [bound noun]	2.1.2.4	41
김 [→–는 김에]	'as long as you're at it'	8.2.6	393
까? [→–(으)ㄹ까?]	sentence ending – suggestions, tentative questions	9.9	432
까지	particle of extent – 'up until'	3.3.3.5	144

–껏	derived adverbs	11.2.1.2	474
–께	object honorific particle	6.2.2.2	278
–께서	subject honorific particle	6.2.1.3	276
나	first person pronoun	→2.3.1.1	74
나 [→(이)나]	particle of approximation/optionality – 'about/or/just'	3.3.5.2	155
나 [→–고 나–]	'after finishing'	5.3.1	242
나 [→–(으)나]	contrastive connective – 'but'	7.2.2	313
나 [→–(으)나 마나]	'whether or not'	7.2.3	314
–나?/–(으)ㄴ가?	sentence ending – dubitative interrogative	9.3	424
–나/ㄴ가 보–	'look like'	5.5.1	250
–나/ㄴ가 싶–	'think it might'	5.5.2	250
나름 [→–기 나름이]	'depending'	2.2.4.1	52
내– [→–(아/어) 내–]	'finish, achieve'	5.1.3	228
–냐 [→–(으)냐, –느냐]	plain style question	6.1.4	266
–냐고 하–	quoted question	10.2.2	450
–냐니(까)	'upon telling'; 'I told you . . .'	10.4.1	464
–냔다	quotation question – reduced plain style	→ 10.3.2	461
–냡니다	quotation question – reduced formal style	→ 10.3.2	461
–냔 말이–	'I mean . . .'	10.4.6	468
–냈어(요)	quotation question – reduced past tense	→ 10.3.2	461
너	second person pronoun	→2.3.1.2	75
–너라 [→–거/너라]	plain style command	6.1.4	268
–네	familiar speech style	6.1.5	270
–네	sentence ending – evidential exclamations	9.5	428
놓– [→–(아/어) 놓–]	'do all the way'	5.1.4	229
누구나	'anyone', 'everyone'	→3.3.5.2	155
–느냐	plain style question	6.1.4	266
–느냐고 하–	quoted question	10.2.2	450
–느니	contrastive connective – 'rather than'	7.2.14	323
–느라고	causal connective – 'what with . . .', 'because of'	7.1.11	308
는/은	topic particle	3.3.2.1	132
–는	present dynamic modifier	8.1.2	380
(는/은)커녕	particle of extent – 'far from'	3.3.3.10	151

–는 가운데	'in the middle of'	8.2.1	388
–는 길(에)	'on the way to'	8.2.7	394
–는 김에	'as long as you're at it'	8.2.6	393
–는 대로	'in accordance with'	8.2.10	395
–는 데	'in the matter of'	8.2.11	396
–는데도	'although'	→7.3.12	339
–는데도 불구하고	'in spite of'	→7.3.12	339
–는 동안/사이에	'while'	8.2.12	396
–는 둥	'may or may not'	8.2.13	398
–는 듯	'just like'	8.2.14	398
–는 듯하–/듯싶–	'seem like'	8.2.15	399
–는/–(으)ㄴ 마당에	'in the situation where'	8.2.19	402
–는 모양이–	'seem like'	8.2.21	403
–는 바람에	'because of . . .'	8.2.23	404
–는 반면(에)	'on the other hand'	8.2.24	404
–는이상(에(는))	'since';'unless'	8.2.28	410
–는 일/적이 있–/없–	'ever/never'	8.2.29	411
–는 줄 알–/모르–	'think/know . . .'	8.2.31	412
–는 중에/도중에	'in the middle of . . .'	8.2.32	414
–는 중–	'be in the middle of . . .'	8.2.33	414
–는 척하–	'pretend'	8.2.38	418
–는 체	'pretend'	→8.2.38	418
–는/–(으)ㄴ 탓에	'due to'	8.2.39	419
–는 통에	'because of'	8.2.40	419
–는 한–	'as much as'	8.2.41	420
–는가	plain style question	6.1.4	266
–(는)구나	sentence ending – exclamations	9.4	424
–(는)구만/구먼	sentence ending – exclamations	9.4	424
–(는)군	sentence ending – exclamations	9.4	424
–는다	plain style statement	6.1.4	264
–(ㄴ/–는)다고 하–	quoted statement	10.2.1	448
–는대	quotation statement – reduced	→ 10.3.2	461
–는댔어	quotation statement – reduced past tense	→ 10.3.2	461
–는데 [→–(으)ㄴ/는데]	additional connective – background information	7.3.12	339
–는지 [→—(으)ㄴ/는지	oblique questions – 'whether'	7.4.4	349
–니	plain style question	6.1.4	266
–니 [→–(으)니]	causal connective – 'so', 'because'	7.1.4	297

Form	Cross-reference	Meaning	Section	Page
–니까	[→–(으)니까	causal connective – 'so', 'because'	7.1.3	297
–님		honorific suffix for titles	→ 1.3.2	34
–다		dictionary form	4.1.7	175
–다		plain style statement	6.1.4	264
–다	[→–ㄴ다; –는다]	plain style statement	6.1.4	264
–다 보–		'after trying doing'	5.2.2	240
–다 주–		'run an errand'	5.2.3	241
–다(가)		additional connective – 'and then'	7.3.11	335
–다(가) 보면		'if . . . and then'	7.5.4	360
–다고 하–	[→–(ㄴ/–는)다고 하–	quoted statement	10.2.1	448
–다는데		quote as background information – 'I heard'	10.4.4	466
–다니(까)		'upon telling'; 'I told you . . .'	10.4.1	464
–다마다		'of course'	→ 9.6	429
–다 말–		'stop after'	5.2.1	240
–다며		'I heard . . .'	→ 10.4.2	465
–다면		'if you say that'	7.5.2	358
–다면서		'I heard . . ., right'	10.4.3	465
–다시피		'just as'	7.8.2	375
다음에	[→–(으)ㄴ다음에]	'after . . .'	8.2.9	395
–단 말이–		'I mean . . .'	10.4.6	468
–단다		quotation statement – reduced plain style	→ 10.3.2	461
–달라고 하–		quoted commands with 주– – reduced	10.3.1	459
–달라고 하–		quoted commands with 주–	10.2.5	454
–달래		quoted commands with 주– – reduced	10.3.2	461
–담/람		sentence ending – disapproval	9.7	429
–답–		verb-deriving suffixes	10.3.2.3	504
–답니다		quotation statement – reduced formal style	→ 10.3.2	461
당신		second person pronoun	→ 2.3.1.2	75
당신		reflexive pronoun	→ 2.3.3	81
당하–		passive deriving support verb	4.4.1.3	210
대–	[→–(아/어) 대–]	'do repeatedly'	5.1.6	231
–대	[→–ㄴ/–는대]	quotation statement – reduced	→ 10.3.2	461

-댔어 [→-ㄴ/-는-댔어]	quotation statement – reduced past tense	→ 10.3.2	461
대로	('in accordance with') [bound noun]	2.1.2.5	41
대로	particle of comparison – 'in accordance with'	3.3.6.6	163
대로 [→-(으)ㄴ대로]	'in accordance with'	8.2.10	395
-댔어(요)	quotation statement – reduced past tense	→ 10.3.2	461
-더	observed/perceived past tense	4.3.1.3	189
-더니	causal connective – 'seeing as', 'since'	7.1.13	309
-더라	observed/perceived past tense, plain style	4.3.1.3	189
-더라고	observed/perceived past tense	4.3.1.3	189
-더라도	contrastive connective – 'even though'	7.2.6	319
-더라면	conditional connective – 'if'	7.5.5	360
더러	'to'	3.2.4.5	115
덕분	'thanks to' [bound noun]	2.1.2.6	41
-던	continuous past modifier	8.1.4	384
-던데요	observed/perceived past tense, polite style	4.3.1.3	190
-던가요	observed/perceived past tense, polite style	4.3.1.3	190
-던 길(에)	'on the way to'	8.2.7	394
데	'place' [bound noun]	2.1.2.7	42
-데요	observed/perceived past tense, polite style	4.3.1.3	190
도	particle of extent – 'also, even'	3.3.3.6	146
도 [→-(아/어)도]	contrastive connective – 'even though'	7.2.5	315
도 [→-이라도]	copula + -(아/어)도; 'even' or 'at least'	→7.2.5	315
도 [→-(아/어)도 되-]	'be allowed to'	7.2.5.1	317
-도록	causative connective – 'so that'	7.6.3	368
-도록 하-	causative	4.4.2.3	221
	'make sure'	→7.6.3	368
도중	'middle' [bound noun]	2.1.2.21	47
도중 [→-는 도중에]	'in the middle of . . .'	8.2.32	414
동안	'during' [bound noun]	2.1.2.8	42
동안 [→-는 동안]	'while'	8.2.12	396
되-	passive deriving support verb	4.4.1.2	209
되- [→-게 되-]	'turn out so that'	5.6.1	251

되– [→–(아/어)야 하–/되–]	'must, have to'	5.7.1	253
되– [→–(으)되]	contrastive connective – 'but'	7.2.4	315
두– [→–(아/어) 두–]	'do for future reference'	5.1.5	230
둥	('may or may not') [bound noun]	2.1.2.9	43
둥 [→–(으)ㄹ/–는/–(으)ㄴ 둥]	'may or may not'	8.2.13	398
뒤에 [→–(으)ㄴ 뒤에]	'after . . .'	8.2.9	395
–든가	optional connective – 'whether . . . or . . . not'	7.4.3	348
–든지	optional connective – 'or'	7.4.2	347
들	plural particle	3.3.1	129
들 [→–(으)ㄴ들]	contrastive connective – 'even though'	7.2.9	321
듯	('as if') [bound noun]	2.1.2.10	43
듯 [→–(으)ㄹ/–는/–(으)ㄴ 듯]	'just like'	8.2.14	398
듯 [→–는 듯하–/듯싶–]	'seem like'	8.2.15	399
–듯이	comparison connective – 'as if'	7.8.1	374
–디	observed/perceived past tense, plain style	4.3.1.3	190
따라 [→–기에 따라–]	'depending on	2.2.4.22	69
따라	particle of comparison – 'unusually'	3.3.6.5	162
따름	'only, alone'	2.1.2.11	43
때	'when' [bound noun]	2.1.2.12	43
때 [→–(으)ㄹ 때]	'when . . .'	8.2.17	400
때문	'reason' [bound noun]	2.1.2.13	44
때문 [→–기 때문에]	'because'	2.2.4.2	53
–라 [→–(으)라, –아/어라]	plain style command	6.1.4	268
–라면	'if you say that'	7.5.2	358
–라면서	'I heard . . .'	→ 10.4.3	465
–라고	quoted command – reduced form	10.3.1	459
–라고 하–	direct quotation	10.1	446
–라고 하–	quoted command	10.2.4	453
–라는데	quote as background information – 'I heard'	10.4.4	466
–라니(까)	'upon telling'; 'I told you . . .'	10.4.1	464
–라면서	'I heard . . ., right'	10.4.3	465
–라셔	quotation command – reduced honorific	→ 10.3.2	461

-란 말이-		'I mean ...'	10.4.6	468
-란다		quotation command – reduced plain style	→ 10.3.2	461
-랍니다		quotation command – reduced formal style	→ 10.3.2	461
랑	[→(이)랑]	comitative particle – 'and/with'	3.2.6.3	126
래	[→-(으)ㄹ래]	sentence ending – feel like	9.11	436
-래		quoted command – reduced form	10.3.2	461
-랬어		quotation command – reduced past tense	→ 10.3.2	461
-러	[→-(으)러]	intentive connective – '[go come] to [do]'	7.7.1	369
-려고	[→-(으)려고]	intentive connective – 'with the intention of'	7.7.2	370
-려면	[→-(으)려면]	'if you intend to'	7.5.3	359
-려무나	[→-(으)려무나]	granting permission; orders	9.15	439
-(으)련마는/-(으)련만		sentence ending – will, would	9.14	438
련마는/련만	[→-(으)련마는/-(으)련만]	sentence ending – will, would	9.14	438
-렴	[→-(으)렴]	granting permission; orders	9.15	439
로	[→(으)로]	instrumental particle 'by/with/as'	3.2.5.1	119
로부터	[→(으)로부터]	particle of movement – 'from'	3.2.4.8	117
로	[→(으)로서]	instrumental particle – 'as'	3.2.5.2	121
로	[→(으)로써]	instrumental particle – 'by'	3.2.5.3	122
로 하여금	[→(으)로 하여금]	particle of movement – 'to'	3.2.4.7	116
-롭-		Verb-deriving suffixes	10.3.2.3	504
를/을		object particle	3.2.2	100
-리-		passive verb deriving ending	4.4.1.1	205
-리-		causative verb deriving ending	4.4.2.1	215
리		'reasons' [bound noun]	2.1.2.14	45
리 없-	[→-(으)ㄹ 리 없-]	'no way that'	8.2.18	401
-ㄹ 지 모르-	[→-(으)ㄹ지 모르-]	'might'	→7.4.5	351
마	[→-(으)마]	sentence ending – promise-like futures	9.16	440
마나	[→-(으)나 마나]	'whether or not'	7.2.3	314
마다		particle of frequency – 'every'	3.3.4.1	152
마련	[→-기/게 마련이-]	'be bound to'	2.2.4.3	54
마저		particle of extent – 'even'	3.3.3.8	150

만	particle of extent – 'only'	3.3.3.1	139
만큼	particle of comparison – 'as ... as'	3.3.6.3	160
만하– [→–(으)ㄹ 만하–]	'worth...'	8.2.20	402
말– [→–고 말–]	'end up'	5.3.2	243
말고	'rather than'	→4.2.3	184
말고 [→지 말고]	'instead of'	→4.2.3	184
말락 [→–(으)ㄹ락 말락 (하–)]	'on the verge of	7.4.7	353
말할 것도 없고	'without saying anything of'	→3.3.3.6	146
–맞–	verb-deriving suffixes	11.3.2.3	504
–망정 [→–(으)ㄹ망정]	contrastive connective – 'even though'	7.2.12	322
–며 [→–(으)며]	additional connective – 'while'	7.3.9	333
–면 [→–(으)면]	conditional connective – 'if'	7.5.1	353
–면 고맙겠– [→–(으)면 고맙겠–]	'would be grateful if'	7.5.1.2	356
–면 되– [→–(으)면 되–]	'be enough/sufficient'	7.5.1.4	356
–면 안 되– [→–(으)면 안 되–]	'not allowed'	7.5.1.5	357
–면서 [→–(으)면서]	additional connective – 'while'	7.3.7	332
–(으)면서부터		7.3.8	333
모르– [→–는 줄 모르–]	'think/know ...'	8.2.31	412
모양이– [→–(으)ㄹ|–는|–(으)ㄴ 모양이–]	'seem like'	8.2.15	399
못	short negative	4.2.1	179
무렵	'around the time' [bound noun]	2.1.2.15	45
무엇이나	'anything; everything'	→3.3.5.2	155
–므로 [→–(으)므로]	causal connective – 'so', 'because'	7.1.9	305
–ㅂ니다	formal style	6.1.2	258
–ㅂ니까	formal style question	6.1.2	260
–ㅂ디다	observed/perceived past tense, formal style	6.1.2	260
–ㅂ디까	observed/perceived past tense, formal style	6.1.2	260
–ㅂ시다	formal speech style proposal	6.1.2	261
바	'thing' [bound noun]	2.1.2.16	45
바 [→–(으)ㄹ 바에(는/야)]	'rather ... than'	8.2.22	403
바라– [→–기를/길 바라–]	'hope'	2.2.4.20	66
바람에 [→–(으)ㄴ|는 바람에]	'because of ...'	8.2.23	404
밖에	particle of extent – 'except for'	3.3.3.3	141

반면에	[→-(으)ㄴ|는 반면에]	'because of . . .'	8.2.24	404
받-		passive deriving support verb	4.4.1.3	210
버리-	[→-(아/어) 버리-]	'do completely for regret or relief'	5.1.7	232
보-	[→-(아/어) 보-]	'try doing'	5.1.8	233
보-	[→—다 보-]	'after trying doing'	5.2.2	240
보-	[→-고 보-]	'do and then realize'	5.3.3	244
보-	[→-(으)ㄹ까 보-]	'think it might'	5.4.1	246
보-	[→-나/ㄴ가 보-]	'look like'	5.5.1	250
보이-	[→-(아/어) 보이-]	'seem'	5.1.9	236
보이-	[→-게 보이-	'seem'	5.6.2	252
보고		'to'	3.2.4.6	116
보다		particle of comparison 'more than'	3.3.6.4	160
부터		particle of extent – 'from'	3.3.3.4	143
부터	[→(으)로부터]	particle of movement – 'from'	3.2.4.8	117
빠지-	[→-(아/어) 빠지-]	'lapse into a negative state'	5.1.10	236
뻔하-	[→(으)ㄹ 뻔하-]	'nearly . . .'	8.2.25	405
뿐		'only, just, nothing but'	2.1.2.17	46
뿐		particle of extent – 'only'	3.3.3.2	141
뿐	[→-(으)ㄹ 뿐]	'only'	8.2.26	399
사이에	[→-는 사이에]	'while'	8.2.12	396
-상		adverb deriving ending	11.2.1.2	474
서	[→-(아/어)서]	causal connective – 'so', 'because'	7.1.1	293
서라도	[→-(아/어)서라도]	contrastive connective – 'even if it means'	7.2.8	320
서야	[→-(아/어)서야]	'only after'	7.5.8	364
서로		'each other' – reciprocal pronoun	→2.3.3	82
-세요	[→-(으)세요]	polite speech style honorific	6.2.1.1	273
-소		semiformal speech style	6.1.6	272
수		'case, circumstance' [bound noun]	2.1.2.18	46
수	[→-을/ㄹ 수 있-/없-]	'can/cannot'	8.2.27	408
수록	[→-(으)면 ...-(으)ㄹ수록]	'the more the . . .'	7.5.9	365
-스럽-		descriptive verb deriving suffix	10.3.2.3	504
-습니다		formal speech style statement	6.1.2	259

-습니까		formal speech style question	6.1.2	260
-습디다		observed/perceived past tense, formal style	6.1.2	260
-습디까		observed/perceived past tense, formal style	6.1.2	260
시작	[→-기 시작하-]	'start'	2.2.4.5	55
-시-	[→-(으)시-]	subject honorific marker	6.2.1.1	273
-시오	[→-(으)시오]	formal speech style command	6.1.2	260
시키-		causative deriving support verb	4.4.2.4	221
십상	[→-기 십상이-]	'it is easy to'	2.2.4.6	56
-십시오	[→-(으)십시오]	formal speech style command (honorific)	6.1.2	260
싶-	[→-고 싶-]	'want to do'	5.3.4	245
싶-	[→-(으)ㄹ까 싶-]	'afraid it might'	5.4.2	247
싶-	[→-나/ㄴ가 싶-]	'think it might'	5.5.2	250
쌓-	[→-(아/어) 쌓-]	'do repeatedly'	5.1.11	237
씨		title-word	→6.3.2	284
씩		particle of frequency – 'apiece'	3.3.4.2	153
아/야		vocative particle	3.2.7	127
-아/어		infinitive form	4.1.6	173
-아/어		intimate 'panmal' style	6.1.3	261
-아/어		causal connective – 'so', 'because'	7.1.2	296
-(아/어) 가-		ongoing activity 'away'	5.1.1	227
-(아/어) 가지고		additional connective – 'and','so'	7.1.5	298
-(아/어) 봤자		contrastive connective – 'even though'	7.2.15	324
-(아/어) 오-		ongoing activity 'towards'	5.1.2	227
-(아/어) 내-		'finish, achieve'	5.1.3	228
-(아/어) 놓-		'do all the way'	5.1.4	229
-(아/어) 두-		'do for future reference'	5.1.5	230
-(아/어) 대-		'do repeatedly'	5.1.6	231
-(아/어) 버리-		'do completely for regret or relief'	5.1.7	232
-(아/어) 보-		'try doing'	5.1.8	233
-(아/어) 보이-		'seem'	5.1.9	236
-(아/어) 빠지-		'lapse into a negative state'	5.1.10	236
-(아/어) 쌓-		'do repeatedly'	5.1.11	237
-아/어 있-		continuous states	4.3.3.1	200
-(아/어) 주-		'perform a favour'	5.1.12	237

–아/어 지–	passive deriving verb ending	4.4.1.4	213
–(아/어) 치우–	'do rashly'	5.1.13	239
–(아/어)도	contrastive connective – 'even though'	7.2.5	315
–(아/어)도 되–	'be allowed to'	7.2.5.1	317
–(아/어)서	causal connective – 'so', 'because'	7.1.1	293
–(아/어)서라도	contrastive connective – 'even if it means'	7.2.8	320
–(아/어)서야	'only after'	7.5.8	364
–(아/어)야	conditional connective – 'only if'	7.5.7	362
–(아/어)야 하–/되–	'must, have to'	7.5.7.1	363
–(아/어)서인지	'perhaps that is why'	7.1.3	297
–아/어요	polite style	6.1.1	256
아니–	negative copula	4.1.3	169
안	short negative	4.2.1	179
안 ...면 안 되–	'have to'	7.5.1.6	358
알– [→–는 줄 알–]	'think/know ...'	8.2.31	412
–았/었–	simple past tense	4.3.1.1	186
–았/었었–	past-past tense	4.3.1.2	187
–(았/었)더니	causal connective – 'seeing as', 'since'	7.1.13	309
–(았/었)더라면	conditional connective – 'if'	7.5.5	360
–(았/었)던	discontinuous past modifier	8.1.5	385
–(았/었)던지	'had done'	7.4.6	352
–(았/었)으면 좋–	'hope', 'wish'	7.5.1.1	355
–(았/었)으면 하–	'should be grateful if'	7.5.1.3	356
–(았/었)을	past prospective modifier	8.2.18	401
야/아	vocative particle	3.2.7	127
야 [→(이)야]	particle of focus – 'if it's'	3.3.2.2	138
–야 하–/되– [→–(아/어)야 하–/되–]	'must, have to'	5.7.1	253
야말로 [→(이)야말로]	particle of focus 'indeed'	3.3.2.3	138
어디나	'anywhere'	→3.3.5.2	155
어디서나	'[happening] anywhere'	→3.3.5.2	155
언제나	'any time'	→3.3.5.2	155
에	particle of movement and location – 'to/in/at'	3.2.4.1	106
에게	particle of movement – 'to'	3.2.4.4	113
에게서	particle of movement – 'from'	3.2.4.7	116
에 관하여	'regarding'	→3.2.4.1	106
에 대해서	'about'	→3.2.4.1	106

에다가	particle of movement – 'in/on'	3.2.4.2	109
에 따라	'in accordance with'	→3.2.4.1	106
에 의하면	'according to'	→3.2.4.1	106
에서	particle of movement and location –	3.2.4.3	110
–오	semiformal speech style	6.1	255
오– [→–(아/어) 오–]	ongoing activity 'towards'	5.1.2	227
–오	adverb deriving ending	11.2.1.2	474
와/과	comitative particle – 'and/with'	3.2.6.1	123
–요 [→–아/어요]	polite style	6.1.1	256
–우–	causative verb deriving ending	4.4.2.1	215
–우	adverb deriving ending	11.2.1.2	474
우리	plural first person pronoun	→2.3.1.1	74
위하– [→–기 위하–]	'in order to'	2.2.4.7	56
–(으)ㄴ	state/result modifier	8.1.3	381
–(으)ㄴ 것	way of creating nominal forms	2.2.6	72
–(으)ㄴ 김에	'as long as you're at it'	8.2.6	393
–(으)ㄴ 나머지	'as a result'	8.2.8	394
–(으)ㄴ 다음에, 뒤에, 후에	'after . . .'	8.2.9	395
–(으)ㄴ 대로	'in accordance with'	8.2.10	395
–(으)ㄴ 둥	'may or may not'	8.2.10	395
–(으)ㄴ 듯	'just like'	8.2.14	398
–(으)ㄴ 듯하–/듯싶–	'seem like'	8.2.15	399
–(으)ㄴ 모양이–	'seem like'	8.2.21	403
–(으)ㄴ 바람에	'because of . . .'	8.2.23	404
–(으)ㄴ 반면(에)	'on the other hand'	8.2.24	404
–(으)ㄴ 이상(에(는))	'since'; 'unless'	8.2.28	410
–(으)ㄴ 일/적이 있–/없–	'ever/never'	8.2.29	411
–(으)ㄴ 줄 알– /모르–	'think/know . . .'	8.2.31	412
–(으)ㄴ 지	'since'	8.2.35	416
–(으)ㄴ 채(로)	'as it is'	8.2.37	417
–(으)ㄴ 통에	'because of'	8.2.40	419
–(으)ㄴ 한–	'as much as'	8.2.41	420
–(으)ㄴ가	plain style question, written form	6.1.4	266
–(으)ㄴ가?	sentence ending – dubitative interrogative	9.3	424
–(으)ㄴ/는데	additional connective – background information	7.3.12	339
–(으)ㄴ/는데도	'even though'	→7.3.12	339
–(으)ㄴ/는지	oblique questions – 'whether'	7.4.4	349

–(으)ㄴ들	contrastive connective – 'even though'	7.2.9	321
–(으)나	contrastive connective – 'but'	7.2.2	313
–(으)나 마나	'whether or not'	7.2.3	314
–(으)냐	plain style question, descriptive verbs	6.1.4	266
–(으)냐고 하–	quoted question	10.2.2	450
–(으)니	causal connective – 'so', 'because'	7.1.7	304
–(으)니까	causal connective – 'so', 'because'	7.1.6	300
–(으)되	contrastive connective – 'but'	7.2.4	315
–(으)ㄹ	future/prospective modifier	8.1.1	378
–(으)ㄹ 거	future tense	4.3.2.2	196
–(으)ㄹ게	promise-like futures	9.9	432
–(으)ㄹ 겸	'with the combined purpose of'	8.2.4	392
–(으)ㄹ 계획	'plan to'	8.2.5	392
–(으)ㄹ 따름이–	'only'	8.2.16	399
–(으)ㄹ 둥	'may or may not'	8.2.13	398
–(으)ㄹ 듯	'just like'	8.2.14	398
–(으)ㄹ 듯하–/듯싶–	'seem like'	8.2.15	399
–(으)ㄹ 때	'when ...'	8.2.17	400
–(으)ㄹ리 없–	'no way that'	8.2.18	401
–(으)ㄹ 마음	'have a mind to'	→8.2.5	392
–(으)ㄹ 만하–	'worth...'	8.2.20	402
–(으)ㄹ 모양이–	'seem like'	8.2.21	403
–(으)ㄹ 바에(는/야)	'rather ... than'	8.2.22	403
–(으)ㄹ 뻔하–	'nearly ...'	8.2.25	405
–(으)ㄹ 뿐	'only'	8.2.26	406
–(으)ㄹ 생각	'thinking of'	→8.2.5	392
–(으)ㄹ 셈	'plan to'	→8.2.5	392
–(으)ㄹ 수 있–/없–	'can /cannot ...'	8.2.27	408
–(으)ㄹ 예정	'plan to'	→8.2.5	392
–(으)ㄹ 작정	'intend to'	→8.2.5	392
–(으)ㄹ 적에	'when' [bound noun]	→8.2.17	400
–(으)ㄹ 정도로	'to the extent that'	8.2.30	411
–(으)ㄹ 줄 알– /모르–	'think/know ...'	8.2.31	412
–(으)ㄹ 즈음(에)	'when'	8.2.34	415
–(으)ㄹ걸	sentence ending – presumptions, regrets	9.8	430
–(으)ㄹ까?	suggestions, tentative questions	9.10	433
–(으)ㄹ까 보–	'think it might'	5.4.1	246

–(으)ㄹ까 싶–	'afraid it might'	5.4.2	247
–(으)ㄹ까 하–	'think of doing'	5.4.3	248
–(으)ㄹ라	causal connective – 'so', 'because'	7.1.14	310
–(으)ㄹ락 말락 (하–)	'on the verge of	7.4.7	353
–(으)ㄹ래	sentence ending – feel like	9.11	436
–(으)ㄹ지	oblique questions – 'whether'	7.4.5	351
–(으)ㄹ지도 모르–	'might'	→7.4.5	351
–(으)ㄹ지라도	contrastive connective – 'even though'	7.2.10	321
–(으)ㄹ지언정	contrastive connective – 'even though'	7.2.11	322
–(으)ㄹ망정	contrastive connective – 'even though'	7.2.12	322
–(으)ㄹ수록, [→–(으)면 ...–(으)ㄹ수록]	'the more the ...'	7.5.9	365
–(으)ㄹ테니	causal connective – 'so', 'because'	→7.1.8	304
–(으)ㄹ테니까	causal connective – 'so', 'because'	7.1.8	304
–(으)ㄹ텐데	additional connective – background information	7.3.13	344
–(으)ㄹ텐데	sentence ending – I'm afraid	9.12	436
–(으)라	plain style command	6.1.4	268
–(으)라고	quoted command – reduced form	10.3.1	459
–(으)라고 하–	quoted command	10.2.4	453
–(으)랴	two-shaped ending	7.1.12	309
–(으)랴	'could ... really?'	9.13	437
–(으)래	quoted command – reduced form	10.3.2	461
–(으)랬어	quotation command – reduced past tense	→ 10.3.2	461
–(으)러	intentive connective – '[go come] to [do]'	7.7.1	369
–(으)려	intentive with modifiers	8.1.7	387
–(으)려던 참이–	'just about to'	8.2.36	416
–(으)려면	'if you intend to'	7.5.3	359
–(으)려무나	granting permission; orders	9.15	439
–(으)련마는/–(으)련만	sentence ending – will, would	9.14	438
–(으)렴	(granting permission; orders)	9.15	439
(으)로	instrumental particle – 'by/with/as'	3.2.5.1	119

(으)로	instrumental particle used to derive adverbs	11.2.1.2	474
(으)로 인해(서)	'due to'	3.2.5.4	123
(으)로부터	particle of movement – 'from'	3.2.4.8	117
(으)로서	instrumental particle – 'as'	3.2.5.2	121
(으)로써	instrumental particle – 'by'	3.2.5.3	122
(으)로 하여금	particle of movement – 'to'	3.2.4.9	118
–(으)마	sentence ending – promise-like futures	9.16	440
–(으)며	additional connective – 'while'	7.3.9	333
–(으)면	conditional connective – 'if'	7.5.1	353
–(으)면 고맙겠–	'would be grateful if'	7.5.1.2	356
–(으)면 되–	'be enough/sufficient'	7.5.1.4	356
–(으)면 안 되–	'not allowed'	7.5.1.5	357
–(으)면 ...–(으)ㄹ수록	'the more the ...'	7.5.9	365
–(으)면서	additional connective – 'while'	7.3.7	332
–(으)면서도	'even while'	→7.3.7	332
–(으)면서부터	'ever since'	7.3.8	333
–(으)므로	causal connective – 'so', 'because'	7.1.9	305
–(으)세요	polite speech style honorific	6.2.1.1	273
–(으)시–	subject honorific marker	6.2.1.1	273
–(으)시오	formal speech style command	6.2	272
–(으)십시오	formal speech style command (honorific)	6.2	272
은/는	topic particle	3.3.2.1	132
(은/는)커녕	particle of extent – 'far from'	3.3.3.10	151
을/를	object particle	3.2.2	100
–음	nominal form	2.2.5	69
–읍시다	formal speech style proposal	6.2	272
의	possessive particle	3.2.3	103
이/가	subject particle	3.2.1	98
–이	nominal form	2.2.1	50
–이–	copula	4.1.4	170
–이	adverb deriving ending	11.2.1.2	474
–이–	passive verb deriving ending	4.4.1.1	205
–이–	causative verb deriving ending	4.4.2.1	215
–이	suffix attaching to given names	6.3.1	283
–이가	suffix attaching to given names + subject paricle	→6.3.1	283

이것	'this thing' – demonstrative pronoun	→2.3.2	80
(이)나	particle of approximation/ optionality – 'about/or/just'	3.3.5.2	155
–이라는	'a . . . called . . .'	10.4.5	467
이라도	copula + –(아/어)도; 'even' or 'at least'	→7.2.5	315
(이)랑	comitative particle – 'and/with'	3.2.6.3	126
이상 [→–는이상(에(는))]	'since'; 'unless'	8.2.28	410
(이)야	particle of focus – 'if it's'	3.3.2.2	138
(이)야말고	particle of focus – 'indeed'	3.3.2.3	138
일 [→–는 일이 있–/없–]	'ever/never'	8.2.27	408
일쑤이– [→–기 일쑤이–]	'be apt to'	2.2.4.9	58
입–	passive deriving support verb	4.4.1.2	209
–자	plain style proposal	6.1.4	268
–자	'upon doing'	→7.3.10	334
–자고	quoted proposal – reduced form	10.3.1	459
–자고 하–	quoted proposal	10.2.3	452
자기	second person pronoun	→2.3.1.2	75
자기	reflexive pronoun	→2.3.3	81
자네	second person pronoun	→2.3.1.2	75
–자니(까)	'upon telling'; 'I told you . . .'	10.4.1	464
–자마자	additional connective – 'as soon as'	7.3.10	334
자신	reflexive pronoun	→2.3.3	81
자체	reflexive pronoun	→2.3.3	81
–잔 말이–	'I mean . . .'	10.4.6	468
–잔다	quotation proposal – reduced plain style	→ 10.3.2	461
–잖아	sentence ending – 'you know	9.17	440
–잡니다	quotation proposal – reduced formal style	→ 10.3.2	461
–재	quoted proposal – reduced form	10.3.2	461
–쟀어	quotation proposal – reduced past tense	→ 10.3.2	461
저	humble first person pronoun	→2.3.1.1	74
저	reflexive pronoun	→2.3.3	81
저 것	'that thing over there' – demonstrative pronoun	→2.3.2	80

저희		humble plural first person pronoun	→2.3.1.1	74
적		'event' [bound noun]	2.1.2.19	46
–적		adnominal suffix	11.3.2.4	506
적 있–/없–]	[→–는적이	'ever/never'	8.2.29	411
전	[→–기 전]	'before'	2.2.4.10	58
정도로 정도로]	[→–(으)ㄹ	'to the extent that'	8.2.30	411
조차		particle of extent – 'even'	3.3.3.7	149
주–	[→–다 주–]	'run an errand'	5.2.3	241
주–	[→–(아/어) 주–]	'perform a favour'	5.1.12	237
줄		('the way, the fact') [bound noun]	2.1.2.20	47
중/도중		'middle' [bound noun]	2.1.2.21	47
중	[→–는 중에]	'in the middle of . . .'	8.2.32	414
중	[→–는 중–]	'be in the middle of . . .'	8.2.33	414
지		('. . . since') [bound noun]	2.1.2.22	48
지	[→저]	reflexive pronoun	→2.3.3	81
–지–		processive verb deriving ending	4.4.3.1	223
지	[→–(으)ㄴ 지]	'since'	8.2.35	416
–지		sentence ending – tag questions	9.18	442
–지–		descriptive verb deriving ending	11.3.2.3	504
–지 않–		long negative	4.2.2	180
–지 않아도 되–		'don't have to'	7.2.5.2	318
–지 않으면 안 되–		'have to'	7.5.1.6	358
–지 말–		negative commands and proposals	4.2.3	182
–지 못하–		long negative	4.2.2	180
–지라도	[→–(으)ㄹ지라도]	contrastive connective – 'even though'	7.2.10	321
–지만		contrastive connective – 'but'	7.2.1	311
–지언정	[→–(으)ㄹ지언정]	contrastive connective – 'even though'	7.2.11	322
짝이 없–	[→–기 짝이 없–]	'very'	2.2.4.11	59
쪽		'side' [bound noun]	2.1.2.23	48
쯤		particle of approximation – 'about'	3.3.5.1	155
채		'just as it is'	2.1.2.24	49
채 채(로)]	[→–(으)ㄴ	'as it is'	8.2.37	417

처럼		particle of comparison – 'like'	3.3.6.1	158
척하–	[→–는 척하–]	'pretend'	8.2.38	418
체	[→–는 체]	'pretend'	→8.2.38	418
–추–		causative verb deriving ending	4.4.2.1	215
치우–	[→–(아/어) 치우–]	'do rashly'	5.1.13	239
치고/치고는		'with exception', 'pretty ... for a...'	3.3.3.9	150
커녕	[→–기(는)커녕]	'far from'	2.2.4.15	62
커녕	[→(는/은)커녕]	particle of extent – 'far from'	3.3.3.10	151
테니까	[→–(으)ㄹ 테니까]	causal connective – 'so', 'because'	7.1.8	304
테니	[→–(으)ㄹ 테니]	causal connective – 'so', 'because'	→7.1.8	304
텐데	[→–(으)ㄹ 텐데]	additional connective – background information	7.3.13	344
텐데	[→–(으)ㄹ 텐데]	sentence ending – I'm afraid	9.12	436
통에	[→–는| – (으)ㄴ 통에]	'because of'	8.2.40	419
하–		support verb	4.1.2	167
하–		processive verb deriving	4.4.3.2	223
하–	[→–(으)ㄹ까 하–]	'think of doing'	5.4.3	248
하–	[→–(아/어)야 하–/되–]	'must, have to'	5.7.1	253
하고		comitative particle – 'and/with'	3.2.6.2	125
–하고 하–		direct quotation	10.1	446
하여금	[→(으)로 하여금]	particle of movement – 'to'	3.2.4.9	118
한–	[→–(으)ㄴ|는 한–]	'as much as'	8.2.41	420
한테		particle of movement – 'to'	3.2.4.4	113
한테서		particle of movement – 'from'	3.2.4.5	115
후에	[→–(으)ㄴ후에]	'after ...'	8.2.9	395
–히–		passive verb deriving ending	4.4.1.1	205
–히–		causative verb deriving ending	4.4.2.1	215
–히		adverb deriving ending	11.2.1.2	474

Index of translation equivalents (English)

English pattern	Korean equivalent	Section	Page
'about' [particle]	쯤	3.3.5.1	154
	(이)나	3.3.5.2	155
'[in] accordance with'	-는|-(으)ㄴ 대로	8.2.10	395
'[I'm] afraid . . .'	-(으)ㄹ텐데	9.12	436
'afraid it might'	-(으)ㄹ까 싶-	5.4.2	247
'after . . .'	-(으)ㄴ다음에, 뒤에, 후에	8.2.9	395
'[only] after'	-(아/어)서야	7.5.8	364
'after finishing'	-고 나-	5.3.1	242
'after trying doing'	-다 보-	5.2.2	240
'allowed to'	-(아/어)도	7.2.5.1	317
'[not] allowed to'	-(으)면 안 되-	7.5.1.5	357
'[do] all the way'	-(아/어) 놓-	5.1.4	229
'also [is, does]'	-기도 하-	2.2.4.16	63
'also' [particle]	도	3.3.3.6	146
'and' [comitative particle]	과/와, 하고, (이)랑	3.2.6	123
'and' [additional connective]	-고	7.3.1	325
	-고서	7.3.2	328
	-거니와	7.3.6	331
'and then'	-다(가)	7.3.11	335
'apiece' [particle]	씩	3.3.4.2	153
'apt to'	-기 일쑤이-	2.2.4.9	58
'around the time'	무렵	2.1.2.15	45
'as . . . as' [particle]	만큼	3.3.6.3	160
'as if' [comparison connective]	-듯이	7.8.1	374
'as it is'	채	2.1.2.24	49
	-(으)ㄴ 채(로)	8.2.37	417
'as long as you're at it'	-(으)ㄴ|는 김에	8.2.6	393

'as much as'	–(으)ㄴ|는 한–	8.2.41	420
'as soon as'	–자마자	7.3.10	334
'at [static]'	에	3.2.4.1	106
'at [dynamic]'	에서	3.2.4.3	110
background information connective	–(으)ㄴ/는데	7.3.12	339
	–(으)ㄹ텐데	7.3.13	344
'because' [causal connectives]	–기 때문–	2.2.4.2	53
	–기에	2.2.4.21	68
	–아/어	7.1.2	296
	–(아/어)서	7.1.1	293
	–(아/어)서인지	7.1.3	297
	–(아/어) 가지고	7.1.5	298
	–(으)니	7.1.7	304
	–(으)니까	7.1.6	300
	–(으)ㄹ테니까	7.1.8	304
	–(으)므로	7.1.9	305
	–길래	7.1.10	306
	–느라고	7.1.11	308
	–더니	7.1.13	309
	–(으)ㄹ라	7.1.14	310
	–(으)ㄴ|는 바람에	8.2.23	404
	–(으)ㄴ|는 이상(에(는))	8.2.28	410
	–(으)ㄴ|는 탓	8.2.39	419
	–(으)ㄴ|–는 통에	8.2.40	419
'[it's] because'	–거든	9.2	423
'because of'	때문	2.1.2.13	44
'before'	–기 전–	2.2.4.10	58
'bound to'	–기 마련이–	2.2.4.3	54
'but'	–지만	7.2.1	311
	–(으)나	7.2.2	313
	–(으)되	7.2.4	315
	–거늘	7.2.13	323
'... called ...'	–이라는	10.4.5	467
'can /cannot'	–(으)ㄹ 수 있–/없–	8.2.27	408
causative	–이/기/히/리/우/구/추–	4.4.2.1	215
	–게 하–	4.4.2.2	219
	–도록 하–	4.4.2.3	221
	시키–	4.4.2.4	222

causative [particle]	(으)로 하여금	3.2.4.9	118
'[with the] combined purpose of'	–(으)ㄹ 겸	8.2.4	392
'[do] completely for regret/relief'	–(아/어) 버리–	5.1.7	232
continuous tense	–아/어 있–, –고 있–	4.3.3.2	202
-cum-	겸	2.1.2.2	40
'decide to'	–기로 하–	2.2.4.16	63
'depending on'	–기 나름이–	2.2.4.1	52
	–기에 따라	2.2.4.1	52
derivational suffix: adnominal form	–적	11.3.2.4	506
derivational suffix: adverbs	–이, –히, –오/우, –게	11.2.1.2	474
derivational suffix: causative verbs	–이/기/히/리/우/구/추–	4.4.2.1	215
derivational suffix: descriptive verbs	–겹–, –답–, –맞–,	10.2.2	450
	–스럽–, –롭–, –지–		
derivational suffix: nominal form	–이, –개/게, –기, –음, –는 것.	2.2.1	50
derivational suffix: passive verbs	–이–/–기–/–히–/–리–	4.4.1.1	206
derivational suffix: processive verbs	–지–	4.4.3.1	223
	–하–	4.4.3.2	223
'direction'	쪽	2.1.2.23	48
disapproval	–담	9.7	429
'don't have to'	–지 않아도	7.2.5.2	318
dubitative questions	–나?/–(으)ㄴ가?	9.3	424
'during'	동안	2.1.2.8	42
'each other'	서로	2.3.3	82
'easy to'	–기 십상이–	2.2.4.6	56
'end up'	–고 말–	5.3.2	243
'even' [particle]	도	3.3.3.6	146
	조차	3.3.3.7	149
	마저	3.3.3.8	150
	이라도	→7.2.5	315
'even [is, does]'	–기도 하–	2.2.4.16	63
'even after'	–고도	7.2.7	320
'even if it means'	–(아/어)서라도	7.2.8	320
'even though'	–(아/어)도	7.2.5	315
	–더라도	7.2.6	319
	–(으)ㄴ들	7.2.9	321
	–(으)ㄹ지라도	7.2.10	321

	–(으)ㄹ지언정	7.2.11	322
	–(으)ㄹ망정	7.2.12	322
	–(아/어) 봤자	7.2.15	324
'ever'	–(으)ㄴ/–는 일/적이 있–/없–	8.2.29	411
'every' [particle]	마다	3.3.4.1	152
'except for' [particle]	밖에	3.3.3.3	141
exclamations	–(는)군, –(는)구나, –(는)구만/구먼	9.4	426
	–네	9.5	428
'[to the] extent that . . .'	–(으)ㄹ 정도로	8.2.30	411
familiar speech style	–게, –네	6.1.5	270
'far from [being, doing]'	–기(는)커녕	2.2.4.15	62
'far from' [particle]	(은/는)커녕	3.3.3.10	151
[perform a] favour	'–(아/어) 주–	5.1.12	237
feel like	–(으)ㄹ래	9.11	436
'finish [doing]'	–(아/어) 내	5.1.3	228
'[do] for future reference'	–(아/어) 두–	5.1.5	230
formal speech style	–ㅂ니다/습니다	6.1.2	260
	–ㅂ니까/습니까		
	–(으)십시오		
'from' [location, object]	에서	3.2.4.3	110
	(으)로부터	3.2.4.8	117
'from' [time, location]	부터	3.3.3.4	143
'from' [human, animal]	에게서/한테서	3.2.4.7	116
future tenses	–겠–, –(으)ㄹ 거–, –(으)ㄹ게,	4.3.2	193
	–(으)마	9.14	440
'[should be] grateful if'	–(았/었으면 하–	7.5.1.3	356
'[would be] grateful if'	–(으)면 고맙겠–	7.5.1.2	356
'have to'	–지 않으면 안 되–	7.5.1.6	358
	–(아/어)야 하–/되–	7.5.7.1	363
'he'	그 사람, 그 남자	2.3.1.3	78
'[I] heard . . .'	–라면서	10.4.3	465
'him/herself'	자기, 자신, 저/지, 당신	2.3.3	81
'hope'	–기를/길 바라–	2.2.4.20	66
	–(았/었)으면 좋–	7.5.1.1	355
'I'	나, 저	2.3.1.1	74
'if' [conditional connective]	–(으)면	7.5.1	353
	–(았/었)더라면	7.5.5	360
	–거든	7.5.6	361
'[only] if'	–(아/어)야	7.5.7	362

'if ... [and then]'	–다(가) 보면	7.5.4	360
'if it's' [focus particle]	(이)야	3.3.2.2	138
'if you intend to'	–(으)려면	7.5.3	359
'if you say that'	–다면/라면	7.5.2	358
'in'	에	3.2.4.1	106
'in accordance with'	대로	3.3.6.6	163
'indeed [does, is]'	–기는 하–	2.2.4.12	60
'indeed' [focus particle]	(이)야말로	3.3.2.3	138
–ing [→nominal form]	–이, –개/게, –기, –음, –는 것.	2.2.1	50
'in order to'	–기 위하–	2.2.4.7	56
instrumental particle	(으)로	3.2.5.1	119
	(으)로서	3.2.5.2	121
	(으)로써	3.2.5.3	122
[with the] intention of	–(으)려고	7.7.2	370
	–고자	7.7.3	373
[go/come with the] intention of	–(으)러	7.7.1	369
'in the middle of'	중/도중	2.1.2.21	47
'in the middle of [doing]'	–는 중/도중	8.2.32	414
'[be] in the middle of ...'	–는 중–	8.2.33	414
intimate speech style	–아/어	6.1.3	261
'itself'	자체	2.3.3	81
'just [do something]'	–기나 하–	2.2.4.12	60
'just' [particle]	(이)나	3.3.5.2	155
'just as' [comparison connective]	–다시피	7.8.2	375
'know how to	'–(으)ㄹ|–는|–(으)ㄴ 줄 알–/모르–	8.2.31	412
'lapse [into a negative state]'	–(아/어) 빠지–	5.1.10	236
'like' [particle]	처럼	3.3.6.1	158
	같이	3.3.6.2	159
'[just] like'	–(으)ㄹ|–는|–(으)ㄴ 듯	8.2.14	398
'look like'	–나/ㄴ가 보–	5.5.1	250
'may or may not'	–(으)ㄹ|–는|–(으)ㄴ 둥	8.2.13	398
'[I] mean ...'	–단/냔/잔/란말이–	10.4.6	468
modifier endings	–(으)ㄹ, –는, –(으)ㄴ, –던	8.1	377
'more than' [particle]	보다	3.3.6.4	160
'[the] more the ...'	–(으)면 ... –(으)ㄹ수록	7.5.9	365
'nearly ...'	–(으)ㄹ 뻔하–	8.2.25	405
negatives	안, 못, –지 않–, –지 못하–, –지 말–	4.2	179
nominal form	–이, –개/게, –기, –음, –는 것.	2.2.1	50

'no way'	–기는	2.2.4.13	60
'no way that . . .'	–(으)ㄹ 리 없–	8.2.18	401
object particle	을/를	3.2.2	100
oblique questions	–(으)ㄴ/는지	7.4.4	349
	–(으)ㄹ지	7.4.5	351
observed/perceived past tense	–더–	4.3.1.3	190
'of course'	–고 말고	9.1	421
'[place something] on	에다(가)	3.2.4.2	109
ongoing activity "away"	–(아/어) 가–	5.1.1	227
ongoing activity "towards"	–(아/어) 오–	5.1.2	227
'only [is, does]'	–기도 하–	2.2.4.16	63
'only' [particle]	만	3.3.3.1	139
	뿐	3.3.3.2	138
'[be] only'	–(으)ㄹ뿐	8.2.26	406
'on the other hand'	–(으)ㄴ|는 반면(에)	8.2.24	404
'on the verge of'	–(으)ㄹ락 말락 (하–)	7.4.7	353
'on the way to . . .'	–는|던 길(에)	8.2.7	394
'or' [particle]	(이)나	3.3.5.2	155
'or' [optional connective]	–거나	7.4.1	345
	–든지	7.4.2	347
"panmal" [→intimate speech style]	–아/어	6.1.3	261
passives	–이–/–기–/–히–/–리–	4.4.1.1	205
	되–	4.4.1.2	209
	당하–, 입–, 받–	4.4.1.3	210
	–아/어지	4.4.1.4	213
past-past tense	–았었/었었–	4.3.1.2	187
past tense	–았/었–	4.3.1.1	186
'per' [particle]	씩	3.3.4.2	153
plain speech style	–다, –ㄴ다, –는다	6.1.4	263
	–(으)냐, –느냐, –니		
	–(으)ㄴ가/–는가		
	–자		
	–(으)라, –아/어라		
'plan to. . .'	–(으)ㄹ 계획	8.2.5	392
plural particle	들	3.3.1	129
polite speech style	–(아/어)요	6.1.1	256
possessive particle	의	3.2.3	103
'pretend to'	–는 척하–	8.2.38	418

quotation as background information	–다/라는데	10.4.4	466
quotations – direct	하고, 라고	10.1	446
quotations – indirect	–다고, –냐고, –자고, –라고	10.2–10.3	448
'[do] rashly'	–(아/어) 치우–	5.1.13	239
'rather than'	–느니	7.2.14	323
'rather . . . than'	–(으)ㄹ 바에(는/야)	8.2.22	403
'[do and then] realize'	–고 보–	5.3.3	244
regret	–(으)ㄹ걸	9.8	430
relative clauses [→modifier endings]	–(으)ㄹ, –는, –(으)ㄴ, –던	8.1	377
'[do] repeatedly'	–(아/어) 대–	5.1.6	231
	–(아/어) 쌓–	5.1.11	237
reported speech – direct	하고, 라고	10.1	446
reported speech – indirect	–다고, –냐고, –자고, –라고	10.2–10.3	448
'run an errand'	–다 주–	5.2.3	241
'. . .'s' [→possessive particle]	의	3.2.3	103
'–s [→plural particle]	들	3.3.1	129
'seem [to be]'	–(아/어) 보이–	5.1.9	236
	–게 보이–	5.6.2	252
'seem like'	–(으)ㄹ/–는/–(으)ㄴ 듯하–/듯 싶–	8.2.15	399
	–(으)ㄹ/–는/– (으)ㄴ 모양이–	8.2.21	403
'[it] seems that . . .'	modifier + 것 같–	8.2.2	388
semi-formal speech style	오, 소	6.1.6	272
'she'	그 여자	2.3.1.3	78
'[time]. . . since'	–(으)ㄴ 지	8.2.35	416
'so that' [causative connective]	–게	7.6.1	366
	–게끔	7.6.2	367
	–도록	7.6.3	368
'start . . .'	–기 시작하–	2.2.4.5	56
'stop after'	–다 말–	5.2.1	240
subject honorific particle	께서	6.2.1.3	276
subject honorific verb ending	–(으)시–	6.2.1.1	273
subject particle	이/가	3.2.1	98
'[be] sufficient'	–(으)면 되–	7.5.1.4	356
suggestions	–(으)ㄹ까?	9.10	433
'supposed to'	–기로 되–	2.2.4.19	65
tag questions	–지	9.18	442
'thanks to'	덕분	2.1.2.6	41

'the fact that . . .'	modifier + 것	8.2.2	388
'think it might'	–(으)ㄹ까 보–	5.4.1	246
	–나/ㄴ가 싶–	5.5.2	250
'think of doing'	–(으)ㄹ까 하–	5.4.3	248
'[I] thought [but was mistaken]'	–(으)ㄹ|–는|–(으)ㄴ 줄 알– /모르–	8.2.31	412
'to' [location, object]	에	3.2.4.1	106
'to' [human, animal]	에게/한테	3.2.4.4	113
'to' [human] – honorific	께	6.2.2.2	278
'[I] told you . . .'	–라니(까)	10.4.1	464
topic particle	은/는	3.3.2.1	132
'try [doing]'	–(아/어) 보–	5.1.8	233
'turn out so that'	–게 되–	5.6.1	251
'unless'	–(으)ㄴ|는 이상(에(는))	8.2.28	410
'until'	까지	3.3.3.5	144
'unusually' [particle]	따라	3.3.6.5	162
'upon telling'	–라니(까)	10.4.1	464
'very'	–기 짝이 없–	2.2.4.11	59
vocative particle	아/야	3.2.7	127
'want to'	–고 싶–	5.3.4	245
'we'	우리, 저희	2.3.1.1	74
'what with . . .'	–느라고	7.1.11	308
'when'	때	2.1.2.12	43
	–(으)ㄹ 때	8.2.17	400
'whether' [→oblique questions]	–(으)ㄴ/는지	7.4.4	349
	–(으)ㄹ지	7.4.5	351
'whether or not'	–(으)나 마나	7.2.3	314
'while'	–(으)면서	7.3.7	332
	–(으)며	7.3.9	333
	–는 동안/사이에	8.2.12	396
will, would	–(으)련마는/–(으)련만	9.14	438
'wish'	–(았/었)으면 좋–	7.5.1.1	355
'with' [→instrumental particle]	(으)로	3.2.5.1	119
'worth [doing]'	–(으)ㄹ 만하–	8.2.20	402
'you'	너, 자네, 당신, 자기	2.3.1.2	75
'you know'	–잖아	9.17	440
'you see'	–거든	9.2	423

General index

adnominal form 506
adnouns 469
adverbs 472
    conjunctive adverbs 481
    degree adverbs 485
    derived adverbs 474
    manner adverbs 486
    onomatopoeic/mimetic adverbs 488
    proper adverbs 472
    sentence adverbs 468
    time adverbs 482
Altaic hypothesis 1
articles, lack of 1, 37
aspiration 32
assimilation 26
auxiliary verbs 226
bases, consonants 172
bases, verb 172
bases, vowel 172
bound/dependent nouns 39
case particles 97
    comitative particles 123
    instrumental particles 119
    object particle 100
    particles of movement
        and location 106
    possessive particle 103
    subject particle 98
    vocative particle 127
causal connectives 292
causatives 292
Chinese characters 9
clausal connectives 292
    additional and sequential 325
    causal 292
    causative 366
    comparison 374
    conditional 353
    contrastive 272
    intentive 369
    optional 345
comitative particles 123
commands 268
    in formal speech style 260
    negative commands 182
    in plain speech style 268
    in quotations 453, 454, 464
    use of honorifics in 272
comparison, particles of 158
complements, position of 6
compliments, responding to 61, 171
conditional connectives 353
consonant bases 172
consonants 9
    aspirated consonants 20
    basic consonants 17
    tensed consonants 20
continuous tense 200
    continuous actions 202
    continuous states 200
counters 84
demonstrative pronouns 80
dependent nouns 39
derivation
    adnominal forms 506
    adverbs 472
    causative verbs 214
    descriptive verbs 504
    nouns 498
    passive verbs 205
    processive verbs 223
descriptive verbs 164
dictionary form 175
dictionary order 10
direct quotations 446
ditransitivizing 215

elliptical language 8, 80
exclamations 426, 428
familiar style 270
first person pronouns 74
formal style 260
future tense 193
gender, lack of 1, 38
genitive [see possessive]
"genitive s" 34
  interrogatives 6, 155
Hangul 10
  Hangul dictionary order 10
  Hangul letter names 10
  Hangul pronunciation guide 13
hearer honorifics 255
  familiar style 270
  formal style 260
  intimate style 261
  plain style 263
  polite style 256
  semi-formal style 272
honorifics 254
  hearer honorifics (speech styles) 255
  honorific kinship terms 286
  honorific nouns 279
  honorific titles 284
  referent honorifics 272
hoping, expression of 255
hortative [see proposals]
imperatives [see commands]
indirect quotations 447
  quoted commands 453
  quoted proposals 452
  quoted questions 450
  quoted statements 448
  reduced indirect quotations 458
  special patterns with indirect quotations 463
  the verb chu- in quoted commands 454
inferential expressions 190, 195, 198
infinitive form 173
instrumental particles 119
intentions, expression of 194, 359, 387
interrogative pronouns 82
interrogative word order 6
interrogatives [see questions]
intimate style 261
kinship terms 36
letter names 10
location, particles of 106
locatives [see location, particles of]
long negatives 180
mimetics 488
modifiers 377
  dynamic modifier 380
  future/prospective modifier 378
  past prospective modifier 387
  past retrospective modifier 387
  retrospective modifier 385
  sentence patterns with modifier clauses 388
  state/result modifier 381
movement and location, particles of 106
nasal assimilation 26
negatives 179
  expressions that require negative verbs 184
  long negatives 180
  negative commands and proposals 182
  short negatives 179
negative verbs 169
nominal forms 49
North Korea 1, 9
nouns 36
  bound/dependent nouns 39
  lack of articles 36
  lack of gender 38
  lack of number 36
number, lack of 36
numbers and counting 84
  counting and naming periods of time 90
  pure Korean and Sino-Korean numbers 84
  sentence patterns with numbers 88
object honorifics 277
  object honorific particle 278
  verbs with special object honorific forms 277
object particle 100
obligation, expressing lack of 364
obligation, expression of 253
oblique questions 349, 551, 352
one-shape verb endings 167
onomatopoeic/mimetic adverbs 488
ordinal numbers 89
palatalization 30
panmal style [see intimate style] 261
particles 96
  case particles 97
  special particles 129
passives 205
past tense 185
  observed or perceived past tense 189
  past-past 187
  simple past 186
permission, denial of 317, 357

permission, expression of 317, 358
plain style 263
plural particle 129
polite style 256
possessive particle 103
postpositions 5, 96
predicting 200, 457
prefixes 494
processive verbs 164
promising 236, 432
pronouns 74
  demonstrative pronouns 80
  first person pronouns 74
  interrogative pronouns 82
  reflexives and reciprocals 81
  second person pronouns 75
  third person pronouns 77
pronunciation 13
pronunciation changes 21
  aspiration 32
  assimilation between r and n 28
  assimilation of r to n 28
  h reduction 32
  n addition 31
  nasal assimilation 26
  palatalization of t and t' 30
  reinforcement 33
  re-syllabification 24
  simplification of consonant clusters 23
  syllable-final consonants 22
proposals
  in formal speech style 260
  negative proposals 182
  in plain speech style 263
  in quotations 452, 461
  use of honorifics in 255
pure-Korean numbers 84
questions
  dubitative questions 424
  in formal speech style 258
  in plain speech style 263
  in quotations 450, 459
  tentative questions 433
quotations 446
  direct quotations 446
  indirect quotations 447
  quoting verbs 455
  reduced indirect quotations 458
reciprocals 81
referent honorifics 272
  object honorifics 277
  subject honorifics 273
reflexive pronouns 81
regret, expression of 430
reinforcement 33
reported speech [see quotations]
re-syllabification 24
Romanization 9
script 9
second person pronouns 75
Sejong, King 9
semi-formal style 272
sentence endings 421
  dubitative interrogatives 424
  exclamations 426, 418
  tag questions 442
short negatives 179
Sino-Korean numbers 84
special particles 129
  particles of approximation and optionality 155
  particles of comparison and contrast 158
  particles of extent 139
  particles of frequency 152
  particles of topic and focus 131
  plural particle 129
speech styles [see hearer honorifics]
statements
  in formal speech style 260
  in plain speech style 263
  in quotations 448, 458
subject honorifics 273
  subject honorific marker 273
  subject honorific particle 276
  verbs with special subject honorific forms 275
subject particle 98
suffixes 498
  adnominal suffix 506
  adverb-deriving suffixes 504
  noun-deriving suffixes 498
  verb-deriving suffixes 504
suggestions 433
support verbs 167
tag questions 442
teknonymy 39
tense and aspect 185
  continuous tense 200
  future tenses 193
  past tenses 185
terms of address 282
  kinship terms 286
  names 283
  titles 284
third person pronouns 77
titles 284
topic, particle of 132

transitivizing 215
two-shape verb endings 164
verbs 164
  attaching verb endings 175
  copula 170
  dictionary form ' 175
  ha– verbs 167
  infinitive form 173
  negative verbs 169
  processive and descriptive verbs 164
verb bases 172
vocative particle 127
voicing 20
volunteering 198, 200
vowel bases 172
vowels 13
  Compound Vowel 의 16
  simple vowels 13
  W-Vowels 15
  Y-Vowels 14
wishing, expression of 355
word classes 2
word order 3